Into Temptation

Into Temptation

The Spoils of Time: 3

Penny Vincenzi

ORION

First published in Great Britain in 2002 by
Orion Books
an imprint of The Orion Publishing Group
Orion House, 5 Upper St Martin's Lane,
London, WC2H 9EA

A CIP catalogue record for this book is
available from the British Library.

ISBN 0 75283 202 6 (hardback)
ISBN 0 75283 203 4 (trade paperback)

Typeset by Deltatype Ltd, Birkenhead, Merseyside

Printed and bound in Great Britain by
Clays Ltd, St Ives plc.

For Emily and Claudia,
who really did get me through.
With much love.

ACKNOWLEDGEMENTS

The roll-call of thank yous seems to get longer and longer with each book; but this one must be headed once again by my agent Desmond Elliott, who is a living breathing archive of the publishing industry; not only in England but New York as well. Other gurus of the New York publishing scene coloured up the book beautifully: Larry Ashmead of HarperCollins and Alun Davies of Simon & Schuster were most generous with both their time and their wonderful anecdotes (not to mention lunches) and I would like to thank Patrick Jansson Smith for leading me to them, and for some stories of his own. Also in New York, enormous thanks to Edna McNabney who spent a whole day showing me a very special New York and of course to wonderful Mike Berkowitz, who collected me from the Algonquin at dawn (literally) and drove me for hours around the Village and Chelsea, taking us both into bars long before they were open, and filling up three sides of tape with marvellous stories. A book in himself, Mike is; he should write one. While I am still (notionally) in America, lots of thanks to dear Betty Prashker, for a new set of stories, and to Caroline Upcher, who entertained me so royally in the Hamptons while I explored. And huge gratitude also to John Dadakis, who gave so generously of his time and legal expertise to steer me through the complexities of inheritance law, USA version.

Back in England, also on the legal front, Natalie Bryant gave me a crash course in both inheritance and company law, English version; her knowledge and her patience were limitless. Alan Martin was the most wonderful source of information on the subject of company finance; Mark Stephens on injunctions; and Sue Stapely continued to amaze me by knowing something about everything I asked her.

Thank you too, once again, to Ursula Lloyd for information on all things gynaecological in the far off days of the 1950s, and Roger Freeman for psychiatric detail in the same era.

More crash courses, one on vintage wine, came from Nicholas Fraser; and another on company investment from Victor Sandelson. And thank you to Felicity Green and Ian Hessenberg, for knowledge of and research into the photographic and modelling scene of these elegantly golden days.

Several wonderful books have helped me too: *Another Life* by Michael Korda, *From Rationing to Rock* by Stuart Hylton, *Elizabeth's Britain* by Philip Ziegler and perhaps most of all *In Vogue* by Georgina Howell.

Once again, enormous thanks to Rosie de Courcy, whose brilliance and sparky inventiveness as an editor are only exceeded by her patience and tact as deadlines come and go. Also for reading so fast, so I don't have to wait in agony for her judgement, and for crying in all the right places in the book. Very important.

Thank you Emma Draude of Midas for so efficiently telling the whole world about it, and for getting as excited as I do over pieces of good news and reviews.

Thank you to the Orion team, for yet another piece of stylish publishing; the list of names is long, but headed by Susan Lamb, who masterminded it, and finishing with Dallas Manderson and Jo Carpenter who saw it into the shops with their usual skill and determination. And in between Juliet Ewers for seeing the whole thing through with immense efficiency and patience, Lucie Stericker for yet another gorgeous cover, Richard Hussey for not being defeated by the tightest deadline yet, and Malcolm Edwards, for all manner of clever contributions and suggestions, and not least saying how much he liked it.

And finally, all the friends who are so supportive and listened so patiently to my endless wails that it would never be finished; and most of all, and as always, my family, my husband Paul and my four daughters, Polly, Sophie, Emily and Claudia, who have had to live with me through three years of The Spoils of Time. I suspect they may be glad we are now leaving the Lyttons behind; I shall miss them, especially Celia, most dreadfully.

Penny Vincenzi August 2002

The Main Characters

LONDON
Lady Celia Lytton, *senior editor at Lyttons publishing house*
Lord Arden, *her new husband*
Giles, *twins* Venetia *and* Adele, *and* Kit, *her children*
Jay Lytton, *their cousin*
Boy Warwick, *Venetia's husband*
Elspeth Warwick, *their daughter*
Keir Brown, *Elspeth's boyfriend*
Geordie MacColl, *Adele's husband*
Clio, *their daughter*
Noni *and* Lucas, *Adele's children by Luc Lieberman, deceased*
Sebastian Brooke, *bestselling author published by Lyttons*
Clementine Hartley, *another Lyttons author*

COUNTRY
Billy Miller, *brother of Barty*
Joan, *his wife, and their sons* Joe *and* Michael

NEW YORK
Barty Miller, *head of Lyttons New York*
Jenna Elliott, *her daughter by Laurence Elliott, deceased*
Cathy Patterson, *a schoolfriend of Jenna's*
Charlie Patterson, *her father*
Jamie Elliott, *brother of Laurence and Jenna's trustee*
Kyle Brewer, *a literary agent and Jenna's trustee*
Marcus Forrest, *editorial director of Lyttons New York*
Isabella (Izzie) Brooke, *Sebastian's daughter*
Mike Parker *and* Nick Neill, *copywriters, Izzie's employers*

Part One

'Rich with the spoils of time . . .'
Thomas Gray
Elegy Written in a Country Churchyard

CHAPTER I

Lady Celia Lytton had been close to death several times in her long life. Not always literally – although there had been occasions, a cycle ride through a Blitz-torn London night, a long jolting car ride while enduring a miscarriage, when the Grim Reaper had appeared to have her very clearly in his sights – but also by repute. And there was no more outstanding example of the latter than the spring day in 1953, Coronation year, when she announced not only her engagement to her old flame, Lord Arden, but her retirement from the House of Lytton. Most of literary London promptly concluded that she was (at very best) in the early stages of a terminal illness. They then raised their lunchtime glasses of gin and tonic, or Martini, or champagne, to her dazzling memory, expressed their huge regret at the ending of a life that had so enriched the literary and social scene for almost five decades, and settled down to speculate over what the death certificate might eventually say, and who exactly might step into her always elegant shoes.

They were hardly surprising of course, those reports. For as long as anyone could remember, Celia Lytton had declared firmly and publicly that only death would separate her from the publishing house of Lytton, truly the greatest love of her life. This was in addition to another of her favourite maxims: that for her, at any rate, no man could possibly replace work as a source of happiness.

Indeed she *was* Lyttons to most people; she embodied it, with her brilliant innovative mind, her flawless editorial judgement, her unique style, her perfect taste. It had always been so, since she had joined the company almost fifty years earlier as a very young girl; but since the death of Oliver Lytton, her husband, a year earlier, she had become more than a figurehead, more than an inspiration, she was its life force. The younger generation might hold shares in it, care passionately about it, bring skill and talent and a great deal of hard work to it, but they trailed behind her in authority. No major book was acquired or published, no editorial innovation considered, no financial investment made, no senior member of staff hired, without her agreement.

3

Not even the theoretical requirement to gain the approval of Lyttons New York for all major developments had dented her glassy supremacy; 'I know what they – or rather she – will feel about it,' she would say whenever anyone raised the matter, and of course she was perfectly right. There were, as was well known, very good personal as well as professional reasons . . .

Lady Celia herself, who would have greatly enjoyed the furore had she been able to witness it, was sitting on a chaise-longue set in the window of her sitting room in her house in Cheyne Walk, looking, as always, perfectly groomed and extraordinarily beautiful, surrounded by her large family, some of them more visibly distressed than others, with the manuscript of her youngest son's new book (delivered two months late the previous evening, to her deep displeasure) on the table beside her.

It was Venetia Warwick, one of her twin daughters, who spoke first.

'Mummy, are you really sure about this?'

'To what exactly are you referring, Venetia? My engagement or my retirement?'

'Well – both. But more especially, I suppose, the retirement.'

'Absolutely.' Lady Celia's voice was brisk. 'Where could there be any doubt? You've been working for Lyttons, Venetia, for – what? Fifteen years. With considerable success, I would add. You must agree it's time I moved over. Even I can see that. Heavens above, you've told me so in more ways than one over the past few years. In your position I would feel relief, if not a keen sense of anticipation. Which I am quite sure is what you, Giles, must be feeling. And don't waste time denying it, because we shall both know you're lying. Now then, you must all excuse me, I'm going to meet Lord Arden for luncheon. I think I deserve a little fun after the rather dreary morning I've had. But I want you all to dine here tonight, so that we can discuss everything more fully.'

It was only when she walked into the dining room of the Ritz, on the arm of her newly affianced, known to his intimates as Bunny, accepting congratulations on her engagement here, expressions of regret at her retirement there, that people began to realise, with a sense of considerable disbelief, it was just possible that not only was she in very good health, but she had actually meant what she said. She was simply going to retire.

The sense of disbelief, both within and without the house of Lytton was hardly surprising. Her office, on the first floor of the new Lytton House, in Grosvenor Square, was still the heart of the company; Giles Lytton, her eldest son, might be Managing Director, Venetia Warwick might be in charge of sales and development and of that strange new science – or was it an art? – marketing, Jay Lytton might be Editorial Director, but it was to

Celia they all deferred, with varying degrees of grace. And Giles might grumble and resent that deference, and Jay might kick against it at times, and Venetia might question the need for it in her particular area, but none of them seriously considered setting it aside.

And now here she was, announcing that she was giving it all up, was walking away, not just from Lyttons, but from the thing which had mattered most to her for the whole of her life: her work. And this in order to marry – only a year after the death of her husband and the ending of their legendary, almost fifty-year marriage – to become the Countess of Arden (though she declared she would not entirely relinquish the name of Lytton), to take up residence in Lord Arden's dazzling vast eighteenth-century house in Scotland. Dazzling it might be, said everyone, as this fresh shock reached the ears of literary society, but it was a very long way from London. Of course Lord Arden had a house, and a very fine one, in Belgrave Square, but he spent a lot of time at Glennings, as Glenworth Castle was more familiarly known.

Indeed, since the death of his first wife, with her well-known penchant for stable lads, he spent far more time there than in London. He was a countryman. He liked to ride and hunt and shoot and fish, and although he enjoyed the opera, had a box at Glyndebourne and would even visit La Scala and the Paris Opera to hear the divine Maria Callas sing, he was never actually happier than when standing up to his waist in the freezing water of his own river, in pursuit of salmon, or taking the hideously dangerous fences of his own estate in pursuit of Scotland's foxes. What on earth was she going to do up there, everyone wondered, the pampered, perfectly dressed and coiffed Lady Celia, that most urban of creatures as she seemed to be – forgetting that she had grown up a country girl herself, on her own father's estate, and, indeed, had first met Lord Arden when she was quite a young girl, not in the hothouse atmosphere of a London nightclub but at a house party in Shropshire where she had gone out with the guns in the driving rain and bagged more birds than he had.

Of course there had been other chapters in their saga, which had taken place in extremely sophisticated and indeed infamous surroundings; but in her late sixties and her new, raw loneliness, Lady Celia Lytton suddenly found herself possessed by a profound longing to return to her roots. And Peter Arden was miraculously able to lead her to them.

'Want to—?'
    'Of course.'
    'Berkeley Square?'
    'Montpelier would be—'
    'Yes, it would. I'll follow you.'
The Lytton twins as they were still referred to, despite being married women with a large number of children between them, still communicated

thus: in the strange, incomprehensible shorthand speech which they had employed since childhood and which drove all around them, but particularly their husbands and their children, to distraction. It was not purely habit that made them cling to it; it was also extremely useful.

They drew up outside Adele's house in Montpelier Street at almost the same time, Venetia in her rather stately Jaguar, Adele in the dark-green MG convertible that was currently her pride and joy. The house was quiet; Adele's two older children were at school, and her small new daughter was out with the nanny.

'But let's go up to the studio. They might—'

'Let's. You're so lucky, so peaceful—'

'Yes, well, if you wanted peacefulness, having six children was not the way to go about it.'

'I know, I know. Shall we—?'

'Be nice. I'll get some. Geordie put a case of Sancerre in the cellar last night. Grab some glasses and go on up.'

Adele's photographic studio, occupying the whole of the third floor of her house, with its glass roof and uncurtained windows was dazzling in the April sunshine. Venetia grimaced and started pulling blinds down.

'Can't cope with this sort of light. Not at my age. Desperately unflattering.'

'Venetia, you're so vain. Anyway, no one's going to see you except me.'

'Geordie might come up.'

'He won't. He's lunching with some old lady who lived through the First World War. For the latest book.'

'Well he's bound to come back.'

'Not for ages,' said Adele confidently. 'Sure to bump into someone who's heard the news. Here, give me the glasses.'

'It is quite—'

'I know. Truly so.'

'I mean, the thought of Lyttons without—'

'I bet you quite—'

'In a way. In a way truly not.'

Adele looked at her. 'I s'pose. What do you think—?'

'God knows. Tired, maybe?'

'When was Mummy ever—?'

'Never. Ciggy?'

'Mmm, thanks.'

Adele took a cigarette, lit it and inhaled heavily. 'The really big question is—'

'I know. I know. Why—'

'I mean, when—'

'All those years. And Kit and everything.'

6

'Of course,' said Adele, 'he is a real honey.'

'I suppose you should know. Your escape, and everything.'

'Well yes. But still—'

'I know. Still doesn't – Why him? Why not—'

'Well one thing's quite certain,' said Adele, taking a large sip of wine, 'she won't tell us. Or indeed anyone else.'

'Except perhaps Kit.'

'And what about—'

'I wonder if she warned him?'

'Doubt it. My God he'll be—'

'Won't he? Absolutely furious. And so hurt. Poor darling.' Venetia's large dark eyes were heavy with sympathy.

'Poor darling indeed,' said Adele. 'It doesn't make any sense at all, does it?'

'Absolutely none at all.'

Of course it would have been Venetia who was singled out for praise that morning by their mother, Giles thought, as he walked back to Lytton House; no word of praise for him, in his caretaking of Lyttons, his successful steering of the house through the difficult post-war austerity, no mention of his best-selling and unique history of the war, told entirely by the ordinary men and women who had fought in it. Just a tart observation that he must be feeling some relief at her departure. Which of course he was: they all were, deny it though they might. To be free at last of her presence, however brilliant, her dominance, however well-earned, her direction, however inspired: free to make their own way, their own successes, their own mistakes, even, to depart from the rigid routes she had set for the conduct of Lyttons and its business would be wonderfully liberating. It had been far worse since his father's death; that had seemed to drive her even harder in her conviction that only she could know what was right for Lyttons, what had to be done.

She seemed to have buried, with Oliver and his gentle restraining presence, any degree of self-doubt; before then she had always had to pit her will against his – as strong in its own way as her own. The day after his funeral, she had summoned them all to her office, and faced them with a composure so steely it dared them to offer so much as a word or touch of sympathy or concern, and told them that they must all continue as Oliver would have wished: and then proceeded to do exactly what she wished herself. At first they felt they could not argue with her, lost as she was in her great and undoubted grief; what they had not foreseen was how swiftly their compliance had been taken for granted, accepted as the norm, and how ruthlessly she would trade on it.

Useless for Giles to point out that they were all on the board, in nominally equal positions, all reporting with equal responsibility to New

7

York on major purchases of books and authors' contracts, the twice-yearly budget and senior staff changes. Useless for Venetia to tell her mother that business practice had changed, that autocracy within a company, however inspired, was no longer acceptable and especially one in which she no longer held a controlling share; or indeed for Jay to affirm that the acquiring of books should not be conducted as an entirely personal process of choice; that was how Celia ran Lyttons, had always run it, and she found any suggestion that things might change quite simply absurd.

She was right of course. Giles had felt a strong sense of relief as he read the announcements in *The Bookseller* and *The Publishers' Gazette* – and what a way to tell not only the world but her own family, and without the faintest hint of it beforehand – that she was leaving the world of publishing from that day forward. It had been Venetia who had alerted him to it, to the announcement, had telephoned early that morning, her voice sounding at the same time excited and strained; he had rushed to pick up his own copies, still lying on the breakfast table, neatly folded with his post by Mrs Parks, the housekeeper, and read them, shaking his head in disbelief before sitting down rather heavily and staring slightly blankly at Helena. Helena had questioned him and then said with a note of satisfaction in her brisk voice, 'And about time too Giles. At last you'll get your chance.' And then most uncharacteristically, had burst into tears.

He had been touched by those tears; Helena had fought most fiercely for him and his right to run the company ever since she had married him over twenty years ago. The fact that her efforts had often been tactless, useless and indeed even counter-productive did not change the basic fact that she loved and admired him and was permanently angry that his talents were not given any proper recognition. Which made Giles forgive her a great deal else; her lack of humour, her overbearing manner, her increasing tendency to treat him like one of the children. It was said that Helena Lytton had even been heard to tell her husband across a dinner-party table to talk less and get on with his food.

For some reason, the success of Giles's book, *The People's War*, published by Lyttons in 1949, had not particularly pleased Celia; she saw it as a rather unnecessary distraction for him from the proper business of running the company. In fact, Giles knew that very little he had done properly pleased her (with the possible exception of his Military Cross). It was a very hard thing for him to bear.

He went over to Helena and patted her rather awkwardly on the shoulder; physical contact of any kind between them, not simply sexual, had long since ceased.

'There there,' he said, 'don't cry. No need for that.'

'I know there's no need,' said Helena, sniffing and wiping her eyes on the back of her hand, 'I just can't help it. I'm so happy for you Giles.

You've waited so long. Of course you still won't have what is your right but – well, at least, you are the Managing Director. It's marvellous. I wonder who her shares will go to?' she added, the 'her' taking on a vicious note. Helena and Celia had always disliked one another; in the year since Oliver's death, the dislike had turned to something more insidious, more ugly. In both of them.

'God knows.' In fact he had not even thought of them.

'They should go to you. As the senior member of the family.'

'I don't suppose they will. Anyway, we only hold – individually at any rate – such a nominal amount, it's not as if we still owned the company. It hardly matters, does it?'

'But Giles—'

'Helena, please. Don't start. Not now. I dare say she will hold on to them. Whatever she says about retirement.'

'Well she has no right to.'

'She will think she has every right,' he said and sighed.

There had been no mention of the shares; no doubt Celia would use them as a weapon to declare her favouritism, to indicate the area she saw as most important. It wasn't quite true that she held so few they were scarcely worth considering; due to Barty's considerable generosity, the family still held 32 per cent of the London company shares. Given the great success Lyttons London (as it was now called) had enjoyed over the past five years, those shares were certainly worth having. Thirty-two per cent, the number so easily and charmingly divisible into four: one quarter each for Giles, Venetia, Jay and for Oliver and Celia jointly. It had been most graciously done; so graciously indeed, that Celia, for one, found it easy to overlook the fact that any generosity had been displayed at all.

Giles, all too aware of the need for gratitude, and of the intense discomfort of the situation, still found a wry pleasure in it. Who would have thought, all those years ago, that Barty would come to hold such power over them . . .

He turned his thoughts from Barty and switched back to the present. It would be marvellous; absolutely marvellous without his mother. Of course, he and Venetia and Jay often had their differences of opinion but those differences could now be resolved by discussion, by reasoned, informed debate, taking in factors like profitability, the competition, an author's track record. As from this afternoon, this very afternoon, he could set up new financial systems, processes of evaluation, long-term planning. Venetia would be pleased, he knew; she found her mother's conduct within the company anarchic. The only difference between them was that Venetia adored Celia, and fiercely admired and valued her talents. It was a very important difference.

But the greatest puzzle of all, of course, was why Bunny Arden? When everyone had thought, with Oliver dead—

'Well Cousin Giles.' Jay walked into his office an hour later. 'Pretty exciting, isn't it?'

'What's that?' said Giles cautiously.

'Oh come on, old chap. We know each other better than that. Celia leaving us to do our job, that's what. Bloody marvellous. Let's be frank. Might even drink to it. I've got a bottle of bubbly next door. How about it?'

Giles nodded slightly wearily, and watched Jay as he went to fetch the champagne. He felt very ambivalent about Jay. Celia adored him, and so did Barty – not that they saw very much of Barty these days of course – and there was no doubt he was everyone's favourite throughout Lyttons. Which was a hard thing to cope with. On the other hand, Giles was unable to dislike him either. Jay was so good-natured, so permanently sunny, his rather bluff manner disguising a brilliant mind and a virtually flawless editorial judgement. He had another quality which made him the company star – an extraordinary ability to win. As well as living out his charmed life at Lyttons as Celia's favourite, he was married to 'one of the most beautiful girls in London' according to *Vogue* where she was frequently featured. Victoria Lytton was tall, slender, blonde, with huge blue eyes and awesomely good legs; as good-natured and charming as Jay, she had already presented him with two sons, and had just embarked on a third pregnancy which she had stated firmly was not only her last, but which would produce a little girl. No one had the slightest doubt that it would.

The extraordinary thing about Jay was that he was not only liked and admired within the company, where his editorial skills combined with a cool financial judgement, and an ability to recognise the strength of business-based arguments, but his authors liked and admired him too. His only fault was that he was inclined to be lazy; life had been too kind to him, too easy, he had long since ceased to be hungry. On the other hand, that very quality gave him an easy, relaxed way with his authors; he always seemed to have plenty of time. He could communicate with them on a deeply sympathetic and instinctive level, and was a most brilliant editor, recognising their sensitivities, valuing their talents, nurturing their hugely individual contribution to the Lytton mix. It was not only the brilliant new young authors – including Kit Lytton himself and a startlingly original female writer called Clementine Hartley, only three years out of Oxford and with two best-selling novels already to her credit – but the older generation too, who found almost to their surprise that they felt valued by and at ease with him: women fiction writers like the great Nancy Arthure, whose success had made Lyttons the envy of the publishing world, Lady Annabel Muirhead, the biographer – and Sebastian Brooke, the venerable elder statesman of the book world, with his elegant time-fantasies written for and loved by children and admired by adults.

Sebastian who had actually had a meeting arranged with Giles and Celia that very afternoon, to discuss the Coronation year edition of his books; Sebastian who had phoned in an appalling rage to enquire why Celia's secretary had seen fit to cancel at half a day's notice so important a meeting; Sebastian who was even now in a taxi travelling to Cheyne Walk, consumed with rage, to elicit an explanation from Celia herself for the true reason behind her announcement; and why she had chosen not to discuss it with him first.

CHAPTER 2

A scream echoed down the stairs, followed by a short silence and then a burst of sobbing. And then footsteps, stumbling over one another and finally, on the first-floor landing, as Adele's family appeared from various rooms to enquire whatever the matter might be, a laugh of sheer triumph.

'That was *Record* on the phone.'

'Didn't hear the phone,' said Geordie, with careful obtuseness.

'That's not the point.'

'Well, Maman, what is? That was a terrible noise, it quite frightened me.'

'I'm sorry, Noni sweetheart. But I was very excited.' Adele gave her daughter a kiss.

'What about?'

'Well—'

'Oh, Mother, do come along, this is very boring.'

Adele looked at her son's impatient face, and smiled.

'*Record*, the American magazine, you know—'

'Yes, Maman, we know.'

'*Record* have asked me to cover the Coronation for them. Be their official photographer. Now then, what do you think about that?'

'Darling, that is amazing. Really quite wonderful. Here, let me give you a kiss.'

'Oh God,' said Lucas, with exaggerated weariness, 'not in front of the children, please.'

He turned away, walked into his own room; Adele looked after him, her mood suddenly punctured.

'Ignore him, darling,' said Geordie. 'He's just being deliberately awkward.'

'Of course he is.' Noni's lovely little face was concerned. 'Stupid boy. Congratulations, Maman, that's so exciting. Wait till I tell the girls at school tomorrow.'

'I don't suppose they'll be terribly impressed,' said Adele smiling at her, thinking of the hugely sophisticated girls in Noni's set at St Paul's Girls' School.

'Of course they will. We all are, aren't we Noni darling? Definitely calls for a bottle of champagne. Come along down, girls, it will start our evening off with a swing,' said Geordie.

'I'll – just see if Lucas would like to join us,' said Adele quickly. 'You go on down.'

She knocked gently on Lucas's door; no answer. She opened it slowly. He was hunched over his books, his thin shoulders oddly vulnerable looking. She went over to him, put her arms round them; he turned to look up at her, his expression oddly blank.

'Darling—'

'Yes?'

He was such a handsome boy, with his dark eyes and hair and long, slightly gaunt face: at fourteen heart-catchingly like his father. His father, who she had loved so much and – Adele switched her mind determinedly away from the past, back into the present.

'Darling, won't you join us downstairs? For some champagne?'

She had thought the sophistication of the offer might move him, but he frowned.

'No, thank you. I'm a bit tired and I have to finish this essay by tomorrow. But of course I'm very pleased for you Mother. Congratulations.'

'Thank you. But Lucas, you will come to the dinner tonight, won't you? Grandmother will be so disappointed if you don't. It's a big occasion for her.'

'I was going to ask you if it was really necessary.' His voice was formal, rather flat. 'It will be so late when we leave, and I'm sure she won't miss me.'

'Lucas of course she will. She adores you, you know she does.'

'Does she? I'm not so sure. Great-grandmama, yes, she was fond of me, well we lived together didn't we? But – no, I don't think Grandmother is specially fond of me. And surely she of all people would understand that I need to work.'

'Yes. Of course.' Adele gave him a quick bright smile.

He turned back to his books, dismissing her.

'Perhaps you could write her a little note. Explaining?'

'Oh Mother, do I really have to? I'm trying to concentrate. I told you, she won't care.'

'I think she will,' said Adele, her voice flat suddenly. 'But – if you don't have time . . .'

'Oh, for heaven's sake—' He pulled a piece of paper towards him, scrawled over it in black ink in his illegible handwriting, and handed it to her. 'There. Give her that.'

13

Adele looked at it. 'Dear Grandmother, Sorry I can't be with you. I have a lot of work to do. Lucas.'

'Thank you,' she said carefully, longing to throw it down again, to say it was outrageously rude, that Celia would be very hurt, that he owed her something better than that. But she had to tread so carefully where Lucas was concerned. He was the typical adolescent, morose, secretive, hostile – all the things that, these days, parents were told had to be understood and humoured.

'I was never allowed to behave like this,' Geordie had said plaintively once when she had begged his forgiveness for some particularly hostile outburst from Lucas.

'I know, darling, and neither was I. But Lucas has had such a difficult time. His history isn't exactly ideal. We have to try and help him through it.'

'It's me that needs the help,' said Geordie with a sigh.

'I know. And I do sympathise so much. But at least we have our own little angel. And Noni adores you.'

'And it's mutual. All right. I will continue to try to apply the damnable American science of psychology to your son. And turn the other cheek. I can tell you, both of them are getting quite sore.'

'Thank you darling. Oh, I love you.'

And she did; she adored him. The second – and last – she so often told him, great love of her life; so different from the first, bringing her a happiness she had never dreamed of finding again – and a great deal of fun as well. There had been the occasional problem, of course. He was, as Celia had remarked more than once, too charming for his own good, one of those people who lift the mood of a room simply by walking into it; life was easy for him, he had great talent, to be sure, but success had come swiftly after the publication of his first book, under Barty's guidance. Men as well as women liked him, he was always the focus of attention (and if he was not he didn't like it), a life enhancer in every way. Adele had always been aware of a slight unevenness in their relationship, a sense that she was more fortunate to have him than he to have her; and she had been half afraid, more than once, that the flirtations he carried on almost compulsively had become a little more serious than was comfortable. But she had never found any real evidence; and when she had taxed Geordie (very gently) on the matter, he had been so shocked, so hurt, that she had felt ashamed of herself.

'It's you I love and you I'm married to,' he said, 'and I'm the luckiest man in England. Would I really risk losing that, do you think? I'm sorry if I've worried you, and I'll try to be less sociable in future.'

Venetia, who was of a rather more cynical turn of mind than her sister, and with rather stronger suspicions, could not help thinking that Geordie's gifts as a writer and storyteller, his way with words and his ability to fantasize, were as much use to him in his marriage as his professional life, but she loved and cared for her sister far too much to say so. If she ever found proof herself, she said to her mother, 'I would kill him. But I think he loves her in his own way, don't you?'

To which Celia replied that she did, that marriages came in all shapes and sizes, and Adele's seemed to fit her very well for most of the time: 'One should never go in search of trouble,' she said, 'if it's there it finds one soon enough, in my experience. As you know yourself,' she added.

'Yes, and look at us now,' said Venetia, 'twenty-five years nearly, despite a fair bit of trouble.'

'Well there you are,' said Celia, as if that settled the matter.

'Lucas is very tired,' Adele said now, walking into the drawing room, 'he has asked to be excused this evening.'

'Well he can un-ask,' said Geordie. 'I shall go up myself and tell him—'

'Darling don't. There's no point. If he comes he'll just sit and sulk and—'

'He needs a good thrashing,' said Noni briskly. Adele looked at her, amused at the archaic language, the stentorian sentiment.

'Noni, really. You don't mean that.'

'I do, Maman. He's a beast. And you spoil him. And it's not fair. Anyway' – her tone altered, became grown up and smooth – 'many, many congratulations. We're very proud, aren't we Geordie?'

'Very proud. Well done. Will that mean you'll have a place at the Abbey?'

'I – suppose so. Goodness, what an honour. Mummy will be hugely annoyed.'

'Will Lord Arden be there tonight, do you think?' said Noni.

'Apparently not. Strictly family, Mummy said. So that we can ask questions, I presume.'

'Sebastian isn't coming either. Izzie rang me earlier for a chat. He's in a huge bait.'

'Well – he's not family either,' said Adele firmly.

'I suppose not. But – he feels like it.'

'What else did Izzie say?' asked Geordie, his face intrigued.

'Geordie—'

'I'm interested. I want to know. Like Noni, I think of Sebastian as family. I guess he must be very upset. About the whole thing. I mean—'

'Geordie,' said Adele, her voice suddenly stern, 'not now.'

'Oh Maman,' said Noni impatiently, 'don't be silly.'

'And what is that supposed to mean?'

Noni's face, so like her mother's, ironed itself out, her dark eyes blank, her mouth set in a sweet smile.

'Nothing,' she said. 'Come on, we'd better go. Geordie, your tie's crooked. I'll just get my coat while Mummy fixes it.'

She left the room; Adele looked after her, then turned to Geordie.

'Do you think she knows?'

'My darling, of course she knows. They all know.'

'But – who will have told her?'

He smiled at her. 'I can't believe we're having this conversation. Again.'

'What do you mean?'

'You were so shocked when you found out that Henry knew. And Izzie.'

'Darling Izzie.'

'Well, yes. Very darling. I adore her too. But she's not a child. Twenty-three now. Of course she had to know. Sebastian's her father.'

'Maybe she told Noni. They're very close.'

'Maybe. Or Henry Warwick, or Roo, or their naughty sisters. Children do talk, Adele.'

'I know but – well, maybe I should talk to her about it.'

'Oh, I don't think so. She doesn't seem too bothered. She's a very worldly young lady.'

Noni came back into the room, a velvet cape draped over her arm.

'Darling you look so lovely,' said Geordie. 'You make an old man very happy. Here, let me help you into that.'

'Geordie! Hardly old. You don't look much older than Henry.'

'What nonsense,' said Geordie, clearly delighted with this tribute. And indeed it was true. With his American preppy looks and style, his long, lean body, his floppy brown hair, his wide grey eyes, he could have been almost any age from twenty-five upwards. In fact he was forty-two, a year younger than Adele; while Henry Warwick, Venetia's eldest son, with his swarthy, dissolute good looks, his already-developing banker's paunch, his slightly fruity manner, did indeed look much older than his twenty-four years.

'Come on,' said Adele, 'this mutual admiration society is making me feel quite jealous. And besides, we mustn't be late. Mummy would never forgive us.'

But in fact dinner was served over half an hour late, and Celia was not in the drawing room to greet her guests; she was repairing the ravages to her face and her composure induced by a long session with a raging Sebastian which had run for over two hours and had only ended when he left the house just as Jay and Tory arrived.

'And the last words we heard were "I wish you well with your fucking Nazi",' whispered Tory to Adele, 'and he was actually crying, tears streaming down his face. Darling Sebastian, I wanted to run after him, but Jay said he was best left alone.'

'Izzie's at home,' said Adele. 'I do know that. She'll comfort him. Oh, poor, poor Sebastian. I just can't bear to think what he must be feeling. Why has she done this, why?'

'Darling I don't know.'

'She really is the hugest mystery,' said Adele with a sigh. 'Always has been. Oh dear. Well perhaps she will explain something of it tonight. Tory that is the most divine dress.'

'Not bad is it? Covers me and the bumpess quite neatly. She's growing awfully fast. I think she'll come out bigger than her brothers. Four months to go and look at me.'

Adele looked at Tory, in her high-waisted, softly sashed dress, her fair hair drawn smoothly back from her lovely face, and thought it was actually hard to tell she was pregnant at all.

'Don't fish for compliments, Tory Lytton,' she said briskly, 'but here's one anyway, you look divine. Now we'd better go in, and do our bit. Thank goodness Bunny isn't here, it would have been hideous—'

'Who's Bunny?'

'Lord Arden. Old nickname, he's called Peter, you see, and—'

'Peter Rabbit! Of course. I didn't realise you know him that well!'

'He helped me escape from France. In 1940. Got me – well –' she hesitated '– more or less got me – a place on one of the very last boats from Bordeaux. We travelled back together. Me and him, and the children of course.'

'I hadn't realised. It sounds madly exciting.'

'It was terrifying. But he is a sweetie.'

'So was Oliver. Your mother seems to attract gentlemen.'

'He's a much softer touch than Daddy,' said Adele. 'He wasn't anything like the pushover he seemed.'

'So Jay always tells me. Not my observation, but—'

'No it's true. His will was as strong as Mummy's and he was just as awkward in his own way, but he kept it well under wraps. Boy, darling, hallo, how many of your dynasty have you brought with you?'

'Only four,' said Boy Warwick, giving them both a kiss. 'God, I don't know which of you girls is more beautiful. Adele my darling, let me get you a drink. I'm acting as hostess for the time being.'

Adele relaxed; if Boy was in charge of things, then there was no need to worry. Of all his virtues, his ability to make any event run sweetly smooth was, in her view, the greatest.

Suddenly, absurdly, she longed for her father; sitting in his wheelchair by the fire, dispensing the odd mixture of charm and detachment that had been so uniquely his. There would have been no tantrums had he been

17

there. But then there would have been no cause for any, not this evening at any rate, she thought, shaking herself mentally, no shocking announcement to make, no well-buried griefs to disturb . . .

'I know,' said Venetia, giving her a kiss. 'I just thought that too.'

'How did you know—'

'I saw you looking at his place. And thought—'

'It seems so soon,' said Adele, 'that's what I keep thinking. So soon. A year, that's all. And—'

'When you get to my age, Adele, years are in shorter supply. You might think about that. It is one of the things I was going to speak about later.'

Adele turned. Her mother was smiling at her, apparently good-naturedly. Celia was pale but perfectly composed; she showed no sign of the intense emotional trauma she had just endured.

'I have just heard that Kit can't come. Such a pity. But – he's very busy.'

And very, very shocked and distressed, Venetia thought; hardly surprising that he had refused to attend.

'I'm – afraid Lucas can't come either,' said Adele. 'I'm so sorry. He's working terribly hard at school, and he's tired and – here, he's written you a note—'

Celia looked at it briefly, her face absolutely expressionless, then walked over and tossed it in the fire.

'Very rude,' she said, returning to Adele, 'to you, as well as to me. He has no manners Adele. You should teach him some.'

'Mummy—'

'Adele I don't want to hear yet again about Lucas's tragic childhood, the loss of his father, all that rubbish. Noni had exactly the same, with the difference that she could actually remember her father. Lucas trades on the whole thing quite disgracefully. And you shouldn't allow it. Tell him we didn't miss him for a single moment. Boy, dear, I think we should go in at once, everyone's here.'

Everyone except Kit, thought Venetia, following her mother into the dining room, taking her usual place in between her and Jay. With Giles at the other end of the table and Helena next to him, it was all so clearly prescribed by Celia that they never questioned it. The only changes came with death. Once Jay's mother had sat where he was now, and Oliver – of course – opposite her mother. Kit's place remained empty; Celia told Mrs Hardwicke, the housekeeper, to leave it.

'He may still come,' she said briefly, and then as Mrs Hardwicke continued to hover over it, 'Mrs Hardwicke, I said leave it laid.'

She didn't like Mrs Hardwicke very much; she couldn't forgive her for not being Brunson, the butler who had looked after the household for almost fifty years, and who had died, as if it was the only decent thing to do, a very few weeks after Oliver.

★

18

But Kit would not come. He was too angry, too shocked, his last shreds of faith in his mother's virtue finally destroyed.

'I don't feel I can ever meet her or speak to her again,' he had said to Izzie on the telephone, his voice raw with pain. 'I simply cannot understand her, Izzie. Is she absolutely wicked or absolutely mad?'

'Neither,' said Izzie, 'she's just your mother. Doing what she feels she must. A law unto herself.'

'A bad law. How is Sebastian?'

'Very very upset. And baffled, like you.'

'Should I come—'

'I don't know. I could ask him. If you like.'

'Yes. Would you, Izzie? Thank you.'

Izzie put the phone down, went into her father's study. He was sitting at his desk, staring out at the darkening sky, white, drawn, his eyes red-rimmed.

'Father—'

'Yes, what is it Isabella? I don't want to be continually disturbed, I know you mean well, but—'

'Kit's on the phone. Would you like him to come and—'

'No, no.' He shook his head, sighed heavily, managed to smile at her. 'I don't think so. But thank him for offering. I just want to be alone. Maybe in a day or two. Shut the door would you?'

'Yes father.'

Kit was getting drunk, he told her.

'Oh Kit. Shall I—'

'No. No, better not. Stay there with—'

'Yes of course. But tomorrow we could—'

'Yes, fine. About one?'

They communicated in half-sentences, rather like the twins. It was interesting, especially to those who did not know their history.

'Now I hope you will understand.' Celia had risen to her feet; dinner was over. 'And forgive what appears to be my rather shocking haste. As I said to Venetia, time is in short supply at my – our age. I loved Oliver very much. Very, very much. We had a fine marriage. And I think I made him happy.' She looked round the table, daring anyone to dissent. 'I certainly tried. But – now he is dead. And I am very lonely.' She paused; clearly feeling very strongly the need to explain, thought Adele. Celia hated admitting to any kind of weakness. And she would certainly perceive feeling lonely as that.

'But I do know,' said Celia, 'Oliver would have wanted me to be happy. Generosity was one of his many virtues. And I am quite certain that I shall be. I have known Lord Arden for a long time, I am extremely fond of him, and we have a great deal in common. We can have a few – I hope not too few – very good years. And having decided it was the right thing for me –

for us – to do, I also decided there should be no delay. As you know, having made a decision, I like to act. You are all adults; how I arrange my private life should not greatly affect you.'

Another silence; someone should say something, thought Venetia; even as the thought drifted into her head Boy stood up. 'I think we should all raise our glasses to you Celia. You deserve every happiness. To Celia.'

'To Grandmother,' said Henry Warwick, smiling, 'from our generation.' Celia smiled back at him, blew him a kiss down the table. A dutiful murmur of 'Grandmother' went round the room.

'Thank you,' said Celia. 'Now, there are some practical details. We plan to marry very quickly – perhaps even within the month. Just a quiet ceremony, in a register office, family only. Anything more would be – distasteful, we thought.'

And when did she ever do anything quietly, thought Helena. She'd manage to make a grand opera out of it somehow; tell half the press, invite a hundred friends . . .

'And I also wanted to explain more fully why I am leaving Lyttons. I feel I owe it to Lord Arden to be at his side, sharing his life fully. That is what he wants, that is why he asked me to marry him.'

God, thought Giles, she sounds like some foolish girl, not a matriarch of nearly seventy. Does she really think we're all going to believe in this claptrap? He felt almost sick with it, and wondered if he was the only one.

'And besides, I feel it is time for me to go. Oliver and I created Lyttons, in the same way we created this family. Together.'

A bit too far, Mummy, thought Adele. This borders on nauseating. She'd be weeping in a minute.

'I find doing it alone, running Lyttons without him, rather – unsatisfactory.'

And that's how she sees it, Jay thought, as 'doing it' still. Running Lyttons. After – what? He'd been there fourteen years. The implication being that they all, still, did what she said. Even if it wasn't quite the way things really were, it was strangely emasculating. He felt Tory's hand slide into his under the table; he squeezed it and smiled at her quickly. She always understood.

'Anyway, you can take it on now. You – three. I won't interfere, I assure you.' She looked round the table again, looking for dissent, her eyes amused. 'I dare say you will find that a little hard to believe. Time will convince you, I hope. And I won't be here much of the time. I intend to spend a lot of time in Scotland, and Lord Arden and I plan to travel a fair amount.'

So odd, the way she refers to him as 'Lord Arden', thought Venetia. As if we were children. She was reminded sharply and sadly of Celia's own mother, who had always addressed and referred to her own husband as 'Beckenham' throughout their entire married life.

'Obviously you will be wondering,' said Celia, 'about my share of Lyttons. Which Oliver and I held jointly until his death and which he left to me. I have thought long and hard about this. Whether I should relinquish that share. It would clearly make things easier for you. Otherwise you would always know that I could exercise my voting rights whenever I wanted to. Continue to interfere. Of course I do realise –' she paused, an expression of strong distaste on her still-fine features, '– that they only represent a tiny fraction of their old value. In purely financial terms. But from the point of view of the day-to-day running of the company, they are important.'

So for the love of God, let them go, thought Giles. And give them to me, let me at last, finally, at the age of forty-nine, as your oldest son, take my rightful place at the head of this publishing house. Running it, as my father did. She was looking at him now, yes, that must mean, mustn't it, it was to be his. God, it had been a long wait, but worth it—

'Now I'm not at all sure that is what your father would have wished. Lyttons was always his first concern; he would have wanted it, I know, to remain mine.'

Well, we know what that means, thought Venetia, it means that you're not retiring at all. You'll still be there. Day after day. This retirement is a farce. And she wondered why she felt a perverse and very slight stab of relief. Celia reached for a cigarette, lit it, inhaled deeply, and then smiled; an odd, self-satisfied little smile. 'On the other hand, Oliver always found it more difficult to move forward than I did. To recognise the need for change. I recognise that need now. I can see it would be hard for you to accept my decision to leave Lyttons while I still hold my shares. And I do want you to accept it – very much. So – I propose a compromise. What might be called a short-term solution. For just one year, I shall keep my shares. During which time I will play no part in the conduct of Lyttons. Either from an editorial or a commercial point of view.' She half smiled again; an ironic, self-mocking smile. 'I realise you may find this hard to believe; you will simply have to trust me.'

Very, very hard: impossible in fact, thought Giles.

'And after that year?' he said, as calmly as he could.

'After that year, I will distribute the shares.'

'Provided we run Lyttons to your satisfaction, I presume. And to Barty's, of course.'

That at least had hit home, had hurt. Celia visibly flinched; then 'I really don't think we have to consider Barty too much in this,' she said finally, her voice ice-edged. 'New York has always been perfectly happy to leave us to our own devices. Indeed they have very little choice, in my opinion. I shall distribute my shares after a year. I have very little doubt that I shall feel happy by then to do so. You are all extremely well equipped to run Lyttons, you have considerable talents and you complement one another.'

'But that's not quite enough,' said Jay. He was almost surprised to hear the words; he hadn't meant to speak.

'I'm sorry?' said Celia.

'You don't regard our talents as quite sufficient. To take over now, from the start of your retirement.'

'Jay, you haven't been listening,' said Celia patiently. 'I want you to take over now. Immediately. I am tired, I want to do other things with my life. Lord Arden and I want to travel, to spend time on the estate.'

Had it really happened, wondered Venetia. Had she really, finally, tired of it, the ebb and flow of the publishing year, the balance of it all, seeing the new books making their faltering way against the background of the great stalwarts, discovering the literary works required to maintain the gravitas of the house, searching constantly for new biographical subjects, meeting the need to get out the new catalogues, fighting the battle for bookshop windows at Christmas . . . all the things that Celia had seemed to regard as more important and indeed more exciting than anything else in the world? Were they really to be set aside in favour of trips down the Nile with an elderly peer, or even days on the moors peering down the barrel of a gun?

'Let me try to explain more fully,' said Celia, stubbing out her cigarette, reaching for another. She smokes too much thought Adele, it isn't good for her.

'This is not a game I'm playing. I am absolutely serious. I'm sixty-eight years old. For almost fifty of those years I have sat in my office at Lyttons. Enthralling, exciting, rewarding years. But with perhaps as little as ten left, I suddenly feel – what shall I say – daunted by what I have not done and not seen. I would go so far as to say it seems a dereliction of duty. A failure to discover and explore as much as I can. You will not find me at my desk tomorrow morning, nor on the telephone, nor at any publishing meetings, and nor will I be checking out Lyttons' position in any bookshops. I dare say I shall continue to take an interest in the overall publishing business, it would be difficult for me not to, but that is as far as I intend to go.'

'Then why not let your shares go?' said Giles.

'Because I feel I would be betraying your father's trust. He left his share in Lyttons to me; he was very clear about it. Almost his last words –' she stopped suddenly, her voice close to breaking, inhaled fiercely on her cigarette, '– his last words were about the company. How proud of it he was and –' her voice had steadied, and she looked around the table at each of them in turn, her dark eyes defiant, '– and of me. Of what we had done together. I cannot walk away entirely. Not yet. I have to reassure myself that Lyttons is in good hands and in good shape.'

Against their will they found themselves swung by her argument. It always happened, thought Venetia; you could go in to see her, ready to fight her, absolutely knowing you were right, and come out shaking your head, thinking how foolish you had been. Feeling guilty that you had dared to question her. She would have been a brilliant barrister . . .

'So in a year's time, possibly – probably even – I shall redistribute my shares. Does that seem reasonable to you now? Have I made my position clear?'

'Quite clear,' said Giles. His voice was quiet and deathly weary. He could see that once again he was beaten. That once again, he must wait. Wait for his birthright, wait to take his place at the head of Lyttons.

'Good. Well now, another toast. To Lyttons. Its future.'

'To Lyttons,' said everyone obediently.

'Good,' said Celia, briskly. 'Well I'm glad you are all – happy with the situation. As I am. Although,' she smiled again, the same self-mocking smile, 'I am sure you will understand this too, it will not be entirely easy for me.'

Good, thought Giles; I hope it's quite horribly difficult for you, I hope you are wretchedly unhappy with Lord Arden, I hope—

'Giles, we must go.' Helena was standing up, her face frozen with disapproval. 'Celia, do forgive us. Thank you for a very – interesting evening. George, Mary, say goodnight to your grandmother.'

She's very upset, Adele thought, watching her leave the room, and who could blame her really. She had spent the whole of her married life waiting for Giles's success and it had never come, not properly. The nearest had been the publication of his book, so well received and well reviewed; but that was in the past now. Poor Giles; white-faced, wretched, kissing his mother as only he could, quickly, hardly touching her face. And the children, the dreadfully dull George and Mary, kissing her dutifully too: but at least they had come. Had not sent rudely dismissive notes. She had got something terribly wrong with Lucas; and she didn't know how to put it right.

They were all gone by ten-thirty; Celia had expected that, had known – of course – that they disapproved of her and what she was doing, known too that she could not properly explain. It could not have been a Lytton evening, one of those endlessly warm, bright occasions, fuelled with gossip and literary allusion, with fierce argument and fun. They would never be the same again, those evenings. Not quite. She could see that now. Unbelievably, after half a century at the heart of the family, she had moved herself out from it. By choosing to marry Lord Arden, that was what she had done. She had shocked and saddened the family, she could see that very clearly. And she had lost Sebastian too: perhaps for ever. Even possibly, it seemed, Kit. Which was harder still.

But given the the savage and shocking degree to which she missed

Oliver, the discovery that she did not want to grow old alone, and neither did she want to find her way in the strange new world that publishing was fast becoming, or to slither into a position where she was regarded with pity or derision or both, and given that Bunny was sweet and funny and affectionate and rich – and impotent – she still felt she had served herself – and them – rather well.

CHAPTER 3

'I shall do what I like and you can't stop me. You're a witch, a wicked, wicked witch and I hope you die in a car crash today—'

'Thank you for that. No doubt you'll hear about it if I do. If not I'll see you later.'

Barty picked up her briefcase and walked out of the kitchen and across the hall; she was just opening the door when she heard footsteps running after her and felt a pair of small arms winding round her waist.

'Wait, stop, I didn't mean it, I love you really.'

'Jenna—'

'No, no, listen to me, it's true, I do, I do, so, so much.'

Barty turned round to look at her; at this difficult, dazzling eight-year-old who was at once the light and the blight of her life, whose two-year-old's temper tantrums had never eased, whose adoration of her was irresistible and whose hatred of her in the face of any opposition was alarming.

'Well I'm glad to hear that, Jenna. And I love you too. But you are not going to host a sailing party at South Lodge. And that is the end of the matter.'

'But why not?'

'Because sailing is dangerous. And I am not going to be held responsible for the possible drowning of a dozen little girls.'

'We wouldn't drown. That's so silly. We would be very careful. And it wouldn't be on the ocean, it would be on the creek.'

'Jenna,' said Barty, setting her briefcase down, realising reluctantly that she had to give this her full attention, 'you were going to be very careful when you got on Lee's pony last autumn. But you fell off and broke your arm. You were going to be careful when you went down that run in the Catskills in January and broke your ankle. You were going to be careful when you climbed that tree at South Lodge last summer and fell out of it and concussed yourself. You can't be careful for yourself, let alone twelve other people. Sailing is potentially a very dangerous thing to do. Now you can have a weekend party, everyone can stay, and you can all go riding on

25

the shore, but you are not going out in sailing boats and that is all there is to it. All right?'

Jenna looked at her; her lovely little heart-shaped face grief-stricken, her extraordinary green-blue eyes filled with tears.

'But Mummy, I've told them now. I shall look so stupid. Please, please, just two of us at a time. And over at Sag Harbor, of course, not the ocean—'

'Jenna no. You'll have to un-tell them. And look stupid. It's not fatal. In any case, I would put money on their mothers all refusing to allow them to come. Now, why don't you get your bag and I'll give you a lift to school.'

Jenna gave it a last shot.

'Please! Don't you love me at all?'

'Very much. So much that I want you and indeed your friends to live to grow up. Come on. Or you'll have to walk with Maria.'

'I like walking,' said Jenna, 'I'm not ready.'

She might have recognised defeat, but she wasn't prepared for total surrender.

'Fine. See you tonight. Love you.'

Silence. Barty walked out of the door of Number Seven, the house on the Upper East Side she had bought when she and Jenna had moved to New York, and closed it very firmly. She was fifty yards down the street when the door opened again, and she heard Jenna shout.

'Love you too.'

She had won then: this time.

She reached her office at Lyttons New York in its brownstone in Gramercy Park and felt calmer even as she looked up at it; many other publishers were in huge modern buildings now in midtown, but Barty adored the gracious mansion-style setting of her workplace, with its iron railings and wide steps running up to the huge front door. She was also extremely excited about her recent acquisition of the house next door to accommodate Lyttons' slow but steady growth. Five senior editors now, each with their own team; as well as an editorial director, Marcus Forrest, with whom she had an interesting love-hate relationship; a fine list, of both non-fiction and fiction; a steady presence in the best-seller lists; along with a reputation for publishing both popular and literary books. And of course, overall control of Lyttons London, not merely financial but editorial – although that was a discipline rather lightly exercised. Budgets were one thing and she was required to approve them; purchases of books, of authors, promotional plans and scheduling quite another. She walked into her office on the first floor and sank slightly wearily at her desk; she found her run-ins with Jenna extremely exhausting. Exactly as those with Jenna's father had been . . .

Her secretary, Cindy Phillips, appeared with a steaming mug of coffee; she knew what her boss's priorities were. No offer of any book, however exciting, no review however brilliant, no sales figures however good – or bad – were given a moment's consideration until the first coffee of the day was on Barty's desk. She picked it up, smiled at Cindy gratefully. 'Thank you. Anything urgent?'

'Not really.'

'Fine. I'll buzz you in a minute.'

She sat drinking the coffee, looking at the picture of Laurence in its silver frame on her desk. Laurence: who Jenna resembled so absolutely, in every way; whose tantrums had been as powerful and exhausting, whose love had been as suffocating, whose emotional blackmail had been as threatening. Who she had loved so very, very much. Who she still missed quite dreadfully . . . She flipped through her post: the usual letters from bookshops and agents, invitations to functions, circulars from various professional bodies – and one from England. Addressed in Geordie MacColl's unmistakable scrawl. Geordie, who she still felt a most proprietary affection for, having discovered him – what was it, God, almost twenty years earlier – Geordie, whose books still sold and sold, Geordie, who everyone loved, even Celia.

Dearest Barty,

Just to let you know *Wild Horses* is at No. 5 in the *Sunday Times*, Bumpus has given it an entire window and it is going to be the *Evening Standard* Book of the Month for May. Everyone is very delighted with it.

Everyone is not in the least delighted with Celia however. The family is shocked, Sebastian is not speaking to her, Kit refuses to go to the house (which she has said she will continue to live in from time to time, and what does that say for Lord Ardent – the family's name for him – and his ardour I wonder). I do so hope you will come to the wedding. She would be heartbroken if you did not (if, indeed, she has a heart to break which I know is something constantly under debate), and if you could bring Jenna then that would be quite wonderful.

Adele sends her best love, and so does your beautiful and brilliant god-daughter. And mine to you.

Geordie

Well, thought Barty, it would perhaps make up for the non-sailing party. Going to London, a month before the Coronation. Staying on for it perhaps. And she really did not want to break Celia's heart. On the other hand, it did rather feel like disloyalty to her beloved Wol.

'I have some lovely news,' said Izzie. 'Barty is coming over for the wedding. And bringing Jenna with her.'

Sebastian scowled at her. 'I'm not sure I like that, I would have expected more loyalty from Barty.'

27

'Father really! Barty is the loyallest person in the world. And her loyalty obviously takes in Celia. She always says she owes her everything.'

'Through gritted teeth. Of course she doesn't. What Celia did to Barty was of very questionable virtue. It did more for her own ego than it did for Barty—'

'Oh, Father.' Izzie sighed, put down her orange juice. 'You really can't go on like this. Celia is going to marry Lord Arden, and I know it's terrible for you—'

'Absolute nonsense. It is nothing to me who she does or doesn't marry.'

Izzie ignored this. 'Well anyway, do you really think Barty would be head of Lyttons if she'd been left where she was all those years ago with her eight brothers and sisters in the slums of London?'

'Quite possibly yes,' said Sebastian, 'she is hugely talented.' Then he met Izzie's eyes and smiled reluctantly. 'Oh all right. Possibly not. But the fact is that Celia may have given Barty everything she thought she needed, but she deprived her of the one thing that really mattered. Her family.'

'Yes Father.' Izzie had heard this many times before.

'Anyway, I'm very pleased that she's coming to London. Although I'm not sure if I look forward to meeting that dreadful child again. Typical American, free-ranging, undisciplined—'

'I think Jenna's lovely. Not undisciplined at all.'

'Rubbish,' said Sebastian. He smiled at her, his fierce old face suddenly tender. 'What would I do without you, my darling? I don't know. Now, you write back to Barty and say she can stay here if she wants to. That'll annoy Celia.'

'Yes, Father, all right. I must go.'

She went over to him and gave him a kiss. He had visibly cheered up at the thought of seeing Barty. He felt such a very strong bond with her. She supposed it was partly because of their similar circumstances . . . lone parents, in the face of dreadful grief. Only Barty had adored Jenna from the beginning; she had not set her apart, to spend her earliest years in an atmosphere of isolation and dislike . . .

Thank goodness, just thank goodness, Izzie thought, as she started up her small Austin Seven, she didn't work at Lyttons. Just thinking about the torn loyalties made her shudder. She almost had; there had been a lot of pressure on her, after Oxford, to join the firm. Celia had been very keen and so had her father. But she had resisted, wanting (like Barty she supposed) to make her own way.

She worked for Michael Joseph where she was the publicity manager and showed considerable flair; she was rather a pet of the great Michael Joseph (known in the firm as MJ), and spent quite a lot of time in his office, at the back of the house in Bloomsbury Street being briefed on various projects. 'We want elegant copy,' he would say, and elegant copy Izzie produced, for book jackets and catalogues, and for advertisements which she secretly thought should be much more lively, but which said things like 'The New Monica Dickens' or 'C.S. Forester. His new book.' What Izzie secretly yearned to write was the kind of advertising copy so popular in the United States, hard-hitting plays on words. But there was no way anything like that was going to come out of her department at Michael Joseph.

Still, it was a wonderful first job, and she was very happy there. She was already a modestly well-known figure in the publishing world. Although this was due in part, as she was the first to admit, to being the great Sebastian Brooke's daughter, she had won a place in it in her own right, through her own talent and her own graceful way with words. She was also very popular; everyone loved her, she was so gentle and sweet-natured and, with her long golden-brown hair and her huge dreamy eyes, she looked rather like a poet herself. And of course like her mother, as those in the literary world who had met Pandora during her brief marriage to Sebastian, frequently remarked.

Izzie was terribly pleased that Barty was coming to the wedding. She adored her. She had been one of the people who had been kindest to her and shown her affection during the first few lonely years of her life; when she had gone away to New York for the first time, Izzie had felt her heart would break. She could still remember standing at the window with her nanny, watching Barty walk down the road after saying goodbye and crying until she could cry no more and then falling asleep on Nanny's lap.

Her joy when Barty had – well – taken the Lyttons on and beaten them at their own game had been intense. Not that she wasn't fond of the Lyttons, she was, she had adored Wol, as Barty had called Oliver, and she loved the twins, especially Adele, and of course Noni. They had all lived together for a while, during the war, at Ashingham, Celia's parents' estate, and Adele had stood up for her when Kit was being so unkind to her, when he had first come back from the war. And had helped her through the other most difficult time in her life ... which even now she could hardly bear to think about.

She was going to supper with Adele that evening; it would be fun. She loved them all; Adele and Noni were both like sisters to her, and Geordie – well, she adored Geordie, had a bit of a crush on him in fact. He was so charming and handsome, and he had such gorgeous clothes, and he flirted with her just about enough, not so that she got embarrassed, but so that she felt attractive and interesting. And he still looked so young – younger than Adele, if the truth were told. She just hoped Lucas wouldn't be too much in evidence. He cast such a blight over everything. Beastly little boy.

'I'm going to change publishers,' said Kit. He smiled in Sebastian's direction: it was not an entirely pleasant smile.

'Really?'

'Yes. I just feel I have to make some kind of a protest. Something which will hurt my mother.'

'But it won't. Surely. I had the same thought. But it would hurt Lyttons, and Giles and Venetia and Jay, not Celia. She's gone, walked away.'

'But she hasn't, has she? Not really. She's still got her shares. And she'll be terribly angry. And hurt.'

'Kit—' Sebastian hesitated. He hadn't thought he could be saying this. 'Kit, is hurting her terribly really what you want?'

'Yes,' said Kit briefly, 'it is. I can't bear this marriage. I'd finally learned to trust her again, to accept what she had done and why—'

'What we had done,' said Sebastian quietly.

A silence. Then, 'Yes. Yes, all right. Both of you. And somehow this negates that trust. It's ugly. It distorts everything. You must see that.'

'I do,' said Sebastian. 'Of course. But—'

'There aren't any buts. She is absolutely amoral. And I'm going to leave.'

'Well – I suppose it's your decision. I'm still not sure it's a wise one.'

'It's not meant to be wise,' said Kit. He sounded suddenly like a sulky small boy. 'It's meant to be – well, a strong statement.'

'It's certainly that. Where will you go, do you think? Look out, old chap, you nearly knocked my coffee over.'

'Sorry. Wasn't looking.' He smiled suddenly, a nicer smile. 'Funny how I still use those words. I don't know where . . . I thought I might talk to Izzie about Michael Joseph.'

'It's an idea. They have some fine authors. I'm sure they'd be very pleased to talk to you. Your track record is pretty good. Five big sellers now. It will cause a big stir, Kit, in the publishing world.'

'I know,' said Kit, 'not all of it very tasty, either. I'm afraid I can see the articles now, can't you? And there'll be a lot of schmaltz too. I'm such good copy, aren't I? The war hero and – well all that. God I hate it. Still, I'm not stupid.' He sighed. 'Schmaltz sells.'

'Kit you mustn't be bitter. It's your books that sell.'

'Sebastian, I do assure you I try not to be bitter. And I know in some ways I'm very lucky. But it's still – hard. Terribly hard.'

'Of course it is,' said Sebastian. His voice was very gentle as he looked at Kit.

There was a long silence: then, 'Well anyway, I've made up my mind. I'm going to see them all this afternoon. I must go. Friday all right?'

'Of course,' said Sebastian, 'what would Friday be without our dinners, Kit? Here, let me help you. You've left your hat behind.'

'Have I?' He sounded surprised. 'I'd forgotten I'd worn one. I'm not quite the thing today, I'm afraid. Thanks.'

He put his hat on, picked up his stick, made his way across the room.

''Bye Sebastian. Thanks for listening. And let me know when you see the first article, won't you? I wonder what it will say? New battlefield for war hero author? War hero deserts Lyttons? Oh, they'll have a field day.'

'I think,' said Sebastian, his voice suddenly more cheerful, 'it will say "Publishers battle over Christopher Lytton." You'll get a lot of offers, Kit, mark my words. Now here's Marks with the car.'

'Good. New Lytton House please, Marks.'

Sebastian watched the car drive away. It was one of Kit's biggest extravagances; he was slightly embarrassed about it, his lifestyle in other ways was so modest, his small mews house in Kensington, his rather shabby clothes . . . But the car made his life so much easier and more efficient. Everyone told him it was worth it.

Sebastian went back into the house, the house on the edge of Primrose Hill which he had bought with the proceeds of the first *Meridian*, and out into the garden. Thinking that he too had once threatened to leave Lyttons, with exactly the same intention as Kit. To hurt Celia. And in the end had not been able to. It was all so very long ago . . .

Adele walked into the house and threw her bag down on the hall table.

'I'm back!'

Silence. Everyone was obviously out. Damn. She so wanted to tell them all about it. She went into the kitchen, filled the kettle, stared out at the tiny garden, smiling. Then she turned round and jumped.

'Lucas! I didn't see you. Didn't you hear me come in?'

'Of course. But I was busy.'

'Yes, I see. Going well, your essay?'

'All right.'

She sighed inwardly. Then, 'I've just come from the palace.'

'Oh yes?'

'We were being briefed about the Coronation. It's going to be so wonderful, Lucas. I still can't believe it. We have the most marvellous access to everything, both inside and outside the Abbey. It's going to be such a wonderful day, Commander Colville, he's the Press Officer, says we must all pray for good weather, but I can't believe it will rain on such a day. It's June after all, and—'

'Mother, I'm sorry, but I really am trying to work. Perhaps we could discuss the Coronation later.'

Adele sighed. 'Yes of course. Sorry Lucas. You must get on.'

She went upstairs with her coffee, tears rising absurdly in her eyes. He had such capacity to hurt her. What was she going to do with him? What?

'That is terrible news,' said Jay, walking back into the board room. The other two looked at him. There was no need to reply.

'I just don't understand it,' said Giles finally. 'Why's he done it?'

31

'Oh Giles,' said Venetia impatiently, 'it's to get at Mummy of course. It's all he can do. Apart from refusing to see her or talk to her.'

'But she's gone,' said Giles, 'it's a meaningless gesture. That's what's so odd about it. Everyone will think he's going because she won't be here any more.'

'Not meaningless to him. He won't care about what everyone will think. It's her he wants to hurt. He knows she'll be upset. Which she will be, with him walking out on the family firm. And anyway, she hasn't gone. She's still got her shares.'

'I suppose so,' said Jay, walking over to the drinks cabinet. 'But – it's not straightforward, is it? She might even be pleased. Think he's the first in a long line of authors walking out. That Lyttons can't go on without her. Venetia, drink?'

'Yes, please. Gin and tonic.'

'Same for me,' said Giles. 'Jay, she can't think that.'

'Of course she can. She knows Lyttons won't be the same without her. She *is* Lyttons. She embodies it, its style, its history. And now it will change.'

'I trust it will. It has to. We have to move with the times,' said Giles stiffly. 'Our mother was fairly adept at not doing that.'

'That's not fair,' said Venetia. 'I can still remember raging rows with Daddy when she was trying to persuade him to go into paperbacks, to take on popular authors, to recognise changes in public taste. She was marvellous at moving with the times. And so was your mother, Jay, to a lesser degree. I can still hear Daddy saying "not you as well, LM" when she took Mummy's side. Not that it did either of them any good. If anyone was stuck in the past it was Daddy.'

Giles said nothing, drained his glass.

'I do fear that people might take their cue from this,' said Jay soberly, 'and what about the authors she did edit, Lady Annabel, for instance, Sebastian of course—'

'Sebastian won't go,' said Venetia firmly. 'I know he won't. He feels part of Lyttons too. He's an honorary Lytton, always has been.'

'Have you talked to him about it? After all, Celia has always edited him.'

'No,' she said, sounding slightly less confident.

'I think you should.'

'Shouldn't you? You're the editoral director.'

'Possibly,' said Jay with a sigh. 'I've been putting it off.'

'Well anyway, Kit is going,' said Venetia, 'and it's bad. He's always the big lead in the Christmas books for children, and with Sebastian only doing his Coronation edition this year . . . Anyone who takes Kit on will make sure there's a lot of publicity about it. It's all so perfect. He's the publicist's gift. War hero. Lady Celia's youngest son—'

'Blind,' said Jay.

The other two stared at him. He looked back at them, smiled slightly shame-faced.

'Well it's true. I don't know why everyone pussyfoots round it. It's part of his myth. You know it is. It's a wonderful story. It's always been part of his legend. *Jeunesse dorée*, Battle of Britain pilot, giving his sight for his country, all that sort of thing. I mean—'

'I hope you're not implying he makes capital out of it,' said Giles stiffly.

'Of course I'm not. I know part of him hates it. But it does him no harm professionally.'

'I think that's a very crude remark,' said Giles, 'if you don't mind me saying so.'

'Oh stop it,' said Venetia. 'Both of you. It's irrelevant to this discussion.'

'Not entirely,' said Jay. 'It's all part of his capacity for generating publicity. Which will be very bad for us. Look, I'm only speaking frankly. I suppose no amount of money could persuade Kit to stay?'

'He said it wouldn't. Surely you heard that.'

'I know. But there's a difference between saying something and meaning it. If we made him a really huge offer—'

'Jay, it wouldn't make the slightest difference. Honestly. This is absolutely about principle. And besides, he has more than enough money. And it's not as if he has a family to support or anything, poor darling. You do have to get that into your head. No, we're going to lose him. And you know what happens when a major author leaves. All the others watch him, wondering why. It could be quite dangerous. For Lyttons and for all of us.'

CHAPTER 4

She had been afraid it would be ghastly and it was. Awkward, stiff, even sad: a day to be forgotten as quickly as possible. Exactly what a wedding day should not be. But at least it was over, Barty thought, sinking down on to her bed: for that everyone was grateful. Waiting for it, trying not to mind, pretending it was actually perfectly all right, fearing it was going to deteriorate, that had been the worst part.

Boy Warwick had, as always, done much to keep things not only calm, but comparatively easy: 'She's going to do it,' he said one evening over dinner to the twins, 'and there's no point there being some dreadful family rift over it. He's a perfectly decent chap, with luck he'll make her happy, there's absolutely nothing wrong with him; in fact he was jolly good to you, Adele, wasn't he?'

Adele nodded; her escape from wartime France and indeed Bunny Arden's part in it was something she tried not to think about too much, bringing back memories that were not only terrifying but which filled her with remorse and shame.

'Jolly good, yes,' she said finally.

'There is something wrong with him, though,' said Venetia soberly, 'you know there is, Boy. You hated it at the time.'

'I know, I know. But we all make errors of judgement.'

'Boy! It was a bit more than that. He was a leading appeaser. Best buddies with Oswald Mosley. Guest of Goering even. He influenced Mummy horribly. And it didn't help Adele much either, did it, Luc being Jewish and everything?'

'Well – he repented.'

'And so did Mummy,' said Adele, 'she was very brave, came to Paris specially to apologise to both Luc and me. And he did then help me, of course he did. I wouldn't have got home without him. So—'

'Exactly. So we should accept him and make her happy. Three-line whip now girls, all children present, *all* – Adele, don't look like that – including Lucas.'

'Yes, all right. It's just that—'

'What?'

'I know,' said Venetia, 'mine too. All of them have said it.'

'What?' said Boy wearily.

'How can she be getting married again so soon. I wonder too, you know. Daddy only died a year ago. I mean, why marry Lord Arden? They can be friends. Who'd care anyway?'

'I am marrying him,' Celia said firmly to Barty over dinner soon after she had arrived, 'because I want everything cut and dried. I don't want a lot of gossipy speculation. About him or indeed anyone else. I don't like disorder, Barty. As you know.'

'Yes, I do know,' said Barty. 'But—'

'I loved Oliver very much,' said Celia, 'very, very much. He was a marvellous person, and his courage was extraordinary. He was a superb father, and particularly so, I would say, to you. Even more than to his own children. Of course I shouldn't say that. I never have before and I never will again. But I think it's important we should both acknowledge it. I know how much he meant to you. And I think I know how this marriage must offend you.'

Barty met her eyes steadily. 'It does,' she said, 'a little.'

'Barty, I am getting older. Not old, of course, but older. Another fact I don't often acknowledge. And I find I don't like, these days, being alone. It astonished me, as a matter of fact. I have always enjoyed my own company. As much as I have enjoyed my work. Perhaps the loss of those two enjoyments go hand in hand.'

'Celia,' said Barty, 'I absolutely cannot believe this loss of enjoyment in your work is permanent. Work, Lyttons, is your life. It always has been.'

'It took me by surprise as well,' said Celia, and she looked suddenly vulnerable. 'I thought it was temporary; grief, weariness after Oliver's death, so much change in the industry. I scarcely recognise it, you know, there are hardly any firms left in family ownership, they're all run as public companies by wretched conglomerates, none of them with any personality. I would never have dreamed that Collins would sell shares to the public. Or Longmans. It's absolutely appalling.' She spoke as if they had sold state secrets to the KGB rather than sought essential capitalisation for their companies. 'The fact is, as of course you know, Barty, once you are answerable to shareholders, you lose the ability to do what your instinct tells you is right.'

Barty managed not to point out that without her own intervention Lyttons too would have had to seek recapitalisation and moved out of family control. Which, she supposed, it had in a way. She smiled rather coolly at Celia, waiting for some kind of acknowledgement; it did not come.

'And all this other nonsense, Penguin forming exclusive agreements with certain other publishers, it can't be right. They should be completely independent, to decide what they want. And this talk of marketing! Research into why people buy books. People buy books for one reason and one reason only: because they want to read them. Michael Joseph said something very similar only the other day. You know what they say about the camel, I suppose?'

Barty said she did not.

'The camel is a horse designed by a committee. I tell you Barty, a lot of camels will be published in the next few years. Instinct is the only thing that should guide a house, editorial instinct. Anyway, it doesn't matter to me in the very least. As I said, I have lost interest in the whole business. I can take no real pleasure in it. It is rather dreadful, actually,' she added, 'it's like losing my identity, like becoming a different person. Or losing one of my senses. I hope it never happens to you.'

Barty was silent.

'Anyway, I have made my decisions. And I feel happier and easier. Bunny Arden – have you met him, I can't remember?'

'No,' said Barty, 'I don't think so.'

'He's very sweet. I hope you like him. And he is what I need at this stage in my life. I have absolutely no doubts at all. I expected them, to be frank with you, but they have not arrived. I feel at peace with myself. I intend to be a good wife to Bunny, supportive of whatever he wants to do.' She smiled at Barty, a wry, conspiratorial smile. 'It's a novel sensation. Now, I don't expect you to rejoice at what I am doing. But I would like you to understand, and to try to approve.'

'I will. Of course I will,' said Barty carefully. She found Celia's protestations deeply unconvincing. It was rather as if she had suddenly embraced a different faith or announced her intention to vote Labour and to give everything she had to the poor. She took a deep breath. 'Anyway, Celia, I am very glad that you're keeping your shares. I feel that if you do – recant—'

'A strange word,' said Celia.

'Perhaps. Well, anyway, if you do start missing it all – which I still think you might – you can get back without too much difficulty. The others probably wouldn't like to hear me saying that,' she added.

'Probably not. Of course it won't happen, and I know I won't miss it, but I'm very touched that you feel like that. Touched and surprised.'

'Celia, I'm not a complete idiot,' said Barty. 'I value you more than anyone or anything else in the company. You know I do.'

'Well, thank you. Now what else did you want to say? I can tell there's something.'

'Well –' she hesitated, '– well, I just feel that Wol would be—'

'Distressed? At my remarrying so soon?'

'Yes. A bit.'

'Barty, I really don't think he would. I honestly believe that. I think he would be quite happy to see me become Lady Arden. And indeed to be leaving Lyttons.'

Another silence. Then Celia leaned forward, put her hand over Barty's.

'Now I can tell you what *would* have caused him distress. My marrying – well, marrying someone else.'

Barty looked at her. 'Do you really think so?'

'I know so, Barty. Absolutely. That would have hurt him very badly. Very badly indeed.'

Just the same, Oliver's gentle, charming presence haunted the marriage ceremony at Chelsea Register Office and later the reception in Lord Arden's house in Belgrave Square. There was something chilly and joyless about the whole day, however much champagne went down, however amusing and flattering Boy Warwick's speech, however determinedly everyone smiled and joked and kissed, however beautiful and happy Celia looked: and she did look both. She wore a dazzling suit from Balenciaga – 'Well one doesn't get married every day' – in palest blue shantung with the new bloused jacket, and a hugely wide feather and straw hat by Simone Mirman, and when the registrar declared them man and wife, Celia smiled and leaned forward to kiss Bunny and knocked the hat crooked. It was one of the few spontaneously joyful moments of the day.

Celia had been very hurt by the polite refusal of her invitation from both Oliver's brothers.

'I don't believe she really thought either of them would come,' said Adele. 'Apart from anything else, Robert is quite old now and it's a frightful journey for him, even by plane.'

'I know, but I don't think she minds quite so much about him. It's Jack, you know how she loves him.'

'Well that's a long journey too, all the way from California, and Lily's very frail, isn't she? With her arthritis, poor old darling.'

'All those high kicks in her youth, I expect,' said Venetia with a sigh. She and Adele both adored Jack's wife; Lily had been a chorus girl when she met Jack, and a very briefly twinkling star of the silver screen in the Twenties. They had returned for a short while to England to live, but the climate had been bad for Lily; and without all their friends in Hollywood they had been lonely and bored. But Celia had loved Jack, who was the same age as her to the day, and she had really thought he would make the trip for her, had even offered to pay the fare, knowing he and Lily were far from well-off. But a charmingly firm note had come back, saying it would be quite impossible, and wishing her every happiness.

'I'm afraid they both disapprove dreadfully,' Venetia said, 'and, I must say, one can—'

'I know, of course one can. But it doesn't hurt her any the less. Oh dear. She's paying quite a price, isn't she?' said Adele.

'Quite a price. Too high, if you ask me.'

'Just to—'

'I know.'

Kit had absolutely refused, despite everyone's pleading, to come. And so had Sebastian. Two great brooding absences, darkening the day. Celia had not expected Sebastian to come, of course, although she had insisted on inviting him, but Kit, her beloved Kit, she had hoped until the last possible moment that he would arrive. Each time the bell rang she jumped, paused in what she was saying, every time the drawing-room door opened, she looked at it, frozen-still, her dark eyes hopeful, and each time when it was only more flowers, another telegram, her smile became brighter, more brittle, and her face beneath its crown of osprey feathers became wearier, and paler.

'Did she really think he was going to come?' whispered Adele to Venetia, looking at her as Celia finished her own small speech, thanking everyone for coming, and for making it such a happy family occasion, her voice faltering over the word 'family'.

'You know Mummy. If she wants something really badly, she gets it. And she wanted this really badly. I think he might have come, I must say. If only for half an hour. Boy went round last night, you know, and begged him. Kit said he was amazed Boy could even think such a thing.'

'So where—'

'I should think, wouldn't you?'

'Yes.'

And what would LM have made of this? Barty thought, watching Lord Arden and Celia cut the cake; LM, Oliver's older sister, his partner in the great early days of Lyttons, with her fierce morals, her unbending loyalties. How would she regard this extraordinary occasion and would she indeed have been there herself, or stayed at home, making her own quiet, loyal protest? She suddenly found Jay next to her, smiled at him rather wanly. He grinned back, refilled her glass.

'Lord Arden's butler's a bit slow on the glass charging. I thought I'd take over. We all need it.'

'I was just thinking about your mother,' she said.

'Yes. Me too.'

'She'd have hated it, wouldn't she?'

'I'm not sure,' he said, surprising her. 'She was a very pragmatic old bird, you know. And she adored Celia. She'd have wanted her to be happy.'

'Yes, but Jay, I don't think she will be. He's – well, he's an idiot.'

He grinned. 'He is a bit. But there's no doubt he loves her. And you know what, he's got a superb model railway upstairs. I've just seen it. So

38

dear old Gordon would have approved of him as well. The hours we spent playing with his, it annoyed Mother so much. She always said she was going to cite Hornby as co-respondent in their divorce.'

'I miss Gordon,' said Barty with a sigh, and it was true, Gordon Robinson's tall, erect figure was another great loss in the room.

'Not as much as I do. He might not have been my dad, but he was a wonderful father,' said Jay. 'The trouble was, he missed Mother so dreadfully that it was half a life he was leading. Now look, Tory's doing her bit for family togetherness, flirting away with old Bunny. Come on Barty, drink up and let's go and join them. You might find he has hidden depths.'

'I doubt it,' said Barty with a sigh. 'Hidden shallows more like it. But if anyone can bring out the best in him, Tory can. You did well marrying her, Jay.'

'I know it,' he said with a touch of complacency in his voice.

Adele had been right; Kit was with Sebastian. Izzie had been invited to the wedding, but had written a sweetly firm note to Celia, saying she knew she would understand that her attendance was almost impossible. Celia had telephoned her to say she did indeed understand, but she hoped that Izzie would at least wish her well.

'I wish you very, very well, dear Celia,' said Izzie. 'I hope you are very happy. And I would have loved to be there, but I'm glad you understand. Perhaps I could come and see you some time soon and meet Lord Arden; I hear he's very sweet.'

This was a complete untruth, she had heard nothing particularly good about Lord Arden at all, even Henry Warwick declared him a silly old buffer, but she knew it would please Celia. She had gone thankfully to work that day, casting a nervous glance at her father's study door; she came home to find him and Kit completely drunk, singing, for some reason neither of them could clearly understand, 'Lili Marlene'.

She phoned Kit's driver, asked him to come and fetch him and managed somehow to get her father up to bed. He looked up at her from his pillows, clearly focussing with great difficulty.

'Silly fucking bitch,' he said almost cheerfully, then turned on his side and fell instantly asleep. But she woke in the night to hear him moving heavily around, and when she went downstairs early in the morning, he was sitting at the kitchen table, his head in his hands.

'Don't even begin to ask how I'm feeling,' he said glaring at her, 'it won't make pretty hearing. Make me some tea, would you, and bring it to my study. I've got work to do. *McCalls* magazine want a short story within the week, bloody inconsiderate, but I said I'd do it, God knows why.'

It was the last time he spoke to her for several days, apart from roaring orders from his study for more tea, toast, coffee, whisky; she could only offer silent thanks to the editor at *McCalls* and his lack of consideration.

CHAPTER 5

'And now the kiss.' The sombre, almost reverent voice broke into the moment; after the splendour, the ritual of the occasion, the simple fact of the husband bending to kiss his wife, was deeply moving.

'She looks so young,' whispered Venetia. 'So terribly young.'

'And he's so handsome,' hissed Jenna. 'Like a prince in a story book.'

The choir launched into another anthem; there was a stir in the Abbey. In the front pew a tiny figure, dressed in white silk, watched with wide-eyed awe.

'He's so sweet, the little prince,' said Izzie, 'so tiny.'

'He's very good,' said Venetia briskly. 'I can't imagine any of mine sitting through that in silence at four years old.

'Yes, well, he's probably not been spoilt from conception,' said Boy lightly. 'More champagne, everyone?'

'Please,' said Geordie, waving his glass at him, 'Oh, isn't this music wonderful?'

'It's all wonderful,' said Venetia. 'What a day. And just think Adele is there, in the Abbey, it's just unbelievable.'

'So are Lord and Lady Arden,' said Boy just slightly tartly. 'Shall we see if we can spot them? Look, they're passing the peers' gallery now.'

They looked at the small black-and-white screen, at the sea of faces.

'There they are,' said Jenna. 'I saw them. Look, there, look.'

'Jenna, you can't possibly see anything,' said Barty, laughing.

'I can. And I did. I saw Aunt Celia, I—'

'Yes all right. If you say so.'

'I do say so.'

'I saw her too,' said a determined voice. It belonged to Lucy, the youngest Warwick, just six years old. 'Didn't I, Jenna?'

'Yes, she did.'

Jenna and Lucy had formed a strong bond; Lucy saw the eight-year-old Jenna as virtually an adult, a view which Jenna fervently encouraged.

'Well that was marvellous. Really marvellous. You know, don't you, that the Earl Marshal and the Archbishop of Canterbury both fought long and hard to keep the cameras out of the Abbey?'

'Not really!' said Barty.

'Really. Apart from the fact it meant tradesmen would have to be in the Abbey—'

'Tradesmen?'

'Yes, cameramen and so on. Don't look at me like that, Barty, it's true. And also, of course, it meant people might be watching it in unsuitable places like pubs.'

'I heard that one,' said Henry, 'and that the men might not even take their hats off.'

'So there you are. Now, Venetia, my darling, shall we have some food? I think they can manage without us for a few minutes. Then we can watch the procession from the balcony.'

Boy had recently acquired a large building in St James's and had not yet sold it on; it had provided a perfect base for family viewing of the Coronation. Even Giles and Helena had been unable to resist the opportunity; Giles had originally said that he had no interest in the event whatsoever, but his family had overruled him.

'You needn't come, Father,' the rather lumpy Mary had said, 'but George and I are going, and Mother said if we went she would feel it was rude not to come too.'

Giles had been astonished, Helena was the last person in the world he would have expected to be caught up in Coronation fever; he made a pompous little speech about jingoism and the Coronation being an anachronism and said he had no intention of going. But he had joined them in the end.

'We've commissioned a book on the thing, I can't afford to ignore it.'

'Of course not,' said Helena.

They had all been in the building since seven; the routes into the capital had been closed at eight. They had watched the procession to the Abbey, in the damp drizzle, waving their flags and cheering. A wave of affection and happiness had swept over London; thousands of people had slept on the streets all night, uncomplaining in spite of the rain. It was as if all the hardship and loss of the past fifteen years were justified by this one heady day. A young and beautiful woman had been crowned, the mystic spectacle watched by millions, thanks to the new wonder of television, and as people everywhere were saying, England had never been greater than with a queen on the throne. And the news that morning that Everest had been conquered by Sir Edmund Hillary and his British team had come as an extra piece of glory on this day when the country was celebrating its very existence.

'The colours are superb,' said Geordie, looking out of the window. 'It's better in its way than if the sun was shining, it's as if the red, white and blue had been painted on a black-and-white photograph. Adele will make a lot of that.'

'I wonder where she is? A better view than Mummy, from all accounts.'

'I look forward to the comparing of notes,' said Boy lightly.

'I just wish we had a royal family,' said Jenna, 'it's so romantic. It's dreadfully dull, just having presidents. Elizabeth is just beautiful, and Philip's so terribly handsome. Mamie Eisenhower is just so, so plain.'

'Jenna!' said Barty, 'that is no way to describe your president's wife.'

'It is because it's true,' she said coolly, with a toss of her red-gold hair. 'How would you describe her?'

'Plain,' said Geordie, laughing. 'Sorry, Barty. It would be wonderful to have a dazzling young First Lady. Maybe we will some day.'

'Unlikely, I'd say,' said Barty. 'You'd need a dashing young president for a start, and where on earth would he spring from?'

'Oh, look, isn't she marvellous!' cried Izzie.

'Who's that?' Sebastian scowled at the screen; he had been asleep for the past hour.

'The Queen of Tonga. Look at her, what a wonderful woman, sitting there in her open carriage in this pouring rain.'

'Half the country is out there in the pouring rain. At least she's in a carriage with an umbrella over her.'

'Oh Father, don't be such an old grouch. And look at the Queen! Doesn't she look beautiful, in that crown, waving, look—'

'Izzie I can see perfectly well, thank you.'

'Father, you're spoiling it for me.' She sounded suddenly genuinely upset; she had longed to join Boy's party, had refused the invitation, knowing that her father and Kit would want to spend the day together, Kit listening on the radio, knowing that any kind of national celebration half-distressed him.

'Izzie don't be silly—'

'No, it's true.' She felt tears rising to her eyes. Absurd, she knew, for an intelligent young woman of twenty-three to be so emotionally engaged with this day; but she was, she had been caught up in the wave of national excitement, with the preparations, the dressing up of the city, the endless articles in the newspapers and magazines, the parties being held every-where. She wanted to be a part of it, part of the celebration – not just of the event, but of this dazzling demonstration of English pageantry, the importance of the Constitution, the divine right of kings. If you were English, you had to care about it; Izzie was very English. And here she was, alone with a bad-tempered old man and a morose young one. It wasn't fair. The phone rang sharply; it was Henry Warwick.

'Izzie? We've all been talking about what we might do tonight. I thought a party in my flat. Want to come? It won't be the same without you.'

'Oh – Henry I'd love to. Thank you.'

She knew she shouldn't; knew she shouldn't ever do anything to encourage Henry's feelings for her. He had always liked her ever since she had been tiny, and she had adored him, toddling round after him and Roo in their big noisy nursery, so different from her own silent top floor. In her adolescence, just after – well, when she was seventeen and he nineteen, they had had a bit of a teenage romance. It had ended rather abruptly when she had caught him kissing another girl at a party he had taken her to and she had quite literally attacked him, slapping his face: 'Hey, steady on,' he had said, laughing, trying to tease her out of it, 'we're not married, Izzie. You know I like you best.'

'No you don't,' she said and had made him take her home there and then, and in spite of his importunings the next day, flowers, apologetic notes, she had refused to have anything more to do with him. Over the years they had eased back into friendship; Henry had had countless girlfriends, was permanently engaged to one or another of them, and she had had one very serious love affair; he had comforted her over its ending in a very brotherly and proper way. But a few weeks later, he had taken her out and told her that he still adored her and asked her if she would consider going out with him again. Rashly, lonely and hurt, she had agreed. But it hadn't worked. Henry was too bland, too conventional for her, his only real ambition was to make a lot of money and head up his grandfather's bank. He lacked subtlety; he was good-looking, charming, and great fun; but she knew a serious relationship with him was absolutely out of the question. And so she had extricated herself from it, telling him he was too good for her; he had reluctantly allowed her to go and had been engaged twice since, while constantly telling her, whenever he was drunk enough, that he was really only waiting for her.

'Good,' he said now. 'Look, it could be difficult getting across London. I could try and—'

'Henry, don't try anything. I'll come on my bike.'

'Your bike . . .' Izzie's bike was a family joke; she loved it and frequently pedalled to work on it, negotiating the ever-increasing London traffic without a qualm. 'It's much nicer than being in the beastly tube, or stuck in traffic,' she would say. Sebastian had told her that her mother too had loved cycling 'all over Oxford, always getting her skirt caught in the wheel'. Izzie didn't wear a skirt on her bike, she wore the new calf-length trousers, and tore down the busy streets, her long hair flying out behind her.

'Well as long as you wear those rather splendid trousers,' said Henry, 'I'll be very happy. Are you sure? It's quite a long way.'

'Henry, it's not. It'll take me twenty minutes. Straight down Baker Street and Park Lane and through the park. It'll be fun.'

'Well, OK. Get here as soon after seven as you can.'

'Will – will Clarissa be there?'

Clarissa Carr-Johnson was Henry's latest girlfriend; bosomy, tiny-waisted, giggly, with a fine line in practised flirtatious behaviour. She was everything Izzie was not.

'Hope so. But her pa's giving some reception tonight, he's some incredible city bigwig you know, she may not be able to get away.'

'Oh dear,' said Izzie quickly. She needed Clarissa to be there; on the other hand it would be much nicer if she was not.

Celia smiled at Lord Arden; they were finally back in his London house in Belgrave Square, exhausted by their long day, but very happy.

'Marvellous, wasn't it?'

'Absolutely marvellous. I enjoyed it so much. Dear Lord Arden.'

'My very dear Lady Arden.' He bent and kissed her hand; she tried not to feel irritated.

'Do you remember the last one?' she said, pulling off her long white gloves.

'Of course. It was magnificent too. And to think that dear little girl is now the Queen.'

'And that sweet young woman has become the Queen Mother. It's happened rather quickly, hasn't it?'

'Very quickly. That's why we were so right to get married, Celia. Life is chancy.'

'Indeed it is,' she said soberly. Wondering what the others were all saying and doing now, how Kit in particular had got through the day, what Sebastian had done . . .

Don't think about Sebastian, Celia, don't.

'More champagne?'

'Yes please. And then—'

The phone shrilled.

'My dear!' said Lord Arden. 'How lovely to hear from you. Wasn't it, yes, absolutely incredible. Yes, of course.'

He passed the phone to Celia.

'It's Adele.'

'Hallo Mummy. I just wanted to compare notes. I feel so excited I think I could fly. Now I wonder if you saw anything I might have missed, that I could add to my story. What? Would you mind? Oh, that would be wonderful. Thank you, Mummy, I'll come right away. I'll walk, it's the only way. I'm not far from you, I'm in the Mall. Oh and you've still got your robes on haven't you? I want a picture of you in them, both of you.'

Celia put the phone down, smiling. It would be wonderful to share the day with just one member of her family.

Barty left Jenna at the Warwicks' for the night, at Jenna's insistence, and went back to her hotel. She had refused to stay with anyone, preferring to remain neutral. She loved the Basil Street Hotel, with its old-fashioned ways, and Jenna found its proximity to Harrods and Woollands extremely satisfactory. Already she was an alarmingly determined shopper. She was a great collector, an odd thing in so young a girl. She collected all manner of things: teddy bears, toy horses, farm animals, furniture and people for a magnificent dolls' house that had once been her aunt Maud's, commissioned by Robert Lytton. It was an almost perfect replica of their house in Sutton Place, New York. And then hats – she loved hats – shoes, sweaters and that great American passion, T-shirts. Jenna had T-shirts in every conceivable colour and combination of colours, some of them much too big for her that she was waiting to grow into, some too small that she had grown out of and refused to part with. She dressed, not surprisingly, in a style which was fairly distinctive. If she had to wear dresses, they were plain, in strong colours, and worn with long stockings, usually black.

'I will not wear those gross white socks any longer,' she had announced firmly to her mother when she was quite small. Barty, who had already adopted a policy of acceding to Jenna's will whenever it was not actually dangerous or anti-social, agreed that she need not. Jenna wore her hair long, scooped back from her face, and the pretty seed pearl and coral necklaces favoured by most little girls of her age were absolutely shunned. On the other hand, she liked to wear a watch: she had learned to tell the time soon after her fourth birthday, and was never without one on her wrist. So far they had been plain, childish watches, but she was beginning to show an interest in more unusual varieties: another opportunity to collect. Barty had bought her a plain square silver one with a black strap which she had seen in the window of a second-hand jewellery shop and hidden in her cabin trunk for Jenna's next Christmas present.

Next week they were going to Ashingham, to see Billy; apart from wanting to see her brother before they went back to the States, she felt it was important for Jenna to meet the other part of her family, as dynamic in its own way as the super-rich, glamorous Elliotts were. Not only Billy and his wife, but the two little boys, growing up into their own heritage, a large farm in the heart of the English countryside. Much gratitude for this was due to Celia's mother, Lady Beckenham, who had left it to Billy in her will. 'Lady Beckenham had bought her son out, paid over the odds for it at a time when he needed the money,' Billy wrote in a letter to Barty, 'and it was hers to do what she liked with. Or her half anyway, Joan and I owning the other half.'

That he had been able to buy half the farm years earlier had been entirely due to Lady Beckenham advancing him some money from her own estate; an act of both great generosity and foresight. Billy and Joan were superb farmers.

'It's such a beautiful place, Jenna, you'll love it,' Barty said. 'Lots of horses and ponies, and places to play, and you'll like the boys, I'm sure.'

'And they're my cousins?'

'They are. Joe and Michael, I haven't seen them for three years now, not since Lady Beckenham died. They'll have changed a bit. Joe is named after Lady Beckenham, her name was Josephine, goodness knows how Billy knew, nobody else did, she was Lady Beckenham to everyone.'

'Even her husband?'

'Well – I think so. Nobody knew his name either, she always called him Beckenham, anyway. In front of people, that is.'

Barty was silent, remembering that infinitely sad funeral, and the death of the indomitable old countess. She died exactly as she would have wanted, falling off her horse on the hunting field and never regaining consciousness. The funeral had been one of the very few occasions Barty had seen Celia near to breaking down.

'And Joan, is she nice?' said Jenna.

'Joan is just lovely. Very warm and gentle but as tough as old boots at the same time. The dairy herd is her responsibility, so she needs to be, often up all night delivering calves, Billy says, and she's won county prizes for her furrowing—'

-'What's furrowing?'

'It's making straight lines with a plough, for planting crops. Used to be done with horses, but now they use tractors.'

'I'd like to drive a tractor. I've seen photographs, Adele has taken lots, she showed me, clouds of birds follow you over the fields. I might try it when we go there to visit.'

'Jenna,' said Barty firmly, 'there is no way you're going to drive a tractor.'

'I don't see why not,' said Jenna, smiling at her with appalling sweetness. 'Anyway, when are we going? I can't wait.'

'Next Thursday.'

'It must be lovely for your brother, having his own farm. I might have one when I'm grown up.'

'What a good idea,' said Barty.

'Kit, won't you let us publish you in New York?'

'No, Barty, sorry. I can't. You must see that would negate my decision.'

'Not really. Here, have some more champagne. It's very good, isn't it?'

'Very good.' He smiled at her. 'But you needn't think it's going to change my mind.'

'Of course I don't. Although your thinking is a bit confused. A lot of people seem to think you're leaving because your mother won't be there any more.'

'As I keep saying, I don't care what a lot of people think. She knows why I've done it and that's all that matters.'

'Kit, you're going to have to forgive her some time,' said Barty gently.

'Don't you start on it, for God's sake. I can't ever forgive her. Or understand what she's done.'

'No, all right. Sorry. Let's just concentrate on having a nice lunch. Did you ever come here when –' an imperceptible pause '– when you were a little boy?'

'You mean did I ever come here when I could see? Yes, of course. My mother felt she had to take me to all the smart restaurants. It was part of my education.' He sighed. 'I specially liked it here, actually, because of the view of the river. A lot of the others seemed rather boring. I mean the Ritz, all that gilt! So unamusing. I liked Simpsons too, I remember, because of the great big covered silver salvers on wheels and the huge joints of meat. I used to love watching the waiters carving them. The only place she never took me to was Rules. I was always asking her, because I loved the cartoons. Boy took me sometimes. But she wouldn't.'

'No, she never took me there either,' said Barty casually. She had a shrewd idea of the reason; she had once suggested she and Sebastian went there, and he had refused.

'Sorry Barty,' he had said firmly. 'Rather not. Bad associations.'

'Bad?'

'Well – you know. Painful. A bit, anyway.'

'So,' she said now, 'scallops? You always like them.'

'I do. Or have they any asparagus? I might like that.'

'It's on the menu, yes.'

'Good. Where's Jenna?'

'With Lucy. The Warwick nanny has taken them both to the zoo.'

'Poor woman.'

'Yes, I shall be surprised if she survives the experience. Still, she insisted.'

'She's an extraordinary child, Barty. Incredible conversations I've had with her. I do wish I'd met Laurence.'

'You don't need to,' said Barty laughing, 'he's been reborn in his daughter, I cannot believe how alike they are. I sometimes think there's no Miller in her at all.'

'Her voice is like yours,' said Kit.

'Of course it's not. She speaks American.'

'She has that lovely huskiness you have. I've always loved your voice.'

'Oh Kit,' she said, laughing, turning on a Scarlett O'Hara twang. 'You certainly do know how to flatter a girl.'

'I wish I did,' he said heavily. 'I'm not doing very well in that direction. Thirty-three and still a bachelor. Bit sad, wouldn't you say?'

'Well—'

'Go on,' he said, his voice heavy suddenly. 'Go on, admit it. It would be pretty nice to have a girlfriend. A wife. Children.'

'Kit, you will. It's just—'

'Just what? A matter of time? At this rate, Barty, I'll be a hundred before I even meet someone.'

She sighed. 'You're very down, aren't you?'

'No. Well – yes, I am a bit. It's not just this wretched business of my mother. And leaving Lyttons, which in many ways I don't want to do. I feel a bit—'

'Stuck?'

'Well, yes. That's about the size of it. I feel I've conquered all the demons I could, I've found a career for myself, I can support myself, I've got my other interests, music and so on. Is that it, Barty, do you think? Is there going to be any more?'

'I don't know,' she said carefully. 'I wish I did.' She paused, then said, 'Look, Kit, why don't you come and stay with us for a bit? In New York. And no, before you say anything, this is in no way a bid to coerce you, undermine your determination to leave Lyttons. Or even a silly attempt to "buck you up", in quotes. It's just that I'd love it, Jenna would love it, and you'd love New York.'

'What would I love about it?' he said slightly wearily.

'It's so – exciting. So fast. So busy. And everyone is so alive, so enthusiastic about everything.'

'Would I be able to join in?'

'Of course you would. Look, think about it. Please. I promise you'd have a good time.'

He was silent; then he said, 'No, Barty. It's very sweet of you. But I don't think I want to do that. It's a difficult time for me professionally, as well as personally. I'm trying to decide which publishers to go to.'

'What did you think of Michael Joseph?'

'I loved it. But I think actually I preferred Wesley. They're so new and young and – well, so enthusiastic. They had such plans for me and the books. And – well, I'm not sure about working with Izzie.'

'Why ever not? Surely you don't still—'

'No, no. Of course not. But we're – very close. Even now. We get on so, so well. We think alike, almost spookily so, love all the same things, and – I don't know, someone might – well, put two and two together and make four and a half. And I don't want to risk it. For her sake, not mine. Incidentally, what's the situation with Jenna and her inheritance? I seem to remember Father saying you were wondering about trying to get her some more.'

'Oh I've decided against the whole thing. I'm going to waive the claim legally. It means going to court—'

49

'Court! To ask not to have something!'

'Yes. Odd isn't it. I have to plead my case before a judge. I suppose because they want to be sure I'm acting in Jenna's interests. But that's all right. I just don't want it for her. Fighting, almost certain unpleasantness, for money she simply doesn't need. We have more than enough. I don't want her to have millions of dollars—'

'Millions?'

'It would be. Many more millions. Obscene isn't it?'

'It is a bit.'

'I really think so. Millions of dollars neither she, nor even I, have earned. I think it would be terribly corrupting. And the lawsuit, fighting for it, more so.'

'I think you're right.'

'I'm so glad you agree. Of course it isn't straightforward, because if Laurence had known about her, then he would have wanted her to have some of it. Not all, because he was very fond of his other children. But – well, he didn't. And it's all gone to them.'

She was silent; Kit took her hand again.

'I'm so sorry. That must be your biggest regret. That he never knew Jenna, I mean, not about the money.'

'It is. Yes.' She fished in her bag for a hanky, blew her nose. 'In some ways, the only one. I mean of course I miss him terribly every day, I loved him so much, Kit, so, so much – oh dear—' She heard her own voice tremble, stopped talking. 'Sorry. It's the champagne talking.'

'No it's not,' he said gently, 'it's you. Go on. If you want to.'

'Well – I think so much about it. That last lovely time, that was so sad and so wonderful, when he was in London you know, during the war, and—'

'And you got married.'

'Yes. And we got married, and didn't tell anyone. It was so extraordinary. So intense. And even the last time I saw him, saying goodbye to him for ever – only I didn't know it was for ever of course – it was so absolutely joyful, in its own way. And then, then there was Jenna, and he never knew and he would have loved it so much. Loved her so much of course, but just knowing she – existed. He never had that happiness. And it's so cruel. Such a – huge, dreadful loss for him. Even though he wasn't aware of it. Everything else I can come to terms with. And God knows what sort of marriage we would have had, once the war was over. He was absolutely impossible.'

'Go on. Tell me about him. You never have. Please. I really want to know.'

'He was the most extraordinary mixture,' she said slowly, 'of good and bad. He behaved quite appallingly, a great deal of the time. Not just to colleagues and employees, but to the family. Maud. His brother Jamie. To Robert—'

'Who's still alive. Amazing.'

'Yes. Dear Robert. He's even still working. He loves Jenna so much. Says she looks exactly like her grandmother. It's true actually, I've seen pictures.'

'It must have been hard for Laurence,' said Kit, 'having to accept a stepfather. And a new sibling.'

'Kit, I can't make too many excuses for him. Of course it was hard. Other people have to endure hard things. Like you.'

'I didn't always behave very well,' he said heavily.

'I know. But you weren't wicked. Laurence set out to – well, to defraud Robert, to wreck his business. He persecuted Jamie dreadfully, simply because he was nice to Robert and Maud—'

'Just a minute,' said Kit, 'how do you know all this? Family gossip I suppose.'

'No,' said Barty simply, 'he told me.'

She could remember it still, listening to Laurence by the hour, while he told her about all the dreadful things he had done – and then giving her the excuses, the rationalisation for them. His terrible childhood, his father's death, his mother's remarriage to Robert Lytton, the birth of Maud and of the second child that had killed her. She could remember wondering how she could possibly love this man, who had deliberately wreaked such harm on people; and wondering that she did.

'He even,' she said now, 'threw away a telegram telling me about Wol's first stroke, because he didn't want me rushing back to England—'

'What? Surely not.'

''Fraid so. Oh, Kit, there's lots more. But – I loved him. I loved him so, so much. I fought it and fought it, but I couldn't help it. Always. From that first moment.'

A long silence; the waiter refilled their glasses.

'Oh dear,' she said, picking hers up, 'I'm sorry, Kit. Bit heavy, all this.'

'No,' he said. 'No, no, I'm so very pleased you're telling me.'

'I – haven't told many people. Obviously. Sebastian knows. He was so marvellous, he helped me through it. Both times, when I first left Laurence, and the second time when he –' her voice shook '– he left me.'

'He knows about grief,' said Kit, 'he told me once that when Pandora died, his only wish was to die too. For years, that's what he wanted. He said grief was the only thing he knew. Until – well, until he accepted Izzie. That was the turning point.'

'Dear, darling Sebastian,' said Barty. There was another silence; then, 'But you see, Kit, I'm not sure that we would have been exactly happy,

Laurence and I. That it would have worked very well. I'm not exactly pliant myself.'

'True. Very true. But I'm sure you'd have managed something. And I'm sorry you're so unhappy.'

'Kit, I'm not.' She sounded surprised. 'I'm really not. I like my life. New York is wonderful, Lyttons New York is wonderful, I have a great time. I'm really happy. I just – miss him. That's all.'

'Of course you do.' He sighed, then said, 'Anyway, back to Jenna. I think you're absolutely right. She shouldn't be exposed to lawsuits and lawyers and greed. It would be bad for her. Have you ever met the other children?'

'No. Now *their* mother really had a bad time. With Laurence, I mean. He only married her to—' She sighed. 'Enough of this. I can't have you thinking entirely badly of him. He had so many virtues. He was loyal, and generous and brave and – well, lots of good things. Anyway, I wrote to Annabel, that was the first wife, when I moved to New York. I felt I had to lay some ghosts, say some things, put what I feared were some misconceptions right. She was surprisingly generous and courteous to me. And we very occasionally meet, at some benefit concert or other. But she's pretty steely. I don't see her parting with any of the money. It's all been left to the children, in trust anyway, and she gets the income. Anyway, I'm afraid I'm boring you.'

'Of course you're not.'

'It's just so nice talking about Laurence. I don't often get the chance. And please think about coming to New York.'

'I'll think about it,' he said, 'if you like. But I really can't come.'

Barty took a taxi back to the Warwick house to collect Jenna; everyone was out and she sat in the drawing room drinking tea and trying to recover her equilibrium. Disturbing memories, vivid, violent memories, were always painful. Not to mention thinking about Jenna, and hoping, as she did almost every day, that she was doing the right thing in claiming nothing for her. And confronting her fear: that one day Jenna might come to think for herself that she was entitled to some of her father's fortune.

'And this is Jenna. Jenna, this is your uncle Billy, and your aunt Joan.'

'How do you do.' Jenna held out her hand to each of them in turn, smiling politely. However unsuccessful Barty's attempts at discipline had been in other areas of Jenna's life, she had at least succeeded in drilling her in perfectly formal, English manners.

'Pleased to meet you, Jenna.' Billy shook her hand. 'You're bigger than I expected.'

'Everyone says that. I'm told my father was tall, too. You didn't meet him, I suppose?'

Her voice was hopeful; so few of her mother's friends and family had met her father, he was still a mysterious, shadowy figure, familiar to her only through photographs – and her mother didn't even have very many of those. Her uncle Jamie talked to her about him, of course, but only in a rather careful, formal way, and Grandpa Robert was very difficult to draw on the subject. She wished passionately that she knew more about him; as she grew older it seemed increasingly important. To say there was a mystery about him was going a bit far; but it was certainly true that there were a lot of blank spaces in the picture she was trying to build up of him.

'No, I'm afraid I didn't. I'd have liked to, of course. But he never got down here—'

'Silly him.' She looked round her and smiled; she was enchanted by it, by the square stone house, the rather untidy garden and the great stretch of countryside that went with it, the big fields, the hedges, the woodland, and, just below the house, the large stable block. 'It's lovely here, I really like it.'

'Good. Well we think it's lovely too.'

Jenna smiled at her. She liked Joan. She was large and cosy, with big strong arms and a tangle of dark hair, flecked with grey. She liked Billy too, but he was less smiley, and he had a way of studying you carefully as if he was making up his mind about you.

'Where are your boys?'

'They're at school. They'll be home at half past three. Sorry about that, bit boring for you, but by the time we've had lunch and Billy's maybe shown you the horses, your mum says you like horses—'

'I do, I love them. I ride in Central Park and of course on the shore on Long Island.'

'Well, we can probably manage a ride for you here. If you'd like that.'

'Oh, yes please. And I'd really like to drive a tractor.'

'Jenna –' said Barty warningly.

Joan laughed. 'Drive a tractor? Well now, that might be a bit awkward, you not having done it before. But one of the boys could give you a ride, I dare say.'

'Do they drive it?'

'Well, Joe does. Never too young to drive a tractor, that's what Bill says, isn't it, love? Once you can reach the pedals, of course.'

'How old is Joe?'

'He's nearly twelve. But he's a big lad. Now then, are you both going to come along in, have something to eat?'

'I'd rather see the horses,' said Jenna, 'and have a ride.'

'Jenna, not before lunch,' said Barty firmly. 'We've only just arrived.'

Jenna scowled at her. 'Joan said Billy would show me the horses.'

'Yes, when it suits him. I'm sure he's busy now.'

'No, I'm not,' said Billy. 'Not specially, anyway. Don't know about a ride now but we can take a look.' He grinned at Jenna. She grinned back, and then triumphantly met her mother's eyes.

There were over a dozen horses in the yard; a couple of very big hunters, two or three smaller ones, some ponies of various sizes and beyond them, in the paddock, two great shire horses.

'That one belongs to Elspeth Warwick,' said Billy, pointing to a very pretty little bay. 'She comes down and rides him whenever she can.'

'He's lovely,' said Jenna. 'What's his name?'

'Florian. Bit fancy is Elspeth, but she can't half ride. Like her ladyship, I always tell her.'

'I like those,' said Jenna, pointing to the shires, 'they're like giant horses.'

'They are indeed,' said Billy. 'We used them in the war, when petrol was so scarce. The grey, we called him Lord B after his lordship. Although they're getting on a bit, I still work them sometimes.'

'For furrowing?' said Jenna.

'How do you know about furrowing?'

'My mother told me.'

'I didn't know she had any knowledge of such things. Just her books and so on.'

'Oh my mother knows about everything,' said Jenna airily.

Over lunch, the conversation turned to Lord Arden; Billy asked what he was like. Her mother said carefully that Lord Arden was very nice, very charming.

'Yes, yes, but what's he really like?'

'Billy—' said Joan in a certain voice. And Jenna knew what that was about: not in front of the children.

'He's OK,' she said, cutting in, 'quite kind and smiling. But he doesn't say much.'

'I don't suppose the poor chap gets much of a chance,' said Billy, laughing. 'All those Lytton women round him.'

Jenna smiled at him.

'It's not that,' she said. 'I don't think he has much to say, even if no women at all were there. I don't actually think he's very clever,' she added, and then looked anxiously at Joan, who appeared to be having a coughing fit.

Her mother said 'Jenna' in the voice she used when she was about to be cross, but wasn't quite; Jenna looked at her.

'What? He's not here, he can't hear me saying that. He's not nearly as clever as Aunt Celia, really he isn't.'

'Jenna, I've told you before not to talk about people.'

'But—'

'Come along Jenna,' said Billy, standing up. 'Let's go and get this pony saddled up.'

She had a wonderful ride on a pretty little pony called Coffee; Billy led her round the paddock once, but she managed to convince him that she was perfectly able to handle him herself.

'And you can't find it easy running with your false leg,' she said.

Billy grinned at her. 'Don't ever think about it,' he said. 'Part of me, that leg. Don't know what I'd do if the other grew back.'

'Might it?' said Jenna. 'It must be quite – sad for you without it.'

'Not a bit of it. I owe everything to losing that leg, hasn't your mum ever told you?'

'Yes, she has. How Lady Beckenham looked after you and gave you a job in the stables. I wish I'd met her.'

'You remind me of her,' he said, 'just a bit.'

She was flying around the paddock on Coffee when she heard a shout; the boys had arrived at the gate and joined their father. She reined the pony in, cantered over to them, sat smiling at them. 'He's so lovely, I'd take him back to America with me if I could. I'm Jenna.'

'You'd better not,' said Joe. 'I learned to ride on him. He's mine.'

'Joe –' said his father.

'Of course I can't,' said Jenna earnestly. She studied Joe. She liked him. He was a big, rather gangly boy, with light-brown untidy curly hair and blue eyes, like his mother; his face was smiling and comfortable like hers as well. Michael looked more like Billy, darker and more serious, with the same way of studying you intently and summing you up.

Michael trailed after her and Joe as they walked towards the paddock where the big old shires were. Jenna was fascinated by them; she had never seen such huge animals in her life.

'I've got some carrots,' said Joe. 'Here, give them a piece. Hold your hand flat.'

'I know,' said Jenna coolly. She looked up at the horses. The grey bent its great head over her small hand and took the carrot gently. She smiled.

'He's a real gent, is Lord B,' said Joe. 'Nice manners, Dad says.'

'I wish I could ride him.'

'You'd never even get up. Anyway, he's not got a saddle.'

'I could ride him bareback.'

'Course you couldn't.'

'I could.'

'You're mad,' said Michael.

'I'm not.'

'You are. And you're a girl,' he added, as if that settled matters.

'Well I'll show you,' said Jenna.

She climbed up on to the gate, stood swaying slightly, grasped Lord B's mane and half slithered, half jumped on to his back. He trembled slightly, and she felt his muscles quiver under her. He was so huge that her short legs were spread almost straight across his back. She grasped the mane further up, wriggled a bit and looked down at the boys triumphantly.

'I told you so.'

All might have been well had not a large horsefly suddenly settled on Lord B's rump. He jumped, kicked out with one of his back legs and swished his tail. In a smaller animal the movements would have been slight; for him they were considerable. Jenna felt him lurch, and started to slither sideways; she clung to the mane, looked down. The ground looked a long way away. She tried to haul herself up again, but couldn't regain her balance; she was pulling quite hard now on Lord B's mane. He began to find it irritating, and moved forward; she clung on, pulling harder still. Lord B blew through his nostrils and launched into a brisk trot. For ten, maybe fifteen seconds, Jenna managed to stay on him, then slowly and quite gracefully she fell to the ground. As she fell, she put out her hand instinctively to save herself and fell awkwardly on her wrist. Very awkwardly.

Two hours later, after having her wrist set quite painfully in the local cottage hospital, facing one round of her mother's wrath, and knowing there was more to come, after being ticked off quite severely by Billy as well, and enduring the double misery of hearing Joe being unfairly told off, she still felt the whole episode was entirely worthwhile as she heard Joe say to his father, 'She's the bravest girl I ever met. Even if she is stupid.'

She found it quite easy to ignore everyone's wrath after that; and when she got on to the plane to New York three days later with her arm in a sling, his words were still ringing in her head.

Record were very pleased with Adele's Coronation photographs. They gave her fourteen pages, and the cover.

'Maman, let me see.' Noni reached out her hand for the magazine; as it was passed across the table, Lucas lifted the newspaper he was reading to turn to another page and knocked the coffee pot over.

'Lucas, you oaf. Oh, God, that's awful, Mummy I'm so sorry, all over it. You stupid idiot, how did you do that?'

'Quite easily.' Geordie's voice, usually so level and good-natured was icy cold. 'I saw that Lucas. Apologise to your mother.'

'It was an accident,' said Lucas sulkily.

'Even if it was' – Geordie's voice made it plain he didn't think so – 'you can still say you're sorry. That is her first edition, and the only one she has at the moment.'

'She can get another. It's a magazine, not some priceless painting. No doubt there'll be a dozen in the house soon. What does it matter?'

'It matters a great deal,' said Geordie. 'Please apologise.'

'I don't see why I should.'

'Well I do. Lucas—'

'Geordie, it's all right.' Adele gave him a quick, anxious smile. 'Honestly. It was an accident.'

'It is not all right, and I don't believe it was an accident. Lucas, if you can't apologise, please go to your room.'

'No. I don't have to do what you say. You're not my father.'

'Lucas!' said Adele. 'That was very rude.'

'It was true.'

'Please apologise to Geordie.'

'I won't. And I'm going to school now. Where people care about slightly more important things than yet more photographs of that bloody Coronation.'

'Lucas—'

But he was gone. Geordie stood up; he was white with rage.

'Geordie—'

'Adele, just leave this to me, will you? I will not tolerate this behaviour.'

'It won't do any—'

But the door had closed behind Geordie; there was shouting from the hall, then a loud slam as the front door banged. Adele and Noni looked at each other.

'Oh, Maman —'

'Oh, Noni —'

'My dear, whatever is the matter? I hate to see you so distressed. Please tell me.'

'Kit absolutely refuses to come and visit me,' Celia's face was swollen with crying as she looked at Lord Arden. 'And I can't bear it. I really can't. I love him so much and—'

'Go on.'

'No. No, that's it.'

How could she tell him? That she had wanted so badly to explain to Kit exactly why she had married Bunny. The tortuous, difficult reasons. And that he had refused all her invitations to hear any of them.

'He'll get over it, Celia. Of course he will. He's young, they always come round in the end.'

'He's not that young, Bunny.' She wiped her eyes, reached for a cigarette. 'He's thirty-three. And he's very – steely. Always has been.'

'And – your favourite?'

'What? No, no of course not.'

He was: of course. Being the youngest, the most brilliant and beautiful, the most charming, the one who had loved her the best. And—

'Yes he is. Come on, you can admit it to me. It's not a crime. Any fool can see you don't get on with Giles. And the twins, they obviously come first with each other, always will. No, Kit has your heart, Celia, and I don't wonder at it. I still remember him as a little chap, sitting on your knee, telling you you were pretty, making you laugh.'

'He wouldn't tell me I was pretty now,' said Celia, managing to smile.

'Well, never mind. As I say, I'm sure he'll get over it.'

'Bunny, don't keep saying that, please.'

Her tone was sharp; Lord Arden looked at her nervously. He was coming to know that tone very well. It hadn't been something he had really heard before they were married. He decided to go to his club. She'd calm down. And when she did, he would tell her of the trip he had arranged, to hear Callas sing in Vienna. That would take her mind off her troublesome family. That and a piece of jewellery he had spotted for her in the window of Aspreys. He didn't normally like modern jewellery but this was exquisite, a diamond and sapphire bracelet, so wide it was almost a cuff. He might go and secure it now, on the way to his club.

Kit leaving Lyttons had been bad enough. He had been right, of course, he knew her so well; she had seen it as a dreadful blow. She might have physically left the firm, but she was still absolutely a part of it, she had created it, it was hers, as much as one of her children. And Kit was part of it, too. It had made him, as good publishers do make authors, however brilliant their work; shaping them, presenting them, building their reputations, guiding their futures. Kit's first book had been clever, original, witty; but it had still needed care, creativity, style, in order to achieve the absolute success it had found. And Lyttons, the Lyttons she had made, had provided all those things just as it provided them for other authors; an absolute concern for quality, a total attention to detail, an instinctive sense of the moment. In other hands *Childsway* would have been a different book, and Christopher Lytton would have been a different author, just as successful, perhaps, but different. He had allowed Lyttons to give birth to his career as an author – and was now rejecting them. And rejecting her. His leaving was a rejection of her. She knew him well enough to recognise that. At first, she had struggled without a great deal of success, to look upon it as a piece of personal loyalty. But then his letter had arrived, typed on his special typewriter, telling her that he wanted to avoid any further connection with her.

'People are still saying, of course, that you are Lyttons, and because that is so undeniably true, I have no wish to be any part of it whatsoever. Please don't telephone me, or try to see me. I really have no wish for that.'

And then, the awful, final rejection, not the messy, scrawled signature, but a formally typed 'Christopher Lytton'.

Her only comfort, looking at that name, was telling herself that he was, in some ways, still something of a child.

At first Celia had thought Kit would come round: that he would agree to see her. That she would be able to make him understand at least a little. But he had instructed his secretary to return all her letters – three of them now, each more importunate than the last – had refused to speak to her on the telephone, had rejected all her invitations. The third one she herself recognised would be the last.

'Please, Kit, I beg of you,' she wrote, 'please come. I want so much to try and explain. I cannot allow you to walk away like this.'

The tersely typed answer telling her that it was she who had walked away finally forced her to accept defeat that day.

She had lost Kit. And she didn't know how to bear it.

CHAPTER 6

'Just go away. Get out of my room.'

'But darling—'

'Mother—'

'All right. I'm going.'

She went; later she tiptoed up, heard the unmistakable sound of weeping. Male weeping. An awful, literally heartbreaking sound. But – she had agreed. That he should go away. Geordie had persuaded her.

God, Lucas hated Geordie. Hated him for his smarmy charm, the way he could wrap his mother round his little finger, the way he tried to order Lucas about, to play the heavy father, tell him what to do: when he had no right to, no right at all.

But most of all he hated him for something quite different. Something that was nothing to do with Lucas.

He longed to tell his mother but he couldn't. It would hurt her too much and, besides, he had absolutely no proof. He had tried telling Noni, but she refused to listen, left the room, told him he was disgusting, just making it up to excuse his own behaviour. She thought Geordie was wonderful too, she adored him. It was pathetic.

The first time, he hadn't wanted to believe it himself. It had been at Christmas, the Christmas after his grandmother had married again; they'd spent it with the Warwicks. It had been pretty grim; Lucas hated most of his cousins, they were so noisy and uncivilised. They didn't show any interest in the arts or literature or anything like that, Henry only cared about making money, and Elspeth and Amy were very pretty, but their only interests seemed to be boys and hunting; he had nothing to say to any of them. He'd spent most of the day reading, had even tried to get on with his book over lunch until Boy had removed it forcibly from him.

Anyway, that evening they were all playing charades because his grandmother insisted on it and he'd gone to the lavatory; he'd stayed as long as he could, just in the hope that someone would take his turn. And as he came out of the lavatory, with his book stuffed up his jersey, he'd seen

Geordie slipping into Boy's dressing room. Which was odd: odd enough to make Lucas want to know why. He'd walked very quietly along the landing, and stood outside the door which wasn't quite shut, and he'd heard Geordie saying, 'Oh, darling, I'm missing you too.' Then a silence and then, 'Well, only two more days. And then we'll have one of our wonderful long lunch hours.' Followed by his awful, creepy laugh.

Lucas had felt sick; so sick he had had to go back into the lavatory and sit there a bit longer. He tried to tell himself that Geordie had been talking to his sister, or someone he worked with, but he knew he wasn't. Lucas was quite a precocious fourteen; he read adult fiction and spent a lot of time at the cinema. A clear instinct told him that it had not been a business liaison. He rejoined the party finally and sat staring at Geordie in disgust as he acted *From Here to Eternity*, with embarrassing enthusiasm.

The second time was worse, because Geordie had realised he knew. Adele was out and he heard Geordie come in whistling; Lucas was in the kitchen making some coffee. He'd looked at Geordie, and at first he couldn't believe it, had to look again to make sure, but there it was, definitely, a great smudge of lipstick on his collar; and he just couldn't help it, he said, 'Better change that shirt, Geordie, before my mother comes home.'

Geordie had glanced in the hall mirror, and then blushed dark, deep red, before grabbing Lucas's wrist and saying, 'You can just keep your nasty thoughts to yourself, you little creep.' And then he had run upstairs and slammed the door to the bedroom. From then on, it was outright war.

And because Lucas simply could not be polite to him, because he couldn't even bear to think his mother was so stupid as to love and trust this dreadful man, things had gone from bad to worse, until finally Geordie had said that either Lucas went away to school, to learn some manners, or he would leave home himself.

He meant it; Adele knew him well enough for that. He was sufficiently angry at Lucas's treatment of her – and sufficiently hurt himself, he said – to finally insist. Geordie was very sweet-natured, terribly easygoing; but there was a point beyond which he could not be pushed. And that point had come. Adele loved Geordie too much to risk losing him. Of course he would not actually have gone, she was sure; would not have actually left her and the small, beloved Clio. But he would have read her refusal as a rejection of him, and she was terribly afraid he would have retreated from her, spent more time in New York – which he loved – moved away from her emotionally. Adele had been lonely before in her life; she couldn't face it again. And so, finally and very reluctantly, she agreed; and Lucas was going to Fletton, in Bedfordshire, currently fashionable for its exquisite buildings and its reputation for the arts and its avant-garde approach to education.

'We think you'll enjoy it,' Adele had said brightly. 'It's the most beautiful place, and—'

But Lucas had turned dark and angry eyes on her and said he was quite sure he would hate it.

'But Lucas! It's a marvellous school.'

'So is Westminster. And I'm happy there.'

'Then you might have tried to behave as if you were happy,' said Adele briskly, 'and treated us all with some degree of respect. I'm afraid you have only yourself to blame.'

She seldom came even close to rebuking Lucas; he was clearly startled. But he said nothing.

And now it was the night before his departure. And Adele, racked with remorse, longing to make her peace with him, had tried three times to be allowed into his room. And failed.

Even Noni was doubtful of the wisdom of what they were doing.

'I'm afraid he may do something drastic.'

'Noni, like what?' said Adele, trying to sound light-hearted, firmly pushing down that self-same fear.

'Run away. Refuse to cooperate. Stay in his room—'

'Of course he won't. Noni, he's only a boy. He'll do what he's told.'

'He hasn't done that here.'

'Yes, well, he's not afraid of us, we have no proper authority over him.' She hesitated. 'He clings to the memory of your father, that's why he won't accept Geordie.'

'I know, Maman. And I think he's awful, honestly. Poor Geordie has been so patient. So have you. So have I, come to that. But Lucas is in a mess. He feels – oh, I don't know, rejected, I suppose.'

'Rejected! But Noni, who's rejected him? No one. Your father is dead, he died ten years ago, we left France in 1940.'

'I suppose that was it,' said Noni quietly, 'you did leave. You didn't stay.'

'No. But—' And then she stopped. Adele could never properly explain why she had left; it was too cruel to the children, too defamatory to their father's memory. She had always simply told them that he had insisted they went, that because he had been Jewish and they had been English, because the Germans were about to occupy Paris, the danger was too great. When really . . .

'I know. But don't you think, from Lucas's point of view, you should have stayed? Maman, don't look like that, that's not what *I* think. I know how brave you were, I can still remember that journey, bits of it, you know I can, and I remember how you always told us how wonderful Papa was, how much you loved him. But – well, I think Lucas sees it differently.'

That, and a strong genetic inheritance, Adele thought. Every year, every month, even, Lucas became more like his father. The same selfishness, the same self-obsession, the same built-in sense of grievance. And the same conviction that he was owed whatever he wanted.

Noni had endured the same hardships, the same sorrows, the same disruption as Lucas, but she had survived, was level, loving, merry-hearted. 'She is a Lytton,' Geordie had said once, when Adele had remarked on it, 'a Lytton like you, my darling. Which is why I love her so very much.'

'And she loves you,' said Adele, and it was true, Noni adored Geordie, they were the best of friends. He had never tried to be her father; indeed he had told her at the outset that he would like to be her friend.

'That is how I regard you,' he said, smiling at her, 'as a very dear and special friend. I know I am a little older than you, but I have friends who are many years older than me and the friendship is none the worse for that. Better, indeed, in some ways.'

But his attempts to charm Lucas in the same way had failed absolutely. Lucas had been wary from the very beginning, when Geordie was no more than a visitor. He greeted the news that his mother was to marry him with an intense, dark hostility that was chilling in a child and fought to be allowed to stay away from the wedding. It was only when his great-grandmother, one of the very few people Lucas respected, told him he was making himself look ridiculous and that his father would have been ashamed of him, that he agreed to go. Indeed she had done much in the early days to ease the relationship along. But when she died Lucas descended into a dreadful grief and anger. And bitterness that yet another of the few people he had properly loved was gone from him.

He had only been ten at the time; Adele could scarcely remember him so much as smiling at her since. With an almost adult intensity, he had set about making himself awkward, uncooperative, casting a shadow over her new happiness with Geordie.

'Give him time,' she kept saying, as Geordie's amusement at Lucas's behaviour turned to impatience and finally to a deep, slow anger. Geordie had not encountered much hostility in his life; his charm, his capacity to be interested by, and to like everybody, had made his own life easy, amusing and agreeable.

But time had only made things worse.

Adele drove Lucas down to Fletton alone; Geordie would have made things infinitely worse and while she would have appreciated Noni's company, she felt there was more chance of communication with Lucas without her. She was wrong; he sat in an icy silence the entire journey, and refused her offer of stopping for lunch.

'I'd rather just get there,' he said when she asked him if he was hungry, 'there's no point trying to make this journey pleasant.'

Those were the last words he spoke directly to her until a sullen goodbye as she left him with his housemaster on the steps of the famous West Front of Fletton.

She drove away in tears and had to stop several times on the way home because she was crying so hard that she could not properly see, not just from sadness at the parting, for she loved Lucas dearly in spite of his awkwardness, but from guilt and remorse as well. In failing Lucas, as she so obviously had done, she felt she had failed his father. She could imagine only too clearly what Luc would have said about her abandoning his son, as he would undoubtedly have seen it. Never mind that Luc himself had failed her all those years ago.

'Are you all right, my darling?'

Geordie came in, sat down on the bed, tried to take her hand. Adele snatched it away. He looked hurt, and surprised.

'Darling. What is it?'

'Geordie what do you think it is, for God's sake? I've just had to take Lucas to a place he is clearly going to hate, somewhere that I feel pretty unhappy about too. He refused even to kiss me goodbye. I've never seen him look so wretched and frightened. Do you think that's going to make me feel good?'

'Darling, we did agree—'

'Did we?' Adele looked at him, and felt angrier still. 'I don't think we did, actually, Geordie. You delivered an ultimatum which left me very little choice in the matter. Now you may prove to be right, but at the moment it doesn't look like it, and I have just had a day of sheer hell. I think I'd be better on my own for a bit, if you don't mind.'

Kit was now published by Wesley. He liked the set-up, the size of the house, the fact that it was new, hungry, and much talked about as being imaginative and exciting. He also very much liked his editor there, a woman called Faith Jacobson, who had an extraordinarily sensitive editorial approach; his agent had secured him a very good contract for his next three books.

'I feel much happier altogether,' he had told Sebastian, 'and they have a high visibility in America, which is very good. You should come and join me.'

'I couldn't,' said Sebastian with a sigh. 'You know what they said about Mary Tudor having Calais written on her heart, I've got Lyttons. In a way I'd like to get away of course, but – well, I just don't feel I can. Lyttons is much more than your mother, it's a lot of people I'm fond of, Jay and Venetia and poor old Giles—'

'Everyone calls him poor old Giles,' said Kit, slightly irritably. 'I can't quite see it. He's got a job – and a company, for that matter – that he almost certainly wouldn't have if he wasn't a Lytton.'

'Hey, steady on! Harsh words.'

'They're true. I'm sorry. It's the one thing I do agree wholeheartedly with my mother about. Giles is not up to that job. He's also not a very good figurehead for Lyttons.'

'You should tell her,' said Sebastian lightly.

But he knew it wouldn't happen; Kit had not even written to Celia to tell her about Wesley. He had quite simply cut her out of his life.

He was doing it again: staring at her across the silence of the Bodleian. In that blatant, almost insolent way. Elspeth frowned, looked away and started making furious notes from the book on *Paradise Lost* she was studying. Five minutes later, she looked cautiously up again; he was still staring. And worse, she saw a half-smile twitching at his mouth. Damn. He had noticed. Noticed that she had noticed him. Been waiting for her to respond. She should have resisted the temptation. It was just that he was rather − attractive. She couldn't deny it. He had very large brown eyes, and very dark curly hair that looked as if it didn't get brushed very often. He tended to wear big shaggy sweaters, and baggy cords, rather than the sports-jacket-and-tie look favoured by his contemporaries. He was moderately tall, just shy of six foot, Elspeth imagined, and he had rather long arms and very large hands which gave him an ungainly look. His name was Keir Brown; he was known to his detractors as the Glasgow Gorilla.

Elspeth didn't like him much: what she knew of him, anyway. He made no attempt to be polite, to get to know her in the usual way, by asking her if she wanted to come for a cup of coffee, or even striking up a conversation after a lecture. He just nodded at her, quite tersely, said 'hallo' occasionally and then proceeded to ignore her, as if it was up to her to make the effort. And it annoyed her, this meeting of her eyes in that I-know-you-fancy-me-and-I-fancy-you way. Of course boys had done that to Elspeth ever since she had been old enough to notice; she was very pretty, she had a wonderful figure, and she was quick-witted and sharp and great fun. She wasn't quite as much of a sexual honeypot as her younger sister Amy − their father said Amy still shouldn't be allowed out unchaperoned − but men did fancy her, and what was more they admired her, for her clear, bright mind.

She had had a wonderful first two years at Oxford; she was reading English, was expected to get a First and had already expressed, to the great delight of her grandmother, a desire to join Lyttons. She was very much one of Celia's favourites; she resembled her physically, with her dark, rather dramatic beauty, she was hugely ambitious − and she was also a fine and fearless horsewoman.

Women were still in a minority at Oxford; anyone half attractive rode through their time there on a wave of heady popularity. Had Elspeth been less committed, less serious about her future, she could have been seriously distracted by the social life; as it was she had worked extremely hard, and, what was more, enjoyed doing so. She also had the inestimable gift of an almost photographic memory; exams were consequently not the nightmare for her that they were for so many of her peers.

So far her social life had been predictable; several romances, a few of them serious, with the kind of boys she was familiar with, bright, well-mannered public-school boys. She was still a virgin and had not yet felt the desire to cease being one strongly enough to undergo the risks. Not just of pregnancy, but of being known as cheap, 'easy', a tart. You had to be very much in love, very, very sure that the feeling was reciprocated, to take more than the most faltering step down that road.

There were of course a few very bohemian girls at Oxford who bed-hopped seriously and tended to sneer at their more conventional sisters; but Elspeth had decided at the outset of her time there that she was not going to be one of them. Apart from anything else, you risked being sent down and what moment of sexual rapture could be worth that?

Keir Brown was one of the new breed of student; he was from a grammar school, he had no money and he spoke with quite a strong Scottish accent. He had made no attempt to modify the accent and for that Elspeth admired him; most of the grammar-school boys tried to adopt an Oxford accent, but it never quite came off, and everyone recognised it for what it was. There was a fairly brutish element among the establishment which made a point of mocking such boys; it required courage to face them down.

She had not been very much aware of Keir Brown during her first two years. Initially, he had kept a fairly low profile and had then become very involved with a girl a year below him who had suddenly left the university. It was rumoured she had been pregnant, but the official reason was that she had simply never settled to university life.

Keir was two years older than most of his peers, having done his National Service before going to Oxford; it had given him a self-confidence that many of the grammar-school boys lacked, and enabled him to cope better with the Oxford snobbery.

And this term he had clearly set his sights on Elspeth. And she was quite determined to resist him.

As she walked out of the room, she managed to drop one of her files; papers went everywhere.

'Damn,' she hissed through the silence; several people looked up, frowned, a friend moved to help her pick them up.

Flushed and flustered she finally moved out of the building and into the street.

'Here,' said a voice, holding out a small clutch of papers, 'you left these.'

It was Keir; he was still not smiling, still those dark-brown eyes were looking at her in that slightly contemptuous way. Just the same, there seemed no harm in saying thank you.

'That's all right,' he said and turned away. She was just thinking how extremely oddly mannered he was when he looked back.

'Would you like to go for a coffee?' he said.

Slightly to her own irritation, Elspeth heard herself saying she would.

Lucas had expected to be miserable at school; he had expected to feel homesick – though getting away from Geordie MacColl would certainly be some kind of recompense for that – he had even expected the kind of bullying and sexual unpleasantness he had heard about but never experienced at day school. What he had not expected was to feel totally disorientated.

From the first moment when he was shown to his dormitory – a bleak, cold room with six beds in it, which clearly afforded absolutely no privacy to anyone – he had felt he had no real idea where he was or what he was supposed to be doing.

It got worse: supper that night, in the huge dining room, with its long tables and horrible food, assumed the proportions of a nightmare. And then at bedtime, lying in the hard, lumpy bed, with its thin bedclothes, being told to be quiet, that lights were going out, as if he was a small child, rather than fifteen years old (at a time when at home he would have settled down to hours of reading); being woken in the morning – woken by a bell rung loudly somewhere in the corridor, dressing in the freezing cold and following the other boys (none of whom seemed remotely agreeable or interesting) down to a breakfast, which was as disgusting as it was inadequate; and then into Assembly in the Great Hall with its high, high ceiling and glass rotunda, where he felt the great mass of boys almost like a physical pressure against him, and so into lessons, where he had expected to shine, but found himself bewildered by new teachers, different approaches – through all this he felt absolutely confused. Confused and cold and angry.

How had this happened to him, to Lucas Lieberman, so clever that he had won a scholarship to Westminster, so confident that on his first day there he had felt not a shred of nervousness, so musically accomplished that he was given a trial for the string section of the school orchestra in his first term, so arrogantly mature that he had become, after his two years there, the member of a small but intensely intellectual little clique that people fought to be allowed to join? How had he become a helpless, incompetent creature, his brain as numbed by the cold as the rest of him, shunned by his peers, mocked by his seniors, already beaten twice by the prefect he fagged for, for forgetting to light his fire and acquire bread for his toast? What was he doing out here on this freezing October morning, wearing nothing but shorts and singlet, doing some form of PE, a punishment inflicted by the senior boys on the juniors, his throbbing arms above his head as he jumped up and down? Where was the music his mother had promised him, the art, the culture? Lost somewhere in this nightmare; this nightmare of hearty games, absurd rivalry, vicious hostility.

Of course the place itself was ravishing, and its beauty was the one single source of comfort to him, impossible to ignore. And he could have done better, he knew, could have made friends, but he was not prepared to, not prepared to lower his standards by taking part in conversations about things he cared nothing about, not prepared to try, even to pretend to try, to be good at games, not prepared to tell smutty jokes, to sing filthy songs, to admire the school heroes – mostly great oafs playing rugby – not prepared to suck up to the masters. It was a tradition that you sat next to them in turn at supper and made polite conversation: if his housemaster thought he was going to try to be agreeable to him when only four hours earlier he had been beating him, then he was very much mistaken.

His first experience of being beaten had shocked Lucas more than he would have believed possible; the humiliation, the attack on his body by someone he despised, the pain of the first blow even through his trousers, the continuing assault of five more – the desperate struggle not to cry out or to cry, and then walking out of the room, head held high, past the queue of boys waiting for similar punishment – it was all such an assault on his psyche that the physical pain, the bruises which developed, were as nothing.

He was beaten constantly; his personal disorganisation grew with his misery and he was constantly late for lessons, for games, for meals, for assembly, garnering so many defaulters that they added up with horrifying speed to beatings. He was insolent to the masters too; there was only one man he admired intellectually, the history master, and he only taught the senior boys.

Lucas slept badly, worrying over the events of the day and then was tired the next day, increasing his inefficiency. Terrified of his own tendency to sleepwalk – he had often in Montpelier Street woken to find himself in a different room – and of getting lost in the cold darkness of the great house, he at first tied his foot to the post of his bed with his tie, but one of the boys discovered it and told the others. They mocked him so ruthlessly for being a baby that he gave it up and lay awake for hours, worrying instead.

He was unlucky in that he had been placed in a dormitory of rather hearty boys, whose parents lived in the country and who boasted endlessly about how much shooting land their fathers had got, and how they were going to roger the girls at the next hunt ball; there were other, more civilised boys, interested in the things he was, even in his year, but he so quickly gained a reputation for arrogance and unfriendliness that nobody bothered with him.

What he longed for was time on his own: time to think, to read, to cry even, cry for his mother, for the house in London that from here looked so warm and so happy, for the school he had loved, for the friends he had lost. But there was none; the only place was the lavatory and even there time was short, people banging on the door telling you to buck up and asking if you were having a wank.

The older boys, the house captains and prefects who could have made his life better, all disliked him for his insolence, for his refusal to buckle down to the school traditions, and tormented him further, putting him on extra duties, giving him almost unearned defaulters; by the end of the first half term, life seemed to have become a long weary cold procession from one wretched day and place to the next.

And for it all, Lucas thought, he had Geordie MacColl to blame; his hatred of him grew and grew like some vicious brooding creature. One day, one day he would get his revenge; that thought was one of the few things which kept him going in his misery.

'So are you going to ask me to this party, then?'

Keir's eyes on Elspeth were probing, half contemptuous, half amused as usual; she met them coolly.

'If you want me to, I will. I just don't think it's a good idea, that's all.'

'And why not? Do you not think I'll fit in with your grand family and friends? Are you ashamed of me?'

'I am absolutely not ashamed of you. You know that. And I think you could fit in if you wanted to. If you'd make the – the effort. I'm just not sure that you would.'

'Well, thank you for that.'

'Oh Keir, don't be so awkward. You know perfectly well being social is not exactly your thing. And while I wouldn't specially mind if you stood in a corner sulking all evening, because someone had said something to upset you, my parents would. It would be – unfair to all of you. Perhaps.'

'Perhaps. Any other reasons?'

'Yes. There will be the full roll call of Lyttons there. My grandmother, the absolute head of the family, I know you'd like her and she would like you, but she is an appalling snob and as for her new husband, Lord Arden – well, I don't see that one, Keir. My mother and her twin sister are pretty strong medicine, talk in riddles all the time, never stop fooling around and talking and flirting with everyone. My brothers – the older ones – are what you'd call public-school poofs. I mean I love them, but I don't think they'd become your best friends. The person I'd like best in the world for you to meet, Sebastian Brooke, the writer you know, won't be there.'

'Why not?'

'He and my grandmother have had the most fearful falling out. I can't tell you why, let's just say family politics. And then there's Giles Lytton, my mother's brother, dreadfully dreary, he'd get you into a corner and bore on about the war all evening, and his wife Helena is worse. She behaves like she's the Queen Mother. Honestly, they're a desperate lot. Some of them are nice, my cousin Noni is heavenly—'

'Heavenly, Elspeth? In what way? Does she have wings?'

'Keir,' said Elspeth tartly, 'I don't comment on your accent and correct your turns of phrase. I don't see what right you have to comment on mine.'

She had discovered quite early on that, like all bullies – and he was a fearsome intellectual bully – he responded to being stood up to.

They had moved quite swiftly from the coffee bar to a drink in the Turl, to a meal at the Vicky Arms; from walks along the river to cosy smoky evenings in pubs; from slightly awkward chat to long, deep conversations, taking in a lot of personal history and philosophy; from standing rather self-consciously clear of each other to holding hands and kissing, and from kissing to a journey far further along the road towards full sexual experience than Elspeth would ever have imagined.

'It's no use, Keir,' she said, pushing his hand away as it embarked on its tirelessly hopeful journey into the country between her stocking tops and her thighs, 'I'm not going to do it, and that's all there is to it.'

'Oh God,' he said rolling on to his back, staring up at the ceiling, lighting a cigarette (they were in his room at Wadham, risky even at lunch time but less so than hers). 'This bloody virginal rubbish. Just exactly what are you saving yourself for, Elspeth?'

'Love,' she said very seriously. 'Love and the man I probably want to spend the rest of my life with.'

'I thought you rich girls were more unconventional than that.'

'Some of us are. I'm not. Sorry.'

'Mummy told you it was wrong, did she?'

'Not wrong, stupid. Dangerous. And I agree with her. OK?'

'Of course not,' he said. 'Look, if it's getting pregnant you're scared of, I can make sure you don't.'

'Oh yes? An awful lot of girls have heard that one. Girls who've then had to get married or have back-street abortions or—'

'Girls who sleep with ignorant wankers who don't know what they're doing.'

'Don't Keir. I'm not going to.'

'Oh have it your own way,' he said and stood up, glaring down at her, then slammed out of the room; she lay there for a while on his bed, then finished the paper cup of appalling cold red wine he had poured her and left. She didn't care if that was the last time she saw him; she really didn't.

But she knew deep down that she would. Keir Brown had a strange and strong effect on her; he invaded her consciousness, he took her over. She found it hard to explain; she realised that she was experiencing sexual desire for the first time, that the shoots of sensation that soared through her when he was kissing her, even sometimes when he was just looking at her across the room, were a new and very powerful thing, but it was more than that; when he was around, everyone else was wiped from her consciousness. She could be talking to, even flirting with, men far more good-looking, much more charming, and certainly more suitable than Keir Brown, but he would appear, walk into the room or the bar or the party, and it was as if she were there quite alone with him, incapable of concentrating on anything else. Quite a lot of the time she felt she didn't even like him very much. He made no effort to amuse her or to flatter her, he wasn't particularly witty, not in the least charming, often truculent, and absolutely not the sort of man she had ever imagined herself being involved with. But she was: completely involved, and almost against her will. She fought it sometimes, told herself she didn't want to go on with it, didn't want to see him any more even; and then he would come over to her after a lecture or at a party and give her that look of his and half smile at her and the resolve would just wash away.

She wondered if this was love and decided it couldn't be. It was too uncomfortable.

He certainly hadn't told her he loved her. He told her she was gorgeous, that she was clever, that she was interesting, and of course that she was extremely sexy, that he wanted her very badly, challenging what he called her ridiculous chastity.

'It's so pathetic,' he said, sighing, turning on to his back and lighting a cigarette after one particularly determined assault on her. 'What do you think is so wrong about it?'

'I don't think it's wrong,' said Elspeth, considerably disturbed and upset herself, 'I just think it's – stupid. To do it like – like this.'

'But why? It's a natural instinct. You want it, I know you do, I can feel it, I certainly want it, what's going to happen to you? I've told you, you won't get pregnant, so what's the big deal? You're flying in the face of nature, Elspeth.' He added, half smiling now, 'And it won't do. You'll give in one day, why waste time? And deny yourself – and me – a lot of pleasure. It's absolutely ridiculous.'

'Not to me,' she said firmly.

'I know what it is, you want it all dressed up in white lace and roses. With Mummy and Daddy smirking in the background. Pathetic, that's what it is, Elspeth. It's not worthy of you.'

So far she had managed to resist him; him and his arguments. But it was getting more difficult.

He was, of course, a ferocious inverted snob. Mocking her background, never missing an opportunity to take a shot at her accent, her education, her terms of reference. It was so stupid. It didn't matter to her, in the very least, that his parents ran a corner shop in Glasgow – she teased him sometimes that he wasn't proper romantic working class with a father who went down the pit or a grandmother who had been in service. Why should it matter to him that she lived in a big house and her brothers had gone to Eton, and she rode to hounds occasionally on her own horse? (This last had provoked a particularly strong attack.) Why couldn't they put such rubbish out of the way? But he couldn't, he was obsessed by it. When he found out that she had been presented at Court, he ridiculed her for about five minutes, without pausing for breath; finally she turned on him.

'I wonder how you'd feel, Keir Brown,' she said, 'if I launched this kind of attack on you. On your accent, your background, your home and family, and everything that mattered to you. But that would be cruel, wouldn't it, not funny, not fair game. You have a very odd sense of values, it seems to me.' And she walked away from him, quickly, before he could see that she was crying; he ran after her, but she shook him off and refused to see him for at least a week. It was a measure of his remorse that he actually apologised to her; and after that, he was more restrained on the subject. Most of the time.

It was the only thing they did clash seriously about; such a stupid, unimportant thing. Of course they argued about quite a lot – politics, (although she was beginning to go along with some of his arguments there, and to admit that socialism did perhaps have some right on its side), religion (although he did at least now listen to her arguments in favour of the Church), their respective groups of friends, he found hers arrogant and two-faced, she found his graceless and aggressive – but they agreed about a lot of other things which really mattered, like work and ambition and family. Rather to Elspeth's surprise, Keir was as keen to have a family as she was, but he thought two children would be quite enough. She passionately agreed with him. They had both grown up in a family of six; and while she had clearly not had to share a room with two brothers and quite often a baby as well, she knew how much parental time and attention was rationed amidst such a mob.

His ambition, he told her rather reluctantly, was to go into publishing, to be an editor; he seemed to have a feeling for the book trade, he worked in bookshops in Glasgow in the vacations and had had several articles published in *Isis*. He also wrote book reviews for the literary section: Elspeth found them rather florid and over-written, but was impressed nonetheless by his uncompromising judgement on what he had read. He either liked or loathed a book, there was never a shred of indecision; her grandmother had often told her that was the sign of a true publisher.

'Well I think you should invite me,' he said finally, as she finished outlining the full horrors of her family, 'and I promise not to eat peas with a knife or spit or take up a seat when an old lady's standing up. It'll be better than not being there, thinking about you, wondering what's going on, what stupid

72

poofter you're dancing with. But there's to be no mention of my interest in publishing.'

'Why on earth not? They might be able to help you and—'

'I want none of that kind of help,' he said, scowling at her, his dark eyes defensive and wary. 'I'll make my own way, and if I can't do that, I won't do it at all.'

'Fine,' said Elspeth, thinking that if she did not find Keir talking publishing to Celia by the end of the evening she would be very surprised indeed. 'I promise. And I'm very pleased you're going to come. Only don't blame me if you hate every minute of it. You'll have to stay to the end, though. And you'll have to wear a dinner jacket.'

'Well I've got used to that over the past two years. Now as my reward, will you take that horrible girdle thing off?'

'You haven't done anything worth rewarding yet,' said Elspeth firmly, 'and no, I won't.'

'Darling, it's so lovely to see you, we've missed you terribly, haven't we Noni? We have such wonderful plans for half term, starting with Elspeth's party tomorrow of course, that's going to be such fun and everyone is just longing to see you there. How is it all? I wish you'd write more, but I suppose you're too busy. Come and sit in the front with me and tell me everything.'

'I'd rather sit in the back,' said Lucas, 'thank you.'

Adele fielded his hostility like a physical blow; she had half expected it, of course, but she had hoped, hoped so much that he might have come to appreciate her and home more, would have come to terms with the decision to move him, even seen why it had happened and resolve to put things right.

'Well all right, darling. Tell us about it anyway. What's it really like, do you—'

'I loathe it,' said Lucas, 'it's vile, and I don't want to talk about it.'

'Darling, in what way is it vile? It can't be that bad, surely, the other boys all seem very nice and—'

'They're not nice, they're unfriendly oafs.'

'But you must have some friends—'

'I don't. I don't want any friends. They're not worth even talking to.'

'But darling, why? They can't all be bad.'

He shrugged. 'Mother, for a few days I'm not going to be there. I don't want to spoil the time here with talking about life there and why I haven't got any friends.'

A silence. Then, 'All right,' said Adele. 'What would you like to do for half term? Noni and I thought we might do some theatres and take you out to lunch tomorrow. Jay said he was longing to hear about it all, he can still remember his first term at Winchester, he says, and he'd love to swop notes with you, he'll be at the party of course—'

'I don't want to swop notes with anyone. All right? And I certainly don't want to go to any parties.'

'But Lucas, it's Elspeth's twenty-first.'

'I really don't care, I'm afraid. I'm not going. I don't see why I should. She hasn't written to me, none of them have. All I want to do is stay at home and read and possibly see some of my old friends. Now if you don't mind, I might have a sleep, I'm awfully tired.'

'Adele, of course he must come to the party. It would be the height of rudeness not to.'

'Well Geordie, I'm afraid he won't. I can't drag him there physically.'

'You must tell him he has to go. He's only a boy and you are his mother.'

'You know perfectly well that doesn't mean a thing. And any influence I might have had over him once is gone. Largely because—'

'Yes? Because of what?'

'It doesn't matter.'

'I suppose you blame me for this rift between you and your son, Adele.'

'Yes,' she cried, tears rising to the surface, after a long day of rejection and hostility from Lucas, 'yes, Geordie, I do. You insisted he went away to school, he's desperately unhappy there. If he was still here, I could be maintaining some kind of relationship with him, the lines would have been open at least, he would have come through this difficult patch—'

'It's been a long patch, Adele. Very long. He's been rude and hostile to me for years. And to you. Even Noni agrees.'

'Yes and even Noni agrees that he's desperately unhappy, and is worried about him. It's been a disaster, Geordie, and—'

'It is far too early to say. He's been there half a term.'

'I don't think it's too early at all. He looks dreadful, so white and thin, and haunted looking. He seems to be living in another world half the time. And—'

'Adele, this is an absurd conversation. We are talking about a boy who has not yet settled at his excellent new school, not someone locked up in some kind of prison.'

'I think that is exactly how he sees it, a prison.'

'Then it's time he grew up,' said Geordie.

'How can he be expected to grow up, in an environment so unsuited to him?'

'Adele, I would like to know what environment *would* suit him. A loving home where he is treated with courtesy and understanding certainly doesn't. Perhaps you could come up with a better suggestion. And he is to come to the party tonight, if I have to drag him there myself by the roots of his hair.'

'You are not to try to force him, Geordie. It's not fair, when he's so clearly upset and only just home.'

'And it's not fair of you to allow him to hurt and insult your sister and her family. I will not have it. Now shall I go up there and talk to him or will you?'

She was silent.

'Oh for Christ's sake,' said Geordie. 'I'm going out. But if he's not ready and in a dinner jacket at seven-thirty this evening, I can tell you his sulky little French backside will become extremely sore.'

'That's it, isn't it?' she shouted. 'It's jealousy, all this, jealousy that he's Luc's, that you think I still love Luc, that's what it's all about.'

'Oh for Christ's sake!' said Geordie again. 'I'm amazed you could be capable of such stupidity. Both now and, I might add, in the past. I'll see you later.'

The front door slammed. Upstairs, Lucas quickly moved into his bedroom from the landing where he had been listening to his mother and Geordie quarrelling. He hadn't felt so happy for a long time.

'Happy Birthday, Elspeth, my darling. You look absolutely beautiful, doesn't she, Boy? You must be so proud of her.'

She always did that, thought Venetia, it was always Boy, not she, who was congratulated, as if she had played some subservient role.

'Thank you, Granny,' said Elspeth, leaning forward, kissing Celia. They were almost exactly the same height, and at that moment, looked quite extraordinarily alike.

'Now I have a present for you here,' said Celia, producing a small package. 'Are you opening them now? No, I'm glad to hear it. Such a vulgar thing to do, I always think. I hope you like it. It's from Bunny and me. He is so sorry not to be here, but he hosts this shoot every year at this time and it was set in stone, or rather peat, long before he knew about your birthday.'

'Darling Granny, that's all right,' Elspeth kissed her grandmother. 'It's so wonderful of you to come. All the way from Scotland.'

'I wouldn't have missed it for the world,' said Celia. 'It's just too exciting for words to think you're twenty-one. I'm only sorry that – well, that everybody in the family couldn't be here.' She smiled brilliantly at Elspeth, but her dark eyes were shadowed. She had been hoping against hope that Kit would come, but he had simply said he couldn't contemplate it and that was all there was to it. It had been a very heavy blow for her.

'No sorrier than me,' said Elspeth. 'But—'

'I know, I know. Now, how is Florian?'

'Marvellous. I went down there last weekend again, with Mummy and

Noni, we stayed at Home Farm and I was out with him on both Saturday and Sunday. It's so nice of Billy to let me stable him down there, and he looks after him so well.'

'Of course. How is Billy?' said Celia.

'Fine. Really fine. As he keeps saying, not bad for fifty and with just the one leg. Dear Billy. He and Joan are making such a success of the farm, and the two boys are really helpful. Apparently Jenna caused an absolute riot down there and—'

'I had heard,' said Celia tartly. 'That child needs some firm discipline.'

'She's awfully interesting, though,' said Elspeth, 'and very sweet.'

'Not a word I'd choose. Now off you go,' said Celia, 'you've done your duty, talked to your grandmother for at least three minutes. I hear there is some rather special young man here from Oxford. I would like to meet him before the evening is over.'

'Well Granny, you can meet him. But you've got to be nice to him.'

'My darling Elspeth, why shouldn't I be nice to him, for heaven's sake? I'm not in the habit of being unpleasant to people, surely?'

'Of course not, but – well – he's – well –'

'He's what, Elspeth? Hunchbacked? Stupid? Ugly?'

'No,' said Elspeth, thinking that any of those defects might be preferable. 'No, he's – well he's –' there was a long pause '– not very posh,' she said quickly. 'He – well, he's at Oxford on a state scholarship. From a grammar school. His parents keep a – a shop.'

There was a pause; then 'How absolutely fascinating,' said Celia. 'Where is he? I can't wait to meet him. Oh, not that desperately attractive young man over there, standing and scowling by the fireplace? He looks very uncomfortable. Take me over, Elspeth, and introduce him to me. I'll have him at his ease in no time.'

'And the extraordinary thing was that she did,' said Elspeth, sitting bleary-eyed on her bed next morning, talking to Amy. 'I thought she'd be wildly patronising, I was terrified, but an hour later they were still talking. He told me she was a fine and interesting woman, and very attractive for her age, and she told me he was a very interesting and attractive young man and extremely well mannered – and in spite of him swearing he wouldn't even mention it, she had him telling her all about his ambitions to be a publisher.'

'Why didn't he want it mentioned?'

'I think he felt we'd laugh at him.'

'How horrible. Of course we wouldn't.'

'No, I can see it. Here we are, great literary clan at the top of the mountain; and there's him, at the bottom, staring up. Bit intimidating. Anyway, apparently she suggested he read some manuscripts for her. You know that's how she checks people out. I must say no one would think she'd retired, hearing her talk last night.'

'No, Mummy says she's slithering back, as she puts it, keeps appearing with manuscripts and books from the competition.'

'Well, they all said she would. Anyway, Keir told me he didn't know if he wanted to do it for her, but of course he will. It was amazing. Honestly, I think they'd have spent the whole evening together, if Daddy hadn't broken them up.'

'Well, good for both of them,' said Amy. 'I think he's absolutely wizard, Elspeth. Very, very sexy. Have you – I mean –'

'No, I haven't,' said Elspeth firmly, 'and not with anyone else either, nor am I going to, until I get married.'

'Oh, you're so old-fashioned. I'm just waiting for the first really good offer I get. All right, all right, only joking. I say, Adele and Geordie looked pretty glum, didn't they? Apparently they keep having the most frightful rows over the terrible infant. Noni says it's absolutely horrid and she keeps getting caught in the middle, because she can see all sides. Poor Noni.'

'Poor Noni. Let's ask her over for lunch today. Your new beau can cheer her up.'

'Oh he's not staying for lunch,' said Elspeth quickly, 'we thought the party would be quite enough for him. He's off back to Oxford quite early.'

'Honestly Elspeth, you're mad. Anyone would think he had four legs. Or rather we all did. I bet you ten bob he wants to stay. He had a lovely time.'

'Done,' said Elspeth.

Ten minutes later there was a knock at her bedroom door; it was Amy. 'You owe me ten bob,' she said cheerfully. 'I just met young Master Brown on the stairs and he most definitely wants to stay for lunch. And Mummy says yes of course we must ask Noni. So – cash or cheque?'

'Cash,' said Elspeth, slightly vaguely. The one thing she hadn't expected was that Keir would fall in love with her family. It made her feel rather odd.

CHAPTER 7

'Mother, I've found you a new beau.'

Jenna had taken to calling Barty 'Mother' lately. She said she was too old to say Mummy.

'Really?' said Barty, slightly wearily.

'Yes. He is just darling. And so handsome. And he's lonely, on his own, like you.'

'Jenna, can we just get one thing straight. I don't think I want a new beau. Thank you all the same. I have quite enough in my life with you and the business. And—'

'Oh nonsense,' said Jenna airily. 'Think how often we're on our own here in the evenings, and anyway, I heard you telling Billy you felt quite lonely sometimes. So you don't have enough in your life at all. Now let me tell you some more, his name is Charlie and he's tall, dark and handsome, and—'

'Jenna, can we stop this right now?' said Barty briskly.

'But why?'

'Because, as I said, I am not looking for a beau and if – if I was, I would consider myself capable of finding one all by myself.'

'But you're not. Otherwise you would have done. Now the whole point about Charlie is that he's a widow like you.'

'Widower,' said Barty automatically.

'That's what I said. His wife died five years ago of cancer. And he has a daughter called Cathy who is in my class and my absolutely best friend—'

'Jenna, your best friend is Melissa—'

'No she's not, she's absolutely vile and I hate her more than anything in the world. Cathy is quite perfect, she's new this semester at the Chapin, but I didn't really get to know her before. She is so sweet, Mother, and she has very long fair hair, and really wonderful blue eyes, and she says she looks exactly like her mother. I told her I look exactly like my father. She misses her mother dreadfully but I just know she'd love you. So you see how perfect it would all be. Anyway, you're going to meet Charlie very soon.'

'I am?' said Barty.

'Yes. Because Cathy has asked me to tea on Thursday and I'll stay on until later, and then you can collect me, instead of Maria, it really makes sense. She lives down in Gramercy Park, isn't that really great, and then if you and Charlie wanted to go out for dinner, we could just wait for you at their house.'

'Jenna,' said Barty, 'can I say again, I don't want a beau, even if he is lonely and handsome and the father of your best friend and even if I met Charlie – Charlie what, by the way?'

'Patterson. He's in real estate, but he's not doing so well, mostly because he's so unhappy, Cathy says.'

'Charlie Patterson, all right. I certainly won't be having dinner with him. And it would still be better if Maria met you, because that's her job—'

'Mother,' Jenna looked at her, her face at its smoothest and most innocent, 'that is just absolutely the dumbest thing I ever heard. Of course you must collect me. And meet Charlie.'

'Jenna, I am not going to collect you. Or meet Charlie.'

'Hi, I'm Barty Elliott. Jenna's mother. I do hope she's been good.'

'She's been absolutely angelic. Or so I'm told. Hi. Nice to meet you. Charlie Patterson. Here, let me take your coat. Can I offer you a drink?'

'Oh – no, thank you. We have to get right off. Jenna has homework to do and piano practice—'

'Done it,' said Jenna, appearing in the hallway with a little girl who did indeed have the largest blue eyes and the most sweetly innocent face Barty had ever seen. Trouble if ever I saw it, she thought, and dynamite when combined with Jenna.

'You must be Cathy.'

'Yes, I am.' She held out her hand. 'It's so nice to meet you, Mrs Elliott. And we've done our homework and our piano practice, it's true, and we're right in the middle of watching a TV special, so there's plenty of time for you both to settle down and relax over a drink.'

Charlie Patterson looked at Barty and smiled, clearly embarrassed.

'Would you like a drink, then? Just a small one? Or a coffee, maybe?'

'A – a coffee would be very nice. Thank you,' said Barty. She felt irritable at being manoeuvred by two over-clever little girls and yet at the same time slightly intrigued by Charlie Patterson. He did seem rather charming and interesting. And although not quite as handsome as Jenna had suggested, he was very pleasant-looking, with dark, quite close-cropped hair and smiling brown eyes behind tortoiseshell-rimmed glasses.

He reminded her of Geordie, and like Geordie, he was hard to age, but she would have put him in his late thirties. He walked with a slight limp; Jenna had told Barty it was the result of a riding accident. He was wearing jeans, and a sleeveless pullover over a blue and white striped shirt and no tie: all of them quite clearly rather old, the jeans washed out, the shirt slightly frayed at the cuffs. Jenna's pronouncement that he was not doing terribly well at his real estate was – like so many of her pronouncements – clearly accurate. Barty wondered how he afforded the fees at the Chapin.

The apartment, on the first floor of a large brownstone, was charming: warm and lived-in, with a wood-panelled hall and a country-style kitchen-breakfast room with a big scrubbed pine table. The living room, into which he brought the coffee, was filled with good furniture, most of it clearly old, big, heavily cushioned sofas, long red velvet curtains, a slightly threadbare Indian carpet, and it had a great many interesting-looking pictures on the wall, many of them maritime. Beside the chair where Barty was sitting was a small round table, covered with photographs in silver frames; mostly of Cathy, from babyhood, but also several of Charlie and someone who she could only assume was Cathy's mother, an ice-blonde, very pretty, with a stunning figure and the same angelic smile as her daughter.

Charlie saw her looking at them as he handed her the coffee. 'That's Meg, my wife.'

'She's lovely.'

'She was,' he said and smiled at her sadly. 'Sugar?'

'No, thank you. That's great. I'm so sorry about – about your wife.'

'Thanks,' he said. There was a silence. Then, 'So – you're in the publishing business.'

'I am. Yes. And you are in real estate.'

'Correct. The girls have done their homework well.'

They both laughed; awkwardly.

It was quite an awkward occasion altogether; Barty was relieved when she had drunk a second cup of coffee and was able, without being rude, to say they really had to go.

Well, she had done it, she thought, as she swung her car out of Gramercy Park and headed uptown along Third Avenue, she had done what Jenna had wanted, met Charlie Patterson. Now the little girls could just continue as friends and there would be no need for any further meetings between the two of them. And she fancied that he, as well as she, would be hugely relieved.

The press had made a great fuss over the fact that Kit was now being published by Wesley. It was of course a wonderful story, on every level: professional, personal and familial. Most of the stories had been in the trade press, which had not been too harmful to Lyttons, but an interview had appeared that spring in the *Manchester Guardian*, in which Kit had stated that he had felt very strongly the need for a change of publisher, that he thought most authors did from time to time, that Wesley were young and stylish and seemed to be so clearly au fait with all the changes in publishing at that time, and that of course his decision had had nothing to do with his mother's retirement: 'Rather the reverse.'

This upset everyone dreadfully; Jay and Venetia for its implication that Lyttons had failed him editorially, Giles because it was such a strong statement of comparison in Wesley's favour, and Celia because it seemed to her he was saying, with a hostility which quite literally winded her, that he would have left Lyttons whether she had been there or not.

'I don't understand him,' she said to Venetia over lunch the day the article appeared, 'how he can be so cruel. And so disloyal. He seems – well, he seems not at all the person I imagined.'

And Venetia, watching her grief helplessly, could only try to explain that from Kit's point of view it was Celia who had been cruel and disloyal, not the other way around.

'Well I can't imagine why,' said Celia, poking viciously at the *sole meunière* with her fork. 'When did I ever put Kit anywhere but first in my life?'

'Never, Mummy. Except maybe now.'

'And why shouldn't I have a little happiness, a few years of doing what I want for a change?'

This presentation of herself as a self-sacrificing victim had become Celia's latest and most frequently played role; in the face of her history of most ruthlessly pursuing whatever she wanted, the family found it rather hard to take seriously. Venetia decided this was not the moment to argue with her.

'Mummy he's dreadfully hurt. He forgave you—'

'Yes? He forgave me for what?'

Venetia sighed. This was another difficulty when confronting Celia's grief; that she had never formally admitted to the facts surrounding Kit's birth. If only Venetia could have said to her then: look, just think for a minute why do you think he feels like he does? How confused he must be by the great chasm you've created, between what he's had to accept over these past few years and what you've done in the past few months. But she knew she couldn't; this was her mother's territory and absolutely out of bounds.

'I'm sure he'll get over it,' she said finally, 'just give him time.'

But Kit needed a lot more than time.

The second term was no better; but Lucas supposed it was no worse. At least he knew what to expect. At least he was beginning to learn how to work the system – and, moreover, to be grudgingly willing to do so – and he no longer had to endure the overtures of the other boys, trying to be friendly. Everyone disliked him, and that was that. He was bullied and beaten no less or more because of it; there was no one to console him in the intervals between such events, but he wasn't looking for consolation. He was simply looking for time to pass. He felt he was living in a long, cold nightmare; the holidays – apart from the satisfaction of seeing his mother and Geordie growing increasingly cool with one another – were little better than the term, simply because he knew they had to end. He viewed each return to school with a nauseous dread: the first thing he thought of each morning, and the last each night. There was no escape anywhere; and his rage and misery grew.

He would talk of it to no one; his disbelief that his mother, whom he loved so much, could inflict this on him had set up a festering hostility towards her, worse in its way than the more straightforward hatred he felt for Geordie. And while he could see that Noni felt for him, struggled to understand and to express that understanding, his jealousy of her poisoned his relationship with her as well. That she should continue to be allowed to attend her day school, returning home each evening to the warm house, the privacy, the gentleness of her family, while he must endure the cold, the brutality, the absolute hostility of his environment, seemed to him an outrage of such immense proportions it could hardly be borne. As for Clio, the spoilt baby, with her entourage of nanny and nursery maid and two adoring, doting parents, he could hardly bear even to think about her.

And this term there was a new and ugly torture; there was a rising tide of anti-semitism in the school, and with his dark, unmistakably Jewish looks and his surname, Lucas attracted a great deal of it.

'Lieberman the Jew boy' or simply 'Jew Boy' became his nicknames, hissed across the dormitory in the darkness, hurled across the classroom or even the dining room if no masters were present. A few of the boys found it hugely amusing to say 'Shalom' and there were interminable jokes about his foreskin along with attempts made to study his penis to see if it was there. One night he came into the dormitory to find a crude paper *koppel* on his bed; he was held down while it was fixed to his head with paper clips; one of them dug so deeply into his head that in the morning there was blood on his pillow. He was accused of having been the cause of the last war and even the death of several of the boys' fathers; violent savage taunts that hurt him almost beyond endurance. But he did endure them and he managed to remain silent; he had learned that response, defence, counter-attack were all useless. But the hurt and the misery became ever more ingrained; and he sometimes wondered, as he lay awake in the darkness, just how much longer this was going to have to go on.

'Is this Barty Elliott?'

'It is.'

'Charlie Patterson.'

'Oh – good morning.'

'Good morning. Look, I wondered if I could collect Cathy this evening. From your house.'

'Well – you can, of course. But I thought she was staying the night. It makes more sense, we're a long way uptown from you.'

'I know that. But she has a dental appointment first thing in the

82

morning, I'd quite forgotten, down in Gramercy Park and I really need to have her down here in good time.'

'Well that's easy,' said Barty, 'I start work very early. I'll bring her down in the morning. You can meet her at Lytton House, if you like. Far better than battling uptown this evening.'

'How early is early?'

'Oh, I'm always at my desk at eight-thirty.'

'That is early,' he said. 'I can remember doing that. Such a good time of the day. No phone calls, clear head—'

'But now?'

'Well now, I have to get Cathy to school.'

'Yes, I see.' And take her to the dentist and the doctor and stay home and look after her if she was sick – and goodness knows what he did in the school vacations.

'They have no maid,' Jenna had reported wide-eyed, clearly seeing this as something on a par with having no clothes, or not going to school.

'Anyway,' said Barty, 'come to Lytton House, we're just south of the Block Beautiful—'

'I know where you are,' he said. 'Cathy insisted we go and look at it.'

'Oh.' Barty felt slightly disconcerted; she wasn't sure why; she decided not to bother to try and analyse it. 'Well, then just ring the door bell. There'll be no one on reception or anything, I'll come down.'

'Thank you so much. It's extremely kind of you. And it means I'll be able to work late tonight as well. A treat.'

Poor man. Was it any wonder his business wasn't exactly booming?

Barty wasn't too sure if she liked Cathy. She was very sweet and beautifully mannered, but she had a slightly secretive nature; she had taught Jenna to whisper. Barty didn't approve of that, she preferred Jenna's openness, however noisy and disruptive. The first time she caught them whispering at the supper table, she was very firm.

'Girls, don't whisper. It's a very rude thing to do in front of other people. If you have anything to say, say it. Otherwise wait until you can discuss it together.'

Cathy turned her immense blue eyes on her.

'Sorry, Mrs Elliott. We were only talking about – about the weekend.'

'Oh yes? What aspect of the weekend? I can't think why that should be anything to whisper about.'

'I want her to come to South Lodge,' said Jenna, 'and see everything there. She'd love it. Can she, Mother, please?'

'Well, I should think so,' said Barty, wishing she could think of a reason why not, rather disliking the thought of Cathy's presence in that very special and private place. But then several of Jenna's other friends had been to stay there, and she had enjoyed having them; she was just being mean.

'Yes, of course she can, as long as her father doesn't need her in the city and won't be too lonely.'

'He could come too,' said Jenna. She smiled sweetly at her mother.

'No, I don't think that's at all a good idea,' said Barty.

'Oh all right.' They both looked rather disconsolate, obviously disappointed at the failure of their match-making.

'This is so very kind of you, Mrs Elliott—'

'Please call me Barty.'

'All right. If you will call me Charlie. It sounds a wonderful place you have out there.'

'Yes, it is,' said Barty, 'we love it. It's a very long drive, especially for a weekend, but it always seems worth it once we're there. My husband had it built to his own design, and it has always been one of my favourite places in the world. We try to spend all the time we can there, especially in the summer.'

She was silent, thinking of the lovely house on the shore at Southampton, built high above the dunes, which Laurence had declared so especially hers, where he seemed closer to her, easier to remember.

'Well – of course Cathy would love to come. Is there anything I can send with her?'

'Oh, just a lot of old clothes. Jenna spends most of her time there up trees or playing on the shore. She likes to ride, so if Cathy has some old blue jeans and would like to have a lesson, I can arrange that. She'll be perfectly safe, you don't have to worry,' she added quickly, thinking that in his position, she would be envisaging Jenna haring down the shore on a runaway horse, or drowning in the breakers after an unsupervised walk.

'I wouldn't worry for a moment, if she was with you. It will be such a wonderful opportunity for her. I'm really grateful to you. And so glad they're such friends.'

'Yes, it's nice,' said Barty carefully.

They left for the Hamptons on the Friday afternoon, as soon as the girls had finished school. As they left Manhattan in the early spring evening, looking up at the pink-blue light dancing off the almost unearthly beauty of the Chrysler building, setting her car on its familiar route through Queens and towards the Long Island Expressway, Barty felt her heart lift as it always did.

Jenna felt it too; South Lodge was hers and she loved it in exactly the same way and nothing would have made Laurence happier than to know that. It was a thought which at once saddened and comforted Barty.

It was dark when they arrived; when they were alone Jenna usually dozed off, but the girls were making each other increasingly excited. They drove through the town of Southampton, dark and sleepy as it never was later in the year, down South Main Street and turned left along Gin Lane, with its tall dense privet and beech hedges which kept the perversely named cottages – with their myriad bedrooms, their vast living areas, their swimming pools, their staff and guest quarters – quiet and private.

'Oh my God,' said Cathy, her already huge eyes visibly enlarging as she gazed up at South Lodge from the bottom of the drive. 'Oh, it's beautiful.'

'Isn't it?' said Jenna, 'Hi Mrs Mills, Mr Mills, nice to see you. This is my friend Cathy, she's come to stay.'

'Welcome, Miss Cathy.' Mills took her small overnight bag. 'Come into the house, it's all ready for you.'

The Millses had worked for Laurence Elliott from the day he had first moved into South Lodge; twenty years on, in late middle age, they were only a little less effective and Barty made sure they had all the help with heavy work in both the garden and the house that they needed. She loved them both; she was determined that they would stay at South Lodge for the rest of their days.

'It's your home as much as mine,' she had said gently to Mrs Mills when she burst into tears on hearing that Barty was moving back to the house and wanted them both to stay. 'And I want you here in it with me. As Mr Elliott would have done, I know.'

'Come on Cathy, come on,' Jenna was running through the door, leading the way into the hall and up the stairs, along the corridor, into a room with bunk beds built in the style of a castle, with both the American and English flags waving from the corner. 'This is my room, the bunks are so I can always have a friend and not be lonely. Now look, out here is a balcony, come out, come out and you can see, wait a minute – there, there is the ocean. Do you hear it, and that other noise, that rustling sound, that's the wind in the grasses on the dunes. Isn't it lovely? We'll go down there in a minute, it's great on the shore in the dark.'

'You will not go down anywhere in a minute, Jenna,' said Barty firmly. 'It's much too late.'

'But it's so beautiful, and I want Cathy to experience that. I don't want her to miss anything.'

'No,' said Barty. 'No no no.'

God, she was like Laurence.

'Oh, you're so mean. Well – tomorrow night, then. Do you like it all, Cathy? Say you do, please say you do.'

'I love it,' said Cathy, and was quite silent over the supper Mrs Mills had prepared for the three of them in the kitchen. Indeed she was subdued until the following morning, when she appeared to come to herself again and followed Jenna about on the treasure trail of pleasures that Southampton could offer.

★

'I'm afraid she's rather tired,' said Barty apologetically to Charlie Patterson when he collected her late on Sunday evening from Number Seven. 'Jenna doesn't know the meaning of the word and she was absolutely determined that Cathy should experience every possible delight open to her. They have walked and ridden their bicycles, and Cathy has had a riding lesson—'

'You must let me know what I owe you for that,' said Charlie Patterson quickly.

'Oh, for heaven's sake. A few dollars, really, it was nothing.'

'I'd still like to settle with you,' he said, his dark eyes watchful, and she felt suddenly shocked at herself, she who had had to spend so much of her life being grateful.

'Of course,' she said quickly, 'well, three dollars, with the hat hire.'

'Fine.'

'Their house is just gorgeous,' said Cathy, her great eyes shining. 'Quite big, with a verandah running around it, and a big lawn that goes right the way to the beach. And we went to a wonderful place in Southampton for lunch on Saturday, it was called Sip 'n' Soda and it was just so great. It's such a pretty town, you'd love it, Daddy. Lots of grand buildings, and lovely shops too. There's even a Saks Fifth Avenue there, can you imagine? And we took a little boat out on a lake, just me and Jenna—'

'Only on a pond,' said Barty quickly. 'It's called Wickapogue Pond, and Jenna has a small tub she rows about there. They both had life-jackets on and Mr Mills was on hand to haul them in—'

'As I said,' said Charlie Patterson, 'I really wasn't worried about her for a moment. I knew she was in good hands.'

His dark eyes smiled at her through his spectacles; again she had the same sensation of being drawn to him and yet not quite at her ease. Silly, probably; she was just out of practice at feeling anything at all for a man . . .

'And this morning we walked for miles along the shore, with Barty—'

'Cathy, I told you, Mrs Elliott—'

'No, I told her to call me Barty. It's silly not to.'

'Stop interrupting. Miles along the shore. And we jumped where the ocean came in and then ran away from the surf. And Jenna got knocked down and soaked—'

'I always do,' said Jenna.

'And then we went back and had lunch in the kitchen, and soon after that we had to get ready and it was just *horrible*.' The word was very drawn out.

'And can she come again soon, please?' asked Jenna.

'Please,' said Cathy.

'We'll see,' said Barty and Charlie in absolute unison.

Finals were over; Elspeth and Keir and their fellow undergraduates – 'Only maybe we're graduates now,' said Elspeth wonderingly – spilled into the streets of town exhaustedly elated, filling the pubs, determined to celebrate with as much fervour as they had been working. By mid-afternoon they were drunk; by nightfall they were very drunk.

'Come on,' said Keir, taking Elspeth's hand. 'Let's go and have a little rest.'

'Where?'

'In my rooms.'

'But Keir, we might—'

'Might what? For God's sake, woman, we've finished here. And do you think they'd bother where we were and what we were doing there today of all days? Even the dons have more compassion than that.'

'Well – all right.'

She felt very odd; she never drank much. Not because she disapproved, but because she didn't like it, didn't like losing control. It was another thing she shared with her grandmother.

She lay down on Keir's bed, smiled at him rather confusedly, and shut her eyes. The room proceeded to spin, slowly at first, then faster and faster; she told him about it, articulating with some difficulty.

'Put one foot on the floor,' he said, taking her hand, kissing the fingers, one by one. 'It helps.'

It didn't help; after thirty minutes, while Keir tried repeatedly to kiss her, Elspeth rushed to the bathroom and was sick.

'Poor lass.' His voice was unusually sympathetic.

'Never mind. I feel better now.'

'Is that your first time?'

'First time for what?'

'Drinking till you were sick.'

'Yes. Yes, I think so. Amy's always doing it, and the boys used to, when they were younger, of course, but I never have—'

'I think you should let your little sister give you a lesson or two,' he said, holding out his arms. 'Here, come and have a cuddle.'

'Yes, all right. Oh, dear, maybe not . . .'

It was a couple of hours before she felt all right. 'Ready for the next bout,' as he said, cheerfully. 'Come on, we're all meeting at the Vicky Arms.'

'Oh Keir, I couldn't.'

'Of course you could. And it would spoil my celebration if you didn't.'

'You go.'

'Not without you.'

'That's absurd.'

'No it's not. I don't want to.'

'Do you really mean that?' she asked curiously. Keir's hard-drinking bouts with his fellows were famous.

'I really mean that. I don't want to go without you.'

'But why not?'

'Because I love you,' he said.

'Oh,' she said, and it was like a physical blow, she was so shocked. She sat up, staring at him.

'Well, don't look so surprised. You must have known. Why else would I have put up with it all?'

'All what?' she said indignantly.

'You keeping your legs together. Those weekends with your family—'

'Keir! You like my family. And they're always very nice to you.'

'I know. But it's not exactly relaxing, is it? Wondering which of us is going to say something unfortunate first. Me asking where the toilet is, your sister's boyfriend talking gibberish to me about being in – what was it, oh yes, Pop at Eton, your brother being terribly charming about how marvellous the grammar schools are—'

'You're so terribly touchy,' said Elspeth, lying down again. 'Nobody means you any harm, everyone likes you—'

'Oh I know. But they're still a bit – surprised at the fact that they do, wouldn't you say? I can just hear your mother saying to your father how charming I am, just that little bit surprised.'

'You're being ridiculous. You've never heard any such thing.'

'No, I know. But I'd bet you a tenner to a sixpence they've had that conversation.'

'Well, it's a pretty safe bet,' said Elspeth irritably. 'I mean, we're not going to find out, are we?'

'Maybe not. But I bet you'd be paying up if we did. The one I like best is your gran, at least she's open about it. She actually said to that husband of hers in front of me, "Bunny, Mr Brown's parents keep a shop, isn't that too fascinating?" She doesn't pretend it's something she and all her friends might do, she's genuinely interested.'

'Well – good,' said Elspeth, wondering at the same time how Celia might react to being referred to as her gran. She didn't ask him if he had had any more conversations with Celia about his ambitions; the ground was much too dangerous. But she did know he had read a few manuscripts for her and sent reports back.

'Anyway, like I said, I can put up with it all because I love you. How about you?'

He had said it again. It was – well, it was literally shocking. She felt dazed with it, dazed and incredibly excited and happy at the same time. She stared at him.

'You mean what do I have to put up with?' she said, playing for time, still not daring to quite believe it.

'No, you fool. I meant how do you feel about me? Now I've made my confession. I thought you'd go all doolally when I told you.'

'I did,' she said finally. 'Absolutely doolally. I'm just a bit – well, surprised.'

'I can't think why. I've known it for months. Where's your female intuition, Miss Warwick?'

'A bit tentative,' she said. 'And why did you wait so long to tell me?'

'I didn't want to distract you,' he said, 'from your studies.'

'Oh really?' she said laughing.

'But they're over now. Come on, Elspeth. Do you reciprocate this fine emotion I'm confessing to?'

'Oh – you know. I quite like you. Considering everything.' She smiled at him, reached up, stroking his hair, allowing emotion to break through. 'Oh Keir, of course I love you. I've loved you for – well, ever since I first got to know you. I love you very, very much. I can't believe how much I love you.'

'Well that's all fine then,' he said, his voice filled with satisfaction. 'But why did you not tell me before?'

'How could I? It's for the man to say it first, isn't it? Only fast girls – well, take the initiative.'

'Oh aye? Well, I've often wished you a bit faster, Elspeth. As you know.'

'I do know,' she said.

'Now come on, and give me a kiss.'

She did; and even in her frail condition, the familiar surge of sexual feeling for him invaded her, pushing into her consciousness, into every area of her body. He felt it, pulled away from her and smiled into her eyes.

'I really do love you,' he said again.

She kissed him again; felt his hands moving over her, to the places that were allowed (her breasts, her legs – to a certain point), then to the ones that were not (her stomach, her thighs), felt too frail and too happy to protest. And then suddenly, his fingers were inside her pants, seeking out, with infinite care and tenderness, a place that – 'Oh God,' she said, as desire whipped through her suddenly, out of control. 'Oh God, Keir, no, please don't, please please—'

'For God's sake, woman,' he said, in between kissing her mouth, her throat, her breasts. 'For God's sake. You're twenty-one. You've finished at university. I love you. You love me. You're not some silly little girl. What are you keeping it for, Elspeth, what?'

And what indeed, she wondered, what? When it was what she wanted, so terribly terribly wanted, and it was true what he said, she was a woman, about to take her place in the world, an adult, a successful, sophisticated adult. Why on earth was she messing about like this, like a silly teenager, when the man she wanted and who wanted her had just told her he loved her.

'I don't know,' she said quite humbly. 'I really don't know. Just – be careful, Keir, won't you? Be very, very careful.'

'I'll be careful,' he said. 'I promise.' And yet again, he told her he loved her.

He was careful; he hardly hurt her at all. And careful in other ways too, turning away from her, putting on the – well, the thing that was going to keep her safe. She turned away too, at that point, kept her eyes shut. She didn't want to see. Even at this stage of things, it seemed a bit embarrassing. Careful too, in the time he took, the long, long time leading her into her excitement until she could hardly wait, hardly bear it. Entering her very slowly, very gently. 'Tell me when to stop,' he kept saying, 'and I will.' And he did; when finally he was there, in her, and it was lovely, so very lovely, she felt herself easing around him, her entire being concentrated there, in that place, and he was pushing and urging her, and she felt herself moving with him, moving somewhere she didn't quite recognise but somehow forwards, into greater and greater pleasure, and she suddenly felt a great rush of triumph, of joy at her own courage and the fact that she could feel such pleasure, and pulled away from him, looked up into his eyes.

'I love you so,' she said, and 'I love you too,' he said, 'so much.' And then they moved on into another country altogether.

He was very skilful; she could see that. Even in the sweetness, the gathering and breaking of her first orgasm – 'Not many people accomplish that,' he said, smiling at her as she lay back, sweating and panting with relief, 'not the first time' – she couldn't help wondering where that skill had come from and whether it mattered. She decided it didn't.

'Really?'

'Really. I'd say you were a natural, Miss Warwick. Well, I knew you would be,' he added, with a touch of complacency.

'Did you?'

'I did. Bet your gran was a bit of a goer,' he added, 'in her day.'

'Keir! What a thing to say. And how can you possibly know?'

'Same way I knew about you. Masculine intuition. Now give me a kiss and let's have a wee kip. After that, I fancy you'll need feeding. How would you like to have supper at The Trout with your lover?'

Fancy me having a lover, she thought, how very grown up. She smiled sleepily at him and fell straight to sleep.

'Mummy? I thought you'd want to know as soon as possible. Elspeth's got a First. She'd have phoned you herself, but she's with a friend in Devon and didn't like to ask if she could make another long-distance call.'

'Oh my darling, how marvellous. I am so very proud of her. As you must be, and Boy of course. Give her my best love. I can't wait to see her. Tell her I'm writing. Goodness, it reminds me of the day Barty got hers.'

It would do, thought Venetia savagely, she never missed an opportunity to remind them of it. And how they had not got Firsts. None of them. Not Giles, and of course Kit had never finished at Oxford. Just bloody Barty.

And then she struggled to remind herself that they all owed Barty a lot. This never failed to half amuse and half irritate her either, that Barty, who had grown up owing them everything had turned the tables so beautifully – and sweetly – on them all.

'Now darling, I'm coming to London next week. So boring up here, and I want to go to Wimbledon. Bunny's off to Henley as well—'

'Aren't you?'

'Of course not. Dreadful, his friends. They just get drunk and talk about the old days. And he rows in some veterans race, it's all too embarrassing.'

'Oh I see.' Poor Bunny. 'How was Cairo?'

'Very hot and very dull. The whole thing was a disappointment.'

'Even the cruise up the Nile?'

'Oh absolutely. I told Bunny I didn't want to do that, but he insisted, and of course I was right. And there were the most dreadful people on the boat – that reminds me, Venetia, what about Elspeth's young man?'

'What about him? Oh, he got a First too.'

'How splendid. Good for him. With all those disadvantages. Just shows what Oxford can do. But – shopkeepers. Who would have thought it possible once? How times have changed. I might write him a little note too. He'd be thrilled, I'm sure. What are his plans?'

'I really don't know, Mummy. You'll have to ask him yourself.'

'Am I going to see him?'

'If you're coming to London next week. He's coming to stay for a few days. Then Elspeth is going up there, and they're going walking in the Highlands with a group of friends.'

'A group of friends? I hope you're sure about that, Venetia. That they're not going off on their own.'

'Of course I'm sure. I trust Elspeth absolutely.'

'How very unwise of you,' said Celia.

Celia travelled down to London a few days later, spent a few days shopping and visiting and then found herself sitting gazing out of the window at Cheyne Walk, wondering what she could do next. She was hating this; absolutely hating it now. The days of idleness, of too much time, time to read, to shop, to lunch with her friends, to do all the things she had thought she might enjoy. Even riding had lost some of its charms, no longer a stolen pleasure, eased out of an impossibly tight schedule; she had been down to Ashingham for a few days in the spring to stay with her brother, and had ridden almost every day. On the last she had returned to London early, saying she was tired, despite the fact that tiredness was the thing she was most impatient of in other people.

Travelling with Lord Arden, so exciting the first time, moderately pleasing the second, had become a bore on the third. She never wanted to get on another plane or ship or train: unless it had a clear purpose, not just another few weeks filled with vapid amusement. She had always loved business trips, with sightseeing snatched out of the working day, each place more intensely interesting for its professional associations, the experience given a tautness and – well, a point. But just looking at places had come to depress her. And she was faced with an eternity of it, as far as she could see.

She had moved into Cheyne Walk 'for a few days', her excuse being that Lord Arden was having several friends to stay for Henley week, and the staff needed a clear run to get it ready. She doubted if anyone would believe this, but she didn't actually care. Always reluctant to admit her mistakes, and confronted with the biggest one in her life, she found herself careless of people's awareness of it. It had been a piece both of personal and professional misjudgement.

And she missed Kit – and Sebastian – almost more than she could bear. She and Sebastian had never been apart so long, there had never been more than a few weeks when they had not met, talked, just been – close. She had never thought it would come to this. Some days it was a physical pain, the missing him: on others, a dreadful bleak nothingness. And she was missing Lyttons more dreadfully than she would ever have believed. The ebb and flow of the publishing year, the preparation of catalogues, the publication of the spring and autumn lists, the commissioning of covers, the panic over late manuscripts, it was all so ingrained into her psyche that she could not look out on a summer morning without thinking of a fresh crop of titles, or on an autumn mist without fretting over the cover of a Christmas catalogue. The only thing she still did was read the unsolicited manuscripts that came in. She had found herself insisting on it, had said that was the one thing she was not prepared to relinquish entirely – and had passed some of them on to Keir Brown, whose reports had impressed her – but it hardly filled a great deal of her time.

And so here she was, in the second year of her new life, knowing that if it went on much longer she would die of boredom. A somewhat convoluted thought, she reflected, but who could be surprised at that? Senility seemed to be stalking her as closely as her own shadow.

She picked up the copy of the *Publishers' Gazette* which had arrived that morning, and leafed through it as she drank her coffee. Pretty poor stuff it was, she thought, grimacing, like everything else that Mrs Hardwicke produced: virtually tasteless. If she was going to spend much time at Cheyne Walk she would get rid of her, and hire a new cook-housekeeper. How absurd it was to expect one person to do the job of both, she should never have allowed herself to be talked into that one . . .

'Oh my God,' she said aloud, and put her coffee cup down, read the item again.

WESLEY SIGNS UP 'DAZZLING' NEW NOVELIST

David Johnson, the author of *Lock and Key* which is tipped to win this year's Somerset Maugham award, has been signed by Wesley, who continue to make waves in every area of publishing. Johnson, whose work was described last year as 'dazzling' in a rare tribute by Michael Joseph, had so far eluded any long-term arrangement. *Lock and Key* was published by Macmillan, but although several houses have offered for his second book (so far untitled), he had not signed with any of them. However, his agent, Curtis Brown, now announce a three-book deal with Wesley.

'They excel in every field,' Johnson told the *Gazette* earlier this week. 'They seem to me to have the most imaginative editors, the most forceful publishers, the most energetic sales force. I am very happy with the deal.'

Johnson is only one of a series of young writers who have gone to Wesley; starting with the defection of young Kit Lytton from the family house, Caroline Barker has moved from Macmillan with her sagas, and Ann Yorke, the brilliant young crime writer, from Michael Joseph. Who next?

'Who next indeed?' said Celia aloud, picking up the phone, and dialling Lyttons number.

'Jay? Have you seen the *Gazette*? Well, you should have done. Go and get it, find page eleven. Didn't I tell you to sign that boy up last autumn? Now look where he's gone, to Wesley, of all places. And Ann Yorke too, I told you she could be bought from Joseph. Does nothing at all get done unless I do it myself? For God's sake, Jay, are you running a publishing house or a bookbinding warehouse? I warn you, at this rate you'll be losing Nancy Arthure as well, I heard she was very unhappy about her last cover and indeed her sales. And as for Clementine Hartley, I heard she and Kit had lunch last week. Did you know about that? Yes, of course they're friends, but I don't suppose their conversation was entirely confined to the weather and Clementine's forthcoming holiday.

'I have to tell you I'm very seriously considering coming in tomorrow and calling a meeting myself. What? Well I know that, but I am still on the board, I would remind you, and I still hold shares. I don't exactly relish seeing their value dwindle to nothing. I cannot believe you have allowed those two, not just one but two, slip through your fingers. What is going on there, Jay, any work or any thinking at all? I'm sorry? Well I'm afraid it seems to be rather a lot to do with me. In fact, I would suggest you do call a meeting for tomorrow morning and I shall attend it, as it is my perfect right to do. Yes. Yes, please do. I shall hold the morning free. Oh, all right, and the following two mornings as well. Thank you.'

She put the phone down and smiled at it. They weren't going to like this one bit.

She suddenly realised she felt about twenty years younger.

CHAPTER 8

Izzie put the phone down, and tried to pretend she didn't care. Didn't care that the rather charming, good-looking young writer she had met at a publishing party the previous week had just telephoned to cancel a supper date. With what had seemed like a very slim excuse.

It happened to her rather a lot; she was slowly facing up to the fact that she just didn't seem to be very attractive to men. Elspeth and Amy Warwick had always had dozens of boyfriends; Amy had been engaged twice already and Elspeth was now so happily and implacably in love with her Scot that all other men hardly seemed to exist. While he was away in Glasgow, Elspeth behaved like a married woman. Probably she'd be announcing her engagement next, Izzie thought gloomily. And most of Izzie's friends seemed to have steady boyfriends, and a social life that was a lot more hectic than her own.

She supposed she just wasn't – sexy.. She had never mastered the art of flirting; whenever she tried she felt embarrassed and could see perfectly clearly that it didn't work, didn't suit her, any more than rather obviously sexy clothes did. She knew she was pretty, and everyone was very fond of her – indeed, if she heard Kit or Sebastian telling her once more that everyone loved her, she thought she would scream. She didn't want everyone to love her. She wanted just one person to be passionately in love with her, wanted them to be trying to get her into bed, wanted to be sent flowers and given jewellery and be taken to nightclubs and – well, just to have a really good time. Instead of which she was twenty-five years old, still a virgin and spent a great many evenings at home with her father.

She wondered if her mother had been sexy; she suspected not. Now that she was really grown up, she could see it was true what people like Barty and the twins were always telling her, that she was like her in every way. She could see her father, on the other hand, must have been very sexy in his youth; so astonishingly handsome and romantic-looking – like a film star, a blond Rudolph Valentino, as Celia had once told her when she had had rather too much to drink. Izzie had discouraged that particular conversation, she found it embarrassing and upsetting, but she had looked out some old pictures of Valentino and could see what Celia had meant. And he had clearly had a pretty wild youth, marrying so young, and then – well, anyway. She was clearly not in the least like him.

She sighed; what could she do about it? She knew she was too serious to attract young men; she tended to like older ones – again, rather like her mother she supposed. Her father had been twenty years older than her when they married – and older men also liked Izzie, but most of the ones she knew or met were married. She was a deeply moral person, and knew she could never, ever have an affair with a married man. She had seen first-hand what terrible unhappiness that caused.

She sighed, sat staring out of the window at the rather bleak October garden; now she not only had to spend Saturday evening alone, but tell her father that she wasn't going out after all. He would be sweet and clumsily sympathetic and consoling and suggest they got Kit round and there she would sit, having supper with them, with a label saying 'wallflower' hung almost visibly round her neck.

The phone rang again; she jumped, picked it up hopefully. Maybe the young man had been speaking the truth, maybe his father really hadn't been very well but he was better now, maybe—

'Izzie? It's Henry. What are you doing tonight?'

'I – don't know,' she said carefully. 'Supposed to be going out with some boring man but – well, why do you ask?'

'I'm having a few friends round. To my flat. Want to come?'

If she hadn't been feeling so rejected, so very undesirable, common sense would have told her to say no. But – well at least Henry liked her. Always had. Even if he was engaged to Clarissa Carr-Johnson, he kept telling her it was only because Izzie had turned him down. Of course he didn't mean it, but—

'Well –'

'Oh go on, Izzie. Bring the boring man if you like.'

'No. He's too boring. You'd have hated him anyway. Look – I'll get back to you. I might just cancel him. It was only – only a drink. Are the others going to be there?'

'The girls are. Noni's probably coming. Roo's out of town, at some house party. Look. You don't have to say now. Just come if you want to.'

'Yes, Henry, all right. I might. Thank you.'

She arrived at Henry's flat at eight, a bottle of Spanish Rioja tucked under her arm. It was the new thing to do, arrive with a bottle. Henry looked at it, and screwed up his face. 'Phew, Izzie. Bit rough. I'll have to give you a crash course in wine. Never mind, sweet of you. I'll bring it out later when everyone's well and truly plastered.'

'Thanks, Henry,' she said tartly. 'You're such a charmer.'

'Oh – sorry. Didn't mean to be rude. Now come on in, lots of people

96

here you know, here's Bobby Cousins, you remember him, he works with me, and Freddy Whittaker, we were at school together. Freddy, this is Izzie Brooke, honorary cousin of ours, she's in your line of business, writes wonderful advertisements for books. Freddy works for – what is it, Freddy?'

'J. Walter Thompson,' he said, 'on the account side. Greatly admire you creative people of course, but I'm just not safe with a pencil.'

He went into a braying laugh; Izzie tried to join in.

'Honorary cousin, eh?' he said, looking at her. 'How's that, then?'

'Oh – just the daughter of a – a close family friend,' she said quickly. She often wondered what people would say if she started telling them the rest of the story. Of how very close the family friend had been, how extremely close she herself had come to the family; the thought did sometimes tantalise her, especially when she could see she was boring her audience. As she clearly was now. She could see Freddy was already dying to get away from her and back to a girl he had been chatting up; Izzie made an excuse, went across to the drinks table, and poured herself a glass of wine.

'Izzie, hallo. How lovely you could come. You look great.'

Amy's tone was enthusiastic rather than convincing; she looked wonderful in a low-cut black top and very full skirt, her hair was done in the new curly Elizabeth Taylor style, her eye make-up heavy, her mouth full and bright red. She looked far older and more sophisticated than Izzie. Izzie always wore very little make-up, and was dressed in a simple red sheath dress; it had seemed rather splendid in Woollands' changing room, here it had suddenly assumed an almost homely air, too long and too body-skimming. Amy, like most of the other girls, was all bosom and hips. Izzie felt suddenly like a maiden aunt.

'Thanks, Amy. How's college?'

'Oh – fine. Terribly hard work. And I'm the most hopeless typist ever. Ten thumbs, I've got.'

Amy sighed. She was at Queens secretarial college, after a year at finishing school in Paris and a year doing the season, having decided against university; she was by her own confession lazy, and wanted simply to have a good time. She had had a triumphant season as a debutante, and her grandmother had insisted on giving her a ball at Cheyne Walk; now, as she kept saying, everything was on hold until she got engaged. Barty had told Izzie that Amy was so like her mother at the same age it was quite spooky.

'Silly, funny, so attractive, absolutely determined not to do anything more difficult than catching a husband.'

Which seemed to be quite difficult actually, Izzie thought; and here she was, five years older than Amy, and not even a boyfriend in sight.

She smiled at her. 'I'm sure you'll get better at typing.'

'I hope so. I want to go and work in a bank or something. Lots of lovely men.'

'Is Noni here?' said Izzie, looking hopefully round the room.

'No, she isn't. Spending the evening with her mama. Says she's trying to cheer her up, she's missing Lucas terribly. I wouldn't miss him, little beast. Apparently she – Adele, I mean – and Geordie are having endless rows about him, there were the most frightful scenes when Lucas had to go back this term, Geordie threatening to thrash him, it's absolutely horrible there. Good for Geordie I say, putting his foot down finally. Oh, there's Porky Cavanagh, 'scuse me, Izzie darling, he promised to get me an invitation to Sandringham after Christmas. Or do you want to come and meet him? I know he'd love you.'

Porky Cavanagh was predictably plump and pink-faced; Izzie shook her head.

'No, honestly Amy. Is Elspeth here?'

'She's over there. You should marry Henry, Izzie, you'd be so good for him. And he's still in love with you, he's always saying so. And the whole family would love it.'

'That's not quite the point though, is it?' said Izzie.

She moved over to talk to Elspeth who hugged her.

'Izzie, I'm so glad you're here. Between you and me I'm not mad about Henry's friends. How are you?'

'Oh – fine. Yes. Thank you. How's Keir?'

'Oh – all right; I haven't seen much of him for a few weeks. He's living up there in Glasgow, trying to get a job, coming down for interviews and then haring back again.' She sighed. 'I'm afraid it's not going terribly well.'

'I'm sorry.'

'So am I. It's not helping our relationship, I can tell you. It's so unfair, he's so clever. But – oh well. I'm sure in time it'll be all right.'

'I'm sure too. How's Lyttons?'

'Oh Izzie, I love it. That doesn't help with Keir either, of course. That I've got the very thing he hasn't. Of course I'm doing the most basic things, reading manuscripts, copy-typing, sending out rejection slips – so many of them – running errands, but it's just so exciting to be there.'

'It certainly must be at the moment,' said Izzie.

'You mean with Granny back in charge? It's priceless, Izzie, they all pretend she's just dropped in, and of course she comes in more and more, day after day, calling meetings, sending memos, it's driving them all mad. Just when they thought they'd got rid of her.'

'Well it was silly of them to think so,' said Izzie.

'I suppose so. Anyway, it is quite edgy altogether at the moment, they're very aware they need to find some brilliant new writers, they've lost quite a few, you know, and of course they don't grow on trees—'

'I don't suppose they do.'

'What does Sebastian have to say about it?'

'Not a lot. It's not something we – well, we've discussed very much.

And of course Jay is his editor now, as much as anyone is, he's getting awfully grand in his old age, won't have anything changed at all. As you probably know.'

'No, not really,' Elspeth sounded awkward; there was a silence, then, 'I must go, I promised Mummy I'd have supper with her, Daddy's away. Izzie, darling, see you very soon. Maybe we could have lunch one day. Now go and talk to Henry, he's looking frightfully down in the mouth. I do wish you'd marry him, we'd all like it so much.'

'Not you too,' said Izzie laughing. 'Don't be silly, he's engaged to Clarissa.'

'I know, but she's such a pain. I wonder where she is anyway, she was supposed to be here hours ago.'

An hour later, Izzie was dancing with Henry; 'Secret Love' was on the gramophone and he held her closer than she would have liked, but he was, on the other hand, clearly distracted, talking little and keeping one eye, notionally at least, on the door. Clarissa had not arrived, had not even telephoned; even Amy thought it was odd and said so.

'On the other hand, she's so full of herself,' she added to Izzie, 'and thoughtless too, I suppose it's not so surprising. I do hope Henry doesn't marry her, she'd lead him a terrible life.'

'Dear Izzie,' said Henry, as the record ended. 'I'm so pleased you came. Enjoying yourself?'

'Oh – very much,' said Izzie carefully. It wasn't true; apart from Henry and the girls no one had bothered to talk to her and she had spent quite a lot of the evening standing alone by the gramophone, changing records. Still, at least she wasn't at home in Primrose Hill . . .

'Henry! Telephone. It's Clarissa.'

'Ah. Please excuse me, Izzie.'

'Of course.' Half an hour later he hadn't reappeared; Amy, wide-eyed with distress came back from searching for him.

'He's really upset, Izzie. Almost in tears. I don't know what's wrong but – well – maybe he'll talk to you. He's in his bedroom. Would you – that is . . .'

'Oh I'm sure he'd rather be alone,' said Izzie quickly.

'I'm sure he wouldn't. Go on, Izzie, be a brick.'

Not sure if she liked the role of brick, Izzie went rather reluctantly along the corridor to Henry's bedroom and knocked on the door.

'Who is it?' His voice sounded thick, odd.

'It's Izzie.'

'Oh – Izzie. Just a minute.'

He appeared at the door, looking strained, pushing a hanky into his pocket, his eyes suspiciously bright. He was holding a bottle of wine in one hand, a glass in the other; he smiled rather feebly at her.

'Mind coming in here for a bit? I don't feel quite like going back to the party.'

'Of course. Henry, what is it, what's the matter?'

'Oh –' he sighed, a heavy, rather shaky sigh '– it's Clarissa. Should have seen it coming of course – but it's always a shock. She's just – well, she's just told me she's not sure about – about our getting married.'

'What, just like that?'

'Yup. Just like that. Says she's afraid we're not really compatible after all. Wants some time to think about it. Oh shit.' His voice shook slightly; he smiled weakly at her. 'Sorry Izzie.'

'Henry, I'm so sorry. How beastly. And just on the phone too, she could at least have come to see you.'

'Well – she said she had wanted to, that it wasn't her fault I'd asked so many people round.'

'I see. And – is that all she said?'

'More or less.'

'Well –' she struggled to find something comforting to say '– maybe she's just being cautious. That's not such a bad thing, is it? To want to be sure?'

'No, I suppose not.' He sighed. 'I'd say it was more likely she's met someone else, that's usually what happens, isn't it?'

'I – don't know,' said Izzie quietly. She put her hand on his arm.

He sighed. 'Better now than after we're married, I suppose. But, Izzie, what's the matter with me, do you think? Third time it's happened now. Have I got BO or something? Tell me, there's a good girl.'

'Henry it hasn't happened yet. And you do not have BO,' said Izzie smiling. 'I can promise you that. Or bad breath. And neither are you boring or stupid or any of those things.'

'Well then. Why won't any of these girls marry me? They start out all right, every time. Mustard keen. Then suddenly it's over. Just like that. There must be something.' He blew his nose hard, poured himself another glass of wine.

'I don't know,' said Izzie rather helplessly. 'I suppose people do change their minds. Find out more about each other and – decide it's not a good idea. Gosh, look at Amy, twice already. It's just something girls seem to do.'

'You don't,' said Henry morosely.

'No. No, I know I don't.' Her tone was suddenly disconsolate. He looked at her.

'Here, have some wine. Share my glass.'

She took a sip obediently; it tasted nice, soothing and comforting. Usually she didn't like wine very much. She took another.

'I'm really sorry for you Henry,' she said, 'but I'm sure in time you'll find the right girl. She's out there somewhere now, I expect, looking for you.'

'I hope so. I really do. Oh God, I don't know. This has been pretty bloody hurtful. Last time we met, Clarissa was talking about where we might live.'

'Poor Henry.'

'I'm really awfully fond of her, you know,' he said suddenly, after a silence. 'Really fond. She's a great girl. Lot of fun.'

'Yes,' said Izzie carefully. It was difficult to know what to say.

'And my parents like her. And I got on pretty well with hers. We were talking about wedding dates, Izzie. It wasn't just a brief romance.'

'No, I know.'

'Pretty bad show all round. I'm going to look no end of an idiot. Here, have some more wine. Poor old Henry, they'll be saying, can't keep a girl. Wonder what's wrong with him—'

'Of course they won't.' She had another drink; she seemed to need it, it was helping her through this difficult conversation. The bottle was nearly empty; Henry looked at it.

'Better get another. Won't be a tick. Don't go away now, will you?'

'No, I won't.'

He disappeared, came back with another bottle and two clean glasses. He filled one to the brim and handed it to her.

'Drink up. Now where was I?'

'You were saying people would be thinking there must be something wrong with you.'

'Well, they will, won't they?'

'I shouldn't think so for a moment,' she said. 'Just look at all the romances you've had. Dozens it seems like to me.'

'But none of them last. That's exactly the problem. How about you, Izzie?' he said suddenly, looking at her intently.

'What about me?'

'Well, I mean, you haven't got anyone – sort of permanent, have you? Or have you? Are you keeping him from us?'

'Absolutely not,' she said. 'I wish I was.'

She stopped. She didn't really want to have this conversation with Henry. It was humiliating. And at this particular moment, slightly dangerous.

'What do you mean?'

'Oh nothing,' she said quickly. 'Nothing at all.'

'Izzie, come on. There is. You look upset. What is it?'

'I don't want to talk about it.'

'Why not? I've been baring my soul to you. Come on, tell me. Tell your big brother.'

'Don't be ridiculous,' she said. 'And you're not my brother.'

And then, partly because of the wine, and partly because the evening had been in its various ways upsetting, and she suddenly couldn't help it, couldn't help thinking of that other relationship, that other, so unbrotherly relationship, far more dangerous and threatening than the one with Henry, she started to cry.

Henry was horrified; he put his arm round her, fished a handkerchief out of his pocket, handed it to her.

'Here. Come on, Izzie, don't cry. Tell me what the matter is, please.'

'Oh it's nothing. Really. It's just that –' suddenly she succumbed to the temptation of talking about it, talking to Henry, who at least, she knew, found her attractive, and made it therefore less humiliating '– well, I don't seem to have much success with men. They just don't seem to like me. At least girls like you, fancy you, want to marry you. Even if they sometimes go off the idea later. And actually I don't often fancy anyone either. I don't know about there being something wrong with you, but I think it's more likely there's something wrong with me.'

'There's nothing wrong with you. You're terribly fanciable, terribly pretty. You know what a torch I've always carried for you for a start.'

'Oh Henry, don't. Don't start being kind.'

'I'm not being kind. I think you're gorgeous, always have done. You can't have forgotten our little romance. Now who ended that, you or me?'

'Me,' she said and in spite of herself, she smiled at him, a reluctant, awkward smile.

'Well, there you are. In fact, you started it, you were the first to set me on my downward spiral. So don't start giving me any sob stories.'

'Sorry,' she said meekly. 'Sorry, Henry.'

'Come here,' he said suddenly, setting down his wine glass. 'Give me a hug. We seem to be in a bit of a sorry state, both of us.'

She let him put his arms round her. 'You silly girl,' he said, kissing her cheek gently. 'You silly, silly girl. Lovely, silly Izzie.'

And then suddenly, and she was never sure afterwards how it happened, she kissed him back quite gently but on the mouth, and against her lips she felt his change, felt them become harder and more urgent and seeking. And also quite suddenly, it was welcome, rather than otherwise, and comforting and reassuring, and she began to return his kiss; and then his arms tightened round her, and he turned her to face him, and moved one of his hands up to her hair and started stroking it and pushing through it, loosening it from its clasp.

'Lovely Izzie,' he said. 'Lovely, lovely Izzie.'

Emotions roared through her, difficult, confusing, dangerous. This was in some ways so exactly what she wanted, to be held and desired and found beautiful; and in some ways so exactly what she didn't, knowing that they were both drunk, upset, feeling lonely. But—

'Oh Izzie,' he said. 'Izzie, you are so silly. And so beautiful.'

And then his mouth was on hers again, and she couldn't help it, she leaned back on the pillows, feeling dizzy, not just with the wine, but with emotion and pleasure and the sweet, strange reassurance of being desired and desirable, and she pushed him away from her and smiled up at him, her eyes probing his.

They were very dark, his eyes, and very serious, and so was his face; and his voice, when he spoke, was shaky, but in a quite different way: 'You really are lovely, you know,' he said again. 'And so very – desirable.'

After that everything happened rather quickly.

She could never have said afterwards that she didn't want it: she did. She wanted it, and wanted Henry, as she had not wanted anyone since – well, since she could remember. She could not pretend she had discouraged him; she did not. She did not just allow him to caress her, to stroke her breasts and smooth her legs, and kiss her neck, she encouraged him; she did not protest in the very least as he began to undress her. She did not say once that he must stop, rather she urged him on; in between kissing him, holding him, she sat up, pulled off her dress, allowed him to remove the rest of her clothing.

She did not tell him – of course, how could she – that she was a virgin, that she had never done this before; choosing instead to let him discover it, thinking, confident indeed that he must be experienced enough to deal with the fact beautifully . . . Disappointment there; he lacked skill, even she could recognise that, and it was awkward, painful even. Her own pleasure and excitement faded as his increased, and by the time he had finished – horribly soon – and rolled off her, breathing heavily, she felt nothing at all except considerable discomfort and even pain. Shocked into sobriety she found herself simply appalled at what she had done.

After a few minutes Henry turned away from her, reached for a pack of cigarettes and lit one. He offered her one; she shook her head.

'No thank you.'

He was silent for a while, drawing heavily on his cigarette; then he said, 'I hope – that is, I hope that was all right for you, Izzie.'

'Yes,' she said, quickly. 'Yes, of course it was. Thank you.'

'I – didn't realise. That – well, you know . . .'

'No. I'm sorry, I should have told you.'

'Of course you shouldn't,' he said in an attempt at gallantry, 'don't be silly. Anyway – well, it was jolly nice for me.'

'Good,' she said, trying to sound cheerful, light-hearted, as if the whole incident had simply been a piece of rather unimportant fun.

'I really am sorry,' he said again, and then turned and smiled at her, his dark eyes moving over her face, the old charm and confidence quite restored.

'Honestly, Henry, there's nothing to be sorry about. Really there isn't. I – well, it was my idea quite as much as yours.'

'I suppose so.'

Another silence; then, 'I think I might get dressed,' she said, 'get back to the party. People might wonder what's happened to us.'

'Good idea. Yes. Want the bathroom? It's just next door. But of course you know that.'

'Yes,' she said. 'Yes, I know that.'

She felt she now knew something else too, without having any experience to base the knowledge on at all; the reason girls might break off their engagements to Henry Warwick. There must be a great deal more to sex than that. Surely, surely there must.

Keir sat in his parents' kitchen, staring at the letter that had just arrived for him. He knew he hardly had any need to open it. 'Macmillan', read the name on the envelope. It would no doubt contain another rejection. So far he had had six. All the big houses, Hutchinson, Michael Joseph, Collins, all had given him an interview, all so far had turned him down. He knew why, of course; and they would never admit it, of course. He was an ideal candidate – on paper. He had a First in English from Oxford, he wrote well, he had reviewed books for *Isis*, he had worked in bookshops, he was very widely read, not only in the classics, but in contemporary fiction as well. He really should have got a job. But – he couldn't. Or not the job he wanted. Time and again, he was told to come back when he had some experience. 'And how do I get that?' he said in despair, 'if no one will give me any in the first place?'

At first he had suspected it was because of his accent, his grammar-school education, indeed, would have welcomed that in some perverse way, it would have given him something to be angry, rather than despairing, about; but it was not. It swiftly became clear to him, that his First in English from Oxford was qualification enough. It was a simple case of supply and demand. For every editor's job, there was a very large handful of applicants; it was as simple as that.

He was offered other jobs in the publishing houses; in production, administration, accounts, publicity, even as a trainee rep. But he regarded those as insults; he wanted to be an editor. And being Keir, he was not prepared to settle for anything else; and being Keir, he took it as a personal insult.

It made him angry and aggressive with everyone: including Elspeth. Especially Elspeth. She had sympathised with him at first, had even suggested, very gently, that she might speak to one of her uncles about him, but he had turned on her, his face contorted with rage.

'Don't even think such a thing. That I would take charity, betray myself like that. Good God, Elspeth, have you no sense of any kind?'

She retreated hastily, said she was sorry, she was only trying to help, was so clearly distraught for him that he had forgiven her. But the fact remained, she had the job he wanted. Had acquired it with the absolute minimum of effort – whatever she might say about the family insisting on a good degree – and it hurt. It hurt badly.

He went upstairs, opened the letter, skimming through its contents: 'Dear Mr Brown, thank you so much for coming to see us . . . very impressed . . . excellent qualifications . . . however . . . wonder if you have considered Sales . . .'

He sat there for a while on his bed, staring at it; then he tore it up into very tiny pieces and put it in his waste-paper basket. And after a while he went downstairs and said to his mother, as if he were announcing he was going to the shops: 'I've decided against publishing. I don't think it would suit me, anyway. I'm going to take up teaching. Far more worthwhile.'

Izzie had managed to persuade herself it had all been for the best. This was, after all, the 1950s, and sex to their generation was not quite what it had been to their parents and grandparents. She was no longer a virgin which was wonderful; her small, but extremely heavy burden had been lifted. The fact that it had not been lifted with any degree of care and skill perhaps didn't matter too much either; indeed if it had been, she might have found herself nurturing romantic notions about Henry which would have been dangerous for both of them. Amy had seen her a few days after the party and told her that Clarissa had telephoned Henry that morning and said she would like to see him.

'Turns out she just had a fit of pre-nuptial nerves. He's like a dog with two tails. They're having dinner tonight. So it's probably all on again. Of course we'd rather it was you, Izzie, but there's no hope of that, we know. And he was wretched about it, poor old boy.'

'Yes,' said Izzie, forcing some laughter into her voice. 'I could see that. And no there's no hope of it being me, as you put it. 'Bye Amy.'

So really, it was all very much for the best. Very much for the best. Of course it was.

'Is it true, Lieberman –' the voice was very measured across the study, very drawling '– is it true your father died in a concentration camp?'

'No,' said Lucas firmly. 'No it's not.'

'But he's not alive? He never brings you down.'

'No. He's not.'

'Well –'

He was silent; there were two boys in the study. The small one, Forrester, was sitting by the fire behind him; he gave Lucas a sharp kick on his backside.

'Answer when you're spoken to you little squirt. You little Jewish squirt.'

'I did answer,' said Lucas steadily.

'You did not. We want to know how he died.'

'Why should you want to know that? It's nothing to do with you.'

'Oh but it is Jew-boy,' said Armitage, the other boy. His back was to the window and it was a brilliantly sunny day, Lucas couldn't see his face clearly. It was unnerving. 'We want to know if he was a traitor, if he collaborated with the Nazis.'

'Of course he didn't.'

'Well if he didn't die in one of the camps, what happened to him? How did he escape? Must have collaborated, it seems to us.'

'It's nothing to do with you,' said Lucas steadily.

'Yes it is. We don't want some filthy Nazi sympathiser's son fagging for us. Come on, tell us.'

'No,' said Lucas.

He could still remember his mother telling him what had happened to his father; still remember the small, sad service she had held in the chapel at Ashingham, and being bidden always to remember how brave his father had been.

'Nazi!' said Forrester. 'Jewish Nazi-boy.'

'Shut up,' said Lucas suddenly. 'Shut up, shut up!'

'Now then,' said Armitage, 'don't lose your temper. We just want to know, Jew-boy, that's all.'

'I'll tell you, then,' said Lucas. He stood up from where he had been tending the fire, slowly faced Armitage. He felt very odd, everything seemed to be in slow motion. 'My father was shot by the Nazis. Not in a concentration camp, but on the streets in Paris. He'd been hiding for years. They'd just found him, were rounding people up early one morning.'

'And – do go on, Jew-boy. This is very interesting. A history lesson. A Jewish history lesson.'

He seemed to be at the end of a very long, bright tunnel; Lucas fixed his eyes on the sneering face.

'And there was a little girl, hiding in the doorway, her parents had been dragged out. My father saw her, tried to grab her, hide her in a cart. The Nazis saw him and shot him, then and there on the street. That's how he died. All right? Is that clear enough for you?'

'Pretty clear.' Armitage walked towards him. 'If it's true.' He grinned at Lucas, his blue eyes hard and mocking. 'It's a pretty good story certainly, Lieberman. A hero, then, for a father. A Jewish hero. Bit unlikely, I'd have thought. Not many of them, I believe. Most of them came to heel snivelling.'

And then it happened; the white heat in Lucas's head exploded into something so violent and so strong he had no idea what he was doing. He seized Armitage by the throat and punched him in the face twice, saw him reeling backwards, yelling, felt Forrester grab him from behind, knee him so hard in the buttocks that he shouted with pain, and then Armitage came at him again, punching him in the mouth once, twice—

'Boys, what on earth is going on in here? What are you doing? Lieberman, Armitage—'

'He hit me first, Sir,' Armitage wiped his hand across the bloody nose that was evidence.

'And Forrester, let him go. Let him go at once.'

'I was only trying to save Armitage, Sir. Lieberman went berserk Sir.'

'And why exactly did he go berserk? Would you like to enlighten me?'

'I don't know Sir. He just got upset. He was talking about his father and how he died. Maybe he felt we weren't sympathetic enough Sir. We were, Sir, really, it was a tragic story.'

'Yes, all right Forrester. Lieberman, go and get cleaned up and report to your housemaster. And you two, I'd like some more details from you.'

An hour later, Lucas was doing his prep in solitary confinement, sentenced to two hours' extra defaulters. His housemaster had said that while he was sympathetic to his distress, there was never any excuse for violence. Lucas's reputation for surly, aggressive behaviour with everyone, staff and boys alike, did not help him; there was no one with a good word to say for him. Everyone agreed he was difficult, ill-mannered, hostile to the school and all its efforts to integrate him. His housemaster looked at him sternly.

'While I can see it was very tragic how your father died, Lieberman, you were a very small child. The memory can hardly be a fresh one. Nor can I see why Armitage and Forrester could possibly have wanted to torment you over something like that. It was heroic behaviour, there was surely nothing derogatory they could possibly find to say. I think you must have over-reacted to whatever it was they said. For which they have been quite severely chastised, I do assure you. We do not tolerate bullying or any kind of abuse in this school.'

Lucas said nothing; just clenched his fists and tried to concentrate on the pain in his jaw and eye which was considerable. It was preferable to the agony of listening properly to this claptrap.

'Now, do you have anything to add to your defence?'

Silence.

'Lieberman?'

'No.'

'No Sir.'

'No Sir.'

That night he locked himself in one of the lavatories and cried like a child; somehow respectful of what was clearly genuine grief, the others left him alone. And in the morning, waking after a very few hours with a throbbing head and an aching jaw, he had decided what he would do.

'Izzie? You all right?'

'What? Oh yes, I'm fine.'

She smiled at Noni across the supper table; they were spending the evening at the house in Montpelier Street as they did most weeks. Noni was having trouble with her maths and was coming up to her School Certificate; Izzie, who had a rather surprising facility for the subject, had offered to help her. Afterwards she would stay on for supper and they would chat; sometimes Adele would join them, sometimes Geordie, increasingly rarely both of them.

'Good. You seem a bit − distracted.'

'Oh − not really. Few problems at work.'

'Like what? Tell me.'

'Oh, nothing, Noni. You wouldn't understand.'

'I might,' said Noni.

'No you wouldn't,' said Izzie. She sounded quite sharp. Noni sighed. Another grown-up out of sorts. Life was much less nice these days.

'Isabella, are you all right?'

'Of course I'm all right, Father. Why shouldn't I be?'

'You're very quiet.'

'I'm quite a quiet person, really. Father, I'm fine, please don't fuss. I'm just tired.'

'Is that job too much for you? Because I—'

'No Father, it's not too much for me. Can we talk about something else, please?'

'Sebastian says you're tired.'

'Kit, I'm fine.'

'You don't sound fine. You sound awful.'

'I'm fine. Stop fussing and leave me alone. If I'm tired there's nothing you can do about it, anyway.'

'Izzie, Henry and Clarissa have named the day. And of course she wants us all to be bridesmaids. Won't that be fun?'

'What? Oh, yes, great fun.'

'You don't sound very excited.'

'Amy I'm trying to do some work. All right?'

'Sorry.'

'If you try to make me go back this time,' said Lucas, fixing his large dark eyes on his mother, 'I shall kill myself. I mean it. Other boys kill themselves at school—'

'Darling, surely not.'

'They do. A boy whose brother was at St James's did. He hanged himself in his study. And I shall do the same.'

'Lucas, this is nonsense. Of course you won't kill yourself. Now let's talk about it all some more and then—'

'I don't want to talk about it any more. I can't stand it. I'm going to kill myself if you send me back. I would rather be dead.'

'Lucas—'

'Mother, don't say any more. Just believe me.'

'Geordie, we have to let him leave. He's desperate. He says he's going to kill himself.'

'Melodramatic nonsense,' said Geordie, quite cheerfully. 'I said something very similar when I was sent back to my prep school. What I meant was I wanted more tuck.'

'Geordie!' said Adele, staring at him, her face white and quite shocked. 'Geordie, I can't believe you just said that. Made a joke about Lucas's misery. I really believe him. I don't like the way he looks at all.'

'I haven't liked the way he's looked for a long time,' said Geordie, 'since you mention it.'

'Don't diminish what he's going through, please.'

'And what about what you and I have had to go through? Before he went and now when he's home. It's absurd, the whole thing. Of course he won't kill himself, people who say they will never do, it's a bid for attention, a cry for help and—' he stopped suddenly, as if realising what he had said. Adele pounced.

'Exactly. A cry for help. Which you're denying him. Geordie, please, please let him come home. Please. I will make him behave better, I promise. I can't bear seeing him suffering like this, I really can't.'

'No,' said Geordie, and his face was absolutely serious, rigid in its determination. 'If we give in now, he'll know that next time there's something he doesn't like, he can do exactly what he wants. You don't seem to understand, this is the only way we can help him in the long run. He's his own worst enemy. He can't go through life being rude and disruptive. Look at his last report, it said, over and over again, that he was uncooperative, aggressive, insolent—'

Adele walked out of the room without even looking at him.

Izzie was trying to concentrate on her book that evening when she heard the phone ringing.

'Isabella! It's Noni.'

Oh God. More problems with the maths.

'Hallo Noni. Look I'm—'

'Izzie, can I come and see you? Please please, I'll get a taxi, or could you come down here?'

'Well – I could—'

'It's Geordie. He's moving back to New York. I heard him shouting at Mummy.'

'But why, what's wrong? To – oh, Noni, that can't be right. Geordie would never leave your mother and Clio. Or you, for that matter.'

'Well he is, he is. Mummy phoned Fletton and told them Lucas wasn't coming back, he's been horribly bullied about – about being Jewish, I don't understand. And then she told Geordie and they had the most terrible awful row, screaming at each other, and finally he said, "Well I told you, Adele, it was him or me. You've made your decision. Now you'll have to live with it." And she said, "Where are you going?" and he said, "Back to New York," and she started screaming at him, and then I heard the door of his study slam and I couldn't hear any more. Oh, Izzie, it's so horrible and it's all Lucas's fault. I hate him, I hate him so much. And he came into my room and said, "There, you've got your dear brother back," and he looked so pleased and almost proud of himself. I do know he has had the most horrible time, but I love Geordie so much and—'

'He probably doesn't mean it,' said Izzie soothingly. 'They were just having a row.'

But it seemed that Geordie did.

CHAPTER 9

It was only physical pain. Nothing else. It was only happening to her. Nobody else. It didn't matter. It was worth it. Of course it was. It meant that it would soon be over, very soon now, and no one else need ever know. Or be troubled by it.

No shock, no shame, no conflict; just a nice clean ending. Her father would never have to know, Kit would never have to know, perhaps most important, Henry would never have to know. Of all her terrors, that had been the greatest. That Henry would find out, and feel bound to offer to marry her. To break off his engagement to Clarissa, and marry her instead. He would, she knew, if he suspected. He was too much of a gentleman not to. Far too much. He . . .

'Quiet,' said the woman sharply. 'I said no noise. And keep still.'

Izzie shut her eyes more tightly; she could feel the sweat on her forehead, cold and clammy, feared she was going to be sick. Half of her wanted to sit up, push her away, this horrible ghastly woman. Get off the bed, run. But she couldn't. She was held there anyway, with her legs in the straps, and besides, she lacked the strength and nothing would then be solved. She would still have the baby . . .

From the very beginning, when the vague drifting worry had become something huge and terrifying that dominated her life, when she had dreamed every night that she was bleeding and woken with a dreadful dullness to the reality of her stubbornly white pants and sheets, when she had become obsessed with her own stupidity and a sense of panic so great that she could hardly think, as she sat over her diary for hours, fretting, counting, she had tried not to think of it as a baby. It was a non-event, something that hadn't happened: no more than that. It was nothing real, there, in the depths of her treacherous body, not something alive and growing, looking for nurture from her. It was simply a lateness, a refusal to bleed. That was all.

She tried everything of course; hot baths, gin, quinine – she had heard somewhere that quinine worked very efficiently. But it didn't. Nothing did. Days passed into weeks, and absolutely nothing happened. She went to her diary over and over again, praying that she had somehow miscalculated; over and over again it only served to show her that she had been in bed with Henry on what she knew to be the most fertile part of her cycle. How could she have been so stupid and irresponsible? How, how? It never occurred to her to think that Henry had been stupid and irresponsible too, and far more so than she . . .

Her greatest dread, after Henry finding out, was that her father would somehow get to know of it. Imagining his rage and grief made her feel so frightened that she physically shook. There had not been many times in Izzie's life when she had longed for a mother; she had no experience of what such a being might do for her. But now, in this all-absorbing, intensely female predicament, endured by women from the beginning of time, she longed for her. She even thought – very briefly – of telling Adele, to whom she was closest in the family; but she didn't dare. Adele was incapable of keeping anything from Venetia, and Venetia was Henry's mother. Izzie simply had to manage alone. There was nothing else for it.

She dreaded seeing Henry, dreaded that he might in some way guess. But she had only seen him once, at a party, when he had given her an embarrassed kiss and hug, expressed an over-hearty hope that she was all right. She was spared that at least.

She knew abortions could be carried out discreetly and painlessly in sterile conditions in clinics – usually abroad. A girl from school had disappeared for a week to Switzerland, sent by her parents; the official reason had been appendicitis, but she told several of her friends the real reason. But the parents were rich; such places were terribly expensive and Izzie had no money. To give this woman what she asked – £150 – she had had to sell one of her most precious possessions, a gold and pearl necklace left her by her grandmother. She took it to a jeweller in Hatton Garden; he offered her £200 for it. It was worth twice that she knew, but she didn't argue with him; it provided her with enough, and that was all she cared about.

The woman had been recommended by an old friend from Oxford, who had used her services, and who assured her she operated under fairly sterile conditions.

'It's not for you, is it?' the girl had said, and 'No,' Izzie said. 'No, for a – for a friend of mine. Honestly.'

'Tell your friend it does hurt. Quite appallingly. But it doesn't last for too terribly long, although it seems like it. Only for about two minutes. While she – well, while she dilates the cervix –'

Even hearing this over the telephone made Izzie wince.

'And then it hurts like hell while it all – comes away. But you know it's ending by then.'

'How – how much does it hurt, then? Just – just so I can tell her.'

'Oh – quite badly. Yes. Like a very, very bad curse, I suppose. No worse than that. But it's bearable. Quite honestly, I was so relieved, I didn't care. I took loads of pills. Tell your friend she should have someone with her if she can.'

'I'll be with her,' said Izzie.

The waiting time had been very frightening. She found herself counting the days, then the hours. She wondered how she would cope with the pain; she hadn't ever really experienced anything serious before. But it was still better than the terror: that someone would find out, someone would guess . . .

The night before the abortion she sat looking at the money, turning it over in her hands, counting it over and over again; it was like Judas's forty pieces of silver, she thought, money with which to betray herself. And the – no, don't think that, Izzie, not about a baby, Izzie. It's not a baby. It's so small, an absolutely tiny blob, it doesn't look like a baby, it isn't a baby. It's a mistake you made and you're putting it right. That's all it is, a mistake you're putting right . . .

The room which the woman led her up to in her house in North London was small and cold, with a bright, unshaded light, thick curtains, and a lino-covered floor. The bed was quite high, and very hard; she was told to remove her lower garments and climb on to it. Her teeth chattered, with terror as much as cold, as she did so. There was a handle on the wall above her head, as bright and shining and hard as the instruments that lay on a small table, terrifying-looking things; she tried to keep her eyes away from them. The woman told her to hold on to the handle as she pushed Izzie's legs apart, strapped her feet into something resembling stirrups.

'You've got to keep still. Is that clear? Otherwise there's a risk of damage.'

Damage: from those awful sharp things, the bright light. Damage. It was suddenly a more dreadful word than she had ever imagined . . .

She heard a scream; it couldn't have been her, of course, but it had coincided with a stab, an awful, deep piercing agony, so cold and hard and deep a pain that it negated the rest.

Someone was telling her to be quiet, though; so maybe it was. Maybe—

'Right. It's over.' She felt a pulling, that was almost pleasure, so mild was the pain of it; she let go of the bar, tried to turn on her side, whimpering, biting her fist.

'You can stay there for half an hour,' said the woman, releasing her legs, pulling the sheet over her, moving over to the wash basin, rinsing the instruments. Was that all she did to them, Izzie wondered, between one desperate patient and the next, were they just washed under the tap like teaspoons, not sterilised properly? She wondered if she had the courage to ask, knew she did not, and besides, what would be the point, what could she do about it now? She closed her eyes, tried to calm herself, to still the awful trembling that had taken possession of her.

Her fear, only ten minutes earlier, had been simply of the pain she was about to endure; now it was of something uglier, things she had read about and heard of, of haemorrhaging, of septicaemia, of sterility even. Somehow until then, getting rid of the – the blob – had been her only consideration; worth any risk. Now she was not so sure. Now it was too late.

'Is your friend coming for you?'

Izzie nodded; there was no friend. Who could she trust, who could she burden with this horror, this vile piece of lawlessness?

'Put this on.' The woman handed her a sanitary towel and belt. 'You may bleed a little.'

'Only a little?' She was relieved, she had heard stories of pints of blood.

'A little today.' The woman's voice was impatient. 'Tomorrow, maybe the next day, you'll bleed a lot. Stay in bed, get plenty of towels in. Take something for the pain, and whatever happens, don't go to hospital or to a doctor. Don't forget you've broken the law, you're liable to criminal charges.'

'I won't,' whispered Izzie. 'I promise.'

'Good. Now take one of these pills as soon as you get home, another tomorrow and if nothing happens, take the third. If you're lucky that won't be necessary. They may make you vomit. I'll leave you for now.'

Izzie lay on the bed, feeling the pain slowly ease. She felt very sleepy suddenly, and very cold. She pulled the thin sheet more closely round her. It was over; at least it was over.

Somehow she got herself home; hobbled to her little car, managed to drive it. A hot knife-like throbbing was invading her; she literally crawled upstairs, calling to Mrs Conley for some hot milk.

'You all right, my dear?'

The voice was gentle through her clamouring pain as she lay in bed.

'Yes. Yes, I'm fine. Well – bit of a tummy ache, you know.'

'Time of the month, is it?'

'Yes,' said Izzie, through chattering teeth, pulling up the sheets.

'Bless you. Always have trouble, don't you? I'll fetch you a hotty. Got some aspirin?'

'Yes. Yes, thank you.'

And a bottle of her father's whisky hidden under her bed; she would add that to the milk. It had always helped in the past, when she had had bad period pains. Why not now?

'Just heard from Mr Brooke,' said Mrs Conley, coming in again, smiling at her, stroking back her hair. She had known Izzie since she was a baby; had looked after Sebastian long before that. 'He sent his love. He definitely won't be back till Friday. Staying in Cambridge. But you know that.'

She did indeed know it; that had been the reason she had chosen today and tomorrow. She would be alone in the house; Sebastian need hear nothing, see nothing, know nothing. There would be no reason for Kit to come round. There would be no other visitors. And Mrs Conley was hard of hearing, and slept like the dead. She would be safe. Safe to get it over with. Alone. Quite alone. She was already bleeding: quite heavily. It would soon be over.

Venetia had worried about Elspeth working at Lyttons. Of course it was a family firm, that the younger generation should move in was part of its philosophy. But just the same, Elspeth was young, raw, she might prove untalented, unworthy of her opportunities. What then? Could she be fired, or worse, remain on sufferance, rather as Giles had done for many years? Would the other staff say she should not have the job, that others should have been given the opportunity, that at the very least there should have been some selection process?

She wondered if her mother had ever felt these things about her; but the firm had been smaller then, totally under family control. She had even voiced some of these fears to Celia, who had looked at her in something approaching disbelief.

'Venetia, she's a Lytton. Of course she should have the opportunity. Why ever not?'

'It doesn't seem quite – fair,' said Venetia.

Celia looked at her, clearly baffled.

'What an extraordinary thing to say. It would be very unfair if she wanted to work at Lyttons, having grown up with it, and then was told she couldn't. There have to be some advantages in heredity, heaven knows they're getting fewer all the time, with all these crippling death duties, and appalling taxation, there's not much we can do for our children any more. Of course she must come to Lyttons. She'll be excellent, I know it.'

And Elspeth was not disappointing them. She was efficient, she worked extremely hard, came in early, stayed late and undoubtedly had an eye for a promising theme, a latent talent. Perhaps more important still, she showed a considerable grasp of the market. It was Elspeth who pointed out to Giles that university bookselling was clearly seasonal and although there might be an increasing demand for books at the beginning of the scholastic year (due to the number of people now going on to higher education), it could not be sustained and should therefore be looked on as a one-off in the publishing cycle. And it was with Elspeth that Celia found herself most easily able to discuss the year's most famous libel case, when Frederic Warburg himself stood for trial by jury, on publication of Stanley Kaufman's *The Philanderer*. Celia had long said that she thought the obscure laws on obscene libel an anachronism. 'We are moving into new, freer times, people will look for more openness in their literature.'

Elspeth spoke out vigorously for her when called into a meeting to discuss the publication of the latest novel by Clementine Hartley which was quite sexy in its theme – the decision of a young woman to leave her husband and live with another man – with passages which veered on the explicit.

'The point is,' she said, her brilliant dark eyes darting just slightly anxiously towards her mother, 'we, that is our – my – generation – we're beginning to question all the old, established standards. We really don't think a mistake in a marriage, for instance, should be for life. And we think that – well, sex doesn't absolutely have to belong inside marriage. And in a book like this, where the heroine is taking such a huge risk, for – well, not just holding hands with someone – then that kind of passion has got to be clearly expressed. If you see what I mean.'

'We do. Very good,' said Celia. 'Then we will risk this book as it stands, Giles. No more editing. After all, as Mr Justice Stable said over *The Philanderer*, are we to take our literary standards as being the level of something suitable for – what was it – yes, the "decently brought up female of fourteen"? And as he also said, of course we are not. That judgement was deeply important to the whole of our industry. It freed not only publishers but booksellers from the fear of prosecution.'

'Mother, I have to disagree,' said Giles flushing. 'I still feel deeply uncomfortable about this book.'

'Well you shouldn't,' said Celia briskly. 'We're talking about sexual desire going on in a woman's head, not a detailed description of her orgasm. Oh don't look at me like that, Giles, for heaven's sake. Jay, you'll agree I'm sure.'

Jay nodded, avoiding Giles's eye. Celia's return might have robbed him of a degree of authority, but it had also brought what he could only describe as grit back into the Lytton oyster. Life was tougher but more interesting. And it was a lot easier and less troublesome to side with Celia against Giles and the rest of the old guard than to take up arms himself. The demands of marriage and particularly of fatherhood – Victoria was pregnant yet again, a fact neither of them was entirely delighted about – had increased Jay's predilection for the easy route, the circumnavigation of obstacles.

Afterwards, Celia invited her granddaughter out to lunch.

'We'll go to the Berkeley, just the two of us. Much more fun and it will rattle the others. Princess Margaret might be there – so dreadfully sad for her, giving up Townsend, but absolutely right of course. Anyway, I want to hear more about your young man, how he's getting on. I'm sorry he's given up the idea of publishing. I was very impressed with those reader reports he did. He makes extraordinarily clear judgements. I would say he has real talent. Teaching, such a waste of his brains. I suppose it's his background, the working class always has this reforming zeal. Come along darling, quickly, get your coat before anyone catches us.'

Elspeth also privately thought Keir's brains were being wasted teaching. Of course it was the most important job anyone could possibly do, everyone knew that, and teaching other working-class children, which of course was Keir's new ambition, opening up their horizons, letting them know exactly how much of the world could be theirs, was a wonderful achievement. But Keir was never going to buckle under to some headmaster, never going to stop defending his own theories. He was doing temporary teaching jobs now and, as far as she could make out, spent his life arguing vociferously with the other staff. He was going to get himself into serious trouble at this rate. On the other hand, he cared so passionately about his cause, she couldn't see him dropping it. And he had a new passion now, for the much-vaunted comprehensive system of schooling.

'The eleven-plus system is divisive and unfair,' he said, biting off, without a moment's misgiving, the educational hand that had fed him and led him to his place at Oxford. 'What of the children who fail, condemned to a second-class education, a life of knowing they're failures? All our children should be educated together, the bright along with the less bright, so that there can be the same high standards for everyone.'

Elspeth tried to explain this to Celia, who was extremely dismissive.

'He's young,' she said, lighting a cigarette. 'He'll learn in time that the only thing which happens when you try to bring all abilities together is a drift – or rather a rush – towards the lowest common denominator. The bright children like Mr Brown' – she refused to call him Keir – 'will find themselves stifled by a lot of dolts who don't want to learn and who drag everyone down to their level. How extraordinary he should think like that when he's been able to improve his own situation so dramatically.'

Elspeth didn't feel able to argue with her on the comprehensive system, as their views exactly coincided; but she did defend Keir's desire to be a teacher.

'He wants to make a difference to the world, Granny. To really help children who were in his situation.'

Celia said nothing for a moment, then, 'He'll learn,' she said briefly, adding, with apparent irrelevance, 'I do think he's extremely attractive. And clearly has a very good brain. Such a pity if it was wasted. I wonder if he would have the time to do some more reading for me, at least?'

Elspeth said she was sure it was worth asking him; she had a fairly clear inkling of the direction her grandmother's thoughts were going. It was a delicious notion. Unfortunately, she knew that Keir would never agree.

Keir spent quite a lot of time pouring scorn on the publishing profession and what he called – most unfairly – its social apartheid. Elspeth held her tongue; she sympathised too much with his experiences and, besides, felt her own privileged position uncomfortable. But now that he had changed direction, he appeared to have forgiven her that and indeed had assumed a rather lofty superiority over her and her work. 'Teaching is the finest and most important job in the world,' he said one evening. 'Anything else has to be regarded as second best. I feel really privileged to be a part of it.' It appeared to be a genuinely held view; Elspeth, relieved at his new contentment, nodded an earnest agreement she did not feel but was happy to assume.

She was very happy, both in her work and, even more importantly, with Keir; what she felt for him was an unswerving love. He was difficult, he made her angry, he quite often made her upset, but he also made her feel absolutely happy. And something she could only describe as involved with him. Everything she did, everything she thought, was to do with him; he had become a part of her, and she could not imagine her life without him. They argued a great deal, fought quite often, but they intrigued and interested one another to an intense degree. And their sex life, conducted during his weekends in London, at the flat her father had bought for her and Amy, gave her enormous pleasure.

She had taken the precaution, like all modern girls, of having herself fitted with the latest in contraception, a dutch cap; it had a very low failure rate, the gynaecologist had told her, and it was nice to be in charge of that side of things, and not have to ask Keir every time they went to bed if he had 'got something with him'. It was also more discreet, she could fix herself up before he even arrived, and there was none of the dreadful fumbling which she so hated, just as she was feeling really excited and longing to get on with it.

Sex with Keir wasn't just a physical pleasure, it was an absolutely complete one; it absorbed all her feelings, all her thoughts. As time went by, it became more intense, not less; it left her afterwards quite shaken by the depths and distances they travelled together. And he felt the same; he had, almost reluctantly but very sweetly, told her so. They were very happy.

They had a great deal in common, as well as differences, enjoyed a lot of the same things – the theatre, the cinema, reading and books inevitably – and they had also developed an interest in cooking. Suddenly food was changing; the birth of the cheap package holiday took people other than the rich abroad for the first time and it also brought at least a nod in the direction of continental cooking. Hotels on the Costa Brava and in Majorca might serve chips with everything, but people also came back talking of dishes like paella and pasta. Keir bought a cookery book, donned a chef's apron and served up spaghetti bolognese and steak Diane, having gone shopping with Elspeth to one of the new supermarkets for the ingredients.

'Supermarket shopping is a completely new experience,' said Elspeth, laughing, to her mother. 'You whizz round with your trolley, a bit like a pram, get everything in no time and then stand in a queue for hours to pay, at this thing called a checkout.' Venetia said she couldn't imagine anything worse and what was wrong with Harrods delivering everything? Elspeth said Keir thought supermarkets were going to change the shopping patterns of working-class people for the better, and they had to be encouraged.

'I'm surprised he approves of them, when his parents have their little shop.'

'I know, and they say it's just a passing phase, but Keir thinks they're wrong. They serve a very small neighbourhood, so they're not actually under threat, not for now, anyway.'

'Yes, I see.'

Just occasionally, Venetia allowed herself to ponder the possibility that Elspeth might want to marry Keir. She didn't find it entirely unappealing, she liked him very much; he was intelligent and attractive and of course times were changing and class differences were not what they had been, but when she reached the wedding day itself and thought about walking down the aisle of St Margaret's, Westminster on the arm of Mr Brown, she flinched. Elspeth would find someone else, someone more suitable. There was plenty of time.

In any case, she had something much more important to worry about, more important than Elspeth's future, far more important than her mother's return to Lyttons and the daily conflicts that had set up, even more important than the fact that Lyttons were losing authors and winning no seriously important new ones: and that was Adele and her unhappiness. Which was dreadful.

Venetia could imagine no worse conflict than that between your husband and your child. She and Boy had had their differences and problems, God knew; but nothing ever like this. It was a nightmare.

'I feel like a rabbit in a trap,' Adele said to her, her voice shaken and exhausted with endless crying and pain, 'and there's no way out of it. If I give in to Geordie, send Lucas back, I truly believe he might do something drastic. So does Noni. He has had the most terrible time, truly terrible, he's been bullied, beaten, tormented over being Jewish—'

'Surely not.'

'Oh yes, he has. And he's at the end of his tether. At the same time, I have Geordie saying he's going to leave if I give in to him. I just can't make him see what Lucas has gone through. He's terribly stubborn, it's his greatest fault. And Lucas doesn't help himself, he goes on being rude and hostile to Geordie—'

'Can't you—'

'Oh God, I've tried. But he sees Geordie as being to blame for the whole thing, and he just hates him for it. And I can – well, I can see it from his point of view. But oh, Venetia, I just can't imagine life without Geordie, I love him so much, so terribly much. But he says – he says that if I really love him, I'll put him first, stop inflicting Lucas's appalling behaviour on him. And I can see that too.'

'What about a different school? Eton? It's much nearer home, I always thought—'

'I've suggested that. Lucas says he won't go, says he can't face trying again.'

'That's not helpful.'

'Venetia, none of it's helpful.'

'Can't Noni help?'

'No. She's tried, poor darling. Lucas has turned against her as well now, says she's just taking our side. It's so awful, and I feel so guilty. What can I do? Lucas actually turned on me the other day, said I should never have left his father, never taken them away from him, we should have stayed in Paris, a family, that I was a coward and—'

'You should tell him the truth,' said Venetia decisively.

'How can I? Tell him his father was cheating on me, that he'd gone back to his wife. It's a huge rock in Lucas's life, knowing his father was a good brave man who died a hero. I can't have him thinking he was – well, rather different.'

'I think he's old enough to be told,' said Venetia thoughtfully, 'after all, Luc did still die a hero. And he was a brilliant publisher, Lucas must surely feel proud of that. Identify with it, even. The only bad thing Luc did was cheat on you. I know it was bad, but don't you think it might help Lucas a bit to know the truth?'

'No,' said Adele. 'I can't do that, I can't tell him. It would be too cruel. Especially at the moment.'

Venetia sighed. 'Poor darling. I just wish so much I could help. What exactly is Geordie saying?'

'Well – that unless Lucas goes back to school, he's leaving. That he can't live under the same roof. That it's wrong of me to ask him to do so. He did say he'd go back to New York, but I don't think he'd leave Clio. Not permanently. But I think he'll spend much more time there. He still thinks of it as home. Oh God. It's so unfair.'

'Yes,' said Venetia, taking her in her arms, stroking her hair. 'Yes, it is unfair. Terribly. The one person totally not to blame is the one being most hurt.'

The days and weeks of the autumn term dragged on. Adele had written to Fletton, telling them Lucas was not going back; she was having him tutored at home as a compromise, rather than ask Westminster to take him back. That she knew would end any hopes of Geordie giving in. In any case, she was not at all sure that they would. Lucas skulked in his room, refusing to join the family for meals if Geordie were present; he had thanked his mother for her support, but that was his only compromise.

Adele's tears and pleading, even her threats to send him back to Fletton if he continued to make no effort with Geordie, had no effect on him. He knew she wouldn't send him back and he was enjoying the furore.

He could also see that Geordie meant what he said; if Lucas continued in his present pattern of behaviour, he would leave.

Which suited Lucas just fine.

'He's not really so bad,' Noni said earnestly to Izzie one night. 'He has had a truly dreadful time, I think I know more than anyone what he's been through. And, rightly or wrongly, he does blame Geordie for it. He hates him, and he wants him to leave my mother. He's very mixed up, I think he ought to have some help, actually.'

'What kind of help?'

'Well – psychiatric help. I think he needs someone completely outside the family to talk to, to try and sort him out. I suggested it to my mother, but she seemed frightened by the idea. She just wants to cling to the idea that it'll all be all right in the end, that it's just a family tiff. Oh Izzie, it's so awful. I love Geordie so much, and I can't bear to think of him going. But I think he will. It just all seems so hopeless.'

She started to cry; Izzie put her arms around her and held her tight. It sounded quite hopeless to her too.

Izzie was beginning to wonder if she didn't need psychiatric help herself. A dreadful dull weariness had overtaken her. She had recovered, physically, as far as she could tell, quite quickly. The hours of terrible pain had ended, finally. She had burnt in the kitchen boiler – forbidding herself so much as a glance at them – all the towels and rolls of cotton wool which had been so drenched in her blood, and she lay in her bed recovering over the weekend, weak and exhausted, telling her father when he returned that she had had some stomach bug and that there was no need to call the doctor.

She went back to work a week after the abortion; she felt tired and frail, but she was not in any real pain. She had not been feverish, she clearly had no infection. She had been terribly, terribly lucky. And it was over.

Absolutely over. No one would ever need to know.

She waited to feel happy, released, and felt neither. She felt at first simply depressed, then more violently unhappy. She would start to cry for no reason, a sudden rush of misery rising in her, so strong that there was no withholding the tears. Forced to explain it in the office, she said that a relative was very ill and refused to elaborate; within the family she met any questioning, any concern, with an entirely uncharacteristic irritability.

'I'm all right,' she would say fiercely to her father, to Kit, to Noni. 'Just leave me alone, for heaven's sake.'

The rest of them she managed to avoid.

She had terrible dreams: about bare rooms and bright lights, about gleaming instruments and about blood. She was afraid to sleep and read far into the night, but in the end the dreams would claim her. She often woke weeping at dawn, and then fell into a heavy second sleep from which she could scarcely rouse herself to go to work.

Her work suffered; she became slow, careless, lacklustre in her ideas. That depressed her further.

Henry's marriage was like a nightmare in itself, slowly coming nearer. The date was set for March; there was talk of fittings, hair styles, shoes. She tried to show an interest, at least. It was not, after all, Henry's fault. And certainly not Clarissa's. So why did she feel so hostile towards both of them?

It was her own fault; her own, stupid, reckless fault. She had been forced to end a human life because of her own lack of responsibility. However hard she tried to hang on to the concept of the blob, she found herself forced to recognise what she had done. She had had a baby growing inside her body, sheltered, safe, warm, it had had a head and arms and legs and a beating heart (she had forced herself, with the courage of the insane, to study a book on obstetrics in the library) and she had dragged it out and killed it. It was perfectly simple. She had murdered her baby. A baby that in a few months' time now would have been born. A live, smiling baby. It was her fault. And she would never, ever, be able to forget it or forgive herself.

CHAPTER 10

She clearly wasn't at all well. The slight feverishness and tickly throat, lightly dismissed earlier in the day as being of little importance, had developed into a full-blown temperature of one hundred and three (and rising) by early evening. Clearly, not only the doctor but also her father had to be informed.

Barty sighed. She wasn't exactly worried about Cathy, she was pretty sure she just had the strep throat infection that had laid half Manhattan low; but the illness (and responsibility) of someone else's child was always a greater concern. Selfishly, she felt irritated; she had planned to work much of the weekend, Marcus Forrest had commissioned a book on Jennie Churchill, Winston's American mother, and was now regretting it. He had asked her to look at the outline and a novel had come in from a completely unknown author, set in the Depression, which she thought wonderful, but which nobody else liked. She wanted to re-read it, make sure she wasn't completely mad. It now looked increasingly unlikely she would get anything done at all.

She dialled Dr McCarthy's number; he had cared for Jenna several times, and she liked him. He said he would come at once. He looked like the caricature of the old family doctor, white-haired and moustached, carrying a battered old leather bag; he always reminded Barty of Dr Meade in *Gone With the Wind*.

He checked Cathy over, confirmed it was the strep bug, prescribed some penicillin and plenty of fluids, and told Barty to call him again in the morning if she was no better.

Barty sent Mrs Mills out for the penicillin and slightly reluctantly called Charlie Patterson. He sounded only a little worried: 'I'm sure she's in good hands. If she gets worse, call me at once, and I'll drive out there. Or do you—'

'No,' said Barty, quite sharply, 'there's really no need. Dr McCarthy is quite sure she's fine, and once the penicillin has got to work, I'm sure—'

'Is that my dad?' Cathy had appeared in the doorway. She was very flushed, swaying slightly as she clung to Jenna's hand. 'May I speak with him?'

'Of course you may, Cathy, but really you shouldn't be out of bed—'
'Please!'

'All right. Come and sit down here, by the phone. But don't be long.'

'I won't. Dad –' her voice had changed totally, became faint and shaky '– Dad, I feel so awful. So terribly awful. What? Yes, he came, and he said my throat looked really dreadful. No, not yet. They haven't got it yet. Dad I wish you were here, I feel so bad. So hot and kind of scared. What? Could you? I know I'd feel better if you – yes, yes of course. She's right here. Barty,' she held out the phone, 'he wants to speak to you.'

Little bitch, thought Barty, taking the phone.

Charlie Patterson arrived very late that night. He looked slightly wild-eyed, standing on the porch. His car, a rather battered T-bird, still had its lights on and the driver's door hung open. Clearly Barty's attempts to reassure him had failed.

'Charlie, honestly, she isn't so bad. I wish I hadn't let her speak to you. She's actually better already, penicillin works so quickly, especially with children. They're watching TV—'

'Isn't she in bed?'

'Yes, of course she's in bed,' said Barty, trying not to sound defensive. 'Jenna has a small set in her room. There's some comedy show on, I thought it would cheer her up.'

'Aren't you worried Jenna will get it?'

'I'm afraid it's too late for that. She's bound to, it's all over the school. No doubt that's how Cathy got it.'

'I suppose so. Well—'

'Follow me.'

As they opened the door, they heard a distinct giggling; it was muffled as soon as Cathy saw her father. She lay back on her pillows, holding out her arms.

'Daddy, Daddy, I'm so glad you're here. I feel so bad.'

'I'll leave you two together,' said Barty. 'Come on, Jenna, downstairs.'

'But Mother—'

'Jenna. Downstairs.'

Down in the den, she gave Jenna a hot drink. Jenna snuggled up to her mother, smiled at her.

'Isn't it nice Charlie's here? And he can see South Lodge and everything. He's been dying to come out for ages, Cathy said, but he didn't like to ask.'

'Really?' said Barty drily.

She lay awake in the darkness for a long time, in the great room which had been Laurence's, with its wall of windows opening on to the ocean, and felt very unhappy. She was hating this. South Lodge was hers, a precious, private place filled with precious, private memories; only the most intimate beloved people were invited there. Wol and Celia, of course, had been, Sebastian and Izzie, Geordie and Adele, and Robert Lytton and Jamie and Maud, of course, and a very few other very close friends. But Charlie Patterson, about whom she felt . . . well, what do you feel, Barty? Come on, maybe this is the time to confront it.

She felt fond of him. Really you couldn't not, she had told herself repeatedly, he was so charming and good-natured and thoughtful and considerate. And undoubtedly attractive, sexy, even, with his quick, anxious smile, his large brown eyes behind their tortoiseshell-rimmed spectacles, his way of concentrating very intently on what she said. He reminded her – just very slightly – of John of whom she had been so fond during the war, indeed had almost married. He had the same gentle charm, the same rather old-fashioned manners. She liked the way he dressed too, he had a strong sense of style and on his long, lean body, the shabby but well-cut jackets, the button-down cotton shirts, often frayed at the cuffs, his washed-out jeans, always looked good. He dressed Cathy beautifully too, very simply, in plain little dresses or skirts and blouses for best, well-worn jeans and T-shirts and big sloppy jumpers for the weekend. A lot of them, he said slightly ruefully, came from the thrift shops and Barty liked that, liked the sense of it, liked too that he could find such things among the jumble of bad taste that made up 90 per cent of thrift-shop stock.

He was fun as well; he had asked her and Jenna to supper a couple of times, 'You must let me repay you a little', and had served up a very good chicken pie. Afterwards they had played Scrabble and she had thought how wonderfully good he was, not only with Cathy but with Jenna too. Imaginative and jokey and in no way condescending.

And then somehow after that, it had only been one step to his inviting her out to dinner: that had been fun too, after the initial slight awkwardness of finding themselves together without the children. He was easy to talk to; and, for the first time, had talked about his wife and how much he still missed her.

'Really seven or eight years is nothing in terms of healing, when you have loved someone that much.'

'I know it,' said Barty. 'Neither is ten, or eleven, I'm sorry to have to tell you.'

'So – your husband was killed in the war?'

'Yes. He was – well, he was in France, after D-Day, with Eisenhower. He never even knew about Jenna.'

'That must be hard.'

'It's very hard. But I do at least have her. I'm very lucky.'

'I feel the same about Cathy. And she was so marvellous after Meg died. She was only three, you know, maybe that helped in a way, too little to understand properly. She was so sweet and brave and so very companionable. We're everything to each other now. In fact I worry that we're too close. That she'll have trouble forming other relationships. It's one of the reasons I'm so glad she and Jenna are such good friends. She's never had a really close friend before. It's very good for her. Although, of course, I miss her sometimes. Especially at the weekends when she goes out to Southampton with you,' he added, and then after what was just fractionally too long a pause, 'but I don't begrudge it to her for one second. And of course I do manage to get a lot of work done.'

'I don't know how you manage at all,' said Barty, carefully ignoring the slightly heavy hint. 'It must be so very hard, always working with an eye on the clock, presumably having to cancel meetings if Cathy's ill.'

'It is,' he said, 'and the income has dropped, I'm afraid. But I decided at the very beginning that Cathy must come first and I've stuck with it. But it ain't easy. It's the getting of clients that's hard; I can deal with servicing them. And hey,' he said with his most boyish grin, pushing his glasses up his nose, 'we're not starving.'

'What exactly do you do? I mean rentals, development, what? My brother-in-law is in your business, so was my father-in-law, I know a little about it.'

'Oh they are? That's interesting. I'm very much on the service end, put apartments and people together. But as I can only afford a very small office and one secretary, it's difficult.'

'Maybe you should meet Jamie. You never know, there might be an area you could collaborate on—'

'That'd be great.'

Jamie took him out to lunch, told Barty he was a nice enough guy, 'but I don't see there's anything we can do together. We're dealing with such a different end of the market.'

'And – what did you think about him?'

'I thought he was very nice, Barty. Very nice. Touch too laid back, maybe. I don't see him burning the midnight oil, but—'

'You mean he's lazy?'

'That would be a bit of a harsh judgement, on the strength of one lunch. Let's say he just seems to me to be a bit of a coaster. Anyway, is he a new beau?'

'No,' she said firmly. Too firmly probably. 'No, he isn't.'

'You could do worse. And he thinks a lot of you. Says you're the most attractive woman he's met for a very long time.'

'Well, he would, talking to you, wouldn't he?' said Barty, disproportionately pleased nonetheless. She was five years older than Charlie; it was very good for her ego if nothing else that he found her attractive.

Charlie said he had liked Jamie a lot. 'If your husband was anything like him, he was a nice guy.'

'He wasn't, actually,' said Barty, laughing. 'Neither like Jamie, nor specially nice. Not in the conventional sense, anyway. But let's not get into that now.'

'He told me he was one of the trustees in some trust fund you'd set up for Jenna.'

'Yes, that's right,' said Barty. 'It worries me a bit, her only having me.'

'You've got quite a substantial set-up to worry about, haven't you?' he said. 'Pretty complex, all of it.'

'Well, yes. Quite complex. That's why I try to keep it well in order.'

She changed the subject; it always worried her when Charlie tried to talk about her financial situation. However casually.

After two more dinners à deux, Charlie had kissed her. She wasn't sure how she felt about that either. She hadn't had any kind of relationship since Laurence; she had assumed herself to be sexually quite dead. She certainly didn't see stars; but it was nice enough. In fact, it was very nice. But she had no desire to take it any further.

And that night at South Lodge she led him firmly to the spare room and closed the door on him, without even kissing him goodnight.

He was out on the verandah when she came down in the morning, holding a steaming mug of coffee, staring out at the ocean.

'Good morning. Your nice Mrs Mills made this for me. Can I get one for you?'

'No, it's fine. I'll get one for myself.'

'It's glorious here. So very special.'

'I'm glad you like it.'

She was hating this; him being here, standing on the verandah, Laurence's verandah, looking at the ocean across the dunes. Laurence's dunes. He had no business there, he was intruding, she wanted him gone.

'How is Cathy?' she said carefully.

'Oh, much better. As you said, penicillin is remarkable. They're both out cold. She woke up just long enough to say, "Hi, Dad", and then went back to sleep. Could we – could we take a walk along the shore?'

'Oh – you go,' she said quickly. 'If that doesn't sound too unfriendly. I really have too much to do. Work, you know. I got a bit held up yesterday. We can have breakfast when you get back.'

'OK.' He smiled, but his brown eyes were slightly puzzled. 'If that's what you want. It'd be more fun with you, but – well, I guess I won't get lost.'

She felt guilty then, said, 'I'm sorry. Maybe later in the day. I'll drive you around a bit, show you the Hamptons.'

That wouldn't be so bad; it was just South Lodge, she couldn't bear him being there.

'Sure. Well – I'll see you later.' He bent to kiss her lightly on the cheek; she pulled back. This time he looked hurt.

'Sorry,' she said, and hurried into the house.

Around mid-morning, after one of Mrs Mills's enormous brunches, she suggested a drive. She still didn't want to, but she felt she had been rude.

'That'd be good. Do we take the girls?'

'Oh I don't think so. Cathy should stay indoors. Mrs Mills will be here—'

'It's all right,' he said, smiling at her. 'I'd much rather go without them.'

They pulled out of the drive, headed up towards the Hampton Road. 'It's so pretty here.'

'Isn't it? And we have culture too. The Parrish, our own museum, not some tinpot little thing, either, we have some very fine examples of eighteenth- and nineteenth-century American paintings. And see, there's our very grand town hall. Pillars and all. Now I thought we could go across to Sag Harbor, it's so lovely there, and then we can make a circle back through Easthampton. That'll give you a pretty good idea of the place. Jackson Pollock, the painter, lives in Easthampton now, you know. I might even give you a glimpse of The Creeks. It's on Georgica Pond and it's the most important house in the whole of the Hamptons. People practically murder to get an invitation there. It even has its own theatre, where Isadora Duncan was supposed to have danced. We could maybe grab a coffee in Easthampton, or even—'

'Barty,' he said very gently, 'you don't have to do this.'

'What?'

'Show me around. In this rather frenetic way.'

'Yes I do,' she said. 'I'd like to.'

'I do understand,' he said gently, 'at least I think I do.'

'Understand what?'

'That it's hard for you, me being here. It was obviously a very special place, for just you and Laurence. We had one, Meg and I, not our own, of course, but a place we always went to, up in Connecticut. It was there I proposed to her, there we went after we were married, and we took Cathy there, right after she was born, as soon as Meg was strong enough. I've never been back there except on my own. So – I know how this must feel for you. Having to share it.'

Then she really did feel ashamed.

He left with Cathy mid-afternoon; she stood with Jenna on the steps waving him off.

'He's just so nice,' said Jenna, and this time she was not conniving, it was clearly genuinely meant. 'Don't you think so, Mother? And it was great him being here. Can he come again?'

'We'll see,' said Barty, 'we'll see.'

★

128

Geordie had gone. He had packed all his things up, his clothes, his books, his beloved portable typewriter, and moved into a small flat in St James's.

'It's comfortable and quite big enough and it has a spare bedroom for Clio when she comes to stay. I'd like to have her most weekends. But I hope we can be civilised over arrangements. Noni can come and see me too, if she wants too.'

'Of course she'll want to,' said Adele wiping her streaming eyes. 'Oh Geordie, don't do this, please, please don't. I love you so much—'

'Not enough, it seems,' he said, his grey eyes quite steely as he looked at her. 'Not enough to put me first.'

'How can I put you before my own son when he's so desperately unhappy? How can I? It's an impossible thing to ask.'

'Well, there's no point running over it all again. And I haven't noticed any improvement in his attitude towards me, even since he was allowed to return to Westminster. Had there been, I might have – well, never mind. I would never have believed, Adele, it could come to this. But—'

'Don't you think,' she said, for the last desperate time, 'you're just – well, over-reacting?'

'No, I don't. And it proves how little you understand, that you should still be talking in such terms. I have been made to feel miserable and unwelcome in my own house, have sat feeling angry and uncomfortable at my own dinner table, have been forced to witness a division in my own family.'

'What's that supposed to mean?'

'How do you think it is for Noni? Forced to observe this, to take sides? Or rather not to take sides? What does it feel like for her, do you think, to sit through every mealtime in an atmosphere of tension? I've watched her trying to ease things, to make conversation, to crush arguments before they begin, and it's extremely sad. No, it's best if I go, since Lucas clearly never will. I hope you and he are well pleased with your work.'

She missed him dreadfully; as well as being her husband, and her lover, he was her best friend, proud of her, supportive of her work, creative in his suggestions for it. He had been a superb stepfather to Noni, and adored the small Clio, who adored him in return. She called him Darling, rather than Daddy, having grown up hearing her mother address him thus; when, on the third day after Geordie had left, she turned to her mother and said, 'When is Darling coming home?' Adele had to leave the room and cried until she could cry no more.

Her only consolation was that she knew she had had no option: there was no way she could have sent Lucas back to Fletton. As, gradually and painfully – for he had felt shame as well as misery – the details came out, she became increasingly angry on his behalf, and more fiercely protective. She felt too that some retribution was due to him, that if he could be given his heart's desire, after all that he had had to endure, then he deserved it. So

Westminster were approached, had the position explained to them – and they did agree to take him back.

'He is an exceptional boy, Mrs MacColl,' said the Head. 'He has an exceptional brain and he and the school can still, we feel sure, do a lot for one another. But it won't be easy for him, he should understand that. He can't expect just to walk in and take up where he left off. There will be bridges to be built, and of course his friends will have changed, moved on.'

Adele explained all this to Lucas; he looked at her with his great dark eyes – Luc's eyes – and said simply when she had finished, 'I know, I won't regret it.'

'This – hasn't been easy for me, Lucas. The cost has been quite high.'

'That's not my fault,' he said, and didn't even smile at her. 'He' – Lucas never referred to Geordie by name – 'he should have listened to me.'

'If you had been more courteous to Geordie, Lucas, then he might have done.'

'He didn't want to,' said Lucas, and got up to walk out of the room; Adele seized his arm.

'At the very least, you owe me some gratitude. This could all have been accomplished with much less pain, if you had made more effort.'

There was a long silence, while his pride and his hurt plainly struggled with his love for her. Then he said, 'I'm sorry. And I do thank you. But—'

'No buts. I don't want to hear them. What I do want is some outward sign of your gratitude. It is too late, I am very much afraid, for any courtesy to Geordie to make any difference. But your attitude to your grandmother, in particular, and to Venetia and, indeed, to all the Warwicks, has left a great deal to be desired. I hope I shall see an improvement in that.'

Silence.

'Lucas!'

'Yes,' he said finally, the words clearly dragged out with an immense effort. 'Yes, I will – try.'

'Thank you.'

And he did; and after Henry and Clarissa's wedding, a most splendid affair, five hundred guests and a reception at Claridges, Celia was heard to remark to Adele that she had observed a great improvement in his manners.

'I still don't agree with your giving in to him, and I think it's quite tragic what has happened to your marriage—'

'Mummy, what choice did I have? Tell me truthfully what would you have done?'

For she had told her mother what Lucas had had to endure, in all its grisly detail.

And greatly to her surprise Celia said, 'Probably exactly the same.'

From which Adele drew great comfort.

★

Celia's attention at the wedding had actually been largely focussed on Izzie. The girl looked dreadful, she thought, white and exhausted, under her rather heavy make-up, and she had lost a great deal of weight. The pale-pink meringue of her dress seemed to engulf her; and even her lovely golden-brown hair, under its crown of sweetheart roses, looked dull and lifeless.

She moved about the room chatting dutifully to people, but with clearly so great an effort that Celia could hardly bear to watch her; after the speeches, when Henry and Clarissa had gone upstairs to change, she beckoned her over.

'You look very tired.'

'I am a bit. Weddings are tiring, aren't they?'

They shouldn't be, Celia thought, for girls of twenty-five, chosen to be one of the two chief bridesmaids, they should be a whirl of happiness.

'How's your father?' she asked abruptly. That might be the reason for Izzie's distress. Sebastian was no longer young, he pushed himself dreadfully –

'Oh – he's fine. Yes, very well. He's in Scotland at the moment, doing some kind of lecture tour.'

'Yes, I heard. Which provided a mildly graceful excuse for his absence today.'

'Celia—'

'Oh, I know, I know. Let's not go down that road. Tell me, have you seen Kit lately?'

That did hurt: having to ask, having to speak his name, even. Not a day passed but she felt the hurt of his loss to her life, not a night ended without her waking to the memory of it and grieving for him.

'Yes. He's absolutely splendid, he's very happy at – oh, sorry.' She bit her lip and flushed.

'At Wesley, yes, yes, I know. But – there's no trouble between you, nothing like that?'

'No, of course not.' She looked away; of course Celia had known, known about – that. But they had never spoken of it.

'You're still good friends?'

'Very good. We have supper quite often.'

'Good. So, then, what is the matter?'

The question took Izzie by surprise; she stared at Celia in silence, her great brown eyes brilliant with tears.

'Nothing,' she said finally, 'nothing, honestly, I'm just tired.'

'Isabella, there is clearly something very wrong. Everyone is worried about you.'

'How do you know?' she said sharply.

'All the girls tell me you don't seem to be yourself, Noni is particularly upset about it, Adele has been very worried, you know how much she loves you, and Venetia too, of course. Unfortunately, I have no idea whether your father is concerned or not. I feel sure he must be. But –' she peered into Izzie's eyes, handed her a handkerchief '– there's clearly something wrong. And you need to tell someone. It might as well be me. There's nothing in the world that could shock me, my darling, I do assure you, and you never know, I might even be able to help. I won't tell anyone, anyone at all. Now, come along, we have to wave them off. That girl is certainly very pretty. And Henry is a good-looking young man. Thank God he's married at last, though, and we can hear an end to all this nonsense about him marrying you. It did irritate me so much. You too, I expect.'

'Quite a bit,' said Izzie, trying to smile, and then she suddenly broke down entirely and ran from the room, with Celia's handkerchief held to her lips. Celia looked after her, deeply distressed. Surely she couldn't have actually wanted to marry Henry?

Izzie telephoned her next morning; she was sorry she had never said goodbye, 'and that I made such a fool of myself yesterday.'

'You didn't. Nobody noticed. Now, do you want to come and see me? Come for luncheon, Lord Arden isn't here, I've sent him back to Glenworth.'

'Well –'

'Isabella' – she and Sebastian were the only people who used that name – 'don't be stubborn. Come and see me. You obviously need to talk to someone. And as I said, there's certainly no one in the world I will tell. Whatever it is.'

Two days later, Izzie wrote to Barty.

I wonder if I could take you up on your invitation to come and stay for a while? I would try not to be a nuisance, maybe I could look after Jenna or something? I haven't been terribly well, one too many chest infections this winter, and I've been a bit depressed, as well. I saw Celia's doctor, who said he thought a complete change of scene would be a good idea. I won't stay for too long, just a couple of weeks, but I'd so love to see you and to go out to South Lodge again especially. Let me know what you think.

A telegram arrived:

Wonderful, wonderful news. Room always ready for you. Jenna beside herself with excitement. Come soonest, stay longest. Writing. Best love, Barty.

★

Izzie asked Michael Joseph if she might take her holiday and add an extra couple of weeks unpaid.

He looked at her fondly across the desk. 'You take as long as you want. Regard it as a sabbatical. You can come back any time, in three, six months, even a year. If you're going all that way, you might as well make the most of it. We'll miss you, but you don't look well, a proper break will do you good.'

Izzie thanked him and wondered why everyone was being so kind.

The twins both thought it was a wonderful idea; Noni was rather sweetly sad.

'I shall miss you so much, Izzie. Don't stay too long.'

It was like history repeating itself, Izzie thought, hugging her, when Barty had left her to go to America for the first time.

'I promise I won't. Promise. Now, how are things with you? I've been so wrapped up in myself lately, I've neglected you dreadfully. I hear you see Geordie quite a lot.'

'I do. Often on Saturdays, and we have supper nearly every week. But it's still horrible without him at home, I miss him so much. So does Mummy, she cries all the time. As for poor little Clio – oh Izzie, why do they all have to be so silly? So stupidly, stubbornly silly.'

'It's not always easy to be sensible,' said Izzie soberly.

Elspeth and Amy were both terribly excited by her plans.

'I'd give anything to be going,' said Amy. 'I hear American men are just heavenly. Well, look at Geordie. And Jack Kennedy. I wonder if Barty could find room for me as well.'

'Amy,' said Izzie, laughing, 'you've just got a new job. I thought you loved it.'

'I do. But look at me, nearly twenty-two now and not even engaged.'

'You were.'

'I know, I know. But I'm not any more. It just didn't feel right. It keeps not feeling right. All the men I know are so – so boring. You never know what a change of continent might do.'

Keir was very envious. 'I'd love to go over there,' he said, 'it's such a true democracy.'

Izzie didn't like to tell him that, according to Barty, upper-class Americans could teach even the English a thing or two about snobbery.

Kit was sweetly supportive. He said he'd miss her terribly, but she deserved some fun, and that he might even come out soon himself.

'Wesley's have just started an American office. They say they think my books could do quite well over there.'

'Oh Kit, do come. It would be such fun. I mean I'm probably not going to be there terribly long, but Barty seems to think I might even get some work.'

★

133

Only her father blighted her happiness. He growled, sulked, told her it was an appalling idea, and that she'd hate America, implied she was going to be a burden on Barty, asked her repeatedly why she was going.

'I want a change, Father. I feel I'm stuck in a bit of a rut.'

'Oh rubbish. If you've got some problem here, it's no use running away from it, I can tell you that. Change your job, if you must, but don't just walk out on everything. Whatever Joseph says, he won't really keep things going for you. He can't afford to.'

'He's promised he will.'

'Well, he doesn't mean it. I think you're making a shocking mistake, and one that you won't be able to put right so easily, I can tell you. People's memories are short, you know, you may find you can't get another job so easily. And if you're thinking Barty's going to be able to find you a job, you really are deceiving yourself.'

'Father, of course I'm not.'

'Good. Well that's something. And there's something else. I fancy you think you're going to have a wonderful time out there, make lots of new friends. The Americans are very insular, you know, they pretend to be welcoming and so on, but I've always found that a complete sham. I've been very lonely and miserable in New York. And Barty will be busy, she can't just drop everything to nursemaid you.'

Izzie burst into tears and fled to her room. Shortly afterwards, Noni phoned; she told Adele she could hear that Izzie was crying.

Celia was having supper with Adele; she telephoned Izzie next morning.

'What's the matter? Is something wrong?'

'I – I think maybe I shouldn't go. I'm so worried about Father, I think he's going to miss me so much. He says it's not that, but—'

'I hope,' said Celia, her voice icily quiet, 'he hasn't said as much.'

'Not exactly. But I can see that it is. And he keeps putting obstacles up, says I'll hate it, that Michael Joseph won't keep my job open, that I'm going to be a nuisance to Barty. I don't know what to do.'

'Go to New York,' said Celia. 'Your father is a selfish old man. Ignore him, Isabella.'

'I'll try. But I am worried about him, he looks so old sometimes and—'

'He is getting old. He's also a consummate actor. Now I don't want to hear any more about this. Just get on with your packing. I saw a very pretty suit in Harvey Nichols this morning, navy blue, in this new A-line. I'll buy it for you, if you like it. Goodbye my darling.'

'Goodbye Celia. And thank you for the offer. But—'

'But what?'

'I'm still worried about Father.'

Celia put the phone down and sat looking out of the window at the river. She was staying at Cheyne Walk as she did increasingly these days. Then she lit a cigarette, drew on it heavily, and dialled Sebastian's number.

'You,' she said when he answered it, 'are a wickedly selfish, disagreeable old man. Now, I hope you're not going out this morning, Sebastian, because I'm coming to see you. It's time you and I had a little talk. What? Oh don't be so ridiculous. This is nothing to do with you and me, I certainly wouldn't be bothering to make the journey if it was, it's Isabella I have to talk to you about. What? Well cancel it, Sebastian. Postpone it. This is much more important.'

'You'll never guess who came to see Mr Brooke this morning,' said Mrs Conley to her friend Rose, her eyes wide with excitement. 'Lady Celia. Well, Lady Arden, as we're supposed to call her now. Oh, she looks so beautiful still, and so young. I have missed her. She just said good morning as if it was quite normal she was there, and that she'd come to see Mr Brooke, and then told me to take some strong coffee into the study. I heard him shouting at her straight away and her shouting back, and at one point he opened the door and started walking out through the hall, but she just said, "Sebastian, how dare you insult me in front of the servants", and he looked at her in that way he has when he's cornered, then just scowled and walked back into the study and slammed the door so hard that the house shook. I didn't like to take the coffee in after that, but Lady Celia came to get it. "He's impossible, Mrs Conley, I'd forgotten," she said. Anyway, it went on being noisy for quite a long time, and then slowly things quietened down. She was here for about an hour, or even longer. When she left, he saw her to the front door. He was still looking – well, irritable, but quite different. And after she'd gone, he got his stick and said, "I'm going for a walk, Mrs Conley," quite cheerfully. And after lunch, I actually heard him singing. Well, what passes for singing with Mr Brooke, talk about tone deaf. Goodness knows what she said to him. I think she's got a bit of witchcraft in her, I really do.'

That night, over supper, Sebastian told Izzie that he was sorry he'd been so hostile to the idea of her going to America.

'I was just – jealous, I think. Wishing I was young enough to go gadding off, doing exactly what I wanted. Stupid of me, I'm sorry, Isabella.'

It was only the third time in her life he had ever said those words to her; she could remember the other two very vividly. The first was at Ashingham, when she was just a little girl and for the first time in her short, sad life he had made a friendly, affectionate gesture towards her, had seemed to be able to forgive her for living while her mother died in childbirth. She would never forget that rush of joy, of pure happiness and excitement. The second time – well, that had been rather different. She tried not to think about it. But now – she stared at him; he was smiling at her almost ruefully.

'Father, you don't have to apologise. I've been so worried that you – well, that you'd be lonely.'

'Lonely! When did I mind being lonely, for God's sake? Breath of life to me, a bit of loneliness. I won't have to listen to that dreadful music coming out of your room, either. Anyway, I've got a lot of work to do, the new book's late and I've got a series of lectures to deliver. I tell you what, though' – his brilliant eyes soft suddenly, as he looked at her – 'I might be able to come out and see you, when Kit comes. What would you think about that?'

'Oh, Father, I'd think it would be wonderful,' said Izzie, feeling quite light-headed in her relief, and then, as a dreadful suspicion slithered into her, 'You haven't been talking to Celia, have you?'

'Celia!' said her father, scowling at his soup. 'For God's sake, Isabella, how could you even think such a thing. You know perfectly well—'

'Sorry, Father,' said Izzie hastily.

Mrs Conley was able to report to Rose the next day that Mr Brooke had suddenly appeared in the kitchen while she was serving up the dessert to say that on no account was she to mention that Lady Celia had been there that day.

'Of course I said I wouldn't. I noticed that he didn't call her Lady Arden, either,' she added inconsequentially.

CHAPTER II

'Miss Lytton, hallo.'

'Oh – good morning, Miss Hartley.'

'Please call me Clementine.'

'Oh – well – well, all right. Thank you. But only if you call me Elspeth.'

'Of course. I wondered if you were free to come and have a bite to eat.'

Elspeth felt rather overwhelmed. Overwhelmed and uncomfortable. Here was Lyttons' leading young novelist – probably its leading novelist, actually, now she'd outsold Nancy Arthure on her last book – inviting her, the most junior member of the editorial staff, not only to call her by her Christian name, but to have lunch with her. It was – well, it was difficult.

'I – I'd love to, but . . .'

'Oh, it doesn't matter, if you're too busy.'

'I'm not too busy, it's just that – well, shouldn't Jay – I mean Mr Lytton . . .'

'Jay's got to go to the printers. Don't worry, he bought me a very over-sumptuous lunch last week. We've covered all the necessary business this morning. And anyway, I'd rather have lunch with you.'

She smiled at Elspeth; she was a pretty girl, with a round, rather baby-shaped face, a small snub nose and rosebud mouth, and a mass of reddish curls.

'Come on. Nothing grand, we could pop into that new little place in Duke Street. My treat.'

'Oh, no, I couldn't allow that, my mother would kill me—'

'Don't be silly. Your mother won't know. Or your grandmother. Anyway, I want to thank you. That's what it's about.'

'Thank me!'

'Yes. Your wonderful grandmother told me that you'd spoken up about the sex scenes in my new book. Swung opinion right round in my favour. I think I owe you an omelette or something at the very least.'

'Oh. Gosh. Did she really say that?'

'Lady Celia? Yes, of course. She thinks you're marvellous. And it would be nice to have lunch with someone from here so near my age. Are you enjoying being out in the great world? Or are you pining for Oxford? Do you know, I miss it still.'

'Oh, so do I,' said Elspeth. 'If I didn't love it here so much, I'd try and do some kind of research fellowship or something, just to be there again.'

'I tried that,' said Clementine. 'But it wasn't the same, everyone there regarded me as a sort of dinosaur, a million years old, you know. No, they should just be preserved in aspic, those years, kept exactly as they were and left undisturbed.'

'Mmm,' said Elspeth, and said very little more until they were sitting at a table in the restaurant.

'You're very quiet,' said Clementine Hartley.

'Yes, I know. Sorry. I was just thinking—'

'Yes?'

'Well, that you could write a wonderful novel about being a woman at Oxford. And call it exactly that.'

'Exactly what?'

'*Oxford in Aspic*. It could be about the whole thing of growing up there, dicovering men—'

'Discovering sex!' Clementine's big blue eyes were dancing.

Elspeth flushed. 'Well – yes. And the friendships and the dreadful bluestockings and—'

'Do you know, I love it. Really love it. I haven't got a theme for my new book yet. I'm going to think about it. Thank you so much.'

'That's all right,' said Elspeth and smiled at her rather awkwardly. She felt slightly out of her depth, at the receiving end of such fulsome praise from so luminary a figure.

'Celia told me you were destined for great things. She said you'd be a junior editor in no time.'

'She did? Well she might have told me.'

'Oh, you know what they're like. They think it's good for us to be kept humble.'

'And grateful.' Elspeth giggled. 'Gosh, how thrilling.'

'And who knows, one day maybe you might edit me. That'd be fun. After all, you've got your grandmother's example to follow. How things have improved since she came back, incidentally!'

'It is wonderful,' said Elspeth. 'She's so – modern, somehow. In her thinking. It's funny, when she's – well, certainly not young.'

'I tell you,' said Clementine, 'she seems a lot younger to me than Jay Lytton. Much more up to the minute. I love her. Why doesn't Kit ever see her any more?'

'Oh – because he left Lyttons,' said Elspeth quickly, 'but I'm sure he'll get over it.'

'It seems to be more on his side than hers. Anyway, he's a sweetheart, isn't he? I adore him. And he loves being published by Wesley, says they're absolutely wonderful.'

'Yes,' said Elspeth slightly sadly. 'Yes, I know.'

When she got back to the office, her grandmother had the page proofs of *Time to Fly*, Clementine's last book, on her desk; she was frowning over them.

'Is there a problem with those?' asked Elspeth.

'Oh – not really. It's a marvellous book. What a clever girl she is.'

'And so nice,' said Elspeth. 'We – we just had lunch,' she said carelessly. Celia looked at her.

'Lunch? I didn't know you were on those sort of terms.'

'Nor did I. But she asked me to say thank you. For speaking up for her sex scenes,' she giggled.

'Oh really? How very nice.'

She returned to the proofs; Elspeth hurried to her own office, afraid she might have broken some complex office etiquette by having lunch with Clementine. Celia had clearly been a little surprised. Oh dear . . .

There was something not quite right about this book, Celia thought. It was a brilliant theme, it was beautifully written, but every now and again, it seemed to stumble. The dialogue became awkward. And certain scenes, essential to the development of the relationship, delicate, subtle scenes between the woman and her lover, seemed very short. She knew what that meant – or thought she did. She reached for the buzzer on her phone.

'Could you get me the manuscript of *Time to Fly*,' she said to her secretary. 'I need to make some notes.'

'Well she's arrived safely,' said Sebastian. He scowled at Celia. 'I miss her horribly. House seems dead. I hope you're pleased with your handiwork.'

'Sebastian, it's hardly my handiwork. Merely a suggestion that she try a change of scene. She was clearly not well and not very happy. Anyway, we don't need to go over all that again.'

'I suppose not. I still don't see why she wasn't happy. She's got everything going for her, she's young, pretty—'

'And she didn't have a boyfriend.'

'A boyfriend! Oh, for God's sake, I didn't expect to hear you trotting out such feminine claptrap. Just because she doesn't get engaged every five minutes, like that absurd cousin of hers.'

'Amy is extremely silly,' said Celia, 'I grant you that. She's so exactly like her mother at the same age, I can hardly believe it. Anyway, it's Isabella we're talking about. And it is not feminine claptrap, Sebastian, everyone wants someone to love and to be loved by. Even you should know that.'

'Oh for heaven's sake, Celia. Below the belt, I'd say.'

'Sorry, Sebastian. I'm very sorry.' Briefly, very briefly, she put her hand on his; he stared down at them, at their two hands, as if he had never seen them before.

Then she withdrew hers. 'But the fact remains,' she went on hastily, 'Isabella's heart was very painfully broken when she was sixteen; she hasn't given it properly to anyone since. She's disappointed with life, worried by her inability to attract men – and I have to say it is odd, that no one has found her. She's lovely, and extremely interesting. And she's – what, twenty-five. It's hardly surprising she's depressed.'

'Oh God.' He took off his spectacles, rubbed his eyes hard, looked at her intently. 'What damage have we done her – them – you and I? How can we begin to put it right?'

'By letting Isabella follow her heart,' said Celia briskly, 'and by encouraging her in everything she wants to do. Now, I hope you've written her a nice cheerful letter, telling her how busy you are and that you haven't had time to miss her at all yet. If you haven't, then I suggest you do it this afternoon. I don't want her worried about you. It'll spoil her trip.'

'All right, all right. I will. Anyway, you know Kit and I are going out, don't you? In the autumn. She knows how much I'm looking forward to that. I suppose she'll still be there.'

'You and – Kit?' She spoke quietly, but the pain in her voice was very raw. 'You're going to New York with Kit?'

'That's the idea. Yes. You hadn't heard?'

'Sebastian, how would I have heard? Who would have told me such a thing? Damn. Damn.' She rummaged in her bag for a handkerchief. He looked at her, got up and left the room, returned a moment later with two large ones of his own.

'Here,' he said gently, 'let me at least resume that much of our relationship, supplying you with handkerchiefs. I'm so sorry Celia, I really thought you would have known.'

'No,' she said, 'I didn't know. Oh dear.' She got up, walked over to the window, stared out for a few moments. He watched her, his face very sad.

'I have – tried, you know,' he said. 'God knows why I should, but I have. It's no use. He's very stubborn. And still very angry and upset.'

'Is he? Well it's to be expected I suppose. I've written and phoned. He – well, he just won't see me. Oh, it hurts so much, Sebastian, every hour of every day. But' – she visibly straightened her back, took a cigarette from her bag and lit it – 'what a wonderful idea. Going to New York, I mean. What fun you'll have.'

'I think we will.'

There was a silence; then, 'How – how is he?'

'He's very well. Very well indeed. Doing splendidly at Wesley, but that much you must know.'

'Yes, thank you.'

'And – how is the noble Lord?'

'Shooting grouse. Oh, Sebastian. It really was one of my bigger mistakes.'

'And the only one I've ever heard you own up to. Well, it makes me very happy.'

'What, that I'm miserable?'

'Well – yes,' he said grinning at her. 'Yes, it does, actually. In fact, I propose a toast. Mrs Conley –' he opened the door '– Mrs Conley, bring in a bottle of champagne, would you?'

'That's an appalling and very cruel idea,' Celia said, blowing her nose again. 'I want no part of it. I'm going to the lavatory, and then I'm going to leave.'

'Of course you're not.'

'Let us drink,' he said, raising his glass to her a little later, as she returned, composed, her still lovely face freshly made up, 'let us drink to your misery. Which is not, as we both know, really too terribly serious. Especially now you have returned to the true love of your life. By which I mean Lyttons, of course. And also to my returning happiness. Don't look at me like that. You owe me a little of that at least, don't you think?'

'Yes, Sebastian,' she said, smiling at him over her raised glass. 'Yes, I think perhaps I do.'

'Oh Barty, it's so lovely here,' Izzie turned back towards Barty from the verandah at South Lodge, smiling happily. 'So very lovely.'

'Isn't it? I love it more than anywhere on earth. It's why I never come back to England to live. I could leave Manhattan, but I could never leave South Lodge. It's going to be blistering today,' she added, 'I shall have to be very careful with Jenna, keep her in a bit, she burns so easily.'

'You'll be lucky. She and Cathy have plans to take a picnic out on the pond, in the boat. I heard them talking about it.'

'Well, it'll have to be a very early picnic. Oh dear. Another battle ahead. How are you feeling, Izzie? Not too tired?'

Izzie had arrived to such dire warnings from Celia about her physical condition that Barty had half expected an invalid to be lifted off the plane on a stretcher, rather than the smiling, if rather thin girl who bounded up to her in the arrivals lounge and hugged her ecstatically. She had since noticed that Izzie was indeed very easily tired and prone to becoming low and even tearful at certain times, but decided to ignore it. Barty had absorbed from Celia a capacity for not intruding; they were both known for their ability not to question the cause of any distress, while at the same time making it clear they had both noticed and sympathised with it. Indeed, Celia had broken the rule of a lifetime in dealing with Izzie's unhappiness; and then only because it seemed to her a matter of almost frightening urgency.

Even then she had waited most patiently for over an hour while Izzie had wept and prevaricated and denied that there was anything really wrong before saying quite abruptly, 'Isabella, forgive me, but is it something to do with Henry? Henry and you? And are you pregnant?' The shock of that had released everything, and because she trusted Celia's discretion absolutely, Izzie had suddenly found herself able to reveal every hideous, painful, ugly detail. Celia's only comment on the whole affair was to say that she wanted her to see her own gynaecologist.

'She is the soul of discretion, and you must be checked out, Isabella. It is quite vital to your future health and happiness.' Apart from that her advice had been calm, practical and constructive.

Barty adopted precisely the same tactics; she neither questioned Izzie as to why she had felt a sabbatical was suddenly so necessary, or why she was so clearly frail and unhappy – even when she came upon Izzie weeping one evening over some old photographs of herself with the Warwick clan.

'I've been rather lonely,' was all she said, then, 'and this has reminded me of how happy I was then.'

'Well I know about loneliness,' said Barty briefly. 'I'm the perfect shoulder to cry on about that one.'

But further explanation was not forthcoming; all Izzie said, her large eyes soft with sympathy, was, 'I suppose you are. Poor Barty. Is it still very bad?'

'No, not really. And of course I'm not lonely as such. But—'

'Have you never – well, felt even remotely for anyone else?' said Izzie gently.

'Not really. Although, since we have a long evening to ourselves, let me tell you about one slightly unremote feeling. You'll probably meet him – in fact, you're bound to, he's the father of Jenna's best friend. Look, let's open a bottle of wine and if you can bear it, I'll tell you about him. I just don't know what to do or what I feel. It's very difficult. Very difficult indeed.'

Izzie was to meet him that very evening, as a matter of fact; school was out for the summer, and Barty and Jenna had moved out to South Lodge for several weeks. Izzie and Mrs Mills were to be in charge of Jenna if Barty had to go in to Manhattan.

'Which I'm trying not to, I deserve a vacation for God's sake, but I may have to. Things aren't entirely easy at the moment.'

Izzie was delighted. 'I can at last earn my keep, I've been here for weeks and done nothing except chat, and meet all your lovely friends.'

She especially liked the gently beautiful Felicity Brewer and her son the still-dashing Kyle: growing a little portly in his middle age.

'If he wasn't so old, I'd think there could be a romance there,' Barty said.

'He's clearly very taken with you, and he's never remarried after his divorce.'

'Oh, Barty no, he's not my type. But it's not because he's old. I've realised that I like older men. Apart from – well, apart from once of course. I'm like my mother, obviously. I just find them so much more interesting and sensitive and – well, more fun. But Kyle is a bit jolly for me. Although I do agree, awfully handsome.'

Kyle had become very close to Barty over the years, an integral part of her life. He was now a hugely successful literary agent, writing, as he put it, half the contracts in New York. His twenty-year background in publishing had provided a superb bank of contacts and company knowledge; the business instinct, inherited from his father, had provided the remaining skills.

Barty had asked him years earlier to be one of the trustees of a fund she had set up. Uneasy at what she called the 'untrammelled money' running around, the income derived from both her Lytton shares and those left her by Laurence, she had put half of them into a trust fund for Jenna. 'She's so alone in the world. She needs taking care of. If anything should happen to me I want everything very carefully organised. And I want Lyttons' interests properly represented as well; a set of stuffy old lawyers isn't going to understand what's best for them. Please Kyle, will you do that for me, be a trustee? I've asked Jamie as well, he's agreed.'

Kyle had kissed her and said it would be an honour.

'Only I don't want to find myself in a position where I actually have to do anything very much. You take care of yourself.'

Charlie Patterson was driving out to South Lodge that evening to collect Cathy, who he was taking to visit her grandmother – against a background of tantrums, sulks and threats to kill herself if he made her leave Jenna.

'I'm afraid she's picked up some of Jenna's tendency to histrionics,' Barty said apologetically as they were forced to witness a performance from Cathy that would not have disgraced Cleopatra when the trip was first mentioned.

'Oh don't believe it,' he said grinning. 'She's always had a great talent in that direction.'

'So you'll meet him,' Barty told Izzie, 'and you can see what you think. I mean, he is just so charming and nice and we get on so well, and he makes me laugh and he's good-looking and attractive and I like him very much and—'

'Well, what on earth are you waiting for?' said Izzie, laughing. 'He sounds perfect.'

'I know. He does. But – I suppose what I'm waiting for is feeling easy.

Not with him, which I do, but about him. There's just something – I don't know, see what you think.'

'So you must be Izzie. Daughter of the famous Sebastian Brooke. Your father is a genius. And he's got me through many a long night with Cathy, when she's been ill or unhappy. Do please tell him that.'

'I will,' said Izzie who had been given this message to pass to her father countless times. 'He'll be so pleased.'

'And how do you find New York?'

'Oh I love it. I've been before, actually.'

'Oh, you have? I hadn't realised.'

'Only once. When I was just sixteen.'

'Too young to appreciate it properly. And – out here, to Southampton?'

'To Southampton, yes. And this bit especially –' she gestured towards the shore and the ocean '– seems to me the nearest I'll ever get to heaven. Until it's the real thing and then I suspect it won't quite match up.'

'It is glorious. Oh, Barty, bless you. Just how I like it. She mixes the best Martini in Manhattan, you know,' he said to Izzie, raising his glass to her.

'Charlie, don't be absurd. Anyway, Laurence always said no woman could make a Martini.'

'Well Laurence is – was wrong.' He took a sip. 'So, you lucky girls are staying here, are you? While we swelter in Manhattan?'

'Yes,' said Barty, and even as she smiled, Izzie thought she looked uneasy. 'Yes, we are. Anyway, I thought you were going up to the Heights.'

'No, I'm leaving Cathy behind with her grandmother.'

'I'm not staying,' said Cathy. 'I hate it there, I hate her too, she's horrible and boring and that horrible poky little—'

'Cathy, be quiet, please.' His voice was light, but his eyes were suddenly quite hard. He's quite tough on her, thought Izzie; rather like Father was with me. The thought warmed her towards Charlie Patterson.

He stayed for an early supper, then left, packing the wailing Cathy and her bag into the battered old T-bird.

'Come back soon or I shall die of misery,' wailed Jenna, as the door was finally closed.

'I will, I will if I'm allowed.'

'Of course you're allowed,' said Barty and Charlie in unison, then laughed. He bent to kiss her briefly.

'Thank you again.'

'My pleasure – again. I'll see you soon.'

'If you do come into the city, call me. We'll have dinner.'

'I will. Now enjoy the trip on your own,' she said quietly. 'Are you going up to Connecticut?'

'Where?' he said and looked puzzled.

'To – to Connecticut. I thought that was the idea.'

144

'Oh – oh yes.' he smiled at her quickly. 'Yes, yes, that's the idea. Now Izzie – goodbye. It was just delightful meeting you. I look forward to seeing you again.'

'Me too,' she said, allowing him to kiss her cheek.

'Barty,' Izzie said, as the car went out of sight and Jenna fled sobbing noisily to the den, 'Barty, he is just heaven. I can't think why you're not madly in love with him. He obviously is with you.'

'Oh don't say that, Izzie. Don't.'

'But why?'

'I'm – frightened by people being in love with me. I can't help it. But – you really like him?'

'I really like him.'

'Would you trust him?'

'Oh absolutely,' said Izzie. 'He seems transparently nice and kind and gentle. He's terribly attractive. And he's a wonderful father. You can see that.'

'Well, I can. But at the same time, Cathy is –' she looked warily at the door of the den, beckoned Izzie into the kitchen, '– Cathy is a horror. I find it hard to like her. Oh, I know she seems very sweet, and her manners are lovely and she's bright and cute. But she's so manipulative. Terribly bad for Jenna. I've tried to break up the friendship just a bit, encourage Jenna to have other friends too, but it's hopeless. And she's secretive, which I hate. Almost sly in fact. That has to come from somewhere.'

'Oh, I don't know. She's had a tough time. I feel for her, I must say. And then of course you don't know what her mother was like.'

'Maybe. That's what I keep telling myself. But – so is Charlie, just a bit. Manipulative, I mean. He always says the right thing, never trips up.'

'Well what's wrong with that?' said Izzie laughing.

'Nothing. Of course. But somehow – oh, I don't know. It's too right. I can't fault him, can't ever catch him out. I feel he tries just a bit too hard to please. And to appear too good as well. But, yes, you're right, he is a wonderful father. And he has a hell of a struggle, has to fit in working around Cathy. He manages marvellously, works short days, stays home when she's ill.'

'But isn't that nice?' asked Izzie.

'Yes of course. But he does like to make sure I know about it. Oh, I'm being horrid, why shouldn't he?'

'And – do you find him attractive?'

'I suppose I do. Of course he's not Laurence. That was kind of blinding, you know. But yes, Charlie's certainly the first man I could even contemplate fancying, as they say over here. So – oh Izzie, I don't know.'

'I do,' said Izzie. 'I think you really, really like him and you're frightened of it. Think it's disloyal to Laurence.'

'Maybe. But whatever the reason, I do feel it, I can't help it. Anyway, none of it matters, we quite suit each other and he's fun to have dinner with and so on. Now – another woman-made Martini, before we turn in?'

'No, I don't think so. I'm a bit tipsy.'

'Cup of tea?'

'Now you're talking,' said Izzie, smiling.

Later Barty sat in bed, pretending to read, thinking about Charlie. There had been something that evening, something that had troubled her, something tangible this time. He had clearly not known why she had mentioned Connecticut, his own 'special place', the one he had talked about so movingly, where he and Meg had been so happy. Oh, she was just being silly. It had come at him unawares, she had probably spoken out of turn anyway. Why couldn't she just enjoy him, accept what Izzie said? Instead of turning her back on a piece of happiness?

Keir was having trouble getting a teaching post. The younger headmasters who interviewed him agreed with him that the comprehensive ideal would solve the educational problems of the country at a stroke, but disapproved of his deep conviction that the old disciplines were best applied to early reading and mathematics; while the older ones, who found this music to their ears, were inevitably in favour of grammar schools and eleven-plus selection. This combined with the fact that he was very inclined to express criticism and to be incapable of arguing a case without becoming first excited and then belligerent, meant that he left every interview empty-handed. By the start of the new school year he still had no proper job, only some supply teaching which left him frustrated and miserable. Elspeth tried to comfort him, and indeed to offer help.

'I can't understand it,' he said gloomily, when she arrived to stay with him and his parents, 'I even did as you said, and managed not to talk about the comprehensives, listened politely while he went on and on about the scholarship, and how several boys moved into the grammar school each year. Then I discovered the boys weren't doing any proper games, just a bit of PE with an old biddy in the playground twice a week and—'

'And—'

'Well, I told him boys of that age needed a lot of physical exercise and should be taught football properly, that it was a vital part of education.'

'And—?' she asked again. She refilled her teacup from Mrs Brown's large earthenware pot; the tea was treacle-strong. They were sitting in the kitchen, which the Browns had tactfully vacated. She could hear their radio turned up to full volume in the next room; it was hard to concentrate.

'So, he said, "I am most interested to hear your views, Mr Brown, but perhaps you would be kind enough to tell me where I might find the budget for a full-time games master. We are not in the private sector here, you know." As if I thought that was the ideal. I'm afraid that did set me off on the comprehensives and – well, he told me he didn't think I was quite right for his school.'

'Oh Keir,' said Elspeth, 'you really have to learn to keep your mouth shut. The thing is once you've got a job, once you're in a school you can put your theories into practice. But till then—'

'Well it doesn't look as if I'm going to get a job,' he said gloomily. 'I'm a failure, Elspeth, a bloody failure.'

'Of course you're not,' she said fiercely. 'It's just a matter of time. A matter of finding the right school and the right head. Why don't you come down to London, try there? There must be more schools, and it would be so nice if you were nearer me.'

'Oh yes? And where do you think I would live? At least I get cheap board and lodging up here with Mum and Dad.'

'You could live with me for a—'

'No. Oh no. I'm not going to take the Lytton shilling. I'll pay my way, whatever I do. And anyway, what would your family think?'

'They needn't know,' she said rather feebly.

'Oh, don't be so bloody stupid. Of course they'd know. And anyway, I'd know. And I wouldn't like it.'

'Well – well, all right. Now I have some news,' she said, unable to keep it to herself any longer. She could see it might be tactless, but it was so important; and he was supposed to love her, he should be pleased for her.

'Yes? What?' He scowled at her.

'I'm – well, I'm going to be an editor. A junior one, of course.'

It had been the most wonderful surprise; Celia had called her in and told her that she thought she showed considerable talent and she wanted her to start immediately, under her personal supervision.

'There'll be a lot of proof correcting, of course, a bit of cover copy, all the dogsbody tasks. But you will also start editing. On the fiction side. And I have a particular idea in mind for you,' she had added, 'but you'll have to wait for that.' And she refused to be drawn any further.

'Oh yes?' said Keir now. His tone and expression were non-committal. 'Granny fixed that for you, did she?'

'Keir, that was horrible. Apologise.'

He did: half-heartedly. But it was an empty apology; for they both knew the truth behind it. Elspeth might be very talented: but she was also a Lytton. To say it was an advantage was an understatement of considerable proportions.

Keir refused to discuss it any further, to share her happiness, to acknowledge her cleverness, just returned to the subject of his own lack of employment, the stupidity and blindness of the teaching profession. His voice went on and on against the background of Elspeth's hurt and the nine o'clock news in the next room. She felt near to tears. She had come a long way to visit him, had taken Friday off from work, and so far it had been a complete waste of time.

They weren't even going to get a chance to go to bed together as far as she could see. She was in his bed and he was banished to the couch in the front room. Although she liked Mr and Mrs Brown very much, and they treated her as if she was made of china, she didn't really want to spend the whole weekend with them. And then Keir was so self-obsessed always, she thought, so ungracious. So uninterested in her, diminishing her own achievements. All right, he'd had a hard time, had failed at getting into publishing and whatever he might say about it being a second-rate profession, he must still care about that. But at least he was doing what he wanted now.

And he appeared quite untroubled by their continued separation, by the vast distance between them. Sometimes, much as she loved him, she wondered if it was worth it. There were other men she met these days, easier, more charming, more – well, more like herself. Men she could see fitting into her life, men who worked in publishing, in advertising, the arts. Men who were impressed by her, men who invited her out to dinner, told her how clever she was. When Keir came down to London, he either cooked himself, which took all evening, or expected her to do it. He never wanted to go out. Not even to the theatre or the cinema. He was too tired, he said, by the journey, by his week, by his wretched, wretched job, or rather the lack of it. She resigned herself now to a miserable weekend and decided she would tell him she had to leave first thing on Sunday. He didn't even seem to care.

Three weeks later he came down to London on the coach to stay in her flat. She had thought it would be better, but he was still truculent, dissatisfied with his job, tired by the long journey.

'You should have come on the train.'

'I couldn't afford the bloody train.'

'I would have –' she stopped.

'For God's sake, Elspeth, I've told you before, I will not take your charity.'

'It's not charity, I love you. I want to help you.'

'Well, you don't help me by reminding me how bloody hard up I am. And what a lot of fucking money you've got.'

'Don't swear like that at me.'

'Sorry.'

She tried to change the subject.

'Would you like to go to the cinema?'

'No,' he said briefly.

'Well, I would. *The Seven Year Itch* is on, you know how you love Marilyn—'

'I said no. I want to stay in with you.'

'And talk about you,' she said bitterly. 'You, and how you haven't got a job and absolutely nothing else. I'm really, really sick of it.'

He stared at her, clearly shocked.

'That's not like you.'

'Maybe it is. Maybe you don't know what I'm like any more. You don't exactly try to find out, do you?'

There was a silence; he saw she was close to tears.

'Oh have it your own way,' he said irritably. 'All right, we'll go to the bloody cinema.'

'Keir, I don't want to go to the bloody cinema as you put it. I want to enjoy things with you. Not drag you somewhere against your will.'

'Well why suggest it?' he said with supreme logic.

'Because I want to stop you being so miserable.'

He was silent suddenly, studying her with his dark eyes and then, as he could do at will, changed his mood, smiled at her, the old raw, arrogant smile. 'I know what the matter with you is, Miss Elspeth Warwick. Not enough sex. Now there's a good way to spend the evening. I'll open a bottle of wine and—'

'No you won't,' she said, her voice quite harsh. 'I don't want to go to bed now, any more than you want to go to the cinema. Sorry. We seem to be rather out of sync. Why don't you just carry on telling me about your career, or rather the lack of it, and I'll cook the dinner. That's what you really want, isn't it?'

'No,' he said, coming over to her, kissing her cheek, her neck, her ear. 'No, of course it's not. What I really want is to make love to you. I miss you so much. You have to make allowances for me, Elspeth, it isn't easy for me. I'm sorry. Look – let's go to bed now and then maybe later we can go to the cinema. How would that be?'

'Well –'

She knew she was beaten. And they never got to the cinema.

'I have some interesting news,' said Sebastian to Celia.

'Oh yes?'

They were lunching together; had taken to doing so once a week. Always at his house in Primrose Hill, always followed by a walk on the Heath. Sebastian was convinced that nobody knew about it, or hardly anybody, and if they did, they didn't care. Celia, who saw things rather more clearly, knew that it was the talk of literary, and indeed social London. She also saw no point in telling Sebastian so.

'Kit has been talking to Clementine Hartley. About the possibility of her going to Wesley.'

'What?'

'Yes, I thought that would stop you in your tracks. Apparently she's very seriously considering it. She's so impressed with what they've done for him, with their fresh approach to everything—'

'Perhaps you'd like to tell me precisely what is so fresh about their approach?' said Celia icily.

'Oh – the way they promote their books. And distribute them. They can get them out to the shops so much faster, they have their own fleet of vans. And they're talking about doing their own paperback imprint.'

'Oh really?'

'Yes, interesting, isn't it? I don't think it'll happen yet, but it's a measure of how forward their thinking is. And their advertising is interesting. They actually gave a hint as to what Kit's new book was about in the last poster, didn't just say, "The new Christopher Lytton". Izzie would approve of that.'

'Sebastian, I hope you're not thinking of defecting.'

'Of course I'm not. You know I never would. Or could. I tried once but – well, I don't need to remind you about that.'

'No,' she said, smiling at him, her eyes soft suddenly. Thinking of a time when Sebastian had saved Lyttons by his own loyalty. So very long ago – and yet . . .

'But I seriously think Miss Hartley might go. I thought you ought to know. She's planning her new book and hasn't signed a contract yet.'

'No, I knew that. But I thought it was a formality. Very stupid of me,' she said. 'I think I should take Miss Hartley out to lunch. Now Sebastian, I want to talk to you about something quite different . . .'

A week later Jay was sitting reading the manuscript of a new novel and trying to convince himself the author was the new Graham Greene, when Celia walked into his office and shut the door.

'Jay. We have a serious problem.'

'Oh really?' He smiled at her. He was tired; the new baby had proved difficult and noisy and he couldn't quite afford the under-nursemaid that Tory felt to be necessary.

'Yes. It's Clementine Hartley. She's on the brink of signing with Wesley.'

'Oh, what nonsense. She wouldn't dream of it. I have the draft contract right here. What's more, it's very generous.'

'I dare say it is. She's actually not interested in money, Jay. I've been talking to her. She has quite a lot of her own. She's much more concerned about promotional opportunities, about cover design – she hated the way her views weren't taken into account last time – and about editing.'

'Editing! For God's sake, Celia, I edit her.'

'Precisely.'

'Well I'm the Editorial Director, for God's sake. What more does she want? She gets every consideration, if she doesn't want to change something, we don't force her, she writes exactly what she likes, she's spoilt to death. God preserve me from successful authors.' He smiled at her.

'A more immediate force than God may do that, Jay, if you're not careful. The point is, she needs, in my opinion, a woman editor. A young one.' She smiled at him. 'You're a brilliant editor, Jay, but you must seem extremely old to her. And you're a man. It really doesn't make sense, your editing her. I blame myself, I should have thought of it before.'

She watched him struggling with his own pride, saw him acknowledging the sense of what she said. He managed a rather rueful smile.

'Well, the view of this old man is that even if you're right, Celia, who? We don't have any senior women editors. Except you.'

'We have young women editors, Jay.'

'Well that's absurd. Clementine can't be entrusted to one of them. Young women editors don't have the experience, they don't—'

'They have a gut instinct for what's going on. A sympathy with their authors and their readers. You're falling into the middle-age trap, Jay. You mustn't do it.'

'Oh Celia, really.' He smiled at her again, his most charming smile. 'I'm the first to be aware of new trends, of what the young are doing.'

'Good. Then you'll sympathise with Clementine's request for her new editor.'

'And who is that?'

'Elspeth.'

'What? That's absurd. Elspeth is a child, she's only been here a year or so—'

'She's very talented. She has a real feel for fiction.'

'Are you saying you go along with this ridiculous idea?'

'Yes. I do. Obviously with some reservations. I think we have to. Otherwise Clementine will go to Wesley.'

'Well she'd better go,' said Jay after a pause. 'I'm not being held to ransom by some girl of twenty-seven.'

'A very important girl of twenty-seven. She outsold almost everyone last year with her novel. She's pretty and charming and very well connected, She also gets a lot of publicity. We can't afford to lose her, Jay. We really can't.'

'But Elspeth will have no idea what she's doing.'

'I think she will. It transpires she even came up with the theme of Clementine's latest book. And the title.'

'What, *Oxford in Aspic*? Clementine told me it was her idea.'

Celia shrugged. 'Whatever she told you, she wants to work with Elspeth. I think we have to go along with it. We can keep an eye on things. Make sure they don't run away with themselves.'

'Celia, no.'

'Jay, yes. Or it's say goodbye to Miss Hartley. For good.'

CHAPTER 12

'I've got a job! I just can't believe it. And not just any job, but the job of my dreams. Oh, I could fly, I'm so happy—'

'Well before you take right off, would you like to tell me what it is? You look as if you're about to burst.'

'I *am* about to burst. It's a job writing advertising copy, Barty. For an agency in New York, an agency specialising in books. I absolutely cannot believe it. Anyway, I didn't tell you until I'd had the interview and that was today, and I got it, I got it, oh Barty, can I buy you dinner to celebrate?'

'You certainly can. I'm longing to hear every single little detail.'

'Don't worry, you will. My only worry is Father. It means I'll be here much longer and—'

'I don't think you should worry too much about your father, Izzie. From what I hear, Celia and Sebastian have made up friends, as Jenna would say, and are spending quite a lot of time together. And he's cheered right up.'

'Really! He never said anything to me in his letters. What on earth could have brought that about? And what does poor nice Lord Ardent have to say about it?'

'I have no idea. Anyway, you can sound him out when he gets out here next week. Now, talking about Lord Ardent, that reminds me of Geordie. It was Geordie who called him that originally, you know. Anyway, Geordie's coming out just before Christmas to promote his new book. And staying for a while.'

'Did Adele tell you that?' asked Izzie, her face suddenly sober.

'No, I had a wire from Geordie this morning. He hadn't been too sure, he didn't want to leave Clio. But he's decided he has to and rightly, I think. It's a brilliant book.'

'You said. What's it called? I'm still waiting for my copy.'

'*Growing Down*. Very, very clever. One of his best. We need something good,' she added. 'I'm extremely tired of seeing *Peyton Place* on the best-seller list.'

'Maybe I can write the copy for Geordie's book,' said Izzie.

'Maybe,' said Barty carefully.

Izzie's job sounded a great deal more glamorous and exciting than it really was. The agency, Neill & Parker was situated in an unfashionable area of Manhattan, on the edge of Chelsea, where property was extremely cheap.

It was headed up by two men called Nick Neill and Mike Parker who ran it on a shoestring; the idea had come from Nick Neill himself, when he was working as a clerk for *Harpers*. He had been called up to a meeting with some proofs one day and heard one of the executives saying to the other, 'I cannot believe the crap the advertising department turns out. It's always the same. We need some fresh thinking and where's it going to come from?'

Twelve months later, Nick had a bank loan, an enthusiastic colleague and a tiny office in one of the old wood-framed houses in the meat district. The address on their mail was a box number; since they always went to their clients or met them in hotels, nobody had to know where the sharp, often original copy they turned out was written. Their agency was a fairly new concept, and what they turned out were new concepts too; they did modestly well. Only modestly; most of the big publishers still used their own departments, but they still got enough work to finance the move to Chelsea in 1955 – and now to take on Izzie in 1956.

'What you'll be doing mostly,' said Nick Neill, 'is going to sales conferences, hearing what the editors have to say about the books to the reps and trying to pick up on something new. Not too new mind you, these guys are not Coca-Cola.'

Coca-Cola was already leading a whole new style of Manhattan advertising. Izzie said she realised that.

'Oh and you'll be quoting from reviews, good and bad. You'd be surprised the good things you can pick out of a bad review.'

'Like what?'

'Well, some smart guy writes in the literary pages that such and such a novel is perfect for the small-minded shop girl. Or that the characterisation is unbelievably two-dimensional. So you pull out "Perfect" and "Un-believable characterisation" and add the name of the reviewer. Believe me, there is no review so bad you can't write a real good ad out of it.'

Izzie laughed; and then thought rather soberly of what her father and indeed Michael Joseph might have to say about such a practice. She liked both the boys, as everyone referred to them; they were in their late twenties, born and bred in Brooklyn with accents as thick as treacle, Jewish, sharp, sexy, and absolutely focussed on their task. Nick Neill was tall and extremely skinny, with a way of waving his hands about theatrically when he got excited; Mike Parker was shorter and already stout, with a mournful face and a penchant for dirty jokes which he rather touchingly felt Izzie would not understand. Neither of them was married or even had a serious girlfriend, which puzzled Izzie, as they both seemed rather sexy to her; they said they couldn't afford either the money or the time. They lived together in a one-bedroom apartment in SoHo.

'OK, so people think we're a couple of nancy boys,' said Nick cheerfully, 'so let them. It saves the rent.'

No job was too small for them, too dull, too painstaking; they would cheerfully work through the night in order to meet a deadline (usually as a result of one of their rivals having turned in copy so dull they were resorted to in desperation). They put up with the most appalling treatment from their clients and warned Izzie she must do the same. 'They'll treat you like shit, honey; just remember that's what you're there for. Everybody needs someone to shit on.'

Izzie said she would remember and again wondered what Michael Joseph might have to say to such a philosophy.

She was under no illusion as to why they had taken her on; even in downtown Manhattan they had heard of her father, they could boast about her. And she was prepared to work for a salary so small it was derisory.

'But I tell you what,' said Nick Neill, 'you can look up at the stars. You know that quotation?'

Izzie said she didn't.

'I'd have thought you would. Don't they teach you anything at Oxford any more? How's it go, Mike?'

'It goes, "we are all in the gutter",' said Mike Parker, ' "but some of us are looking at the stars." It's our company motto. When we're big and famous, we're going to put it on all our stationery.'

'I think maybe you should do it now,' said Izzie. 'Who wrote it, anyway?'

'No, everyone would laugh. You've got to be big to show sentiment. It's Oscar Wilde. You like his stuff?'

'Very much,' said Izzie carefully.

They constantly surprised her.

The other reason they had taken her on, but which she failed to appreciate at first, was because she patently had class. Not just literary class but social class. They might be clever, they might be hard-working, but neither of the boys would ever seem anything but what they were: working-class Jewish. And a lot of their would-be clients in the big houses, they explained, were WASPs, 'what you'd call posh, I guess. People like Harcourt, Brace, Scribners, Doubleday, they're all still owned by the people who founded them. Publishing is an occupation for gentlemen, who've all been to the same schools and summered together in the same places and dine in one another's clubs and—'

'Same in London,' said Izzie.

'So we hear. And twenty years ago even, we wouldn't have stood a chance. But times are changing. Simon & Schuster, Random House, Viking, they're all mainstream Jewish firms. Pretty gentlemanly Jewish, but still. And they think different, faster, more interesting. In some of these places it's even kind of smart to use Yiddish words.'

'Yes, I see,' said Izzie.

'You can talk about chutzpah at Simon & Schuster, they know what you're talking about. But then again, we do need a bit of class, and a bit of old-fashioned English class would be best of all. You ever met Queen Elizabeth? Or the Prince?'

Izzie said she was afraid not. They were clearly disappointed.

'But I do know some people I think you'd call upper class,' she said, anxious to restore their faith in her.

'What, like earls and stuff like that?'

Yes, she said, a couple of earls, a countess, stuff like that. 'I knew it,' said Mike Parker in tones of great satisfaction.

She introduced them to Barty, who was enchanted by them, promised to give them some work.

'We need some new ideas,' she said, and she also promised to introduce them to Kit when he came over the following month.

'What about Sebastian Brooke, your dad? You think he'd like to meet us?' asked Nick hopefully.

'I know he would,' said Izzie.

There was a ring at the door; Lucas opened it. Geordie was standing there. Sometimes Lucas found he had almost forgotten how much he hated Geordie; he had only to see him at close proximity to be reminded.

'Oh,' he said, 'it's you.'

'Yes, Lucas, it's me,' said Geordie, his face a cold blank. 'How are you?' Lucas said nothing, gave a shrug.

'Are you going to invite me in?'

'Please do come in.'

He wasn't going to be rude to him today; he was not.

'I wondered if you and I might have a talk,' said Geordie. 'I hear you are much happier at school and it seems to me that the two of us might be able to communicate a little better as a result.'

Lucas looked at him.

'I am happier at school, yes,' he said, 'but that's no thanks to you, is it? It was my mother who got me out of that place. If you'd had your way I would have had to rot there for two more years. Things were so bad there I would have killed myself if it had gone on any longer. I suppose that would have solved all your problems, wouldn't it? Got me completely out of the way.'

'Lucas don't be absurd. You're exaggerating. Shall we continue this discussion in a more civilised way? In the drawing room, perhaps—'

'There's nothing to discuss. Not that I can see. I shall never forgive you for what you did to me, never. And nor will my mother. She said so.'

'Lucas, I find that very hard to believe.'

He shrugged again. 'Please yourself. It's true.'

Adele came running up the steps of the house, and walked into the drawing room, her face alight at seeing Geordie there.

'Geordie, hallo.'

'Hallo Adele. I'm afraid I'm a little early.'

'Well, that's all right, it's nice to see you, isn't it Lucas?'

Lucas said nothing, turned and walked out of the room.

'Lucas –' she called after him, '– Lucas, come back at once.'

At the rear of the house a door slammed; Geordie looked at Adele.

'Such a charming boy, your son. Now I want to ask you something.'

'Yes?'

'Did you or did you not say you would never forgive me for sending Lucas to school? Say it to him?'

She flushed, was silent. 'Did you, Adele?'

'I – well I don't know. How can I remember? I'm sure I said – well, a lot of silly things. At the time. We were all upset, weren't we, and—'

'Lucas certainly has the impression you did. Say it, I mean. I find that rather hard to take, Adele. It seems to me a very aggressive, uncompromising thing to say. Especially to him.'

'Geordie—'

'No, it's all right, I just wanted it established. And there is no future in going over it all again. What I wanted to discuss was my trip to the States. I shall be away for at least six weeks. And I want Clio to be upset as little as possible. We must handle the situation very carefully, don't you think?'

'Yes,' said Adele quietly, 'yes, very carefully. Of course.'

It was such an absurd and hopeless situation, she thought, watching him drive away with Clio; that their happy marriage should have become this absurd separation, simply because of the bad behaviour of a sixteen-year-old boy. And yet – there really did seem to be no solution. Even her mother agreed. If she was not prepared to send Lucas away again, and she couldn't persuade him to treat Geordie with courtesy – and both seemed equally impossible – then Geordie could not be expected to return to the house. They were all in an entrenched position, and all of them, to an extent, had right on their side. That was what made everything so absolutely impossible.

Maybe in another two years, when Lucas went to university – then maybe Geordie would come home. That was the new hope, to which she clung these days.

Adele was very unhappy. She wasn't even working much. Loneliness and a sense of injustice and resentment had made her depressed, lethargic, even; she found it almost impossible to become enthusiastic about taking photographs for anyone. It seemed a foolish, trivial occupation. Her mother was always telling her that she would feel better if she thought about something other than Lucas and Geordie, that forcing herself to work, however impossible it seemed, would create its own energy, drive some of the demons away. But Adele was less driven than her mother, less even than her sister, and the traumas of the war, her sense of absolute isolation in Paris, the terror she had lived through on the long road south, and indeed on the rest of her journey home, the shock and grief of hearing about Luc's dreadful death, had all left her frail, vulnerable – and with an appalling sense of guilt. It was this above all, increased by the knowledge of what he had endured at school, that kept her so firmly on Lucas's side, convinced her he was in the right, however bad his behaviour. No child should have to endure what he had endured, first as a terrified toddler, then as a wretchedly insecure teenager. And on both occasions, she had, to a large extent, been to blame. Restitution was undoubtedly due to Lucas; and Adele felt bound to pay it.

Sebastian and Kit had arrived in New York.

Kit looked wonderful, fit and tanned – he had spent most of August in a villa in the south of France belonging to the chairman of Wesley, his latest book had had rave reviews and he was visibly excited about being in New York.

Barty also noticed the name 'Clementine' cropped up fairly frequently in conversation.

They were both very busy for the first few days, seeing people, doing interviews, visiting bookshops; a trip out to South Lodge was planned for the weekend.

'I really long to see that place again,' said Sebastian the night before they left, 'it took hold of my heart.'

'It certainly has a hold of mine,' said Barty, 'it's so very precious to me. Oh Sebastian, it's lovely to have you all here. I've so enjoyed having Izzie, and when Geordie arrives it really will feel like being at home.' They were alone, that evening. Izzie had taken Kit out to dinner with the boys to a restaurant in Greenwich Village.

'Yes. Poor Adele, she's having a rough time. Celia is quite worried about her, thinks she's heading for some kind of breakdown and she certainly looks dreadful. I could kill that boy for doing this to them, but as Celia says, they both have right on their side. And you know, I never quite –' He stopped.

'Never quite what?'

'Oh – I don't know. I was going to say never quite trusted Geordie.'

'Sebastian, that's a dreadful thing to say. Everyone loves Geordie, he's so charming and sweet and—'

'Oh I know all that. Of course he's charming and sweet. But I did always feel exactly that, that he was a touch lightweight, not up to it when – if – the test really came.'

'I think you're wrong,' said Barty stoutly, 'he put up with Lucas for ages.'

'He did. But then he didn't use much subtlety. It was as if he was tired of that game and wanted a new one. Demanding that Lucas was sent away, refusing to consider any alternative when it was so clearly a disaster – I felt it rather suited him to be a martyr. He does like to star in a drama, our Geordie, if you ask me.'

'Well I feel very sorry for him. And for Adele. For all of them, actually. It reminds me of Laurence and his situation as a child, you know. I do understand how hard Lucas must find it.'

'Precisely my point. Maybe you should have talked to the wretched boy. Celia says his behaviour is definitely improving, but then Geordie has gone.'

'Give it time. Things may improve. Now Sebastian, I seem to be hearing a lot about Celia,' said Barty, her eyes dancing suddenly. 'I understand there's been a rapprochement.'

He glowered at her, suddenly his old self.

'Yes, well, there was a certain amount of misunderstanding. We've addressed that. And it's very nice to have her – friendship again.'

'It must be.' She gave him a quick kiss. 'I'm so glad. And so is Izzie.'

'How is she? She seems happy.'

'She's wonderfully happy. She likes her job, she loves being here, she's made some friends, and we all get on so very well. Jenna adores her.'

'Where is Jenna this evening? It seems very quiet.'

'It is. She's out with her friend Cathy. Who you will met, she's coming to Southampton with us. She comes nearly everywhere with us,' Barty sighed.

'Don't you like her?'

'Oh, she's all right. She keeps Jenna happy. It's always a worry with an only child, you know.'

'I never worried about Isabella.'

'I don't suppose you did. Poor child. Only teasing, Sebastian, don't look at me like that. Anyway, her father is bringing her over tomorrow, before we go. It's a school holiday and—'

'Her father?'

'Yes. He's a widower.'

'Nice chap?'

'Very nice,' said Barty quickly. She avoided Sebastian's eye.

'Barty. I sense something – interesting here.'

'Oh – not really. Goodness, he's—' she smiled at him quickly then saw his eyes probing hers and said, 'No, actually, Sebastian, you're right. And

I'm very glad you're going to meet Charlie. I'd so like your opinion of him. *In loco parentis*, so to speak.'

'Heavens Barty. Sounds very serious.'

'It is – a bit. He's – well, he's asked me to marry him.'

She still couldn't quite believe it herself. It had been a shock so profound that she was still shaking the following morning. And she wasn't at all sure how they had arrived there. Via bed, of course; and why had she allowed that, she wondered, cursing herself for what seemed, with hindsight, infinite foolishness. And yet – also with hindsight – she couldn't pretend it hadn't been extremely good. Really extremely good. Not wonderful, of course, but then she had not expected that. Wonderful sex belonged in another life, another country, with Laurence; Nothing could touch that, nothing reach it; it was hers, and it had given her happiness, wonder, absolute fulfilment – and Jenna.

But now, twelve years later, she was lonely; getting to know Charlie had made her realise that, had reminded her of how many evenings she had sat alone, unable to discuss work, problems, anxieties, joys; and failures, successes, plans, hopes. How many nights she had lain alone in the great bed at South Lodge – and in her smaller one in Manhattan – feeling isolated, uncared for, growing older, all alone. How many days and weeks and years she had spent, just with Jenna, loving her, wondering at her, watching her – and watching her grow up. How many years she saw ahead of her, with Jenna gone, herself quite alone.

She had been quite unprepared for it, for her desire to go to bed with Charlie. They had been out to dinner; Cathy was staying at the Manhattan house, they were leaving for Southampton in the morning; the girls were both asleep when they let themselves in. Maria too had gone to bed; the house was quiet. Dangerously, awkwardly quiet.

'Do you want a nightcap before you go?' she said.

'That'd be nice.'

'Bourbon?' It was his favourite.

'Yes. I'll get it. I know where it is.'

'All right. I'll be in the den.'

She put the radiogram on, kicked off her shoes, settled on the couch. He came in with the bourbon and two glasses.

'That's nice.'

'Isn't it? Haydn.'

'I didn't mean that. I meant you. So relaxed.'

'Aren't I usually relaxed?'

'No,' he said very seriously. 'No, you're not. You're always just a touch edgy around me.'

'Well I can't think why,' she said with a quick laugh. 'You don't make me feel edgy, Charlie—'

'I think I do,' he said, handing her a glass, sitting beside her, giving her a quick kiss, 'and I think I know why, too.'

'Oh really?'

'Yes. It's because of Laurence. All those memories getting churned up, you fighting them off, hating me for disturbing them . . .'

He was right, she realised, as always he had read her perfectly. She was just drunk enough to tell him so.

'From that very first time at South Lodge, when you understood about – well, how I felt about you being there, you seem to know me. Really know me.'

'And do you think you know me?'

'Actually, no,' she said, sitting back, looking at him carefully. 'I really don't think I know you at all. Well, not in the same way. You're a bit of a dark horse, Charlie Patterson.'

'Really?' he said, and his eyes behind their spectacles were pained. 'I try not to be. I'm a very simple sort of guy really. Most of the time I just tick over, doing my best for Cathy, trying to do my job . . .'

He was silent; then he suddenly said, into the near-darkness, into the music, 'So you couldn't have known I'd fallen in love with you, then?'

'No,' she said, genuinely astonished – although afterwards, the next day, she realised that she must have known, at least suspected, but had crushed it, like every other emotion. 'No, Charlie, I couldn't have known.'

'Well,' he said, sitting apart from her now, his face heavy, avoiding her eyes, 'well I have. I didn't want to, it was too difficult, impossible even—'

'Why impossible?' she asked, genuinely surprised.

'Barty! You can't be that stupid. You really cannot.'

'I'm sorry, Charlie, but I obviously am. You'd better explain.'

'You're a very rich, very powerful woman. You might live behind this façade of being just Jenna's mom, and a single one at that, and caring for her and taking the girls for wonderful weekends and sailing and riding with them, but we both know that's not the real you.'

'Yes it is.'

'No, Barty, it isn't. You have an extraordinarily successful career; you've had what was clearly a wonderful marriage—'

'Not all wonderful,' she said soberly.

'Well – extraordinary, anyway. Your life-story is exceptional. You own one of the most important publishing houses in both the United States and in London. You mix with the rich and famous. It's just that to me – well, obviously, we see these things differently. As we both know. I worry about not having money, you seem to worry about having it.'

She looked at him; it was such a difficult area, this, and he was very proud. He never mentioned his own financial situation, except to tell her that Cathy's grandmother paid her school fees; she had once offered, quite light-heartedly, to invest some money in his business and he had been really angry.

'I would so absolutely hate that,' he had said. 'Please, please don't mention anything of that sort ever again. The balance of our relationship is difficult enough as it is.'

'I don't see why.'

'Well you should,' he had said, sounding almost truculent, and the evening had ended early and uncomfortably. It was the first and last time money had been mentioned. Until now.

'And then,' he said, 'your family background is also powerful and moneyed—'

'I've told you, Charlie, it's neither.'

'Yes, yes,' he said impatiently, 'I know all about the poverty and the slums. The fact is that from the age of two, or whatever you were when Lady Celia took you home, you grew up amidst fabulous wealth. I'm afraid it won't wash, the other story, Barty. And how can I compete with all that?'

He looked so genuinely wretched, so nervous that she was quite shocked. And suddenly she saw herself through his eyes, as a rich and very spoilt woman, wielding considerable power, both domestically and professionally, a woman not unlike Celia, in fact; she had become exactly the person she would once have wanted not to be, and so shocked was she by this perception of herself, that her eyes filled with tears.

'Hey,' he said, putting his arms round her. 'Hey, Barty, don't do that. I didn't mean to upset you, I was just—'

'Charlie,' she said interrupting him, and suddenly she was angry as well as sad, 'Charlie, you have simply got to understand. I was born in a slum. Do you have any idea what that means? No, of course you don't. It means a big family.

'I was the fifth, you know, living in a basement room crawling with damp, half underground; it means four children having to sleep head to toe in a bed, babies, like me, having to sleep in a crate, toddlers – like me – being tied to a chair all day in case they hurt themselves crawling about.

'It means women slaving all day and most of the night, on too little food because the children and the men must have it, it means washing hanging permanently across the room, it means your father coming home drunk and knocking your mother about. And then your mother knocking you about, because she's too exhausted, too desperate, to cope any longer. It means babies not being wanted, being dreaded, it means –' she hesitated, then went on '– it means babies being born malformed through malnutrition, and dying immediately, it means dreading infant deaths, not so much because of any sorrow, but because of paying for the funeral. It means no hope for the future, little education, no break in it anywhere.

'And yes, I was taken away from all that, and do you know what that meant, Charlie? It meant that I was well-fed and well-clothed and educated, but it also meant I lost my family, everything I knew, it meant my brothers and sisters all rejected me, except for Billy. It meant I felt awkward and lonely, not sure who I was all the time I was growing up, condemned to permanent gratitude and a sense of inferiority. Now then, do you really think I have led a life of such privilege? That I am so removed from reality now that I am out of touch with ordinary people, with ordinary worries and concerns? Because if you do, then you do me a great injustice. Very great indeed.'

She was crying now, crying hard, all the old hurts crowding back in on her, adding to the new one of Charlie's view of her. He sat in silence for a long time, staring at her; then he moved nearer to her, put his arms round her.

'Of course not,' he said. 'Of course I don't think that. I – I guess I just hadn't realised quite how – how bad it was for you.'

'Well then,' she said, 'now you do.'

'Yes. Yes, I do. And I admire you more than ever. What you've done, what you've achieved. It can't have come easy.'

'No,' she said, sniffing, 'no it didn't. That's for sure. Not even Laurence and – and –' she waved her hand rather helplessly round the room '– all this came easy. Rather the reverse. I didn't want it, not really. I'm glad more of it didn't come to me.'

'What do you mean?'

'I mean that most of Laurence's money went to his other children. In trust. What we – I – have is the tip of the iceberg.'

'Some iceberg,' he said quietly.

'Yes, I know. But, well, he didn't know about Jenna, she got nothing, of course. I got the houses and a few – well quite a lot of shares. It seemed enough somehow. It is enough. More than enough.'

'You didn't think of fighting for more? Not even for Jenna?'

'Charlie! Whatever for?'

'Well,' he said, 'because you should have it. That's what for. It's yours.' He looked quite distressed; she was surprised.

'Does that matter?'

'I – don't know,' he said. And then, seeing her eyes on him, said quickly, 'No. No, of course not. I guess you don't exactly need it.'

'Charlie,' she said, 'there's something I want to say to you.'

'Yes?'

'I hope – well, I do very much hope – that you can see through it all. Can see me, the real me.'

'Of course I can.' He smiled at her suddenly. 'It's the real you, that I – love. That's what's so special about you, that I can see through it. Am I really going to love some terrifying kind of tycoon? I'd give anything for you not to be that person. So that I could—'

'You could what?'

There was a long silence; then he said, 'So that I could feel you might – love me back.'

'Oh Charlie. You haven't been listening to me. I'm me, Barty Miller, I'm very uncomplicated really.'

'And what does that mean? That you – do love me?'

'No,' she said quickly, too quickly she supposed, but she couldn't let him think for a single moment that she was in love with him, 'I'm not saying that. I'm terribly, terribly fond of you, I love being with you, but I'm not in love with you. I'm sorry.'

'Ah,' he said.

'Oh dear,' she said, taking his hand, leaning forward to kiss him gently, 'you look so very sad.'

'I feel pretty sad,' he said. 'That was a fairly powerful rejection.'

'It wasn't.'

'Barty, it was. You should have heard yourself: "No, Charlie, I don't love you. No, I probably never will love you. But I do like being with you. So will that do?"'

'What about Meg?'

'What about Meg?'

'Don't you still feel a great loyalty to her?'

'Yes, I do. But it's been a long time, I've moved on. And she wouldn't mind, I know she wouldn't, if I was going to be happy. Would Laurence mind?'

'Mind?' she said, laughing. 'Charlie, he'd send a thunderbolt down. Two to be on the safe side, and kill you, no hesitation whatsoever.'

'That would be kind of mean.'

'He was kind of mean. He was very far from perfect. But what I felt for him and what he felt for me was perfect.'

'Well,' he said, and his voice was very sober, quite heavy, 'maybe I should stop seeing you. Just stay out of your life altogether. It'd be better, I guess. For you and for me. We could manage the girls' friendship without actually meeting, I think.'

There was a silence; Barty felt suddenly chilled. Looked at her life without Charlie, without the endless meetings over the girls' arrangements, the laughing discussions about school, teachers, homework, ballet class, the other girls, the imminence of the dreaded adolescence, without the weekly dinners, the trips to the cinema and the skating rink with the girls, the easy chats about everything. It looked empty and very bleak; she felt almost afraid.

She took a deep breath. 'I – don't think I'd want that,' she said, 'not seeing you any more.'

'Yes but—'

'I know, I know. I'm asking you to take all the risks. Saying maybe one day, all that kind of thing. But I – well, I'm asking you, Charlie. If I honestly thought there was nothing in it for you, ever, I'd say. I'm quite – strong, you know. Quite honest, too.'

'Oh yes,' he said with a touch of a smile in his dark eyes, 'I had observed both those qualities.'

'Sorry. They're not necessarily very attractive.'

'Everything about you is attractive,' he said, 'I think. Everything. I think you're beautiful, and clever, and I love the way you laugh, and your quite bad jokes—'

'They're not bad,' she said indignantly.

'They're quite bad, that's what I said. And the way you dress, and the way your hair is always untidy—'

'It's not!'

'It is, but it suits you. And the food you cook and the games you play with the girls, and the way you're so astonishingly hopeless at Scrabble, and the way you get drunk so easily, and the way you care about your work, and a hundred more, I love all those things.'

'Oh,' she said and felt touched, infinitely warmed by what he said, the intimacy, by his knowledge of her. 'Oh Charlie—'

He kissed her suddenly, on the mouth; harder and with more passion than he ever had before. Something in her moved then; something she had supposed long-buried, not forgotten but certainly dead just as Laurence was dead, a flicker, a warmth, a leaping, a reaching out. It was sexual desire; and slight as it was, it felt important and strong.

'I think,' she said, 'I think I would like us to go upstairs. If you would like that too.'

'I would,' he said. 'I would like it very much indeed.'

He was wonderful; careful, patient, tender. He led her, waited for her, led her some more; talked to her gently and sweetly, listened to her, smiled at her, told her he loved her. She did not quite come; something held her back, cut her off, frightened her almost. But as he did, she relaxed and received him absolutely; and afterwards, as he held her, she first smiled and then laughed with sheer joy. And after that, each time, it got better.

He had not exactly asked her to marry him – at first. He had mentioned it, mentioned that he couldn't help thinking about it, and thinking too how absurd a notion it was, how wonderfully, gloriously ridiculous. And she had said why, why absurd, why ridiculous, asked him if she had not become more real to him, less of an object. To which he had replied yes, she had, but even so, he had too little to offer even to consider it. She had grown almost irritable then, had said what mattered in a marriage were intangible things, tenderness, humour, acceptance, 'And sex. Of course.'

Then, afraid of the conversation going further, growing out of control, she had suggested they went to bed. She did that quite often; having rediscovered sex, she was hungry for it, wanted it more than she would have believed. Her early fears of guilt, self-distaste, thunderbolts even, did not materialise. Sex with Charlie made her happy, relaxed, easier. If it did not quite scale the heights she could remember, it still carried her a long way, took her deeper and deeper into their relationship.

And then one night he did it; got very drunk, told her why he was very drunk – 'I have to summon up my courage somehow' – and then after a long pause while he fiddled with his cuffs, pushed back his hair, adjusted his glasses, cleared his throat, told her yet again that he loved her, said, after a long silence, that although there was no point in doing it, he still couldn't stop thinking about marrying her. 'One day, maybe. When I'm a millionaire, own half Manhattan.'

Barty looked at him, very steadily. 'Do you really think that would make any difference to me?' she asked.

'No,' he said, 'probably not. But it would to me.'

A very long silence; then, 'Maybe I should think about it too,' she said.

A longer one. Finally, 'Oh, Barty,' he said, 'if only, if only you would.'

'He's being very sweet,' she said to Sebastian now. 'Very patient and understanding. But I do have to give him an answer soon. And I don't know what I want it to be.'

'Do you love him?'

'I'm really not sure,' she said slowly. 'Certainly not as I loved Laurence. But then – I love being with him, he's gentle and funny and easy and all the things Laurence wasn't. It's quite – different, so I don't feel too disloyal. And I'm much happier in a way with him. No, not happier. That *is* disloyal. But more comfortable. And certainly not lonely any more. And we get on so well, we like the same things, we think the same about the girls, how we bring them up, about an awful lot, really. But Sebastian, no, I don't love him. Not as I understand love, anyway. And so maybe I shouldn't marry him, maybe it's wrong. Unfair to him.'

'Let me meet him,' he said, understanding everything she said. 'Let me meet him and tell you what I think. I shall give you my full and frank opinion of him and quite possibly we will never speak again as a result of it. Mind you, it's a heavy burden of responsibility. I hope the whole thing won't hang on my judgement.'

'Of course it won't. I'm a bit more sure of myself than that. It's just that – well, no one I care about or whose opinion I value has met him, except Izzie. Who does love him. But then she loves most people.'

'No one in particular, though?'

His voice was casual, but his eyes were watchful; Barty smiled at him and patted his hand.

'No one in particular. I wish there was. She needs to be loved.'

165

'We all do, don't we?' said Sebastian.

'Yes,' said Barty, 'yes, I suppose we do.'

'Keir,' said Elspeth. He was staying with her for a week, it was half term.

'Yes?'

He scarcely looked up, he was deep in an article in the paper about the uprising in Hungary and its brutal suppression by the Soviets. 'I've half a mind to go out there,' he said. 'A lot of young people have, you know.'

'Keir, please! I need to talk to you. I don't want to have to compete with the newspapers.'

'You were pretty bloody well engrossed in that rubbish about Grace Kelly marrying some ridiculous Ruritanian prince. As if I cared.'

'Oh don't be ridiculous,' she said irritably. 'You're so vicious about everything. It's like the royal family here, what harm have they done you?'

'Same as they've done to all of us,' he said, 'lived at our expense in absurd style while perpetuating the worst of the class system in this country. You know what John Osborne said about them.'

'No,' said Elspeth rather wearily.

'That they were the gold filling in the mouth of decay in this country. I think it would have been a good idea if she'd married Group Captain whatever his name is. Margaret, I mean. And gone to live in a semi-detached with him as plain Mrs Group Captain. Step in the right direction.'

'Yes, all right, Keir. If you say so.'

'Now then, I want to go to the pictures. You'd like that, wouldn't you? You're always complaining I never want to go out. There's this film called *The Blackboard Jungle*, it's about violence in an American school. What do you think?'

She said nothing; he looked at her sharply, put down the paper.

'What's the matter?'

A long silence; then 'I'm late,' she said.

'What for?' He looked genuinely puzzled.

'Keir! Don't be dense.'

'I'm not.'

'You are. I'm late.' Her dark eyes were large, bright with fear. 'My period's late. Nearly two weeks. I – well, I went to see a doctor today. I might be pregnant, Keir, I'm really, really scared.'

CHAPTER 13

The door slammed: he was home. Cathy switched off the television quickly and ran over to the table, rifled through her books, pulling a couple out, opened one, leaned over it.

Her father came in, smiled rather wearily at her.

'Hi, darling.'

'Hi, Dad.'

He looked terribly tired; he often did these days. She knew he was worried about something, but she didn't know what. He wouldn't tell her.

'Homework done?'

'Almost,' she said, 'almost finished.'

'Practice?'

'Yup.'

'You might have to give up your piano lessons,' he said.

Cathy stared at him. 'Why?'

'Can't afford them, poppet. They're so expensive. Would you mind very much?'

Cathy wouldn't have minded in the least, she hated practising, and she could play well enough now to do what she and Jenna called jam sessions. But she saw an opportunity here to milk things. Her blue eyes filled effortlessly with tears; she bit her lip, fumbled for her handkerchief.

'No,' she whispered, 'of course not.'

'Oh for God's sake,' he said and his voice was quite different suddenly, 'don't make things worse.'

'Sorry. Sorry, Daddy.'

'It's not bloody fair,' he said, sitting down, pulling her on to his knee. 'Sorry, sweetheart, shouldn't have said that, rude word, but it's not, is it? Why shouldn't you have whatever you want? Why shouldn't I, for that matter? When so many people do.'

'I don't know.'

'I've tried so hard,' he said, 'tried to do my best for us both. Worked so hard.'

Cathy was silent; she didn't actually think that was true. She had observed someone working hard, and that was Barty, starting early, working late, both at the office and then at home, even at the weekends at South Lodge. Much as Cathy loved her father, she could see he did nothing of that. He often came home, saying he had work to do and then just sat in front of the TV, drinking beer and eating pretzels, until it was time to get the supper and then he said he was too tired to do any more. He was always home when she got in from school, or came to meet her from the bus; of course she liked that, all the other girls envied her having such a handsome father who was free in the afternoon, and then when he said they could go to the movies, which he quite often did, that was incredible. But it didn't add up to working hard.

'You should marry Barty,' she said slowly, anxious to offer him a solution, to cheer him up. 'Then we could have everything, couldn't we?'

'Oh Cathy,' he said, 'believe me I'd like to. And yes, yes, I guess we could.'

'So why don't you ask her?'

'I'm afraid,' he said, 'it isn't quite as simple as that.'

She was disappointed. She and Jenna had talked a lot about how wonderful it would be, had agreed it was getting more likely, that their parents seemed terribly fond of one another.

'I'll get the supper,' she said, sliding off his knee; he looked miserable suddenly. 'You just sit there; can I get you a beer or something?'

'Yes. If there are any.'

'I'll look. Spaghetti OK?'

'Absolutely OK.'

She found him some beer and even a bottle of wine, which he drank most of with his spaghetti, but he was still out of sorts. After supper they sat and watched TV together, his arm round her on the sofa. She looked up at him; he was half asleep, half gazing into the distance, not concentrating on the TV at all.

'Daddy, is something the matter?' she said. 'Really really the matter?'

'You could say that,' he said, his voice slurry as it often did get after supper, his eyes focussing on her with some difficulty. 'You could say something was the matter. I'm running out of time, Cathy, that's what it is. Running out real fast. I don't know that I can hang on much longer. I really don't.'

'Shall I – shall I talk to Jenna about it?' she said, and then was frightened by the speed with which he seemed to come back to life, to be sober, to look really scared.

'No,' he said, gripping her arm suddenly, gripping it really hard, his face sharp and angry, his eyes almost black. 'No, you will not. About any of it, ever. Not to anybody, and especially not to Jenna. Do you understand that, Cathy?'

She said she did; and she stood up and went to bed very quickly and quietly. It was the only thing to do on such occasions.

'Oh this is such fun.' Barty smiled round her dining table. 'All my favourite people.'

'What about Charlie?' said Jenna.

'Charlie will be here later,' said Barty quickly. 'Just look at us all, Izzie, Sebastian, Kit, and now Geordie. It's wonderful. A toast, Geordie, welcome to New York. And every possible success with the book. Not that you need much help from anyone. It's already riding high. Scribners have a window full of it, Barnes and Noble too, and the requests I've had for interviews – endless. It's all terribly exciting.'

'It is. And it's lovely to be here. Thank you. Here's to Lyttons.'

'I just wish you'd stay with us,' said Barty. 'Is it really so much less comfortable than the Algonquin?'

'Much more. But the Algonquin is so very central. And I'm going to be keeping some odd hours. And of course it's publishing heaven.'

'Mike told me such a funny story about the Algonquin,' said Izzie, 'apparently, when impoverished English publishers and agents come here, they tell all the New York publishers they're staying there, it being absolutely the place, only really they stay down the street at some really cheap place and just go up to the Algonquin to meet people for tea. Every now and again, they get caught because someone from Simon & Schuster or Doubleday calls the Algonquin to change an appointment and of course the hotel says they've never heard of them.'

'I heard that too,' said Geordie, smiling at her. 'You must introduce me to these people you work for, Izzie, they sound great. Maybe they could come to my launch party, Barty.'

'I don't see why not.'

'Oh my God,' said Izzie, 'could they really? They'll be so thrilled. I can't wait to tell them. You'll love them, Geordie. And maybe we can do some work for you—'

'Maybe. You'll have to ask Barty.'

'I already did. She said Lyttons had quite a lot of stuff in place, but there could be the odd little thing, and it was up to you. They are just so talented—'

'You're beginning to sound like a New Yorker, Izzie,' he said, smiling at her. She smiled back.

'I take that as a huge compliment.'

'Oh really? Well that's nice. And you're looking stunning. Isn't she, Barty? So – well, so grown up.'

Izzie smiled at him again, flushed slightly, pleased to be flattered by him. 'I should look grown up, Geordie. I'm twenty-six.'

'Good Lord, are you? I always think of you as—'

'Dear little Izzie. I know.' She sighed. 'Everyone does.'

'Well you're not any more,' he said. 'Not to me, anyway.' There was a slightly odd silence.

'Why didn't you bring Adele?' said Jenna suddenly.

'Jenna,' said Barty warningly.

'But—'

'She couldn't come,' said Geordie easily. 'She's very busy with her photography. Maybe next time.'

'She's doing a lot of work for *Vogue*, I heard,' said Izzie.

'Yes, quite a lot.' Another silence.

'How's Noni?' said Jenna. She was clearly yearning to be part of the grown-up conversation, thought Barty; well, she was growing up, fast, and she and Cathy spent as much time now drooling over Frank Sinatra and Elvis Presley and grieving over the newly deceased James Dean as they did over their dolls and their ponies.

And she was beginning to look grown up, too; she had developed a waist, her legs and arms were less gangly looking and, unmistakably on her flat chest, were two tiny budding breasts. She was obviously going to be beautiful; while Cathy's synthetic prettiness had hardly changed, Jenna had acquired cheekbones, a fuller mouth, and the clear, freckled skin of childhood was changing to a pale translucency. The red-gold hair, the blue-green eyes, were not blighted by the pale lashes and brows usual in her colouring; Barty's only visible legacy to her were very dark, very thick eyebrows. 'Like Liz Taylor's, you're so lucky,' Cathy would wail, while Jenna, who hated them, would tug at them mercilessly with her mother's tweezers until the skin around them was red and sore-looking. Their twice-weekly dancing lessons at the Colony Club (attended by suitable boys from Buckley and St Bernard's) now required up to an hour's worth of preparation. 'I reckon we have one, or maybe, if we're lucky, two years left,' Charlie had said to Barty. 'After that – mayhem. We'll have to lock them up.' Barty hadn't said anything, but she was hoping that the intense friendship would have eased a little by then; she planned to send Jenna to boarding school when she was thirteen, preferably to Dana Hall, which was very sporty and single-sex. She felt that Jenna and boys should be kept apart for as long as possible. She knew she would miss her horribly, but she wanted a more academic education for her than she was getting at the Chapin school where Jenna was now coasting through most of the lessons. Dana Hall was also extremely expensive; she doubted very much if Charlie, or rather Charlie's mother-in-law, would be able to afford it. Unless . . .

Barty switched her thoughts very firmly away from that and returned them to her dinner table.

Elspeth faced her mother bravely. Venetia had not been as angry as she had expected, but she had been quite horribly upset; 'I don't know how you could have been so stupid,' she kept saying, 'in this day and age, surely—'

'Mummy, I was careful. Honestly, I was. I went to see someone, right at the beginning of our relationship. But—'

'All right, all right. And now what do you want to do about it? You say you want to keep the baby—'

'I do, I do,' said Elspeth miserably. 'And I want to marry Keir. But he's being so difficult—'

'Oh he is, is he?' said Venetia. 'Well, we shall have to see what your father has to say about that. He can talk to him. If that's what we decide is best.'

Elspeth didn't like that 'we'. It seemed to imply that the baby was her parents' problem, rather than her own.

'Are you quite sure –' Venetia hesitated '– quite sure that having it is the best thing? I mean these days . . .'

'Mummy! How can you even consider such a thing? This is a baby, mine and Keir's, we couldn't possibly just get rid of it. It's a disgusting idea, it's murder, I—'

'It is indeed a baby, Elspeth. That's the whole point. Babies need homes, set-ups, nannies, money. Above all they need parents. Two of them. And if Keir is being difficult . . .'

'Oh, not difficult like that. He's very – pleased about the baby.'

'Oh really?'

Elspeth hesitated; then 'Yes,' she said firmly.

It wasn't quite true; Keir's first reaction had been 'Christ!' and then, 'What on God's earth are we going to do about it?' She had been so upset she had screamed at him that she hated him and told him to get out of her flat and out of her life; two days later a letter had arrived from him, remorseful, loving, telling her it had just been a shock, that he would have been delighted and proud for them to have a baby together if they were ready for it, but surely she could see that they were not.

Elspeth had written back and said that they might not be ready to have a baby, but the baby was certainly ready to be had. 'It's ours and our responsibility. If you're not prepared to face up to that fact, I'll do it for both of us.'

He came down to London again the following weekend and said he had been thinking very hard about it; he loved her, he cared about her, and he thought they should get married. Elspeth stared at him, so patently astonished that he had laughed.

'Am I really so much of a rotter?'

'Yes. No. I thought you were, that's all.'

'Well, you were wrong.'

'Oh Keir.' She flung herself into his arms. 'I'm so, so happy.'

'But there's just one thing –'

'Yes?'

He looked at her warily. 'Quite a big thing.'

'What?'

'You have to come and live in Glasgow. On my salary. I'm not being kept by the Lyttons, in any way. My wife and the mother of my child is my responsibility and mine only. Is that quite clear?'

'Yes, of course,' said Elspeth. She smiled at him as wholeheartedly as she could, hugged him, told him she loved him; but an icy fear was trickling into her which she did her best to ignore. There was no doubt he meant it. He was immensely proud and immensely stubborn. And it was of course a perfectly reasonable thing to say. Wives did follow their husbands – wherever they led them. But – she thought of living up in Glasgow, in some tiny house, which would be the best she could hope for, or even worse, with his parents, of giving up her flat, giving up her work, leaving her friends, her family . . . she felt quite sick. Or rather, even sicker than she did already.

'That's all right, is it?' he said, watching her closely.

'Yes, of course,' she said. 'Perfectly all right. It's just that – well, I have got a flat, in London, and quite a well-paid job—'

'No Elspeth,' he said, 'oh no. You marry me, you live with me. And I don't want you working. And don't think you can talk me round. We'll manage. The baby will have a perfectly adequate roof over its head. So will you. But it won't be in bloody Chelsea and you won't be swanning off to Lyttons every day, leaving our son with a nanny. I don't approve of it, and that's an end to it. Children should be with their mothers.'

'It's perfectly ridiculous,' Venetia said, when Elspeth explained this. 'Totally selfish. How can he expect you to go and live in some hovel in Glasgow? On a teacher's salary? Your father will have to speak to him.'

'Oh no!' wailed Elspeth. 'No, don't let him, that'll just make matters worse. He's so proud, Mummy, surely you can see that. He can't be asked to live off his wife.'

'He should be grateful for the offer,' said Venetia tartly. 'Most young men in his situation would leap at it.'

'I don't think they would. And if he did, you wouldn't admire him for it, would you?'

'I don't admire anything about him at this particular moment,' said Venetia.

It had been the most wonderful few days Izzie could remember. Barty had suggested they all went out to South Lodge for Thanksgiving: 'It'll be awfully cold, but wonderful. And very romantic.'

'Romantic?' said Jenna. 'Are you going to ask—'

'Not in that way,' said Barty firmly.

'Is there another way to be romantic?'

'Of course there is,' said Geordie. 'Long walks on wild beaches, sitting by huge log fires, listening to wonderful music—'

'Elvis?' said Jenna hopefully.

'Rachmaninov,' said Geordie. 'Barty, we accept, don't we, Izzie?'

'Of course,' said Izzie.

It was very cold; and the red sun sank into the ocean by five each afternoon, and they sat by the fire for hours, drinking, telling stories, having dinner, drinking some more, playing games. Geordie was brilliant at games, always the first to guess or know anything, to find a word containing both x and q in Scrabble, a natural actor in charades. Izzie, who wasn't really very good at them at all, was openly impressed, so much so that Barty actually said one evening, 'Izzie, do stop flattering him so much, he's big-headed enough already.'

Not even that annoyed Geordie, he just smiled easily at her and said, 'One can never be big-headed enough, in my opinion. You carry right on, Izzie.'

Barty couldn't help noticing that he didn't seem very distressed by his separation from Adele; indeed when she questioned him about it, he simply said he hoped it was temporary, that he missed Clio dreadfully, and changed the subject as fast as he could. She was surprised and even a little shocked; Sebastian's words about his being a lightweight kept coming back to her. Then she thought that men really didn't like talking about emotional matters and he was probably just embarrassed.

One day Geordie and Izzie went for a walk, just the two of them, and misjudging the time, found themselves walking in total darkness along the shore, with the wind howling round them and snowflakes in the air. She only had a light woollen coat on and became seriously cold, shivering violently, teeth chattering.

'Here,' he said, 'take my coat.'

'Geordie don't be silly. You'll freeze. I'll be all right. You could lend me your scarf, if you like, I can tie it round my head.'

He did it for her, knotting it firmly round her throat, gave her a quick kiss.

'You really are terribly cold,' he said. 'Let me warm you up a bit.'

He put his arms round her, held her in a bear hug, wrapping his own sheepskin coat round her as well.

'That's lovely,' she said, pressing herself into the warmth of him, and then, suddenly awkward, without being quite sure why, 'come on, we'd better get back. They'll be worried.'

Thanksgiving Dinner was wonderful; Izzie had not experienced one before. It was a bit like Christmas, without the fuss of presents. There was the wonderful turkey feast, the decorated house, the feeling of solidarity with the whole country, thinking of everyone in homes of every size and in every town and city and tiny village, all doing the same thing, celebrating being American.

'A bit fraudulent, as we're nearly all English,' said Barty, refilling everyone's glasses for the umpteenth time, 'but it's still lovely.'

'Geordie's American,' said Jenna, 'and I'm American, and you're sort of American, Mother. Sort of deep down.'

'I suppose so,' said Barty, and realised, to her surprise, that it was true.

'And Cathy is American. Poor Cathy, she's having a horrible time.'

'Now, how do you know that?'

'Because she's not here, and Charlie's not here. They were so hoping you'd ask them.'

'Well we couldn't,' said Barty carefully.

'Yes, you could. There are plenty of bedrooms.'

'Jenna, this is a family party.'

'Cathy and Charlie are just as much family as Geordie and Izzie.'

'They are not. Much as I like them.'

'But—'

'Jenna! What did I say about staying up with us?'

'I can't remember.'

'Yes, you can. I said only if you behaved really well. Which means not arguing.'

Jenna fell silent, clearly with a great effort; the party resumed, with a game of Monopoly, which she loved. But a shadow had been cast over the evening for Barty; she didn't like the idea of Charlie hoping he'd be asked for Thanksgiving and being disappointed. It made her feel at once irritable and guilty.

'I may have to leave the Chapin,' said Cathy. Jenna stared at her in horror.

'Why?'

'My dad can't pay any more fees.'

'Oh my God, Cathy, how do you know? Did he tell you?'

'Of course not. No, I found a letter. From the school. Saying that the bank hadn't honoured his cheque.'

'What does that mean?'

'It means he didn't have enough money in the bank to write the cheque.'

'Oh. Oh, I see. But I thought—'

'What did you think?'

'That your grandmother paid your school fees. Your dad's mother.'

'Why on earth did you think that?'

'Well I—'

For once in her life, Jenna was lost for words. Her mother had once told her that, in a rash moment, and forbidden her ever to mention it: 'Charlie hates talking about money. And I'm sure Cathy does, too. I shouldn't really have told you.'

'She couldn't possibly pay my fees,' said Cathy now.

'Why not?'

'Because she's dead. She died before I was even born. And my other grandmother, my mom's mom, she's terribly mean, she wouldn't pay for anything. And my dad hates her.'

'Hates her?'

'Yes. He thinks I don't know, but I heard him one night when he thought I was asleep, on the phone, telling her she was a mean old witch.'

'That doesn't sound like Charlie,' said Jenna. She felt rather shocked; it was very rare for Cathy to divulge family secrets, she was always rather reserved on the subject.

'No, well she – she upsets him. He did tell me that once. She thinks it was his fault my mother died.'

'How could it be? She died of cancer.'

'I know. I guess she's just crazy. That's what my dad says, anyway.'

'But – what will happen about your school, Cathy?'

'I don't know. I really, really don't know. I expect something'll turn up. It usually does, Daddy says.'

Jenna felt very impressed by such calm in the face of what seemed to her a disaster.

Elspeth was distraught; apart from feeling wretched, she couldn't see any solution. She was a realistic creature; she knew that being on her own all day in a cramped flat in Glasgow, with a baby, would drive her very quickly mad. But the alternatives were hideous. An abortion was absolutely out of the question; she could not imagine how anyone could even consider such a thing. It was murder. Perfectly simple. Taking a human life. Wicked. Horrible.

She could, of course, not marry Keir, have the baby and look after it herself with the aid of a nanny; she had the means, or rather her parents did, and it would be greatly preferable to the Glasgow scenario. But it would be a terrible thing to do to a child, any child, condemn it to grow up out of wedlock. It would be a social outcast, tormented at school, damned by society, officially a bastard; she just couldn't do it. And her own position would be hideous, she would be branded that most dreadful thing – an unmarried mother. Even if she did have money and a flat and a career and the might of the Lytton and Warwick empire behind her. Just thinking about what her father would have to say made her feel quite faint. And anyway, she did love Keir. She loved him terribly. She wanted to marry him. Enough even to move to Glasgow. It was his baby too, and he had a right to say how it was brought up.

Only – and then she was back on the treadmill again, desperate with worry and with no idea what to do.

Celia found her one day, slumped at her desk, pushing a spoon miserably round in her coffee.

'Elspeth, you don't look very happy. Are you having trouble with that manuscript? Do you want to tell me about it?'

Confronted by the one person she knew who was absolutely pragmatic and non-judgemental, Elspeth did.

'Mummy's been quite nice about it,' she said, blowing her nose on her handkerchief after the initial storm of tears had passed. 'Really not too terribly angry at all.'

'So she should have been,' said Celia briskly.

Elspeth looked at her. 'Why?'

'Let us just say,' said Celia smoothly, 'she has learned some wisdom. After having six of you. What about your father?'

'Furious. Horrible. Especially about Keir.'

'Really? Well, we shall have to see what we can do about that. Now you're determined to have it, are you?'

'Granny, of course. I wouldn't even consider having an abortion. It's wrong and besides, it's terribly dangerous.'

'It need not be,' said Celia carefully, 'under the right conditions. And it's a matter of opinion whether it's wrong or not.'

'In my opinion, it's murder,' said Elspeth, 'and I wouldn't commit it.'

'Very well. As long as you've thought about it properly, aren't being swept along on a sentimental tide. Babies are demanding, exhausting and expensive, Elspeth. They don't lie slumbering sweetly in their cots living on air, you know. Your life will change for ever, in a way you cannot begin to imagine. And your work will suffer considerably, and you know how much that matters to you. It's important you understand all that.'

Elspeth looked at her doubtfully. Her mother had often told her about the large nursery staff her grandmother had employed, and that Celia had continued to work seven days a week for the whole of her life, from Giles's birth onwards. It was hard to imagine how her life had been blighted in the way she described.

But she smiled at her dutifully and said she would remember what she had said.

'What about your young man? What does he want to do?'

'That's the real problem,' said Elspeth, bursting into tears again. 'What he wants is – well, it's a bit difficult.'

'And that is –?'

Elspeth told her. 'And Mummy and Daddy are being ridiculous, they say it's absolutely out of the question, that they won't allow it—'

'Very helpful of them,' said Celia briskly. 'Well, I have to say I admire his spirit. And his independence.'

'Do you?' said Elspeth, looking at her through tear-smudged eyes. 'Do you really?'

'Yes, of course. Although I don't suppose you exactly relish the idea?'

'No I don't. But I don't seem to have much option.'

'Not at the moment, no. You don't. If you really want to have this baby and to marry Keir.'

'Yes, I do. Of course I do.'

'Then I have to say I admire you also. Now listen, darling, try not to fret too much. You never know what might happen in the future. One never does.'

'Like – like what?' said Elspeth, blowing her nose.

'Oh – I don't know,' said Celia vaguely, 'but meanwhile, I'll have a word with your parents, if you like.'

'I wish you would. It might make all the difference. Oh, Granny, we're so lucky to have you.'

'Not a view everyone would agree with,' said Celia. 'Now you get on with that manuscript, it's already late.'

Elspeth looked after her fondly, wondering how many grandmothers would have received such a piece of news without expressing any shock or passing any word of judgement. Not many. She wondered if anything comparable had ever happened to Celia. No. Not in her day. It was unthinkable.

Celia knew exactly how to solve Elspeth's problem; the only thing was she didn't think Keir would agree with her. But she felt it was worth trying. She took him out to lunch and offered him first her congratulations and then a job at Lyttons, as an editorial assistant.

'It's a great opportunity. There are young men all over England who would kill for it.'

'I dare say there are. But I'm not one of them, Celia, sorry. I'm doing something much more important now. And I'm not taking your charity. My wife's charity. If I couldn't get a job on my own merits, I'm not taking one on someone else's.'

'Hardly charity, Keir. You'd have to work extremely hard. More to the point, you'd be a great asset to the firm. I have an instinct for these things, I genuinely feel you have talent.'

'Yes, and a great asset to Elspeth as well. Sorry, Celia. The answer's no. I'm not even going to say I'm flattered, because I'm not. I can see exactly where this offer has come from, and why.'

'I hope you don't think Elspeth had anything to do with it.'

'Of course not,' he said. 'If I did, I'd have no more to do with her, bairn or no bairn. She has more integrity than that.'

'You won't even – think about it?'

'I won't.'

'Well,' she said, 'I was pretty sure you wouldn't. And I admire you for it.'

'You do?'

'Of course I do.'

He looked at her and grinned.

'You're quite something, Celia, aren't you? Why make me the offer, then?'

'Because I know it would be the best possible solution for all of you. And it seemed worth a try.'

'Oh you do?'

'Yes, I do. I've learned quite a lot of wisdom in my rather long life. However, you have yet to see that. And I warn you, I never admit defeat. I shall make the offer again. And again.'

'And my answer will be the same. Again and again.'

She smiled at him.

'Well, we shall see. Now then, would you like a brandy? Or will your pride prevent you from accepting even that?'

She also had a fairly brief and forthright discussion with Boy and Venetia; as a result they agreed, with enormous misgivings, that Elspeth should marry Keir and go to live in Glasgow with their blessing.

'And be nice to Elspeth about it. She's being awfully brave, and I admire her tremendously. You should be proud of her.'

'Yes, Mummy,' said Venetia.

The party for *Growing Down* at the Waldorf-Astoria was a great success; a large – but not too large for exclusivity – affair with guests ranging from reviewers and editors to buyers and bookshop owners, including the great Mr Scribner himself, a rare coup, as Barty hissed to Sebastian. Two of the most powerful women in literary Manhattan were also there – Helen Strauss from the William Morris Agency and Phyllis Jackson from the Ashley-Famous.

Word had got round that Geordie MacColl was worth courting. Endless bottles of champagne were drunk, some extremely expensive and elegant canapés were toyed with, Geordie made a charmingly modest speech, Barty made what was, for her, a rather fulsome one, and the social editor of the *New York Times* interviewed Izzie and Sebastian on the difference between the literary scene in London and in New York.

It was towards the end of the party that it happened; such a small thing, so apparently unimportant, but actually of immense significance, a small, still moment that gave no warning of the tumultuous events which followed in its wake. Looking back on it afterwards, Barty always thought of the old nursery rhyme about the lost horseshoe nail, which had led to the loss of a rider, a battle and then with dreadful inevitability to the loss of a kingdom.

Izzie was standing with her father, chatting to a small group of journalists and fiddling with the string of pearls she was wearing, a habit of hers when she was nervous or over-excited. A passing waiter knocked her arm with a tray of canapés, and caused her to pull on them so sharply that they broke; she clutched at them with both hands, caught some of them, but a cascade fell on to the floor.

Flushed, more embarrassed than distressed, she stood watching helplessly as half a dozen people bent to retrieve them; in no time at all they had all been gathered up and given to Sebastian, who put them in his pocket.

Thanking everyone effusively, charmingly confused, she had thought the incident was over, and was taking a sip of champagne when Geordie appeared, having observed the slight fracas from across the room. Izzie was just explaining what had happened, reassuring him that everything was absolutely fine, when he suddenly said, 'Excuse me, Izzie, I have a little fishing to do,' and very gently put his fingers into the cleavage of her dress to pull out a last recalcitrant pearl.

'My goodness,' she said, smiling up at him, against a background of laughter and applause, 'how extremely observant of you, Geordie, to spot it.'

'Not really,' he said, smiling back. 'I've been transfixed by its location all evening.'

It was, of course, the sort of thing he was always saying; but he was exhilarated by his evening, an outstanding success even by his own standards. He had had several glasses of champagne and his eyes, meeting Izzie's, were very serious suddenly, boring into her, disturbing her. And Izzie was looking, she knew, quite sexy. She had known it as she studied herself in the mirror before leaving the apartment, had scarcely recognised the chic woman in the black satin, full-skirted, tight-waisted cocktail dress, one of the new half-hats with a tiny veil perched sexily on her piled-up hair; the woman with darkly dramatic eye make-up and full, brilliant mouth, the woman who seemed to have become, at last, the creature she so wanted to be.

It was odd, she thought, as she accepted fulsome compliments from Barty and her father, how a changed appearance could change everything; for as she had sat in one of the long fleet of cars driving up Park Avenue, as she had emerged gracefully from it towards a small crowd of press cameras, as she had walked into the ballroom and taken her first glass of champagne, she felt like that woman in the mirror, self-confident, glamorous – and very sexy.

As she stood laughing up at Geordie, holding the pearl he had retrieved from her bosom, still feeling, vividly, his fingers between her breasts, her thoughts and her pleasure took her no further than that moment, in all its extravagant, happy sexiness; and she reached up and kissed him, very gently, on the lips.

It was only Barty, watching her from across the room, who felt a sudden catch at her heart, and remembered hearing Izzie's own voice saying, 'I've come to recognise I like older men.'

CHAPTER 14

'There's a cable for you, from New York.'

'Oh – goodness. Let me see. Yes. Thank you, darling. I'll – maybe I'll look at it later.'

'Maman, you can't look at cables later. That's the whole point. You look at them straight away. Shall I read it to you?'

'No. Yes. Oh I don't know. Maybe he's coming home sooner, that would be lovely, wouldn't it? Yes, you open it, darling. Thank you.'

Noni tore open the envelope, pulled out the cable. Her hands were shaking. She hoped her mother hadn't noticed.

'It's – well, yes. It's from Geordie.'

'Yes, I see. And—'

'And he's not – that is, he is – oh, I'll just read it to you. "Delayed in States a further two weeks. Tour extended to West Coast. Will wire exact return date. Love to girls. Geordie." Oh Maman, don't cry. I mean it's wonderful his book is doing so well, isn't it, and he's so – oh, dear, here, come on, let me hold you –'

Noni sat there, holding her mother's thin body, stroking her hair, their roles reversed, she the comforter, the strong one, her mother, clinging to her, weeping and frail.

'Maman, please! Don't be so sad. It's all right. He will be back. It's only two weeks. And then maybe he'll come home. Really home, I mean. Maybe being over there, with Barty and Izzie and everyone, will bring him to his senses. You know how fond he is of both of them, and he's bound to talk to them about it—'

'I don't know that I want him talking to them about it,' said Adele fretfully. 'It's nothing to do with them.'

'Well – maybe not. But Barty is so wise. And Izzie is one of our very best friends. There's nothing like a change of scene for seeing things differently. Now, aren't you supposed to be at *Style* by now?'

Noni looked at her mother anxiously; it was one of the manifestations of her depression that she had become vague and inefficient. Once so dynamic, so absolutely in control, she had become worryingly ineffectual, often late, occasionally forgetting appointments altogether. This job today was important; she had let *Style* down once already and it was only her long association with them that had persuaded them to give her another chance.

'Oh my God, so I am. The models are arriving at eleven and I have to work out the lighting and the props as far as I can before then. Oh, dear, I'll be late, I've got to get all my stuff into the car, then unload it the other end—'

'Shall I come with you? I'm not specially busy. I've got all the vacation to do my work. I can help carrying stuff in and so on. And I'd love to see the studio. Where is it?'

'Soho Square. Bit of a trek. But as long as the traffic's not bad – yes, darling, if you really wouldn't mind. Thank you.'

'It's fine,' said Noni, giving her a kiss. Anything was better than standing by helplessly while her mother cried.

Style House, in Soho Square, was a tall and elegant early Victorian building, hopelessly inconvenient in many ways, but suited visually nonetheless to its role as home to one of the principal fashion advisers to the nation. Vogue House in Golden Square, half a mile away, occupied a very similar building; it was not unknown for photographers and models going for briefing or casting sessions to become more than slightly confused as to which building they were actually in.

As well as housing editorial, advertising and publishing staff, both had studios on the top floor; beautiful and beautifully dressed women stalked the corridors, many of them as giraffe-tall and elegant as the models they worked with. It was virtually impossible to work for either without a private income; salaries on both publications were extremely modest and it was essential to dress the part.

'I wish darling Cedric was still here,' Adele said with a sigh, as she led Noni into the studio. 'He was so beautiful and such heaven to work with, just looking at him made one feel inspired. I do miss him.' Cedric Russell had been a wonderfully exotic photographer in the Thirties and had given Adele her first job as his stylist; he had continued to take credit for most of her subsequent success.

'I brought her to life,' he would say complacently, smoothing down his golden curls, picking a speck of dust off his immaculately tailored jacket, 'I am her muse.'

They had been best friends for years, long after her marriage to Geordie; when he had died of septicaemia following a burst appendix, she had felt a truly dreadful grief, and had never quite recovered from the loss of one of the greatest sources of pleasure and fun in her life. It was a long time before she could even enter the *Style* building without her eyes filling with tears.

'He was heaven, I know,' said Noni, aware, as her mother seemed not to be, of how late they were running, 'but we must hurry, Maman. Take this bag and I'll carry your cameras. Come on!'

She followed Adele into the studio, set down the bag of cameras and film, and looked round interestedly. She was used to the one in the house, of course; but this was busier and more colourful, filled with racks of clothes, the walls covered with photographs by all the greats: Norman Parkinson, Irving Penn, the brilliant English photographer John French, famous for never actually pressing the camera shutter himself but directing his assistant to do so by a series of lightning-fast taps on the floor with his elegant feet and autocratic cries of 'Now!'.

And the great models of the day were there too on the walls: Barbara Goalen, Fiona Campbell-Walter, Bronwen Pugh, haughtily perfect, ballerina-graceful, fêted like film stars, never seen anywhere without immaculate hair and make-up, or perfectly elegant clothes.

In the corner was the dressing room, one wall all mirror, surrounded with lights, with a long bench of a make-up table set beneath it; a girl sat with her back to them, gazing into the mirror, studying her face with immense devotion.

'Adele, there you are. I was expecting you earlier.'

It was Duncan Lloyd, the studio manager, bustling about in oddly incongruous clothes, a neatly tailored suit, a white silk loose shirt and a pair of ballet shoes.

'I know, Duncan, I'm so sorry. Anyway, we're here now, are the models here?'

'Only one.'

'Oh well, I expect the other will be along soon.'

'I don't think so.'

'Why not?'

'Because she wasn't booked.'

'What? Of course she was booked, I did it myself.'

'You didn't, Adele, I'm afraid. I've checked all the records. Only one girl was booked. Look, Hope Lumley Agency, Marella Cope-Brown. No one else.'

'Oh God.' Adele sat down abruptly. 'This is terrible. It's absolutely essential we have two girls, the whole feature is about mirror images, black dress, white hat, and vice versa; well, I don't know why I'm telling you. We'll just have to get someone else.'

'Fine. Good. Well, Marella is doing her make-up now. Maybe she can make some suggestions.'

Marella said she couldn't; she looked at Adele down her elegant nose and said she couldn't think of anyone she'd want to work with, who was of sufficient calibre. Adele began to phone the agencies, her voice raw with panic, but she knew it was hopeless. Top-quality girls were simply not available at half an hour's notice.

Laura Proctor-Reid, the fashion editor, appeared; she was tall and impossibly thin, wearing a perfectly tailored black suit and a hat resembling a very large mushroom, made of black ostrich feathers. She looked more as if she was going to a funeral than a fashion session; she was followed closely by her assistant, who was almost invisible, her arms piled high with shoe boxes and sweaters.

'The rest are on the rail, Adele, I expect you've looked at them. I want to start with the suits, then the sweaters and skirts. There's a lovely John Cavanagh suit, absolutely stunning, maybe we could do that first, pair it with the Stiebel – where's the other girl, by the way?'

'She – there – that is –'

'Your daughter has a lovely look,' drawled Marella, painting in the outline of her lips with a lipbrush and brilliant red lipstick. 'Very French. Maybe she could—'

The fashion editor ignored her. 'Hasn't she turned up? These girls are appallingly inefficient. I shall have a word with Peter myself. We shall dock her fee. We don't pay them £3 an hour for not being here.'

'Laura – that is – I'm afraid there's been a mistake. The second girl was never booked. It was – well, it was my fault. I'm so sorry.'

'Never booked! But the whole point of this session was the two girls—'

'I know, I know. Laura, I'm absolutely – appalled at myself. Really.'

Laura Proctor-Reid's expression made it clear she was equally appalled at Adele.

'And there's no one else?'

'No. I've tried. I just don't know what to do—'

'There's very little any of us can do. We'll just have to postpone the session,' said Laura Proctor-Reid icily. 'A very expensive mistake, Adele. Very expensive. We'll still have to pay the agency, the studio time will have to be charged, the studio assistant – I'm very surprised at the whole thing. I don't quite understand—'

'Laura, I was just saying, Adele's daughter has a lovely look. Wonderful eyes. And the colouring is perfect.'

'Marella, we are not using some raw amateur in the pages of *Style*. We'll have to book a re-shoot. Possibly with another photographer, if Adele isn't free.'

It was clear that whether Adele was free or not, she would not be shooting the session.

'You could try,' said Marella, picking a row of false eyelashes out of her make-up tray with a pair of tweezers and coating the edge with glue, 'that's all I'm suggesting. Look at her, she's the right height, she's very slim, she's got marvellous hair—'

They all turned and stared at Noni; she stood feeling like a prize cow in a cattle market.

'Turn round,' said Laura Proctor-Reid. 'No, not like that, slowly, for heaven's sake. This isn't a ballroom-dancing class. Pull your hair back. Yes, now stand over there. Just stand still, relax. She is – quite attractive, I suppose.' She removed the black ostrich mushroom, laid it carefully down on a chair.

'Adele, let me have your camera. No, no, the Hasselblad. I want to see how she looks through the lens. Look this way, dear, would you? No, not at my face, at the camera lens. God, why am I even considering this? Pull your skirt up, would you, let's have a look at your legs. Mmm. Smile. Now turn sideways. And then the eyes to me. No, no, the lens, that's better.'

She stood for a while, staring down into the camera viewfinder, tapping her foot; then she said, 'I don't know why I'm agreeing to it, but we'll do one shot. We can get an idea of how bad it is. After that we can make a decision. Get the lighting set up, Adele, I thought you were going to have it ready. Go into the dressing room, dear – what's your name?'

'Noni,' said Noni, wondering if it might occur to anyone at any point, even her mother, to ask her if she would agree to being camera fodder, and deciding it wouldn't.

'Noni, yes. Do you actually have French blood?'

'Yes, my father was French, he—'

'I thought so. Now go into the dressing room. I'll do your make-up, you won't be able to manage yourself. And you –' she said to the assistant, who appeared to have no name '– go and get a model release form, we'll have to get the girl signed up. Quickly, we haven't got all day.'

Duncan Lloyd said he would go; he had been standing like a petrified rabbit throughout the entire exchange, his small feet in their ballet shoes turned rather incongruously out in first position.

'Well, go and do it, then,' said Laura, 'and while you're about it, Duncan, re-book Marella at the first possible opportunity, will you? I have no faith in this exercise whatsoever, I don't know quite why I've allowed myself to be talked into it.'

She dragged Noni's hair back from her face with a band and peered into it.

'Your skin's not bad,' she said, 'but your eyebrows are frightful. They'll have to be plucked. Tweezers!' She snapped her fingers like a surgeon in an operating theatre. 'Quickly please.'

The assistant, pale with terror at the morning's drama, hurried over with a pair of tweezers. Noni submitted herself to them as resignedly as she could. Anything for her mother . . .

'And then she said we might as well do another shot. And then another. And in the end we did all five. She kept shouting at me and getting terribly cross because I put the wrong foot in front and I thought it would be over and then she'd say, "That's not bad", or "It could be worse", and we'd be off again. The model, Marella, was fantastic, not nearly as terrifying as she seemed. She kept whispering that I was doing really well. La Proctor-Reid's last words were that she was quite sure they'd all end up in the dustbin, but Mary Louise said she'd never have gone on if she hadn't wanted to and thought it was worth it.'

'It sounds madly glamorous,' said Amy wistfully. 'I wish I could do it. So much more fun than beastly typing.'

'Oh Amy, don't be silly, it would get awfully boring after a bit. And you'd never meet a husband, they're all queer, photographers and so on. Anyway, you're engaged, for heaven's sake, to lovely Richard, you can't start modelling now.'

'Are you going to do it again? Leave Oxford and be a top model? I would. Can I be your agent?'

'No you can't,' said Noni, 'and no, I'm not. I don't expect the pictures will ever be used.'

'But if they were, would you want to do it again?'

'I'm not sure. Maybe. It's terribly tedious. But exciting too, trying things on, making the clothes work, as Miss Proctor-Reid puts it. And Marella was telling me she sometimes even gets sent abroad on jobs. Only usually not, and she's modelling sundresses on the beach in January here and fur coats in July. She does like it, though. I suppose it might be useful for making some pocket money . . . But as a full-time job, no thanks!'

Just the same, Noni had enjoyed it enormously. It had been such a relief to have some fun. She was beginning to find the situation at home so extremely depressing.

'Hallo? Yes. Oh – oh Geordie, how are you? Me too. Pretty bad. What? No, I haven't seen it. Just a minute – here it is, yes, I've – oh my goodness. I'll ring you back. Yes, of course it's funny. Very funny . . .'

It was, of course it was. Three pictures of herself and Geordie at the party, right across the top of the social page in the *New York Post*. Captioned 'The Pearl Fisher'. The first showing Geordie's fingers down her dress; the second him holding the pearl aloft; and the third her reaching up and kissing him.

Well – that was all right. It had only been a bit of fun. He had only been retrieving her pearl. And she had only been saying thank you. She started to read the article:

Geordie MacColl, whose new book, *Growing Down*, has topped the best-seller lists for several weeks on both sides of the Atlantic, was in romantic mood last night at his launch party. Isabella 'Izzie' Brooke, daughter of the famous children's author Sebastian Brooke, and an old friend of Geordie's, showed her gratitude in no uncertain terms, when Geordie rescued part of her broken string of pearls from the interior of her dress.

Geordie, who lives in London and is visiting New York without his English wife, later sat next to Izzie at the private dinner given by his publishers at the Italian Pavilion. They left together at the end of the evening.

'Oh no,' wailed Izzie. 'Oh no, no.'

'What's the matter, sweetheart?'

Nick Neill peered at her across the room.

'Oh Nick, it's terrible. Look at this, read it, it's so awful.'

'Let me see – hey, those are some nice pictures. You look very classy, Izzie.'

'I don't look classy,' said Izzie. 'I look like a trollop.'

'No way, you don't. You couldn't. Pity they didn't mention the agency, but there you go. Don't worry about it. It's only a bit of newsprint. Wrapping up garbage tomorrow. No one takes any notice of those things.'

'Oh Nick, they do, don't be silly. Whatever would Adele say if she saw it?'

'Adele, who's she?'

'Geordie's wife. One of my best friends.'

'Well, if she's got any sense she'll say it's a load of baloney and put it out with the garbage as well.'

'But you don't understand, they're separated at the moment and—'

'Well if they're separated, what's it matter anyway, for God's sake? And it's perfectly obvious he fancies you.'

'Of course it's not,' said Izzie.

'OK,' said Nick equably. 'He's just play-acting. Now look, Izzie, I hate to mess with your personal publicity campaign, but those ads just came back from Joanie.'

'Oh dear,' said Izzie, closing the newspaper with a great effort. Joanie Morell was the advertising manager at Cleveland & Marshall, a modest publisher specialising in romances and thrillers. She was the bane of their lives, demanding, rude, impatient – and one of their biggest accounts.

'Yeah. Old bitch. Look what she did. I stapled on a note saying "OK?" and she's crossed the whole thing out and written, "OK to do over" all in red ink.'

'Yes, I see,' said Izzie. She still didn't move.

'Honey, come on will you? We don't have very long. Joanie wants this back after lunch, latest.'

Izzie put the paper aside and turned her thoughts to Joanie's ad. Nick was right. It was much more important.

Lucas was never sure afterwards which of the two things had meant more to him: singly, neither was actually of very great importance. But coming together as they did, in a well-orchestrated sequence, they represented something very important, and what he thought of as the beginning of the end: of the anger, the sense of injustice, the feeling of alienation.

He had been walking down one of the corridors at school when he heard his name called by Mr Blake, one of the history masters.

'Lieberman! I'd like a word with you, please.'

Oh God; more trouble. Westminster might be immeasurably better than Fletton, but it was never quite the same as it had been in the early days. Friends had moved on, changed, his place in the centre of his own clique was lost to him, he had become odd, not quite an outcast, but still not quite one of the crowd. And he had not managed to shed the attitudes he had developed at Fletton, of distaste for authority, and something that was not quite insolence but certainly not courtesy. He was not popular, either with the pupils or with the masters; it was a vicious circle, reinforcing his difficult behaviour.

'Yes, Sir.'

'I enjoyed hearing your views on the monarchy very much today. They were highly original.'

'Thank you, Sir.'

Lucas was astonished; he would have been less surprised if he had been rebuked for so forcibly expressing his views: that not only should England become a republic, but that the House of Lords should become a second chamber of elected peers, rather than hereditary ones. They were not sentiments very often voiced at leading English public schools.

'I think you have a genuine talent for debate. I wonder how you'd feel about being one of Westminster's representatives in an inter-school competition next term?'

'I—' more astonishment. Had they got the right person? 'Thank you, Sir. Yes, I think I'd like that.'

'Good. You've never joined the debating society, have you? Can't think why not. Anyway, it's never too late. Come along next week. Lunch time, Thursdays.'

'Yes, Sir.'

He walked on to his next lesson in a state of rather happy bemusement; he had always known he was clever, he was confident about getting into Oxford, but there were a great many boys at Westminster with similar gifts. This was something rather different: something special, something that not everyone, very few people indeed, could do, and moreover, in some strange way, something new, a fresh start, something that would make people think well of him, rather than badly.

It was a very pleasing thought.

There was a group of boys in the classroom when he went in; they were discussing a party to be held the next Saturday. Lucas, with his rather morose presence, didn't often get asked to parties; he pretended not to care, but like every other rejection, it hurt.

'You free on Saturday, Lieberman?' asked Mark Davies. He was one of Lucas's friends from the early days, who had more or less stuck by him.

'Not sure. Why?'

'Wondered if you'd like to come.'

'What, to the party?'

'What else, you idiot?'

Lucas shrugged, slung his books down on the desk, said nothing. This was proving an extraordinary day.

'Well, would you or not?'

'I – suppose so. Yes. Thanks.'

'Don't thank me. It was my sister's idea.'

'Your sister! Why should she want me to come to your party? I've never met her.'

'No, but she saw you at that service last week, in the Cathedral. Hasn't stopped talking about you since. I told her she ought to have her eyes tested, but – well, no accounting for taste. She's bringing a few friends along. Should be quite fun.'

Lucas went home that night feeling strangely happy. It was as if after years of isolation, of living in a hostile foreign country where he understood almost nothing, he had at last begun to learn its language and to feel welcome there.

'Heavens!' said Barty.

'What?'

'Noni is going to be in *Style* magazine.'

'Really? How interesting. In what capacity?'

'As a model.'

'Surely not? She's never shown any inclination for that sort of thing.'

'No, I know. But apparently Adele forgot to book a model one day and Noni was there and she got roped in. Well, I always did think she was the most beautiful girl. So unusual. Aren't you intrigued, Izzie?'

'Yes, very,' said Izzie. She didn't sound very intrigued. She sounded completely uninterested. Barty looked at her sharply. She didn't seem quite herself at the moment. In fact she wasn't at all herself, distracted, jumpy. Barty was just a little anxious about her; about what just might be going on. She had seen the *New York Post*. Of course it was ridiculous, unthinkable: Izzie was the most deeply moral person. Adele and Noni were her dearest friends. She often said she didn't know what she would have done without Adele in the various crises in her life. So – there couldn't possibly be anything to worry about. Just the same, she was very glad Geordie had gone: down to Chicago and then San Francisco. And then he was going home. So she could relax and concentrate on her own problems. Which were quite pressing enough . . .

★

Sebastian had been very frank, as she had begged him to be, told her exactly what he thought, after warning her she wouldn't welcome it.

'I think he's a perfectly nice chap. Very nice, in fact. But not good enough for you, Barty. Really not.'

'In – in what way?'

'He's – oh God, I just don't think he's good enough for you. He's a lightweight. Very charming, easy, all the things you said. But – well I don't see this as a marriage of true minds at all. I don't think he's that – bright. And then . . .'

'Go on,' she said.

'Well – he seems to me a bit lazy.'

'How on earth could you tell that?'

'Just listening to him. He was telling me about his business, how he's never really managed to get it going since his wife died, how he's had to sacrifice it to look after Cathy. I don't think that washes, you know. She's eleven now, not a baby—'

'Sebastian, you really don't know what you're talking about. You always had Nanny, and Mrs Conley. Charlie can't afford anything like that.' Barty felt fiercely defensive of him suddenly. 'Children go on being demanding, you know, go on being ill, having problems at school—'

'I know, I know, but the child clearly spends a lot of time with you, including weekends. And it's a really boom time in his industry. Everyone knows that. Dear old Robert was telling me. I just don't think he's making the most of it.'

'Oh, Sebastian, that's not so important. It isn't for me, anyway. Anything else?'

She knew she sounded defensive; she couldn't help it.

'Oh Barty, I knew you'd be cross.'

'No I'm not,' she said, trying not to sound it.

'You are. But you did ask me. I just don't quite – trust him. Don't ask me why. I couldn't tell you. Oh, darling, don't cry. I shouldn't have started on this. You obviously care about him a lot. So if my criticising him has made that clear to you, it's something.'

'I just wanted you to like him,' she said fretfully, 'and that you'd think it was a good idea.'

'Barty – it's you who would marry him, not me. For God's sake, you know him an awful lot better than I do. If you want to marry him, then you should. You've been alone for twelve years—'

'Most of my life, it feels like,' said Barty with a sigh. 'It wasn't exactly a very long time we had together, Laurence and me.'

'There you are. If you've found someone you think you can live with, far be it from me to stop you. God in heaven, Barty, you're – what are you?'

'I'm forty-eight,' she said. 'I can't believe it, but I am.'

'Well then,' he said, 'you may seem a child to me still, but you're much too old to be taking advice on whether you should get married or not.'

'Sebastian,' she said, 'if I hadn't needed your advice I wouldn't have asked for it. Thank you. And I shall heed it. So there.'

But what did heed exactly mean? Not the same as taking. She could listen to Sebastian, to Izzie, to Jenna, to all of them, she still had to make up her own mind. It was her life. People kept saying that. And it was true. She just wished she could decide if she liked how it was or not. And whether she would like it any better if she married Charlie Patterson.

'Izzie?'

'Geordie!'

'How are you?'

'Fine. How are you? And how's Chicago?'

'Cold. Windy. Lonely. I wish you were here.'

'Geordie! Don't be silly.'

'I'm not.'

'Where – where are you going next?'

'Oh, across to the West Coast. Should be fun. Ever been there?'

'No. No, I haven't.'

'Pity. It would suit you.'

'Well –'

'I just wanted to say goodbye, really. If you're not prepared to come down to Los Angeles and see me. It's back to England after that.'

Izzie felt a pang: then, 'Well, give my best love to Adele. And Noni, of course.'

'I will. And thank you for a wonderful time, it's been such fun.'

'Oh—' She stopped, gathering her new sophistication around her with a great effort. 'Oh, no, Geordie, thank *you*. It *was* huge fun. Bye.'

She put the phone down and sat staring at it, her eyes very soft; Nick Neill, watching her from across the room, felt his heart contract with a mixture of very complex emotions.

She had decided; she was going to tell Charlie. Tell him that she couldn't marry him. That she was terribly fond of him, that their time together had been absolutely wonderful, that she hoped they could still be friends, but she couldn't marry him. It just wasn't fair on him, she didn't love him enough, he deserved something better, someone who really adored him, someone much younger possibly, who could give him more children. It would be selfish and wrong of her to marry him; and she must tell him immediately, so that he could get on with his own life.

She had expected to feel better, having made her decision, but actually she felt worse. Irritable and depressed and absolutely exhausted. And frightened, terribly frightened of being quite alone again, of saying goodbye to what might be her last chance of happiness. But it had to be done.

Maybe, when she had told him, it would be better. Maybe that was the reason for her misery, having it hanging over her. It was going to be terribly difficult; from now on, until Jenna went to a different school. She had sounded Charlie out about Dana Hall and she was right, he couldn't possibly afford it. Or rather, Cathy's grandmother couldn't possibly afford it. Well if there was one thing that would be an improvement, it would be the removal of Cathy from her life. Barty liked her less and less as she grew up. Her obsession with boys, with her nails and hair – even Jenna was a bit irritated by that – her tendency towards secrecy, Barty didn't like any of it. Maybe she could send Jenna to Dana before next fall. It would certainly be more comfortable. She would make some enquiries; the thought of almost a year of having to see Charlie while she collected and delivered Cathy, of having Cathy with them at South Lodge throughout the next summer—

'Barty, can I come in?' It was Sebastian, standing in her office doorway; he smiled at her.

'Oh, yes. Yes of course.'

'I wondered if you'd like to have dinner with me.'

'Oh – no, Sebastian, it's awfully sweet of you, but I'm already booked for dinner.'

With Charlie. To tell him she wasn't going to marry him.

'Pity. Izzie and Kit are having dinner with the boys, as Izzie calls them. They asked me to join them, but I said I couldn't. I thought I'd be a bit of a blight. Old chap, spectre at the feast.'

'Sebastian, you should have gone.'

'No, no, I'll go home and have dinner with your daughter. Who are you dining with? Charlie?'

'Well – yes. I'd ask you to join us but—'

'I wouldn't dream of playing gooseberry.'

'Don't be silly, Sebastian.' Her voice was sharp. 'You wouldn't be. But I just want to talk to him, that's all. About—'

'You don't have to tell me.' He smiled at her. 'I don't want to hear, in fact.'

'No, I'd like to tell you. I've decided – well, I've decided I'm not going to marry him.'

'Oh God.' He sat down abruptly in the chair opposite her desk. 'I feel dreadfully responsible.'

'Don't. It's not for any of the reasons you said. In fact, you almost swung it in the other direction. You're so wrong about him, Sebastian. He isn't lazy, and he's totally to be trusted.'

'Well then—'

'No. It's because he's – well, he's not Laurence.'

'Now that's silly.'

'No. No, it isn't. I mean it might sound silly, but it's not. The point is, I loved Laurence so much, and I know that what I feel for Charlie just isn't enough. It wouldn't be fair. So I'm going to tell him tonight. Which will be awful. He'll be so upset.'

'Poor chap. Well – if you want to have a quick drink first? Get up some Dutch courage?'

Barty looked at him consideringly. It wasn't such a bad idea. She had been going to meet Charlie for a drink straight from work, but somehow the idea of postponing that, even for an hour, was quite attractive. Cowardly maybe but still . . .

'Yes,' she said slowly. 'Yes, maybe that would be nice. Can you wait, for half an hour or so? I have some letters to do.'

'At this hour? Barty, it's a quarter past six. Doesn't your poor secretary ever go home?'

'Yes,' said Barty, irritability rising in her again, 'of course she does. When I've finished doing my work. Now if you can't wait, Sebastian, never mind.'

'I can wait,' he said mildly, pulling some papers out of his briefcase.

Barty's stalwart secretary of almost nine years' standing was away sick and a temporary was doing her job. She looked at Barty in horror when she said she had some letters to give her.

'Can't they wait till tomorrow, Miss Miller? I have a date and it's already –' she looked at her watch '– after six.'

'No,' said Barty sharply, 'they can't. They're important. Now, the sooner you get on with them, the sooner you can leave. Get your pad and bring it in to my office.'

'Yes, Miss Miller.'

It was three-quarters of an hour before the letters were typed; Barty signed them, and told the secretary to get them in the post.

'Now, I must just go and tidy up a bit,' she said to Sebastian, 'and then I'll be with you. Sorry I've been so long.'

'That's OK. I've been reading Kit's new synopsis. It's awfully good.'

'Well, I'm pleased to hear it,' said Barty tartly, 'how nice for Wesley that they're being allowed to publish it.'

'Barty! That doesn't sound like you. It's not my fault Kit left Lyttons.'

'No,' she said, suddenly remorseful, 'no, I know it isn't. It's just that – oh, Sebastian, I'm awfully tired. And fed up. And dreading this evening.'

'Of course you are,' he said, standing up, holding out his arms to her, 'I feel very sorry for you. Come and have a cuddle.'

'No, I'm – Sebastian, I do hope I'm doing the right thing. I'm awfully scared.'

She went over to him and stood there with his arms round her, trying not to cry, her face buried in his chest, and failed to notice the temporary secretary glance in through the half open door.

Cathy heard her father come in and quickly slid the magazine she was reading – *Hollywood Secrets* – under her homework. He didn't like her obsession with film stars and their private lives. She need not have worried; he hadn't realised she was there. Well, she wouldn't have been normally, but her piano lesson had been cancelled, her teacher wasn't well. Or so she had said; she seemed perfectly all right to Cathy. Old witch. She hated her anyway; she'd be really glad not to have any more lessons.

She heard Charlie go into the room where he worked; he had given up his office on Third Avenue a few weeks ago. She wasn't supposed to tell Jenna that. She had, of course, but had sworn Jenna to secrecy.

She decided to make him a cup of tea; he always liked that when he came in. He said it reminded him of when her mother had done it for him.

Sometimes Cathy wished she could remember her mother more clearly; but she was only three when she died and of course she had been a pretty hazy memory for the year before that. She'd been at the clinic, and Cathy had never been allowed to go there and visit her. She'd accepted it at the time, but now she quite often wondered why not. Surely if you were very ill, if you were going to die, you'd like to see your little daughter. That whole period was a bit hazy, of course. Whenever her mother came home from the clinic, she'd looked pretty well all right. And then when she'd actually died, it had been terribly sudden. She'd just gone, gone from the house in an ambulance, Cathy did remember that. She also dimly remembered her mother lying on the floor in the hall while they waited for it to come and two days later her father told her her mother had gone to be with the angels.

Everything Cathy had read since she had been able to understand such things, told her that when people died of cancer they suffered horribly, were in terrible pain for a long time. Her mother didn't seem to go through that. When she was home she seemed fine. So she'd obviously been lucky.

Cathy did remember how pretty she had been; and how she'd played with her, taken her to the park, combed her hair endlessly and put pretty ribbons in it. Except when she was ill, of course; those days she just lay in her room and Cathy wasn't allowed near her. Her father had to stay home and look after her. But it didn't usually last too long.

Cathy went out into the hall quite quietly; she'd surprise her father, give him a piece of the cake she and Jenna had baked at the weekend. His study door was open; he was sitting at the desk, dialling a number. She tiptoed past, went into the kitchen, boiled the kettle, made some tea in the small pot and laid out the cake and some cookies on a tray for him, even put a lace cloth on the tray to make it special. Then she opened the kitchen door; she could hear his voice. He sounded upset; she wondered what the matter was. He'd been looking very tired lately, and worried, and he was always on the phone.

As she got nearer the study, she could hear him more clearly.

'I know, I know, for God's sake,' he was saying, 'but she still hasn't made up her damn mind. What? Yes, I'm still hopeful, of course I am, I wouldn't have taken out that last loan if I wasn't, but I can't get any more out of them. No, I can't do that, she'd—'

And then he saw Cathy and slammed the phone down.

'I've told you before,' he said and his face was more strained and harsh than she had ever seen it, 'you are not to listen to my phone calls. And I don't want any cake just now. Leave it in the kitchen, I'll help myself when I'm ready.'

Cathy went back into her room, feeling very upset.

Barty went along the corridor to the ladies' room. Sebastian was waiting for her downstairs, she had promised to be very quick. Both cubicles were shut; she started brushing her hair and inspecting her face, wishing she didn't look so tired and – well, so old. What had happened to the Barty who had first come to New York, who Laurence had fallen in love with, the Barty he had said was so beautiful, the Barty who he had loved so much, with the lion's mane of hair, with her tall, strong body, her joyous energy. She was gone, leaving behind this white-faced, thin, worn-looking woman, staring at her with haunted eyes. Maybe some more lipstick – or would that make her look even more raddled, paler still? She—

'Old witch,' came a voice from one of the cubicles. 'She is just such a slave driver. I had to do five long letters before she'd let me go.'

It was her temporary secretary; Barty stood there, ice-cold, afraid even to move.

'Well, I suppose she doesn't have much of a life,' came another voice, less familiar. 'Her husband's supposed to have been killed in the war, but that's kind of a neat excuse, isn't it? I mean, he could just as easily have walked out on her.'

'She's got that old man from England here. I saw them just now, smooching in her office.'

'What! You didn't! At their age? How gross.'

'I know. Well, I suppose if you're both old, you don't notice the other person's wrinkles and so on. He must be older than her, though.'

'Maybe a bit. Well certainly no one younger'd want her, I mean would they? Sad really. It must be really lonely for her, bringing up that child all on her own—'

'Serves her right, if you ask me. It's the kid I feel really sorry for, mom with a temper like that. The other day—'

There was the sound of a lavatory flushing; Barty fled, silently, ran into her office, slammed the door shut, stood leaning against it, breathing hard, fighting down the panic and the tears.

Two hours later, she sat in the Four Seasons and told Charlie Patterson she would like to marry him, very much, if he would still have her.

Part Two

CHAPTER 15

'Ladies and Gentlemen, a toast! The bride and groom.'

The champagne glasses were raised; a murmur of 'the bride and groom' went round the room; the bride smiled radiantly, the groom just slightly awkwardly.

She kissed him; he kissed her back and then rose to his feet, looking rather serious.

He was very handsome, Venetia thought; and very sexy too. She had always been able to see the attraction. It was all that rather violent, suppressed energy. And he was immensely clever; her mother kept pointing it out. She knew it was partly to annoy her; Celia was taking a perverse pleasure in the whole thing. But he was. There was just no doubt about it. Completely wasted in his chosen career. Still—

'So I would just like to thank Mr and Mrs Warwick for welcoming me to the family and to assure you I will do everything in my power to take care of Elspeth.'

Pity he hadn't done a bit more four months earlier, Venetia thought savagely; she was finding this very hard.

'And I would also like to thank my own parents for all they have done for me, and the sacrifices they have made. I propose a toast to them: my parents, Dora and Robert Brown.'

There was a momentary awkward silence; then 'Dora and Robert! Congratulations. Jolly well done.'

It was Lord Arden's voice, cutting into that silence, saving the mood just in time. Celia, looking at him across the table, remembered sharply, for the first time in several months, why she had wanted to marry him. Or at least why she had thought she wanted to marry him. She rose to her own feet, smiling first at him and then at the Browns.

'Dora and Robert,' she said firmly. The rest of the room followed, raising their glasses. The Browns sat looking proudly embarrassed, but smiling properly for the first time that day.

'Bunny, that was very well done,' Celia smiled at him across the drawing room. 'We were all a bit slow on the uptake, I'm afraid.'

It was six o'clock, the bride and groom had departed for their honeymoon – a week in the Scottish Highlands – the Browns for the small hotel where they were spending the next two days with their two younger sons, in order to experience the wonders of London for the first time. Venetia had gone upstairs for a rest, to recover from the traumas of the day. Boy was dispensing drinks to the remaining guests.

'What's that, my dear?' said Lord Arden. 'Oh, the toast. Yes, well, they're very sweet people. Very sweet. I particularly liked Dora. Very bright woman. We had a most interesting chat.'

'What about?' said Celia. 'I was most intrigued, Bunny, I must say, you seemed to be getting on tremendously well.'

'Suez.'

'Suez?' said Boy, astonished.

'Yes. Our Dora is very well-informed. She says she has a lot of time to read the paper while there aren't any customers in the shop. She thinks it's a very good thing Nasser has nationalised the canal. I was very impressed, I can tell you.'

'How extraordinary,' said Boy.

'Not at all,' said Celia, 'you're so stupidly narrow-minded, Boy. I'm surprised at you. Why shouldn't Dora Brown be intelligent? Keir's brains must have come from somewhere. Just because someone is poor and ill-educated doesn't mean they're stupid. Barty's mother could hardly write and her father couldn't even read, but look at Barty.'

'Yes,' said Boy, 'just look at Barty.'

Barty's announcement that she was going to get married again had caused considerable division in the family.

The romantics thought it was wonderful, that she deserved some happiness; the realists were deeply sceptical, given that her husband-to-be had no money, no job worth talking about, was younger than she was and had a daughter he was raising on his own.

Sebastian and Kit, who had congratulated Barty most heartily when she told them, and expressed huge pleasure at being the first to know (after the girls, who had gone into a state of stratospheric excitement), only discovered on the flight home how extremely uneasy they both were about it, and indeed about Charlie Patterson himself.

Izzie, on the other hand, being the leading romantic, and who pointed out, with perfect truth, that she knew Charlie better than any of them, said she thought it was absolutely lovely, that Charlie clearly loved Barty very much, and that it was absolute nonsense that he was marrying her for her money.

This unthinkable, unsayable thought was first expressed with great forcefulness by the boys.

'Well he's certainly a very smart guy,' was all Nick Neill said; Mike Parker was more outspoken.

'So he's got no money, no job—'

'He has got a job,' said Izzie indignantly, cut off abruptly in her rhapsodising.

'Oh pardon me. I forgot. A real estate business run during school hours with no secretary, OK, what you could call quite a modest job, and he's marrying a woman who has millions? Nice work, Charlie. There's one born every minute. Although I wouldn't have thought Barty Miller was one of them.'

'Mike, that is just so unfair. Charlie is the sweetest man—'

'I never said he wasn't sweet,' said Mike, 'I just expressed a view that he was smart.'

'Anyway, Barty's wealth is hugely exaggerated. She didn't get much of her husband's fortune and neither did Jenna, he died without knowing—'

'Yeah, yeah, we know. Listen, a mansion in the Hamptons, a house in the Upper Eighties and a publishing company based in New York and London don't come exactly cheap. Get real, Izzie. Now Charlie Patterson may be the sweetest man on God's earth, he may be closely related to the angels, he may be standing right behind Billy Graham in God's line-up, I certainly don't know that he isn't, but it don't alter the fact that he's got very, very lucky.'

'I think you're both horrid,' said Izzie. 'And I shall tell Barty to strike you off the post-wedding party guest list.'

'Now that's really very mean. You wouldn't do that, would you?'

'I would. If you go on talking like this. Now I'm going to do some work. I have to leave on time tonight.'

'Ah. Do we have a hot date, Lady Isabella?'

This was their new name for her, ever since they had heard her father calling her Isabella.

'No I don't,' said Izzie. 'I'm looking at apartments, that's all. And don't call me that stupid name.'

'I love you. So very, very much.'

'And I – love you.'

She heard the hesitation herself; however slight, it was there. It always was. He smiled. If he did hear it, he was not acknowledging it, and he should certainly not mind. She had made it clear, that first evening, that it was vital they entered this marriage on clear, honest terms. She did not love Charlie as she had loved Laurence; that was impossible. But she cared for him very deeply, she loved being with him, she wanted to spend the rest of her life with him. It was very simple; he must understand that.

Charlie did. He said it was fine that way; that he was very, very happy to be cared for deeply, and that she should love being with him. He was going to make her happy; that was his only concern.

Reminding herself that whatever else Laurence had done, he had very seldom made her happy, she went to bed that night in Charlie's arms, deeply content.

They told the girls first; they sat and listened, their eyes growing larger and starrier by the moment, clasping one another's hands, looking alternately at their parents and at each other. Neither spoke for a long time; then Jenna said simply, 'So now Cathy can be my sister. And come to Dana too.'

Charlie had looked at Barty quizzically, sweetly, and she had liked him for it, for reading her so well, as he always did, and had said, taking his hand, 'Yes, of course she can,' and had not felt anything but delight that she could do so much for both of them.

Then she told Sebastian and Kit; they had been wonderful, absolutely happy for her, had shaken Charlie by the hand, offered to buy them all lunch. Charlie had said that sounded great, but Barty said she had lunch with an agent which had taken her months to fix: 'I can't cancel it, I really can't. Let's all have dinner instead.'

It was only afterwards, sitting in the cab going downtown, that she realised she must have sounded exactly like Celia . . .

She sent a cable to Celia; she felt she must tell her as soon as possible, before there was any danger of her getting a whiff of the news from someone else. She wasn't sure what reaction she might get; when it came, by way of a cable, it was of course totally predictable.

'Delighted. Inform date of wedding soonest. Letter follows. Love Celia.'

No questions asked, no surprise expressed – Barty had never forgotten Celia's mother, Lady Beckenham, saying it was common to appear shocked or surprised by anything – just an assumption that she would be at the wedding. Which of course she would have to be. Only. . .

'It means I have to ask them all,' she said to Charlie.

'Why?'

'You don't understand. You don't have just one Lytton, to anything.'

He was silent for a moment; then said, 'You did want it small and private.'

'Yes, I did. What about you?'

'That's what I wanted too.' He hesitated. Then, 'Suppose – suppose we just had mothers? And the girls and Izzie of course.'

'Neither of us has a mother.'

'No I know. But Lady Celia is the nearest you've got. And I could ask Meg's mother. And with the girls, that'd be very neat. No awkwardness asking cousins and great-aunts and old college friends.'

She thought for a minute.

'It's a lovely idea. I really like it.'

'Good. Now I have another idea. I don't know how you'd feel about it.'

'What's that?'

'Suppose I ask Jamie to be my supporter?'

'Jamie!'

'Yes. I thought it would be nice. He's been so kind to me, and I just thought—'

'Don't you have a closer friend you'd want to ask?' Barty asked, trying to give herself time to think, wondering how exactly Jamie had been so kind to Charlie. As far as she knew he'd done nothing to help him at all.

'Not really. You know I lost touch with them all over the past few years. And I thought it would be nice for you, too. I know how fond of Jamie you are, how important he is to you.'

'Yes,' she said and now that the idea was settling, she found she liked it, that it reconciled the past with the future. She was indeed terribly fond of Jamie. And he was so different from Laurence, so easy, so sweet, there would be no – no what? She pushed the idea of exactly what aside.

'Yes,' she said, kissing Charlie. 'Yes, I think it's a really nice idea. Thank you. And he'll love it.'

'Good. Now – where?'

'Not – not South Lodge,' she said quickly, and then felt ashamed of herself.

'Well, of course not,' he said so gently, she felt even worse. 'I would never, ever have thought of such a thing. No, no. The Waldorf? The Plaza? My place?'

She kissed him, laughing.

'Your place. No, let's have it here. We can get married at the City Hall and then have just a family lunch. And a party later, maybe. How would that suit you?'

'It'd suit me very well.'

'Good. I can't wait for you to meet Celia.'

'I can't wait to meet her. I hope she likes me.'

'Now on that,' said Barty, 'all bets are off. She is a law absolutely unto herself. There is no logic to her likes and dislikes. Never has been.'

'Will she bring the noble Lord?'

'Who? Oh, Lord Arden. I shouldn't think so. We can't tell her not to. But Sebastian says he's not allowed to go anywhere much with her these days.'

'Can't he insist?'

'No he can't,' said Barty. 'Believe me.'

'Tell me—' he said casually.

'Yes?'

'Celia and Sebastian – they seem to have a rather – close relationship.'

'They're great friends,' she said carefully. 'Lifelong friends.'

'No more than that?'

'Charlie, I don't think I want to talk about it.'

'Why not? It's intriguing.'

'It's – off-limits,' she said. 'Sorry. Not my story to tell.'

'So there is a story?'

'Everyone has a story,' she said with a stab of irritation. He had become more pressing since she had said she would marry him, she was noticing it more and more; only over small things, of course, but not letting subjects rest, asserting his choice over films they saw, restaurants they ate at. Well, that was probably good for her . . .

'Yes, and this one is intriguing, I suspect.'

'It's one you're not going to hear. Unless Sebastian or Celia tells you themselves. Which is hugely unlikely. Now let's change the subject, shall we?'

He smiled at her, his most open, guileless smile. 'Sorry. Now then, the only thing about this plan is, what about your nice brother? Shouldn't he be invited?'

'I very much doubt if he'll come. He runs a farm. Not easy to get away. Oh dear, you're right, he should be invited, though. He and Joan. Maybe we should have it in England. But then—'

'No, let's have it here. And then visit England.'

'Yes, all right. But I do want you to meet Billy. You'd like him so much.'

They set the date for the wedding in January.

'That will give Celia time to get over here. It seems silly to wait, when we could do it tomorrow. But—'

'January's only a month away. I can wait that long. To make you Mrs Patterson.'

She hadn't thought of that. She felt a stab of alarm at no longer being Mrs Laurence Elliott. She called herself Barty Miller at work, but domestically, socially, she was Barty Elliott. It was important to her, linked her still to Laurence. But – she had to give something up, for God's sake. And she had to move forward. It was a bit like South Lodge; she could no longer keep that for herself. And professionally, of course, she was still Barty Miller. That wasn't going to change . . .

'Noni, that was *Style*.'

'Oh yes?'

'They want you to do another job for them.'

Adele sounded slightly irritable; she would have preferred it to have been her. The pictures had been very good, she knew. Despite some rather grudging praise from Laura Proctor-Reid, they had had a very strong dramatic quality, and Noni had looked marvellous, no one would have known she wasn't an experienced professional. She had a natural grace, in any case, and had immediately picked up the rather exaggerated angular poses *Style* wanted. And what Marella had insisted on calling her French look, her dark hair and eyes, her rather white skin, her narrow frame, had suited the clothes very well.

'Well – are you going to do it?' Adele's voice was impatient.

Noni looked at her thoughtfully. She was so touchy, these days, so easily upset. Geordie's extended absence had made her worse; now that he was coming home in a few days, she was raw with anxiety. It probably wasn't a very good idea to do the job for *Style*, encroaching on her mother's territory, a territory she was no longer very confident about. And there was no way she really wanted to be a model; it was a pretty silly way to make a living. But she had been fascinated by what had been done that day, a few quite ordinary-looking garments turned into a brilliant visual idea. And it had been fun too—

'Noni! Do concentrate. They're waiting on the phone.'

'Oh – sorry. I'll speak to them, shall I?'

It was the downtrodden assistant, Mary Louise; Noni had rather liked her. She was clearly used to being kept waiting.

'Oh that's perfectly all right,' she said in her nervous near-whisper. 'It was just that Miss Proctor-Reid would like you to work for us again. She wants to do a feature on spring jackets, couture, mainly, and she wants to shoot them in Paris—'

'Paris!'

'Yes. Next week. Just before the real Christmas rush starts. I realise it's short notice, but Miss Proctor-Reid really wants you.'

'I'm not sure—'

'Oh Miss Lieberman, please say yes.'

'Noni, I do rather need the phone. Please hurry up.'

Noni looked at her mother. She was on edge; Geordie was coming home in just a few days, war would be breaking out again, her mother crying, Clio upset, Lucas sulking . . . although Lucas was changing, was somehow happier, a bit easier these days, beginning to grow up at last. But he wasn't going to welcome Geordie.

Adele banged down a coffee pot very loudly, turned the cold tap on full.

Noni looked at her tense, aggressive back. 'Yes, all right,' she said, 'I'd like to come, very much, thank you.'

Adele walked out and slammed the kitchen door.

Elspeth was working hard at telling herself that she was very lucky really; she was having a baby, a much-wanted baby, she had a husband who loved her, she had her own home. Thousands, millions of girls all over the country would have envied her. Of course the home wasn't very big, in fact it was very small, a one-bedroom flat in one of the new high-rise, council-owned developments which were replacing the slums and the bomb-damaged areas on the outskirts of Glasgow, but it was modern, and only on the third floor of the building. When she had first seen it, when Keir had proudly shown it to her, she had been so appalled, she hadn't been able to disguise it. He had stopped short in his guided tour, had been first upset then angry.

'Of course, it's not what you're used to, I can see that. It's not a plush flat in Chelsea. But I have to pay for it and it's the best I can afford. You know about that, Elspeth? Paying your way? It's an odd notion, I give you that. Maybe you'll learn in time. It's not a rich publisher you're married to, it's a struggling supply teacher. Sorry. Perhaps you should go home to Daddy and the Lyttons right now and admit you were wrong.'

'Keir don't. I'm sorry. Very sorry. I can't – can't help being a bit worried.'

'Oh indeed. What are you a bit worried about? The neighbours? Not quite your style? The decor? Sorry about the curtains. Or rather the lack of them. You'll have time on your hands for a bit, perhaps you could lower yourself sufficiently to make a few up. My mother will help you. She offered to make them, as a matter of fact, only I thought you'd want to do it yourself.'

'Keir, stop it,' she said, fighting back the tears. 'Don't be so angry. I'm sorry. Of course I like it, it's – it's sweet. But it is a bit – small.'

'I don't see that. It has a bedroom, a living room, a kitchen and a bathroom. You're lucky, I looked at a few with an outside toilet.'

'Yes, but – but where will the baby sleep? There's no room for a – a . . .' 'Nursery' was the word struggling to get out. She crushed it just in time. 'For its – his room.'

'Well, he can sleep with us. What's wrong with that?'

'With us! Keir, we can't have a baby in our room.'

'And why not? He won't take up much space. He'll still be able to sleep and breathe, all that sort of thing.'

'Well because – because –'

'What you mean is that your sort, people like you, don't have babies in their rooms. They have nurseries and nannies. Well, I've told you, Elspeth, if you want that sort of thing, you've married the wrong man. This is the best I can do. If it's not good enough for you, then I'm sorry.' She saw, suddenly, a dangerous brilliance in his dark eyes, realised how upset he was. She went up to him, put her arms round him, kissed him.

'Keir, I'm so sorry. It's all right, really. You have to forgive me, make allowances for me. I'm just a spoilt brat, as you're always saying. I love the flat, really I do. It's sweet. And I'll make curtains, and – and everything. It'll all be fine. Please forgive me, Keir.'

She was crying herself, now; he looked down at her and relented, smiled suddenly at her.

'All right. I forgive you. And I'm sorry it isn't – bigger. When I'm a headmaster, I'll buy you a fine house. Meanwhile, maybe the bairn can sleep in the living room at night. I'm told cots are quite easily transportable.'

Danger was averted: for the time being.

But now they had moved in, into the tiny space, where she felt like a caged tiger, pacing up and down much of the day, for want of anything else to do. Naturally energetic, intensely hard-working, she was desperate with boredom. She had hoped to be able to carry on with her editing in a freelance capacity, but even Celia had found herself unable to convince Jay that this would work and especially not with a book as important as the Clementine Hartley novel; that had hurt her almost more than anything else.

She cleaned the flat each morning, carefully and energetically at first, then with increasing listlessness, and usually found herself at ten or eleven o'clock with endless empty hours ahead of her. She would have gone for long walks, had she been in London, but it was hardly walking territory, endless streets, leading to more endless streets; and then the neighbourhood was not exactly rough, but it was very lower class, and she was already teased by the children in the block. They called out 'hoity toity' when she walked past them and stared and giggled at her, and their mothers regarded her, she knew, with a mixture of curiosity and scorn. She had tried to be friendly at first, but it hadn't worked, they assumed she was being patronising and, at best, ignored her, at worst, were outwardly rude, staring at her from their cosy groups of three or four, standing at their doorways in the block's long concrete corridors or in the shops. And there was the problem of understanding what people said to her; their accents were very thick and unfamiliar; she had to keep saying, 'I'm sorry?' or 'What did you say?' and it emphasised horribly the difference between them.

Shopping, trips to the greengrocers and the butchers and the corner shop, had become a dreaded ordeal; she had tried to do it at times when the shops were empty, leaving it really late until the children were home from school and having their tea, or early in the morning before most of the mothers were about, but they were almost always about and anyway, she was even more nervous in the dark evenings.

She had already told Keir that next time they went down to London, she was going to bring her car up with her; she told him it was so that she could be more efficient with the shopping and so on, but it was actually so that she could feel less of a prisoner. He had argued with her briefly and then given in; she resisted the temptation to point out that he too would benefit from having the car.

She felt quite frightened by her loneliness and isolation; she felt she had somehow landed in a completely foreign country, where she knew nothing of the customs, didn't speak the language and had no point of contact with anyone. Sometimes whole days went by when the only person she spoke to was Keir; she tried to tell herself it would pass, that it would get better, but she couldn't see how. She filled the hours with reading, and writing letters to her mother and Celia, but the awful emptiness of her life provided very little material for that and she was horribly aware of their forced cheerfulness and increasing brevity.

The only outings she actually enjoyed were to the ante-natal clinic at the hospital. There, among other young women in the same situation as herself, nervous, excited mothers-to-be, many of them for the first time, she managed to cut through the barriers of class, of her accent, her clothes, and to feel one of a group, discussing the problems of sickness, sleeplessness, heartburn, the baby's kicking, the anxiety about the pain of labour, the debate over breast-versus-bottle feeding.

She thought of asking a couple of these girls, with whom she became genuinely quite friendly, to visit her in the flat, but rejected the idea. At the hospital they were on neutral ground, in her home where, modest as it was, there were expensive ornaments, family photographs in silver frames, piles of books with no shelves to put them on, she knew she would be branded immediately as different, posh, stuck-up. Safer to keep things as they were, herself at a distance.

But visits to the infirmary were only monthly; she was wretched most of the time, her loneliness and boredom emphasised by a visit home. Keir had insisted that they spend Christmas alone together, in their own home, and he had been right, it had been surprisingly and sweetly happy, but they did go to London for New Year. There, in the warmth and busyness of her family, she had looked at the icy solitude of her new life and wondered, for the thousandth time, whether she was actually doing the right thing. She dreaded going back as if it were to some ordeal. As indeed it was.

The worst thing, of course, was the effect it had on her relationship with Keir; depression and a sense of isolation hardly made for a happy atmosphere. She tried to be cheerful, to express interest in his day (not often very happy either, but at least busy), and always had supper ready for him. But after that – which he liked, and she hated, to have early, at six – he disappeared into the bedroom where he had a small desk, to do his marking and preparation work for the next day, leaving her to face another two hours of solitude. She became resentful and irritable with him, which in turn increased his truculence, his constant references to the difference in her circumstances, his observations that she was not enjoying her new life; and as for sex, a continuing nausea, and the discomfort of the growing baby, made it something she dreaded rather than welcomed. Which shocked and distressed her more than anything.

She was unable to regard her marriage as a success: to put it mildly.

'Oh,' said Lucas. 'Oh, hallo.'

Geordie nodded at him briefly.

'Good afternoon, Lucas.'

They stared at one another: hostilities had already resumed. 'Good trip?'

'Yes, thanks. I've come for Clio.'

'Right. I'll call her—'

There was no need: 'Darling, Darling –' she threw herself into Geordie's arms; he hugged her tight, kissed her dark curls.

'Did you miss me?'

'So, so much.'

'I missed you. Coming out with your old daddy?'

'Yes please!'

'Go and ask Nanny to get you into your hat and coat.'

She ran upstairs.

'She misses you,' said Lucas.

'Well, I'm glad somebody does. How's your mother?'

'Fine,' said Lucas. 'Much better, I'd say.'

He knew this was completely untrue; but he refused to give Geordie the satisfaction of thinking anything else.

'Good,' said Geordie. 'Ah – here she is. My best girl. Tell your mother I'll bring her back in the morning. OK?'

'OK.'

Adele was upset that she had missed Geordie. She had been out shopping and had got held up in traffic. She phoned him later that evening.

'I'm sorry I missed you. Everything all right?'

'Perfectly all right.'

'Could we – could we meet, do you think? For lunch or – or tea?'

'If you like.' His tone was the opposite of warm. 'I'll see you when I get back, won't I? Won't that do?'

'I meant not here. You know. Let's have tea, Geordie. At Browns, perhaps? About four? It's nice and quiet there.'

'Yes – all right. Now Clio and I have a date with Pooh and Piglet. Sorry. 'Bye, Adele.'

''Bye, Geordie.'

She wanted to talk to him; to explain that Lucas was going up to Oxford next year. To ask him if he would consider coming home then. She really thought he might.

She had supper alone with Lucas that night; Noni was away, in Paris. Lucas was changing: it was wonderful. He had grown up, just in the past few weeks. He seemed to be moving, at last, from sulky adolescent to someone more talkative, easier, even at times quite cheerful. He was happy too; he actually talked to her about his new passion, the debating society at school, where he was clearly becoming a star; it seemed very odd to her, broody, silent Lucas. Although of course he had always been articulate when it had suited him, swift with the right – or rather the wrong – words, the withering put-down, the tart observation. And more surprising, his social life seemed to be developing; he seemed to have friends of both sexes, was suddenly in demand for parties; girls obviously liked him and she could see why. He was going to be very sexy, with his dark, brooding looks, his unmistakable French style. He was, in fact, exactly like Luc. Except, she hoped, nicer . . .

She told him her plan; she felt she must, and she didn't want him to think he was being pushed aside – again.

'It's just that you won't be here,' she said earnestly, 'and so you won't have to live with one another. It'll be quite different, don't you see?'

He sighed. 'While I'm away, I suppose. Yes. But I'll be back, won't I, in the vacations? I honestly think, Mother, if this is what you want, and if he agrees, I should find a flat. Geordie and I could never live together. Not now.'

'But Lucas—'

'No, Mother, we couldn't. But that's fine. I quite fancy a bit of independence.'

'But you're much too young to live on your own.'

'Oh I don't know. I quite like the idea.' He smiled at her.

Adele didn't; she contemplated Lucas living alone in London, unsupervised, his burgeoning sexuality untrammelled, and knew it was out of the question.

'And you don't feel you could even try? In the vacations?'

He looked at her for a moment, then said, 'No. I don't. It wouldn't work.'

'This isn't just about school, is it? Not any more?'

He hesitated. 'No. Not really. I mean, I'll never forgive him. For what he did to you, as well as me. I know I was difficult—'

She half smiled. 'Just a bit.'

'But I was only a kid. He's a grown man. Supposed to be. We could have worked something out. Still. Blood on the tracks now. I'm sorry about it all.'

'Oh, Lucas, don't. And of course I don't want you to leave.'

'Well – I'd have to. If he came back.' She could see this was different; not emotional blackmail. He hesitated for a moment, then said, 'There's something else, though, Mother. He's just not good enough for you. Honestly.'

'In what way?'

Just for a moment she felt he wanted to tell her something; but all he said was, 'Oh – he just isn't. I suppose I'm a bit biased. No, you do what you can with him, Mum. I'll get out of your hair.'

Anyway it didn't work. She came home, ran upstairs, locked herself in her room, weeping. They had moved too far apart, Geordie said, he didn't think he could even contemplate coming back now.

'It's not just Lucas, Adele. It was what it revealed – about us. And the value you put on our relationship. It's natural, I suppose, that you should put your son first. But I tried so hard, Adele. So very hard. You gave me no credit for that. You didn't seem to care how miserable I was, or lonely, or about my separation from Clio, and Noni's distress – you just went on, knowing you were right, knowing what was best for all of us. And I'm afraid that destroyed rather a lot for me. But –' his voice had changed; she looked up, saw the old Geordie suddenly, smiling gently at her, infinitely sad '– I'll always love you. Always. But I can't fight your love for your son. And we can't turn the clock back. I only wish we could.'

Noni came home from Paris, excited, happy, ran into the house, calling to her mother. Lucas came out to the hall, shook his head, indicated the closed door. She went up, heard the muffled weeping, tried to find the strength to go in and comfort her, and somehow – just couldn't. Later she and Lucas sat discussing it, over a bottle of wine.

'Geordie's so ghastly,' he said. 'Utterly ghastly. She just can't see it.'

'Lucas, he's not ghastly. When will you let it rest, why can't you make more effort?'

'Noni,' he said, 'it's not just me. It was never just me. He's a spoilt brat. Even more of a spoilt brat than I am. He likes life easy. Comfortable. Geordie-shaped. Everything going his way.'

For the first time, he told her about the overheard telephone conversation, the lipstick-stained shirt; she stared at him in horror.

'Oh God,' she said, 'God, how horrible. You don't think, do you, there's anyone else now?'

He shrugged. 'I don't know. Possibly. He's been over in the States quite a long time.'

'Yes, but he's been working.'

'Every night? Every day?'

'Oh God,' she said again. 'Maybe I should write to Izzie, see if she knows anything, has heard any gossip.'

She went upstairs again; her mother was asleep. Lying fully clothed on the bed, surrounded by dozens of discarded tissues. It would all start again in the morning. Noni sighed. She was getting very weary of it; very weary indeed. She seemed to be the only person not getting any consideration. Everyone was worrying about her mother, about Lucas, about Clio; and the burden was falling most heavily on her.

She made a decision that night: to leave Oxford and take up modelling full time. She supposed she was running away from reality, but she just didn't care. It was her way of getting through it all; and she was going to take it.

CHAPTER 16

'She's not coming? But I don't understand. How could she refuse? I thought she was so special to you, I thought Cathy loved her—' Barty stared at Charlie; she felt genuinely upset.

'Not so much these days. The words Old and Witch hang heavy in the air.'

'Yes, but still. All these years, she's been very good to you, paying the school fees, and Cathy's been to stay so regularly—'

'I'm baffled, too. I really thought she'd want to come. But she's refused. Maybe she's ill, I don't know.'

'Does she say she's ill? Can I see the letter?'

'There isn't a letter, she phoned. She was pretty abrupt.'

'Surely she'd have said if she was ill.'

'Barty —' he hesitated.

'Yes?'

'I – I actually think it's a bit more complicated.'

'Oh really? In what way?'

'Her mother, Meg's grandmother, had dementia. She was totally confused apparently, always running away from the care home, wandering round in her night clothes or less. I think maybe Sally, that's her name, is going the same way. I've noticed she's changed a lot lately.'

'Oh no! That's dreadful. How old is she?'

'Not so young. Seventy-five.'

'Quite young for dementia. Poor lady. Is she having good medical care?'

'Yes, I think so. I hope so, anyway.'

'Well – presumably money isn't a problem. I mean she must be pretty well off to pay the school fees.'

'Oh yes. She's very comfortable.'

'Maybe we could go and see her, after the wedding, take some photos—'

'That's a lovely idea. You're a nice person, Barty.'

'I try to be.' She gave him a kiss. 'I must go to work. What are you doing today?'

'Oh – a few clients to see. Then I thought I'd meet the girls from school, take them skating. They'd like it.'

'Have you got time? They're perfectly all right, just coming back here. They have a lot of studying to do.'

'I know. But it'd be fun. And it is nearly Christmas. I told you, Cathy's just slightly knocked off her perch by all this. Moving out of the apartment and so on. Even though she's so happy about everything, it's a pretty drastic change. And readjustment.'

'Yes, of course. Well it was your idea to give up the apartment.'

She had been slightly surprised that he wanted to do that before the wedding. Surprised and, even though she didn't like to admit it, irritated. It seemed a little presumptuous. On the other hand, his lease had almost run out, there were only six weeks to go, and it did simplify life a lot. He had suggested – sensing her discomfort – that he and Cathy move into a hotel, but she had said, of course, that they mustn't think of it.

She had suggested he and Cathy move into the guest suite on the top floor. There were two bedrooms up there, a small sitting room, which Charlie could use as an office, and a bathroom; they would be self-contained and they could preserve the fiction to the girls that there was no impropriety going on. He came over to her, ruffled her hair.

'You know, I've been thinking.'

'Yes?'

'Next year, when the girls are safely installed at Dana Hall, shall we take a long trip?'

'Oh – I don't know. I mean – we are going to England, aren't we?'

'That's just to meet the family. I meant a real long trip. See something of the world.'

'Charlie –' she stared at him '– Charlie, how long a trip?'

'Oh – couple of months.'

'I can't go away for a couple of months,' she said. She felt disorientated, almost scared. 'I've been worrying about the two or three weeks in England as it is.'

'Why, for heaven's sake?'

'I have a business to run. A very complex, demanding business. You don't seem to understand.'

'Darling, I do understand. I understand something else too. You look tired, worn out, you seem very stressed. You need a really long vacation. I want to see you relax, enjoying yourself.'

'But I do enjoy myself. I enjoy myself running Lyttons.'

'Yes, but there's more to life than that, surely? You must see that. You tell me all the places in the world you've seen, Barty.'

'Well – England. Scotland. France—'

'And America. There you are. What about India, China, Egypt, the rest of Europe? Don't you have any curiosity about those places, don't you long to see them?'

'Well –' she hesitated '– well I suppose so. But I've always—'

'Always what?'

'Had too many other things to worry about. Jenna, Lyttons—'

'Jenna will be away at school. She's really happy about us. She's settled down a lot lately. I've noticed.'

'Jenna didn't need to settle down,' said Barty. She was beginning to feel seriously irritated. 'She's always been – Jenna.'

'Of course. Adorable. But very naughty, very – wilful. Sweetheart, you're always saying it.'

'I know but—' It was all right for her to say it; not for him.

'Anyway, they're both going to be fine. Taken good care of. So we could head off, without worrying about them. And we ought to have some time on our own. Just – getting to know one another.'

'I think we do know each other pretty well,' said Barty.

'Well – yes and no. Heavens, Barty, we're getting married, surely we deserve a honeymoon.'

'I never think anyone deserves anything, in that sense,' she said – God, she was sounding more and more like Celia. 'And there is absolutely no question of my taking a long trip in the foreseeable future. I'm sorry. Lyttons is too important. I've neglected it lately, I've missed two important books I should have bid for – you don't seem to understand, this is a full-time, more than full-time, job. I have to read the *New York Times* every day, really read it. I aim to get an idea for a book at least once, possibly twice, a day. I need to lunch regularly with agents, I need to see new young authors, I need to know absolutely what is being published out there. These are tricky times, the market is changing, there are new types of books being published, the paperback market is becoming increasingly important, I need to talk to the bookshop owners, I—'

'Yes, yes, all right,' he said, 'I get the idea. I'm still surprised you can't set it aside for us, just for a little while.'

'Charlie,' she said, and she was angry now, 'that company provides—' She stopped; just in time. Only just in time.

'Provides what?'

Money: money for the houses, for the school fees, for the cars, for travelling. For him now as well as for her.

'Provides me with work and responsibility for the next hundred years,' she said.

'So, do I have to wait a hundred years?' He was smiling at her carefully; he had sensed her anger, had pulled back. 'Well, it'll be worth it.' He kissed the top of her head. 'You get along to your important work. No, don't glare at me like that, I understand, it is important and I love you for it. And I'll stay home and bake an apple pie. Talking of apple pie, sweetheart, could you lend me ten dollars? I forgot to go to the bank last night, and I have to take a client out for breakfast first thing.'

'Yes of course,' she said, absentmindedly, pulling a note out of her wallet. 'Here—'

'Honey, I don't want fifty.'

'Take it. It's all I've got. And ten dollars won't last a minute. I keep meaning to open a joint account for us. Would that be a good idea, do you think?'

'It'd simplify things a bit, sure. Then I could take care of things like the household accounts for you.'

'I can –' Barty stopped '– take care of them perfectly well,' she was going to say. But at least Charlie could do that; it would be a good idea. It was a bore, all the insurance and regular bills, paying Maria and the cleaner and the food suppliers. 'Yes, that'd be good,' she said. 'I'll fix it today.' She gave him a kiss. 'I won't be late. Give the girls my love and tell them they must do their homework the minute they get in from skating.'

'I will. 'Bye honey. Have a good day. I'll miss you.'

She had felt very odd as she sat in the cab, driving down Fifth Avenue; as she passed Elliott House she looked up at it, at its vast, rather stolid grandeur and felt a rare pang of regret for it. It was a museum now; she would have loathed to live there, infinitely preferred Number Seven. But suddenly she felt a longing for it, for its reassurance, for what it represented, the days when Laurence had been in love with her and she had at least been sure of how she felt and what she was doing. However difficult and uncomfortable.

Without knowing quite why, she stopped the cab at 50th, and walked through to the Rockefeller Center and the ice rink, stood leaning on the wall, looking down at it, and at the vast Christmas tree just above it, thinking of Charlie skating there that afternoon with the two girls, while she worked far into the evening, wondering if they would miss her or indeed think of her at all.

Well, even if they didn't, she had no real choice. And besides, she had about as much desire to spend her days skating and shopping and lunching as she did to – well, to go travelling. How could any of that compare with finding a book, a potentially successful new book, the thud of the heart that accompanied it, honing and shaping it, seeing it come to life, watching it jacketed, displayed, sold, reviewed . . .

'God, Barty,' she said aloud, turning back towards Fifth Avenue and the glittering row of over-lit, over-dressed over-sparkling stores and buildings that were Manhattan at Christmas time, 'you're getting more and more like Celia.'

And then she thought, to her immense surprise, that she was looking forward to seeing Celia more than she would ever have believed possible.

Celia with her clear vision, her withering judgements, her absolute shattering honesty.

Only of course by the time she arrived, it would be too late.

It was Keir who made the suggestion: over dinner with Celia one night, during his visit with Elspeth to London.

Celia had said she was worried that Lyttons was not keeping up with the trend towards increasing realism in publishing and the theatre.

'Look at the success of *Look Back in Anger*, an absolute revolution, young people speaking out against the old order, nobody else in the place seems to feel a need for change, but I do.'

'By which you mean working-class stuff, I suppose?' said Keir. Elspeth looked at him anxiously, but he was smiling at Celia.

'Not entirely,' she said coolly. 'What I really mean, and I don't see why you have to be so eternally touchy on the subject, Keir, is books about real people, on every level. The Kingsley Amis book, *Lucky Jim*, hugely interesting, I thought. A lower-class but very real heroine, I liked that.'

'So, exactly, working class.'

'No. Real life. Life now.'

And he had come up with it: a book about the colour problem in Britain. He phoned her the next day, to discuss it further. Told her she'd need to be very courageous.

'Courage is one of my virtues,' said Celia.

'Right. Well now. They're arriving here in thousands. From Jamaica, mostly. Friend of mine from Glasgow works at a school in Brixton, I saw him at a meeting of the NUT a couple of months ago. I tell you, those kids could tell you some stories. Make your hair stand on end.'

'Such as?'

'They can't get anywhere to live, for a start. People, landladies and so on, just won't take them in. Say they'll get a bad name. They put notices in the windows saying "no coloureds". How do you think that makes a lad feel? A coloured lad?'

'It's a most curious description, that,' said Celia thoughtfully.

'Of course it is. As if the rest of us were albino or something. Anyway, they're living five families to a house, some of them. Ten blokes to a room. One lad in my friend's class, he and his parents share a flat, a flat, mind you, with two other families. He sleeps under the dining-room table.'

'How extraordinary,' said Celia. 'That's how the Millers lived when I first met them.'

'The who? Oh, yes. You'd have thought society might have moved on since then. But at least the Millers didn't have to contend with prejudice. Another lad, his dad can't get work, he applied for a job on the railways, but he was told "no coloureds". My friend asked his mum about it when she came to a parents' evening, she said it was because the white staff object. The excuse is the coloureds don't work so hard. A fine excuse. And then there are pubs which put up signs, saying "no coloureds" as well. A man can't even go out for a drink in the evening without being desperately insulted. Think of the social problems all this is going to cause. It's terrifying.'

'Indeed. I had no idea.'

'So, there's your book. If I were you, I'd commission one.'

'Really?' said Celia drily. 'And what would you suggest we did for a plot?'

'Oh that's simple. Black man, white girl. Dynamite. But like I said, you'd need to be pretty damn courageous.'

There was a long silence. Then, 'God knows what Giles will have to say about it,' said Celia, 'but it sounds like a very good idea to me.'

There was a silence, then she said, 'Keir, could I just suggest once again—'

'Celia,' said Keir, 'the answer's no. Once again. Sorry, but no.'

CHAPTER 17

'So Mummy, tell. What was he like? Did you like him, did Barty seem happy, was anyone else there, was the daughter nice?'

Celia lit a cigarette, inhaled deeply, and picked up the glass of champagne Venetia had poured for her.

'I thought he was absolutely dreadful,' she said.

She had been very upset by her visit. Barty had met her at Idlewild herself, driven her home, talking furiously, clearly anxious to avoid any questioning.

She had looked tired, Celia thought, and very thin, not at all as she should have done; she commented on it and Barty laughed it off, said she had been working too hard, it had all been very difficult. 'But now I'm terribly, terribly happy.'

Charlie was there to greet them on the doorstep, a little girl on either side. Jenna threw herself into Celia's arms, covered her with kisses; she had grown and grown up, Celia observed approvingly, was less bombastic, less argumentative, with an alarmingly adult sense of humour. The only sign of eccentricity was a watch worn on each wrist.

'You remember I collect them. I have so many, I have to wear two at a time.'

The other child charmed her less; she was very pretty, and nicely mannered, but there was something sly about her. Celia was surprised she could be Jenna's best friend.

And then there was Charlie. Her first reaction to Charlie was one of complete horror; he was standing there, so carefully posed with the girls, smiling an open, beguiling smile, holding out his hand to her, telling her how terribly, terribly pleased he was to meet her at last, how Barty never stopped talking about her, had told him everything she had done for her – Celia didn't like that for a start, being cast so firmly in the role of benefactress, it made her feel old and rather like the Queen Mother. She said so, wanting to see how he would react; he simply smiled and told her he had also heard how she was the cleverest woman in the world. 'And one of the most beautiful.' She hated that even more – as if Barty would have said such a thing – and swept past him into the house.

By the end of dinner, she couldn't imagine how she was going to get through the five days of her visit. He was appalling, so perfectly courteous, so charmingly deferential, hanging on her words, begging her to tell him more about England, about the early days of Lyttons, about Barty as a little girl, about her parents, about what he called her 'other children'.

'I think you must be under a misconception,' she said firmly. 'There was never any question of Barty being one of my children. She was always a Miller, I went to great lengths to keep her in touch with her own family.'

'Of course. She told me that too, how much she appreciated it.'

Celia looked at him.

'Now tell me about yourself, Mr Patterson.'

'Charlie, please.'

'Charlie. Yes. I presume your name is Charles? I think I prefer that. Until I know you slightly better.'

'It sounds a little formal.'

'I am a little formal, Charles. I come from a formal generation. I was born a Victorian.'

'I cannot believe that's possible, you look so young.'

She ignored that. 'Anyway, do tell me about yourself. You are an estate agent, I believe?'

He told her about that: a little. About how hard it had been, carrying on with it after his wife died. He told her about his wife, that she had died of cancer, that he and Cathy had been on their own for over five years before he met Barty.

'After that I didn't really feel alone any more.'

He told her he had plans now to develop the business: the girls would be away at school, it would be easier for him.

'And of course you will have the benefit of Barty's maid, when they are home.'

'Well – yes.' He grinned at her; clearly determined not to be deterred by her outspokenness.

'That was what convinced me that he was an absolute charlatan,' said Celia to Venetia, 'any normal person would have begun to be riled by me, but he went on playing his bland, easygoing role.'

She could scarcely sleep the first night; fretting over Barty, over the appalling mistake she knew she was making. In the morning she and Barty travelled to Lyttons together by cab; Charlie saw them off, smiling, from the doorstep. He was planning to take the girls over to New Jersey to visit a school friend. In Barty's car. 'Is that OK? Mine is acting up.'

'Of course. You should get rid of that old thing, Charlie, it's always letting you down. We'll get a new one.'

'Oh, I'm so fond of it, though. But maybe you're right.'

★

'You don't like him, do you?' said Barty. She didn't speak aggressively, she sounded calm and rather unemotional.

'No,' said Celia, 'since you ask me so directly. I don't especially. He is not the sort of person who appeals to me. But I don't dislike him. And I'm not going to marry him.'

'Do you know why?'

'He tries too hard. That always irritates me.'

'Don't you think that's natural? He's very nervous about meeting the whole family, and you especially.'

'Absolutely natural. Of course. And I hardly know him. You presumably know him very well. So—'

'I'm not sure that I do,' said Barty, 'actually.'

'Well that's rather serious,' said Celia after a pause. 'You should know the man you're entering into a long-term relationship with.' She looked at Barty. 'Perhaps you should wait a little longer.'

'Celia, I can't.' She sounded distracted. 'Everything's planned. You're here. The girls are so excited.'

'Not good reasons. Plans can be dismantled. Young girls get excited over anything. It could be new dresses tomorrow. I can go home again.'

'Oh – please, please don't. It's just pre-wedding nerves I expect,' said Barty. 'I was hoping you'd settle them for me.'

'What does Izzie think of him?'

'Oh, she adores him. And really, you know, he's the sweetest man. Gentle, thoughtful, very understanding.'

'What about the money?' said Celia abruptly.

'What about it?'

'Well – what arrangements are you making?'

'I haven't made any – yet. Apart from the fact that we are each becoming legal guardian of each other's child. That seemed only sensible.'

'Yes, of course. But Barty, you must sort out the money. It's terribly important. Believe me. This is not a criticism of Charles in any way, it's a simple fact.'

'Oh I see. Well I – I suppose I should have, but it's a delicate area. I don't like to raise it. He's very proud.'

So proud, thought Celia, he's already living in your house, using your car and apparently doing no work whatsoever.

'When I married Oliver,' she said, 'he didn't have two pennies to rub together. My father bought the house in Cheyne Walk for us, and it was always understood that if I died first, the house would go to the children. Oliver wouldn't hear of having it on any other terms. I admired him for that, as I did for so many other things. I really would advise you to sort all that out.'

'Yes,' said Barty, 'yes, you're right. I will.'

Celia changed the subject; her role, she felt, was to remain detached. She enjoyed her day at Lyttons immensely; although she and Barty met twice yearly, usually together with Giles or Jay, for editorial and financial review, this was rather different. She was alone with Barty, for a start, uninhibited by the presence of the others, free to listen to new publishing gossip, and to observe the New York market. She was fascinated by the success of *Marjorie Morningstar* a year earlier; it intrigued her that the novel, with its Jewish heroine, could combine romance and social realism, so succesfully.

'There's a wonderful story about *Marjorie Morningstar*,' said Barty. 'The red cloth binding, you know, wasn't quite waterproof. Girls were taking it to the beach, and getting their white swimsuits stained. Lots of complaints. Still, it hasn't done it a great deal of harm, I must say.'

The book seemed to Celia to echo her own pet project of the moment, Keir's idea for a love story between a white girl and a black man in England. Barty had backed the idea from the beginning.

'It sounds wonderful, and I've loved what I've seen. Of course I don't think we could do that here. Colour prejudice is far too strong.'

'It was Keir's idea. You haven't met him yet, you'll like him, his parents are the most ordinary people, yet he's a brilliant and charming young man, an ideal husband for Elspeth. I have, let us say, hopes for him.'

'Really? With Lyttons? How intriguing. I must certainly meet him. Does he know?'

'Of course not,' said Celia.

Barty was lunching with one of the top women agents that day, had arranged for Celia to come too.

'Unless you're tired?'

'Of course I'm not tired,' said Celia.

'She's called Ann Friedman. I thought we'd go to the Mamiton. It's one of the most "in" places at the moment. We're meeting her at twelve-thirty.'

'That's extremely early.'

'I know. Lunches are earlier here. She'll have been there since twelve, knocking back the Martinis, I'd put money on it.'

Lunch was a great success; the legendary Ann Friedman was delighted to meet the legendary Lady Celia Lytton, and cross-questioned her about the London scene and lists, which books had crossed the Atlantic, why she thought others hadn't, was there the same fascination with religion, many of the non-fiction bestsellers in America had had a religious theme. 'Interesting you should ask that,' said Celia, 'I wanted to do a book with Billy Graham.'

'Very good idea. What happened?'

'He wouldn't.'

'You mean you wouldn't pay him enough.'

'Possibly.'

Ann Friedman also expressed great envy of the greater sexual liberality of literary England. 'We have to be so careful here. We're still living practically fifty years ago. I'll give you an example. Old Mrs Doubleday, you know, lives down in Hawaii and reads every book Doubleday publishes. And they listen to her comments. This is a firm worth two hundred million dollars. What do you think of that?'

'Not a great deal,' said Celia.

They parted on the friendliest terms and with an invitation for Miss Friedman to visit Lady Celia should she come to London.

Celia was less charmed by Marcus Forrest, Barty's editorial director; she found him rather pleased with himself. But she didn't say so; she felt she had done enough criticising for one day.

'I thought we'd stay in tonight,' said Barty, after an afternoon of budgets. 'You must be tired.'

'Barty I am not tired. I was hoping you'd take me to the Stork Club.'

'The Stork Club?'

'Yes. I'm assured by Sebastian it's *the* place. He actually saw both Hemingway and John O'Hara there one night, he must have told you. I hear it's a great favourite of the John Kennedys, such a charming couple, and the Hearsts—'

'Oh there's such a good story about the Hearsts,' said Barty. 'They threw a party there for about two hundred people and Mr Billingsley, he owns it, you know—'

'I do know, of course.'

'He refused to charge them. Said that way he'd never read anything bad about the place in the Hearst papers.'

'Very sensible of him. Anyway, I want to go. We could take Izzie. Does she have a boyfriend? He could join us.'

'No, I'm afraid not,' said Barty. 'I wish she did. She's too lovely to be on her own. She's just got an apartment, she's dying to show it to you.'

'I know, we're going to have an evening out down there just before your wedding. And I am to meet these fellows she works for. Well, what about the Stork Club?'

'I – don't think I could get a table. At this short notice,' said Barty.

'Of course you can. I'll telephone, if you like. I'll say I'm a friend of Hemingway's.'

'Celia!'

'Well, I've met him. Several times. Terribly attractive.'

They went to the Stork Club that night, with Izzie. Celia had acquired a table – although not in the much-prized Cub Room. 'And I didn't even have to play my Hemingway card, just mentioned Lord Beaverbrook.'

She was entranced by the whole thing, by the famous real gold chain across the lobby, the mirrored bar, the large mirror-panelled main room. She sat at their table, drinking Martinis, and studying the crowd.

'This place was a great favourite of the Duke and Duchess of Windsor, you know,' she remarked to Charlie, who was sitting next to her.

'They arrived so late one night that Mr Billingsley had taken his shoes off, and couldn't find them in time. He had to greet them in his stockinged feet. Wallis was frightfully amused.'

'Wallis? Did you know her?'

'Oh yes,' said Celia, airily, putting yet another cigarette in the long holder she used at night, 'they were both great friends of my husband.'

Charlie was for once silent.

She insisted on dancing with him, anxious that Barty should not think she was being judgemental or hostile; he was a very good dancer and she warmed to him slightly.

'I love dancing,' she said. 'My husband, my first husband, that is, had two left feet. I found that rather irritating. Although my mother always said it was common for a man to dance well – reminiscent of a gigolo.'

She had discovered Charlie was something of a snob; it gave her great pleasure to play up to it.

She enjoyed her night out with Izzie and the boys enormously. Izzie was beside herself with pride over her apartment, the first floor of a very pretty house in Greenwich Village, just off University Place. It had one large room, which she used as a sitting room, a bedroom, an apology of a kitchen (carved out of the bedroom) and a rather splendid bathroom with a large rolltop bath and lion's feet. The street was tree-lined and pretty and was full of friendly people, Izzie said.

'It's the most marvellous place to live, every other person seems to be a writer or an artist. And there are the most wonderful bars, with such stories to tell. Right out there, for instance, on University Place, is the Cedar Tavern. People like Jackson Pollock drink there – you've heard of him?'

'Of course.'

'They don't have any money or phones at home, and the Tavern takes messages for them all day long. And they just run up a tab at the bar and pay for it with pictures. It's really pretty, we could have a drink there, if you like.'

'I certainly would.'

'The boys will be here soon, they are longing to meet you. They're rather awestruck by – well, by your title. You mustn't mind.'

'Not as much as their not being awestruck,' said Celia, smiling at her.

The boys were indeed awestruck; they half bowed over Celia's hand as Izzie introduced them to her, and were both very quiet for the first ten minutes.

'Izzie tells me you are extremely clever,' said Celia graciously.

'Well, we try, your – your Ladyship.'

'Do please just call me Celia.'

Izzie stared at her; she must really like them.

'And how's Izzie doing?'

'Oh extremely well. She has great talent. We're most terribly proud of her.'

'And so am I. Well, shall we go?'

'I told Celia we'd take her to the Cedar Tavern.'

'Izzie you can't take Lady – your – er – Celia to a place like that.'

'Why on earth not?' said Celia.

'There's some real rough types go in there. And it's terribly noisy.'

'I am not averse to rough types. And neither do I mind noise. I want to see it.'

She sat in the Tavern in one of the wooden pew-like seats, drinking bourbon, admiring the Tiffany lights and the wooden panelling, and the Jackson Pollocks hanging behind the bar just as Izzie had said.

'Robert Lytton introduced me to bourbon,' she said to Izzie. 'I've always liked it although I wouldn't drink it in England. Can I tempt you, gentlemen, or are you staying with beer?'

'This really is turning out to be some evening,' said Mike Parker.

'I thought they were charming,' Celia said to Izzie at the end of the evening, as the boys went off to find her a cab, 'and clearly very talented. Is Barty using them?'

'A bit, yes. I absolutely love them,' said Izzie. 'They've been so good to me.'

'You realise, of course, that Nick is in love with you?'

Izzie stared at her. 'Celia of course he isn't. Don't be ridiculous. And anyway, they're in love with each other.'

'You mean they're homosexuals? I don't think so.'

'No of course I don't. They couldn't be less so. I just mean they're completely interdependent. No room for anyone else. And the agency of course. Honestly. Now – tell me, Celia, what do you think of Charlie?'

'Oh – he seems perfectly pleasant. I haven't formed much of a judgement yet. Do you like him?'

'Very much. He's sweet. And Jenna adores him, which is important, isn't it? I don't know how I would have coped with a new mother at her age. But maybe a father is different.'

'Maybe. Anyway – this time tomorrow, they'll be married. I understand they're going away for a few days.'

'Yes, up to the Catskills. I think Charlie would have liked to stay at South Lodge, but Barty's awfully funny about it. About him going there. She doesn't seem to mind the rest of us.'

'Well, we're family,' said Celia soothingly. 'Ah now, here are the boys with a cab. It has been so nice to meet you both,' she said, 'and thank you for a wonderful evening. That last bar we went to was splendid.'

The last bar had been the slightly infamous White Horse Tavern on Hudson Street, where they told her she might see Jack Kerouac or Brendan

Behan; she was disappointed in that, but had a wonderful time nonetheless, talking to anyone who would listen, smoking cigarette after cigarette, drinking glass after glass of bourbon. Before that they had gone to Chumleys and she had sat beneath the rows of book covers and signed photographs of Hemingway and O'Neill and Scott and Zelda and before that . . . Izzie couldn't really remember before that.

'She'll be half dead in the morning,' whispered Mike to Izzie.

She was not of course, she was up early, drinking coffee and sipping grapefruit juice when Cathy came into the kitchen.

'Good morning Catherine.'

'Good morning,' said Cathy, slightly warily. She was rather in awe of Celia.

'Well, this is a great day. I understand your grandmother cannot attend.'

'No. No, she wouldn't come.'

'I thought she was ill.'

'No, she's not ill. She just doesn't like—' she stopped.

'Doesn't like what?'

'Oh – big parties,' said Cathy quickly. 'She's a little shy.'

'Oh really? I always think shyness is a form of arrogance. To think that everyone should be taking any notice of you. Do you see much of your grandmother?'

'No. That is – well, sometimes. I used to, anyway.'

'I'd have thought she'd have wanted to keep in touch with you. Have you to stay and so on. I love having my grandchildren to stay.'

'She doesn't have room,' said Cathy after a moment. 'That's the main thing.'

'Is that so? But—' she stopped. It wasn't fair to quiz the child. Puzzling, though; Barty had told her that Sally Norton was very well off, had paid Cathy's school fees.

'Well, I expect you'll go and see her afterwards, show her the pictures and so on.'

Cathy smiled at her, a sickly-sweet smile. Like her father's, thought Celia, exactly the same.

'Yes, I expect so.'

'And where does she live, your grandmother?'

'Oh – in Brooklyn.'

'Does she have a house there?'

'No, she – Oh, hi, Daddy.' She seemed relieved to see him; Charlie kissed her, smiled briefly at Celia.

'Well, we have a lovely day for our wedding. How was your evening, Celia?'

'Quite wonderful. We went to a series of bars, and ate dinner at a restaurant so crowded I couldn't imagine how they got the tables in there in the first place, never mind all the diners.'

'It's fun down there. I admire your energy. You were very late home.'

'Oh I have a great deal of energy,' said Celia. 'I inherited it from my mother. She always said being tired was a form of self-indulgence. She went hunting three times a week, well into her eighties. And ran a school during the war.'

'Really? How fascinating. Now I have to go out and get some more coffee, Maria has been so busy with the lunch menu she forgot the basics. Cathy, you want to come with me, honey?'

'Yes please,' said Cathy.

Celia returned to the *New York Times*; after about five minutes the kitchen door opened and Barty came in. She was very pale and looked upset.

'Is Charlie here?'

'No, he's gone out to get some coffee. Apparently your maid forgot it.'

'No she didn't. We have at least three packets in the cupboard. How odd. Oh well . . .'

'Can I make you some?'

'Yes, thank you.'

'Are you all right? You look rather – strained.'

'Celia I—'

'Yes?'

She appeared to be about to embark on a serious conversation. Celia waited, filling the kettle, ladling coffee into a jug.

Barty looked at her, fiddled with her hair, sat down, stared at her hands. Then she said, 'Celia, I just – well, I just went up to—'

'My darling.' It was Charlie, returned with a packet of coffee. 'You're not supposed to let me see you this morning. Now go on back to bed at once, Cathy will bring you some breakfast on a tray, won't you, darling? What time is your hairdresser coming?'

'Oh – at ten,' said Barty. She still sounded odd: strained and odd.

'Well then, you can have another hour's beauty sleep. Not that you need it. Run along. I can't have a weary bride.'

She walked out dutifully, smiling at him rather wanly. Celia watched her go.

'I'll take her breakfast in,' she said to Cathy.

'No, no, we're both doing it, aren't we Jenna?'

Jenna had appeared in the kitchen now, her red-gold hair tousled, her face still sleepy.

'Yes, it was the plan and then I'll help Mother get ready. That's all right, isn't it, Charlie?' She looked anxious.

'Of course. We can't have our plans disrupted.' He looked at Celia and for the first time he wasn't smiling, his guard was down. 'The girls have been planning today for weeks, Celia, I know you'll understand.'

She decided not to argue.

The ceremony at City Hall was simple and sweet; Barty, composed and happy, looked beautiful in a cream wool suit and hat, carrying a posy of blood-red sweetheart roses. Charlie wore a new dark-grey suit and looked alarmingly handsome; the girls, also in cream, carrying matching posies, watched and listened intently, smiling, holding hands.

When the Justice of the Peace said, 'I now declare you man and wife,' and Charlie bent to kiss Barty, Cathy burst into tears.

Silly child, thought Celia irritably, silly, selfish child, intruding into Barty's big moment.

The lunch at the house was easy and happy; Robert Lytton and Felicity and John Brewer had been asked to join them, and, although Celia was clearly not over-fond of Felicity, their company was, in fact, a welcome and warming addition to the party.

A great deal of champagne was drunk, and Charlie had arranged for a pianist to attend, a surprise for Barty, who was visibly touched and delighted. The large white grand piano – which Celia privately considered rather vulgar – was in the drawing room, but could be clearly heard at exactly the right pitch in the dining room. He played entirely classical music; 'I was afraid if he played anything modern, or even from the Thirties or Forties it would bring back sad memories,' Charlie said to Felicity Brewer.

Robert made a very charming speech, saying what a delight it was to have Charlie and Cathy in the family. Celia rose to her feet at this point, not to be upstaged by another Lytton, and said how honoured she was to have been invited as the sole representative of the English branch of the family, and how she knew Oliver would have been delighted to see Barty so happy. Jamie also made a speech, saying how honoured he was to have been chosen as Charlie's supporter, and how happy he was that Barty and Charlie wanted him to remain part of their family.

He did not mention Laurence by name; he did not have to. Everyone was aware of his presence. Especially Barty.

While she was changing, Celia tapped on the door.

'You looked so lovely, and so very happy. Congratulations, Barty, my darling. I was very proud of you.'

'Thank you. And thank you so much for the glorious bronze figure. Did you get her in New York?'

'No, in London. Adele helped me find her. She's pure Deco, absolutely Adele's thing. Are you – all right?'

She would never have asked so direct a question usually; but she had been so struck by Barty's distress that morning that she wanted to give her a chance to talk before saying goodbye.

'Oh – yes,' said Barty, clearly aware of exactly why she was asking the question, while not acknowledging it. 'Yes, of course. A bit tired, perhaps, but – Celia, could you just help me with these buttons – so silly to choose a back fastening.'

And that was that.

If only, if only she hadn't gone up to Charlie's study, as it already was called, that morning; if only she hadn't found that chequebook, pushed to the back of a drawer, as she looked for the name and telephone number of the limousine company who were to drive them down to City Hall that day. The chequebook on their new joint account, already half used, several of the stubs blank, several filled in with the names of people and firms she had never heard of. Of course it was all perfectly all right, they must be simply – well, suppliers for the wedding perhaps, and for the honeymoon bookings and things for the girls. It was nothing to worry about. She would have asked him about it any other day. It was simply that she couldn't then.

But it did worry her. All day it worried her. And when she finally did ask him, it led to the first real row they had ever had; and certainly the first row of their married life.

CHAPTER 18

Who was that screaming? God, it was her. How awful, how disgraceful, how could she – oh God, here it came again. One pain so quickly after another. She couldn't bear this much longer.

'Now, Mrs Brown, come along. With the next pain, I want you to bear down – try to relax just now – that's right –'

Relax, thought Elspeth, relax? How could anyone relax with this agony going on, tearing your body apart? She had been told that if she did her breathing exercises – much extolled in the clinic – she would remain in control, that the pain wouldn't ever become unbearable, that it would even be quite pleasurable. Pleasurable! This horror, this overwhelming pain, and the woman screaming her head off in the next cubicle wasn't helping . . .

'Right – Now! Bear down. Now! Come along, Mrs Brown, you'll have to do better than that, your bairn will never see the light of day at this rate. Now, a big deep breath of the gas and air, and – Mrs Brown, pull yourself together, this isn't helping anyone, and certainly not your baby –'

And then suddenly in the middle of the pain and the misery and the longing for Keir, for her mother, who had promised to be there, only it had all happened too soon, the baby had decided to arrive early, longing for anyone she knew, anyone other than this fierce, dour woman, suddenly it was all different and she knew what she was doing, and she pushed hard, right through the pain, that seemed to burst into splinters and again and then again and—

'There. A lovely little girl. Oh, she's beautiful, Mrs Brown, quite beautiful, now let me just – there. Oh, her daddy will be proud of her. Such lovely blue eyes. There, there you are.'

Her daddy wouldn't be absolutely proud of her, thought Elspeth, taking the small indignant bundle into her arms, gazing at the furious red face, the screwed-up eyes, the frantically waving frondy fingers. He'd wanted a son, had known the baby was a son – but who cared, she was lovely, perfect.

'I think we should call her Cecilia,' she said to Keir. He was too relieved – after her thirty-six-hour ordeal – and too happy to disagree. Certainly too relieved and happy to wish the baby was a boy.

'Girls are much more fun,' was all he said, taking the baby in his arms, kissing her small now-tranquil face, 'look at your grandmother.' Even in her hour of happiness, Elspeth felt more than mildly irritated that he hadn't said, 'Look at you.'

Even Venetia could do nothing with Adele. Noni was in despair; Lucas was worried, little Clio patently distressed. Adele was tearful, lethargic, suffered terribly from insomnia. The doctor had prescribed sleeping pills, but she refused to take them, said they made her feel muddled and more depressed. 'I just don't understand why he won't come home,' she said, 'when I've explained that Lucas is leaving, going to university. What other reason can there be?'

Venetia felt there very likely was some other reason, but nevertheless appealed to Geordie for help.

'I'm sorry, Venetia. There's nothing I can do. Lucas'll still be there a lot of the time. All the old problems would start again, I'm sure of that. I honestly don't think there's any point—'

'But Geordie, couldn't you just for now – try – it would mean so much to her.'

'I don't think you understand,' he said, 'this is a one-way street: it was her choice that I left. She refused to consider any other solution. Nobody seems to understand how hurt I was by that. Nobody.'

'Of course I do. But—'

'Look,' he said finally, 'I've got one suggestion. Adele could come here for a few weeks. With Clio. Leave Lucas in the house. He's old enough. That might work.'

But Adele refused to consider it. 'I can't do that. Disrupting Clio's life, disrupting mine for that matter. What about Nanny? And of course I can't leave Lucas on his own, he's doing his exams. And what about my studio, my work?'

'But Dell, you're not doing any work,' said Venetia patiently.

'I am. Of course I am. No, it's no good, that's a very hostile suggestion of Geordie's if you ask me. Very hurtful for Lucas. Very destructive all round. I won't do it. Sorry.'

Venetia reported back to Geordie; he sighed.

'I didn't think she'd agree,' he said, 'you know sometimes, Venetia, I think it's that boy she's in love with, not me.'

The strain on Noni was considerable; she felt responsible, while being quite unable to do anything constructive. She tried talking to Lucas about it, but apart from saying he was quite happy to be left at home, and telling his mother so too, he couldn't really help very much. Adele refused to talk to him, saying he mustn't be worried, especially when he had his exams to do.

'It's not because of me Geordie won't come home,' he said to Noni, 'not any more. It's because he doesn't want to, he likes his freedom. He knew she'd never agree to going there. It was just a clever ploy of his. He's a selfish pig, Noni, and she's better off without him.'

Noni didn't bother to argue with him; in any case, she was beginning to feel he was right. She felt a deep unease at Geordie's apparent lack of real concern for her mother's distress.

She spent hours listening to Adele, comforting her, trying to advise her, occasionally attempting to brace her up; without the excitement and glamour of her new career, she would, as she often said, have gone quite mad herself.

And the excitement and glamour were considerable; she adored it.

She was astonished how swiftly she had caught on as the new face of the Fifties, as an article in the *Tatler* had christened her. Every photographer was after her, every magazine and advertising agency; her agency, Ann Knight, chosen with the help of Laura Proctor-Reid, were advising her most shrewdly, cherry-picking jobs, turning down much she was offered.

'The big money, of course, is in advertising,' said Ann Knight, a tough, shrewd woman who looked not unlike a model herself, with her dramatically dark hair drawn back into a tight chignon, her perfectly tailored suits, her long elegant legs, her brilliantly red nails. 'But we have to choose those jobs with great care. The really big campaigns, a cosmetic contract, absolutely fine, but we mustn't over-expose you. I don't want to see your face on hosiery advertisements for instance—'

'Or lingerie,' said Noni hopefully, who had been horrified by an offer of several thousand pounds which had come in that very morning for an exclusive contract with Maidenform bras.

'Well obviously not,' said Ann Knight, 'we leave that work to the lingerie models.' She spoke as if such creatures were only a little better than prostitutes. 'No, we want the glossies, not the weeklies. *Woman's Own* telephoned me this morning asking for you for a beauty shot, I said it was very unlikely, but I would get back to them after I had talked to you. We don't want to get you a reputation for arrogance. And then some really good advertising campaigns, as I said, and I am hoping we can get you over to America as well.'

'America!'

'Yes. Irving Penn has expressed an interest in you, and Roland Klein has wired me, asking to see some of your pictures.'

'Goodness how exciting,' said Noni.

She learned fast; how to do her make-up, changing her look from day to night, how to put on false eyelashes, style her hair. She built up a wardrobe of underwear, shoes, stockings, belts, jewellery, which she carried round everywhere with her in a huge leather bag. This was for the advertising work, rather than the editorial; a fashion editor would accessorize any photograph down to the last button, but even then it was not unknown for a pair of shoes not to turn up from the manufacturer, for a belt to be too big – or too small.

She learned to go on standing in the same pose until her back ached, her legs throbbed, while she got cramp in one of her feet; she learned not to complain when she was tired, cold, hot, knowing that the money she was paid was as much for her ability to perform in the way a photographer asked as for her looks. She learned which photographers were easy to work with, which were unreasonable, which bad-tempered, and how to deal with each of them. She learned how to work with other models, how not to upstage the stars, how to cope with jealousy from the older ones, threatened by her youth. Above all she learned how to develop and project her own style, so that whatever she was asked to wear and do, she remained in some indefinable way herself, instantly recognisable but never predictable.

By April she was an acknowledged star; it was not only her rather unusual beauty, her very dark eyes, her white skin, her lovely graceful body, it was her versatility. She could look as elegant and thoroughbred as Barbara Goalen and Suzy Parker, in ball gowns and couture suits and dresses, but, when required, she could look more youthfully chic in Chanel style, in her pastel tweed suits, complete with camellia, and long loops of pearls; or even like the teenager she was. Indeed, a shot in the April edition of *Vogue*, of her hanging half out of a tree in turned-up blue jeans and one of the huge coarse-knit sloppy-joe sweaters which were the rage that spring, her smile wide and infectious, her hair caught up in a loose ponytail, was bought from *Vogue* and used as the main picture in *The Times* to picture an article on the new freedom of the young. It named her personally: 'Oenone Lieberman, just nineteen years old and a shooting star in the fashion world', and went on to say that she was also to be frequently seen in one or other of the hot nightclubs of the capital.

She had not expected to enjoy the social scene; she and Izzie had in common a dislike of parties and dances, and of what they called chitterchat, and she had flatly refused to do the season and be presented at Court like her Warwick cousins; now she discovered, as her fame grew and with it her popularity, that what she had disliked about dances in particular, was the sense of failure, a lack of conquests, a dread of the familiar pattern of disappearing partners, of withdrawing to the cloakroom, with the other wallflowers, to apply lipstick and perfume for the tenth time in an evening and pretend they were having a wonderful time. Elspeth had told her a dreadful story of a girl in her year whose mother had forced her into doing the season, and shipped her off night after night to dances, often in the country, where she knew no one and where she considered herself successful if she was offered one dance.

But somehow it was different now for Noni: when charming and rich young men invited her to the Mirabelle, with its mid-restaurant fountain and great bank of flowers, or to dine and dance at Quaglino's (known as Quags) or the Café de Paris, with its evening-dress-only rule, and its brilliant cabarets. She saw Noël Coward there one especially dizzy night, and Jack Buchanan, and danced into the small hours herself. Princess Margaret, so incredibly beautiful, was often there with her friends, the exuberant, glamorous Margaret Set, smoking endlessly through her long cigarette holder.

Sometimes, if it hadn't been for the anxiety she felt about her mother, Noni would have thought life was too good to be true.

Being a mother was not too good to be true, Elspeth thought; she was astonished by how exhausted she felt. The week in hospital had been fine, fun even. She had really enjoyed it, the sense of achievement, the way her milk had flowed, the friendship with the other mothers, the comparisons with all the other babies, knowing with total satisfaction that Cecilia was more beautiful than any of them, the sharing of the physical problems and discomfort, the lewd conversations after supper, when the husbands had been sent home.

Elspeth was shocked that these women, apparently so dominated by their husbands, so dependent on them, could also speak about them with such derision, laughing about their sexual demands. But they did; and moreover they were generally completely in control of their households, in control of arrangements, of routine, of budgeting. It seemed the husbands handed over their wage packets and the women then doled out rations for drink, the dogs, and the working-men's clubs they all belonged to.

Elspeth resolved to talk to Keir about this when she got home; she hated the way it was the reverse in their household, her housekeeping money handed over by Keir each week. God knows how she would have managed if she had not had her own money, which of course Keir knew nothing of. It made her feel wretched, beholden to him, without any kind of status of her own.

She went home feeling confident and quite cheerful, with at least a purpose now to her days; within a week she was in absolute despair. The milk, which had flowed so obligingly in hospital, dried up like a spent spring, and Cecilia, instead of sleeping sweetly for three or four hours at a stretch, wailed miserably after two and through much of the night.

Elspeth was sore still, she had had to have several stitches which hadn't quite healed; it hadn't mattered in hospital where the nurses helped her with warm salt baths and comforting words, but now it seemed rather more important and worrying, and her nipples were cracked and sore where the baby sucked endlessly. The pain as her hard little gums took the breast was so intense that Elspeth had to take painkillers before each feed; she would

233

sit there, with her teeth clenched and tears of despair blurring her view of the small dark head.

Keir took a week off to look after them both, but actually did very little, apart from cooking unnecessarily elaborate meals and complaining about the crying, which disturbed his sleep and his work.

She was relieved when he went back to work, but then found herself still in her nightdress when he came home, a pile of nappies waiting to be washed, and a supper unprepared. After three weeks, she began to think she would go mad, frightened by the violence of her misery and by her feelings towards the crying baby. When Cecilia slept she would look down at her, overwhelmed with love, but the moment the dreadful demanding noise began again, frantic anxiety would arise, like bile in her throat. More than once she picked Cecilia out of her cot and shook her in her despair and then stopped, horrified at the look of shock on the small crumpled face, and rocked her for hours, crying herself, and telling her how sorry she was.

It was only the arrival of Venetia, worried by a phone call, that saved both of them.

'Darling, what she needs is a bottle. I'm going out to buy one now and lots of lovely Cow and Gate, and then I'll feed her while you have a bath, and wash your hair, you look quite frightful.'

'Well, thank you for that,' said Elspeth, but she was too relieved to properly protest; an hour later, while Cecilia slept peacefully for the first time in weeks, and she was dozing on her bed, she heard her mother talking to Keir.

'I really think I should take her home for a bit, she's awfully down and absolutely exhausted, and you obviously can't work here. She can come back in a week or two, when she's properly recovered, it's impossible for her at the moment.'

Elspeth waited for him to fly into a temper and say that he wouldn't allow any such thing; then thought she must be still asleep and dreaming when he said yes, perhaps that might be a good idea.

'Here you are, my dearest. Anniversary present.'

'Anniversary? I don't know what you mean, it's not—'

'And I thought you were a romantic. It's three months since we were married. A whole season. A happy, happy season. For me anyway. And I do so hope for you.'

'Of course. Of course it has been. And – thank you. For my present.'

'You don't look very excited. Open it, go on, I've been longing for you to come home all day. And I've booked us a table at the Four Seasons this evening. You know why, of course.'

'No—'

'Barty! It's where you said you'd marry me. How could you forget that?'

234

'I haven't forgotten,' she said, 'of course. It's – it's a lovely idea.'

'Go on – open your present.'

She tried to be generous about it; not to check the cost mentally as she undid it, undid the unmistakable white ribbon round the unmistakable blue Tiffany box. To express delight as well as surprise at the contents (comparatively modest, a gold bracelet with a swinging heart set with a diamond, but still – several hundred dollars), to smile, to kiss him, to thank him as effusively as she could.

'Here, let me put it on. It suits you. Suits your little wrist. If you don't like it you can change it—'

'Charlie, I love it. Really. Thank you.'

'Good.' He kissed her. 'It's me who should be thanking you, really. For making me so happy.'

She was silent.

'Now then. You go and have your bath and change.'

'Where are the girls?'

'Oh – at the movies. They'll be back any minute.'

'The movies! But Charlie—'

'What?' His expression was innocent, his smile easy. 'It is the holidays.'

'I know but – Jenna has a piano exam tomorrow.'

'Yes, and she was practising half the morning. Cathy, here you are. How was the movie?'

'Great.'

Cathy was looking rather grown up, Barty thought, something was different.

'Cathy have you changed your hair?'

'Yes, do you like it?'

'Yes it's – very nice.'

'I love it. I had it done today. Early birthday present from Daddy.' Another present.

'Where – where did you have it done?'

'Kenneth.'

Kenneth! Kenneth, one of Manhattan's top hairdressers. He did Jackie Kennedy's hair and all the other society ladies, what was Charlie doing taking a little girl there?

'It's – it's very grown-up looking. You look –' she struggled to be generous, '– you look like Grace Kelly.'

'You think so? Oh thanks Barty. That's exactly what Kenneth said.'

She did too, with her ice-blonde hair, cut just above the shoulders, the front shorter than the back, waving softly back from her face. She was such a pretty girl, but – well, she was only twelve. Too young to have hair like a film star.

'You wait till you see Jenna's.'

'Jenna's? Jenna's had her hair cut?'

'She sure has. It's gorgeous. Jen! Your mom's home, come and show her your hair.'

Jenna came in slowly, her eyes apprehensive on her mother's face. Her hair, her glorious red-gold hair, Laurence's hair, which had been hanging past her shoulders that morning was cropped short, short as a boy's, with a gamine fringe, high on her forehead. Barty sat down abruptly; she felt quite sick.

'Jenna, what on earth have you done?'

'Don't you like it?'

'Like it? Of course I don't like it. I hate it. And I hate that you've had it done without asking me, I—' she felt tears absurdly in her eyes.

'Mother!' There was a touch of hostility in Jenna's voice, 'I'm twelve now. I'm not a baby. I don't have to get your permission to get a haircut, for God's sake —'

That was not Jenna talking; it was Cathy. Jenna might rant and rave and fall off horses and out of trees, she might take boats out against orders, she might tell Barty she hated her and wished she was dead, but she didn't look at her in that wall-eyed way and tell her she didn't need permission to get a haircut.

Only – maybe she did. Maybe she did now. She was twelve, it was true, and twelve these days was like fourteen, fifteen when Barty had been a child. Just the same . . .

'You shouldn't have let her do that,' she said to Charlie, 'not without asking me.'

'Asking you! I have to ask you if I can take your daughter to the hairdresser? Barty, you're always so busy. I wouldn't dream of interrupting one of your high-powered meetings to ask you about Jenna's hair. It's my job to look after the girls while you're at work and—'

'Yes, and looking after them doesn't mean taking them to an adult hairdresser and completely changing the way they look. It must have cost so much money, what's wrong with taking them to Bloomingdales, where they've always gone—'

'Barty, you're not begrudging them a few extra dollars I hope. That would be mean. What do you spend on your hair, for heaven's sake?'

'That's not the point,' she said and discovered she was shaking, shaking with rage. 'The point is—'

'The point is they're not children any more. They're growing up. They're interested in their appearance and so they should be. The other point is that you were not here, you were working as always, and so I took them to have their hair cut. It's only been cut for God's sake—'

'Yes, and it will grow again.' Jenna was upset now by her mother's distress, went over to her and put her arm round her. 'I thought you'd like it. It's meant to look like Audrey Hepburn's—'

'Jenna, you're a little girl. I don't want you looking like a film star—'

Charlie met her eyes over Jenna's head.

'Darling, if you want to supervise everything Jenna does, you should stay home and look after her. I'm just doing my best in your absence.'

This was so untrue, Barty couldn't even be bothered to argue with him. She stood up, set the Tiffany box aside.

'I'm sorry, Charlie, I don't feel like going out tonight. I have a terrible headache.'

'Oh darling, I'm so sorry. So very sorry. Can I get you anything, some painkillers, a cup of good old-fashioned English tea—'

'No, thank you, nothing. I'll just go and lie down and try and get to sleep.'

'It seems such a shame, to waste the table. You don't think you'll feel better later—'

'No, I don't. Why don't you take the girls instead as you're so keen for them to grow up?'

She hadn't expected him to respond as he did. But he smiled at her, a smile of pure triumph, and then said, 'Hey, that's not such a bad idea. How'd you like that, girls, show off your new hairstyles at the Four Seasons tonight?'

'Oh wow,' they said in unison.

This was how he did it, how he was coping – if that was the right word – with the money. With being permanently placed in a subservient position, of having to ask, to be permanently grateful . . . not that he did a lot of asking. He just took. Whatever he wanted, whenever he wanted it. New suits, a new car, something for the house, clothes for Cathy . . . He always presented it as being for Barty, of course. 'Honey, I thought you'd be thrilled, you said you were so tired of the Studebaker, you wanted something more exciting . . . darling you told me I should get myself smartened up . . . sweetheart, Cathy needed new clothes for the school skiing trip, Jenna is so perfectly kitted out, I knew you wouldn't want her to feel like the poor relation.'

A particularly clever one that: who could begrudge a child new clothes when her stepsister had wardrobes packed with them?

The first row over money had been dreadful, had absorbed two days of their honeymoon. She had confronted him with the used book of cheques, had asked him, reasonably, she thought, why it had been necessary to write so many, without recourse to her. He had been at first defensive, saying he had not expected to be cross-questioned over it, that she had suggested they should have a joint account, that he would financially run the household, and surely she didn't expect him to come to her with every bill that came in, the whole idea was to spare her such detail.

Of course not, she had said, but so many, and so quickly; and then the stubs that were blank, what were they for, and for what amounts? She would need to know when she was checking the account.

He lost his temper then, raged at her, as she could never have believed possible, asking her if she was accusing him of stealing her money, saying that he could not live with her on that basis, having to account for every dollar he spent. It was outrageous, ugly, he felt diminished, insulted . . .

Remorseful at first, genuinely shocked by the violence of his reaction, she apologised; and then in the aftermath of the row, when he was still cool, still morose, she thought again about it, thought how unfair of him to react in that way, that it was unreasonable, that anyone would have expected to account for money they were spending. She thought of Celia, warning her to sort things out financially, wondered what she could do now to inject some order into the whole thing. Perhaps she should make Charlie an allowance, had suggested that, even. It had been worse; another row followed, more accusations of meanness, a lack of generosity not only materially, but of spirit.

'I simply cannot believe this of you,' he said finally, before withdrawing from her again. 'I thought this was what you reassured me would never happen, that your money was unimportant to you . . .'

She would have remained angry herself, but much later in the day he came to her, had clearly been weeping, begged her forgiveness, said he had to explain.

He had had terrible debts, he said; he had been struggling with them for some time.

'But why didn't you simply tell me? I would have done anything to help you, paid them off, made you a loan, whatever you wanted. You know I would. The only thing that's upset me is – well I felt you were deceiving me.'

'I know, I know, I can see that now. But given our financial situation, mine and yours, think about how difficult that would have been for me. Here I was in one breath telling you I loved you, that I wanted to marry you, and in the next that I needed some money – quite a lot of money – desperately. I am so, so sorry, my darling. Please forgive me.'

As always he had expressed things exactly as she would have wished, showing an almost uncanny understanding of her feelings. Remorse flooded her; she took him in her arms, apologised, asked him to forgive her, to promise never to keep anything from her again. He promised.

The cheques when they were presented were large, several thousand dollars; he offered to pay her back 'slowly', she told him not to be absurd, that she was happy to be able to do this for him. After that any attempt to make a formal arrangement, a separation of their finances, seemed clumsy and ugly.

He had a chequebook on the joint account; and although there were no more of his own debts, he used it mercilessly.

But he had never quite forgiven her; and one of the ways he got at her was through the children: spoiling them, taking them to places she disapproved of, sophisticated restaurants and adult movies, encouraging them to look older than they were so they could deceive the box-office attendant, letting them off their homework, their piano practice, buying them jewellery and clothes which were too old for them, buying their affection.

It was horrible. She had worked so hard on Jenna, never letting her think she could coast through life on money, telling her that everything had to be earned. The work of the past eight, ten years was being unravelled before her eyes.

What upset her most was that Jenna fell for it; Barty knew it was unreasonable to expect her to say no, Charlie, I won't come to the movies, I have to do my homework, but a tiny part of her hoped that she would. And she was losing Jenna; she could feel her slipping away, week by week.

'It's so much more fun now, with Charlie,' Jenna said one day, slipping her arm through her mother's as they walked in Central Park, alone for once. 'It used to be really boring after school, on my own with Maria, Charlie works so hard at taking care of us, giving us a good time.'

What could she say to that?

And this was another thing; something she hadn't thought of, she and Jenna were never alone together any more. They had been so close, always, despite the fights, had talked about everything from Jenna's lessons to Barty's best-seller lists, from Jenna's ambitions to be a mountaineer or bareback rider to Barty's to take over Doubleday. They had planned vacations together – not that there had been many, Barty had to admit – worked out what they were going to do about Christmas – always tricky for small family units – and savoured dozens of small pleasures like eating Chinese takeaways out of boxes in the den, giggling over TV comedy shows, cycling round Central Park. And Barty had talked to her, more and more as she grew up, about her father, knowing how important it was that she should get a strong sense of what he had been like. She tried to be honest, to tell Jenna that as well as being loving and generous and clever and talented, he could also be difficult, bad-tempered and hugely possessive.

'No one is perfect: that's what love is,' she had said to her one night, as they cuddled in the den, listening to Beethoven's Fifth (she had decided it was time Jenna was introduced to classical music), 'it's still loving people in spite of knowing the bad things. Never forget it, Jenna, ever.'

Well, Charlie certainly wasn't perfect; but whatever love she had felt for him was waning fast.

They were going to Southampton for Easter; there was no possible reason not to. She had waited for a long time before suggesting it, until the girls did in fact; but as Easter drew nearer, she realised she was dreading it.

It was the first time since they had married, the first time she had to properly share it with him; she even tried the diversionary tactic of proposing a skiing trip. But the girls had already done that, and wanted to go to South Lodge.

'It will be perfect,' Jenna said plaintively, 'getting warmer, lovely for riding, and such fun to be there as a proper family.'

As they drove out, Barty felt increasingly wretched; and she knew why. The girls were chattering and giggling in the back, singing Frank Sinatra songs, Charlie was alternately joining in and talking to her about the arrangements. Could they do an Easter Egg hunt, could he maybe have some riding lessons, what about a party, invite the neighbours, to celebrate their marriage.

Barty's stomach rolled into a tighter and tighter knot; she felt sick, she had to stop several times to go to the lavatory, she thought at times she would scream, especially at the suggestion of the party. She had even postponed telling the Mills about her marriage until a month ago, knowing that they, too, would feel a sense of awkwardness at the arrival of a new master in Laurence Elliott's house: the house he had allowed no one into after Barty had left him.

They arrived at tea time; Mr Mills was out in the drive waiting for them.

'Congratulations Sir,' he said, shaking Charlie's hand, 'and to you Miss Miller.'

She loved him for that; for avoiding the use of her new married name.

She was having tea with the girls when Charlie came down: white-faced with rage in a way she had only seen him once before.

'Can I speak with you?' he said.

'Of course.' She put her cup down; felt her stomach heave. She knew what it was about.

'Not in here.'

She followed him out silently; the girls looked at one another, and clearly by mutual consent went outside and down across the long lawn to the shore.

He was in the drawing room, his eyes almost black with rage.

'Did you know the Mills had put us in the guest suite?'

'Of course.'

'Did you ask them to do that?'

'Yes I did.'

'Barty —' there was a long silence; then, '— Barty you are married to me now. Before, I could understand it – your phobia about sharing this place with me.'

'It is not a phobia,' she said steadily.

'It is a phobia. You can hardly bear to have me in the area, let alone in the house. Your precious house, that Laurence built for you—'

'He did not build it for me.'

'Well, bequeathed to you. Where you were so – so happy together.' His tone was very harsh. 'You and he.'

'Yes. Yes, that's right.'

'His house, his staff – his bedroom.'

'Yes.'

'But not any more, Barty. He's not here. You are married to me and I want to sleep with you in that room. How do you think it makes me feel in front of Mr and Mrs Mills—'

'I don't care how it makes you feel in front of Mr and Mrs Mills. I don't care how it makes you feel at all. I can't and I won't sleep with you in that room. I'm sorry. Now if it's not acceptable to you, you can leave, but I have nothing more to say about it. I'm going for a walk. If you do decide to stay, dinner will be at eight.'

He did stay: of course. He was waiting for her when she got back, with some flowers which he had driven into Southampton to buy, expressing huge remorse, saying all the usual things, the careful, graceful things to which she could not possibly object: that he had felt so hurt, so diminished, it had come out as rage, as tactlessness, that of course he understood, he would have felt the same if it had been Meg's house, Meg's room, it was just his own foolish pride. And jealousy because he loved her so much.

She listened, accepted the flowers, kissed him, said she was glad he understood so well, apologised for any tactlessness on her side; they ate dinner, slept in the guest suite, made love, and Easter passed, if not entirely happily, then tolerably well.

But only tolerably. And this time she felt no remorse.

'Mother, what is this book?'

'What book is that Giles?'

'This book that you've put in the autumn schedule. *Black and White*, I think you've called it.'

'That's a working title. Far too crude, of course.'

'I don't recall our discussing it.'

'You don't? How odd, I'm sure I do. Ask Jay, he knows about it.'

'I have. He says it's very much your baby, but he's happy about it, if I am.'

'And –?'

'Well I'm not very happy. Nor am I unhappy. How could I be, when I don't know anything about it?'

'Oh Giles. I'm sorry. Let me tell you about it. It's a very exciting project. It was Keir's idea—'

'Keir's? Since when did Keir have anything to do with this company?'

'Since he came up with the idea for this book. He's an extremely clever young man, Giles. I'm very impressed with him. I was talking to him one day, and he suggested we commission this book. It's about a young black man, recently arrived in this country, and a white girl, who fall in love and decide to marry.'

'A love story!' His tone was derisive. 'Well, that certainly won't be the Book Society's choice. I thought we were endeavouring to keep Lyttons' literary status in the market.'

To be the Book Society's monthly choice was what every publisher wanted for every major book. It meant a minimum of 15,000 sales; it also meant considerable status. Books were chosen by a distinguished panel, headed by the high-profile reviewer Daniel George, whose brainchild the Society had been; they were bound in buckram, with leather labels on the side, and people placed them on their shelves with great pride.

'It could be. This is a love story which tackles a very important social issue. Do you know how many of these people have come to live here, and do you know the kind of problems they are up against? That we are all up against? I thought not. Let me tell you—'

After a few minutes he held his hand up.

'All right, Mother, I get the idea. Very dreadful, I'm sure. But – a book? About that?'

'Yes. It will attract huge attention. It will get a lot of publicity as well. The colour problem is genuinely a burning issue.'

'And this chap – Hugh Meyrick – who's writing it. Where did you find him?'

'He submitted something else. He's new, but with careful editing—'

'And who is doing that, Keir?'

His voice was raw with derision; she met his eyes steadily.

'Of course not. You're being ridiculous. Although he will be reading it. As will a friend of his, who is teaching in Brixton and who gave him the idea.'

'I see. Well, perhaps the whole thing had better be published privately, by you and this new team of yours.'

'Don't be absurd, Giles. You sound very childish. I think I should edit it personally.'

'You?'

'Yes. It's very much my project after all. I've met Keir's friend, a charming young man. We can work on it together with Hugh Meyrick. I do have a little experience of editing, you know. And you didn't object to my taking over the Clementine Hartley book, after Elspeth left. That will also be a great success this autumn. And will undoubtedly be the Book Society Choice. I do assure you, Giles, I know what I'm doing. I haven't yet quite lost my touch.'

Giles looked at her; and wanted to hurt her, puncture her arrogance more than he could ever remember.

He sat back in his chair, picked up a pencil from his desk, started twirling it in his fingers. It was a habit he had had ever since he had been a small boy; he knew it irritated her.

'You know, of course,' he said, 'that Clementine and Kit are going to be married?'

CHAPTER 19

'Darling, we want to talk to you.'

'Oh. You look very serious.'

'We feel very serious.'

'Oh – well, OK.'

Izzie sat up very straight at her desk, put down her pencil.

'What is it?'

'We're – we're kind of in – difficulties.'

'What sort of difficulties?'

Mike looked at Nick.

'She asks what sort of difficulties! How many sorts of difficulties are there? Only one, baby. The sort that means you can't pay the rent, or your staff, or even for lunch at the deli.'

'Oh. Oh, I see.'

'We've hung on a long time. Things looked better for a while – but well, I guess we just don't have the resources.'

'But Nick, we've been doing more work than ever this summer. Two new accounts, even Joanie has been pleased with us. I don't understand.'

'Let me explain. It's called Cash Flow. You send in a bill, client doesn't pay, you send a reminder, client still doesn't pay, you don't like to get heavy in case they walk out on you, go somewhere else for copy – do you know that Joanie, just for instance, has over a thousand dollars out on invoice to her? Hasn't given us a dime since January.'

'But that's disgusting. She shouldn't be allowed to do that. We're so small and they're so big and—'

'You try telling that to Joanie, darling.'

'Well I'd like to. In fact I think I will.'

'No Izzie, you won't. Won't help. Joanie is our biggest client—'

'And what's the use of that if she doesn't pay?'

'Well, she will eventually. She always does. Anyway, she's not the only one. There's three or four more, all hanging on to their money. And we can't sustain that. It's always been the way. The big boys can wait. We can't.'

'It's terrible.' Izzie was silent, thinking with particular loathing of Joanie Morell, Joanie with her arrogance, her rudeness, the way she had the boys grovelling after her wherever she went. Sometimes when Izzie went to one of Cleveland & Marshall's sales conferences, one of the boys would go too; Joanie would treat him like a personal servant, throwing her coat at him to hang up for her, tapping her long red nails on the table while he pulled out her chair, demanding he get her drinks, sandwiches, taxis (many of which she often forgot to pay for). It was disgusting; she shouldn't be allowed to get away with it.

She looked at them, so downcast, so hopeless, and felt a wave of love for them. They were her family now, as much as her father and Barty; she couldn't fail them.

'Look,' she said. 'I can still afford lunch at the deli. Let me treat you both. No, I insist. As long as we can go to Katz.'

The boys looked at one another.

'I guess we could just about agree to that.'

Katz Deli was at the bottom of Second Avenue, and it sold pastrami sandwiches to kill for, as Nick frequently said. Izzie adored it. She led them in that morning; they were early, even for a New York lunch, eleven-thirty. They went over to the counter, collected their pastrami on rye and their coffees, and sat near the back, gazing gloomily and silent down the great long white-tiled expanse that was Katz, as if it might offer them some sort of solution.

'So,' said Izzie finally, defeated as always by her sandwich.

'So, Lady Isabella. Mind if I have another?'

'Not at all. I'm terribly impressed you can manage it. Go ahead. You could get me a slice of apple pie though. A small one.'

'Ain't nothing small here,' said Nick.

'Anyway,' he said, finally pushing his plate away, picking up his mug of coffee. 'This looks like the end of the road. We have to say goodbye to you.'

'Oh no!' Izzie felt close to tears. 'You can't fire me.'

'We're not firing you, we're letting you go. You'll get another job, easy. With your background and the experience we've given you.'

'I'm not going,' said Izzie firmly. 'I'm just not. You can't make me, you need me to do the work, I have so much in hand and—'

'Darling we can't pay you.'

'So? I'll work for nothing. For a bit, anyway.'

They sat and stared at her for a long time. Then Mike spoke.

'Izzie,' he said, 'we always knew you had class.'

That night, Izzie took Barty out to supper. She was surprised by how willing she was; she had expected to have to wait for her to have a free evening, but Barty said she couldn't think of anything nicer, that Charlie and the girls were going to the movies.

'Don't you want to go with them?'

'Oh – no thanks. It's the latest great epic from Cecil B. de Mille.'

'What, *The Ten Commandments*? Barty, I'd adore to see that.'

'Well go with them then.'

Was she imagining it, or was Barty's voice irritable?

'Of course I don't want to go with them. I want to see you. Shall we eat down here, or in Chinatown?'

'Chinatown'd be good. There's a great new place on Bayard Street apparently. Let's meet there at seven. I'll look forward to it.'

Izzie was shocked by the sight of Barty; she hadn't seen her for weeks, she had got very thin, and – she could only describe it as lacklustre. Her tawny hair, her eyes, even her skin looked dull, seemed to have no life; nor did her manner – or her conversation.

Izzie couldn't bear it; she took Barty's hand and said, 'Whatever is it? You don't look well.'

'I'm fine,' said Barty, smiling at her quickly.

'Or happy.'

'I'm fine. Really. Please, Izzie. Let's not talk about me. I haven't seen you for ages. I want to hear all about the boys, about your job . . .'

'Well – not too good, I'm afraid.'

'Oh, no! What's happened? Tell me about it.'

Izzie did. Barty listened intently, her eyes suddenly brighter, manoeuvring her chopsticks in her long fingers with great skill.

Then she said, 'Let's get some lychees. I still feel hungry, can't think why. Now listen, Izzie. I think I might have an idea . . .'

Celia would not have believed it was possible for anything to hurt so much. All the pain of her life, all the loss and grief and fear, appeared like the over-inflated emotions of adolescence by comparison. That Kit, her beloved Kit, not only her favourite child, but her favourite human being, should do this to her, turn his back on her with such absolute finality, announce his engagement, his love for someone, someone, moreover, who she knew, then plan his wedding, and a whole new life, while barring her from it absolutely: it was unthinkably cruel. She felt as if she would choke, vomit even, the shock a physical presence in her throat and her stomach.

She went home that first day and locked herself in her room; she felt ill, she ached, every inch of her skin felt sore, she was feverish. She lay on her bed, staring up at the ceiling, trying to make sense in some way of Kit's behaviour, to find an excuse for it even, dry-eyed at first, then weeping endlessly, a great flood of grief and pain and outrage. Kit, who she had loved so very much, who had been at the heart of her life from the moment he was born, and who had wrenched himself from it. Kit had done this to her, rejected her with a harshness and a cruelty that was beyond imagination. She relived his whole life that night, the joy of his birth, of his brilliant childhood, the exceptional promise of his youth, and then his brief career as a pilot, and his hideous descent into blindness and despair. And then finally, the triumph, the discovery that there could be happiness for him, and success too. Not a day, not an hour even, had passed that she hadn't thought of him, been concerned for him, cared for him. And he had turned his back on her so absolutely, torn her out of his life with a ruthlessness which was so thorough, so final, that he might as well have died, for all she had left of him. It was truly hardly to be borne.

She refused dinner, paced the house for most of the night, and finally left for the office without breakfast, there to remain for a further eighteen hours. As always, work was her solace.

Lord Arden, as always helpless in the face of her moods, swiftly realised there was no way in which he could help and drove himself up to Scotland, leaving a note to say that she had only to telephone him and he would come straight back to London. He knew she would not.

He also knew – for he was not quite as emotionally inept as he seemed – that, entirely illogically she blamed him for what had happened. If she had not married him, if she had remained single, or had married – well, had married someone else – she and Kit would still be close, still be all the world to one another. The fact that the marriage had been largely her idea was neither here nor there; their relationship had most effectively removed Kit from her life. As, initially, it had removed Sebastian. He had come round, of course; for which Lord Arden found himself relieved rather than jealous. Sebastian absorbed a great deal of Celia's emotional energy, improved her temper and relieved him of the tedium of hearing about Lyttons day after day.

Why a woman with a great deal of money, who could have spent the final decades of her hugely successful life travelling, entertaining her friends, and enjoying the pleasures of the countryside – and she was a superb shot – should choose to lock herself up all day with a lot of silly bickering people and a mountain of paperwork, was completely beyond him.

Still, he had married her, and he had to make the best of it. And when things were good they were still pretty good. When Celia sat at his table at Glennings, after a day's hunting or shooting, her mood steadied by physical exhaustion and being out of doors, charming his guests, flattering him, when she came to kiss him goodnight, bringing his hot toddy with her on a tray, when she stopped fussing and fretting over her London life and her children (he often thanked God he had never had any children, they seemed nothing but trouble), he felt profoundly happy and grateful that she had married him. It was just that most of the time, she did none of those things, working endlessly at Lytton House, entertaining her publishing friends in Cheyne Walk, saying quite truthfully that they bored him and he them, so it was much better that way. He was alone; and quite lonely.

And now, with this dreadful new upset, it seemed unlikely he would see her for quite a while.

It had been very cruel of Kit; Sebastian rebuked him quite harshly.

'I find it very difficult to believe you should have wanted to hurt your mother quite so much.'

'She hurt me quite as much,' Kit said briefly, 'what she did was unforgivable and I can't find it in my heart to include her in my plans.'

'Well, I don't think it was so unforgivable. I've told you her reasons, and she would explain it to you herself if you would allow her to. It may sound very warped to you, and to an extent it does to me, but it makes perfect sense to her, and I suspect it would have done to Oliver.'

'Oh really, Sebastian! Don't talk such rot.'

'I don't think it is rot. There's a logic behind it. If she'd married me, it would have been a public statement that she'd always loved me. It would have looked very disloyal to his memory. And that would have hurt you too. Anyway, I can see there's no point talking to you. But I would beg you to consider inviting her to your wedding. Apart from breaking her heart it will split the family in two, I don't know if you've thought of that . . . What am I, for instance, supposed to do?'

'Well I'm sorry,' said Kit, 'but it was her decision to do what she did, it was she who split the family in the first place. I find it very difficult to understand how the others can have accepted it—'

'Maybe because they are not quite so intimately touched by it,' said Sebastian gently. 'Kit, it was all a long time ago, and—'

'She married Lord Arden a year after her husband died. And no, I will not invite her to my wedding. I don't want her there. She could hardly attend without him—'

'She attended Barty's wedding without him.'

'That's different.'

'Well,' said Sebastian with a sigh, 'I can see it is hopeless. But I think it's very cruel.'

Kit did have a cruel streak; there was no doubt about it. And Sebastian had a horrible idea he knew where it came from. Of course his life and its considerable problems had no doubt contributed to it; becoming blind at the age of nineteen, any prospects of a career at the bar brought to an abrupt end, being abandoned by his sweetheart, falling in love again and having the path to that happiness barred most cruelly as well, through no fault of his own – none of these things were conducive to a sanguine approach to life. And yet he had found success. He did have a brilliant career. And now he was in love again: with a most delightful and clever young woman. Sebastian liked Clementine enormously.

They had had long conversations about Kit, about her life with him, about how difficult it would be; she was brave and blithe about it, convinced that they would be extremely happy together.

'I love him so much as he is, you see, I never knew him any other way. He's Kit to me, and he's what I fell in love with. I know he's difficult and bad-tempered at times, but who wouldn't be?'

Kit had told her about his difficult history, she said. 'He felt I should know and I think he was right. It might have been a hard thing to – discover by chance. I won't tell anyone, of course. But it explains a lot. Poor Izzie; it must have been so very dreadful for her.'

'Yes, it was,' said Sebastian, remembering the savage misery of those terrible days, 'it was. But she has become very self-reliant as a result. And it would have been a disastrous marriage. She would have simply become his slave which would have been very bad for both of them.'

'I suppose so,' said Clementine, 'I certainly have no intention of becoming his slave. I'm a bit daunted by joining that clan, though, I can tell you.'

'Oh they're all right, if you take them individually,' said Sebastian. 'Don't let yourself think of them *en masse*. For the most part, they're not so remarkable. Except Celia, of course.'

'Yes. Poor Celia.'

She had tried, also without success, to persuade Kit to invite Celia to the wedding.

Keir had been offered half a term's supply teaching at a school in Birmingham; it was a much better school than the one in Glasgow and might – just might, he told Elspeth – lead to something permanent.

'The head and I really see eye to eye. I like him a lot.'

'I see,' she said carefully, 'and you'd go and live down there, I presume?'

'Of course.'

'And – what about me?'

'I don't know.' He had clearly not thought about her at all. It made her even angrier. 'I could come home at weekends.'

'At weekends. So I'd be alone all week.'

'You should have made some friends. I don't understand you. And you could spend more time with my mother. She'd love to see you.'

She ignored this. 'You don't think I could go to Birmingham too?'

'Of course not. We couldn't get a place for half a term. No, you'll have to stay here. If I get a permanent job, then you can come and join me.'

Something snapped in Elspeth: something ugly and very strong.

'No, Keir. Sorry. If you take this job – and I agree you should – then I'll go home for the six weeks. I will not stay here, on my own.'

'You've got Cecilia.'

'Keir, I love Cecilia to death. I adore her. But her conversation is limited. I'm bored and dreadfully lonely and I'm not prepared to see it get worse. I'm going home to stay with my mother while you're in Birmingham and that's all there is to it.'

Greatly to her surprise he gave in.

'I think you should see a psychiatrist.' Dr Ferguson smiled gently at Adele. 'I really feel you need some help.'

'That's ridiculous,' she said, 'absolutely ridiculous. I am a bit depressed, of course I am, who wouldn't be, but I do not need to see a psychiatrist. I find the suggestion rather insulting, actually. I'm like my mother, I believe in sorting out my own problems. I shall be quite all right when – when – I'm sorry—'

Her voice became light with tears; she fumbled in her bag, pulled out a handkerchief.

Dr Ferguson watched her cry. 'There's nothing to be ashamed of, in being mentally ill. It's no worse than having flu or appendicitis.'

'Of course it is. It's a weakness, it's not being able to cope.'

'Exactly. Which is what happens when you have flu, your body can't cope. It needs rest, medication, a little help—'

'Dr Ferguson, I am not going to see a psychiatrist. I am not. Now please don't suggest it again. But I would like some more sleeping pills. They are helping.'

Sighing, he wrote her out a prescription.

That night, Geordie telephoned: he was going back to New York, just for a few weeks, Barty wanted to talk about the paperback rights of *Growing Down*, there were people he needed to see. Before he went he would like to see as much of Clio as possible. Adele said of course she understood and tried to sound as if she didn't mind in the least. Afterwards she cried for a long time.

The letter arrived that morning; Lucas had done exceptionally well in his 'A' levels. He went flying up the stairs to tell his mother; she was lying in bed, looking pale and exhausted. But she sat up, flushed with pleasure, and hugged and kissed him.

'Congratulations, darling. I'm so pleased. Off to Oxford then?'

'Yes.'

'Well you deserve it. All of it. You've worked awfully hard.'

'That's true.' He grinned at her and then, slightly more awkwardly, said, 'A friend's asked me to go and stay for a few weeks. In the family place in France. That OK?'

'To – France? Who with?'

'Mark's family. His mother's going to ring you about it. Down in the South.'

'How – how lovely for you. For how long?'

'Oh – a few weeks,' he said again.

'Yes, I see.'

He could see she hated the idea, of him going. He felt bad about it. But what was the alternative? Staying here, helplessly, in this miserable house, with her moping about, crying. And there was nothing he could do to help. He'd tried, God knows he'd tried, always trying to get her out to supper with him and so on, but she never would. It was terribly frustrating. And he did terribly want to go. Mark had a very pretty sister, who would be there and who was extremely sexy; Lucas had kissed her several times at parties, and she had made it very clear that she would like their relationship to develop. Lucas wanted that very much too; he was still a virgin and was determined not to arrive at Oxford one.

'It's not far away,' he said rather awkwardly now, 'I can always come back if – if you need me.'

'Of course. But I won't. It sounds marvellous, darling. Of course you must go.'

He felt terrible, even thinking it, but it really would be a relief to get away.

'It's so exciting! You'll never guess.'

Noni had decided this was the way to play it; to present it to her mother as something so wonderful she couldn't possibly object.

'What's that?'

Adele spoke listlessly; she was having what she called a down day.

'*Vogue* want me to go to California. In a couple of weeks. To shoot some cruise wear.'

'California! But—'

'Yes. But only for two weeks, really quick. I'm so excited. What do you think?'

'I – I'm pleased of course, darling. It sounds wonderful.'

She spoke slowly, as if it was a physical effort to get the words out; Noni felt a pang of remorse. Perhaps she shouldn't go, perhaps—

'Really wonderful.' The voice had changed suddenly, taken on the ultra-bright tone. 'Lucky you. Goodness, what an opportunity. You must go and see your Great Uncle Jack and Lily, they'll be so thrilled.'

Noni smiled at her, kissed her. She didn't sound too bad. Not too desperate about it. She pulled something out of her pocket.

'Look. This is the colour test shot of my very first *Vogue* cover. Isn't it lovely? I'm very excited.'

Adele looked at it; it was lovely. Noni was sitting at a table, out of doors, under a huge parasol; the parasol and the scarf which was wound round her head were the same vivid breathtaking azure blue. Her eyes looked huge in her pale face, huge and brilliant, there was the promise of a smile on her full lips and just one curl of dark hair was escaping from the scarf. 'Who did that?'

'John French. I do adore him. He's so – so elegant.'

Adele felt a rush of pride suddenly for Noni; and after that a stab of something else, something less attractive. It was jealousy, fierce, ferocious jealousy.

She could have done that shot; if only she'd been given the chance. Except no one was giving her a chance any more. It wasn't fair; it just wasn't fair.

'You're what? Investing in what?' Charlie's face wore the narrow-eyed mean expression that Barty had come to hate.

'In Mike Parker and Nick Neill's agency. Not in a big way, just a few thousand dollars.'

'Oh, just a few thousand dollars. Hardly worth mentioning. Well that's fine. I wouldn't expect you to talk to me about it.'

'Charlie, you've just spent five thousand dollars on that cabin in the Catskills. You didn't talk to me about that.'

'Oh, I'm sorry. I should have told you about your birthday surprise before you had it. I suppose it would have been a good idea. You might have been able to tell me then you didn't want it.'

'I didn't say I didn't want it,' said Barty, trying to keep her temper. 'I said I didn't think we would have much use for it. We have South Lodge don't we, for the summer and weekends and—'

'South Lodge is yours. The cabin is ours. Somewhere we can go without any previous associations. I think we'll have quite a lot of use for it. I certainly will. I shall enjoy not feeling like a guest all the time.'

'Charlie – let's not start that again. I'm sure we'll have great fun up there. Anyway—'

'Anyway, you've decided to back these guys. Is that a good idea? You might lose the lot.'

'Well, if I do I do.'

'Oh so it doesn't matter if you lose five thousand dollars. That's fine, we don't need to lose any sleep over that.'

'I don't think we will,' she said. 'I have huge faith in them.'

'Well I don't. How would they have got into that situation in the first place, almost going bust? You should have asked me about it Barty, I would have advised you very strongly against it.'

'And that would have been sound financial advice, would it?' she said. 'I seem to remember you being in a fair old financial mess, shortly before our marriage.'

'That is unfair,' he said quietly. 'There were reasons for that. As you very well know.'

'There are reasons for this, too. Like firms that don't pay their bills, like the big boys can afford to carry a debt, the small ones can't. I could go on. All I'm doing is putting a bit of money in place to tide them over. Improving their cash flow, if you like.'

'So – is this Lytton money? Or Laurence's money?'

'It's my money,' she said; and then bit her lip.

'Oh, your money. Pardon me. I forgot about that. Well it must be nice. Not having any money of my own, it's hard to remember that some people have so much they can just throw it away.'

'Charlie, please. Look, I—'

'Mother! Can we go now? We're starving.'

'You go,' she said quickly, smiling at Jenna, 'I have so much to do. You go with Charlie. I'll see you when you get back. I have an early meeting in the morning—'

'You're always working,' said Jenna, 'it's crazy. You should enjoy life more, Mother, there are other things you know—'

'Jenna,' said Barty, finally losing her temper, 'the fact that I am always working enables us to enjoy life as you put it. They don't come free, you know, all the things you like doing. I—'

'Hey, honey, not now.' Charlie put his arm round Jenna's shoulders, smiled at her, the mean look quite buried suddenly. 'You don't want to start putting guilt on Jenna, I'm sure. She knows how hard you work. Now you stay here if you want to, but we're planning on a real feast tonight, aren't we girls?'

Jenna didn't even answer; she looked sulkily at her mother and walked out of the room. The last thing Barty heard was the three of them laughing as they went out of the front door.

She had meant to talk to him about his settlement that evening. It had become something of an obsession. One night, when she had been feeling happy and relaxed, after they had been out on their own for once, and then come back, high on pleasure, and made love, she had agreed with his suggestion that it would solve a lot of their problems if Charlie did have his own money.

'It would save me having to come cap in hand all the time,' he said. 'I think we would both be so much happier.'

Barty hadn't noticed Charlie coming cap in hand, but she was feeling too content and easy to say so.

'I'll talk to the trustees,' she said, 'see what they have to say. But I – could make over an agreed amount to you. You could invest it, or use it how you like.'

It was the kind of thing, she was sure, that Celia had meant.

'I'd be a really good boy,' he said, 'look after it very carefully.'

She smiled, kissed him. 'Don't make me out to be an ogre, Charlie. I'm really not.'

★

253

The very next day she discovered he'd run up a bit of a debt at his bookmakers. Nothing serious, just under five hundred dollars; but enough to make her think. And worry about turning over a sizeable sum to him. She could hardly say, if it was all wasted, 'Sorry, Charlie, that's it, no more.' It would – it could – become a bottomless pit. He was appallingly extravagant. It shocked her at times, that a man who had lived so modestly, managed so well for years and years, should have become so reckless with money. He had taken to going to wine auctions, bidding for cases of valuable wine, paying absurd amounts of money for them, buying pictures and antiques that they had no room for. When she complained – as mildly as she could – he expressed, as always, resentment at first, telling her he was only doing it for her, and then contrition. But it left her worried; and she kept shelving any action on the settlement. Which he was beginning to grow angry about.

The house seemed very quiet when they had gone. It was nice. The girls were growing noisier every day, playing their records at top volume. At the weekends, Barty could scarcely think against the noise of Elvis. Charlie refused to support her in any request to turn it down.

'They're only having fun. They're almost teenagers for heaven's sake. That kind of music isn't the same played quiet. Anyway, I don't mind, I love it too. I was just telling your mother, Jenna, how much I love Elvis. She was wondering if you could turn it down a little. I don't mind a bit but – I guess she's trying to work . . .'

Casting her again as one of the bad guys: it never stopped.

She fixed herself some scrambled eggs, remembering how she and Giles had loved them as children in the nursery. That seemed so long ago. She tried to imagine Celia tolerating noisy music. Poor Celia. She must be so upset about Kit's wedding. Venetia had written telling her about it, about her mother's grief.

'No one can budge him on it. Little beast. I'm glad I'm not Clementine, I wouldn't marry him. I even told him we wouldn't go if he didn't ask Mummy, but he said that was up to us.'

Barty tried to imagine her own pain if Jenna excluded her from her wedding and flinched.

Now, when was it? She had promised Jenna they could go: that the long-postponed visit to England would take place then.

'And we can maybe spend Christmas in London, with Venetia, or Adele, or even in Scotland at Glennings, as Aunt Celia calls it. That'd be fun.'

'But we'd take Charlie, wouldn't we? And Cathy, we couldn't not have Christmas with them.'

'Of course,' said Barty quickly. She had actually considered going without them; but it was, of course, out of the question. Still – she would like to know the date. So she could start planning. It was June already, the year would fly away with her if she wasn't careful.

She looked through her own desk; no sign of Kit's pre-invitation, announcing the date.

Charlie had been very intrigued by it; maybe he had it. She hesitated for a moment, unwilling to invade his privacy, go into his study. But – she wasn't going to start prying into his things. Just see if the invitation was lying around.

Charlie's study was in chaos; it made Jenna's bedroom look quite tidy. Papers on the desk and on the filing cabinet, books piled on the window-sill, the floor, the shelves half empty, his photographs still piled higgledy-piggledy in a packing case. The photographs of his other life: of Meg, of Cathy as a baby, of his parents – they looked so sweet, his parents, smiling out of their leather frame, a middle-aged couple, clearly quite well-to-do, in front of the house in Summit, New Jersey, where they had lived.

She wondered sometimes what had happened to that house; Charlie had said it had to be sold to pay their care-home bills, but it was a very substantial house, something of it must have been left . . .

Stop it Barty, don't go down that road.

Sally, Meg's mother, now she didn't look quite so nice. Although she clearly was, generous and very loyal to Charlie. But she had a bit of a hard face; not like Meg's. Meg had been lovely, a golden smiling girl. Such a tragedy: such a terrible tragedy.

Suddenly she decided she would like to talk to Sally; she was surprised Charlie hadn't proposed a visit so they could show her the wedding pictures. Maybe she would phone her and fix it; Charlie would have to go then. They would all go; it would be a generous and kind thing to do. Before they went to South Lodge for the summer.

No sign of the invitation. Well, she could ask Charlie. Or Izzie, she had had an invitation too. She wondered how Izzie would feel, seeing Kit marry. Of course it was so long ago, ten years, but still . . . it had nearly happened . . .

She thumbed through Charlie's address book. She knew Sally's name, of course, she had seen the letter Charlie had written to her about the wedding.

Sally Norton. Here it was all alone on the N page. Charlie really did have very few friends. He told her he had lost touch with them during the years he was caring for Cathy. She supposed it made sense.

Quickly, before she could lose courage, she dialled the number. A voice answered almost immediately. A sweet, pleasant voice. Rather as she had imagined Meg's mother might sound.

'Yes?'

'Mrs Norton?'

'No. No, I'm sorry, she doesn't live here any more.'

'Oh. Oh I see.'

Funny, Charlie hadn't said.

'Well – do you have a number for her please? Or maybe she's – that is, is she in a care home?'

'Oh I don't think so. She didn't seem in need of any care. Rather the reverse.'

'Oh. I thought—'

'We moved in here just about a year ago. She was fine then.'

A year ago! This wasn't making any sense.

'So – do you know where she moved to?'

'We have an address for her. For mail. No telephone number, though.'

'Well, perhaps you could give me her address. I'll write to her.'

'Of course. And when you do, tell her we're very happy here in her little apartment.'

'Apartment? I thought – oh, it doesn't matter. Thank you.'

Sally was supposed to have had quite a big house. Not a little apartment. What was this, what was going on . . .

'Now just a minute, my dear. Yes, here we are. Apartment 4, 1429 Avenue N, Sheepshead Bay—'

'Sheepshead Bay!'

She was stunned. Sheepshead Bay wasn't a place a well-to-do lady would live. It was very modest. And some of it quite rough, down in the south of Brooklyn, near to Coney Island. What was this? Why was she living there, why hadn't Charlie told her she had moved?

'God, dear God,' said Barty aloud. She realised she was almost crying: without really knowing why.

It was unutterably wonderful being back in London: back with her friends, with her family, to have help with Cecilia, to be able to shop and chat and gossip and talk publishing, to spend time at Lyttons. Both Jay and Celia had been very welcoming, had asked for her opinion on various books – including *Black and White* (as it was still called), now at proof stage and which she thought was brilliant. The only awful thing was the thought of going back to Glasgow. Or to some other equally terrible prison in Birmingham. That would be better, she supposed. Much nearer London. But still – the same awful dreary monotony of a life. Sometimes she wondered if she still loved Keir at all; at others, when they had had a good evening, talking about the things they both cared about, politics, literature, their future, when they had made love, she knew she did.

She had been terrified of sex for ages, afraid of so many things connected with it, afraid of it hurting, of it not being the same, or of waking Cecilia, but suddenly one night she found herself hungry for it, and he had been so gentle, so careful, so patient that she had relaxed, warmed, flown with him, felt after so long the joy, the leaping, soaring, fierce pleasure – and she had suddenly realised that it was all worthwhile, that she did still want him, wanted to be married to him, to make it work.

'If only, if only he'd just give a bit,' she said to Celia one evening, when she had gone to dinner with her in Cheyne Walk, Lord Arden having been banished to his club, 'just see things my way. But he won't listen, it's as if he's deaf. And blind. And although I do love him, I'm just not sure I can go on like this for very much longer. It's too much to ask. Or am I being very spoilt and selfish? Which is what he always says.'

Celia told her she was not.

'Something will turn up, darling, I know it will. Life is quite good at resolving things, I've always found.'

'Well it's taking a very long time over it,' said Elspeth fretfully.

Adele sat in the psychiatrist's office and stared past him out of the window. She was hating this. She was still not sure it was a good idea. It was Venetia who had finally persuaded her, after finding her hysterical with grief the morning Lucas had left for France.

'You can't go on like this,' she said, 'now come on, you must get help, see someone. I'll come with you.'

'I don't want you to come with me,' said Adele.

But she did agree to go.

He was quite easy to talk to, actually; his name was Dr Cunningham, and he was young, rather vague-looking and very gentle. She started slowly, just telling him she couldn't stop crying and she couldn't sleep, in spite of the sleeping pills; but then when he asked if she knew why she was crying, she said it was because her husband had left her.

'I can't see that's so surprising,' she said, almost defiantly. 'Anyone would cry.'

'And do you know why he left you? Is there someone else?'

'Of course not. He left me because—'

And then it did start to come out; along with a great many more tears. On and on she went, reluctantly at times, at others talking with great speed; trying to explain her terrible guilt, how she felt she had harmed everyone she loved, except perhaps Clio.

'And I know I'm harming her too, her father's left her.'

After an hour, he held up his hand.

'I'm sorry, Mrs MacColl. I only have this one hour for you. And in any case, I don't like my patients exhausting themselves. Now look, I want you to come and see me again, possibly on Thursday. We can talk some more then. And meanwhile I would like you to start taking these pills.' He scribbled out a prescription. 'They're not too strong, they'll just make you feel a bit more able to cope – although it will be a few days before they start taking effect. And I want you to change your sleeping pills, try these instead.'

She looked at the prescription; his writing was terrible.

'Do all doctors write badly so that we can't read what they've said?'

He smiled. 'No. We just do. It's in our genes maybe. The Triptizol is the anti-depressant. And Largactil is a sedative, to help you sleep. Don't get them muddled up.'

'I won't,' she said and went home feeling exhausted, but just slightly less despairing.

Next time she went, she started talking about Luc Lieberman; about their doomed relationship, about how much she had loved him.

'Sometimes I think I've never loved anyone else, certainly not as much.' She talked about how utterly desolate she had been, alone in Paris, with the German army about to invade, when she found he had gone back to his wife – and she talked about her terrible guilt at leaving Paris with the children without saying goodbye.

'But I was so angry, you see, so hurt, I could only think of getting away.'

'Of course.'

'Even so – it was dreadful. He never saw his children again, never was able to say goodbye to them, never even kissed them after that last day. How could I have done that—'

'You did what seemed best at the time.'

'But – I robbed him of them. You don't understand. And then he had to go into hiding, knowing he would never see them again. And when he was shot, trying to save that little girl – he must have thought of them then, probably his last thought – oh, God—'

She broke down then, wept for a long time; afterwards she felt eased by Cunningham's refusal to judge or to probe; he just let her talk. But she was still no nearer to being able to forgive herself. Luc had cheated on her; but was the punishment she had meted out to him really justified? Walking away, without a backward glance, without waiting for explanation, for justification, even. Perhaps she had been cruel to him, less than loving, perhaps he had felt rejected, criticised: who could judge that?

On her next visit she described the journey through France with all the other refugees, the dreadful things she had seen, had subjected the children to.

On the fourth day, she told him about the captain of the boat.

She was feeling better anyway, the pills were beginning to take effect, she was certainly sleeping better. And her sessions with Dr Cunningham had assumed a confessional quality.

'It was so awful, probably the worst thing of all. But – well, I needed to get us on that boat. We'd travelled right through France, arrived safely somehow, I'd got those two tiny children all that way against all possible odds – only to be told there was no room for me on the last boat to England.'

'So what did you do?'

'I slept with him,' she said. Exactly as she had said it to Venetia so many years before. 'I can't describe how horrible I felt; how filthy, how ashamed. I thought I could never tell anyone ever; except my sister of course. And my mother. Well, one has to tell her everything. I've never even told Geordie. And afterwards I was so afraid that I would be pregnant, that I'd get some kind of venereal disease – oh, it was horrible. It's what I dream about, and wake up to, at two in the morning. I can't get away from it. And I never will.'

'But if you hadn't done that,' he said, lighting a cigarette, offering her one, 'is it right to say you would not have got home?'

'Yes. Probably I wouldn't.'

'You'd have been trapped in France: a country occupied by the enemy.'

'I know. I know all that. But it doesn't help. Of course I felt I had to do it. But it disgusted me. And nearly twenty years later it still does. You can't cure me of that, Dr Cunningham.'

'Of course not. I wouldn't try. Now – our time is up. Again. How are you feeling?'

'Better,' said Adele. 'I think.'

She did feel better; that confession had been hard to make. And his calm acceptance of it was healing.

But still it was not the greatest crime; that had been leaving Luc, taking away his children, without any of them saying goodbye.

No one could heal the pain of that.

It really was quite ridiculous, Celia thought; some stupid telephonist at Keir's school refusing to give him a message. She had told her how urgent it was; who she was, even what it was about.

'Staff are not permitted to receive personal calls,' she said, 'or to make them, and that's all there is to it. I will tell Mr Brown you've phoned, and he will get that message at the end of school.'

'But—' Celia stopped. There was clearly no point explaining that she needed to talk to Keir before the end of school, that she must know if she could bring the proofs of *Black and White* up to go through them with him – having been unable to contact his friend at the school in Brixton – that there were certain delicate points the lawyer had raised that could not be settled without his reading them in context. She would just have to go. She had his address, he was hardly likely to be out, she would just go to see him there, with the proofs, and get it settled. She could find somewhere to stay and come back in the morning.

She was rather given to such feverish activity nowadays. It helped her through her misery.

Lucas climbed out of the Davies' swimming pool, and lay down on a chaise longue in the sun; his long lean body was already dark brown.

'Lucas! Hallo. I thought you'd gone shopping with the others.'

It was Mrs Davies; smiling down at him. She was wearing a dark-blue swimming costume; she had a marvellous figure and was extremely fit, spent at least an hour every morning swimming up and down. She looked about twenty years younger than the rather bluff Mr Davies. Lucas liked her; and she clearly liked him. Her husband had not yet arrived, and she had made something of a pet of Lucas, putting him next to her at dinner each night, challenging him to a game of tennis early each morning before the sun got too hot.

'No. I don't like shopping. I'd rather soak up the sun.'

'Like a lizard. Look, there's one.'

He sat up obediently; his wet hair fell in his eyes. Sally Davies reached a brown hand out and pushed it back for him.

'That's better. I do hope you're enjoying yourself, Lucas.'

'I am.'

'Good. I was afraid you might be feeling a little – left out. Now that Tricia's boyfriend has arrived.'

That had been a slight blow; especially as he was a complete twerp.

'Oh – don't worry about me,' he said.

'But I do. I can't help it. I'm a very – conscientious hostess. I like my guests to be completely happy.'

She looked at him, her eyes moving down his face, lingering on his lips. Lucas returned her gaze; he felt oddly relaxed and excited at the same time.

'I am,' he said, 'really.'

He reached for his pack of cigarettes, offered her one.

'Light it for me,' she said.

He did, then took it from his lips, placed it between hers. She smiled at him, a slow, inviting smile.

'Good. Look – it's very hot out here. I wondered if we might go indoors for a while, have a little drink together before lunch. The others will be hours.'

'Yes,' said Lucas, absolutely taking her meaning. 'Yes, I think that would be awfully nice.'

He followed her into the house, admiring the sway of her hips, her taut, high buttocks. He supposed he should feel nervous but he didn't. This was a far better way, after all, experience seducing youth. And it was the French way.

'Izzie? This is Geordie. I'm in New York.'

'Geordie! Oh my God, I didn't know you were here—'
'I just arrived. Didn't Barty tell you I was coming?'
'Yes, of course. But I thought it was next week, I—'
'Would you like to see me? I'd certainly like to see you.'

Celia arrived at Birmingham New Street at five that afternoon. The train journey had been quite short and easy; provided that she found Keir at home, she could be home again by ten. If not, she would stay somewhere and go back in the morning. It was incredibly annoying that he had no phone in his digs; a very nice bedsitting room, Elspeth had said. The landlady had a phone of course, but she was out. Really, the way people conducted their businesses was astonishingly inefficient.

She decided to take a taxi to the address; it was a way from the station, she was told, in Edgbaston, one of the nicest residential areas of Birmingham, but it should only take about twenty minutes. If he wasn't there, she could leave a note and then come back and book into a hotel. She had already settled on one in her mind, the Royal in Victoria Square; she could instruct Keir to telephone her there, or come to see her.

She found her drive through the city centre, still scarred by its massive bomb damage, depressing. It was a bleak, wet afternoon, and the entire city looked grey and raw. Why did Keir have to live and work in such horrible places? Why couldn't he show some sense and move to London? Edgbaston, though, was a pleasant surprise, leafy and spacious, filled with large Edwardian villas. The taxi pulled up outside a slightly less grand example; she got out and paid the fare, looking up at the windows, wondering if Keir had seen her, thinking what fun they would have that evening; she could take him out to dinner. She always enjoyed his company; of course he was a difficult character, and he certainly hadn't made Elspeth's life easy, but he was invariably good to talk to. Maybe she wouldn't go back tonight anyway, maybe she would stay.

She rang the bell. A pleasant woman answered it. No, she didn't think Mr Brown was back from school yet, he was often late, he worked so hard, he looked so tired sometimes – clearly another member of the Keir Brown fan club, thought Celia, irritated suddenly. He got away with too much, and poor Elspeth got away with absolutely nothing at all. It wasn't fair.

'Could I – could I wait in his room do you think?'

'Oh, I don't think so. I can't just let anyone in, it's his home after all. I have to go out again myself now, to meet my husband. You're very welcome to wait in the lounge until he gets back. Or to leave a note, of course. He does know you, I presume, Mrs – er –'

'Lady Arden,' said Celia graciously. 'How kind. Yes, he does know me. He's married to my granddaughter. I'll wait for a little while.'

'Very well. But you'll have to keep an eye out for him, he lives on the first floor, up those steps by the verandah, do you see, with the outside stair? So he doesn't come through the house. You might miss him.'

'I'll try not to,' said Celia. 'Now, don't let me keep you, I'd hate to make you late.'

She sat in the lounge, patient at first, then growing edgy as time passed. What on earth was he doing? Surely he wouldn't have gone out for the evening without coming home first to change. Maybe he would. She began to regret her spur-of-the-moment visit; it could prove the most dreadful waste of time.

After half an hour she wrote Keir a note. She would put it under his door and go back to the hotel. The taxi driver had given her a card with his phone number on, and she had seen a phone in the hall.

She heard voices suddenly, looked up. There was someone coming in at the gate, sharing an umbrella. It was Keir. With a friend. She hadn't expected that. Maybe he would be less pleased to see her than she had thought.

And then she watched as Keir walked towards the house, round to the side and up the iron steps: with his companion who she could see more clearly now. A fellow teacher perhaps, quite possibly indeed. A very pretty one, moreover; Celia studied her with great interest, a girl, with long red hair and very good legs, her hand in Keir's, her face lifted to his, laughing at something he had said. Well, he could be very funny, Celia thought irrelevantly.

They paused at the top of the steps, while Keir got out a key, then disappeared inside. The room was overhead, and she could hear their footsteps and their voices quite clearly: as clearly as she could hear the abrupt silence that followed. And went on.

Celia waited: for five minutes. Five long, silent minutes. Then she picked up her bag and her hat and walked out of the front door of the house round to the side, up the iron staircase and pressed the bell very firmly. Very firmly indeed. And went on pushing it.

Keir's face when it finally appeared, looking cautiously round the door, was actually very funny, a parody of shock and guilt, first flushed and then extremely pale, his dark eyes large with alarm, his jaw rigid.

Finally he said, 'Celia.'

'Yes,' she said, smiling at him sweetly, 'yes, that's right, Keir. It is indeed Celia. I do hope I haven't come at an inconvenient time. I have some editorial matters to discuss with you, rather urgently. May I come in?'

CHAPTER 20

Giles was having a lot of difficulty with *Contrasts*, as *Black and White* had finally been titled. He could not help admiring it; it was superbly written, it was a clever idea – Celia and Keir had been right, the colour question was hotly debated at every level, in every newspaper, round every dinner table – and it had a wonderfully clever ending, leaving the reader to wonder whether the couple were going to continue with their pregnancy or not.

Meyrick hadn't used any cheap tricks; the Jamaican hero was a trained teacher, desperately trying to get a job; the heroine was a nurse, her father a headmaster, refusing to help his son-in-law. It had everything – family, class, snobbery both intellectual and social, love, sex – all set against the background of appalling colour prejudice.

Keir's teacher friend had arranged for Meyrick to talk to two or three of the Jamaican families whose children were in his class; he had visited them in their hopelessly overcrowded homes, seen their disappointment and indeed despair at never being able to make a future, not only for themselves, but for their children.

One man had been living in one room at a rent of £1 a week, with eight others, taking it in turns to find a bed, sofa or even a space on the floor to sleep. The authorities had discovered this and turned them out, claiming health and even fire risks, and then quickly went on to find them council accommodation; local white residents, living in only slightly better conditions themselves, were outraged and this had increased hostility. There were even some calls for segregated areas where the 'coloureds' could be housed.

This man's brother, whom Meyrick had also met, lived in Birmingham and had been involved in a dispute on the buses there. The white employees were 'overwhelmingly opposed' to employing coloured people, in spite of the fact that there were vacancies, and held a strike; banners could be seen all over Birmingham saying 'Keep Britain White'. Even Winston Churchill spoke of the dangers of Britain becoming 'a magpie society'; there were letters to *The Times* warning that most of the two million people in Trinidad and Jamaica were planning to come to England,

and there were rumours of an organisation in Bradford smuggling Indian and Pakistani men into the country, obtaining passports for them for anything up to £400.

The immigrants even found organising a social life with one another difficult; Birmingham City Council barred them from using their school halls for dances, blaming 'misuse' (vaguely described as overcrowding and abusing the toilet facilities), and the immigrants were also frequently blamed for distributing drugs to teenagers.

'It's all very ugly and makes one ashamed,' said Celia after one meeting with Meyrick, adding with her usual ruthless honesty that nevertheless it made for a wonderful book . . .

Giles worried about it endlessly, fearing that the anti-coloured feeling in the country would rebound against Lyttons; Celia, Elspeth and, indeed, Jay, all told him he was talking nonsense, that in literary circles such behaviour would be regarded with distaste and that Lyttons would be seen as occupying the vanguard of liberal opinion.

'We could also,' he said, looking heavily round the boardroom table, 'be accused of capitalising on the misfortunes of these people.'

'I don't think so,' said Jay, 'particularly as two of the men Hugh Meyrick has talked to have very bravely agreed to be interviewed by the press. They're both articulate, reasonable, and right behind the book, as well as happy at being able to have their problems brought into the open. And it's not as if we're showing any kind of bias, the girl's misgivings about her situation are very frankly examined. It's brilliant, Giles, you really have nothing to worry about.'

Giles continued to worry.

His greater problem with the book, of course, was Keir Brown's involvement in it. Keir Brown who, from that August, would be working at Lyttons as an editorial assistant, Keir Brown who had no experience of publishing whatsoever, Keir Brown who was his mother's latest discovery and apparently her new favourite, brought in to assist on copy-editing the book. It was outrageous. Useless for his mother to point out that Keir had worked on *Isis* in his final year at university, that she was very impressed with some readers reports he had done, that he had a feel for words, that the book had been his idea. None of that justified what she was doing for Keir.

Nobody was quite clear how it had happened: that he should, with quite shocking suddenness, without much consultation with anyone, join Lyttons as Celia's protégé. Of course she was getting on a bit, she had always been rather inclined to get ideas into her head, to act quixotically, but this was a rather extreme example of it. No one had actually objected, except Giles, or indeed seemed to mind too much. Jay was delighted; he was short of junior staff, he had always liked Keir and got on with him and Celia's assurance that he would knuckle down and perform the most humble tasks without complaint had proved absolutely correct. Keir was fun and he was funny, he was good-natured, in spite of a tendency to lose his temper at rather unpredictable moments, and everyone liked him. Women in particular.

The person most surprised, perhaps, was Elspeth; when Keir arrived out of the blue on the Saturday after Celia's visit to Birmingham and announced that he had decided after all to accept a job at Lyttons, she had genuinely thought she must be dreaming. After she had asked him for the third time if he really meant it and why, and he had told her he did really mean it, and it was because he had begun to give up hope of getting the kind of teaching job he wanted, she gave up, deciding she was tempting fate. She asked her grandmother what she thought might have tipped Keir over into his decision, but Celia had been rather cool about it.

'I have no real idea, darling, but I certainly haven't pressed him on the matter and it's my advice that neither should you. It can't have been easy for him, and I think you should recognise that. Just be nice to him, make it up to him, he's bound to be feeling a bit – sore. The male ego is very delicate, as I'm sure you know, best to pander to it, I've always found.'

'Granny,' said Elspeth, looking at her intently, 'there's more to this than meets the eye, isn't there?'

'Not really,' said Celia. 'I told you life usually resolved things for itself, didn't I? Obviously it has, once again. Oh and darling, whatever you do, don't even contemplate going back to work yourself yet. That really would be very silly.'

Elspeth, encouraged by the 'yet', promised that she wouldn't.

'There's absolutely no excuse,' Keir had said, twisting his fingers in his thick black hair as he always did when he was upset, 'I know that. I've behaved appallingly.'

'Very true,' said Celia calmly. 'Do have some more wine.'

'Thank you. But – oh, I don't know. Elspeth's changed so much. She doesn't seem to be fun any more. And—'

'Keir Brown, how can you even think that, let alone say it,' said Celia severely. 'Of course she's not fun. Removed from everything she knows, her family, her friends, her work, her home, stuck in what sounds a rather remote part of Glasgow' – she was careful not to criticise the standard of accommodation, even in her hour of triumph – 'all alone, with a baby all day for company. Babies are wonderful little creatures, but they lack conversational skills. When you came home, I'm sure you made a great effort to talk to her, to be interesting and amusing, but Oliver certainly didn't. He worked terribly long hours, it was dreadful.'

Keir was silent. Then he sighed heavily.

'I do still love her, you know. But she won't let me near her half the time. She seems angry with me.'

'Well, I'm not surprised. I would be too. I was angry with Oliver. I remember that vividly. And then, of course, Elspeth is probably very tired. It wasn't an easy delivery, it takes time to recover physically—'

'We haven't had much sex,' said Keir bluntly, 'if that's what you mean.'

'I suppose I do. Partly. Which is no excuse, either, for sleeping with someone else.'

'I know that. But Margaret did come after me. She seemed rather keen.'

'Really? Well you are a very attractive man. I've always thought that.'

'And one thing led to another. I was never going to let it go on, not once I'd left Birmingham. I didn't get that job,' he added and sighed heavily. 'I've really mucked things up, haven't I?'

'A bit, yes.'

'I suppose you'll be telling Elspeth. The minute you get back. And her bloody parents.'

'Now, what good would that do anybody?' said Celia. She sounded genuinely puzzled.

Keir stared at her, took another large gulp of wine. 'Well – I don't know. I just thought—'

'You don't know me very well yet, do you? Discretion is my greatest virtue. I've constructed an entire life out of it. I have very little time for the truth. Certainly not unvarnished. Of course I'm not going to tell Elspeth. It would break her heart, wreck your little family, and make Venetia and Boy unbearably smug. I would hate any of that.'

'So—'

'So what am I going to do? I'll tell you. I'm going to offer you, for at least the tenth time, a job at Lyttons. Which you will not only enjoy, but be very good at.'

'Celia—'

'Which you will accept this time, I feel sure. And move to London.'

'And Elspeth will move back into her bloody flat and her job at Lyttons, I suppose. Where she will be vastly my superior and—'

'Of course she won't go back to Lyttons. I wouldn't have her there. She should be at home, looking after Cecilia, and providing her with some brothers and sisters. Neither will she be moving back into her flat. Amy's in it, anyway, she won't be at all pleased if she has to share it with a baby. Silly child, that one, just like her mother at the same age.'

'And who is Elspeth like,' said Keir rather wearily, 'would you say?'

'Elspeth,' said Celia with great finality, 'is very like me. In a great many ways.'

'God help me,' said Keir, but he smiled at her. There was a long silence; then he said quickly, as if he had quite literally decided to move into dangerous territory, 'All right, Celia, you win. I'll accept your offer. I don't like it though, I don't like blackmail.'

'This is not blackmail,' said Celia, 'it's simple pragmatism. I want you at Lyttons. Always have. And you'll enjoy it, I do promise you that.'

'But there's a deal in the background. I think we're both aware of that.'

'You may be,' said Celia, 'I'm certainly not. I told you. Nothing would make me tell Elspeth what I know. Nothing. I wouldn't hurt her – and therefore you – for the world. I'm just really glad we've been able to work something out to our mutual advantage. Now come along, stop fiddling with your hair like that and eat your steak. It's really very good.'

Giles suggested Lyttons did a paperback imprint.

The family were astonished; it was so absolutely out of character for him to propose anything innovative, anything remotely risky, that Venetia was driven to wonder aloud if he was finally cracking up. On the other hand, for once in his life, he found himself ahead of the crowd.

'I'm not suggesting we do it in a big way,' he said when the idea was discussed at a board meeting, 'just that we put a few books out, from the backlist, say half a dozen, and see how they do. I thought we could launch next spring. I don't see why we should give Penguin or Pan all our best titles. I would like to put it to Barty, get her reaction.'

Celia was particularly excited and offered to help Giles with overseeing the project; he turned her down with unusual firmness.

Elspeth had been afraid that Keir would regret his decision, that he would become bad-tempered and difficult, start talking about returning to teaching, but he didn't. He seemed quite happy, and had thrown himself into working at Lyttons with his usual energy; still faintly disbelieving of her good fortune, but infinitely grateful, she devoted herself to finding somewhere to live that they could afford on his salary, settling on a mansion flat in Battersea, overlooking the park. It wasn't fashionable, of course, rather the reverse, but it was as big as a small house, with three bedrooms and a room which she could turn into quite a grand drawing room. She liked the period features, the cornices and the fireplaces, and the tiny balcony that overlooked the street. It also had the considerable advantage of being almost within sight of her grandmother's house in Cheyne Walk. It was amazing, she thought, the difference in value made by the presence of quite a small stretch of water. On the Chelsea side of the river, the flat would have cost at least five times as much.

Having found it, she began to furnish it, searching out bargains in sale rooms, not only in London, but in Buckinghamshire, near Ashingham, and struggling to make her own curtains with a sewing machine Celia had given her.

She refused to entertain any notion of help in the house, continuing to do all her own cleaning and to look after Cecilia by herself; she had taken very seriously Celia's warning about the vulnerability of the male ego. She wasn't sure how her grandmother fitted into the change in her fortune but she was fairly sure there was a connection; consequently if Celia had told her to walk backwards for the next five years, she would have agreed to do it.

Keir's main role in his first few months was to read: manuscripts, proofs, proposals, and give his view of them; but he also spent a lot of time poring over *The Bookseller*, studying what other publishers were bringing out, and visiting bookshops to see how the Lytton books and the material used to promote them were faring.

'They're a joke those bookshops,' he said to Celia one day, 'you'd never think they wanted to sell anything at all. They look like grocers' shops, dark brown, lots of high shelves you can't reach without a ladder, and as for the windows – they're just a jumble. I don't understand it, especially as they all operate on the self-service principle. You have to really work to find what you want: unless it's a very new book, and even then I saw some horrible things. Two of Lyttons' spring titles just stuck on shelves right at the back.'

'I know,' she said, 'there's nothing more reactionary than the English book trade. They are still living in the Victorian age. You should hear Barty on the subject. Although many of the New York houses are not much better, you'd be surprised. They seem to think that books will sell themselves. The entire business inclines to the view that the overt pursuit of money and sales is vulgar.'

'You don't,' he said, grinning at her. 'Have you always been so ahead of your time?'

'Always,' said Celia firmly.

He became very interested – to Giles's intense irritation – in the packaging of the proposed paperback imprint.

'The only books that look modern, cheer the bookshops up, are the paperbacks,' Keir said to him one morning.

'Really?'

'Yes. Some of the Pan covers are really great. I was talking to a chap called Godwin, very interesting ideas, he's taking over Better Books, opposite Foyles, you know—'

'Yes, I did know,' said Giles shortly.

'Clearing it out, cheering it up. Do you have a name for the paperback list yet?'

'No. No I don't.'

'They all have very strong animal associations, I notice. Animals and birds. I wondered about Centaur.'

'Indeed?'

'Yes. Seeing as the centaur was a mythological creature, half man, half horse—'

'I was aware of that,' said Giles.

'I thought it rather appropriate. It gives the idea of the paperback some gravitas – and then the background colours could be white, or at least light grey, like the centaur, they'd be very noticeable.'

'Keir, I'm sorry, but I do have a lot of work to do this morning,' said Giles, 'and I don't think you can quite appreciate that all these things have to be settled by careful discussion at board level, not by a quick chat in the corridor.'

'No,' said Keir, 'I didn't.' And he went to see Celia.

As a result, and over lunch at the Savoy, Centaur was put forward as a title to Jay, who loved it and proposed it at the next board meeting. In the absence of any feasible alternative, it was adopted; Giles was furious. And most of his fury was directed inevitably at Keir.

Barty was lunching with Geordie at the 21 Club after a meeting with Bantam in the famous 666 building to settle his paperback deal. She was enjoying his visit; she had been missing everyone in England terribly.

'I love it here so much,' she said, looking around the restaurant, 'and there's supposed to be a secret room, you know, a sort of cellar inside another room, the size of a small bedroom with no windows, where the really big contracts are signed. I've never seen it myself, but it's part of publishing folklore. Laurence used to bring me here. Well, he brought me to most places, of course.' There was a silence; she looked down at her hands. Then up at the ceiling. 'One day,' she said, smiling at him quickly, 'one day I'm going to have one of Lyttons' vans hung up there.' It was one of the unique services the '21' provided for its better customers: hanging models of their company trucks and planes from the dining-room ceiling.

'Right. And my racing colours will adorn one of those guys standing on the steps outside,' he said. 'But maybe not just yet.'

'Jenna loves those jockeys,' said Barty, smiling, 'she had her photograph taken with them last year, the maître d' let her climb up on to the balcony and pose with them. By the way, how's Clio?'

'Clio's heaven. Want to see a picture?'

She smiled at the snapshot of the six-year-old Clio, all dark eyes and curls and dimples. 'Geordie, she looks exactly like Adele.'

'I know it.'

'How is Adele?'

'Oh – she's fine.'

He clearly wanted to avoid the subject; as much as she did of Charlie.

'Now, tell me about Lyttons New York. How's it doing?'

'Oh – all right. We need your new book. How's that coming along?'

'Slowly. But it's a good theme. I've gone back to my first love, society murder.'

'Oh that'll do well.'

'I hope so. I'm fascinated by these Kennedys, you know. They really are like a royal family here. Funny, when old Joe was once a bootlegger, and now he's so uppity. Determined to see Jack president, by all accounts.'

'Yes. I wonder if he'll manage it.'

'You bet he will. I met him once, just before they left London. I never saw anyone with such naked ambition in my life. Anyway, the family in my book are not a million miles away from them. Of course no one's in the running for president, that really would be considered libellous, but they're a rich, spoilt, close clan, ferociously ambitious in business—'

'A bit like the Lyttons,' said Barty mildly.

He grinned at her. 'A bit.'

She was worried about Lyttons New York, she said; it wasn't performing as it should, competition was hotting up. Places like Simon & Schuster never stopped signing people and she hadn't had a big popular book for a while. 'Except yours,' she said hastily.

'You mean a really popular book don't you?'

'Yes. That can go into paperback and sell zillions. That's where the money is now. Well I don't have to tell you that. God, they're so powerful, these paperback houses, they seem sometimes to own the world. And it means prices are being pushed up. We're doing all right, but we don't have a lot of money to play with, to buy books. I know they're doing their own paperback imprint in London, I think it's a marvellous idea and I love the name—'

'Isn't it good? Brainchild of Celia's new favourite, Keir, you know.'

'I was very surprised to hear he was working for Lyttons, I thought he was a teacher.'

'He was. But he's made the switch. I can see exactly where Celia's mind is going, and so can some of the others I think. Giles can't stand him.'

'Oh dear. Poor Giles.'

'Poor old Giles.'

'I could do with a bright young spark here, to be honest,' said Barty. 'I'm feeling a bit creaky.'

'What about Marcus Forrest?'

'Well he's wonderful, of course, but we really need new young blood as well.'

'There must be plenty of it about.'

'Yes, I suppose so. But I don't seem able to find it. Marcus is joining us for a drink, by the way.'

'Good.' Geordie liked and admired Marcus Forrest; Barty had hired him as senior editor five years earlier, and he was now editorial director; she had poached him from Delacorte, from right under the nose of the legendary Helen Myer. Geordie could still remember her glee at having accomplished it; he had been in New York and she had practically flown into the King Cole Room at the St Regis, where they were meeting for a drink, and told him. He looked at her now, and couldn't imagine her doing anything like it; the gloss had gone from her, the excitement, the sheer delight in doing her job and running her company. What had gone wrong?

'Anyway, I'm sending the family down to South Lodge this summer and staying here for July, at least, getting my head down. I want a real contemporary tear-jerker – a bit like Celia's *Contrasts* novel, which I think is marvellous, incidentally. I may even have to commission one. Oh, now look, there's Fred Nolan. He publishes the *G Report*, have you ever seen it?'

'No.'

'You'd adore it. It's a gossip sheet about publishing and everyone reads it. I'll send you a copy down to the Algonquin.'

'Thanks.'

'I hear you're seeing Izzie on Saturday,' she said lightly.

'Yes. I'm going down to see her apartment and then take her out to supper. Can you come too?'

'I can't, I'm afraid. Cathy and Jenna are appearing in a school concert. You're lucky I didn't invite you along to that.'

'I wish you had,' he said, 'I'd have loved it. Now, when are you coming to England? The family are beginning to think your husband has two heads.'

Barty wasn't sure why she was looking forward to the trip to England so little. She should have been longing to introduce Charlie to everyone. Whatever his faults, he was very charming, very well-mannered. So was Cathy; she and Jenna would delight everyone.

She had decided – with a degree of relief and what felt like a reprieve – that she couldn't spare the time before Kit's wedding. And they certainly couldn't go twice.

Charlie had become very angry about it, he accused her of trying to keep him from her family, of being ashamed of him even, 'I'm not the success Laurence was, am I, bit of a lame duck, to introduce into your glittering dynasty?'

She told him not to be ridiculous, saying it was quite simply pressure of work, she couldn't take two long trips in one year: he had raged at her, accusing her of putting her work before everything, and then returned remorseful as always, begging her forgiveness.

'You must understand, darling, I do feel I need to meet them. But of course if you're too busy – that's different.'

He never stopped trying to persuade her away from Lyttons, away from work, was constantly coming home with travel brochures, which were supposed to tempt her and actually irritated her beyond endurance. She supposed, to be fair, it was difficult for him, he had very little to do, while she was always working.

But then – he could be working too. She was prepared to back him. She had several times asked him what he would like to do in the long term; he always said vaguely that for the time being Cathy needed him. 'And Jenna too, for that matter.' When they were away at school in the fall, then he'd think about it.

'But not real estate,' he said firmly, 'I am up to here in real estate.'

Beyond that he refused to go.

He had seemed very happy, on the other hand, at the prospect of taking the girls to Southampton for the summer.

'We'll have a great time,' he said, smiling at her, 'do all sorts of things. As long as you promise to come down for August.'

Barty promised she would: without committing herself to quite how much – or little – of August it would be. She was, although she would have hated to admit it, looking forward to the peace and tranquillity. She was going to miss Jenna; but having the place to herself would be awfully nice.

'Venetia! Hallo, it's me. I just had to tell you, I feel so much better today. It's like some clouds have just rolled away and let the sun back in.'

'Oh, darling, I'm so glad.'

'Yes, and that's not the best thing. *Record*, you know, the American magazine, have asked me to do a job for them. I can't believe it. It's only a little job, but – I'm going to do it.'

'What is it?'

'I've got to find some third-class train carriages and photograph them. Preferably in a siding somewhere. You know they've abolished them?'

'I didn't but—'

'Well they have. End of an era stuff. Anyway, it's a very "me" assignment. I've just rung the press office, and they're looking for some for me. *Record* want them within the week. I'm really excited, Venetia.'

'Darling, so am I.'

Barty had written to Sally Norton, but she hadn't replied. She was clearly very odd; there was no point pursuing her. She obviously didn't want to have anything to do with any of them: that was all it meant, nothing mysterious or odd. Barty would just put the whole subject out of her head. For good.

Charlie and the girls were leaving for South Lodge at the beginning of the next week. Term was over; the concert had been a great success. Jenna had played a solo and got an encore; for the hundredth, the thousandth time, Barty longed for Laurence to be able to see her. Every success, every landmark, in some odd way hurt more. So many things about her he would have loved, admired, been proud of. And a lot of things he wouldn't, she thought, reminding herself before she got too sentimental, of the real Laurence; there would have been terrible rows about noisy record players, neglected homework, haircuts without permission, clothes that were too old for her, books and magazines that were too facile, music that was too trashy.

He would have demanded absolute obedience, unwaveringly high standards, devotion to her studies, early nights, a nun-like social life probably, Barty thought, until she was twenty-one. There would certainly have been no mixed parties, jazz clubs, sleepovers, no experimenting with make-up, fashion binges, posters of crooners on her wall. Not without an enormous struggle, anyway. It would have been very, very uncomfortable; on the other hand . . .

'Izzie this apartment is lovely,' said Geordie, smiling, 'really lovely.'

'Isn't it? I'm so thrilled with it. It's a bit of a mess still, I'm afraid.'

She had spent all morning cleaning it, washing the windows, putting flowers in jugs on every available surface, then carefully mussing it up again, a magazine slung down there, a sweater draped over a chair here, lest it look as if she was trying too hard. Which she wasn't. Of course she wasn't.

'You've done it so nicely, I love it. Except maybe for that lamp.' He smiled at her, indicated a bright-pink china table lamp which stood on the side table. 'I hope I'm not offending your sensitivities when I say that it doesn't quite match up to the rest.'

'I know. I got it in the thrift shop. It came free with the table.'

'Expensive at the price, I'd say.'

'One day, when I'm rich and famous, I'm going to have a real Tiffany lamp, you know? With the stained-glass, leaded shade. All in reds and blues. I've seen exactly the one I want.'

'My favourite, too.'

'Really? Can I offer you a drink?'

'He sat down in the big chair by the window in her sitting room, looked down the pretty street.

'It's awfully like London.'

'Celia said that. Maybe that's why I like it. Later I'll show you around the neighbourhood.'

'I know it a bit. I spent some of my youth here. Do you go to Chumleys?'

'Of course I do. I adore it. Haven't seen Mrs Chumley's ghost yet, but I live in hope. I thought we'd go there for a drink later – unless you don't have time, of course.'

'Izzie, I have all the time in the world. For you.'

He was only teasing of course. Of course. She must keep telling herself that. It was just Geordie, being uncle-like.

'How's Noni?'

'Oh fine. Doing terribly well. Look – this came this morning. Adele sent it to my hotel. It's going to be the cover – the cover, mark you – of *Vogue*. She's in California right now with them.'

'Oh my God. It's lovely.' She studied it for a moment, then got up, put the colour test shot on the mantelpiece. 'It looks nice there. So she's enjoying it, is she?'

'So much. And she's turned into a real social butterfly. Spends her life in terribly smart places like Les A and the 400 Club – which she tells me is known as the headquarters of society – with a lot of rather grand young men.'

'Goodness, it doesn't sound like Noni.'

'I know, but it's true. She sends lots of love.'

'And – how's Adele?'

'Fine. Very well. Yes.'

'Good.'

Not quite what she had heard: but he clearly didn't want to talk about it. After a while, she suggested they went out for a walk and visit a few bars; a walk was safe, sexless, would show him she felt nothing for him, nothing at all, except friendship. Which she didn't. And it was obvious he felt exactly the same for her.

CHAPTER 21

'Darling? More coffee?'

'Oh – yes, please. Then I must go. When are you leaving?'

'Mid-morning, I guess. When the young ladies have deigned to give me their suitcases. And made their final phone calls to their friends.'

'Good. Well have a lovely time. I'll try and come out at the weekend. Although it might be better to wait till I can move out for a few weeks.'

'Yes, and knowing you, that'll probably be for Thanksgiving.'

'No it won't,' said Barty smiling, giving him a kiss. She felt very affectionate towards him. They had made love the night before, for the first time for weeks; it had been very good, he had led her into a pleasure so sweetly intense she had wept as she came, wept with delight and release and relief, and she had lain in his arms afterwards, feeling sated, warm and very happy. If they could still accomplish this together, this closeness, this delight, this exploration of one another, then they had more than perhaps she had thought, as much even as she had hoped.

He had told her over dinner that he had an idea for a company he wanted to talk to her about: 'I think you'll like it.'

'What sort of company?'

'I'm not telling you. In the realm of transport.'

He wouldn't say any more; but she was pleased that he was at least thinking of working again. Absurdly pleased.

Was she actually turning into Celia?

This was wonderful. Really wonderful. She had almost forgotten what a marvellous moment this was: when the image slowly appeared in the developing dish, rising from the blank paper, and was exactly what you had hoped for. Or even better. This was even better. Adele wanted to jump up and down and shout for joy . . . only there wasn't quite room for it in her darkroom . . .

The pictures really were good: very, very good. A lot of it had been luck. The Great Western Railway had managed to find her a few third-class carriages in a siding near Dawlish Warren station; the grass was growing tall by the railway line, speckled with great fronds of cow parsley, and she had shot the carriages from a very low viewpoint, through the grass. She had waited until evening, when the sun was low, sending long shadows across the carriages from some nearby trees; they looked abandoned, sad relics already of another era.

She would FedEx them first thing in the morning; *Record* would get them by Wednesday. What a fool she'd been, not working all this time, letting herself get so down; her mother was right (as always), work really was such a cure for heartache, disappointment, despair even. And now she was feeling so much better she felt able to try and get some more work, she might even go and see *Style* this week. Noni had said they were starting a new column called 'Objets', accessories for the home, lamps and mirrors and ornaments, absolutely her thing.

And then things at home weren't really so bad; she was managing on her own, somehow. And maybe, maybe Geordie would come round in time. He had, after all, told her he'd always love her. That last day, when they'd had tea. Maybe all she had to do was be patient. Wait for him to see how much better things could be without Lucas. And maybe when Geordie saw how much more positive she felt about life, he would want to be with her more. It couldn't have been much fun living with her over the past few months. She couldn't believe how much better she felt; it wasn't so much the anti-depressants, she thought, it was being able to sleep. Hours and hours of wonderful deep, dreamless sleep. Too good to be true.

Like her pictures. She went back to admiring them.

Izzie turned her head on the pillow and looked at Geordie; they were in his room at the Algonquin, she preferred to be with him there, she felt less exposed, and less treacherous, without knowing quite why. He felt her move and smiled sleepily at her.

'Good morning. Dear Little Izzie.'

'Good morning, George.'

'Don't call me that horrible name.'

'I will, if you call me Dear Little Izzie. Every single time.'

'All right then. What would you like me to call you?'

'Just Izzie. That's perfectly all right. Or Lady Isabella, which is what the boys call me.'

'Bit of a mouthful. I'll stick to Izzie. Would you give me a kiss, please? And then another. Happy?'

'Of course,' she said. Wishing it was true, wishing for what must be the hundredth time already, that she did feel happy, really happy, more at peace, less guilty. 'Of course I am. And now I must get up, I mustn't be late today.'

She still wasn't quite sure how it had happened: how she had been persuaded to betray a lifetime of friendship with Adele, long years of closeness to Noni. She knew it was wrong, terribly wrong: however much he told her that the marriage was over, that Adele was fine, that he had been as hurt and as angry as she had been over it all, that he missed Clio so much it was like a physical pain, but he could never, ever go back. 'She was so – so unyielding, Izzie, so blind to my misery, so deliberately incapable of understanding what I was trying to do. Which was only to defend her, stop him being so beastly to her. Not me at all.'

She had listened to him talking about it for hours that first day, disbelieving to begin with, then confused, then finally desperately sorry and sad for him. It had been interspersed, of course, with his telling her how much he adored her, how he could still remember the first time he had seen her: 'You were wearing a pink dress and your pearl necklace, the terribly important pearl necklace that brought us together, and you were flirting with Henry and Roo—'

'Heavens,' she said, awed by this revelation, 'I really can't believe that.'

And then she was silent, reflecting that it was also the time he had first met Adele; guilt pierced her happiness suddenly. She said so; he looked at her very intently, then said, 'Izzie, you take life much too seriously.'

It had begun, really begun, when she had knocked some wine over. They were in a small, smoky restaurant just off Washington Square and she had been wondering how she could have been so worried about the evening. It was obvious that he just wanted to be friends. The only thing was – she had a faint sense of anti-climax. Which was ridiculous.

'Penny for 'em,' he had said.

'Nothing,' she said. 'Really, nothing.'

He smiled at her; and there was something about that smile which upset her. It was almost – fatherly. Sweet, tender, but fatherly. It made its own point; that she was little more than a child to him, someone he had always known, someone young, naive, uninteresting. His stepdaughter's friend. Not an interesting, sexy, intriguing woman; not the woman whose pearls had broken, who had flirted with him so recklessly that night, the night of his party. That had been a piece of foolishness, inspired no doubt by his own excitement and success, she had been just another bit of excitement. She was just 'Dear little Izzie,' as he said suddenly, 'dear, dear little Izzie.'

Something snapped in her then, something dangerous.

'Don't call me that,' she said sharply. 'Just don't. I hate it.'

'Sorry.'

'I think I'd like to go now. If you don't mind. I'm very tired and—'

She stood up suddenly, and in standing up, knocked the bottle of wine over, the red wine. It was only a quarter full, but there was an awful lot of it, pouring all over the table, down on to the floor, spilling into Geordie's plate, his lap, a horribly visible red flood, testimony to her clumsiness, her gaucheness, her lack of style.

'Oh God,' she said, standing there, staring at it, 'I'm so sorry, I really am such an absolute idiot—'

And then she started to cry, great, slow tears, tears of humiliation and unhappiness and dejection. He looked up at her, baffled by her reaction and then he stood up too, took her hand and said, 'Shall we go outside?' And they just walked away from it all, out of the restaurant, pausing only to throw a twenty-dollar bill down on to the table, far too much for what they had eaten, and into the street.

'I'm so sorry,' he said, as they sat, later, in her apartment, 'I just forgot. It was meant to be a joke, really. You know how I adore you.'

'Of course you don't adore me. Don't talk like that. It's ridiculous.'

'But I do,' he said, more serious now. 'I do absolutely adore you. In fact, I think I'm in love with you. No, that's wrong, I know I'm in love with you . . .'

'Oh,' she said. The room seemed very quiet. Very still. She could hear the clock ticking, from somewhere outside the silence, and she was aware of the pink lamp casting a very bright light onto a big rug that stood in for a carpet. She noticed suddenly that it was very worn, the rug, threadbare in places. Well it had only cost ten dollars, from the charity shop. What could you expect for ten dollars? And the colours were lovely, all faded, pinks and blues—

'Izzie, are you listening?'

'What? Oh, sorry. Yes.'

They had not gone to bed together that night; awed, dizzy with fear and excitement, she had sent him away.

'I need to think, Geordie, I need to get used to the idea.'

'May I come back tomorrow?'

'Yes. Of course.'

He had returned in the middle of the next day, a huge bunch of red roses in one hand, a bottle of champagne in the other.

'I had to come. I know it's Sunday and a most inappropriate day for seduction but—'

'Most inappropriate,' she said smiling. 'You can have a nice cup of coffee and then you are to go away again.'

'Immediately?'

'Almost immediately.'

'Then, before that, we must go to bed.'

He was looking at her, his eyes boring into her; she felt it physically, felt a deep rush of desire in her belly, so strong, so undeniable, it made her actually squirm. He recognised it, smiled, reached out his finger and touched her lips.

'Come along, my darling, darling Isabella.'

How could it be, she wondered? How could you be lying in bed with a man, who had made love to you, so gently, so tenderly; how could you be experiencing sensations, glorious sensations, how could you be feeling unimaginably intense, sweeping pleasure, how could you be hearing your own self cry out with the violence of it, how could you then be lying in his arms, hearing him tell you he loved you, and at the same time feel remorse and guilt, and a knowledge that it was terribly, terribly wrong?

Every hour of every day from then on, she had resolved to stop it, before it was too late, before more harm was done: she couldn't go on with it, she could not build her own happiness on such cruelty, she would tell him next time he phoned, came to see her, kissed her goodbye; and every time she thought she could not hurt him now, while he was making her laugh, telling her how happy she made him, being so generous, so gentle, so absolutely perfect . . .

And every hour and every day carried her further into confusion, further into frailty: further into what at least seemed to be love.

'Venetia, I've got an idea. Can I sound you out?'

'Of course.'

'Thing is —' Adele sounded shakily excited '— thing is, I just got a cable from *Record*.'

'And?'

'They loved the pictures. Which I thought they would. And now they want me to do some more for them. They're looking for ideas. You know, like I used to do, "Day in the Life of a Village", that sort of thing . . .'

'Darling, that's wonderful.'

'Isn't it? I just feel so thrilled. So — so happy. Anyway, they want a list of ideas. Which of course I could send them. I wondered about a story about the coloured children, at Keir's friend's school.'

'Well, it's no use asking me about that, you'll have to talk to him.'

'Of course. But they also say if ever I'm in New York, they'd love to see me. And — well, and this is the idea, I thought, why not? Geordie's there, after all, and I could see him, which might be really good, away from all the pressures here. And I could see Barty and Izzie for that matter. I could even go and see some other American magazines maybe, and — oh, it's so wonderful to feel like me again—'

'Adele—'

'Anyway, it would have to be pretty soon. Like this weekend. If I can get a flight. Geordie's only there for another two weeks. I thought I might not tell him I was coming. Just turn up at the Algonquin and surprise him. Do you think he'd like that?'

'I expect so,' said Venetia carefully, 'but I always think that sort of surprise is a bit hard. He might be out, or something, you should ring first.'

'Well — maybe. I just think it'd be more romantic as a surprise.'

★

Celia was less than enthusiastic.

'I know she's feeling better,' she said to Venetia, 'but it's a very fragile recovery. Only due to those pills, nothing's really been solved. Except that she's working again. She seems rather over-excitable to me. Not really stable at all. And it's a long and tiring journey, on the plane. I'm going to suggest she asks her doctor at least.'

Adele didn't like this idea at all. She had set her heart on the trip and was already notionally on the plane.

'Honestly Mummy, I feel perfectly all right. I'm sleeping, you see, that's what's made all the difference, not the other pills at all. Sleeping and getting back to work. You of all people should appreciate that.'

'Of course. Maybe I should come with you.'

'No,' said Adele firmly, 'I don't want to sound ungrateful or unfriendly, but I want to go on my own. For the first time for months, I feel I can stand on my own two feet, and I want to do it. Sorry Mummy.'

'That's perfectly all right,' said Celia coldly, 'I'm growing used to rejection.'

Charles Donald Patterson, the letter said. Forwarded from the old address in Gramercy Park. On the back of the envelope was printed: St Anthony's, Thorncliff, Westchester Co., and underneath that, Care for the Care-less.

It was a good copy line; Izzie would have admired it. Barty supposed it was an appeal. Only – whoever it was from obviously knew Charlie personally. It didn't say The Occupier, or even just Mr C. Patterson. Only a very few people knew Charlie's middle name. He hated it so much, he kept it very quiet. In the early days she had teased him about it.

But – maybe it was a care home and maybe it was where Sally Norton was now. Maybe she had left that other address, in Sheepshead Bay. In which case, the letter should be opened. They might want money, they might want to contact Charlie, Sally might be ill. Barty had agreed to save his post, and take it down to South Lodge at the weekend. Only it was beginning to look now as if she wouldn't be going, she was terribly busy. A quiet weekend on her own would clear a vast backlog, of neglected manuscripts, letters, thinking, even.

She wondered if she should phone him, ask him what he would like her to do. But that would mean a protracted argument about her not coming. Not today. Maybe tomorrow, when she had quite made up her mind . . .

She put the letter down on the kitchen table, on the top of the pile of newspapers, and went to work.

When she got home, both the pile and the letter was gone; she asked Maria what she had done with them.

'Thrown them out with the garbage, Mrs Ell—Patterson.' Like the Mills, Maria had problems with her new name. Like the Mills, she didn't seem to like Charlie very much.

'Oh Maria! There was a letter on the top, didn't you see it?'

'I did, yes, but I thought as you put it right there, along with those old envelopes, you didn't want it.'

'Well, I did,' said Barty, distressed. 'You really shouldn't have done that.'

'Mrs Patterson, I am very busy today. I have one of my heads, and how I am supposed to know what you thinking?'

'Maria, it's not very difficult to know a sealed-up letter shouldn't be thrown away.'

'It was not for you. Was for him. For Mr Patterson. I thought—'

'Yes all right. Well, where is the garbage, have you put it out?'

'In the garbage bin.'

'Can you see if it's still there, please? I hope the dustcart didn't come today.'

Maria shrugged, went out of the back door, looking upset. She came back a few minutes later, holding the letter. It had bits of raw carrot and onion adhering to it.

'Here,' she said, holding it out to Barty disdainfully, 'here is.'

'Thank you, Maria. Very much. Oh, dear, it's a bit of a mess.'

Maria shrugged again.

And since the letter obviously was going to be illegible within a very short space of time, liquid from other pieces of unpleasantness having seeped on to it, Barty decided she should open it. It couldn't be that personal or that important after all.

Only it was.

Adele was flying out of London on Saturday, had booked herself into the St Regis Hotel. She didn't even tell Barty she was coming.

'If I do, she might let it slip to Geordie, and I do want it to be a surprise,' she said to Venetia. 'It'll be more fun that way, he won't be able to get all defensive or anything. I'll telephone her the minute I've seen him, obviously. I'm longing to see her. And Izzie of course. And to meet Charlie, what a lot of excitement. Now, it'll be hot over there, won't it? Lots of nice silk dresses and things, I think. I can do some shopping, what bliss. And maybe go out to South Lodge for a few days, that'd be lovely. I just can't wait.'

Barty arrived at South Lodge late on Friday night. She had told Charlie she was coming, she didn't want him accusing her of being underhand, of sneaking up on him.

The girls rushed out when they heard the car, hugging her, kissing her; they both looked tanned and well, Jenna's face covered with its summer uniform of small, dusty freckles. Charlie came over to her as the girls released her and gave her a hug.

'Darling, it's so good to see you, I was afraid you wouldn't come at the last minute. We have some supper waiting, don't we girls, and such plans for the weekend.'

She didn't want to spoil her arrival with any kind of uncomfortable conversation; she sat in the kitchen with them, eating clam salad and crusty bread and drinking soda. She had refused wine, although the bottle of Muscadet which Charlie had on ice for her looked terribly tempting; she wanted to keep her head clear.

After she had finished, she sat with them in the den for a while, discussing the next day – sailing, a picnic on the shore, maybe a ride – and then stood up.

'I'm really tired. And it sounds like we have a busy day tomorrow. Would you excuse me? Charlie, are you coming?'

The girls kissed her, and said goodnight; she led the way upstairs to the guest room. She had been half afraid, had been dreading, indeed, that Charlie might have moved into the main bedroom in her absence, but the door to it was shut firmly; his things were scattered round the guest room in their usual disarray.

'You are so untidy,' she said, smiling, kissing him, so that he didn't get defensive.

He raised his hands in a gesture of surrender and grinned back.

'I confess. I am. But you knew that. Darling you look so tired, why don't I run you a bath, so you can relax before we go to bed—'

'Yes, maybe. Later.'

'Later?' He smiled at her again. 'You have plans right now?'

'I do – yes. But not—' she stopped. 'I want to talk to you about something.'

'Yes?' He sat down on the bed; he was holding a glass of bourbon on ice, he looked totally relaxed. She thought how perfectly and quickly he had assumed the summer uniform of the Hamptons, the Madras shirt, the khaki shorts, the boating shoes. He looked in fact very handsome, tanned, his hair cropped shorter, the dark brown already streaked with the sun.

'Charlie,' she said abruptly, 'what exactly does being an old boy of St Anthony's, Thorncliff mean?'

And the tanned face turned white, the dark eyes no longer smiled, as he looked at her; he took an enormous slug of his bourbon and stood up, went over to the window.

'How did you find out?' was all he said.

It was actually a very sad story; his parents were not the charming middle-aged couple standing in the garden at Summit, New Jersey. That was a family he had worked for as a gardener while he had been at college. His mother, Nanette, had been a waitress in a bar in Queens, his father a drunken, unemployed labourer who had beaten her up several times before leaving her, just a year after the wedding, on hearing that she was pregnant with Charlie.

Nanette had waited several weeks before accepting that he was not coming back; in any case, being a good Catholic girl, as she put it, there was no question of an abortion. Charlie was born in the state hospital and for almost three years she managed, somehow, to support the two of them. Not without difficulty; Charlie was left alone every night in the room she rented, while she went to work in the bar; during the day she took a cleaning job and paid someone to care for him. She went without food herself to support him; but after a horrendous interlude when he managed to tip over the cot into which he was tied every night for safety and fell, pinioned and screaming in pain from a fractured leg, she gave in and delivered him to St Anthony's, a Catholic orphanage in Thorncliff, Westchester County, recommended by the priest at her church.

It wasn't a bad place, a big house in the country, cold and sparsely furnished, but there was no physical abuse, as there was in so many Catholic institutions, and Charlie was adequately fed and clothed; but there was very little affection. For a couple of years Nanette visited him occasionally; then she managed to find herself a husband, whose only condition in marrying her was that Charlie should not have to live with them.

He was old enough to have developed a strong bond with and love for his mother; he missed her dreadfully. He would sit for hours, weeping, banging his head against the wall by his bed; after her increasingly rare visits he became very withdrawn, would refuse food for days and sit sucking his thumb, his eyes blank wtih despair.

But gradually he settled; one of the younger nuns, a pretty Irish girl who looked after the younger children, developed a great attachment to him, and would nurse him and sing to him at night, when he was crying. Later, as he began to grow up, she continued to take an interest in him and encouraged his fondness for music and for art, and, rather oddly, for cricket, for which she had a passion. When Charlie was ten years old, she died of TB; his grief was terrible.

There were only about fifty children there and they were taught by the nuns; they tried hard, but a lot of the boys ran wild and some of them, as they grew up, got into trouble with the police. Charlie didn't run wild, and he didn't get into trouble; in fact he was discovered to be rather clever. He was often top of the class; this gave him the only real satisfaction in life he had ever known. When he was fourteen, he went to the local high school, where he continued to succeed; at eighteen he won a scholarship to Columbia University, where he studied math and politics. Academic success came easily to him; he never had to work as hard as his peers, he had a superb memory and a gift for encapsulating knowledge, both of which stood him in very good stead at examination time.

Very few of the children at St Anthony's went to college at all; to have acquired a place at such an establishment as Columbia was a truly great achievement. He was very hard up; his scholarship only covered his fees and he lived in a run-down apartment two miles from the university. At night he worked in a bar. At Christmas and Thanksgiving he had nowhere to go, except his room; he worked all the hours he could to stave off loneliness, but it was pretty bleak.

He was moderately happy; he had some good friends. But for the first time he also began to realise how disadvantaged he was. It was not just being poor, it was having no background. No parents, no family, no personal history. He told everyone that his parents had both been killed in a motor accident. It was not entirely convincing. The less kind, better-off students looked down on him, sneered at his cheap clothes, at his accent, at his lack of social status.

It was a friend at college who told him about the jobs to be had on the coast in Maine; he had worked there the year before, in one of the country clubs. 'Mostly in the kitchen, but sometimes I got to work behind the bar. It was a breeze. Hard work, but boy, what a place.'

Charlie made his way to the coast, hitching lifts on trucks, and went from bar to bar until he got a job. And there he discovered a new tribe: indolent, self-indulgent people, Ivy League, old money, who appeared to have so much in return for so little – and he knew that was what he wanted.

He learned fast: how to dress, how to speak, how to get his hair cut, how and what to drink. He was a quick study; in two years he felt he could pass for one of them: or nearly one of them. Certainly not an abandoned child born into poverty and brought up in an orphanage. He was tall, good-looking, and he wore his clothes well; once away from college, he reinvented himself.

The nice couple from Summit, New Jersey, became his parents, both dead; St Anthony's became a modest prep school in Hudson Heights; Columbia remained Columbia, spoken of no longer with pride, though, but with an affectionate disparagement – 'It's a funny old place, everyone there is terribly worried about their future prospects!' And Charles Donald Patterson, bursary student, became Charlie Patterson who soon began to make his way in the real estate business . . .

'So,' said Barty, when he had finished, had refilled his glass for the third time. 'Is there any more?'

'No. You know the rest.'

'Oh, I do?'

'Yes. I met Meg, I married her, we had Cathy, Meg died—'

'Did Meg know? All this?'

'Kind of.'

'What's that supposed to mean?'

A long silence; then, 'She did know, yes.'

'But Cathy doesn't?'

'Of course not. We agreed never to tell her.'

'But why?' said Barty. She felt physically dizzy, weak with shock. 'What's so wrong with it, what is there to be ashamed of?'

'Oh Barty. Surely you can see—'

'No. No, I can't. Look at me, at my background, I'm not ashamed of it.'

'Yes, well you were wanted and loved. Your father didn't desert your mother, he wasn't violent—'

'He was, sometimes.'

'That's not violence. And you didn't grow up in some crap institution, didn't have the occasional friend who ended up in prison. What do you think it would do to a little girl, knowing all that about her father?'

'Not a lot, I would have thought,' said Barty, 'Cathy adores you, she thinks you can do no wrong, I'd have thought she would be proud of what you've achieved.'

'And what's that? What exactly am I supposed to have achieved? A two-bit, mostly unsuccessful company, a minus bank account. Not a great deal to be proud of there. I'm not risking it, and if you tell her, I—'

'Charlie, of course I'm not telling her. I can't believe you said that. How can you even think such a thing?'

'Sorry,' he said. He still hadn't met her eyes.

'So – you told Meg?'

'Yes. Well, she found out after a while. She saw some papers, some letters from my real mother to St Anthony's—'

'Before you were married?'

'Yes.'

'I seem to be rather more gullible,' said Barty. 'But why, Charlie? Why her, why not me?'

'Barty, she was different from you. She was just an ordinary girl, her father was a pretty modest lawyer – modest by your standards, anyway – she was a teacher, not a tycoon, she didn't need living up to, no one could have imagined I was marrying her for her money—'

'Oh Charlie. Does it all matter that much to you?'

'Of course it does, for Christ's sake,' he said, his voice low, a flush rising on his face now. 'How do you think I feel, day after day, living off you, having to be fucking grateful for everything? Charlie Patterson, the failure, who managed to reel in a rich widow. All that's bad enough without being Charles Donald, raised by charity, with a penniless slut of a mother and a brute of a father.'

'None of that matters to me.'

'Well, it does to me. And it would to a whole lot of other people.'

'Other people don't matter.'

'To me they do. They would to you, if you'd grown up like I did. Being looked down on, sneered at, having no proper home, not even a room of my own, no possessions, sharing a few shabby old toys, wearing hand-me-downs . . .'

'I certainly know about being looked down on. Charlie, the only thing that matters to me is that you lied to me. So dreadfully. I – just don't know that I can bear it.'

There was something familiar about all this; a sense of *déjà vu* almost. What was it?

'Well,' he said, 'that's absolutely up to you. Of course. I was just trying – in my own, no doubt peculiar way – to cope with it all. It's not easy, you know. It took a lot of courage to ask you to marry me. Loving you, making love with you even, that was all right. But marrying you, that was different. Quite, quite different.'

'Were you ever going to tell me? Was there really no time when you thought you owed me – owed me your honesty? This person you're supposed to love.'

'Who I do love. Oh, Barty, I don't know. Yes, I suppose I thought I would, one day. When I was really sure of you, when I felt really safe.'

She was silent, trying to take it all in, to make sense of it. Of being married to someone, sleeping with him, sharing the extraordinary day-to-day intimacy of marriage with someone who was not what she had thought, who was so competent a liar, so ruthless a deceiver . . .

'I'm going to bed, Charlie,' she said. 'I'm terribly tired. I'll see you in the morning.'

He looked at her; she saw him recognising what she was saying, that of course she was not going to sleep with him, that she might never sleep with him again, might not remain married to him, even, and that there was absolutely nothing he could do about it.

'Yes,' he said, 'yes of course. Till the morning, then.'

He came over to her, kissed her very gently on the cheek; Barty flinched from him.

'It was only because I loved you so much,' he said quietly, 'I couldn't face the other way. The truthful way. It just got too late. I'm so, so sorry.'

She went then, without a word, to the other room, to her room, to Laurence's room, and lay awake for most of the night, staring out at the vast starry sky, and thinking about John, the one other man in her life, the kind, sweetly straightforward, uncomplicated man who had wanted to marry her, who she had thought perhaps she loved but had finally turned away from, in order to be with Laurence. She seemed to have a lemming-like propensity for trouble.

CHAPTER 22

'Good morning, my darling. What are you doing today?'

'Oh – lots of things. Saturday things. Shopping. Cleaning. Going to the laundromat. Possibly doing some work.'

'That doesn't sound like a lot of fun.'

'Life isn't all about fun, Geordie,' said Izzie primly.

'Oh dear. You sound like Celia. Can I come and see you?'

She thought for a moment. She wanted some time to herself, to think, to plan. She had to do it: had to tell Geordie she couldn't go on. However happy they were together, however wonderful it all was, it just wasn't right. Every day she woke up feeling more confused, more anxious. It had to end before it was too late. But it wasn't going to be easy. He wasn't going to go quietly . . .

'After lunch,' she said, 'how would that be?'

'It wouldn't be as good as before lunch. But it'll do. 'Bye Izzie darling.'

''Bye Geordie.'

She was going to be saying that again – rather less light-heartedly – in a few hours. She was. She had to be. It was the only way.

'Ladies and gentlemen. Please return to your seats and fasten your seat belts. We are now preparing for our descent into Idlewild.'

Adele smiled happily. She had managed to sleep quite a bit on the plane, thanks to her wonderful pills. New York was bathed in sunshine; Geordie was down there, more work was down there, Saks Fifth Avenue was down there; it was all too good to be true.

Barty had decided she had to stay for the weekend; the girls would be so disappointed if she didn't. They had prepared so carefully, so sweetly for her visit. A picnic packed, a bag with towels and swimsuits sitting by the door, a ride booked, a barbecue arranged, steaks and burgers in the fridge . . . she couldn't let them down.

She was woken from a two-hour sleep by Jenna, bearing a tray of tea.

'Hi Mother. What are you doing in here?'

'Oh – I couldn't sleep. I wanted to read.'

'You OK now?'

'Of course. That tea looks awfully good.'

'Breakfast's ready when you are.'

'Is – is Charlie down there?'

'He was.'

A stab of hope; maybe he'd gone back to New York, given her a breather.

'He's gone for a walk. He says we'll leave for Sag Harbor whenever you're ready.'

'I see.'

He walked into the kitchen as she toyed with the fruit salad Cathy had made for her, picked up a bagel, spread it with cream cheese, avoiding her eyes.

'You OK?'

'I'm fine.'

'It's a lovely day. Perfect for sailing. We could go across to Fire Island. Picnic there.'

'Sure.'

He looked at her then; the relief in his eyes was intense.

'I'll go and fetch the life jackets,' was all he said.

Adele checked in at the St Regis at noon. It was very hot and bright in the street, but her room was cool and dim. She thought of phoning the Algonquin right away, to see if Geordie was there, or at least leave a message, but decided to have a rest first. She did feel rather tired. She ordered some iced water – it was so wonderful the way everything in America was iced – and a club sandwich and lay down on the bed. It was very large. She looked at the empty pillow beside her thoughtfully. Maybe, just maybe, Geordie would be sharing it with her before she went home. You never knew . . . Adele fell asleep.

Geordie arrived at Izzie's apartment just after two.

'It's my time now. You said after lunch. This is after lunch. My goodness, it all looks very pristine.'

'Doesn't it? I worked very hard on it.'

'You've still got the picture of Noni sitting there I see.'

'Yes.' She'd left it there, as an instrument of torture for herself: to remind herself how wrong it was, what she was doing, to strengthen her resolve.

'I've brought you a present,' he said.

'Oh, Geordie, no, you mustn't, I—' she was about to say it there and then, or at least hint at it, but somehow she couldn't. Not just then. It was a big box: he watched her unwrap it.

288

'Tiffany! Oh, Geordie, you are naughty, whatever – oh my God!'

How could you tell a man you didn't want to see him any more, when he'd just bought you an utterly gorgeous Tiffany lamp, when he was looking at you in a mixture of triumph and anxiety, lest you didn't like it, when he had remembered so precisely what you'd said you wanted, the shade a mixture of reds and blues.

'It's so beautiful. I love it, I absolutely love it. Thank you so, so much.'

'Let me put it in place for you. There. Isn't that glorious?'

'Absolutely beautiful. But you—'

'No buts. I thought you might like to show me your appreciation. In the usual sort of way.'

'Oh Geordie—' The very thing she had resolved so absolutely not to do: no more lovemaking, no more anything. Just – goodbye Geordie. Before any real harm was done.

'Please, Izzie! I want you so much.'

She wanted him too. For the last time, the very last time, she told herself, she would agree. And then—

It was very lovely, their lovemaking, that hot afternoon, with the sun shafting in through the blinds, the noises from the street as background, children laughing, people talking, birds singing in the trees, the occasional rather sleepy-sounding car lurching along. She found herself concentrating absolutely on every moment, every movement, every word, every response, etching it in her mind so that she would never, ever forget it; it made the experience still more intense, sweeter, richer.

'I love you,' she heard him say, somewhere outside the tumult and the crying out that was her orgasm, and 'I love you too,' she said, as she fell slowly into the deep sweet peace of afterwards.

Adele woke feeling very confused. Her head ached and she couldn't work out at first where she was. She rang for some tea, and sat sipping it, while the St Regis receptionist tried to connect her with the Algonquin.

'Algonquin Hotel. Good afternoon.'

'Oh – yes.' Why did she feel so nervous? 'May I speak to Mr MacColl, please?'

'I'll try his room for you. Please hold the line.'

A long silence; then, 'I'm sorry, he doesn't appear to be in. May I take a message?'

'Yes, please. Er – do you have any idea when he might be back, did he say?'

'I'm afraid not.' The voice sounded just slightly disapproving.

'Very well. Could you say that his – that is, Mrs MacColl rang. And would like to speak to him.'

'At which number, Mrs MacColl?'

'I'm at the St Regis.'

'Very well. Thank you, Mrs MacColl.'

How frustrating. Now what was she going to do? She really hadn't expected this. She had somehow thought Geordie would be there, that he would be totally available for her: how stupid. He was no doubt seeing some journalist or publisher even now.

On a Saturday? Surely not. She felt her mood begin to sink; felt very alone, suddenly, in this strange city. With no one to talk to, no one to say come round here, we'd love to see you. Just a lot of receptionists and waiters and maids and—

Don't be silly Adele, this is your own fault. This is your blow for your own independence. You wanted to arrive unannounced, you could have had Barty greet you at the airport, Izzie inviting you round for dinner. It was your idea to surprise everyone. How could they all be expected to be in on a sunny Saturday afternoon? Geordie had probably just gone for a walk. Or to meet some friends or something. He would surely be back in time for dinner. And even if he was having dinner with someone, maybe she could join them.

Meanwhile, she could amuse herself, for heaven's sake. She could go and take some photographs: New York street scenes, perhaps. But you needed quite a lot of energy to do that, and she was rather tired. And it was very hot. Maybe she should go and do a bit of the shopping she had promised herself. There was no great rush, after all, to see Geordie. As long as he was still in New York – which she knew he was – tomorrow would do. Or even the next day. She suddenly wondered if he might be away for the weekend. Away with Barty, even, in the Hamptons. Now, that would be a pity. Well . . . Adele stood up, brushed her hair, reapplied her lipstick, picked up her bag and set out determinedly for Saks Fifth Avenue.

It was a perfect day for sailing; brilliant, with a strong breeze. Barty watched Charlie as he pushed *Southern Lady* along, tacking easily and skilfully across the wind, concentrating absolutely on his task. The girls were leaning out over the side, hair whipped by the wind, faces wet with spray, their bare feet tucked under the strap, squealing with excitement and pleasure.

She looked up the length of the sail, up to the blue sky and the scudding clouds, feeling the sun and the water on her face, wishing she could also feel the happiness such a day demanded. Instead of alternately angry and dully miserable, exhausted with the sheer physical effort of smiling, chatting, remaining upright, even. What she really longed for was to be lying somewhere, somewhere preferably dark, dark and still and quiet, where she could think about it all. About Charlie, about Charlie lying to her, so consistently and over so long a period; they might not actually amount to much, those lies, they were not fraudulent, not strictly speaking, at any rate, not dangerous even, but they were of a deeply important nature. Presenting himself to her as someone he was not; upgrading himself, denying his past, denying his parentage, all for what? To impress her? To ingratiate himself with her? To make himself more acceptable to her?

Whatever his motives, she was horrified; that he could have gone into their relationship in a deception so wilful, so careful, so beautifully rehearsed, that only by a very slight quirk of fate had she discovered the truth about him.

She felt stupid as well as hurt, mortified as well as angry; she had known Charlie for almost three years; and in all that time had watched and listened to this presentation of himself and suspected nothing in it. Looking back now, of course, there had been clues: the lack of friends, the fact that his well-to-do parents should have left him nothing; but she had cast only glancing suspicions at them.

She felt something else, too, something strange, something unexpected: a fierce jealousy that Meg, his first wife, the mother of his child, had known all this, had lived with the truth, had been married to the real Charlie, while she had married a fake one, and lived with him in ignorance, foolish, foolish ignorance . . .

'Mother! Wake up. Charlie says can you take the tiller?'

'Sorry.' She jerked back to concentration, took the tiller, steered the boat in the direction Charlie was indicating; and then as they reached the lee of the land, as the wind dropped, watched herself in awe as she jumped out, laughing, swam right into shore towing the *Lady* behind her.

And still more in awe as she sat on the rocks at the back of the cove, eating cold chicken and drinking Coca-Cola and chatting and laughing with the girls, fussing over Jenna burning, Cathy's forgotten sunhat, a graze Charlie had got on his knee as he scrambled up the rocks and slipped.

'You're such a good sailor, Charlie,' said Jenna, biting into a piece of French bread. 'Where did you learn?'

'Oh – on the coast off Maine. When I was at college. I used to vacation down there, bummed my way through the summer. I had a friend with a boat, not unlike this one.'

'It must have been fun,' said Jenna, 'did you spend all the vacations down there?'

'Yes, I did. And it was fun. I worked some of the time, when I ran out of money, worked behind bars, that sort of thing. But there was still plenty of time for beach picnics and sailing.'

'Like this?'

'Pretty much like this.'

He smiled at her. Barty felt sick. This was how he had done it, it was a perfect example, nothing quite false, nothing quite true either, just a careful making over of the facts . . .

'I'm going to swim,' said Jenna, 'you coming, Cathy?'

'Sure.'

He waited until they were out of earshot: 'Barty—'

'No, Charlie,' she said, 'not now. Later, when they're in bed, I don't want to spoil their day.'

'Of course.' He had brought some wine, had drunk quite a lot of it. He waved the bottle at her; she shook her head.

'No thanks.'

'OK. I think I'll go and swim too.'

She watched him as he ran into the water; he was very slim, very fit-looking and his Madras cotton shorts emphasised his tan. He plunged in, surfaced underneath Jenna, pushed her up on his shoulders; she shrieked with pleasure.

Whatever else, he was very, very good with her; he showed Cathy absolutely no favouritism whatever. It couldn't have been entirely easy. She had that, at the very least, to be grateful for.

Adele returned to the St Regis at five; she had had a good afternoon. She had bought herself a red linen suit with a cropped jacket (not a style she had seen a great deal in London, but much in favour in New York) and a very pretty black silk cocktail dress with a low-cowled back and high waist. She thought she could wear that this evening if Geordie – or Barty of course – invited her to dinner. There was a hairdresser at the hotel; she could get her hair done, it was looking pretty frightful, what with the flight and the heat.

She walked into her room, checked for messages. None. The excitement of her afternoon ebbed a bit; taking a deep breath, she phoned the Algonquin. No, Mr MacColl had not returned. Yes, of course they were sure, and of course her message would have been passed on to him. Adele began to feel a little odd. Lonely. Very alone, actually. She almost – *almost* – wished she had let her mother come with her.

She wondered whether she might go down to the bar and have a cocktail, but it was very much the mark of the single woman, drinking alone in a bar. And she wasn't single. She was just waiting for Geordie to come back to his hotel. Then, at the very least, they would have a drink. She was quite sure of that.

She ordered a Martini from room service, drank it as slowly as she could. She wasn't actually supposed to drink with her pills, but she had discovered that as long as she limited her intake carefully, and didn't bolt the alcohol down, it was all right. Goodness, it was actually time for her pills. She rummaged in her toilet bag, found them, took two. She had been very careful, as Dr Cunningham had told her, to watch the change of time, to make sure she didn't miss any. Or take too many for that matter.

The phone rang; she jumped. It had to be Geordie, it had to. No one else knew she was here . . .

'Darling? It's Venetia. Just checking you're—'

'I'm fine,' she said firmly. 'Absolutely. Probably having a drink with Geordie later.'

'Good. Give him my love. Speak to you tomorrow. 'Bye, darling, better go—'

'Of course. Thanks.'

Another drink? Better not. She wasn't hungry. What was she going to do this evening, if Geordie didn't phone? It was going to be quite – long.

But he would. He was sure to.

She pulled out her cigarette case, one of the Cartier pair Sebastian had given her and Venetia for their eighteenth birthdays so long ago. When her parents had given them the dear little red car that even now was in Boy's garage, driven by the occasional young person. She had been pretty lonely that night: watching Venetia dancing with Boy, recognising that here was something important, something that was going to come between them. She – oh damn. Maybe she had better have a meal in the dining room. That would be all right. Or – room service. She had a good book. Except she just wasn't hungry. Or tired any more. Maybe – maybe she should ring Barty; it was silly not to. Better than spending the evening alone. If – if Geordie hadn't phoned in another half hour, that's what she would do. Definitely. Meanwhile, maybe another slow drink . . .

'Shall we go out for dinner?' said Izzie. She had woken, feeling very remorseful, shocked at her lack of willpower and moral courage. She looked at Geordie; he was half lying on a great pile of pillows beside her, reading intently; he felt her gaze and turned to smile at her, his grey eyes very tender.

'Good sleep? I thought you'd never wake up.'

'Yes, very.' She stretched. 'What are you reading?'

'*A Certain Smile*. By that French girl. Françoise Sagan. It's marvellous. Have you read it?'

She shook her head. 'Not yet. I've been drowning in *Peyton Place*. It's like eating boxes and boxes of chocolates, it's so self-indulgent.'

'You should try the Sagan. I'll leave you my copy.' He put it down, leaned over her and kissed her.

'You're so lovely.'

'Geordie—'

'Now what was that you were saying about dinner? I'm starving.'

'I wondered if we should go out.'

'Good idea. But not yet. Much too early. It's only – let's see – six-thirty. Too hot, too. Why don't we stay here, have a drink, some of that very nice champagne you still haven't drunk and then go out about eight. Would you like to go uptown? I mean we could go somewhere really ritzy, if you like, the King Cole Room at the St Regis, that's pretty nice—'

'No,' said Izzie, 'no, I hate those sorts of places. Let's eat locally.'

'Fine by me. God it's hot. Could I take a quick dip in that very grand bath of yours?'

'Of course. I might even come and join you.'

This was not the sort of thing she should be doing, Izzie thought, as she settled into the bath with Geordie, her legs intertwined with his, laughing as he put great dollops of soap on her nose, her breasts, her belly, leaning forward to kiss him, wondering if they could go back to bed again. God, how could you want someone so much, so terribly much? Thank goodness he couldn't read her thoughts.

'Are you thinking what I'm thinking?' he said suddenly.

'No. I mean, I don't know what you're thinking.'

'Yes you do. Lady Isabella, how very voracious you are. Shall we leave this water to get cold and return to it later?'

Not the last time then, that afternoon, she thought afterwards, lying in his arms, exhausted now, desire most profligately spent, what was she thinking of, what was she doing?

'Barty? No, no, it isn't, is it, I'm sorry—'

'Miss Miller not here. This is Maria. Her housekeeper. Can I help you?'

'Oh, Maria, hallo. You probably won't remember me. This is Adele MacColl, I stayed with Barty a few years ago. Anyway – is – is she around?'

'Gone to Hamptons. To join Mr Patterson and the young ladies.'

Disappointment cut into Adele; another avenue of companionship cut off. 'How – how long is she there for?'

'I dunno. She say she not going at all this weekend, then suddenly, Friday afternoon, she pack and just leave.'

'On her own? She didn't take any friends? Like – well, like my husband, Mr MacColl?'

'She not take nobody, I don't think.'

'Right. Well – well is Miss Brooke there?'

'Miss Brooke, she don't stay here no more.'

'Oh really? Where has she gone?'

'To her own place. Down in the village.'

'Oh. Oh I see.' She remembered now, Noni talking about Izzie moving. Well – Izzie would be a good person to spend the evening with. If she was free. Even if she wasn't, she was pretty sure to invite her along. They had always had that sort of relationship.

'Do you have her phone number there, Maria, please?'

'I will see. Just wait, please.'

Adele sat tapping her fingers on the bedside table, telling herself that it didn't really matter if Izzie wasn't there, she could see her tomorrow, she could just go to bed early, take an extra pill maybe, and sleep; it would seem less daunting tomorrow, being all alone in this great city.

'Yes. Here is. You want address as well?'

'Oh – yes, please, Maria. Thank you. Thank you very much.'

Izzie and Geordie were back in the bath when the phone rang.

'Bloody thing,' said Geordie, 'expecting anyone?'

'No.'

'We'll let it ring.' It rang and rang. And then stopped.

'Great. Now then, shall I wash your back – shit. There's the phone again. Someone's keen to get hold of you. I'd better go –'

He got out of the bath, slipped slightly on the tiled floor, stubbed his toe on the lavatory pan.

'Ow! God that hurt. Shit, don't laugh Izzie, it's not funny. Now the bloody thing's stopped again. Can I take it off the hook? We don't want to talk to anyone, do we?'

'Don't think so.'

'Right, then.'

He came back, smiling with satisfaction.

'Whoever it was will have to manage without us. Now where was I? Moving down to your very charming backside, I think . . .'

So she was out as well. Oh God . . .

Adele's fragile spirits were in free fall; she felt lonely, unloved, almost frightened. What on earth had made her do this, come all this way on her own, to a city where she knew no one, or almost no one, when she could have been at home with Clio, reading her a bedtime story, cuddled up on the sofa? Adele felt tears rising in her eyes, felt the treacherous despair reaching into her. Nobody cared about her, nobody loved her.

She took a large sip of her Martini; it was very strong. It seemed to restore her. Come on, Adele, this won't do, you're here, you have to cope with it.

She would try once more, then just order a sandwich and go to bed, with an extra sleeping pill. She'd be fine; she'd feel better in the morning.

She tried the phone again; it was engaged. So Izzie was there; how wonderful . . .

'Darling I've got a better idea. Why don't we eat here? I'll cook. I can, you know, I've had to learn.'

'I don't believe you. Cook what?'

'I do a real mean chilli con carne. How would that be?'

'Sounds great.'

'I shall go shopping right now. We can sit under your new lamp and gaze at one another while our mouths burn. All right?'

'Very all right.'

She might as well enjoy it; she couldn't do it today; not now. Not when they'd made love twice, and he'd given her this wonderful present. She'd wait till tomorrow.

Still engaged; she'd tried three times now. Izzie must be having a marathon conversation. It would be so nice to see her, to see her apartment, as well. Maybe – no, she had never liked the idea of dropping in on people. Hotels were different, but houses – her mother had always said it was extremely inconsiderate: although she could remember a great many occasions when Celia had just arrived on her doorstep, demanding hospitality. Well, that was fairly par for her mother's course, don't do as I do, do as I say. Anyway – Adele took a deep mental breath. She would go. Why not? She'd go down there, in a cab. She could ask the concierge how far it was, but she was pretty sure it wouldn't take long. And Izzie had been out for ages, and now she was on the phone, Adele had a pretty good chance of catching her. It was worth a try. At worst, it would use up an hour or so. Making it nearer a respectable time for her to go to bed.

'Right. I'm off. You got any wine?'
  'No. All drunk. Except your champagne.'
  'That won't go with chilli. I'll get some, and some beer. 'Bye darling.'
  ''Bye Geordie.'

Twenty minutes, the concierge had said. That was fine. She asked him to get her a cab.
  This would be fun. She could stop on the way, get Izzie some flowers. She'd be so surprised, so pleased to see her.

'Here you are, lady. Number Five.'
  'Thank you.'
  The light was on in the ground floor: what the Americans called the first floor. Maria had said it was the first floor. So Izzie was there. How lovely.
  She paid the cab off, gathered together her bag, the flowers she had bought Izzie, her evening wrap, and rang the doorbell.

Geordie had been very quick. She'd expected him to be at least three-quarters of an hour. Maybe he'd forgotten his wallet or something. And he must have forgotten she'd given him her key – he really was not himself. Any more than she was . . .
  Izzie went to the door smiling, opened it.
  'Now what have you – oh my God. My God, Adele!'

She really, really thought she was going to be sick. She also felt she might fall over; the ground was heaving in a rather alarming way. She took a deep breath, put out her hand to steady herself on the door frame.

'Adele,' she said again. Her voice sounded odd even to her.

'Hallo Izzie. I'm sorry, I've obviously given you a fearful shock. I just suddenly thought of it. Here – these are for you.'

'Thank you.'

Izzie took the flowers carefully, as if they were made of fine china.

'Thank you very much, Adele.'

'The least I can do.' She smiled at Izzie, her most brilliant sparkly smile. 'Aren't you going to ask me in?'

'Of – of course. But I was just – just—'

Izzie was behaving rather oddly. She seemed far more shocked than Adele would have expected. And she was very pale.

'Izzie, are you all right?'

She appeared to pull herself together; she smiled a rather strained smile, and said, 'Of course. Just a bit of a shock, seeing you. I mean, I thought you were four thousand miles away, or whatever London is.'

'Three I think. Maybe four. You know how badly educated I am. Geordie would know. Have you seen him, by the way?'

'Oh – yes. Yes, once or twice. Adele, do please come in. I'm sorry, I – let me take your things.'

Izzie was feeling a bit better now; a bit steadier. But – what was she going to do? What in the name of God could she do? Make an excuse, rush out, try to head Geordie off?

Adele was looking very beautiful, of course. Very thin, but – beautiful. Perfectly groomed, as always, in a spotless white linen dress, her make-up flawless, her long nails perfectly manicured. Izzie cast a mental glance at herself, dressed in her jeans and a big T-shirt from the army surplus store, her hair still damp from the bath, curling wildly round her face. How could Geordie possibly—

'Izzie, this is a divine apartment.' Adele was walking round it, peering at things. 'Really divine. So – so you, isn't it? What a perfectly gorgeous lamp, can I switch it on, so I can see the colours?'

'It hasn't got a plug,' said Izzie quickly, 'it's – it's new.'

'New! Goodness, Izzie, you must be doing well. Or was it a present from someone? I love that chair, it's so pretty. And – goodness.'

For the first time her voice was odd. She looked at Izzie intently.

'How did you get that picture of Noni, on the fireplace? I sent that to Geordie—'

'Yes, well – well, I told you I'd seen him. He showed it to me and I put it in my bag by mistake. The colours are so lovely, they seem to suit the room, do you mind?'

She was talking much too much, rambling, even; she felt a flush rising on her face.

297

'Of course I don't mind,' said Adele. 'But – when did you see Geordie? Not today, I've been trying to get hold of him, he's not at the hotel.'

'Really?'

'No. I've been ringing him ever since I arrived.'

'Adele, it's wonderful you're here but I don't – oh, sorry, would you like a drink?'

Suddenly a drink was what she wanted more than anything on earth. 'I don't know. I've had two Martinis and I'm not supposed to drink at the moment. I'm taking some pills.'

'What sort of pills?' As if she cared.

'Oh – I've been a bit down. Anyway, yes, a little one. What have you got?'

'Only—' Only champagne. The champagne Geordie had brought; the very expensive champagne Geordie had brought. Suppose it was his favourite brand, suppose Adele recognised it . . .

'Would you mind champagne?' she said feebly.

'Not a bit. How lovely. Just a tiny glass, though.'

Izzie went into the kitchen, took the champagne out of the fridge, and cast a desperate glance round the sitting room for clues to Geordie's presence. A sweater, a handkerchief even. Thank God, just thank God it wasn't the winter, there would have been a trail of things, scarves, gloves—

'Here.' She handed Adele a glass; she had carefully left the bottle in the kitchen.

'Thank you, darling. Now I want to know everything, what you've been doing, about your fabulous job, about Barty, about Charlie—'

'Yes, of course. But, Adele, you haven't told me, you haven't explained why you're here . . .'

'It was just a whim. You know how I like acting on whims. I've started working on *Record* again and they said they'd like to see me, and I thought, well, Geordie's there, and you're there and Barty's there and why not? I've been a bit fed up in London. I thought I'd give you all a surprise. Specially Geordie. I do miss him, Izzie. I know we've had our problems and everything, but I still love him so much. And miss him so much.'

She was talking an awful lot, Izzie thought, more than usual, and she seemed terribly over-excited.

'And I thought if I just arrived, appeared on his doorstep, with no children to distract us, we'd be able to talk, you know, really talk and—'

'Adele, I wonder if you could excuse me just for a moment,' said Izzie, 'I've just remembered I've got a letter that absolutely must catch the post, work, you know the sort of thing, I won't be more than five minutes, would you be all right? I can give you a magazine to read and—'

'Darling, of course. Don't be silly. You've got *A Certain Smile*, I see, I've been wanting to read it, I'll make a start. And then when you get back maybe you'll let me take you out to dinner?'

'That would be – lovely. Well, I'll just—'

But it was too late; there was the sound of a key in the lock, of the door opening, the door into the lobby, of the door being pushed closed, too late now, too late to do anything. Izzie stood there, just waiting, waiting—

'Darling, here you are, three bottles of wine, should be enough, put them straight in the fridge, it's—'

And then silence; he stood absolutely still, frozen in time, his eyes dark and horrified in his suddenly white face, just staring and staring at her. And then he said, in a voice that was almost frighteningly normal, 'Adele! What on earth are you doing here?'

CHAPTER 23

Cathy wouldn't stop crying. On and on it went, helpless, hopeless crying; Jenna looked at her in despair. She had tried everything: cuddling her, soothing her, offering her sweets, Coca-Cola, even a glass of wine (Cathy had rather taken to wine that summer). Nothing did any good.

'You don't understand,' she kept saying, 'it was hearing them quarrelling like that, shouting at each other, it was exactly like when Mummy was alive, shouting and shouting, I hated it so much.'

Jenna was surprised; Cathy had never mentioned the quarrelling before; she had always imagined a perfectly happy little threesome. And envied them. Jenna adored her mother and she was very happy now, of course, but she did often wonder what it might be like to live with your two parents, in a normal way.

'I'm so afraid of what might happen,' Cathy moaned, reaching for yet another tissue.

'What do you mean?'

'Well that they might get divorced or something.'

'Cathy, your parents didn't get divorced.'

'They couldn't. My mother died. But people do. I couldn't bear it, Jenna, it's so lovely, the four of us. Daddy's so happy—'

And she started to cry again.

Jenna stood up.

'Where are you going?'

'To get some cocoa. Want some?'

'No thanks.'

Jenna walked down the corridor to her mother's room. The one that had been her mother's room before. Where she seemed to have settled for the time being. She knocked on the door.

'Who is it?'

'Jenna.'

'Oh, Jenna. Just a minute. Wait there, darling.'

There was quite a long pause; Jenna could hear the taps running in the bathroom. What was going on in there?

Her mother appeared in the doorway; she had obviously been crying.

'Hallo,' she said, with the brief smile which meant she was having to try rather hard to produce it.

'Can I come in?'

'Of course. Everything all right?'

'No. Cathy's crying and crying. I can't stop her.'

'Why?'

'She heard you quarrelling with Charlie.'

'Oh. Well, I'm sorry—'

'She says it's like when he was married to her mother and they quarrelled.'

'Really? I'm surprised she can remember, she was only three or so—'

'Well she says they shouted at each other a lot. And she hated it, and I guess it's brought it all back. And now she's scared you're going to get divorced. You're not, are you, Mother?'

Her mother looked at her; very seriously for a long time. Then she said quite light-heartedly, 'One quarrel hardly means a divorce.'

'That's not an answer.'

'All right. We certainly have no plans for divorce. At the moment, anyway.' She managed another smile. 'All married people quarrel, you know.'

'I told Cathy that. But then I began to get worried myself. I would so absolutely, absolutely hate it. It's so great now, all of us together, everyone's happy, everyone's having a really good time.'

'You're very fond of Charlie, aren't you?'

'Terribly. He's so sweet to me, I never feel he's Cathy's dad and not mine. The other night I got my period, you know, and it really, really hurt. Cathy was asleep, and he was just so kind, got me a hot water bottle, and some Excedrin, and tucked me up under an eiderdown in the den and let me watch TV with him. I think he is just the nicest man in the world and I think we're really lucky.'

'Yes,' said her mother, 'yes, I can see that. Well – good.'

'So – everything's all right, then? I can tell Cathy?'

'You can tell Cathy there are absolutely no plans for a divorce. Well, not as far as I know.'

Barty managed a smile; she did look dreadfully tired, Jenna thought, tired and actually a bit – old. She was quite a bit older than a lot of the mothers at school of course. And right now, she looked a lot older than Charlie. They must try to persuade her to stay a few more days, have a rest. She'd been talking about going back on Monday.

Jenna gave her a kiss.

'Night, Mother. Love you.'

'I love you too, Jenna.'

Jenna ran back to their room to tell Cathy the good news.

★

'I think it would be absolutely marvellous,' Celia's voice was at its most peremptory. 'We should do it for the summer. I've already had two meetings with General Dugdale and he assures me he can meet a March deadline.'

'Celia –' Jay hesitated '– Celia, I'm sure the General's memoirs will be marvellous. But do we really want to do them now? It's eleven, no, twelve years since the war ended. Will people really want to read any more about it?'

'Of course. They're still obsessed with it. If you talked to ordinary people, as I do, outside the publishing industry, you would realise that. People are still immensely proud of the way we won the war, of the spirit of this country during the Blitz, the wonderful sense of comradeship that existed through those years—'

'I don't think that's quite the same as wanting to read military memoirs,' said Keir, cutting in. 'I'd agree with you on people's feelings about the war, Celia, but I think you'd do much better with a book about exactly that, what happened here, to people in London – and Glasgow, for that matter – during the Blitz, that sort of thing. Possibly even as fiction.'

Giles's face promptly set in the kind of frozen distaste he reserved for Keir Brown.

'I really can't agree with you,' he said. 'What this country endured during the last war was hardly the stuff fiction is made of—'

'Oh really?' said Celia. 'How fascinating. Would you say that applied to any war?'

'Yes, broadly.'

'So how do you regard *Gone With the Wind*? *For Whom the Bell Tolls*? *War and Peace*, even? As mistakes, aberrations by their publishers? I agree with Keir, it would make a marvellous theme for a novel. We should think about commissioning it. But I also feel very strongly that we should do these memoirs. George – that is, General Dugdale – has submitted a synopsis, and a couple of chapters about his time in Tripoli, before he went out to the desert.'

'So he's a friend of yours, is he?'

'He is. Sebastian Brooke and Nancy Arthure are none the worse as writers for being personal friends. Perhaps you think they are, Giles.'

'No,' he said, 'no, of course not. But—'

'I've brought a copy of the synopsis with me, you can see how well he writes—'

As always, she was right; the writing was vivid, amusing, stirring even, despite some grammatical eccentricities.

'And if you really want proof that the public will buy it,' said Celia, 'look at *A Sailor's Odyssey* by Viscount Cunningham. Hutchinsons have done wonderfully well with that.'

'I'll tell you what I think,' said Jay, 'we should invite the General to come in, discuss terms and dates.'

'I hope you're not going to be penny-pinching about General Dugdale's advance,' said Celia. 'He could command a very large sum and has already been offered ten thousand pounds by Heinemann.'

'We can discuss that with him,' said Jay firmly, 'but I really don't think summer is feasible Celia, it will be a huge book, the editing alone will be a massive task, although I agree he does have a wonderful turn of phrase. I also think' – he looked at Keir – 'that your idea of a novel set in the war is very well worth considering. Let's talk about that in a minute. Now I am a little worried about – yes, Susan?'

Susan Clarke, Venetia's secretary, was standing in the doorway, looking agitated. It was an unbreakable rule that publishing meetings should not be interrupted; flood, fire and haemorrhage, Sebastian had said long ago, were the only acceptable excuses.

'I'm so sorry to interrupt, but – Mrs Warwick, could you come to the phone, please? It's your sister, calling from New York. She says it is very urgent. She sounds a little upset.'

It was very hard trying to soothe a hysterical person across thousands of miles and down a telephone line. Venetia listened, half disbelieving, half horrified, to Adele gasping out words between sobs, trying not to ask her to repeat things, trying to find out what she could do. Finally she said, 'Look, darling, shall I come out there? I could get on a plane tonight.'

'No! No, I want to get away from this horrible, horrible place. I don't want to stay any longer.'

'Have you booked a flight?'

'No. No, I couldn't.' The voice was weak suddenly, whispery. 'I just couldn't seem to – to do it.'

'But—' Venetia stopped. 'Look Dell, where's Barty?'

'Out at Southampton.'

'Well can't you ask her to come back?'

'No. No, I can't, I don't want to tell anyone, I'm so ashamed, so miserable—'

'Darling you've nothing to be ashamed about. What about Uncle Robert? He'll do it all for you.'

'I don't want to tell him either. I don't want to tell anyone. That's what I was doing all yesterday, just trying to manage, trying not to tell anyone—'

'All right. Look, get the concierge to book you on to a flight. Then you don't have to explain anything, just say it's an emergency. And get him to arrange a cab to the airport, everything. Let me know when you're coming, and I'll be there to meet you. All right?'

'All right.'

'And I'm going to ring you in half an hour to make sure it's all fixed. Stay in your room, don't go out, will you?'

'No. No, of course not.'

''Bye darling, darling Dell. I love you.'

'I love you too.' Her voice was very frail; Venetia hoped to God she would cope with the arrangements. Maybe she should ring the concierge herself.

How could she have done that? Izzie, of all people, Izzie, who was so sweet and so good, Izzie, who had always been so close to Adele, who was one of Noni's best friends, Izzie, who Adele had helped so much in her own crises. Who would have thought that behind the angelic face, the soft, sweet voice, such treachery could lie?

Izzie sat at her desk at Neill & Parker, staring at the piece of paper with the brief which Nick had handed her an hour ago. It might as well have been written in Chinese for all the sense it made to her.

She felt very odd: not part of the world at all, cut off from it by some steely, impermeable barrier. On the other side were normal people, lucky, good people who had not done dreadful things, people who had not slept with one of their best friend's husband, who had not betrayed their best friend's daughter. People who could look the world in the face and not be ashamed, people who could walk down a street thinking about ordinary things like their jobs or what they might cook for dinner.

She had completely destroyed her life, in that dreadful, selfish, absolutely treacherous act; there was no one she loved, no one she cared about who would understand, who would be able to begin to forgive her. Not Barty, not her father, not Celia, not Jay, Tory, Venetia, Noni – they would all unite in judgement against her. Never in her life, even when she had lain in agony on the abortionist's table, when she had been in her room, bleeding, it seemed, to death, not even when she had discovered who Kit actually was, had she felt so alone, so utterly isolated and afraid.

Barty was sitting on the verandah when Geordie phoned. She had agreed to stay on at South Lodge for another couple of days, rather than do the great trek back on Sunday night; partly because she felt so exhausted and partly because the girls were still anxious about the row she and Charlie had had, and the ongoing tension between them.

It had been a very bad row; she had not only shouted, she had hit him and scratched his face, overcome by such blinding rage at what he had done that she felt only hurting him physically would ease it. It did; but only briefly.

She knew why she was so angry; just as she could explain the sense of *déjà vu* she had felt, confronting Charlie with what he had done. She was a deeply honest person, and she loathed any kind of dissembling or deceit. It had been Laurence's deceptions that had driven them apart: his secrecy about owning half of Lyttons had shaken her as profoundly as if she had discovered he was having an affair. Still worse had been his inability to understand her rage. At least Charlie could see why she was upset; he had sensitivity enough for that.

She felt confused and she felt uneasy, as if she didn't know who she was any more; and she felt terribly, terribly angry.

And she had no idea what she was going to do about it all.

Geordie's distressed voice, his desperate request to see her, therefore, was something of a relief. He said he would do anything, come out to South Lodge, meet her in Manhattan, but he had to talk to her. It was terribly important, he couldn't discuss it on the phone, but he felt that she would understand.

'I've done something fairly − appalling,' he said, 'and I need your particular brand of common sense to tell me what to do. Even if it's to throw myself into the Hudson River.'

Barty told him not to do that, it was unlikely to solve anything, that she would be back in Manhattan on Tuesday, or, if he was truly desperate, he could come out to Southampton.

'But I wouldn't recommend it, the girls are of an age when any intrigue is almost more than they can bear.'

Geordie said he would wait until Tuesday.

'But I warn you, it may be the last time you'll ever want to see me.'

She knew, even before she put the phone down, that it must be about Izzie. And hoped, desperately, that she wasn't responsible for it, however remotely.

Adele sat in her room, shivering violently. She felt as if she might be sick again. She kept being sick. The concierge had booked her flight, had told her the cab would be collecting her at three to take her to Idlewild, that she should ring when she wanted her luggage taken down, had asked her most gently, clearly sensing her distress, if she would like him to order a meal or a drink from room service.

She had refused; all she could tolerate was sips of cold water. She was furiously restless; if she lay down, she wanted to be up again, pacing the room, and even as she did that, she felt so exhausted she wanted to lie down once more.

She had managed to remember to take her pills: indeed they had come to seem her only friends. During the long hot Sunday − when she had stayed in her room, the curtains drawn, telling herself she could manage, she could bear it, she would survive, no one need ever know about her humiliation, the dreadful, dreadful rejection, she would just carry on as if nothing had happened, would go back to London, saying she had had a good trip, yes, seen *Record*, not seen anyone else, had taken lots of good pictures for her portfolio, no, Geordie had been out of town, and so had Barty, she hadn't seen anybody – she had taken her pills very carefully, these so she could sleep, those so she could face the day, counting them out painstakingly, swallowing them with the large glass of water Dr Cunningham had stressed was important. Her pills: her link with sanity, with courage, with feeling the world was all right. When she knew it was all so hopelessly, terribly wrong.

The phone rang; she picked it up. Maybe Venetia, maybe the bellboy—

'Adele, this is—'

Geordie. She slammed the phone down. She would not, could not speak to him. Ever, ever again. How could he have done that to her, had an affair with Izzie, of all people, betrayed her so cruelly? She couldn't even bear to hear his voice, that light, charming voice; the thought of having to look at him, that smiling, handsome face, made her want to vomit. He had phoned her repeatedly the day before, had come to the hotel, and the concierge had rung up to say he was there. 'Please tell Mr MacColl,' she had said, 'that if he doesn't leave the hotel at once, I shall call the police and have him removed.'

She had felt better for a while after that . . .

She had acted with great dignity on the Saturday night; she could see them both watching her in some awe. It had almost been funny at first, while she was still numbed with shock, seeing their faces, Geordie white-faced, brilliant-eyed, speechless, Izzie flushed, tearful, manically active. Adele had asked them to get her a cab, and Izzie had jumped up and rushed out, clearly grateful to have something to do, leaving Geordie there, standing in the kitchen doorway, speaking only once, to ask her if she was all right. She had ignored the question, had sat stolidly on the sofa in the window, waiting for Izzie to come back with the cab, had only moved once and that was to get Noni's picture off the mantelpiece and put it in her bag.

They had both seen her into the cab, it had been an absurd performance, Geordie holding the door for her, Izzie watching, as if she had spent a happy, normal day with them, both of them asking her yet again if she was all right. She had got back to the hotel feeling odd, but quite normal, quite excited, in a way, by the drama, had gone up to her room and ordered a bottle of wine and a club sandwich and then while she was waiting for it, had begun to realise what had happened.

She still felt no real pain: she was able to contemplate the situation quite calmly and almost dispassionately, thinking what she might do, how soon she could divorce Geordie, what she would tell Noni.

She had had a bath then and sat at the bathroom mirror, studying herself, wondering how old she actually looked now, comparing her drawn, unarguably lined face with Izzie's young one, wondering if people would be able to tell what had happened just by looking at her, see that she was an abandoned wife, a failure.

And then the pain began; so bad she felt at times she could hardly breathe through it; blinding, awful pain, born as much of Izzie's treachery as Geordie's, and a humiliation so deep and so frightful she wondered if she would ever be able to face the world again. Somehow, somehow people must never know. Never know that for the second time in her life she had been deserted by the man she loved, set aside in favour of another woman. Somehow she had to live through this, keep it a secret, never ever tell.

'Darling I won't tell anyone. Ever, I swear. Stop it, Adele, stop being so frightened. No one need know, no one at all.'

Venetia sat on her bed with her sister, holding her; she had taken her straight back home, had arranged for Nanny to take Clio to stay in Berkeley Square. Adele was not well, Venetia had explained, she needed complete peace and quiet, she had picked up some bug in New York and would be in bed for several days.

Although it would take more than several days for her to recover from what had really happened in New York, Venetia thought soberly, looking at Adele's ravaged face, at her thin, shaking body, hearing the pain and humiliation in her voice. How was she going to survive this? How?

A terrible rage began to grow in Venetia as she tried to comfort and to soothe Adele; against not only Geordie but Izzie as well, who had done this thing to Adele, already so frail, so unhappy, who had loved them both so much. If either of them had walked in then, she would have quite simply wanted to kill them.

CHAPTER 24

It was cold on the moors; an icy, creeping cold that seemed to seep into the veins. There was no colour anywhere; just shades of grey. It wasn't raining – quite – but the air was sodden, deadening; even the periodic shouts of the beaters, the barking of the dogs, seemed muffled, almost ghostly. Celia, who had declared herself, at breakfast, absolutely ready for a good day's shooting, was trying hard to resist the temptation to go back to Glenworth Castle, trying not to think of the roaring fires, the deep sofas, the trays of drinks and boxes of cigarettes, the creaking but modestly efficient central heating that the first Lady Arden had had installed in a few of the downstairs rooms.

But that would be admitting defeat; and defeat was not something Celia cared to glance at, let alone embrace. Bunny had told her not to come, had warned her, indeed, that it would do no good to the cough which plagued her, but she had laughed at him, called him an old woman, said that she wanted to come, that it was going to be fun. Which it had been – at first. She was the only woman out with the guns, had done well, bagged several brace, with the help of one of her father's beloved Purdeys.

Lord Arden said it was unsafe, it was so old. Celia had retorted that any gun was safe in the right hands, a slightly below the belt reference to Lord Arden's increasing tendency to miss the birds and hit other targets instead. This was all right when it was trees, but occasionally, and tragically, he hit a dog; and once (rather less seriously, as he was fond of saying over the third round of port) a beater. There was no great harm done, it was only a flesh wound, but Celia told him briskly that the very first time her father did such a thing, her mother forbade him to shoot ever again.

'Well darling, I'm sorry, but I'm not prepared to accept that. There's no real danger to anyone and I enjoy it far too much.'

They had had a very good lunch, brought out by the servants, a marvellous consommé, which was at least half sherry, and some excellent pies. Several of the wives had joined them, but that was a good hour and a half ago, Celia's hip flask was empty, and tea seemed a distant mirage. The rain had started now in earnest and was making its insidious way between her neck and her coat. She started to cough, endlessly; her throat was sore. Damn it, she'd had enough; pride or not, she was going back. Only, how? The Land Rovers had gone back to Glenworth, bearing servants and wives and empty picnic hampers, and the only one left was lost to sight in the mist; she could hardly summon it simply in order to be taken home. It would make Bunny very angry. Well, too bad; she was just going to—

'You all right, Celia?' a voice came out of the gloom behind her; it was Nigel Morrison, one of Lord Arden's great friends. 'Not flagging, are you? God, I admire you. Not many women would stay out in this. My wife wouldn't even come out to see us off on a day like this, I can tell you. Bunny must be very proud of you.'

'Oh, it's absolutely what I love best,' said Celia, smiling at him, fastening the storm flap of her Barbour more tightly. 'Come on, Nigel, we're missing the action here.'

When they finally got back it was almost dark, pouring with rain; she was so cold she felt sick and her head was throbbing, her throat on fire. She lay in the bath, longing to go to bed, but the same pride that had both driven and kept her out, forced her to the dinner table and to insist on the wives staying with the men while the port was drunk. She knew Lord Arden hated that, but she didn't care; at her age one deserved some privileges, and sitting with a lot of dull women (and God, they were dull up here, she hadn't realised how dull) talking about the servant problem and the challenge of keeping a full larder, was not what she wanted to do. But by the time she fell into the great bed she notionally shared with Lord Arden, there was a pain in her side like a knife and her cough kept her awake most of the night.

In the morning, Lord Arden insisted on calling the doctor who diagnosed pleurisy and said she must stay in bed.

'Otherwise, Lady Arden, you'll get pneumonia and probably put yourself in hospital. Your temperature is over a hundred and one, and that throat looks absolutely dreadful.'

'Very well,' said Celia meekly, grateful, in spite of feeling so bad, not even to have to consider preserving her reputation as the most stalwart female gun that day, 'I'll stay. But I have to go back to London tomorrow. It's my granddaughter's engagement party and I can't possibly miss that.'

'Lady Arden, you cannot go back to London. You cannot leave that bed. I'm sorry. I will be back in the morning. Now, you need penicillin, I have some here, but a prescription will need to be fetched, and you must drink plenty of fluids. And of course no smoking,' he added with a glare in the direction of the silver case and lighter on her bedside table.

He had not treated Celia before; had he done so, he would have been less surprised to find her gone from Glenworth in the morning, and to hear she was on the London train.

★

She did feel appalling, she realised, as she sat watching the countryside fly past the window, the dark dankness of the North slowly becoming a sparkling frosty southern morning. Much as she loved Glenworth, the climate was truly awful. But it was hard to appreciate the beauty fully; her head ached so badly she could hardly see, and her throat felt so raw she could scarcely bear to swallow anything, even the weak cool tea which she had ordered as her breakfast. Normally she loved breakfast on the train, wolfed down bacon and eggs and fried bread and black pudding. She also felt quite severely dizzy; and the pain in her side had not really eased, in spite of the penicillin.

She frowned out of the window; she hated and despised illness, saw it as a weakness, and a waste of time. But she had been feeling terribly tired lately, going into Lyttons every day had been an immense struggle, in spite of the excitement of commissioning General Dugdale to write his memoirs under her Biographica imprint and the wild success of *Contrasts*. It had already been reprinted three times, and the Christmas orders were excellent; none of Giles's fears had been realised, the critics and the public had accepted it for what it was, a love story set against the background of a very modern social problem, and had in no way seen it as an attempt to capitalise on the misfortunes of the people it chronicled so vividly. The publicity had been immense; Hugh Meyrick had been interviewed by every conceivable newspaper from the *Daily Mirror* to the *Guardian*, and every journalist had praised his careful research, his lack of sentimentality or sensationalism, his vivid dialogue.

She was also very pleased by Keir's performance in the company. She had been worried, not that he would prove less talented than she had thought, but that he would regret his decision, weary of the work, resent the way she had got him there. He wouldn't leave; he wouldn't dare. But he could stop trying, make it clear that his interest was lukewarm, that Lyttons was second best.

However, he had worked like a demon, stayed late, come in early – she worried sometimes about Elspeth, at home with Cecilia, but at least she was back in London with her friends – turned in ideas with impressive regularity, didn't mind the most menial task, coped with Giles's hostility, capitalised on Jay's goodwill towards him – and displayed no resentment towards her whatsoever. That last must have been difficult, she thought; whatever the crime, the punishment is seldom welcome.

She could not, of course, have recognised the true reason for his behaviour: that at last he was doing what he had wanted so passionately to do when he left Oxford. Far from the price of her silence being high, it had actually proved extremely low . . .

She had other more serious worries; Adele had returned from New York in a state of appalling misery, the cause of which only Venetia knew. Used as she was to the exclusive nature of the twins' relationship, Celia still found this almost unbearable. Adele was clearly no longer mildly depressed, she was in despair; when Celia suggested that Geordie return home to care for her, Venetia simply said that was out of the question.

'And don't ask me any more, Mummy, because I am absolutely not able to tell you.'

'Is it Geordie, has the marriage finally broken down? I always thought—'

'Mummy please. You can't help. I wish you could. I wish someone could. Dr Cunningham comes the closest, and he's seeing her three times a week.'

'She's so horribly dependent on those pills,' said Celia, 'it does worry me. Pills never cured anything.'

'These are doing a pretty good job,' said Venetia firmly. 'And she'd be lost without them. Please leave her be, Mummy. She'll come through it, she's tougher than she seems. Meanwhile, all we can do is be as supportive as we can. All right?'

'All right,' said Celia.

'It's a pity Izzie's not here,' said Noni. 'Mummy was always so fond of her. I miss her dreadfully. I can't believe she's not coming over for Kit's wedding. I don't actually understand it, do you? I mean I know she's busy but—'

'Not really,' said Venetia, who had written a cold note to Izzie, forbidding her even to think of coming near Adele. 'Given her past relationship with Kit, maybe she can't quite face it. God, is that the time, Noni darling, I must fly. Appointment at Belinda Belville with Amy, we're both having the most lovely things made for her party and she has some very interesting ideas for The Dress as well. Try not to worry too much about your mama, she'll be all right in the end, I know she will. And Lucas is home next week, isn't he, that will cheer her up.'

Lucas, always wretched Lucas, thought Noni. None of this would have happened without him. Just the same, it would be good to have him back; he would lighten the atmosphere in the house at least.

Noni was not alone in thinking Izzie's absence from Kit's wedding was strange; Celia was extremely puzzled by it. It was so unlike her, she had always been so very involved with the family, the excuse that she was too busy just didn't make sense. She worried that perhaps Izzie was ill; that the abortion had taken its toll on her health, but a letter from Barty assured her that all was well on that score.

'Izzie is fine,' she had written, 'looking marvellous, working very hard, and doing so well at Neill & Parker. They are pitching for other work now apart from book advertising and have got a few small jobs. It is just that it is an impossible time for her to get away. She is desperately upset about it, but feels there is nothing else she can do.'

That was clearly nonsense, Celia thought; of course Izzie could come over for the wedding, however busy she was, she could be spared for a few days and indeed she wrote to the boys herself, asking if it were possible. A letter came back from Nick, addressed to Lady Celia Lytton, Countess of Arden, almost by return of post, echoing Izzie's own letter, and regretting that she couldn't be spared. She put it away very carefully in a locked drawer in her desk; it was one that she thought Lord Arden probably should not see.

In the end, she decided that perhaps Izzie was finding the prospect of Kit's marriage more painful than she was prepared to admit; she put this idea to Sebastian, who was hurt and angry at Izzie's refusal to come. He scowled at her and said that Venetia had said much the same thing, but he really couldn't believe it.

'She should be feeling perfectly all right by now. It was ten years ago, for God's sake.'

'Sebastian,' said Celia gently, 'is ten years really such a very long time? When it comes to such matters as these? How long is it since you first brought *Meridian* to me? Almost thirty-eight years. Are you telling me you feel all right now? As you put it?'

He was silent; then shook his fine old head and smiled at her.

'Not entirely, no. Do you?'

'Of course not,' she said and smiled back at him, very tenderly.

Her own pain at the wedding plans and her exclusion from them was intense; there were times when she could scarcely even bear to contemplate it, times when she still hoped everything would change and that an invitation would arrive. In fact, that had become a horribly vivid recurring dream: the letter coming through the letter box, or finding it lying on the mat. And there were times when she felt so angry that if the invitation had come, she would have refused it. She felt humiliated too, sleep increasingly eluded her and even work, always her panacea for misery, was ineffectual. As the date drew nearer − only six weeks now − the pain and the humiliation grew daily worse.

Clementine had been to see her, to apologise; 'I've tried everything, Lady Arden, even threatened to postpone the whole thing, but absolutely without success. I'm so terribly sorry. There is nothing I would like more, do please believe me, than to have you there, at our wedding.'

Celia smiled at her, patted her cheek; she was a sweet girl, she thought, so pretty, so charmingly English-looking, with that wonderful pink and white skin and clear blue eyes and deep dimples, and the lovely bouncy red hair. How sad, she thought, that Kit would never see her, never see the beauty. She had the most lovely voice, however, low and melodious, and an exquisite, slightly mannered way of expressing herself; no doubt that had had a great deal to do with his falling in love with her.

★

God, it was getting worse, the pain. She was breathing as lightly as she could, sparing herself every possible exertion lest she start to cough, but it was still extremely severe, a hot searing pain on both sides, now, of her chest.

Celia allowed herself a long time to get ready for the party as well, since every action exhausted her, the bath, dressing, doing her hair, putting on her jewellery even. Oh for a maid, how carelessly she had treated her maid when she had been a young woman, how she longed for one now. But she was ready by seven, and smiled with satisfaction at her reflection, at a still-beautiful woman, in a narrow black crêpe dress, and long black gloves, dark hair drawn back in a perfect chignon, her mother's treble-stranded pearls and heavy drop pearl and diamond earrings the only relief from the black.

She picked up her evening bag, an exquisitely beaded Deco creation, a present from Adele for her last birthday, packed carefully with cigarettes, scent — Quadrille by Balenciaga, her new favourite — two handkerchiefs and a selection of throat sweets and painkillers, pulled her mink stole round her shoulders and walked out to the hall where Lord Arden's chauffeur was waiting for her.

'Good evening your ladyship,' he said; no one would have guessed, watching her walk past him, head high, holding her mink stole round her shoulders, the effort required even to get down the steps and into the car, or how much she was suffering.

'My darling! You look perfectly beautiful. What a lovely dress.'

Amy smiled and leaned forward to kiss Celia; she looked and sounded so exactly like her mother it was almost eerie.

'I'm so glad you like it. I don't often wear pink but it's awfully flattering. You look divine, Granny. I do so adore those earrings.'

'Yes, well I've left them to you in my will,' said Celia briskly. 'As you know.'

She enjoyed such references, enjoyed the flurry of protestations that she looked absurdly young, that she would live for ever; but tonight the joke seemed to be a little less amusing.

'Darling Granny.'

'Is Adele here?'

'Yes. She's over there with Mummy, looking wonderful, I think, don't you?'

Adele had clearly made a great effort; she was wearing a black satin A-line dress, which partially disguised her acute thinness, had had her hair done, and was carefully made up; she was sparkling furiously, over-talking and over-giggling, smoking through a long holder. But her eyes roamed the room constantly, and every so often her guard dropped and she looked so ineffably sad that Celia wanted to go and hold her in her arms, take her home with her.

But that would never do. It was Amy's night, and they were all there to wish her well, her and the Honourable Richard Goodhew, who worked in the family stockbroking business, and was heir to a huge fortune.

'New money, though, darling,' Celia had said when Venetia told her about Richard, bubbling with excitement, 'not to be trusted, no land.'

'Oh Mummy, don't be so tedious. Daddy didn't have any land, for heaven's sake.'

'There was land in my family,' said Celia, firmly and illogically, as if that settled the matter.

'Now then, darling,' she said, taking a glass of champagne, sipping it gratefully, so icy cold, so soothing to her throat, 'you mustn't let me monopolise you. I'll be perfectly all right. Why don't you introduce me to that extremely good-looking young man over there. Oh, Elspeth darling, you look lovely. Now, where's Keir? Venetia my dear, congratulations, Boy, good evening.'

On and on it went, apologising for Lord Arden's absence – he was hosting his shoot, she explained, the most important of the season – kissing, greeting, chatting – until suddenly, as she lit her first cigarette of the evening, stupid really, but she was so desperate for it, thinking it would ease her pain, she began to cough. An agonising, racking cough that seemed to urge every breath out of her body. As she excused herself, asked for water, made carefully for the door through a room which seemed to be hazy now, swaying slightly beneath her feet, nausea as well as pain overcame her, and she sank slowly and gracefully on to the ground, briefly unconscious, silenced at last. Half an hour later she was being rushed to King Edward VII Hospital in an ambulance, where she was diagnosed as having double pneumonia and placed immediately in an oyxgen tent; the family was informed that she was on the danger list, and the consultant, summoned from a party himself to examine her, told them that he would be unable to say for at least forty-eight hours whether or not she would recover.

'I think I should go to England.' Barty's voice was very strained. 'I've just had a cable from Venetia. Celia is desperately ill, with pneumonia—'

'Oh, darling, I'm so sorry, but is that really necessary? I mean, I'm sure she's very ill, but pneumonia isn't what it was, it can be treated these days with antibiotics, and besides, by the time you get there, she'll surely be better—'

'That's not the point. I ought to go. She would want me to be there. I know that. And if she's not better – well, I have to know I did everything I could.'

'Of course. Of course.' Charlie's voice was soothing, as if it was she who was ill, not Celia. Barty was irritated.

'Would you like me to come with you?'

314

'No! No, of course not.'

'Darling, there's no need to sound so horrified. I thought I might be some use.'

He was trying very hard to be supportive; she could see that.

'I'm sorry Charlie,' she said, 'I didn't meant to sound anything. I'm just so worried. Frightened.'

She was slightly surprised, shocked even that she should feel so very worried and afraid; that however ambivalent she might have felt in the past, Celia had become the very centre of her life, a strong, driving, absolutely important force. The prospect of life without that was unthinkable.

'Should I take Jenna, do you think? She's very fond of Celia. As Celia is of her, as you know.'

An honorary grandchild, no doubt about it; as important to her as any of her own.

'It's up to you, darling, of course. I wouldn't have thought so, taking her out of school, away from her studies.'

Which you would do without a moment's thought, Barty reflected, lifting the telephone to make the necessary arrangements; the girls had already been taken out of school for several weekends that term, all for perfectly good reasons on the face of it, but all contriving to make them think that school was less important than having a good time. Jenna, who was athletic, had missed two lacrosse matches, and a swimming gala; Barty had drawn the line, said school must come first. And now here she was, ringing the headmistress again, to take Jenna away from school for possibly two weeks.

But the headmistress was surprisingly understanding; and told Barty that of course she must go to Celia, and Jenna too.

She thought, as she waited at Grand Central for Jenna's train, about when Oliver had had his stroke; and discovering that Laurence had tried to keep it a secret from her. It had been so much harder in those days, no transatlantic flights, she had had to endure a five-day sea voyage, terrified that Wol would die before she got home. He hadn't, of course, he had survived against all the odds; Celia had been sitting there when she arrived, holding his hand, virtually demanding that he should live. Who was going to do that for her?

She supposed she should tell Geordie; and Izzie, of course. She would be dreadfully upset. Poor Izzie; for all that she had done wrong, Barty felt desperately sorry for her. She had sat listening to her for hours, as she poured out her misery and her remorse, tearing at her nails, her eyes swollen, her face ashen. And – was she really so much to blame?

Geordie was clearly the villain, he had told Izzie that the marriage was over, that he wanted a divorce. Who could really blame her, innocent and inexperienced as she was.

'You don't understand,' she wailed, as Barty tried to console her, 'Adele was my friend, that's the whole point. If Geordie had been married to someone I didn't know, or to someone who hadn't meant so much to me, it wouldn't have been so very bad, I agree. But to move in on her marriage, even if I did think it was over – oh Barty. She'll never forgive me, never. Nor will Noni. Or Celia, or Father or—'

She looked so much the reverse of an adulterous woman, sitting there, looked all of sixteen years old again, her great brown eyes wild with remorse, tears streaming down her face, her long hair loose, falling over her shoulders, her hands wringing in her lap. Barty held out her arms to her, as she would to a child.

'Darling Izzie, don't. They will forgive you, maybe not Adele, but of course Celia and your father and – well, everyone, really. They'll come to understand. That marriage has been falling apart for years, it was perfectly plain . . .'

But Izzie was not to be comforted.

Barty blamed Geordie more; he knew what he was doing, knew how inexperienced Izzie was, must have sensed she was in love with him. Of course he had sworn he was in love with Izzie, that he had had no idea Adele was clinically depressed, was seeing a psychiatrist.

'Had I known that, I would have stayed with her, at least until she was better, I swear I would,' he said, pushing his hands through his hair, looking at her out of tormented eyes. But it didn't quite work, that remorse, she thought; he would have to have been fairly thick-skinned to have had no inkling of it. It was quite simply unbelievable.

This crisis, the first real one in his charmed life, was proving too much for Geordie; he wasn't able to cope with it. Always before he had talked, smiled, eased himself out of trouble; this time he could not. He was going to have to pay a high price; Adele would never let him near Clio now, certainly not to spend any more than an afternoon with her, she would make sure that Noni and Lucas were told to have nothing to do with him either, would forbid him the charmed Lytton circle.

And then there was Izzie; Barty was shocked at his treatment of her. He had offered her no support, no comfort, as far as she could tell (Izzie had been staunchly loyal), had simply told her that for all their sakes it was best that their affair ended: and then walked out of her life. Some women could have coped with that; the kind of women to whom adultery was an amusing fact of life. But Izzie, innocent, sweet gullible Izzie, thinking he had loved her, looking to him for help and finding none: she deserved better.

He left New York, moved down to Washington, where he had relatives; his excuse being that it was easier for Izzie. Easier for him, of course, where no one knew her, no one would hear of the liaison, or about how he had deserted his sick wife. Clearly he was hoping to start again, build a new life. And that had a horribly familiar ring to it . . .

Charlie was not very pleased that Barty was going away. He didn't actually object, he expressed a certain concern for her, and for Celia, but he clearly resented it. He was very good at sulking; at the cold, dull silence, the refusal to smile, the well-timed shrug. It was much more noticeable without the presence of the girls. The night before they had eaten supper in silence. She tried to break it, had asked him about his new project – not something she was terribly enthusiastic about – a saleroom for vintage cars, which so far had involved inspecting a lot of suitable premises, mostly very expensive and in central Manhattan, and poring over magazines specialising in such things, but not much else.

She had even showed him, that evening, an advertisement for a showroom in Gramercy Park that seemed very suitable to her, but even this had elicited no response. He sat hunched over his plate, not even reading, and then disappeared up to his study.

She supposed she should have agreed to let him come to England too; but it would be no time to introduce him to the family. And if – well, if Celia was ill for a long time, then he would get bored, restless, start pressurising her to go home again. Not that she would be able to stay long; and certainly Jenna would not.

She had settled down again with Charlie; had forced herself to accept him and what he had done. There was really no reason to leave him, she kept telling herself, to break up her new, happy little family, to find excuses to tell the girls. And there was something else, as well, something she found it difficult to acknowledge; she wasn't at all sure she could face the humiliation, the ignominy of admitting she had made a mistake. Quite a major mistake. That the man she had married, had fallen in love with, was a fraud, not an Ivy League preppy, but an orphan boy, raised in an institution. Not that she cared; she truly did not.

And so (while disliking herself considerably for it) she had finally managed to believe what he said, that he still loved her, he still wanted to be married to her, he had done nothing seriously wrong. She had struggled to accept the new Charlie, the changed, less worthy Charlie, had slowly managed to set aside her distaste, her shock, acting out the charade he had forced upon her.

It wasn't very good; in fact, it was rather bad. She found it hard to enjoy his company any more. Sex had become difficult, too; she tried, she complied, she pretended, but as she lay there, struggling to enjoy it, to draw some response from within herself, visions came streaming into her head like an over-familiar movie, of her discovery, of his explanation, of the rows they had had.

Much of the time she felt hostile, resentful, and depressed. And worse than any of it, a terrible frustration that Charlie was completely unable to understand why she felt it.

But it was the best she could do for now, and the best thing for the girls. And of course much the best thing for Charlie.

Jenna suddenly appeared, breathless and flushed; she hugged Barty.

'Hi Mother. Sorry, have you been waiting ages?'

'Only because I'm phobic about being late for things. How are you, darling? You look wonderful.'

'Yes, I'm fine. School's great, I love it there. I miss you – and Charlie of course, but it's so good there, I'm playing sport all the time, riding a lot, and the other girls are really nice.'

'And Cathy?'

'Oh – yes. She loves it too.'

She sounded odd; not quite herself. Barty wondered what it was.

'I thought we'd just get a cab from here. Out to Idlewild. Rather than bother Clarke.'

'Sure. Good idea. What time is our flight?'

'Four.'

'Any more news of Celia?'

'No. No more news. Which could mean anything, really.'

'I guess so.'

They sat in the cab, moving down Manhattan; Jenna looked out of the window, smiling occasionally at her mother. She was a little quiet; there was definitely something on her mind.

'Are you all right?' Barty asked.

'Yes. Yes, I'm fine. Mother, don't fuss.'

She would tell her sooner or later. Meanwhile, Barty would have to wait. Jenna was increasingly Laurence's daughter: infinitely capable of keeping her own counsel, resenting any intrusion into it.

The plane was delayed: by an hour. Barty and Jenna, settled in the first-class lounge, ordered coffee and sandwiches, opened magazines.

'This is fun at least,' said Barty, testing her out, 'just being the two of us, I mean.'

'Yes,' said Jenna, 'yes it is. But I wouldn't like it always. Not any more. I'm really, really happy with Charlie.'

So she had done the right thing.

A voice came over the tannoy. 'Could Mrs Patterson come to the desk please. Mrs Charles Patterson. Travelling to London, Pan American Flight Zero Seven . . . Could Mrs Patterson come to the desk.'

'Oh God,' said Barty, clutching Jenna's hand briefly, standing up, her heart tight and cold with terror, 'it must be Celia. She must have died.'

CHAPTER 25

'Darling! Not more flowers! You're spoiling me. They're beautiful, red and white roses and – Bunny, go and get them put in water, would you? And perhaps you might like a little walk, you look awfully pale and fed up. Darling, come and give me a kiss. See you later. Don't hurry back, I'm absolutely fine. In fact, why not have dinner at your club tonight, come back in the morning. Do be careful, you nearly knocked that tray over. There really isn't room for more than one visitor at a time.'

'Right oh,' said Lord Arden. He looked relieved.

'No really, don't go,' said Kit half-heartedly.

'Oh Kit, don't be absurd, he's been here for hours. Far better for him to have a break. Isn't it, Bunny?'

'Yes, probably,' said Lord Arden. 'But I'll come back later, Celia.'

'Oh please don't bother. The girls are coming in the early evening and then I'll be exhausted. Kit, settle down and stop fidgeting, there's a good boy. Nurse, my husband is leaving now, and could you bring some tea for my son? Thank you so much.'

Lord Arden left, looking sheepish. Celia frowned as he closed the door.

'So irritating,' she said, 'he just sits and sits, no gossip, nothing at all. I find it quite trying.'

'Mother I'd forgotten how dreadful you are,' said Kit.

'Of course I'm not dreadful. I need amusing, not being bored almost to death. Oh, darling, it's so lovely to keep seeing you. I missed you so terribly.'

'It's lovely to see you too,' said Kit. He smiled at her awkwardly. He still felt rather strange in her presence; the long period of absence from her, followed by the shock of hearing she might actually die, had left him oddly ill at ease with her.

He was ashamed, too, of his initial reluctance to believe the reports, convinced she had, at worst, a bad cold, that this was just another tactic of hers to get him to her bedside; but when Lord Arden had rung him personally, his voice shaken and low, to say she was asking for him constantly, that the doctor had said she was really extremely ill, with

319

pneumonia in both lungs, that she was in an oxygen tent, fighting for her life, he had finally, reluctantly, agreed to go to visit her.

He had remained suspicious, even as Venetia led him up to the room where Celia lay; it was only when the nurse said she had been moved to intensive care that he allowed himself to believe it. And then he felt ashamed of himself; and something else, too. Absolute terror that she would indeed die. It was a revelation, that terror. A revelation of how much he loved her; how much he had missed her; and of how unbearable life would actually be without her. It was one thing to say he never wanted to see her again, when the choice was his; another to have the option taken from him.

They had been told to go home, that there was no point waiting to see her, it would be at least twelve hours before they knew whether or not she would recover, but Kit insisted, and sat bolt-upright in a waiting room all night, as close to praying as it was possible for a committed atheist to be, and when at half past five a nurse came in to say that Lady Arden was just a little better, he stood up and, in a voice that shook with relief and fear at the same time, begged to be allowed to go in to her immediately.

'It was very sweet really,' the nurse reported to her colleagues over breakfast, 'I led him in, he's blind you know, and sat him down by her bed and said "Lady Arden, your son is here." She just sighed and turned her head away, and then he said, "It's Kit, Mother", and picked up her hand and kissed it and she opened her eyes and just stared at him, and almost shouted his name and then clung to him crying and laughing at the same time and kissed his hand, and his arm, and his face and although I had to ask him to leave after a couple of minutes, she just looked so much better. Honestly, you'd have thought he was her lover, not her son. Didn't seem nearly so keen to see her husband, when he was shown in an hour later,' she added.

Three weeks later, Celia had almost recovered; still in the hospital – 'Simply because I don't trust you to rest and not to smoke and, quite possibly, not even to go shooting again,' Dr Peebles told her severely – and very easily tired, but able to read and chat and receive the apparently ceaseless flow of visitors who called at the hospital day after day.

The medical staff said, of course, that it was the penicillin that had cured her; she knew better. It had been the sight of Kit, his face drawn with love and fear, his hand tenderly reaching out for hers, that had done it. She knew in that moment that she would get better because she had to: simply to experience the sweet, pure joy of having Kit in her life once more.

They had not talked much at first; she lacked the strength and any exertion made her cough. He came for frequent short visits; as she recovered, he became less easy with her, his hostility revived. She sensed it, despite his efforts to hide it.

'Kit,' she said one afternoon, 'we must talk.'

'We've done quite a bit of that, surely,' he said, his voice carefully light, fiddling with his signet ring as he always did when he was uncomfortable.

'No, I mean really talk. I know—'

'Mother—'

'No. We have to.'

'I would really rather not,' he said firmly.

'Rather not what?'

'Discuss it.'

'Discuss what?'

'Your – that is, what you've done.'

'My marriage, you mean?'

'Well – yes. I think it's best left. I am happy we've become – friends again. But I can't – obviously – accept your marriage. I just can't. No matter what you say. So is there really any point?'

'I think so, yes,' she said.

'Well I don't. And I find the subject so painful—'

'You think I've been disloyal to your father?'

'Yes,' he said simply, 'to both of them. Very disloyal indeed.'

She was silent. Then, 'Sebastian has forgiven me.'

'I know. I don't understand it.'

'I wish you'd let me try to explain, Kit, please—'

He had stood up and seemed about to leave; then abruptly sat down again.

'All right. But I can't imagine it will help.'

'Let me try.'

He sat there while she tried; and when she had finished, something a little like a smile passed over his face. Then he sighed.

'It's a piece of wonderful double-think, Mother. That only you are capable of.'

'But, can you begin to understand? Just begin?'

'I – I'm not sure. It's very – hard, you know.'

'I do know. Of course. But – I was terribly lonely. So lonely. I missed Oliver so much.'

'I know you did. But – it still seems so wrong. You don't even love him.'

'Kit,' she said, 'Kit, you haven't understood at all. That's the whole point.'

Jenna was very disappointed not to be going to London after all. She was glad that Celia was better, of course; but she had been longing to see them all, the twins, and Noni, who she had specially liked, even the slightly weird Lucas, as well as Lucy and Fergal Warwick who were about her age, and of course she wanted to go down to the farm again and see Billy and

Joan and her cousins. And ride Lord B again, without falling off. That most of all.

The wedding had been postponed. There was now no question of it happening without Celia's presence; and as she was still in hospital a week before the agreed date, it would clearly have to wait.

Clementine said this was a very small price to pay for her happiness and relief at being able to include Celia in her plans; 'It's not as if we're leading separate lives exactly, darling,' she said severely to Kit as he fretted over the delay. 'What difference does a few weeks make? And I'd like to make it early March rather than January or February, which are such beastly cold, bleak months. A spring wedding, how lovely that will be. It's what I always wanted really. And it means we can have the house completely ready. Much better.'

They had bought a house in Oxford: a charming villa on the edge of the city. Kit had wanted a town house, but Clementine said they needed somewhere larger, with a garden. 'I intend to have lots of children, and that means lots of room.'

Kit enquired slightly tartly if she had considered whether he might want lots of children and she said if he didn't she had no wish to marry him.

Sebastian was a little sad that they would be gone from London; but so happy in his relief over Celia and Kit that it seemed relatively unimportant.

'It was worth nearly losing you, to have this happen,' he said to Celia one day over tea in Cheyne Walk, where she had decided to convalesce – 'So much warmer and more comfortable than Bunny's house.'

'I think so. And I am so excited about the wedding. I've promised Clementine not to interfere, even the tiniest bit, although I do think "Jesu Joy of Man's Desiring" is a little hackneyed and I really don't think sweetheart roses for her bouquet. Maybe for the bridesmaids, what do you think? And I did wonder, why Brown's for the reception? So impersonal! I mean, since Clementine's parents have both died, why not here? It's the perfect place—'

'Celia,' said Sebastian firmly, 'if you're not careful you'll find yourself uninvited once more. Leave them alone, for God's sake.'

'Oh – very well,' she said.

He looked at her in surprise; she must still be feeling very far from strong.

Jenna sat in bed, hugging her knees, looking at Cathy. She didn't look any different. But she was; she really was.

Cathy had made her promise not to tell anyone: and of course she never would. Just the same – not a virgin any more. And sleeping with the school gardener . . .

She didn't know how Cathy could have done such a thing; the gardener seemed pretty gross to her. Old – about thirty, certainly twenty-five at least – and sort of leery. But Cathy said he was really sexy.

The whole thing was beyond Jenna; even if Marlon Brando had turned up, complete with motorbike and leather jacket, and gone down on bended knee, she wouldn't have risked her future in the way Cathy had. He would just have had to wait. Life and its hurdles that had to be cleared were surely more important than the gratification of some peculiar feelings. She still couldn't quite imagine those feelings anyway, wanting to do it, even with someone really gorgeous. How could it actually be anything other than – well, embarrassing? Kissing was fine, it was great, she had kissed a few boys that summer, proper tongue kissing and, except for Tony Hardman, who had had the most disgusting breath and acne, it had felt pretty good. But – the other, having a penis put into you – well, no thanks. Not yet, anyway. Maybe if you really loved someone, which was what her mother said made all the difference, but Cathy certainly didn't really love the gardener. She couldn't.

Slowly, very slowly, Jenna was beginning to like Cathy a little less. It had taken a long time, and it was a bit unfortunate, when they were together all the time, and no doubt she'd get over it again, but Cathy really didn't have much to talk about these days. Apart from boys and make-up and crooners. She wasn't doing too well at school; she was clever enough, but she was lazy. Jenna didn't exactly like doing her prep, but she did it. Cathy ducked it, made excuses, said she hadn't felt well, borrowed other people's and copied it, including Jenna's. That annoyed Jenna. She knew it was probably mean of her, but she felt that if she'd worked on an essay for two hours, it was hers, and she didn't see why Cathy should copy the best bits into her own in twenty minutes.

She'd said so once or twice, but Cathy had just told her she was mean and selfish.

'I can't help it if I'm not as clever as you are. I'd have thought you'd have wanted to help me out, not shit on me like that.'

'Cathy, you're just as clever as me, you just don't do the work.'

'Oh listen to you, Miss Goody Goody. You sound like one of the professors. I'd never have thought you'd turn all pi on me Jenna Elliott. What's got into you all of a sudden? Have you been talking to your mother? Because you sound like her, banging on and on about how wonderful and important hard work is.'

'No,' said Jenna stoutly. 'And don't talk about my mother banging on.'

'Well, she does. She's always doing it. Have you done your practice, have you tidied your room, have you read that wonderful book yet? I get really sick of it.'

'Oh shut up,' said Jenna, and went out of the room and slammed the door.

★

'Oh God,' wailed Izzie, 'Oh, God, oh God. Nick, now what am I going to do? My father's asked me to go home for Christmas. I can't, I simply can't . . .'

'Why not, sweetheart?'

'You know why not.'

The boys had become her confidants, having demanded an explanation for her distress and distraction at the end of that first dreadful week. They were prepared to put up with her crying all the time, although it wasn't much fun, but it was making her ineffective and that was something quite different.

'We depend on you. Besides, you're a partner in this firm. If it goes down, you go down. You can't afford it. And neither can we.'

They had been absolutely sweet to her as she slowly and painfully told them the story, had sat one on each side of her in Chumleys bar, plying her with bourbon, for which she was learning to develop a taste, and telling her she had nothing to reproach herself with.

'The guy's a schmuck,' said Mike, 'an absolute schmuck. I always thought so.'

'No you didn't. And don't talk about Geordie like that.'

'OK. He's not a schmuck, he's an asshole. If not, then why isn't he here, taking care of you? Instead of beating it down to Washington, back to Mummy.'

'Mike! Don't.' She stood up, glaring down at him. 'I won't have him criticised, and it's not just him, we were both to blame.'

'All right, darling.' Nick reached up and took her hand, pulled her down again. 'He's a really fine guy, an outstanding human being. We're all agreed on that. But it was his marriage, he knew what was going on in it. You didn't. Or only what he told you.'

'But Nick, he had no idea she was so depressed, that she was seeing a psychiatrist—'

'Well he should have had an idea. Anyway, let's not argue about that. Thing is baby, you got caught with your—' he stopped, looked at Mike.

Mike took a large gulp of beer, and choked on it; Nick suppressed a laugh with great difficulty.

'What is up with you two?' said Izzie crossly.

'Sorry darling. I was just going to say you got caught with your hand in the till—'

'No you weren't,' Izzie glared at him. 'You were going to say I got caught with my pants down. Well I didn't. Not quite anyway—'

She suddenly giggled, then stopped talking, overwhelmed with a mixture of laughter and tears; Nick grinned and gave her a hug.

'That's better. Now look, you've just got to start forgiving yourself. Anyone would think you'd committed murder, listening to you, rather than – well, having an affair with an about-to-be-divorced man. Just what is so terrible about that?'

'What's so terrible about it,' said Izzie, sober again, 'is that his wife was one of my best friends. She's been good to me all my life, right from when I was a little girl.'

'Well that's tough, I can see that. But she sounds pretty mixed up to me. I mean she has this absolutely horrible child and she puts him before her husband, then acts all surprised when the husband says he's had enough. I mean is she stupid or what?'

'Not at all,' said Izzie, 'and there's so much more you don't understand, she had the most terrible time in the war—'

'In the war! Honey, that's over twelve years ago.'

'I know, but—'

Izzie told them about Adele's war and about Luc; they listened politely. Then Mike said, 'So what's with the daughter? Is she all mixed up and nasty to her stepdad?'

'No, she's perfectly lovely to him.'

'Well then. That guy, the son, he most definitely is another schmuck, I think we can all agree on that. And if your friend can't see that, then she *needs* to be seeing a shrink, I'd say. Seems to me, Izzie, this whole thing is not actually your fault, not lover-boy's fault, even, but her fault. She sounds pretty damn tiresome to me.'

'She's not, she's not,' wailed Izzie, 'she's—'

'OK, OK. Don't tell us, she's absolutely lovely, a cross between Mary Magdalene and Joan of Arc. Just – dumb with it. Lady Isabella, you've got yourself trapped in a hornet's nest. You want to get out of it before you get stung. You just let us take care of you, see you don't get into any more trouble. Now come on, drink up, and then let's go and eat. Fancy a plate of chop suey?'

Izzie suddenly realised she was hungry for the first time in days.

'You're so good to me,' she said.

'Sweetheart, our turn. You've been pretty good to us.'

'Why don't you ask your dad over here?' said Nick now, 'tell him you want to have a New York Christmas. We'll join in, if you like. And show him a really good time.'

'He wouldn't come,' said Izzie, slowly, digesting this idea.

'Want a bet?'

'I'm thinking of going to New York for Christmas,' said Sebastian.

'What, to see Izzie? Wonderful idea. I might come with you.'

'Celia, in the first place you're not invited and in the second you're not well enough. I'm not absolutely sure about it myself, as a matter of fact. She says I can have her bed but warns me it won't be comfortable. She says her apartment is really cold as well.'

'It sounds like hell.'

'Yes, but I do rather like the idea. I love New York and I want to be with her.'

'You could stay with Barty.'

'Yes, but that would rather defeat the object. And anyway, I don't think I could take Christmas with Charlie.'

'Me neither. Oh dear, I do hope Barty's all right.'

'So do I,' said Sebastian soberly.

CHAPTER 26

It was ridiculous of course: to be jealous of your own husband. But that was how she was beginning to feel. Professionally, at any rate. And even personally, at times.

Of course life had improved dramatically; it was marvellous to be back in London, the Battersea flat was gorgeous, she had her friends to see, and at least she was no longer isolated and lonely. Cecilia was growing up, she was absolutely enchanting, she was nearly a year old now, scuttling about on her small fat knees, so pretty, with dark eyes and curls, absolutely a Lytton, in fact she looked so like Elspeth as a baby that it was almost eerie. Keir said he sometimes thought she had been created by Elspeth by parthenogenesis and that he had played no part in it whatsoever.

Just the same, looking after her, however sweet she was, wasn't quite the same as working. She sometimes felt her brain must be wasting away, like unused muscle, that it would never regain its strength; she worried about it.

And it was made much worse, of course, by the fact that Keir was doing exactly what she most loved, and was clearly doing it terribly well. Everyone said that he had real talent, that he was going to be a great asset to the company, that he worked so hard, that all the authors liked him; on and on it went, until Elspeth wanted to scream.

She had done exactly what Celia had said, hadn't even mentioned that she might like to go back to work, spent her time building up Keir's confidence, stroking his ego – not that he had ever needed it, in her opinion – and his natural arrogance had never seemed greater. Now, when he came home at night, talking endlessly about this book, that author, the other promotion, as if she understood or indeed knew about any of it, she found it very hard to respond enthusiastically.

She had even talked to Celia about it, had admitted to feeling shut out, resentful; Celia patted her hand and told her to be patient.

'I told you, darling, things usually sort themselves out.'

'Yes, I know, and they have to an extent, of course, but I just feel life is passing me by.'

'I can remember feeling exactly the same at your age and stage of life.

Pacing this house, wondering how I could persuade your grandfather to let me rejoin him.'

'Why weren't you there anyway?'

'I had a miscarriage. After Giles. I was working, too hard I suppose, and one day – well. It wasn't very nice. Then I had the twins, and of course I had to be very careful. But I made a bargain with him.'

'A bargain! Granny, you are dreadful. What was it?'

'I said I'd stay at home for an extra year if he'd agree to Barty coming to live with us.'

'And he agreed?'

'Oh yes,' said Celia. 'After a while, that is. One has to be patient.'

'Why did you want Barty so much? It must have been a bit – daunting.'

'I loved her,' said Celia simply, 'I always had. We had a very special rapport, she used to enjoy my visits to her mother – you know I was involved in doing a report on the family—'

'Yes, yes.'

'And I realised things were getting rather serious, that her father was ill-treating her mother, that Barty herself was being – well, she had a few bruises. I knew I could help. So I did.'

'And you didn't have any doubts about it?'

'Doubts?' said Celia, and she sounded absolutely astonished. 'No, of course I didn't have any doubts. I knew it was the right thing to do, and it was. As you know.'

Elspeth took Cecilia home, marvelling at her grandmother's self-confidence; and wondering what bargain she might be able to strike with Keir, that would allow her to go back to work, even part-time.

Barty was literally ticking off the days to Kit's wedding and the trip to England. It was only with a reunion with her family so near that she realised how much she loved and missed them all. She had bought her outfit – a beige silk suit from Oleg Cassini, who was said to be designing a lot of clothes for the beautiful Mrs John Kennedy – and had taken Jenna and Cathy shopping; it was the longest day she could ever remember. Finally she put her foot down and said it was either the next thing they saw, or they would go in what they had; and in Bonwit Teller they found an A-line dress and jacket for Jenna in green-blue taffeta which almost exactly matched her eyes, and something very similar in palest pink for Cathy.

Charlie had spent a fortune on a morning suit at J. Press and a large additional wardrobe for the trip, from just about every store in New York. When she queried the need for three overcoats and five suits, he looked at her with a certain malice and said, 'I didn't think you'd want to be ashamed of me.'

Christmas had been surprisingly all right. Things had been very cool between them until the girls came home when he suddenly became affectionate and expansive again; on the same day he found premises for a car showroom just off Park Avenue. It was terribly expensive, but she paid the vast deposit without a murmur; he responded by becoming extremely helpful, telling the girls how lucky they all were to have her, and buying her a gold bracelet from Tiffany. With her money. She thanked him effusively. Anything for a happy Christmas . . .

They had stayed in Manhattan; Izzie and Sebastian joined them on Christmas night for dinner. Sebastian had seemed very happy, overjoyed about Kit's reunion with Celia, very proud of Izzie's success – Neill & Parker had just won a pitch for a small chain of art shops, with Izzie's copyline. He seemed completely unaware of any liaison between Izzie and Geordie. Barty supposed she was relieved; but it worried her just the same. She had seen too many secrets, buried for no matter how long, come painfully to light, to believe that any could be kept for ever.

He asked why the boys couldn't have joined them: 'I can see they wouldn't celebrate Christmas, of course, but it would be fun to have them here. I like those fellows so much.' And Izzie told him they had gone home to their mothers for the holiday, like the good Jewish boys they were.

'I was hoping they'd come too,' said Jenna, 'they're just so cute. Lucky you, Izzie, working with them all day. And to have both of them in love with you as well.'

'Nick and Mike,' said Izzie, genuinely astonished, 'in love with me? Jenna, don't be ridiculous, of course they're not, I'm just – just someone who works for them. More like a sister than anything.'

Jenna sighed, looked at Cathy, raised her eyes to the ceiling.

'Dumb,' she said. 'Seriously dumb.'

'Jenna,' said Barty, 'that will do.'

'What a delightful notion,' said Sebastian, smiling at Izzie. 'Is it true?'

'Of course not,' said Izzie firmly, blushing: but thankful nonetheless to be romantically linked, however mistakenly, with two such suitable suitors.

It would be very nice, Barty thought, noticing the blush; it was a notion she had toyed with herself, but then dismissed it. They were hardly Izzie's type, either of them, and it was true what she had said, their relationship was more like brothers and sister than anything remotely romantic. Izzie did seem much better though, still filled with remorse, but healing. Geordie's defection, his failure to support her in any way, had hurt dreadfully at the time, but it had been a cure of sorts.

'I can see what a – a not very nice person he was,' she said to Barty. 'If he'd been really sorry, if he'd been concerned for me and my feelings, I'd have respected him more, of course. But I'd have felt much worse in the long run.'

She was still in a fearful dilemma about Adele; and, of course, Noni, not knowing whether or not she should make some kind of approach – write, telephone, even; Barty advised her to do nothing.

'As Celia says, things very often work themselves out in the end. I've certainly found that to be true. Something will happen to make it right—'

'Nothing could make it right. Not possibly.'

'All right, make it better. Maybe when we all go over for the wedding . . .'

Izzie was dreading the wedding so much she could hardly bear to think about it.

Adele seemed to Venetia to be very ill. Noni was in despair about her, and Lucas was very shocked when he arrived home after a first triumphant term at Oxford. They had all agreed just before Christmas that the effect on little Clio of seeing her mother creeping round the house in her dressing-gown much of the day, added to the loss of her father, was potentially disastrous. She missed him dreadfully; they had been terribly close, and while she had weathered his departure to the Albany, this was something different. He had not been home since the autumn, and seemed settled with his mother in Washington; not surprisingly, Adele refused to contemplate Clio visiting him there and had written to say that if he did come back for Christmas she would change the locks and refuse to let him see Clio. So far, Clio was still displaying her blithe high spirits, probably because she spent much of her life with her cousins in Berkeley Square, but it was bound to affect her sooner or later.

Adele was obsessed with people 'not finding out'. While no one knew what had happened between Geordie and Izzie, she felt, she said, safe. She spent a lot of time staring at herself in the mirror. At the gaunt, dull-haired, hollow-eyed woman whose husband had cheated on her with a beautiful young girl with thick hair and creamy skin and huge brown eyes; a girl who everyone loved and wanted to be with. Was it surprising that he should have left such an ugly middle-aged woman? And the betrayal by Izzie was just as hard: Izzie, who she had loved and cared for since she was a tiny little girl, had nursed through so many heartaches, Izzie who felt both like another daughter and a best friend. How could you do that to someone who loved you so much? How could you take the hand that had literally fed you, and cuddled you and stroked your hair while you cried and grieved and mourned, and not just bite it, but hack it off? Only if you thought so little of her, perhaps, that all that kindness and tenderness was as nothing; only if you despised her, laughed at her, behind her back, only if you had never really loved her at all . . .

In the early stages, Adele clung to Venetia, but even she, unthinkable as it once would have seemed, was drifting away from her. She felt that was hardly surprising either: Venetia was busy, successful, happy, she had a good marriage, she was still beautiful, she still looked young. Why should she spend her days struggling to prop up her boring failure of a sister, when there was no point, when nothing was going to make her feel any better, when she would never again be busy or successful herself?

Noni was very sweet to her, but Adele could sense her growing impatience; Noni had changed, and Adele found it difficult to cope with this beautiful, confident creature, a celebrity in the world where she had once been a star of sorts herself. Only Lucas could cheer her; he would sit with her for an hour at a time, telling her funny stories about his life at Oxford, about his new, outrageous set of friends, making a fuss of her, bringing her a glass of champagne each evening before he went out. But he went out an awful lot. She was very lonely.

Even Dr Cunningham was failing her now; on each visit, she told him the same things, over and over again; on each visit, he asked her if anything had changed, if she felt any differently. He had increased the dosage of her pills, especially the sedatives; but they weren't working, she told him, they did no good any more, she lay awake night after night, crying, fretting, reproaching herself.

Of course there was a good reason for that, which she would not have dreamed of telling him; she wasn't actually taking them. She was saving them up, the pills, her friends, saving them in a drawer in her studio, where no one would ever find them, saving them for a time when they could take her away from it all for ever and ever. She was just waiting; until she knew it really was time, when there was some kind of a sign that she had had enough. And then she would take them all. All at once. And her friends, the pills, would have finally saved her.

Izzie had decided exactly what she would do. She would say she was coming for the wedding, she would even book a flight; and then, at the last minute, she would cable to say she was ill. It was impossible even to contemplate going; but she couldn't go on saying she was too busy. Clementine had written her a very sweet note, telling her the date had changed and saying that now, she hoped, Izzie would be able to come: 'It just won't be the same without you, Izzie. Kit and I both want you there so much. So tell your horrible boss – he must be horrible, to keep you quite that busy – that you're coming and that's the end of it.' How could she not respond to that?

Noni, too, wrote: 'You must, must come to the wedding. It would be horrible without you. Incidentally, I hear from Geordie that' – what had she heard from Geordie, Izzie thought with a pang of terror, her eyes racing on along the lines, but it was all right – 'both the men you work for are in love with you. Lucky you. Bring them along.'

Well, that was a clever piece of gossip, Izzie thought. How did he do it? How had she ever believed anything he said?

★

With a stroke of generosity that surprised even himself, Kit had suggested to Clementine that they should make Celia perfectly happy and have the reception at Cheyne Walk.

'It's the house where I grew up, it's nothing to do with Lord Arden, and it's much nicer really than some hotel. I think we should do it there, unless you mind terribly, of course.'

Clementine, who secretly fancied the idea of being married from the house where the Lytton dynasty had been quite literally conceived, said she didn't mind in the very least and would consider it an honour; Celia was so touched when they asked her that she burst, most uncharacteristically, into tears.

It was not to be a very large wedding, about a hundred guests; the ceremony would be in Chelsea Old Church. Clementine was anxious about wearing a traditional wedding dress, she said she was too old and that she'd look like a wedding cake, but she had finally found something simple enough to satisfy her, and had been growing her rather schoolgirlish red curls as fast as she could, so that she could wear them up.

She was going to look beautiful, Venetia said to Adele (having been given a preview), and it was a terrible shame Kit wouldn't be able to see her. Clementine was the sort of person you could say those things to, she added; Adele, it seemed, was not. She burst into tears and said she thought that was the saddest thing she had ever heard in her entire life. The wedding was upsetting her altogether; Venetia supposed that Kit reminded her inevitably of Izzie.

'Darling don't cry,' she said, calling on all her patience with a great effort, 'it's lovely, he adores her, she adores him, they're going to be terribly happy, and have lots of babies. Who would have thought Kit's story would turn out such a happy one?'

'You never know with stories,' Adele said. 'The happiest ones can turn sad, look at mine.'

Venetia had been to see Dr Cunningham, to tell him how worried she was about Adele. He told her that he was extremely worried too, that she didn't seem to be responding to the drugs any more, and that he was seriously considering giving her electric shock treatment. 'She is really very ill, you know.'

Venetia was horrified; electric shock treatment had always sounded to her absolutely barbaric.

Dr Cunningham tried to reassure her.

'It would be done under a general anaesthetic, she would know nothing about it, and we are achieving remarkable results with it. Anyway, I don't want to broach it with her just yet—'

'Do you think she should be alone so much? It worries me terribly.'

'It's difficult; her home is clearly her refuge, she finds it reassuring, and her children are there, aren't they? As well as the nanny and other staff. Let's leave that a little longer. If she doesn't improve by March, say, I think perhaps we should take her into a nursing home and broach the subject of the electric shock treatment with her then.'

People talked about falling in love; it was so very apt. It did feel exactly like falling; it started slowly, you thought you could save yourself, you tried to steady yourself, grabbed at things, grabbed at sanity, at caution, at common sense, and somehow missed them all. Then things moved faster, you could see yourself losing control, feel yourself going, half afraid you were going to hurt yourself, half unable to even think about it, and then you did fall, you landed, and lay there, looking up, the view absolutely changed, feeling foolish, dazed – and very, very happy.

And it had all begun with what the Americans called a strep throat . . .

'Darling, you'll have to do the presentation today on your own. Think you can manage that?'

Izzie gulped. It was quite a presentation: to their new account, the chain of art shops, on an important new line they were planning for the spring, a series of literally pocket-sized art books about the Old Masters, which could be collected. She had come up with a very good copyline, or so she thought, A Gallery in Your Pocket, but she wasn't very good at presentations.

'Nick, I can't. I really can't. You know how I hate it.'

'Sweetheart I'm sorry, but you have to. Mike's ill. Strep throat. Can't speak, even if he wanted to. And I have to go see Joanie. Do we stand Joanie up? I don't think so.'

'Couldn't I go and see Joanie? It'd be less frightening.'

'And less productive. You know she prefers fellers. No, it's the Lady Isabella show at Art World. OK?'

'Yes,' she said reluctantly. 'Yes, OK.'

She felt quite sure it wouldn't be; but working with the boys had taught her one thing. You had a go.

'There's my girl. You'll be great. Just remember, look up at the stars.'

'I'll remember.'

The team waiting for her was not too formidable: the two sales managers, and the marketing director. Just the same, when she got up to speak, Izzie felt violently sick, so sick indeed that she really felt she might throw up then and there, in the boardroom, couldn't muster a sound other than a rather awkward squeak; her throat seemed to have closed up as well. But they were on her side; the marketing director, whose name was Dick Gross, said, 'You know, you're a lot better looking than the other fellers.'

She giggled and then she was away, flying smoothly confident into her presentation.

And they liked it, liked her copyline, liked the promotional ideas (like getting a half-price voucher with one book to redeem against the next, getting a free poster when the whole set was complete), then took her out to lunch, where they told her they were thinking of doing a modest radio campaign and could they have her suggestions for that?

She arrived back at the office in high spirits, flushed with triumph and rather a lot of wine; Nick was there.

'Hi, darling. You come through?'

'Just about.' She told him; he came over to her, gave her a hug.

'You're a clever girl, Lady Isabella. We must send you out some more. In fact, I think we'll just stay right here in future and see what you can bring back for us. A radio campaign, eh? That is really something. I've dreamed of that for years.'

'I know you have. And I've already thought of an idea.'

'And what's that?'

'Music for each artist. Like, say, Debussy for the Impressionists, Beethoven for Rembrandt. Something like that. And then the tag line is "Listen to the pictures. Or better still, come along and see them." '

He sat there gazing at her in absolute silence. Then he said, 'You really do have it all, don't you? Just wait till I tell Parker about this. Oh, shit, Izzie, let's go tell him now. Might cheer him up.'

So they went round to the apartment they shared, with a bottle of champagne; Izzie had been there before, but never failed to be struck by its appalling state. It wasn't exactly dirty, but the mess was fearsome, they had no furniture except the bed, a clothes rail and a TV. Everything they possessed was in piles on the floor. Books and ornaments in the living room, sweaters and shoes in the bedroom, towels in the bathroom. Only the kitchen made any pretence of being equipped; there was a sink filled with (mostly clean) mugs and plates, a double gas ring and a very old refrigerator, piled high with a mountain of tins and packets.

'It doesn't matter,' Nick had said, seeing her face as she gazed at it all the first time, 'we never cook, except to make coffee.'

It was looking especially bad that day; Mike had the curtains closed, and for the first time she saw them in all their horror: brilliant orange nylon with purple flowers, hanging in sagging loops off the minimum number of rings, about four on each side, with a large hole in one of them and the hem unravelled on the other. Mike was awake, and clearly feeling dreadful, but he struggled to sit up and punched the air when they told him the news. He blew Izzie a kiss, and then snatched the bottle of champagne Nick had bought on the way home and insisted on opening it. Having been rather shaken about, and there being no glasses ready, the contents took on a life of their own, and spurted all over the room, and particularly on Izzie, who was sitting on the bed. Mike lay back on his rather grey-looking pillows and stared at her, appalled.

'Honestly, don't worry,' she said laughing, 'it doesn't stain or anything.'

'Darling, you're soaked,' said Nick. 'Look at your shirt.'

'It doesn't matter.'

'It does to me. Apart from anything else, you'll smell like an old wino and I'm going to take you out to dinner. You'd better have one of mine. Here you are, you like this one? Or this?'

He rifled through the clothes rail that stood at the side of the room, it contained a number of the luridly striped shirts they both loved. She looked at them and said carefully, 'I don't quite see myself in one of those. Look, just lend me a T-shirt, I've got my jacket. I can rinse the shirt out and come back for it, and the rest of my things. Unless of course we're going to the Waldorf or something.'

Nick looked pained.

'Isabella, please. Where else would I take you? Chinatown?'

'I hope so,' said Izzie.

She borrowed a T-shirt, combed her hair, blew Mike a kiss and they left.

They had a good time, drank too much, talked endlessly about life in general and the dazzling future of Neill & Parker in particular. Nick told Izzie a lot of very bad jokes and they went back to the apartment so that Izzie could collect her things. Mike was asleep, sprawled across the bed. Nick stared down at him.

'Poor guy. Looks like I'll be sleeping on the sofa.'

'You don't have a sofa,' said Izzie, looking round the chaotic room.

'OK, on the floor.'

'You can't sleep on the floor.'

'Why not? We have a carpet. And a sleeping bag.'

'Nick! That's silly, I've got a sofa, why don't you come back and crash on that?'

Nick looked at her; she looked at him, and just for a moment, an odd, slightly shaky moment, there was something there, something disturbing, something utterly unexpected. And then it was gone again, almost before she had noticed it, certainly before she could allow it to concern her.

'Go on. You'll be much more comfortable.'

He hesitated; again, just for a moment, then said, 'I'd be proud to sleep on your sofa. Let's go.'

They were both rather drunk; Izzie settled Nick on the sofa, with a lot of giggling while she dragged a couple of blankets out of the bathroom cupboard, kissed him briefly goodnight and went to her room. She suddenly felt terribly tired and lay down on her bed just as she was, fully clothed. Only for a moment; she would just close her eyes and then when she felt better, when the room stopped whirling, she would get undressed.

She fell asleep at once; and then woke at three, terribly hot, very confused, with an aching head and a raging thirst. She pulled off her clothes, still half asleep, unable to find her nightdress in the dark, and then decided she must get a drink of water. She was halfway across the living room, which lay between her bedroom and the kitchen, when she remembered Nick. Remembered him; but then thought he must be asleep. And rather than turn back, she walked on into the kitchen, didn't see him, lying there, looking at her. She filled a jug of water, took a glass and turned back; and then she did see him, and saw he was looking at her, very seriously and sweetly studying her, his eyes moving over her, and too late, she tried to cover her breasts with her arms, and promptly dropped the jug of water.

'Oh shit,' she said, 'oh shit. Nick that was – that was – well, you should have said something.'

'Like what? Like "I can see you?" or "Am I dreaming?" or "That is a truly beautiful sight"?'

'Oh don't joke,' she said, cross now, as well as embarrassed, 'it isn't funny—'

'It certainly isn't,' he said, 'it's very far from funny. Run along, back to bed, I'll clear up the water.'

'But I want the water,' she said irritably, 'that's what I got up for.'

'Then I'll bring you some more. Go on, quick now, before my eyes fall right out of their sockets.'

'Nick!'

She half ran into her room, dived into the bed, and sat with the covers pulled up to her chin; she could hear him moving about, clearing up the mess, then he knocked at the door.

'May I come in?'

'Yes, of course.' He was carrying the jug and a glass, and wearing, she was relieved to see, a shirt and some boxer shorts. 'Thank you. Thank you very much, just put it down there, if you don't mind.'

'I don't mind at all. Shall I pour you a glass?'

'No. No, it's all right, I'll do it.'

'I'm very sorry,' he said, 'if I embarrassed you. I wouldn't have done it for the world.'

He looked so remorseful, his long, rather beaky face mournful, his dark eyes so filled with misery that she smiled at him. What did it matter, after all? He was like a brother to her, they both were.

'It's all right,' she said, 'honestly. Quite all right. It was – well, it was silly of me.'

And then, suddenly, without having the faintest idea why, because it was clearly not quite the best thing to do, she reached up to give him a kiss. Meaning just to show some affection for him, sisterly affection. A goodnight kiss. Only somehow, he didn't kiss her cheek as she had thought he would; his mouth brushed on hers, and she felt her own mouth move, very gently, under it, letting him know what she suddenly wanted. Wanted

336

very much. And then there was another of the shaky, sparky moments; they felt it, both of them, acknowledged it, their eyes met, and then he looked quickly away, stood up.

'I feel this isn't quite what I should be doing,' he said, 'I feel like the kind of guy I don't really approve of. Maybe I should just – just go back to bed.'

'Sure,' she said, 'good idea. Sleep well, Nick. Thanks for the water.'

And then lay awake until it was quite light, feeling alternately foolish and oddly happy, wondering what on earth might have happened if she hadn't sent him away. She heard Jenna's voice suddenly, her clear little voice saying, 'Both those boys are so in love with Izzie', heard her father saying, 'What a delightful notion', and saw the words in Noni's spidery writing, 'I hear the boys are both in love with you.'

Was it true? Could it be true? Of course not. She set the thought aside with a great effort of will. It was ridiculous: quite, quite ridiculous. It was just that he had seemed – well, to find her attractive. But then, what man wouldn't be aroused by the sight of a completely naked girl walking past his bed, and then respond when she invited him to kiss her goodnight? She'd wanted him to kiss her, though: very much. And she'd wanted to kiss him too. It was very odd; she'd never felt anything remotely like that for either of them. And Nick wasn't the sort of man she fancied normally; not in the least good-looking, certainly not well-dressed. Maybe she'd just been drunk. Yes, that was it. What a way to behave; how crass and undignified. Hadn't she learned any lessons at all? She finally fell asleep as the dawn broke, to dream feverishly about walking naked into her presentation, and realising that one of the men in the room was Geordie . . .

In the morning, they were both awkward, embarrassed; she sent him into the shower – 'No, no, you first, I'll make coffee—'

'Please don't,' he said, 'your coffee is deeply revolting, I'll do it.'

He left quickly (having made some very good coffee), saying he must go home to change, that he would see her in the office, thanking her for the use of her sofa. He clearly couldn't wait to get out of the place, regretted horribly what had happened. She had ruined, with her own stupidity and crassness, what had been a perfect friendship. He was no doubt telling Mike about it even now, and Mike would be shocked, horrified, even. In fact she couldn't face the thought of seeing either of them. God, she was an idiot; Izzie sat down on her bed, put her aching head into her hands and burst into tears.

Two weeks before the wedding, Barty came home one evening to find Charlie looking distraught.

'What on earth's the matter, is it the lease?'

He had had endless trouble with the lease on the Park Avenue premises.

'No, no, it's – not that. It's Sally. She's very ill.'

'Sally? Oh God, Charlie, I'm sorry. What's wrong?'

'She's had a stroke. She's in a state hospital. Down in Brooklyn. But – a friend has contacted me. Apparently it's a wretched place, she's terribly disorientated and upset. I just wondered—'

Barty knew what he was wondering; and found it less enraging than usual.

'Charlie, of course.'

'Of course what?'

His eyes were innocently puzzled.

'Of course she must be moved to a private hospital. Immediately.'

'Oh darling! You're so sweet. I didn't mean that.'

'Well I do,' she said briskly, resisting the temptation to say that she knew perfectly well that he had meant it, 'so make the necessary arrangements. All right?'

'All right darling. I'm so sorry to keep taking and taking from you. One day, when this new business of mine takes off – which it will – I'll make it all up to you.'

'You don't have to,' she said, kissing him with something of an effort, 'and I'm just grateful that I can do something for her, when she's been so good to you and Cathy. Do you think we should go and visit her?'

'I will,' he said quickly, 'see how bad she is. If she's up to visitors, then yes, I'm sure she'd love to meet you.'

Barty thought of the unanswered letter to Sally Norton and felt less sure.

Charlie found a private hospital in Brooklyn near the Heights that could take Sally; she was moved in the same day. Charlie supervised the move; he came home looking very sober.

'She's in a bad way, poor woman. It's a very serious stroke, her speech is severely affected, as is the use of her legs and one arm. The doctor isn't sure what the prognosis is. And she's very confused, so there really is no point your visiting her. I'll go again in a day or two, see how she's getting on.'

'All right Charlie. But I'm very happy to go if there's any point. I know a bit about it because of when Wol had his stroke. The thing is, they can hear and know what's going on far better than we realise.'

'I'll see what the doctor thinks.'

The doctor said there was absolutely no point in a stranger visiting Sally Norton.

'Apparently it might even be disturbing, but he thought I should continue to visit, she might benefit from the stimulation.'

Charlie left early to visit Sally most mornings; he said she was best first thing, and then he could get on with the day. As the day seemed to consist largely of looking at increasingly expensive vintage cars, Barty wondered at the necessity of this . . .

At the end of the first week he had gone off as usual, and Barty had stayed behind in the house to do some financial housekeeping. The idea that Charlie might take this over had proved hopeless; she had very quickly learned it amounted to financial suicide. Not only was he hopelessly extravagant, he was also totally inefficient, left bills unpaid, ignored any official-looking letters, and ran up absurd bills gathering interest at stores.

She was halfway through that week's pile – God, the hospital was expensive – when the phone rang.

'Mrs Patterson?'

'Yes.'

'This is the Mount Pleasant Hospital, Mrs Patterson. We have your mother-in-law here.'

'Of course.'

Could this mean Sally had died? Such phone calls often did.

'Mrs Patterson, I wonder if it might be possible for either you or your husband to come in to the hospital?'

'Come in – but I thought –' Oh God. Not again, please not again.

'Yes. We did explain to your husband when he first came to see us that we would need some more nightdresses for her as soon as possible, and anyway, the doctor would like to see one of you.'

'Yes. Of course. Well – yes. I could come down today, if that would help.'

'That would be wonderful, Mrs Patterson. I'm so very sorry to trouble you.'

'That's all right,' said Barty, 'but – well – are you quite sure my husband hasn't been in at all?'

'No, he hasn't been in. Not since the first day, that is. She's only had one visitor so far, a neighbour. I'm sure she'll be very glad to see you.'

'But I thought – well, yes, I expect she would. I'll be down within the hour.'

And all the way down to the city, driving herself through the crawling traffic, over Brooklyn Bridge into the stylish splendour of the Heights, she felt almost too frightened to think that perhaps here were more lies to be uncovered, more secrets to be revealed – and more misery to be confronted. The whirling sense of disorientation took hold of her again, the feeling that she could not be sure of where she was, even of who she was; as she walked into the hospital, she felt most dreadfully frightened.

Sally Norton was on the third floor; a nurse led Barty along the corridor to her room.

'She's rather tired, not too long, please, Mrs Patterson.'

'How – how is she?'

'Oh – not too bad. It's her right side that's affected, as I expect your husband will have told you.'

'Yes, he said it was very serious. And that her speech was affected as well.'

'Well –' the nurse looked puzzled '– not really. She can certainly make herself understood.' She smiled at Barty.

Another lie then; Barty closed her eyes briefly.

She followed the nurse into the room; Sally Norton lay in the bed with her eyes closed. The nurse picked up her hand gently, stroked it.

'Mrs Norton. You have a visitor.'

The eyes that looked at Barty were very blue and very large: Cathy's eyes and Meg's eyes.

'Yes?' she said. 'Who is it?'

Her speech was slurred, but perfectly comprehensible.

'It's Barty, Sally. May I call you that? Barty Patterson. Married to Charlie—'

Sally Norton's sleepy face became alert, sharp, then contorted with rage.

'Well, you can get out again,' she said, 'right out. I don't want to see you, don't want you here—'

'Mrs Norton!' The nurse sounded embarrassed. 'Mrs Patterson has brought you some lovely flowers, look, of course you want to see her—'

'It's all right,' said Barty quietly, 'I knew she was confused. I—'

'I'm not confused,' said Sally Norton, 'did he tell you that? Did Charlie tell you that?'

'Well—'

'Look just get out of here.' The voice was no longer angry, nor was the face, both of them just infinitely weary. 'Go away, stay away—'

She started to weep, silently, great tears rolling down her face; she tried to raise a hand to wipe them, missed the face, hit the pillow. It was an oddly sad sight; the nurse reached for a tissue, wiped her eyes gently.

'There, Mrs Norton, there, there. That's better. Now you don't really want Mrs Patterson to go, do you?'

'I do. I do.' She began to grow agitated again, raising and lowering her hand rather feebly, 'I want her out of here—'

'I'd better go,' said Barty in a low voice to the nurse. 'I'm obviously upsetting her. It's all right, I understand, my – my guardian had a stroke, I know how difficult it is—'

'I'm so sorry, Mrs Patterson. Look – I'll try and calm her down, maybe you could wait for a while, see the doctor then try again—'

'Yes, all right. I've brought some of the things you asked for, some nightdresses and toilet things, and some books she might like and—' She felt dreadful suddenly; she had to get out of this room, away from all this. She walked quickly down the corridor, took a chair by the nursing station, sat there, her eyes fixed on a picture of a flock of birds flying through clouds above the desk. Concentrate on that, Barty, don't think about the rest.

340

A woman pushed through the door from the corridor; she was quite old, shabbily dressed, carrying a plastic bag. She walked down the corridor, towards Sally's room, disappeared into it; after a very short time she came out again, escorted by the nurse. She led her over to Barty.

'Mrs Patterson, this is Mrs Dixon. She's a friend of Mrs Norton. I – I thought perhaps you should meet her. I'm afraid Mrs Norton is rather upset now, still not ready for visitors. Mrs Dixon, this is Mrs—'

'Yeah, I heard who you were.' Mrs Dixon looked at Barty rather intently, as if she was studying a rare species of animal. 'You don't look like I thought you would.'

'How – how was that?' asked Barty.

'Flashy. Fine clothes. Thought you was rich.'

Barty felt a sudden and disproportionate sense of relief that at least she wasn't flashy.

'I – I see,' she said.

There was a silence; she and Mrs Dixon looked at one another. 'You could buy me a cup of tea, if you like,' she said, 'till she calms down. She gets like this, it ain't just you.'

'Oh – oh, I see,' said Barty. 'Yes, tea would be nice. Where can we go?'

'There's a cafeteria,' said the nurse, 'on the ground floor. You can get tea, coffee, it's quite nice—' She sounded relieved, was clearly eager to get rid of them.

'Fine,' said Barty. 'Come along, then, Mrs Dixon.'

They sat at a small table in the cafeteria; Mrs Dixon stared at her, clutching her plastic bag.

'Never met her, have you?'

'No,' said Barty, 'I haven't. I did try, of course, I asked her to the wedding, and I wrote to her, but—'

'She'd never meet you. Never want to.'

'Oh,' said Barty, 'oh, I see.'

'Nothing personal, of course.'

'No?'

'Not really. Just that you married him. Charlie.'

'Did they – do they – not get on?'

'Get on! That's mighty fine! Sally get on with *him*! I don't think so.' Her tone was derisive; she slurped at her tea.

'But – Mrs Dixon, you must forgive me, but I don't understand. Can you tell me why not?'

'Why not? You askin' me why not? That's very fine. Well, I s'pose he maybe won't have told you all of it.'

'All of what?'

'The way he treated her.'

'Who? Sally?'

'Sally? No, I'm not talkin' about Sally; I'm talkin' about Meg. The way she died.'

'I'm sorry.' The dizziness was getting worse. 'You'll have to tell me. She died – she died of cancer, didn't she?'

Mrs Dixon put her cup down, stared at her.

'My. You really don't know much, do ya? Cancer! Is that what he told ya? Well I s'pose it's prettier. In a way.'

'Prettier than what?'

'The truth. She didn't die of cancer, Mrs Patterson, she died of a heart attack. Brought on by alcoholic poisoning. She was an alcoholic, that's what killed her. Poor soul.'

There was a long silence; Barty felt as if she was sitting inside it, inside its shell; outside it, all around it, people chatted and clinked their teaspoons and scraped their chairs, but they were remote, distant from her. Finally she spoke.

'Mrs Dixon –' she took a deep breath '– could you tell me everything please? Because I do rather need to know.'

'If – if that's what you want. But – Mrs Patterson – well, forgive me, this is your husband we're talking about. You sure you want to hear it?'

'I do, yes.'

'Meg married him when she was real young, not quite twenty. I didn't know her then, or Sally, come to that. Meg was the only child, her parents wanted to do well for her, sent her to some snooty secretarial college they couldn't really afford, all that stuff. Paid off, though. She was working as a private secretary to some big-shot businessman when she met Charlie. She was kind of impressed by him, Sally said. They all were, all three of 'em. He was so charming, and he seemed well off, talked big. He had a job in some New York real estate firm, had a big future, he told her. They were two of a kind, maybe, him and Meg, both seeming a bit better than what they were.'

She stopped. 'This sounds very rude, Mrs Patterson. Are you sure you want to hear all this?'

'I'm – quite sure,' said Barty quietly.

'Doesn't seem right somehow, I mean, me tellin' you.'

'Someone has to.'

'OK. Well, she liked a good time, Meg did, she was a party girl, not in any kind of a bad way, just liked to go out a lot, have fun. And drink; she did drink, even then. Too much, Sally said, but she used to say it didn't matter, she could handle it, how could anyone have a good time without it. Turned out her dad liked his drink, and her grandpa, he was a real drunk. It runs in families, drinkin' does, everyone knows that. Anyway, Charlie didn't earn that much, he was on commission, but Meg was on a good wage. They moved into a real nice apartment in Gramercy, more than they could afford, really, but Charlie said it was an investment, he had to entertain clients, all that stuff. Meg liked that, of course; any excuse for a party. Anyway, after a bit, Charlie decided to set up on his own, said that was the only way you got rich, not by working for other people, so he gave up his job, took a small office. Idea was Meg would keep 'em. They were in real debt right from then, Sally said, living beyond their means.'

'Were they – were they happy?'

'Sally says yes, at first. And they were a lovely looking couple, well, you'll have seen pictures, she was a beautiful girl, and he was quite handsome, in his way. Still is, I dare say. But – Meg started drinking more. The worry, Sally says. And then she lost her job.'

'Why?'

'She got unreliable. Late in day after day, hangovers, mostly. It was OK, she got another, but not as good. So – more debts, more worries, more drinkin'. Sally said she begged Charlie to get another job, to help Meg, but he wouldn't. Told her it was crazy, when he'd come this far. It was always just around the corner, the big break, the big money. And who's to say it wasn't, he was certainly clever enough. But then Meg got pregnant. She was real happy, gave up the drink straight away, Sally said, just like that. But of course she couldn't work, not for long. So Charlie had to get a job again. Give up his own firm. He was really upset about that, there were lots of rows. But – Cathy was born, and he just fell in love with her. It was like he lost interest in Meg from then on, all that mattered was Cathy.

'Nothing was good enough for that child. He insisted on moving into another, bigger apartment they couldn't afford so she could have what he called a nursery. He bought her pricey clothes and toys, the best pram, it was ridiculous. It was around then I met Sally; Bob, that's her husband, died and she moved to my neighbourhood. He was a bit like Charlie from the sound of him, talked big, never made any real money. He left most of what he had to Sally, but it wasn't much, and a little bit to Meg, a few hundred dollars. Meg didn't tell Charlie about that, didn't want it to go where she knew it would, into another of his schemes. She kept it quiet, it was their secret Sally said. Anyway, he did get a job and worked really hard, but it wasn't enough. And so Meg had to get a job too. Well, she couldn't work in the day, because of looking after Cathy. Sally offered to help, but Charlie wouldn't let her.'

'Why not?'

Mrs Dixon looked at her. She seemed embarrassed.

'Please do go on, Mrs Dixon, I really want to know.'

'Well – forgive me for saying this about your husband, but he's a godawful snob. The right accent, the right school, all that stuff really mattered to him. He was always trying to make out he was better than what he was, he believed it himself, Meg said. He didn't want Sally round his precious princess of a daughter, said she didn't speak good enough, or some such rubbish. Anyway, Meg wasn't gettin' on with her ma so well at that time, they'd had too many rows about Charlie. So she worked in bars at night. And that wasn't too good, not with her problem. She used to come home drunk, and they'd have awful rows. Real screaming matches. And course it was costing money, the drinkin', by then. She was spending her earnings on it. I liked Meg, she was real pretty, and smart too. Another husband and she'd of been a success, I reckon. And the same goes for him, maybe, I can see you could be good for him.

'Anyway, Meg couldn't cope with any of it. The debts, the rows, Charlie. So she drank more and more. Charlie did try and help, it's important you know that, he tried to make her go for counselling, and to Al Anon meetings. But she wouldn't, said it was all his fault, if he'd work a bit harder, earn some proper money, stop wasting it on all the stuff for Cathy – she just hated him in the end, she was just so angry with him, all the time, said that was why she drank. Mind, she spent half what he gave her for food on liquor.

'And it got real bad for the kid, she was three or four by then, and there was her mom reeling about the place, getting the shakes, vomiting, falling over, shouting at her dad. Last straw came when it was time for Cathy to go to school; she had to have the very best, no neighbourhood schools for her. That was when Charlie had to let Sally help, fetch her from school and that, because Meg couldn't be trusted to be sober. But she had to say she was the maid.'

'Oh God,' said Barty.

'Yeah, I know. She did it for Meg, Meg begged her to go along with it, to keep Charlie happy. She did try to move in with Sally, take the kid, but Charlie said if she went, he'd get Cathy, tell the authorities about her drinking and she'd never see Cathy again. Anyway, cut a long story short, Meg got hospitalised one day, she'd been drinking early in the morning, wasn't eating any, she took some pills, Sally found her with the kid, both of 'em in the bed, Meg unconscious. Stomach pump, all the usual. She pulled through that time but it did awful things to her insides, and her liver. She was an invalid, really, after that. Sally moved in for a bit, tried to keep her away from the drink, but it didn't work none. She'd get her to stop for a week or two, then come in and find she'd been bingeing. She wasn't strong anyway, they found out when she was in hospital that she had a heart condition. Or maybe it was the drink caused it, I don't know. Charlie was doin' his best by then, but he had to work, try and pay the bills. And then one night they had a real bad row, he found out about her money from her dad, and he told her she was a disgrace and not fit to be a mother, and then he went out and left her alone, and she just drank and drank and drank and next day she was in a coma. She died in hospital next day.'

She stopped, wiped her eyes. 'It was terribly sad, Mrs Patterson. Such a waste of a life. It's an awful thing.'

'And how old was Cathy then?'

'Not quite four, I think. Course she didn't understand. They kept the worst from her. Right at the very end, she was livin' with Sally most of the time.'

'Poor little girl.'

'You got it, Mrs Patterson. Poor little girl. She just thought her mom was ill, they kept telling her that. Without Sally she'd'a been much worse off. She saved her, you know, she really did.'

She blew her nose, wiped her eyes again.

'Then right after, he came and took her, and hardly ever let Sally near her again. It was real sad, she'd done a lot for that little girl. And Cathy liked her then. But he turned her against her gran. Charlie, I mean. Told her she was mean and that she didn't like him and didn't want to see them no more. He just wanted to start again, it seemed like, turn himself into someone else. He moved away, got a new apartment and that was that. He got hold of the money Meg'd been left, said he was going to use it for Cathy's school fees. He was obsessed with that child, just obsessed. And with giving her the best. Anyway, Sally reckons he killed Meg. Course he didn't. Lots of ways he tried real hard, I really want you to know that. It was the drink that did it. But – well, I guess he didn't do her no good either.'

'No,' said Barty. 'No, I can see that.'

'You seem nice,' said Mrs Dixon, 'good for Cathy, I'd say. How is she anyway? Sally hasn't seen her once since she was around nine or ten.'

'She's fine,' Barty spoke slowly; she felt as if she was waking from a long troubled sleep. 'She's very pretty and very sweet, and she and my daughter are great friends. They're at boarding school now, the pair of them—'

'Boarding school! Charlie'd like that.'

'Yes,' Barty said. 'Yes, he certainly does.'

She said goodbye to Mrs Dixon after that, asked her to tell the doctor to phone her and that she would pay for anything necessary, and maybe come back another day.

'You sure you're all right?' said Mrs Dixon. 'You look awful pale.'

'I'm fine. Thank you. Yes. But I must go.'

As she reached the reception area on the ground floor, Barty felt so dizzy, so sick, she had to sit down for a moment with her head in her hands. People looked at her curiously, sympathetically, obviously thinking she had suffered a bereavement, had lost someone very important to her, someone she had loved very much. She supposed that in a sense she had.

CHAPTER 27

She would have to get away; not be there, be in a different city, a different country, even. She would leave, take herself off permanently somewhere, where no one would be able to find her, where she would be safe. Only – where?

It had been Noni who had said it, excitedly, over breakfast: 'Izzie is coming, isn't it lovely?'

'Coming where?' she had said stupidly, stabbing butter on to her toast.

'Here, of course. For Kit's wedding. Maman, what is the matter, you look as if you've seen a ghost.'

'Oh – nothing,' said Adele, 'nothing at all. Sorry, I was – I was thinking about something else. Excuse me, Noni, I have to – have to make a phone call.'

Venetia arrived and tried to be reassuring.

'She has told Sebastian she's coming, yes. And Kit. But – darling, don't sound so terrified, is she really going to blurt out all about it to everyone at the wedding? I wish I could make you understand, she's going to be as wretched as you are about it. With good reason. I—' she stopped. Tearing into Izzie wasn't going to help; she had refrained from doing so throughout. She had written to her, that one firm, cold letter, and had felt there was no more she could do.

'Well I can't bear it. I don't know how she can even consider coming. At least Geordie's had the decency to stay away. I think you're wrong, Venetia, I think she'll tell everyone, have them all laughing at me and thinking how wonderfully attractive she is. You know she never got anyone after Kit and thought she was going to be an old maid—'

'Adele, for heaven's sake. Do stop it. You're being ridiculous.' Venetia knew it was wrong to talk to her like this, it smacked of telling her to pull herself together, the one thing Dr Cunningham had said she was incapable of, but she couldn't help it. There was a limit to her patience.

Adele promptly started to cry.

'Now you're angry with me. It's not fair, no one's on my side,

346

everyone's against me.' She stopped. Noni had come into the room, her eyes brilliant with excitement.

'Guess what! Such lovely news. I've got a booking in New York, just the week before the wedding. Absolutely marvellous, a big fashion shoot with lots of other models, Suzy Parker for one, can you imagine, me in a shoot with Suzy Parker? Unbelievable. It's Irving Penn for *Vogue*. And the agency there, Fords, you know, they think they might get me into *Harpers* as well, I'm so excited.'

'Well done, darling. I – I'm just – going upstairs for a moment,' said Adele, and hurried out of the room. Noni looked after her, biting her lip.

'Is she all right? Oh dear, she gets upset sometimes when she hears things like this, almost jealous, I'd think, if it wasn't so absurd.'

'It sounds wonderful to me,' said Venetia, anxious not to spoil Noni's triumph. 'Congratulations, darling.'

'Thank you. And the best thing is I can go and see Izzie, I haven't seen her for so long. This is my first New York booking. In fact, we could maybe fly over together, you know she's coming at the last minute and—'

There were moments when it was absolutely impossible to say anything even close to the right thing. This was one. Venetia gave Noni a kiss.

'Lovely idea, darling,' she said.

'How extraordinary,' said Celia, 'this is a cable, Bunny—'

'I can see that, my dear. Not quite senile yet.'

She ignored him. 'A cable from Barty. She's coming over on her own with the girls. Without Charlie. She doesn't say why. What on earth could that be about?'

'I really couldn't say, Celia. Perhaps he's very busy.'

'Busy! The man doesn't know what busy means. And he couldn't wait to get over here, meet us all. No, there's something behind it. I just wonder what it is.'

'Can't help, my dear,' said Lord Arden, standing up and tucking *The Times* under his arm. 'If you'll excuse me now, got a lot to do—'

'Of course.'

He hurried out of the room; the Lytton women – and he included Barty among them – were so much a law unto themselves, it was very unwise to enter into any conjecture about their behaviour.

Barty had gone straight to South Lodge from the hospital. She had left a message with Maria for Charlie and the girls that she would be there for a couple of days, doing some urgent work, and needed absolute peace and quiet.

She didn't even want to broach the subject with Charlie; she couldn't bear the thought of being in the same room as him, never mind entering into a long and painful discussion with him, which would lead inevitably to a great tide first of self-justification and then remorse. She wanted to be quiet, to think, to try to decide what she actually felt, what she wanted to do.

Once there, on her own, she felt better. The power of the place to ease and comfort her did not fail her. She went for a long, long walk along the shore until she reached the shining sheet of Shinnecock Bay. As she pushed against the salty wind, her eyes fixed on the ocean, on the breakers rolling endlessly in, cutting into the white sand, she felt her mind washed clean again, clear of shock and falsehood and ugly discovery. Later, to her surprise, she managed to eat some supper, cooked by an anxious Mrs Mills, and then she went to the great bed in her room, Laurence's room; she had expected to be awake all night, had left the blinds drawn back so that she could watch the night sky, the extraordinarily brilliant stars undulled by the pollution of the city, but she fell asleep and woke refreshed to see the dawn across the sky.

She spent much of that day in the car, driving around to all the places she loved so much, the ones she had shared with Laurence, first to Sag Harbor, and then on the ferry across to North Haven, she walked there on the shore, then drove back to East Hampton and then to the woods of Amagansett and made her way to Alberts Landing and Accabonac Cliff. She stood looking over to Gardiner's Island, shrouded in mist as it almost always was, remembering the first time Laurence had shown it to her, and told her about the wild turkeys and white-tailed deer who lived there, and its supposedly buried treasure: he had tried – as only Laurence could – to buy it once from the Gardiner family, and failed.

She knew what she was doing, of course; she was reclaiming it all, making it precious again, special again, no longer shared wantonly with someone who did not deserve it.

She came home, as she had known she would, to a dozen messages from them all, from Jenna saying could they please, please come and join her, from Cathy saying could she please, please come back, they had so much to ask her about, they needed her with them, from Charlie, saying he wanted to see her, he needed to talk to her. And then she knew that he had found out, had discovered she had been to the hospital and that she had to return to him, to real life and to what she knew now that she had to do.

But not yet.

'I don't want to spoil the wedding for the girls,' she said, 'I'll take them, of course, and then, when we come back, we can – settle things.'

He was, as she knew he would be, in turn angry, then reproachful, then defensive, and finally very frightened. He knew this time that he was probably beyond help.

Cathy was his weapon, of course.

'You can't spoil everything for her,' he kept saying. 'Hurt me and you hurt her.'

Barty looked at him levelly and said, 'You did this to her, Charlie, not me. You put her into a position where she would be hurt.'

Just the same, she knew that Cathy was her problem now: not Charlie.

He was absolutely right; he was horribly clever. And also quite horribly stupid.

She let him tell the girls whatever he wanted; 'I'm not prepared to lie to them. But I'll go along with what you say.'

'Daddy's not coming,' Cathy said to Jenna, her great eyes filled with tears, 'that old witch of a grandma of mine is about to die and he says he has to stay with her.'

'That is so absolutely like him,' said Jenna, 'he's so kind and good.'

Izzie couldn't ever remember being so miserable: not even after the abortion, after Kit, after Geordie. God, she'd made a hash of her life. A complete hash. The one thing that was really good about it was her job, and she'd messed it up. She was such a fool. A complete and utter fool. Nick had withdrawn from her; he treated her with polite formality, had stopped teasing her, discussed work but nothing else, called her Izzie, not darling or sweetheart or princess or even Lady Isabella. She found it absolutely disorientating, she felt she hardly knew who she was any more. Mike was obviously embarrassed by the atmosphere between them; he had come back two days later, clearly still unwell, but cheerful, and found himself in an atmosphere of icy gloom. It was rather like the pea-souper fogs which had enveloped London in her childhood, Izzie thought, they were all groping round in it awkwardly, bumping into one another with no real idea where they were going any more.

On the third day, Mike could bear it no longer; he took Izzie out for a coffee. 'What's happened to you guys?'

Izzie stared at him.

'What do you mean?'

'Oh baby, come on, it's like the aftermath of World War Three up there. Something must have gone wrong. Well, I know a bit of course but—'

'So – he didn't tell you?'

'Nope. Only that he felt no end of a fool, that he should have stayed with me that night. He kind of left me to fill in the gaps.'

'Oh,' said Izzie. 'Oh, I see.' She wasn't sure if she felt better or worse. 'And – and what sort of things did you fill the gaps with?'

'Darling, I presumed he'd made a pass at you. Something like that. Which you very sensibly dealt with. Being the clever girl you are.'

'Well – it was something like that. Yes.'

'The guy's a schmuck, no doubt about that. Thinking he could – could make it. With you.'

Izzie felt irritated, without knowing quite why.

'I don't quite see why not,' she said, 'actually.'

'Well because he's what he is and you're what you are. You must have enough sense to see that, for God's sake.'

He looked so put out, so baffled, Izzie had to smile.

'I don't actually,' she said. 'I'd have put it more the other way round. But still—'

'Oh Izzie, come on!' He sighed, clearly thought he'd got it right. 'Look, he's an idiot, I know. But it certainly isn't a lot of fun at the moment. So could you just make an effort and put it behind you? Just write it off as inexperience on his part, start acting normal. Please, princess.'

'Of course,' said Izzie, 'I'm sorry. Of course I will.'

In her efforts to act normal, as he put it, she went over the top, laughed too much, talked too loudly, and whenever there was an awkward silence, told them both how much she was looking forward to her trip to England and the wedding.

'Is he gonna be there?' asked Nick, rather coldly, one day. His own behaviour hadn't changed; obviously Mike hadn't made the same plea to him. Or he wasn't prepared to act on it. 'Your boyfriend. Pardon me, your ex-boyfriend. Mr Smooth. The one who was so terribly good to you.'

Izzie flushed; it was her greatest dread.

'I – I don't know,' she said.

Nick said nothing, just walked away and sat down at his desk with his back to her. She stared at that back, that long skinny back, through eyes blinded by tears. Mike gave her an awkward grin and sat down himself.

It was all so horribly, horribly different. And it was all her fault.

They were going to stay at Claridges; Barty felt that was best, despite a flood of invitations. She was already worrying about confronting Adele, with her knowledge of what had happened between Geordie and Izzie standing between them. She knew that Venetia must know, if no one else did, she knew that Sebastian would not, and she knew that moving two teenagers into Cheyne Walk would be a recipe for disaster. The wedding was on 10 March; Charlie drove them to Idlewild on the fifth, kissed and hugged the girls and embraced Barty briefly, kissing her on the forehead. Barty watched him walking away, and wished she felt more; every emotion had left her, anger, sadness, resentment, any sense of foolishness, even. She regarded him temporarily, at least, with a cool distaste, and a sense of slight wonder that she had ever felt anything else towards him at all. She supposed they would return, the violent emotions, but was grateful for the respite.

Cathy burst into tears as he walked away from them and continued to sob loudly until she found herself on the plane, where the excitement of being shown to her seat and strapped in, of watching the earth sinking beneath them as they took off – and of being offered sweets and orange juice by the stewardess, and even champagne – took over.

'No,' Barty said at once. 'Certainly not, Cathy. Nor you, Jenna.'

They both stared at her, shocked by the sharpness of her tone, then nudged each other, raised their eyebrows and finally started to giggle; she sat there, mildly irritated by them, but aware that this was a new burden she was going to have to carry for as long as she had care of Cathy, a new fear in her life: that she would follow in her mother's – and her grandfather's – footsteps and become an alcoholic.

'Darling, I want to talk to you.'

Elspeth's eyes were very tender as she looked at Keir, and handed him his plate, laden with the fish pie that was his favourite. Tender and just a little anxious. He took a large sip of water – they couldn't afford wine, except on special occasions – looked back at her suspiciously.

'Yes? What about?'

'I – I've got something to tell you.'

'Ye-es?'

'I'm – well, I'm having another baby.'

He looked horrified. There was a silence. Then he said, 'Elspeth, you can't be. We've been so careful. I thought. Or –' his eyes on her were very hard '– or – haven't you?'

'Keir that's so horrible. I can't believe you said that. Of course I've been careful, I always, always wear the beastly thing, you know I do. I'd never not. But you know perfectly well Cecilia was an accident, and – well, it seems to have happened again. Anyway, it's really nice you're so pleased. It makes me feel very happy and secure.' She stood up, threw her table napkin down. 'Anyone would think I'd committed some awful crime, rather than making love with and getting pregnant by my own husband. Perhaps you'd rather we abstained completely in future. Then you'd be quite safe.'

'Elspeth don't. I—'

'Don't what, Keir? Don't have it? Don't be upset? What do you expect me to be? I've tried so hard to be a good wife to you, and a good mother to Cecilia. I've done absolutely everything I could, and now you behave as if I was some kind of – of trollop. What do you want me to do, have an abortion?'

'Elspeth! That's a vile thing to say.'

'Well you're being vile. I don't understand it, you love Cecilia, you're enjoying your job, we're managing fine—'

'Oh we are? Some very nasty bills have just come in. Rates, rent, electricity, all gone up. I've asked Giles for a raise, but he won't give me one.'

'Well, there's a surprise. Keir, why didn't you tell me all this, I don't have to be shielded from such things, I could help—'

'No,' he said, 'not if you mean going back to work, no. I'll not have it.'

'Of course not. How could I, anyway, with Cecilia being so tiny and this new little one on the way? But – babies don't cost very much. We've got all the stuff, the cot and pram and everything, and it – he – will be living off me for a while. Although Cecilia does need some new clothes, she's growing so fast, and some shoes now that she's starting to walk. But anyway, we are having another one and that's all there is to it. Don't look so miserable, we'll manage. And you know we have to have the son and heir – I just know this one'll be a boy. Please, please, Keir, be a little bit pleased.'

She sat down on his lap, put her arms round his neck; he managed to smile at her.

'Of course I am. A little bit. I'll be more so, I dare say, when I get used to the idea. It was just – just a bit of a shock, that's all.'

'I can't think why,' she said, 'we've been doing an awful lot of the right things. I'm really excited.'

'How do you feel?'

'Oh – not too bad. Yet. It's very early days.'

He looked at her, hope in his eyes. 'Then – then you could be mistaken?'

'No, definitely not. Once you've been pregnant, you know the signs pretty well. They're all there, I'm tired, a bit dizzy, my breasts are sore, I can't face coffee—'

'Well,' he smiled at her, rather wearily, 'we'll just have to manage somehow.'

'Of course. Of course we will. Look, you finish your supper and I'll make us some tea.'

She went off to the kitchen, humming happily under her breath. First part of the mission safely accomplished. It had worked beautifully, making those holes in her dutch cap. The next phase might be more difficult; but she knew she could do it. Her grandmother would be so proud of her: if she could only tell her. But of course she couldn't. Even Celia wouldn't have been that devious, she was quite, quite sure.

Izzie sat frozen with fear, waiting for Noni to arrive. She had tried very hard to dissuade her from coming; had pleaded first busyness, and then an incipient illness, but Noni was having none of it.

'If you're busy I shall just come and watch you work till you finish, and if you're ill, I'll take you home and look after you. You can't get out of it that easily. What's the matter, don't you love me any more?'

'Of course I do,' said Izzie, aware that even in her misery, she couldn't have Noni thinking that. 'You know I do. I've missed you terribly, it's just that—'

'Just what? Oh, never mind, you can tell me when we meet. I'll be finished at six tomorrow, or thereabouts, I'll phone you, shall I, and then make my way down to you. I'm so longing to see your apartment, Barty says it's lovely. Or – or maybe I could come to your office, I'd love to meet your boys. I've heard so much about them, I'll get a cab and come downtown. Don't you like that, Izzie? I've picked up all the New York lingo already.'

Izzie looked at the boys. They were sitting together, working on an ad for Barty; she had put a lot their way lately. When they had told her she was being too kind, she said not at all, the more work she gave them, the quicker she'd be able to cash in on her investment.

'And of course that's not the only reason, before you get all paranoid. You do the best ads I know. Look what our in-house ad department came up with, did you ever see such – such garbage.'

'Barty,' Mike had said, reading the ad, passing it to Nick, 'I tell you, you don't even know what garbage is. You want to see garbage, I'll show you some. Meanwhile, OK, we'll see what we can do with this. And thanks. Again.'

'Izzie, hallo. Is it all right to come up? The door wasn't locked. Oh it's so wonderful to see you, let me give you a big hug.'

'My God,' said Izzie. The words came out unbidden. 'My God, Noni . . .'

Was it really her? Shy, quiet, rather serious Noni? This tall goddess of a creature, in a mink coat slung casually over a loose woollen sheath dress, gleaming dark hair swept back in a perfect chignon, great wings of eyeshadow and rows of fake lashes emphasising her nearly black, almond-shaped eyes, her mouth a slash of brilliant colour.

'It's me, it's me, I can't believe I'm here, we're together again. Izzie, you look gorgeous, absolutely gorgeous, and now you must be the boys, I've heard so much about you, all about how clever you are, and how madly attractive. Now which of you is which? You must be Nick, I imagine, and you Mike—'

'Wrong,' said Nick coming over to her, holding out his bony hand, 'I'm Nick, I'm the really attractive one, and this is Mike, he's the rather less attractive one—'

'Hi,' said Mike. He appeared equally dazed; they all three stood there, speechless, staring at her.

'Well, aren't you going to show me round? All your offices and everything, and where does everyone else work, goodness it's so exciting—'

'Lady,' said Mike, 'you're standing in 'em, all our offices, and everyone works right here, in fact, you're looking at everyone—'

'You mean you do it all on your own? My God, how amazing. I've spent the afternoon at *Harpers*, you wouldn't believe the fuss they make about every single little thing. Carmel Snow, she's the editor, she goes to church every single morning, they're on Madison and there's a church just two or three blocks up, she says she couldn't do her job without it, and I have to say I think she must need God on her side. It's a nightmare there, there's this woman, Diana Vreeland, who's the fashion editor, and she is just so grand and snobbish—'

'Snobbish,' said Mike. 'You can recognise snobbish?'

'Yes, of course. Why ever not? I'm not used to snobbery at all, except from my grandmother of course and she doesn't count, does she, Izzie? But Mrs Vreeland is just ridiculous, she examined me as if I was a racehorse of some kind, walked round and round me, nodding occasionally, and then she said – not to me but to the art director – "Yes, she'll do." Anyway, you don't want to hear about me.'

'Oh we do,' said Nick, still staring at her absolutely transfixed. 'We most certainly do.'

Izzie saw her salvation.

'Why don't you both come with us? We're only going out to supper, aren't we, Noni?'

'Yes, of course, that'd be divine, please do say you'll come. I thought later we might go on to the Stork Club, what do you think? The other girls will be there, and possibly Richard Avedon. You know who I saw in his studio? Fred Astaire. Mr Avedon photographs him a lot, and he is an absolute darling, so charming and courteous. Richard Avedon's studio is just so civilised, you'd be amazed, there's always music playing and he serves tea in little white cups—'

'I think perhaps not the Stork Club,' said Izzie quickly. The thought of going there, where people like Andy Warhol and Truman Capote drank and talked their nights away, was almost as terrifying as spending an intimate evening with Noni.

'Pity. I know they'd love to see you. Now, I've got some wonderful news for you, Izzie. I've managed to get you a flight back with me. One of the other models was coming with us and now she can't, so I said could you have her place. It's all booked and paid for, you might as well. We can sit and chat all the way to London and it's only a day earlier than you would have flown, I checked with Sebastian—'

'I'm not sure,' said Izzie feebly. 'The thing is, I've got so much to do and—'

'You go, darling.' It was Nick; he clearly couldn't wait to be rid of her. But at least he'd called her darling.

'Good. That's settled.'

They all went to a restaurant in the Village; the boys sat on either side of Noni, listening enthralled while she chattered through the meal. Izzie sat at the end, grateful for the diversion, but faintly embarrassed at the nonsense pouring out, endless nonsense, some of it quite amusing. There was gossip about the other models, who was marrying this millionaire and who was marrying that peer of the realm – 'It's a wonderful way to get a rich husband, Izzie, I tell you that' – about photographers, which ones were homosexual and which ones weren't – 'I prefer the fairies, myself, much better gossip and you can talk about your hair and make-up to them for hours' – which couturiers she liked and which she didn't – 'I actually met Chanel the other day, can you imagine? She is so beautiful still, and so chic. There's a spiral staircase leading up from the salon and while her show is going on, she always sits at the top of it, just out of sight' – what she had bought in which shop in New York – 'Don't you love Bonwit Tellers more than any place on earth?' – about being 'sort of engaged, only don't tell anyone, not even Maman', to someone divine called Percy.

'Percy! Noni, you can't be in love with someone called Percy.'

Somehow in her strung-up state this amused Izzie hugely; she struggled to compose herself.

Noni giggled. 'I know, it's not the best name. But it's a frightfully noble one, he's the son of an earl, which means I'd be Countess of Crowthorne one day, wouldn't Granny love it?'

At this point the boys looked as if they might be about to burst with excitement; Izzie, on the other hand, sat looking at this astonishing new Noni, and thought that, grateful as she was for the reprieve, she had really rather preferred the old one.

At last the meal was over; Noni said she must get back to her hotel, that she had promised Mrs Vreeland she wouldn't be late – 'She says late nights show on the skin' – and then just as Izzie thought she was safe, suddenly started talking about Geordie.

'Have you seen him? He said he'd bumped into you, and that he'd seen your apartment. Maybe we could go back there now, no, I'd better not, maybe another time, I wish I had one, I'm still living at home, you know, can't leave Maman—'

'Is – is she all right?'

'Not really,' said Noni, her voice heavier suddenly, 'she's very depressed. And lonely, poor darling. She's not working, so she's bored too. But she's seeing a psychiatrist now and—'

'A psychiatrist!'

'Yes, yes she is, has been for ages.'

This was getting worse. 'Oh, Noni, I'm so, so sorry—'

'Darling, you're so sweet. I know. It's awful, and she's on loads of pills, anti-depressants and—'

'Nobody told me,' said Izzie. 'Nobody told me that.'

'Well – not many people know. She hates people to; don't mention it when you see her, will you. Of course Geordie knew.'

'Geordie knew?'

'Of course. But he kept it quiet, for her sake. God, it's so awful, all that, if only he'd come back, she misses him so terribly. But I don't think he ever will now, it's all such a mess, and one of those things that really is no one's fault. It's terrible for poor little Clio too, she misses Geordie dreadfully. If he'd only come back to London, it would help, at least he could see her again. What a mess. Perhaps I won't get married. Darlings I must go, sorry you two, so boring, hearing all about my family. Thank you so much for the meal, now I wonder, could you be terribly clever and get me a cab?'

She was gone at last; Izzie stood staring after her, feeling as if she had had a very long illness, and had only just begun to recover.

'She was something else,' said Mike, shaking his head, 'really something else. My God, Izzie, your family—'

'She's not my family,' said Izzie, 'she's nothing to do with me.' And burst into tears.

They were both very sweet. Mike offered to go back with her, but she said, no, it was all right, she was very tired, and she just wanted to go to bed. So they got her a cab and kissed her goodnight, both of them, on the cheek, and saw her into it; the last thing she saw was the pair of them, standing in the street, talking earnestly.

She was halfway back in the taxi when she realised she didn't have her house key. She had the office key, but she had separated them earlier that day and left one with her neighbour so she could let the electrician in to fix a plug. And she'd forgotten. She'd meant to get the spare from her desk; she'd just have to go back for it. The cab driver was not very pleased.

She walked into the office, the quiet, dark, untidy office, where she had spent the happiest times she could ever remember, and sighed, thinking how she had completely messed all that up. She went over to her desk, opened the drawer and retrieved her key. And then sat there thinking, thinking about all this dangerous new knowledge and freshly appalled at what she had done. Not just betrayed Adele, the Adele she thought she had known, but a different, still more vulnerable one, on anti-depressants, in the care of a psychiatrist.

Well at least she could see now that she was going to have to go to London and face Adele. There was no way out. She would tell her herself how sorry she was, that she had not known she was ill, that she had thought her marriage was over. However terrifying the prospect. And it was terrifying. She—

The door of the office swung open; she jumped, terrified. It was an intruder, she'd be murdered, well maybe that would solve a problem or two, probably raped as well.

'Izzie. What are you doing here?'

It was Nick. She stared at him, too miserable even to be embarrassed.

'I left my key behind. What about you?'

'I wanted to do a bit of work.'

'Oh, I see. Well – I'm just going, I won't distract you.'

And then suddenly she burst into tears.

He was very good; he sat down next to her, took her hand and gave her a handkerchief.

'Here, dry your eyes. What's the matter?'

'Oh – everything,' she said, 'absolutely everything. I've just completely messed up. Messed up everything, you've no idea—'

'I haven't, really,' he said, looking at her. 'How about you tell me? I guess it upset you, hearing about your boyfriend—'

'He's not my boyfriend,' she said, 'stop calling him that.' And she started crying again.

'All right, your ex-boyfriend. Izzie, the man's a schmuck, I told you before.'

'I know, I know he is, more than ever. But I didn't know, Nick, I really didn't know Adele was so ill. I would never, ever have – have – oh God—'

'Sweetheart,' he said, and even in her wretchedness it was so good to hear that endearment, 'of course you wouldn't.'

'And I've completely wrecked everything, my friendship with Adele, with Noni—'

'She doesn't seem the best kind of friend for you anyway,' he said.

Izzie stared at him. 'What do you mean?'

'Well – she's kind of ridiculous,' he said finally. 'She's gorgeous, I give you that. But – not too much like you, Princess.'

'She's not really like that,' Izzie said, wiping her eyes. 'She's really very sweet and sensible.'

'You could have fooled me.'

'No, it's true. Oh, I'm such an idiot. You've no idea.'

'Want to tell me? Again?'

'Again! Nick, you don't know half of it.'

'OK. You tell me the other half. Go on, it might help.'

'Well – well, first of all,' she said, blowing her nose on his hanky, 'first of all I had this affair with – with Kit. You know?'

'Sure. Nice guy.'

'Very nice. When I was only sixteen. We were going to run away together, to Scotland, to get married there—'

'Sounds romantic. And? Why didn't you?'

'They stopped us. When we were on the train.'

'Because you were so young?'

'No,' she said flatly. 'No, because he was – he was my half-brother.'

There was a very long, fierce silence; Nick sat staring at her, and she stared back at him, so shocked at herself for telling him, so shocked at telling anyone about this thing she had thought she would never recover from. She had been so afraid of it, always, without being quite sure why, had spent much of the time denying it even to herself. It was so ugly, so horribly shocking; not so much that Kit's father was Sebastian, not Oliver; not even that Celia and Sebastian had been lovers for years, or that Kit had been brought up by Celia and Oliver as their son; but that she had fallen in love with her own brother, had almost slept with him, married him.

'So – just a minute. Sebastian's his dad?'

'Yes.'

'And – Celia led everyone to believe that Kit was her husband's son?'

'Well – yes. She had to, in a way. For a long time she hadn't been absolutely sure, but as he grew up, he looked so like Sebastian, there was just no doubting it.'

'And they never told you? Either of you?'

'Not till – till that day, no. When they stopped us from running away.'

'That was kind of remiss of them, I'd say.' Nick's eyes on hers were very thoughtful.

'They didn't know, didn't realise. That we were – well, in love with each other. I was such a baby, and—'

'Exactly. Such a baby.'

'They didn't tell me even then, actually, they thought I was too young. But I found out, years later, I heard Sebastian and Kit shouting at each other, and I – I realised—'

'Good God,' he said, and he looked absolutely shocked. 'How perfectly horrible for you. My poor, poor darling.'

'It gave me nightmares,' she said, too distressed even to notice the darling, 'for ages. I was so shocked by it. Adele was wonderful, she was the only person who really helped me. I was so angry with Father and with Celia. I got over it, of course, forgave them, as Oliver had. You do, when you grow up, you get to understand things better. But it was – very hard at the time. And knowing lots of the family had known, that there was a sort of conspiracy to keep it from me. I felt so stupid, so naive, such a fool. And then,' she said, a sob rising in her voice again, 'then when I'd got over that, I had to go and sleep with one of the Warwicks. Celia's grandson.'

'Why'd you do that?' he said, his voice very gentle.

'Oh, because he was miserable, I was miserable, I'd never had another boyfriend, I was drunk, he was drunk, you know the sort of thing.'

'Just about,' he said.

'It was only once. At a party. And –' for a moment she was tempted: to tell him the rest, about the baby, about the abortion. It would have been such a relief, such a dazzling, blinding relief. But she couldn't. It was one step too far, one thing too awful, too wrong. '– that just finished me off,' she said. 'I felt so worthless, so cheap, so ashamed of myself.'

'Oh Izzie. I'd say he was a lucky guy. How long did that last?'

'It didn't,' she said flatly. 'It was – just one night. He announced his engagement about a week later. To someone else, I mean. I had to be her bridesmaid.'

'My God. You poor kid.' He shook his head, half smiled at her; his eyes were very soft, very concerned.

'Well – in a way it wasn't really so bad. I suppose.'

Not told this way, anyway, no shining instruments, no terror, no pain, no—

'Sounds quite bad. You poor, poor baby.'

'And then I got so down, I thought I'd never find anyone, anyone who'd love me, care about me, at all. I guess that's why I got involved with Geordie. What a good idea *that* was.'

'How did you get over here? Don't quite follow that bit.'

'Well, it was Celia's idea. She thought it would do me good. She was wonderful, she noticed I was really depressed, and – well of course she knew about Kit, she had always worried about me afterwards – I found myself telling her everything. And she suggested I stayed with Barty for a while. And you know the rest. Everything was so lovely, I met you and Mike, I loved my job. And then what do I do, I go and have that stupid affair.'

'Ye-es. We've probably said enough about that one. That all?'

'No,' she said, and started crying harder than ever. 'No it's not all, is it? I've wrecked things with you as well now, by being so stupid, throwing myself at you, embarrassing you, thinking you . . . well, you . . .'

'That I what?' he said, very gently.

'That you – liked me. That you'd want me, it was so stupid, just because I was drunk, and, and—'

'And what?'

'And I decided I wanted you. I'm so, so sorry, Nick, for spoiling everything, our friendship, our working relationship, I really am such a complete idiot—'

'Now just a minute,' he said, 'can we rewind a little here? You wanted me? That night?'

'Yes. Yes of course I did. But only because I was so drunk and excited about the presentation and—'

'Only because—?'

'Well – well –'

'Izzie,' he said, 'Izzie, never did a girl ever get anything so wrong. I adore you, I think you're quite horribly sexy, I always have, I wanted you so much that night I thought I would expire. But how could I do that to you, take advantage of you? I've been brought up better than that, for God's sake.'

He looked quite indignant; she stopped crying and stared at him, trying to make sense of it all, to disentangle what she had thought from what he was saying.

'You – you wanted – but Nick, in the morning you were so odd, you have been ever since, I obviously embarrassed you to death, I felt so ashamed—'

'I *was* embarrassed, sure I was. Only by my own behaviour. Staring at you like that, letting you walk past me buck naked, not pretending I was asleep, as a gentleman should – I felt so bad. And then kissing you like that, almost letting my feelings get the better of me. I felt terrible—'

'Oh,' she said. Everything had become very still; she just sat there staring at him. Then suddenly she smiled, and put out her hand and stroked his cheek, very gently.

'We seem to have got everything a bit – wrong,' she said. 'Why don't we go back to my place and have a replay?'

They managed to find a cab. 'Just as well,' he said to her, laughing, 'otherwise it would have had to be the office floor,' and went home, home to her apartment.

They said very little then, went straight into her room, lay down on her bed, removing their clothes, kissing frantically, endlessly, greedy, joyful, impatient for the pleasure; and then he stopped suddenly, leaned away from her, smiled into her eyes.

'What?' she said, alarmed. 'What is it, what's the matter?'

'Nothing,' he said, 'nothing at all. But I have to tell you something.'

'What?'

'It's this,' he said, starting to kiss her again. 'I have never seen anything as beautiful, ever, not in any bedroom, not on any night, not in my entire life, as you, walking across that room in there. You know what I thought?'

'No,' she said, 'what did you think?'

'I thought here I am, lying in the gutter, looking up at the stars.'

CHAPTER 28

She looked better than she had; calmer, happier, less exhausted. Celia didn't ask Barty why Charlie wasn't with her, of course; but Barty told her anyway. She invited her to dinner at Claridges, while Jenna and Cathy were at the Warwicks', and said she wanted to talk to her.

'I feel I owe it to you,' she said, raising her glass to Celia. 'You've been so – so generous about everything. I can't just arrive without him and not tell you why. But I'd rather you didn't tell the others.'

'Barty, I am not in the habit of gossiping,' said Celia severely, and then added, a flash of humour in her dark eyes, 'that isn't quite true, of course. But I am not in the habit of breaking confidences. As you very well know.'

'Yes. Yes, I do.'

Barty looked at her; for the first time, Celia was beginning to age. Her illness had taken a severe toll; she was still desperately tired-looking, and her face was drawn, the cheeks gaunt, the lovely eyes even slightly sunken. She was still very glamorous, dressed that evening in one of the new sack dresses in light-navy wool; it might have been designed specifically for her, disguising, as it did, her extreme thinness, hinting at a shape she no longer had. She had been ordered to stop smoking; when she drew out her cigarette case, Barty shook her head, tried to take it from her.

'Celia, really! You are so stupid.'

'Nonsense. I never smoke before dinner. Well, before dinner time. That means I've cut out at least twenty a day. Quite enough. Really, Barty, you can't expect me to get through a day at Lyttons without smoking at the end of it.'

'Is it really so bad?'

'Well – you know, difficult.'

'You've been doing awfully well. The figures are most impressive. Bigger profit than the New York office this year. I shouldn't be telling you that, should I?'

'Of course you should. I can't think why not.'

Barty smiled at her; Celia would never come to terms, she knew, with the fact that she was notionally her superior.

'Well – I have some very good plans in place for next year.'

'Oh really? What?'

'Oh – a historical series. Very big in the States at the moment, history. A marvellous mystery story. I'd like to launch a paperback house, but it's out of the question at the moment, the numbers are too huge. Centaur seems to be doing well. You can do these things on a small scale here. Over there it means millions of dollars investment.'

'My biggest problem is keeping the standard up. It isn't easy. Jay is getting very lazy, I'm afraid, and Giles is – well, just Giles. So dreadfully dull in his thinking. It's Keir I've got my eye on, he's such a brilliant young man. And, of course, one day Elspeth will be back. We have to keep the younger generation with us—'

'Of course,' said Barty soberly, thinking that perhaps that was what she was lacking in New York, someone truly representative of the younger generation. 'But surely, dear Celia, you must be getting tired of it all? Don't you ever wish you could just – walk away from them?'

'No,' said Celia, looking at her as if she had suggested she should take up street walking or joining a convent. 'Of course not. Do you?'

Barty said she did not, of course, either; and then that she would like to try to explain about Charlie.

'It's all dreadfully sad,' she said, 'but you know, I feel much better in a way. Trying to make the relationship work was like pushing water uphill. I was so wrong to marry him. I don't know why I did.'

'I do,' said Celia, 'same reason I married Bunny. You were lonely.'

'Yes, but now I spend my life trying to get away from him.'

'Of course. Exactly the same thing.' She looked at Barty and smiled. 'You've done the right thing,' she said.

'I haven't done anything yet. But I am going to tell him I don't want to live with him any more. I can't. He's a fantasist, and you can't have a relationship with a fantasist. The real problem is the girls, they both adore him.'

'Well, they can still see plenty of him. He doesn't have much to do, as far as I can make out.'

'No, but it's not as simple as that. Jenna's going to find it very hard to cope with, I know. She was so happy for me, happy I wasn't on my own any more. And Cathy is a very complex little person—'

'Barty,' said Celia quite severely, 'you must do what is best for yourself. Not them.'

'But I'm not sure I know what that is. Except that I can't go on accepting all these lies. I can't even bear to discuss it with him. Of course it wasn't all his fault, I'm sure he had a really hard time. In many ways worse than if Meg had really had cancer. But – why keep it from me? Why go on and on in this wretched pretence that he's something he's not? What kind of basis for a relationship is that? Poor Charlie,' she added soberly, 'I do feel quite sorry for him, you know. As well as angry.'

'Don't,' said Celia, 'he doesn't deserve it.'

Jenna was bitterly disappointed that Billy and Joan and the boys weren't coming to the wedding; she found the explanation that they were too busy to leave the farm completely unacceptable.

'It's only one day. And it is a family wedding.'

'I know, Jenna, but you can't just leave a farm.'

'You've left Lyttons. For three weeks.'

'I know, but that's different. There aren't any animals at Lyttons, you can't walk out on a stable full of horses and hope they'll be all right for a few days. Billy just doesn't feel he can get away.'

Jenna suspected this was not entirely true; there was a cowman at the farm, she remembered being told, and a stable lad as well. She looked at her mother.

'Is it because Billy hasn't been asked?'

'Of course he's been asked,' said Barty. 'I've seen his letter to Kit. He just can't come. Now, Jenna, can we change the subject please? I'm getting rather tired of it. You still need to get some shoes, how about—'

'I'm sick of shopping,' said Jenna. 'Mother, is it because he doesn't feel comfortable about coming? All those terribly important people, lords and ladies and so on?'

Barty hesitated. Then she said, 'Something like that, yes. I think it is. To be absolutely honest. And I think the boys would hate it.'

'Why?'

'Boys do hate weddings. They hate getting dressed up and they won't know anybody—'

'Well,' said Jenna, 'I can certainly understand that. But we must go down there, then. I so want to see them.'

'We can't. Not till after the wedding.'

'Why not? It's three days away still.'

'Because we all have too much to do.'

'I don't. Could I go down there at least? Take Cathy, maybe?'

'No. You'd get lost.'

'I wouldn't. I have eyes in my head. I can read a train timetable. I get myself to school and back—'

'Jenna, no.'

Jenna walked out of her mother's room and slammed the door. Then she went down to the hotel reception.

'Do you have a train timetable?' she asked.

Cathy said she wouldn't come, she had more shopping to do. Jenna knew what she really wanted to do was hang around Fergal, Venetia's youngest boy; he was quite gorgeous, she had to admit, seventeen and the most handsome boy she had ever seen, very tall and athletic-looking with dark hair and almost black eyes. His sister Lucy had told her he was terribly brave.

'He's a brilliant rider, Granny says. He went skiing last year and went down all the black runs, that's the very dangerous ones—'

'I know what a black run is,' Jenna said airily; but she was impressed just the same. She was pretty brave herself, but she didn't think she'd tackle a black run. Fergal seemed to quite like her; but he was clearly much more taken with Cathy. Cathy put on her very best performance for him, fluttering her eyelashes wildly, hanging breathlessly on everything he said, laughing hysterically at his rather weak jokes, and getting physically close to him at the slightest opportunity. He'd been standing at the hall table the day before at the house in Berkeley Square, looking at the newspapers; Cathy joined him, leaning against him whenever she could, brushing his hand with hers, and expressing an immense interest in the forthcoming march to Aldermaston by the Campaign for Nuclear Disarmament, which Jenna knew she couldn't care less about, asking Fergal to explain why they were marching and what difference it might make, gazing up at him with her huge blue eyes and telling him how clever he was to understand it all. The ghastly thing was how impressed he seemed to be. Jenna could never understand how boys couldn't see through that sort of thing . . .

It was actually very easy to get to Beaconsfield; first the tube to Marylebone, and then out on the mainline train. She sat on the train feeling terribly excited, not only that she had made her escape, but about seeing them all, Billy and Joan and Joe and Michael. They had somehow come to epitomise England for her, England and family, far more than any of the Lyttons. New York and London were staging posts. Her mother had talked to her endlessly about her own childhood, had said it was so important that Jenna understood about the early days in Lambeth, about the tiny dark rooms in the basement, about her father, all her brothers and sisters, and her much-loved mother; and then about moving into Cheyne Walk, how vast it had seemed, how forbidding, how miserable she had been, how much she had missed everyone.

'You should have just gone home,' Jenna said, but Barty had said in those days children did what they were told and accepted things, and besides, her mother had been so grateful for everything that Celia was doing for her, she didn't really think Barty should come back.

'And then, you see, I became estranged from the others, they were jealous of what I had. In the end only Billy was at all nice to me—'

'So you didn't belong in either place?'

'Not really. Not for a long time. But in the end, I was happy, I was very fond of Giles, we ganged up on the twins and when Kit was born, I was his godmother, I think that was what finally made me feel part of the family. And Lady Beckenham, Celia's mother, being so wonderfully good to Billy, of course; I sometimes think he felt even more part of the family than I did.'

Perhaps they were the links, Jenna thought that morning, Billy and Joan, the links between her and her mother's family, and therefore immensely important. Perhaps that was why she had felt so much she wanted to see them all again.

The train pulled in at a station: 'Beaconsfield! Beaconsfield!' She hadn't expected the journey to be so short; she grabbed her coat and bag and jumped out on to the platform, just in time before the train pulled out again in a cloud of noise and steam, and accosted a porter.

'Where are the cabs, please?'

'The cabs? You mean the taxis. Over there. Where d'you want to go, my dear?'

'Ashingham. Home Farm, Ashingham.'

'Ashingham! That's a long way. A very long way to take a taxi. Can't someone come and fetch you?'

'No, no they can't. They're too busy and anyway, I want to surprise them.'

'It'll cost you a fair bit,' he said, looking at her with concern.

'I don't care, I have lots of money.'

'Well, you're a fine one,' he said. 'Here, Jim, this young lady wants to go out to Ashingham, to Home Farm. Can you take her? She says she has lots of money.'

It didn't seem a very long way to her, used, as she was, to the long haul out to Southampton, only just over half an hour; she enjoyed it, studying the English countryside, thinking how different it was from Long Island, or Massachusetts, for that matter. It was extraordinary that fields and hedges and trees and skyscapes could rearrange themselves so totally from place to place. Rather like features on faces, she supposed; she had always thought it odd that two eyes, a nose and a mouth could form so many millions of variables.

'That's one pound, ten shillings then,' said the driver, pulling up at the top of the lane as she had asked him to; she wanted to walk down and surprise them. 'That all right for you?'

'Of course,' she said. 'Thank you. Here—' she fumbled in her purse '– oh dear, I've only got a five-pound note, would that be all right?'

'I suppose so.' He obviously wasn't very pleased; she handed him one of the lovely five-pound notes Barty had given her, great big black and white parchment-like things, with curvy writing all over them, looking more like an official certificate than money.

'You can find your way all right then from here, can you?'

'Oh yes. I've been here before. Thank you. Here—' she gave him ten shillings back from her change. 'That's for you.'

'That's very nice of you,' he said.

'Not at all. Thank you again.'

She got out of the taxi, started down the lane, turned to wave at him; he was still staring at her. She supposed it must be her accent. The lane down to the farm, little more than a track, was wet and muddy, with a stream running down the side of it, but very pretty with high hedges and primroses just starting to bud. She stopped and picked a bunch; she could give them to Joan. Over her head, willows waved against the blue sky, a dusting of green just starting to appear on them; she lifted her head up to them, smiling, aware of a great happiness suddenly, feeling the first spring warmth of the sun on her face.

She could hear cows lowing behind the hedge; she came to a gate and stood looking in at them; she had always liked cows, with their peaceful faces, their long eyelashes, their sweet breath.

She walked on; another field, ah, she remembered this one, it was just before the big corner that hid the house, it was where – yes! Yes, he was still there, her friend, every bit as huge as she remembered him, munching steadily as if he planned to consume the whole field by lunch time. She climbed up the gate, held out some grass to him.

'Lord B! Hi! Here, come on, remember me? You broke my arm once, come on, good boy.'

He ambled over to her, bent his great head to take the grass she offered him. She patted his nose, smiled, leaned forward to kiss it.

'Hi, beautiful! It's so good to see you again. Here, let me give you a mint, I have some in my pocket, my horse at home loves mints—'

'Hey! You! Get down off there, leave the horse alone, don't you know nothing—'

A young man – not a boy – was running up the lane. He was very tall and thin, with brown hair which looked as if it hadn't been brushed for several days, and fierce blue eyes. It was the eyes that did it; she knew it was him.

'Joe! Isn't it? I'm Jenna, remember me?'

'It never is.' He stared at her, his face wary.

'It is. Hi. It's so nice to see you again.' She clambered off the gate, walked towards him, holding out her hand. He took it gingerly in his own large, bony one, as if it might break.

'Hallo there,' he said awkwardly.

'And Lord B. He hasn't changed a bit. My mother thought he might have died, I was just so relieved he was here—'

'Is she here? Is Barty here?'

'No, she's in London. We're over for the wedding. I heard you weren't coming, so I decided to come and see you down here.'

'Oh yeah?' He nodded, a slight smile easing its way into his face. 'You come on the train, then?'

'Yes. And then a taxi. It was fun.'

He said nothing after that, just stood there, looking embarrassed.

'Aren't you going to take me to the house?' she said after a bit.

'Yes, of course. Sorry. Come on, this way.'

'It's lovely here,' she said, 'so pretty.'

He shrugged. 'It's all right.'

'Are you – still at school?'

'Yes.'

'And Michael?'

'He is too, yes.'

There was a long silence then, as they walked down the lane; Jenna couldn't think what else to say. He walked very fast, and she had to half run to keep up with him. She had dressed carefully for the occasion, in jeans and sneakers, anxious not to appear too townie, as the Warwick children called it, with a big Sloppy Joe under her jacket, but she could see he thought she looked pretty strange. He was walking just ahead of her staring at the ground, and every so often he turned around and looked at her, as if half hoping she might have gone away. Each time he did it, she smiled at him encouragingly, but she had given up any attempt to talk.

They reached the yard in front of the house; there was no one about. It was very muddy, the yard and the house looked more battered than she remembered it; she supposed when you were eight you didn't notice things like paint peeling off doors. It seemed smaller too; she had thought it was huge.

Joe led her round the side of the house, pushed open a door, dragging off his wellington boots.

'In here,' he said, then went in ahead of her, shouting 'Mum! Mum! We got a visitor.'

The kitchen was exactly as she remembered it; big and white-walled, with a quarry-tiled floor and a great table in the middle, covered in an assortment of things, old newspapers, piles of letters, some jars of jam, a few onions, a box of apples, a shotgun, a head collar and, slung down in the middle of it, a hare that had clearly met its end fairly recently.

'A visitor, you say, Joe? Who – well bless me! Jenna, isn't it? My word, you've grown. And grown up. How lovely to see you. Joe, pull out a chair for her, there's a good lad.'

It was Joan, exactly the same, smiling and comfortable, her wide face so lit up with pleasure that Jenna felt close to tears. She went over to her, gave her a hug, then handed her the primroses.

'These are for you. I picked them in your lane, I'm afraid, I hope that's OK. It's lovely to see you, I just had to come. I couldn't wait till after the wedding.'

'Bless you, but how'd you get 'ere? And where's your mum?'

'Oh, in London. I came by myself.'

'By yourself! All that way!'

Joan looked rather as if Jenna had announced she had arrived from the Antarctic or Australia.

'It wasn't very difficult. I just got the train. I'm not a baby any more, you know.'

'I can see that. Quite the young lady you are, isn't she Joe? Oh, but it's lovely to see you. I don't know what Billy'll say. He's out with the horses, but he'll be back in a minute. You want a drink, my love, or something to eat?'

'Something to eat would be lovely,' said Jenna, realising she was starving. 'Just – just a cookie or something.'

'You had any lunch?'

'No. No I haven't.'

'God bless you, you must be hungry. Let me see what I've got—'

She opened a door at the back of the kitchen leading into an enormous pantry, leaned in, produced a large ham on a plate.

'There now, how does that look to you?'

'Lovely. Really great.'

'Right then, and I got some bread and some cheese, I think. Sit down, my lovely, let's feed you up a bit. You're very thin.'

She studied Jenna, her face anxious. 'You ever eat?'

'All the time,' said Jenna, buttering a piece of bread, biting into it gratefully. 'Cathy – she's my stepsister – she's always on some weird diet, but I can't be bothered.'

'Diet! How old is she, then?'

'Same as me. I wanted her to come too, but she wouldn't. She had some shopping to do.'

'Oh yes? Pity. I'd have liked to meet her. And how do you get on with your stepfather? Charlie, isn't it?'

'He's just great,' said Jenna, 'we're really happy, mother and me.'

'But he hasn't come over with you, is that right? That's what Lady Celia, or whatever her name is these days, that's what she said.'

'No, Cathy's grandmother, her mother's mother, is dying and Charlie had to stay with her. He's like that, really kind and good. But you'll meet him soon. I was looking forward to bringing him down here.'

'It's so lovely you came,' said Joan. 'Oh now, here's Bill. Bill, look who's arrived, just like that, it's Jenna!'

'Well I never,' said Billy. 'Well I never did.' He looked just the same, very tall and heavily built, with wide shoulders and thick arms, his hands gnarled from a lifetime of working out of doors, dark hair only a little more grey, moving with extraordinary ease on his wooden leg.

'Little Jenna. Hallo, then. My word, you've grown.'

'Well I would have done,' said Jenna patiently, 'it's five years since I was here.'

'I know. I shan't forget that visit in a hurry. And don't you go riding no horses this time, will you,' said Billy severely.

'Why ever not? I can't wait. I've already seen Lord B, he looked really great. And I want to meet his daughter, and all the others too, Lucy said she had a pony here, and I'm dying to see Fergal's horse—'

'You didn't bring none of them with you then?'

'No,' said Jenna, 'I like doing things on my own. It's so much less bother, nobody saying there isn't time, and let's go tomorrow or the next day.'

'Well where's your mum, where's Barty?'

'She's not here either.'

'She's not here? You came all on your own?' He seemed as astonished as Joan.

'Yes. It really isn't very far.'

'Good gracious! Well, I never! But she knows you're here, I hope?'

'Oh yes,' said Jenna airily. 'I left her a note.'

'I just didn't think you'd care,' she said sulkily, several hours later. Barty had just arrived, was standing in the farmyard, her face taut with rage. The same taxi driver who had brought Jenna was parked at the gate, unashamedly enjoying the drama.

'Jenna, how can you say such a thing? I was worried out of my mind.'

'I thought you said you left a note,' said Billy suspiciously to Jenna.

'I did. It's not my fault if she couldn't find it.'

'Oh really? Stuck into the frame of the bathroom mirror? After I'd left for the office?'

Jenna was silent.

'You really are so naughty, Jenna. I still can't believe you did this.'

'Mother, you knew how much I wanted to come. You knew how I'd been looking forward to it. I didn't have anything else to do. So I just – came.'

'Did Cathy know?'

'Yes,' said Jenna sulkily.

'She didn't tell me.'

'Well, I told her not to.'

'She was certainly obeying orders,' said Barty grimly. 'I couldn't get a word out of her. And she could see how worried I was—'

'Look –' Billy's big face was troubled '– look, I think we're all agreed Jenna's been naughty. But no harm's been done. And I can't help being pleased she wanted to come so much. I think you should calm down, Barty. Why don't you come into the house, have a cup of tea? Joe and Michael can take Jenna up to the parlour. It's milking time, maybe she could even help a bit. Michael's a rare one with the milking,' he said to Jenna, 'he'll teach you.'

'She's not to go anywhere,' said Barty. 'She's coming straight back to London. Now.'

'And where's the sense in that?' said Billy. 'My word, Barty, you looked just like Mum then, when she was in a paddy. You've both come a long way, you have some food and a rest and then you might as well stay the night—'

'We are not staying the night,' said Barty. She sounded disproportionately angry, Jenna thought; what on earth was the matter with her?

'It isn't Billy's fault, Mother,' she said, 'there's no need to be angry with him.'

'True enough,' said Billy, 'and besides, don't you want to see us? Seems to me you don't, all you're bothered about is Jenna and how naughty she's been.'

Barty stood there in the yard, staring at them all, and then suddenly ran into the house. Jenna followed her. She found her mother sitting at the kitchen table, staring in front of her; she suddenly put her head into her hands and burst into tears.

'Mother, don't. Don't cry. I'm sorry I upset you, really I am. I just wanted to come so much, and I thought you were so busy, you wouldn't mind.' She put her arm around her mother's shoulders and thought how much thinner she had got.

'You need some of Joan's food,' she said, 'you're all skin and bone.'

'I'm not,' said Barty, shaking her off; but Jenna knew her rage was easing. In another minute she'd look up at her and half smile; then they'd be friends again.

'I'm really sorry,' she said again, 'it's only because I love your family so much, your family and mine, I just had to be with them.'

Barty looked up at her and half smiled.

'You are so horribly like your father,' she said.

'It's so lovely there,' said Jenna to Cathy after lunch next day. They were sitting in the reception of Claridges, thumbing through magazines, trying to decide whether they would go out shopping yet again, or stay in the hotel and listen to the radio and read. 'I wish you'd come. The countryside is so – so perfect, so green, so many trees and hedges and the fields cut up like a patchwork quilt, well, that's how they look from the top of a hill. And their house is – not pretty, exactly, but so welcoming and warm, and busy. Well, it's warm downstairs where there are fires. Mother and I had to share a bedroom, they only have one spare, and it was just freezing, we piled our coats on to the bed, and even some rugs we found in a cupboard, but it still wasn't very warm. Anyway, we had such fun, Joe and Michael took me up to the milking parlour and showed me how to milk a cow. It's really hard until suddenly you get it, like riding a bike, and—'

'What are they like? Are they good-looking?'

'Sort of. I specially like Joe, he's so serious and really thinks about everything, a bit like Billy—'

'Does he like you?'

'Oh Cathy, I don't know,' said Jenna impatiently, 'if he did he wouldn't say.'

'Why not?'

'Because he's so shy. Anyway, he's my cousin, obviously he wouldn't like me in that way.'

'Oh yes, of course, I'd kind of missed out on that. It seems so strange, you having a cousin here. Do you think I'd like him?'

'Absolutely not,' said Jenna firmly. 'Where was I? Oh yes, so then we had supper in the kitchen and almost everything came off the farm, chicken—'

'Fergal kissed me,' said Cathy in a dreamy voice.

'He didn't.'

'He did.'

'What, properly? French kissing?'

'Yup.'

'What was it like?'

'Great,' said Cathy. 'Really great. We were in what they call the study and he told me I was the prettiest girl he'd ever seen, and tonight we're going to the movies, with some other people as well, of course, Lucy and Lucas, and you can come too.'

'Thanks,' said Jenna, 'can't wait.'

'Anyway, Fergal might be coming to New York this summer, to work with his uncle Robert and I said he must come to South Lodge and—'

'Cathy,' said Jenna, 'you can't just ask people to South Lodge, it isn't yours.'

'What do you mean?'

'What I say. It belonged to my father. Now it's Mother's. Mother's and mine.'

'Your mother is married to my father,' said Cathy, two red spots rising on her cheeks, 'and everything is shared now, between all of us, it belongs to us all. Daddy said so. So I can ask to South Lodge whoever I like—'

'You can not,' said Jenna, realising she felt terribly angry and upset suddenly. 'You can do nothing of the kind. Not without asking Mother and—'

'Oh you're so – so mean,' said Cathy, 'so mean and selfish and – and arrogant. Why on earth shouldn't I ask someone to South Lodge if I want to, it's big enough. Sometimes, just sometimes, I wish I didn't have to live with you, I wish I wasn't your sister—'

'In which case,' said Jenna coolly, 'you certainly wouldn't be able to ask people to stay in my house. And I do assure you I often wish you weren't my sister either. Very often, actually. Anyway, I'm going to my room. And I do hope you enjoy the film and that Fergal kisses you some more. Mind you don't get pregnant, won't you?' she added, in a flash of sweet inspiration.

In her house in Montpelier Street, Adele sat alone in the bathroom, counting her pills. She actually counted them every night; it was the only thing she really enjoyed doing. Making sure she had enough, checking them over, imagining taking them and then drifting away from it all for ever. It had been worth going without sleep all those endless nights to have them; worth lying there alone, staring into the darkness, counting the quarter hours as they were chimed by the hall clock. Just to know that she could finally get away. Away from the hurt and the humiliation, away from the wedding, away from having to face everyone, away from having to see Izzie.

She was definitely coming; Noni had cabled to say they were travelling together. Of course Noni didn't know, although in her worst moments Adele imagined the two of them talking about it, laughing at her behind her back, saying was it so surprising it had happened, really, when Adele was so old-looking and miserable and dull. And who could blame Geordie?

Well, none of it would trouble her very much longer. She could leave them all behind her. Of course, it was dreadful to think of Clio growing up without her; but she was perfectly happy with all her cousins, and Adele was no use to her as a mother any more. She would get over it. The only thing which really troubled her was Geordie reclaiming Clio. That was a dreadful thought. So she had added a codicil to her will, saying that in the event of her death, Clio was to live with Venetia, and not with Geordie. She hadn't asked Venetia, but she knew she wouldn't mind. It would be the last thing Venetia could do for her. That was the other truly dreadful thought, leaving Venetia behind. They had always said they would die together as very old ladies, drive their car off a cliff, the beloved Austin Seven which still sat in Boy's vast garage, stowed behind his Bentley and Venetia's new Aston Martin. Very occasionally they got it out – it always started at once – and drove sedately round the West End, enjoying everyone staring at them, two identical and rather grand middle-aged ladies, packed into a very small pillar-box-red car.

Only of course they hadn't done that for a very long time.

Adele had decided exactly when she was going to do it: while the wedding was actually taking place. That way there was no possible risk of discovery. She would just phone Venetia in the morning and tell her she was ill, and couldn't face it. Everyone remotely involved with the family would be at the church, and then at the reception, even Nanny and Clio, who was to be a bridesmaid, and her own housekeeper, who was helping in Cheyne Walk; she would be quite quite safe. Undiscovered for many hours. And by the time they finally came to look for her, it would be too late. Her friends the pills would have taken her away.

CHAPTER 29

It was extraordinary, she thought: that she should have known him so well, known when he was happy and when he was excited, when he was sad, out of sorts, when he had the stomach ache that plagued him (she kept telling him he should see a doctor, thought it might be an ulcer), when he was tired, when he was hungry, when he was hopeful, when he was in despair, know all those things without having to be told; that she should know all his odd habits, the way he tugged at his ear when he was thinking, wrinkled up his nose when he was about to laugh, took a deep breath when he was going to tell one of his terrible jokes. And that she should have spent so much time working with him, getting cross with him, worrying about him, wanting to please him, laughing at the terrible jokes, being teased by him; had watched him in horror sometimes when he came in for an important meeting wearing one of his most lurid shirts, or had had his hair cut much too short by his barber so that he need not go again for a long time (and spend another two dollars); know what he thought about everything from politics (Democrat) and religion (Reform Synagogue) to the best way to make a pastrami on rye (hot pastrami, cold bread, French mustard) and the best cure for a hangover (prairie oyster); that she had known all these things, and yet had never realised that he was so exactly what she had been looking for, someone funny and honest and absolutely reliable and kind (and, all right, sometimes bad-tempered, and, OK, often argumentative, just for the sake of it, and yes, occasionally arrogant and quite probably fairly selfish); someone she could love and trust and be happy with; and terribly, terribly sexy too.

How had she not seen that at least? How had she just thought of him as funny, mournful-looking, too skinny, badly dressed – no, appallingly dressed – not as someone who could just touch her hand and make her want him, want him so badly, his mouth on hers, his hands on her breasts, his skin against her own, the very centre of her focussed on him, aching, tugging, pulling, softening with desire, so that she was quite incapable of concentrating on anything else at all.

'It's just as well you're going away for a bit,' he said one night, as they lay, happily sated, desire temporarily spent, in her bed, 'otherwise Neill & Parker would be dead in the water. How did I ever get through my life, I wonder, without this –' he kissed one breast '– and this –' he kissed the other '– or this –' as his hand moved over her stomach '– or these lovely things –' smoothing her thighs.

'I don't know,' she said, quite briskly, propping herself up on one elbow, studying him intently. 'I've wondered the same myself, about me, I mean. Well, never mind. We managed somehow. It just wasn't so much fun.'

'It was not. I never had so much fun.'

'Never?'

'Never. Well – maybe once. One time I can remember.'

She looked at him, suspiciously.

'Nick, what are you saying?'

'That I once had nearly this much fun.'

'With? This isn't very tactful.'

'Sorry, baby. Well, it was with this girl. This young woman. Now what was she called? Oh, yes. Mother. That's the one. She was great great fun. She took me to Coney Island for the very first time and bought me balony on a roll, and took me on the big dipper and—'

'And that was better than – than being in bed with me?'

'Oh, not better, I didn't say that. I said nearly as good. In fact –' kissing her again '– it was pretty much the same, swooping and zooming, thinking, oh my God, here we go and I can't stand this, it's so exciting and – hey, shall I try and work through the whole thing with you?'

'No, thank you,' she said firmly. 'I don't think I like being compared with a heap of metal.'

'It's not the metal I'm comparing you with, it's the sensations it evokes. But – no, I just changed my mind. You are definitely better. Well, I think so.'

She lay back laughing. It was wonderful to be so happy.

They had worried at first about Mike – 'It'll be a bit like a divorce for him, really,' said Izzie soberly – but he had been delighted, happy for them both (although telling Izzie repeatedly that Nick wasn't nearly good enough for her).

He was a little sad; of course he was. But they were as careful, as tactful as they could be, ate dinner with him every night, asked him to go for walks, to the cinema, to bars with them, until he said he was beginning to think there might be something wrong with their relationship, if they needed him around so much.

They didn't have very long together, before she went to London: only just over a week. But, as Nick remarked, you could do a lot in a week . . .

She was still worried, of course, about facing Adele, and the others; she asked Nick what he thought.

'Do you think I'm very wicked?' she said; it was the night before she left, and she was very nervous.

'Honeybunch, it wasn't wicked. The guy was separated from his wife, you were quite sure of that when you slept with him. I don't see that as a qualification for going to hell. Purgatory, maybe—'

'How do you know about purgatory?' she said curiously.

'I had a Catholic girlfriend once. Catholics and Jews have a lot in common, you know.'

'Oh.' She hadn't really asked him about his previous romantic life; perhaps it was time. He knew after all, about hers; her brief and heady history. 'How – how many girlfriends did you have? Proper ones, I mean?'

'I only ever was interested in the improper ones,' he said, grinning at her. 'And there were – let me see – only half a dozen of them.'

'Half a dozen! That's a lot.'

'Darling, I'm nearly thirty. You're not in love with a monk, you know.'

'Of – of course not. But – well, what I meant was – well—'

'No,' he said, 'no, I never did love any of them. Even the most improper. Not how I love you, anyhow. I see them as training grounds.'

'How very coarse.'

'I am very coarse. That's one of the things you have to get used to. Oh, I suppose, yes, I was very fond of a couple. This Catholic girl, she was fun, she was Irish—'

'An Irish Catholic, and she let you sleep with her!'

'Did I say that?'

'Well – no. But—'

'You can have a pretty good time with your clothes on, I'd say,' he said, 'look at us, all these months.'

'Yes, but—'

'And a lot of fun trying to get them off. I never did succeed with her. But there was one important girl. You should know about her, I guess. I nearly thought about marrying her—'

'You *nearly* thought about it? What stopped you?'

'I met Mike,' he said laughing, 'and I found his proposition much more attractive. Now stop worrying, Princess. I love you. More than I would have believed possible. OK?'

'OK,' she said.

He came to see her off at Idlewild. It felt awful to be parting from him so soon; she said so.

'It feels terrible. But we'll survive. And you'll have all those smart people to console you, at least. What do I have? Mike. And Joanie.'

'Mike's promised to look after you,' she said, kissing him. 'I asked him yesterday. And while I'm away, go to the doctor. About your stomach ache, OK?'

'I might,' he said. She knew what that meant of course. He wouldn't.

She had bought, at the last minute, something to wear to the wedding, a dress and jacket in dark red wool, far too old for her, but she simply didn't care. It was the first half-suitable thing she could find. No one was going to look at her, after all. And she couldn't spare the time to go looking for anything better.

Noni was late; maybe they'd miss the plane, thought Izzie, with a stab of hope, maybe they'd miss the wedding, it'd be the perfect solution, and it wouldn't be her fault . . .

'Izzie, darling, sorry, so sorry. Oh, hi, Nick, how lovely to see you. Now come along, Izzie, we're late, my fault, overslept, ignored the wake up call . . .'

Halfway across the Atlantic, Izzie could see there was not the slightest danger of Noni even beginning to quiz her about Geordie, or indeed about anything at all. She was absolutely absorbed in herself. The chatter went on and on, an endless stream; then she suddenly announced she was exhausted, put on her eye mask, curled up against Izzie, and slept for most of the remaining journey.

Izzie's father was waiting for her at the airport; he opened his arms and she went into them.

'My darling, you look wonderful, what have you been doing?'

'Oh – you know. Working very hard.'

'Working very hard with one of those divine boys, if you ask me,' said Noni, giving Sebastian a kiss. 'He came to see her off at the airport, terribly lovey dovey they were, you just ask her about it. Now, are you going to take me back with you?'

'Yes, that's the arrangement,' said Sebastian. 'I promised Venetia.'

'How's Maman?'

'Oh – you know.'

'Yes,' she said with a sigh, suddenly solemn again, 'I do know. Well – never mind. Perhaps the wedding will cheer her up.'

They both looked at her doubtfully.

'So is it true, are you really all – what did she say – lovey dovey with one of those boys?'

'Yes,' said Izzie, kissing her father, smiling happily. 'Yes, I am. The tall skinny one.'

'Mike.'

'No, Nick.'

'Oh yes, of course. Well, that sounds very nice. I'm delighted. And are you going to marry him?'

'Not for a very long time. And if I am, you'll be the first to know. Meanwhile, I'm terribly, terribly happy, it's too good to be true. Now, do I really have to go to this dinner tomorrow?'

'My darling, of course you do. Celia would never forgive you if you didn't. And nor would Kit. It really is a three-line whip. I can see you're very tired, but if you get a good sleep tonight, and have a quiet day tomorrow, you'll be fine.'

'But—'

'Isabella, no buts. It's the official pre-wedding dinner, the whole bloody lot of them will be there—'

'And it's at Lord Arden's house?'

'It is indeed, in Belgrave Square. Very grand. Cheyne Walk is already in the grips of all the caterers and florists, dreadful business, the whole thing. Anyway, you go off to bed now and try to sleep. Take a pill, I would. These long flights play havoc with your system. Welcome home, darling, it's so lovely to have you here.'

She felt a stab of guilt; he must be very lonely. Of course he had Celia, but she was, after all, married to Lord Arden, she couldn't spend all her spare time with him. And Sebastian was beginning to look older now, at last, the golden hair quite white, the face heavily lined. Well, he was seventy-five. It always gave her a shock when she thought about that; most of the time she was able to ignore it, he was so full of energy and emotional vigour. But he seemed perfectly well and was very happy. He was delighted about Kit's marriage, he adored Clementine, and although he was sad about their move to Oxford, she had made him promise to go and stay every weekend with them.

'I won't, of course, but I'll go pretty often.'

He was just starting a new book, he said – 'well, what else would I be doing with my time' – and had a couple of lecture tours booked – 'one in America, so that'll be nice, be able to see a bit of you there. And Jack and Lily too, such a pity they can't come over for the wedding, but she's much too frail, poor old soul—'

Izzie refrained from pointing out that Lily was exactly ten years younger than her father.

'Is – is Adele going to the dinner?'

'Oh, I expect so. She's very down, of course, but it's such a special occasion. And Venetia will take care of her.'

'Is she – is she all right?'

'Well, she's under this psychiatrist chap, so I imagine there's some progress being made. She doesn't look too good to me, I must say. Now, off you go to bed. I'll tell Mrs Conley to bring you some hot milk. That still your favourite tipple?'

Izzie said it was, kissed him and went upstairs to her room, wondering how harshly he would judge her when he knew the truth. Which of course he would.

Venetia had written to her; it was waiting for her in her room, a cool, warning note.

I can see you felt you had to come, but I must ask for your complete discretion. No one in the family has any idea what has happened, and that is what Adele still clings to. She is in a very fragile state; I think any kind of confrontation with her would be a grave mistake. Of course you will both be at the wedding, and possibly the pre-wedding dinner, but it should not be too difficult for you to avoid contact with one another. Apart from then, I see no reason for you to meet. Please respect my wishes in this. Venetia.

Not even the sleeping pill helped Izzie through that night.

Barty had been rather afraid she would start to miss Charlie. She didn't: not exactly. But her decision to leave him was already becoming blurred, confused by undeniably happy memories, a sense of regret – and dreadful guilt. The guilt was the worst.

She knew she should not have married him, purely to ease her loneliness, to rescue her from the prospect of a dried-up, widowed old age. She had used him in her own way, as much as he had used her. She would, of course, make him a very good financial settlement so that he could buy an apartment, possibly even set up his wretched classic car business. Charlie would be fine. He was a supreme pragmatist.

No, the real guilt was about the girls; so happily settled in their new lives, with their new parents, in their new school. Would they be able to remain in it happily together now? Probably not. She was going to break into their friendship, trample on it brutally; say right, sorry, but everything is changing again and you're going to have to deal with it as best you can. It was a very tough prospect for them. It would have been tough for two adults; for two rather difficult little girls, one of them extremely vulnerable, it would be very harsh.

But – what could she do? Stay with Charlie, pretend, as parents had done since the beginning of time, that all was well, playing out a polite farce, waiting until the girls were old enough to cope with it? And when would that be? When they were sixteen? Eighteen? Twenty-one? How could you put a timetable on it? On bringing an end to security, happy memories, shared lives. It was hideous; for lack of anyone else to talk to, she invited Sebastian to join her for dinner, told him, falteringly, of the appalling mistake she had made, of Charlie's deception, of her sense of remorse and shame. And asked him what he thought she should do.

He looked at her for a long time when she had finished, then reached across the table and stroked her cheek tenderly.

'My darling. You haven't been lucky in love any more than I have. In fact, I would say our stories are rather similiar. A few months of intense happiness and then long years of loneliness. Only, of course, I've lost the woman I loved twice.'

'Dear Sebastian. Yes, I know. And you've been so brave, you've so much made the most of it.'

'Hardly. Look at poor Isabella, years of neglect on my part. Oh, my darling, I don't know what you should do. It does seem very hard on those poor girls to separate them now. But – you can't stay with him.'

'You don't think so?'

'Not possibly. Nobody can base their life on a lie. Or a series of lies. Let me think . . .'

He was silent for a while; she watched him, his head bent in concentration, breaking a piece of bread into ever smaller pieces. Finally, he looked up at her and said, 'I would suggest – and it is only a suggestion, my darling – a little deception. A bit of dissembling. As you know, I've done quite a lot of that in my time.'

Barty said nothing, simply smiled at him.

'The girls are at boarding school, after all. Perhaps Charlie's business could take him to another city, at least in the term time. I would have thought Los Angeles, for example, would be a splendid place to sell classic cars. You obviously couldn't go with him, not with your career in New York. That way, even in the holidays, you could spend some time apart, the girls could go and stay down there with him, and I feel sure that for a few weeks you could maintain the fiction that you were happy together. He is not after all a disagreeable fellow.'

'No,' said Barty, 'no, he's not.'

'It wouldn't be perfect, and it wouldn't be easy. But I think it would be better than any of the other alternatives. And you could insist on it. You do after all hold what I believe are vulgarly called the purse strings. If Mr Patterson wants to remain in a lifestyle to which I imagine he has become very happily accustomed, then he is more or less obliged to do what you say. Anyway, that's my suggestion, darling. For what it's worth.'

'I think it's worth an awful lot,' said Barty, leaning over to kiss him. 'Thank you, Sebastian. I shall think about it very, very carefully.'

Adele wasn't going to Celia's dinner; she had pleaded exhaustion, and a need to rest for the next day. She had also refused to see Barty. Upset, Barty had talked to Venetia, who told her, rather coolly, that Adele saw her as being in the Geordie camp. 'You are his publisher after all.'

'Well that's ridiculous,' said Barty. 'I'm not in anyone's camp. My relationship with Geordie is purely professional.'

'Oh really? I thought you were quite friendly. Didn't he go to South Lodge for Thanksgiving, that sort of thing?'

'Venetia, you're looking for trouble,' said Barty coldly. 'Let's just say I'd like to see Adele, if she'd like to see me. I can't do more than that.' She went back to her hotel feeling very upset; the power of the twins to upset her, the old enmity and rivalry between them, the ability they possessed to close ranks absolutely against her, all these things were never quite going to go away.

Adele woke up on the wedding day feeling almost excited. This was the day. The day when it would all be over, when she would be safe. For the first time for weeks she got up before breakfast, went down to join Clio and Nanny in the kitchen. Clio was rather subdued; her disappointment at the failure of her father to appear had been intense.

'He wrote and said he'd be coming,' she said, when Adele found her the day before, standing at the window, watching for him, eyes huge and smudged with tears. 'He told me, you know, in that letter to Noni. Why can't he, why?'

'Daddy's not very good at – at knowing what he's doing,' said Adele, struggling to keep the viciousness out of her voice, 'and he's a long way away, it all has to be planned.'

'He's had lots of time to plan it,' said Clio, 'ages and ages. He knew about me being a bridesmaid, Noni told him. Doesn't he want to see me, in my frock, doesn't he love me any more?'

'Oh my darling,' said Adele, her own tears rising, 'of course he loves you and of course he wants to see you. But he can't, he's so busy and—'

'Barty's busy. Izzie's busy. Noni's busy. They've all come. Why can't he?'

Adele couldn't find anything else to say to comfort her, just sat holding her, weeping with her, her anger at Geordie stronger than any emotion she could ever remember. Bastard! Selfish, self-centred, cruel. Rather like Luc. But at least Luc had been brave, had been, underneath it all, a good person; that could hardly be said of Geordie. He was a weak, charming coward; she hated him. She really, really did. Izzie was welcome to him; and, moreover, she deserved him . . .

Clio had gone to bed fairly happy; comforted by Noni, promised that everyone in the whole church would be looking at her and thinking how pretty she looked, promised that her father would be sent lots and lots of pictures of her. But she had woken twice in the night, crying; Adele, lying awake, as always, heard her and was about to go to her, but Noni got there first, and the second time had taken her into her own bed, and cuddled her back to sleep. It was better that way; really, Clio would be so much better off without her. Moping about and crying all the time; it wasn't good for any child to have a mother like that.

'I've told her we can get ready together,' Noni said, 'and I'll do her hair. I've got rather good at hair. Kenneth in New York showed me the most marvellous trick for keeping a French pleat up, shall I do yours, Maman?'

'No,' said Adele quickly. 'No, I'll do my own. Thank you, darling.'

'And you're wearing –?'

'Oh – something new. Pale grey silk.'

She'd known she must get something, had forced herself out to Woollands and Harvey Nichols, or they'd be suspicious otherwise.

'Can I see?'

'When it's on.'

'Hat?'

'Oh –' she hadn't thought of that '– I'm wearing one I got for Ascot last year.'

'Maman, you can't go to Kit's wedding in an old hat.'

'Of course I can,' said Adele, irritation sending her voice up half an octave. 'It's not old, anyway, it's only been worn once.'

'I know but—'

Lucas appeared in his morning dress.

'Thought I'd give you a preview. How's the waistcoat?'

'Darling you look marvellous. Really so handsome. Here, let me just ease that knot a bit—'

Adele smiled at him. It was so unfair, Noni thought, rage rising from somewhere deep within her; he did so little, and yet he had the power to lift her mood and please her, simply by coming into the room.

'We'll go and get ready, then,' she said. 'Come along, Clio.'

'Yes, all right,' said Adele absently. Noni looked back; her mother was already engrossed in Lucas's tie.

Izzie looked at herself in the mirror doubtfully; the outfit really had been a mistake. It was a particularly heavy red and drained her face of colour; it was the wrong length too, too long for her, longer than the fashionable calf-length, just dowdy looking. Even in her misery, she felt angry with the wretched saleswoman at Saks, who had told her how marvellous she looked. Well, at least Nick couldn't see her. He had phoned the night before, to tell her he loved her and he was missing her.

'Although it's very peaceful. Without you snoring beside me.'

'I don't snore.'

'Darling you do, I'm afraid. Quite loudly, sometimes. Has no one ever told you? Not very aristocratic, I must say. You must never go to sleep in presentations. I can't talk any more. Mike says we can't afford it. I love you, Princess. Keep looking up at the stars.'

'I will. And I love you too.'

She put the phone down.

Her father looked in. 'All right?'

'Yes. Yes, I'm fine. You look wonderful, Father.'

He did; astonishingly handsome still, in his black morning coat. 'Put the hat on.'

He put it on, settling it carefully, adjusting it in her mirror; 'You're a vain old thing,' she said, kissing him, 'but you have a right to be. You're going to outshine the groom.'

'Nonsense,' he said, 'no one could do that. You look nice.'

'I know I don't,' she said, 'but never mind. Everyone else will look marvellous, so who's going to look at me?'

'I am,' he said, 'with great pride.'

Were any of the other guests, Celia wondered, sitting in the church, noticing the likeness? Wondering at it, the uncanny resemblance of the set of the head, the width of the shoulders, the same thick, thick hair, the way it grew quite low on their foreheads, the same fine features, the same heavy brows. Probably not; the forty years or so between them had wrought some powerful changes, in colouring, stance, ease of movement. But the voices were exactly the same: deep, powerful, musical, and so were their quick, sweet, almost impatient smiles and their equally quick, ferocious scowls. Not that they were going to be in evidence today. Two quite extraordinary men. And she loved them both, so very much . . .

If he turns round again and smiles at her just once more I shall be sick, Jenna thought; it was revolting, the way they were carrying on. Twice last night she had caught them necking, once before dinner and once after, and the second time Fergal had undoubtedly had his hands on Cathy's breasts. It was disgusting. They hadn't been sitting together at the table, luckily, but he kept smiling at her, making silly faces, and she kept leaning forward so that her cleavage showed, making sure he was looking all the time.

Jenna had been sitting two places along from her, next to Lucas; she really couldn't see why they all thought Lucas was so awful, she found him very interesting, and he had a really odd sense of humour, which she liked, he didn't laugh at any of Fergal's awful jokes, but came out from time to time with really funny one-liners.

He was quite tall and very thin, and he had a rather gaunt, bony face, with deep-set dark eyes and very long eyelashes: very long for a boy, anyway. He was also rather interestingly dressed; he was in a dinner jacket, of course, all the men were, but instead of a conventional black tie, he had on a floppy black cravat. Jenna thought it was very stylish. Cathy, meanwhile, had been drinking unwatered-down wine and she got so drunk that she had to be helped from the table by a laughing Fergal; Jenna saw her mother watching rather anxiously. She supposed she must feel more responsible for her without Charlie being there.

She still wished with all her heart that the Millers were there now, in the church; although there were lots of other nice people there. She loved Jay and Tory and their children and she quite liked Giles even though he was so – so solemn. George, his son, was quite nice, a bit pompous, but interesting underneath. Mary was a terrible pain, just like her mother, neither of them seemed to know that smiles had been invented . . .

And Boy, he was marvellous, so funny and naughty, sent everyone up, even Celia. Jenna really liked him. And some of the Warwicks were all right. She supposed Fergal was just spoilt. Barty had told her he'd been born in the middle of an air raid, in the house at Cheyne Walk and that Celia had rescued Venetia, who was in labour, from Lytton House in the middle of the worst air-raid of the war, that she had cycled through the City of London with a tin hat on her head and bombs falling all round her. She was wonderful; Jenna adored Celia. She knew her mother did, too; in spite of saying she had been a mixed blessing in her life. She thought they were quite alike, in a funny way: funny, because they weren't related at all. But they were both so obsessed with their careers and with Lyttons, both had such high standards, such belief in the power of hard work, both were so passionately interested in an amazing assortment of things.

'And you're both tall and both beautiful,' she had said to her mother; Barty had laughed and said she might be tall, but beautiful, no.

'Of course you are. Terribly. I bet my father thought you were beautiful.'

To which her mother had replied that everyone thought the person they loved was beautiful, and that she had considered Laurence extremely handsome.

'But he was. In all the pictures you've shown me, he could have been a film star.'

Jenna knew she looked exactly like him; and of course that was nice, to carry on his looks even if she couldn't carry on his name, not if she got married, anyway, but she'd actually rather have looked more like her mother. She preferred Barty's colouring, her high cheekbones and her huge tawny eyes. She looked quite wonderful today.

Right. She would get dressed now, and do her hair, then tell Nanny she was having trouble with her hat and ask her to take Clio to the church in the official car and say she'd follow in her own little MG. Noni and Lucas had already gone. If Nanny started to argue, she'd start crying and then Nanny would give up straight away and do what she said. Everyone knew better than to make Adele cry.

Who would have believed this, Venetia thought, smiling at Kit as he sat there, concentrating on the music? Who would have thought that his terrible, tragic youth could have turned into such happiness. And it was real happiness; it shone out of both of them, him and Clementine. She was such a rare combination of cleverness and niceness; despite being immensely successful, Venetia was still, at the age of forty-eight, deeply impressed by any kind of academic accomplishment. Clementine was ferociously clever;

not only a brilliant novelist, but extremely well-read, rather like Barty, only you could chat to Clementine, giggle with her. A bit more like Izzie, actually, Venetia thought, a shadow falling suddenly over her day. Izzie as she had been, before she went to New York, before she had changed and become – well, whatever she had become. It still didn't quite fit; the casting of Izzie as wicked adulteress. She was still too shy, too eager to please, too naive; or maybe just very good at seeming those things.

Now where was Adele? Surely it was getting a little late.

Right. They'd gone. They'd all gone. She had waved them off from the top of the stairs, telling Clio how lovely she looked. She'd wanted to hug her, hold her close for the last time, but she'd decided that would be too dangerous, her resolve might weaken. She had to do it, for everyone's sake, not least for Clio's; she had to be brave and see it through. And really she had no alternative.

She looked at the clock; a quarter to eleven. She had to time it quite carefully. Once the ceremony had started, she must take the pills; when it was over, Venetia, at any rate, would start worrying about her. But she would hardly be able to get away from the reception until after lunch. It was lucky that Clementine and Kit were having a morning wedding and a buffet luncheon. A more conventional afternoon affair, with canapés, would have been over much more quickly.

She took off her grey silk suit, hung it up neatly, and then her silk slip and stockings and put on a dress she had always been rather fond of instead, soft harebell-blue wool. She didn't want to be in her dressing gown; she wanted to look nice when they found her. She brushed her hair too, and sprayed herself with Diorling, her current favourite, and then went downstairs and fetched a large jug of water. She felt calm, very very calm . . .

If only, if only Kit could see her, thought Sebastian, as Clementine came into the church to the strains of 'Zadok the Priest', on her uncle's arm, her face radiant, her red hair caught back in a crown of flowers, her blue eyes fixed on Kit with absolute attention and love. Her dress was very simple, white silk with a modestly scooped neckline and long, tight sleeves, a full skirt and quite a short train; and her bouquet was a mass of tiny sweetheart roses in pale pink. Behind her walked Clio, her small face solemn, and behind Clio, Lucy Warwick, the only grown-up – or nearly grown-up – bridesmaid, both of them in palest pink, with white flowers in their hair.

They walked, very slowly, all four of them. Then, as her uncle released her, Clementine stepped forward towards Kit, and in a brave and lovely break from tradition, she put her hand in his and reached up to kiss him, so that he might know she was actually, finally there, standing beside him.

It was at that moment, when love seemed quite literally to fill the church, that Celia and Sebastian looked at one another: across the aisle, across all the years, and they smiled; and everyone who saw that smile, knowing what it represented, understanding the reason for it, found it as moving and as poignant in its own way as all the rest of the day.

She piled up some pillows, in a great white mound, settled herself on them, on her bed. She had already got the pills ready, had put them on one of her favourite plates, a present from Cedric years ago; it had a small floral pattern on white, with a fine gold rim. There were thirty of the pills: more, far more than enough, she imagined, but she wanted to be quite, quite sure.

She lay looking at them for a while, then reached out and picked the first one up . . .

'. . . and thereto I plight thee my troth.'

Kit's voice, his lovely melodic voice, was slightly unsteady as he spoke; and Izzie felt a pang, sharp and deep, where she supposed her heart must be. In that moment, she forgot everything else, her guilt, her unhappiness, her concern for Adele, and remembered only a day almost ten years earlier when Kit had told her he loved her; when the tenderness and passion in his voice she could hear now had been for her, when she had felt absolutely happy, and absolutely safe. Now, suddenly, for the first time since then, she felt it again, and realised that she was finally free of Kit. She had not been before, she could see that now, she had been looking ever since for what had been given her and then taken away again. And now, there was another man, so very different from Kit, not a golden over-privileged youth with a tragic history, but a grown-up man who had dragged himself up by his own bootstraps and hitched himself to the stars. Not handsome, not romantic either, she supposed; no, that was wrong, he was romantic, funnily, cleverly, touchingly romantic; not an intellectual, but self-educated, and in his way every bit as brilliant as Kit. Nick had become, in just a few days, the absolute centre of her life, the source of all her happiness; she found it impossible to imagine now a time when she had not known him, not loved him, not been loved by him. She hadn't expected it, nor did she feel she deserved it, but there it was, she had it, and as she stood there, thinking about Nick and what they had together, she wanted to share it with her father and to let him know she loved him too. She looked up at him, slipped her hand into his, smiled, and knew that the tears which were suddenly at the back of his eyes were happy ones also, and were for her.

The phone was ringing; she would ignore it. She had started on her journey now, had taken one of the pills, had decided that she needed more than just water, which was a little flat and forbidding, that champagne would be nicer, with its lovely shining colour and taste. So she had gone down to the fridge and found a bottle of Lanson, her favourite, beautifully cold; it had been hard to open, she could never do it, she was struggling with it for ages, but in the end, she was carrying a full glass upstairs with the bottle in her other hand, and had settled back again on her lace pillows to drink it. She was feeling rather tired now; she had a few sips without taking any pills, then thought that, actually, time was passing and she must proceed. She had just picked up the next pill, was almost placing it on her tongue, when the phone began to ring.

She ignored it for a long time; but it didn't stop. On and on, she could hear it quite loudly in the hall. It irritated her; it disrupted her mood of calm resolve. Who would be ringing like that, with everyone knowing today was the wedding? Or − a dreadful thought struck her − had something happened to Clio? That was the only thing she could think of. Had she had an accident, was she lying in the casualty department of some hospital? She waited for three more rings, then left her room again and ran downstairs, her heart thudding, her head spinning slightly. She supposed it was the champagne . . .

'Hallo?' she said.

There was a long silence: then 'Adele? This is Geordie.'

'. . . with my body I thee worship, and with all my worldly goods I thee endow . . .'

What a beautiful thing it was, Barty thought, the marriage service, so familiar and yet so different each and every time: her one regret about her marriage to Laurence was that it had not taken place in a church, with these lovely words, against a backdrop of music and friends, but in a cold and ugly register office. It hadn't mattered then, she had been too happy to care; but sometimes, over the years, she wished she had it to keep as a memory.

Everyone in the family seemed to be fighting back tears; strange how intense happiness could create such raw and tender emotion. Sebastian was wiping his eyes with a handkerchief, Venetia was biting a trembling lip, even Jenna's eyes had filled with tears. Barty smiled down at her, fiercely proud of her, glad, so glad that she was there with her. She glanced at Celia, and smiled: she had never felt so close to her. That was the moment the idea slipped into her head; and would not be dislodged.

'Thereto I give thee my troth.'

Clementine had such a lovely voice, thought Elspeth, so musical, they both did, she and Kit, their children would speak wonderfully . . . God, she felt sick, terribly terribly sick; she just prayed she wasn't going to have to rush out of the church, spoil their moment. Deep breaths, Elspeth, that's it, keep calm you'll be all right . . .

She saw Keir looking at her anxiously; she smiled up at him, squeezed his hand.

'I'm all right,' she whispered. At moments like this she knew she still loved him.

He was being very sweet now, he really seemed quite pleased about the baby and, in a huge concession, had agreed that Cecilia could stay with Tory and Jay's nanny at the back of the church in case she started to cry. But he was still very worried about money, and with good reason. She'd had a look at the bank account and they were very overdrawn; quite soon now she'd be able to make her suggestion. She thought, provided she picked her moment very carefully, he'd agree. He had to, really.

'I don't know what you want, but please get off the phone.'

'Adele, don't. I don't want to upset you but—'

'Well, you are upsetting me. I am trying to get you out of my life, all of our lives and—'

'I want to speak to Clio.'

'You can't.'

'Adele, please. Please.'

'She's not here. She's at the church. It's Kit's wedding day. She's a bridesmaid.'

'I know that. That's exactly why I'm phoning. To wish her luck, tell her I'm thinking of her every minute, even though I'm not there . . .'

'How touching. Well, I'm afraid you're too late. Did you oversleep, Geordie, or were you busy doing something else in bed?'

'For God's sake, I've been trying to get through for hours. It's not easy.'

'Pity you didn't think of it earlier. Rung yesterday, perhaps. When she was crying her eyes out because you weren't here. Because you've abandoned her and abandoned her mother, as well, for that matter. Just get off the phone, Geordie, and leave us alone.'

There was a silence, then a click; the line went dead. Her eyes were streaming with tears. Adele left the phone off its cradle and went back upstairs to continue with her task.

'. . . whom God has joined together, let no man put asunder.'

How lovely the words were, Venetia thought, watching Kit and Clementine through a blur of tears; they had their own music, as rich and as uplifting as the organ, moving now into the lovely cadences of Bach's 'Fugue in D Minor'. They looked so perfectly joyful, the two of them, smiling, their hands still clasped; she turned to look up at Boy and he smiled at her, his eyes very tender; nothing like a wedding either, she thought, for enfolding all the other marriages in the church in its magic and its happiness. They had been lucky, for the most part, she and Boy, and very happy; there had been problems, but they had managed nevertheless to create that most elusive thing, a large and happy family. And then into the warmth and pleasure, there slithered a growing anxiety about Adele. She had warned Venetia that she might not come of course, might not be able to face it; but she loved Kit so much, and it was Clio's so-important hour. Surely she would wish to see her in it?

She felt uneasy, illogically afraid, and felt a sudden desperate longing to be with Adele, to see for herself that she was all right. Perhaps if she ran out of the church now that the important part of the service was nearly over, and drove quickly to Adele's house, she could check she was all right and be back in time to join the crowd outside the church. But − oh, she couldn't do that, couldn't disrupt the service, spoil Kit's and Clementine's day, she was being absurd. She was worried about Adele because she worried about her all the time at the moment, and because the emotion of the moment had intensified her anxiety. As soon as she reached Cheyne Walk she would phone her; but she really couldn't before then. It wasn't fair.

She felt terribly sleepy; she must concentrate. She had only had about four pills, but somehow, the endless sleepless nights, the raw extra misery of talking to Geordie, had left her so, so tired. She had expected it to be easy, taking them, but it was quite hard work, actually, each one an effort, they were quite big. The champagne had been a good idea in its way, but it wasn't ideal for swallowing things; the bubbles made her hiccup. She closed her eyes, just for a moment, felt herself beginning to drift off. Don't Adele, you can't risk going to sleep now, you haven't had enough, and you won't get another chance, not like this one, concentrate, take another, that's right and then another.

They were walking down the aisle now, smiling at everyone, Kit turning to right and left, rather rigidly, Clementine waving here, then there, blowing kisses and half laughing with happiness.

As they passed her, Izzie looked at Clio; she was peering desperately through the crowd, turning her little head this way and that, a bewildered sadness on her face. And when Izzie got outside and looked for her, she couldn't find her.

Everyone was laughing and kissing and saying how marvellous it had been, how beautiful Clementine had looked, how handsome Kit was, how sweet the bridesmaids had been. Izzie began to look more seriously for Clio now, among the crowd, in the porch of the church, even back inside. She wasn't to be seen.

Izzie felt panic rise; where was she? Had someone taken her? Maybe Nanny had whisked her off − but no, there was Nanny, talking to Mrs Conley, who had been sitting at the back of the church.

Izzie walked out to the road, looked up and down it, but there was no small figure there; maybe she had just run away, but where would she start to look for her if she had, in which direction? There was the Embankment just a few hundred yards away, at the bottom of the road. It was dreadfully dangerous and she was so tiny ... maybe she should tell someone, Sebastian perhaps. She started to go back to the crowd, hoping, half expecting, even, to see Clio holding someone's hand, or maybe even scooped up in their arms – but no. She was not to be seen.

'Izzie!'

Ah. Maybe someone had found her, someone who had seen her so obviously searching, had put two and two together: but no, it was Elspeth, looking rather pale, she thought, leaning on Keir's arm.

'Hallo, Izzie, you look marvellous. You didn't leave your bag behind, did you? The verger has one, asked me if I recognised it, I said I thought it was yours.'

'Yes, yes, I did,' said Izzie, 'thanks, Elspeth, where is it?'

'Inside the church, just inside the door. See you soon.'

Izzie walked into the church. It was completely empty now, oddly and rather forbiddingly silent. Her bag was perched on a pile of hymn books; she picked it up, looked round the church. And then she heard it; the sound of sobbing, quite soft, but very clear, coming from behind the font. Izzie walked over to it, and there, sitting on the floor, her arms wrapped round her knees, her head buried in her arms, and her crown of white roses sadly askew in her dark curls, was Clio, weeping.

'Darling,' Izzie said very quietly so as not to frighten her, dropping down on to the floor herself, 'darling, what is it? Tell me, come on, come and sit on my knee.'

'It's Daddy,' said Clio, climbing into Izzie's arms, her voice broken with tears. 'He didn't come. He kept saying he wanted to see me being a bridesmaid, in his letters, and I thought he would, I thought he'd come today, but he didn't, he didn't even ring up, I don't think he loves me any more, I think he's forgotten all about me—'

She stopped, tears drowning her voice. Izzie sat holding her very tightly, guilt rushing at her in a tidal wave, guilt, sorrow, and a sharp memory of how it felt to have a father who seemed not to love you.

'Darling Clio, he does love you,' she said, tears heavy in her own voice, 'he loves you very, very much. More than anyone else in the world.'

'But he isn't here, why isn't he here?'

'Because – well, because he couldn't be. He's so far away—'

'You're here,' said Clio with blinding logic.

'Darling, I know, but ... but—'

'I don't like it here, I want to go home. I want to go home so much.'

'Oh sweetie, don't you want to have your picture taken, with Kit and Clemmie? Don't you want to have a lovely lunch at your granny's house—'

'No, I want to go home, *now*, he might be there, he might, he might have come, and not know where we are, please, please take me home—'

She was crying harder now, sounded almost hysterical, her little body shaking with grief.

'Clio, I can't take you home, I—' She stopped. She could; she perfectly well could, she could get a taxi, and take her home.

She stood up suddenly. 'Yes, darling, all right, I'll take you home. Here, take my hand, and we'll go very quietly, out of that side door, look, so no one sees us. Come on, no more crying now, just do what I say—'

She saw the verger suddenly, went up to him.

'Could you, please, tell one of the wedding party, preferably Lady Arden, that I've taken Clio home, that she wasn't very well—'

And then they were out of the side door and out of the church gate, the small one at the side, and into the road, and the pair of them were running, running as fast as Clio's little legs would go, away up Old Church Street, and towards the Kings Road.

And so it was that when Celia and Venetia reached the house in Montpelier Street just over an hour later, they found Izzie and Clio sitting on the stairs, wrapped in each other's arms, and, in her bedroom, a very pale and tear-stained Adele, lying back on her pillows, with a heap of pills and a half-empty bottle of champagne on her bedside table, and her doctor sitting beside her, taking her pulse and holding her hand.

CHAPTER 30

They were all mad, these Lyttons, Jenna had decided: in their various ways. She was awfully glad she wasn't one.

But at least she was going to be allowed to go and see the Millers again. She was to go down there to stay for a few days. Her mother had a lot of work to get through she said, at the office, 'and various other things'. Jenna didn't know what they were, but Barty had gone off rather mysteriously the morning after the wedding to an appointment somewhere in a place called Chancery Lane. Jenna had hoped it might be in the country and asked if she could go, but Barty had said absolutely the reverse, and that it was going to be a very boring meeting with some lawyers. But they were to be in England for another week, and so, she said, Jenna might just as well be down there where she was happy. Joan and Billy had said she should come for as long as she liked. 'Maybe for ever?' said Jenna, laughing; but she didn't quite mean it. She loved the farm and she loved the Millers, but, like her mother, she felt her heart was very largely in America. 'But mostly at South Lodge. I love it so much. Just thinking about it makes me feel – kind of calm. I know my dad loved it, maybe that's why. It's the most I've got of him.'

'Yes,' said Barty, feeling a catch at her heart, 'it's the most I've got of him too. Apart from you, of course.'

Cathy was staying with the Warwicks: having managed to become Lucy's best friend, in a performance of such revolting cunning that Jenna had felt quite sick, while forced to admire her tactics. Even Barty had been taken in by it; Jenna had felt tempted to tell her, but then realised it might mean Cathy coming to the farm, and she certainly didn't want that, having her thrusting her cleavage at Joe and simpering at him across the cow shed. Not that she'd have gone into the cow shed; she might have got her new, pointy-toed shoes dirty.

Jenna had enjoyed the wedding a lot; she had had a lovely time at the lunch, sitting between Lord Arden, who was perfectly sweet, she thought, and Sebastian, who was even nicer. They both kept telling her it must be very boring for her sitting next to two old men, but she assured them she was enjoying it. It was true; she much preferred talking to Sebastian about his books and Lord Arden about his own farm, to putting up with Fergal's awful flirting. She really couldn't imagine how Cathy could like him. She was disappointed not to be sitting next to Lucas again; but she still had fun.

Anyway, she was off in the morning, for three wonderful days; it would be just – just perfect.

The wedding had gone off pretty well, everyone seemed very pleased. Jenna liked Kit, and Clementine even more. She thought it terribly romantic and brave of her to marry someone blind. She must love him very much.

Of course there had been the fuss about Adele, who'd been taken ill, apparently, and now was in some sort of hospital, but she was all right; Venetia had had to miss the wedding lunch, which was a shame, but she had arrived at the end, looking a bit tearful, to wave the couple off and had said Adele was in good hands.

Poor Izzie had been very upset by it all; she had come back to the wedding halfway through the meal, looking very subdued, but bringing little Clio, also rather pale, but much more cheerful; she said she had spoken to her father and he was coming to see her very soon.

'And I can go and see him in America, he says,' she said to Jenna, to whom she had taken rather a fancy.

'That's good. You can both come and stay with us at our house by the sea. I like your daddy, he's great. I'll take you out in my boat.'

'Have you got a boat?'

'Oh yes,' said Jenna airily.

She had asked her mother what had been wrong with Izzie, but her mother had said it was very complicated, and she couldn't really explain. Grown-ups always said that when what they meant was you were too young to be told about it; she decided to ask Noni, beautiful Noni who talked all the time and wore false eyelashes. She had promised to give Jenna a pair and show her how to put them on; maybe she could talk to her then. But when she asked her about Izzie, Noni said she had no idea, she supposed it had been horrid for her, finding Adele so ill and that she must ask Izzie herself.

Jenna decided that it would have to wait for a while. She found herself missing Charlie, and kept thinking how much he would have enjoyed the wedding; she told her mother who smiled at her rather vaguely.

'You must be missing him.'

'Yes, of course I am.'

'Is he all right? Have you heard from him?'

'No. America is a long way away, phone calls are terribly expensive. But I will ring, just to see how Cathy's grandmother is.'

'Give him my love, won't you?'

Her mother said, as she often did, that she was glad Jenna liked Charlie so much and changed the subject, told her they must go to Lillywhites that day and buy her some jodhpurs and some riding boots for her visit to the farm. 'And a hat. Just in case you fall off again.'

'I won't,' said Jenna loftily.

Izzie wished she was allowed to go and see Adele, but she wasn't. She had to be kept absolutely quiet, she was allowed no visitors except Venetia. But at least she was alive.

It had been one of the most dreadful moments of her life, finding her already half asleep, the pile of pills at her side, the half-empty bottle of champagne held in her thin hand, spilling on to the bedspread.

Izzie had told Clio to go to her room, to find one of her dolls and dress it ready for the wedding lunch, while she made Mummy more comfortable, she obviously wanted a little sleep, 'and then I'll try to telephone your daddy, I'll call you if I get to speak to him.'

To her surprise, Clio trotted obediently off down the corridor. Having established her father was not at the house, looking for her, she had become quite calm and cheerful again.

Izzie began slapping Adele round the face over and over again, trying to make her say how many pills she had actually had, while trying to stab the telephone on her bedside table into life at the same time. It seemed to be dead.

'Off the hook,' Adele had said drowsily.

Izzie left her, raced down to the hall, started to ring 999, and then changed her mind and phoned Adele's own doctor instead. It could be quicker. His number was on the pull-out tray on the telephone, as she had known it would be; everyone kept important numbers there. By some miracle, he was in his surgery and spoke to her.

'Know how many she's taken?'

'She says six, but she's not making much sense. She's very confused.'

'I dare say she is. Now, mix up some mustard in a jug of warm water, about three tablespoons, and try to make her drink it somehow, make her sick. Get her walking about, if you can. I'll be there in – let me see – less than ten minutes.'

Izzie ran into the kitchen, made up the revolting mixture, grabbed a bowl and a glass, and raced upstairs again. Clio was sitting on the stairs now, singing happily, brushing her doll's hair; she smiled at Izzie as she passed.

'We're nearly ready.'

'Good.'

Adele was even drowsier, her head lolling about; when Izzie slapped her face again, her eyes rolled upwards.

'Adele, you've got to drink this, absolutely got to. Come on now, please, please, just a bit.'

She wouldn't swallow it from the glass, so Izzie fetched a big spoon and started tipping it into her; she managed to get a bit of it down her, not nearly enough, she was sure, but then Adele was suddenly sick anyway; Izzie was still cleaning her up, washing her face, trying to get her disgusting dress off, when the doctor arrived.

'All right,' he said, sitting down on the bed, feeling for Adele's pulse, 'well done. I'll take over. As you said, she doesn't seem too bad.'

'Can I – can I help?' She hoped not.

'No, no, you go and look after that dear little thing on the stairs, keep her occupied.'

Gratefully, Izzie did what she was told; five minutes later, Celia and Venetia arrived.

'Apparently, she's going to be all right,' said Celia, coming out of Adele's room. She looked very shaken. 'She's been very sick again, but she seems pretty alert, just horribly upset. Naturally. Poor child. Poor, poor child.'

'Could I see her? Just for a moment?'

'Not now. Venetia wants to be with her. The doctor has phoned some nursing homes, is arranging for her to be taken in immediately. Oh, Isabella,' she sighed; she looked very old suddenly, her face somehow collapsed, 'what a dreadful thing.'

If only you knew, Izzie thought, just how dreadful a thing it was. And that a lot of it was my fault.

She wasn't allowed to see Adele; she was carried off on a stretcher, bound for a nursing home in Kensington, Venetia went with her. Celia said firmly they must go back to the wedding reception.

'We mustn't spoil Kit's day more than is necessary, they'll all be so worried about us. Where's Clio?'

'Listening to her own heartbeat through the doctor's stethoscope. She's giggling, she seems all right. I've promised we'll phone Geordie later, Barty will have his number. Celia, I must tell you something, something important—'

'Not now, darling. After the wedding. There's a time and place for everything.'

Somehow Izzie got through the afternoon, smiling automatically, mouthing platitudes, pretending she was someone she was not, someone nice and kind and good, not an adulteress who had also almost become a murderess. What was she going to do, how was she going to live with herself for the rest of her life? Making someone so unhappy that they had tried to kill themselves. Probably not even Nick would want to know her any more now . . .

Her father had seen there was something very wrong with her; she told him everything as soon as they got home. He was sweetly supportive, although sad that his beloved daughter should have been involved in something so wretched.

'But I, of all people, have no right to judge you, Izzie. And I blame Geordie far more than I blame you. You must have been so unhappy. I wish I'd known.'

'So do I,' she said sombrely, 'even if only to have one confession off my chest. Oh, Father, how am I ever going to forgive myself?'

'You must,' he said. 'From everything you've told me, you were only partly to blame.'

'I don't see it that way, I'm afraid. And now I have to go and make another confession. To Celia.'

'I don't think she'll be too hard on you,' he said, 'she certainly shouldn't be.'

Celia's only rebuke was that Izzie should have told her earlier.

'You know you can trust me. And I needed to know, Adele being so desperate.'

She seemed more upset about that than anything, said it was a terrible indictment of her as a mother. What about me as a friend, Izzie had wailed.

'Of course what you did was wrong,' Celia said. 'You should have known better. But Geordie is very persuasive and charming and clearly very deceitful as well. I'm very shocked at him, I must say.'

'No Celia, I can't let you make excuses for me. I knew what I was doing, I knew how much it would hurt Adele, I just – just – oh dear.'

She started to cry again; Celia patted her hand.

'We all do things we regret, Isabella. I certainly have. The only thing, having done them, is to put them behind us, try to make amends, not let them dominate our lives. I've learned that much at least. You can't undo your actions, or your words; you can only try to limit the harm they do. And you did save her life. Don't forget that.'

'I wish I could see her.'

'I think the last thing you should do is rush over to the nursing home and indulge in a lot of emotional outpouring to Adele. She isn't up to it, and it won't help at the moment. I would suggest you explain everything you can to Venetia, and leave her to judge when and how to tell Adele. Now, I want to hear about your being in love with one of those charming young men.'

Venetia telephoned her the next day.

'Hallo, Izzie. I think we should have a little talk. Would you like to meet at Browns for tea?'

'Yes. Yes, of course. Thank you.'

'Four o'clock, then. Don't be late.'

As if she would. She arrived fifteen minutes early and sat waiting for Venetia, as if for her executioner.

'I thought I should say a few things to you,' said Venetia, her voice rather stern; she was beginning to sound like Celia, Izzie thought irrelevantly. 'I'll pour, shall I? Sugar?'

'No thank you.'

'First of all, I wanted to thank you for saving Adele's life.'

'I didn't. Not really. Well – only by accident.'

'However it was, you did. The doctor said you were marvellous. And for looking after Clio as well. Can't have been easy. We should have spotted how upset she was, in church, none of us did except you.'

'Well—'

'Now don't get me wrong. I think what you did was appalling, sleeping with Geordie. Really appalling. When Adele had been so good to you. I'll never understand it. But—'

'Venetia—'

'Don't interrupt, please. Mummy told me what you'd told her. About having no idea Adele was ill, him telling you the marriage was over. And I do know he's a smooth bastard. He once –' she took a cigarette out of her case, and lit it, blew a cloud of smoke into the air '– he once made a pass at me. I've never told anyone that. He's the only man who ever tried to come between us, you know? Unbelievable, isn't it? My sister's husband.'

Izzie sat very still, almost afraid to blink.

'I tried to tell myself it was just because he was drunk and upset about Lucas. But there was no excuse for it. I'm afraid – he's a bad lot. Not all bad of course, but very, very spoilt and charming and used to getting his own way. Especially with ladies. He's always been the most popular boy in the school, and that's very bad for a person. You end up thinking you can have anything, walk on water. Anyway – where was I? Oh yes. The other thing is that Adele has been ill for a long time. Long before Geordie ever went to New York. They've been suggesting electric shock treatment, as a matter of fact, for ages.'

'Oh God,' said Izzie. 'How horrible.'

'Yes. She's going to have it now, her psychiatrist is very hopeful that it will help. Apparently her problems go right back to the war, to her experiences getting out of France, Luc being shot, never saying goodbye to him, all that sort of thing. She feels terribly guilty about it all. So – yesterday wasn't really just about you. It really wasn't and it would be wrong of us to let you think that. She would have tried it anyway, almost certainly, the psychiatrist said. People don't just decide to do it for one single reason, there are usually several, apparently. Or, of course, a psychiatric condition. He said it was important we all knew that.' She sighed; she looked exhausted.

'So – don't expect me to be your best friend or anything. I'm still shocked at you, at what you did. But – don't blame yourself too much. Oh, and no need for Noni to know. About you, I mean. We've all agreed, the less said the better. Well, goodbye, Izzie. I hope you have a good trip back to New York.'

Izzie watched her tall, elegant back as she walked out of the lounge of Browns and felt deeply comforted.

Barty was feeling very tired, but oddly happy. She supposed it was being back in England, back in the heart of the Lyttons; she wouldn't have chosen to be there for ever, but in her present crisis it was wonderfully restorative, removing her as it did into not only a different country, but into what felt like a completely different world, far from Charlie and the anxiety and guilt he aroused in her. Above all, this visit had given her time, not just away from him, but a realisation that she had plenty of time in which to make decisions, take actions. There was no rush.

And then there was the action she had decided to take, which was making her feel very happy, very at ease. She slept very soundly the night after she had made her visit to the offices in Chancery Lane, better than she could remember for a long time. The result of her visit was now placed under the tray of the small jewellery box she had brought with her. She felt it was safer there; the box had a key which she kept in her handbag, and the box itself was in the hotel safe. There was no danger of Jenna or Cathy finding it.

The whole thing made her feel that her life had somehow come back to order, that things were in a better shape. She planned to tell Celia and no one else what she had done; Celia would be so pleased, so very, very happy.

In this new stage of her life, that had come to seem very important.

'Well,' said Elspeth, 'all's well that ends well. Poor Adele. She must be very ill, to be in a nursing home. But at least she'll get some proper treatment now. And poor Izzie, finding her, having to cope.'

'Yes,' said Keir. He appeared to be hardly listening.

'According to Amy, there was something going on between Izzie and Geordie while he was in New York. What do you think?'

'What do I think about what?'

'Oh, Keir! Do listen. I'm asking you what you think. About whether Izzie and Geordie had an affair.'

'Obviously I have no idea,' he said shortly.

'Well obviously, but do you think it's possible? I mean, do you think people sometimes behave out of character, Keir?'

'Sometimes, I suppose so, yes.'

'Of course love – or whatever you like to call it, sex, I suppose really – does funny things to people. But I just don't think Izzie would—'

'Can we please stop this conversation?' he said, 'I'm not really enjoying it very much.'

'Oh. All right. You look awfully fierce, Keir, what's the matter?'

'I'm – worried,' he said shortly, 'Very worried.'

'What about?'

'What about!' he said. 'I'll tell you what about, Elspeth. Money. We're in a bit of a mess. I had a letter from the bank this morning, we're very overdrawn—'

'Are we? Oh Keir, why didn't you tell me?'

'Because it's the sort of thing I'd rather handle by myself. But – they want some security against the overdraft. And I don't have any. We could move, I suppose, somewhere cheaper, but—'

'Keir, we can't move. We're so happy here. And anyway, we don't own this flat, so—'

'I'm aware of that. I could use it as security if we did.'

'Of course. Sorry. And you're worried about the baby, as well, aren't you?'

'Just a bit. Yes.'

'How would it be if I did some freelance work? Don't look like that. I'm not talking about going out to work. I could do it here, during the evening, or while Cecilia's asleep.'

'No,' he said, 'I won't have it. If I can't keep my own wife and family I'll—'

'You'll what?'

'I'm not sure. Get another job, possibly.'

'Well you could try. But you're doing so well at Lyttons. It's just a question of hanging on. Have you asked Giles again for a rise?'

'No. He made it very clear there wouldn't be one.'

'Keir, please. Think about me doing some editing.'

'I've told you, Elspeth, I won't have my wife going out to work.'

'But that's the whole point. I *won't* be going out to work. No nannies, nothing like that. I'll be here, with the children. And it could make all the difference.'

There was the slightest hesitation before he spoke again; she noted it, marked it down.

'The answer's no. We'll manage.'

Right. This was it. If ever there was a cue, it had been given her then. Deep breath.

'But Keir, we're not managing. That's the whole point. It's not your fault, it's not mine. It's just a fact, it's a very difficult time, when you're young and having babies. It's not as if we were the only ones. Tory told me they're in a frightful pickle—'

'I'm not interested in Tory.'

'Well you should be. I don't know quite why you're so against me working. What do you think your mother's doing, when she looks after the shop for your father? Tell me that, would you please?'

★

399

Two days later, she was able to phone Jay and ask him if he had any freelance editing she could do.

'Like Clemmie's next book. She told me at the wedding she wished so much I could do it with her . . .'

Jay said he would be delighted to give her some editing.

As much as she could handle.

'Wish my wife could do something useful, earn a bit of money.'

'Oh Jay,' said Elspeth with a sigh, 'you might just drop that into a conversation with Keir. Just casually. I'd be really, really grateful.

Noni lay awake half the night, after her mother was taken to the nursing home, thinking about it, about how desperate she must have been, castigating herself for not having realised it and for not doing more. She also wondered how they could all think she was so stupid. That she really didn't know. About Izzie and Geordie. When not only Venetia knew, but all her Warwick cousins, and Barty . . . She had gone along with it, with the fiction, for the time being, because it was easier, it saved a lot of painful discussion, and it saved her from getting involved. And because she didn't quite know what to do about it. The most hurtful comment had come from her grandmother, talking to her mother: which was actually when she had first learned about the affair.

'Of course Noni's too busy being an international beauty at the moment to be very concerned about anything much else . . .'

That had been the phrase and it had hurt Noni more than almost anything she could ever remember. That she should be seen as some sort of empty-headed, self-centred bitch; when in fact she had been so hurt and shocked over everything that had happened over the last few years, ever since Lucas was first sent away, in fact, that she had scarcely been able to bear it. She had seen all of it, from the very beginning. Lucas's bad behaviour, Geordie's growing impatience, her mother's blindness: and then Lucas's desperate misery, Geordie's stubborn selfishness, little Clio's sorrow, Adele's refusal to move in with Geordie – she had seen it all as no one else had. And been unable to do anything about any of it.

She had tried: she had tried so hard, to support her mother, to steady Clio, to dissuade Geordie from leaving, to reason with Lucas. It had all been horribly difficult; she had felt herself slowly drowning in it all, dragged down by the selfishness and in-fighting. When Izzie, her only support for a long time, had gone to America, she had found it almost unbearable; getting into Oxford had been a help, but the oppressive misery at home was counter-productive to her studies. And then it had happened: her modelling career, a sudden and wonderful explosion of relief, a dizzy, starry escape; suddenly she had not felt like the last in line but the first, an important person, to be courted, flattered, worried about, any irritation soothed, her least desire satisfied, her slightest worry removed. It had meant such fun, too: evenings spent dancing at the Café de Paris and Quaglino's, dining at Les A and the Mirabelle, flattered and fawned upon by a lot of funny, charming, well-connected young men, being at the heart of London's most in-crowd, it had been very restorative. Her shyness melted away, her weary anxiety lifted like morning mist; she felt quite literally a different person.

Two days after the wedding, her agency asked her if she would like to do a few days' work in Florence the following week; she accepted without hesitation.

Lucas was also horribly upset. Like Noni, he felt guilt and a heavy burden of shame. He had sat in the waiting room at the nursing home with Noni, waiting to see Adele, white-faced and silent. His behaviour was as responsible for what had happened, he knew, as much as anything else. Always before he had managed to make excuses for himself: tonight he didn't even try. He looked at himself, and he hated what he saw. And when he was finally allowed to see his mother, looking somehow emaciated, lying in the high bed, her dark eyes sunk into her drawn face, trying to smile as he kissed her and took her hand, he found himself weeping, like a small boy.

'I'm sorry, Lucas,' she managed to say, 'so sorry.'

He always said afterwards that was the night he really began to grow up.

Barty was having dinner alone at the hotel when Dean Harmsworth, the company secretary, telephoned her: clearly embarrassed, he had felt, nevertheless, it was essential to contact her. Charlie had been forging her signature on company cheques; several had come in over the past few days; what did she want him to do about it?

'I have to go back to New York immediately,' she said to Celia. 'I've managed to get on a flight in the morning. I'm sorry, we still had a lot to discuss. But—'

Celia said nothing, except that it must be something very important. Barty hesitated for a moment then told her why.

'Only please don't tell anyone, will you? I don't want this getting about, it's bad for Lyttons and, of course, bad for the girls.'

'Of course not,' said Celia. 'Will you take the girls with you?'

'I can't. I can't get them on the flight, and anyway, I don't want them around while I talk to Charlie. Jenna's down on the farm, she's perfectly happy, I could probably leave her there a little longer. They could fly back together next week as arranged, they're quite old enough. And Cathy seems happy with the Warwicks—'

'Very happy,' said Celia coolly, 'apparently she and Fergal are conducting a teenage romance. Venetia found them together in his bedroom only last night. She made a frightful fuss, I'm glad to say, and Cathy is now being kept practically under an armed guard.'

'Oh God,' said Barty, 'that child. Were they, well—'

'Heavens no. Fully clothed. Venetia was going to tell you, she found it quite amusing, if irritating.'

'I can't really ask her to keep Cathy, then, it's an awful responsibility.'

'Of course it's not. Venetia's quite used to wayward girls. She's got the housekeeper on the job when she's at the office, watching them with a very beady eye, and Boy's given Fergal a tremendous dressing down. No, don't worry, Barty, you have more than enough to think about.'

'I'll phone Venetia, apologise. Oh dear . . .'

Venetia was perfectly happy to keep Cathy, she said.

'She's quite sweet in her own way. Just a few too many hormones. Like Fergal. It's their age. Don't worry Barty, I can cope with that. And if Jenna comes up at the weekend, she has enough sense for the two of them. She's an absolute delight; you must be very proud of her.'

'I am,' said Barty simply. 'Terribly proud.'

She phoned Home Farm; Joan answered.

'Hallo Barty, nice to hear from you. Jenna's been a little sweetheart, good as gold. Helping me a lot, riding with Joe – it's wonderful to see them together, she's got him really talking, he never says a word, usually.'

Barty told her what she wanted; she could almost hear Joan beaming down the phone.

'Course she can stay. It'll be a pleasure.'

'Could I speak to her, please?'

'Course you can. They're in the tackroom. My word, she's a worker. You've done well with her, Barty, you really have. I'll just get her. Want to speak to Bill?'

'Well – yes, if he's there.'

Billy's heavy, slow voice came on to the line.

'Hallo Barty. Doing all right?'

'Yes, fine, Billy, thank you. But I've got to go back to New York in the morning, unexpected problems. So I was hoping Jenna could stay a bit longer. Joan said it would be all right.'

'Course it is. We love having her. Got the boys right out of their shells, she has, and she's got a real feeling for the farm. She's a good girl, Barty, you must be ever so proud. I often wished these last few days that Mum could see her. She'd have loved her, she really would.'

'Do you think so? I hope so.'

'I know so. Well, you look after yourself, Barty, and we'll look after Jenna. Come again soon, won't you?'

'I will, Billy, thank you. Thank you.'

Jenna came to the phone; she sounded wary.

'I don't have to come back early, do I?'

402

'No, you don't. In fact you can stay a couple of days more.'

'Oh great! Why?'

'I have to go back to New York early. Trouble at Lyttons. Sorry, darling. But you can fly back with Cathy next week. Is that all right?'

'Of course. I'm having such fun, we've done some riding, I can milk really well, and tomorrow Billy's going to let me have a go on the tractor—'

'Well be careful, Jenna. Don't—'

'I won't. Fuss, fuss. Love you, Mother. See you next week.'

'I love you too, Jenna. 'Bye, my darling.'

She put the phone down feeling oddly bereft; saying goodbye to everybody so soon was unsettling. And yet she felt she had to do it, tie up all the loose ends. There were visits she hadn't even made, people she'd hardly talked to . . .

She rang Sebastian; told him where she was going – and why.

'Oh my darling, I'm so sorry. What a filthy thing. I won't ask you what you're going to do about it, but if I can help in any way—'

'Dear Sebastian, you can't. Except go on listening to me. Thank you for all your listening, in fact. I should have taken more notice in the beginning.'

'Nonsense. No one can tell anyone what to do in this life, I learned that very early on. It's been lovely having you here, darling, thank you for coming. It meant such a lot to Kit, you know, he's so fond of you—'

'As if I'd have missed it. Not for the world. The whole thing has been wonderful. And Jenna's loved it.'

'She's a sweetheart. Lot of sense in that fiery little head of hers. You should be very proud of her, Barty. Very proud indeed.'

She laughed. 'Everyone says that. And I am. She seems – so far – to have got all the best of Laurence and me.'

'Well it's a pretty good result. Now, darling, you take care of yourself and come and see us again soon—'

'I will. And the same to you. You've been so – so good to me, Sebastian. Always. Thank you.'

Now why had she said that? Suddenly?

'You've been pretty good to us,' he said gruffly. 'Funny to think what might have happened if Celia hadn't snatched you up that day. We'd all have lost a great deal, in my view. Goodbye, my darling. God bless you.'

He hardly ever said anything like that: he was a fierce atheist. He must be mellowing in his old age. She smiled into the phone.

'Goodbye, Sebastian. God bless you too.'

She was so tired; so terribly tired. And she hadn't even begun to think what she was going to do about Charlie. What a mess. Well, there was a long flight ahead of her; she would address the problem then. She phoned

Giles; she had hardly seen him except in the office and felt bad about it. The anxious little boy who had been her only friend in the nursery might have become a defensive, rather curmudgeonly middle-aged man, but she still loved him.

'Giles, I'm sorry we've had no time together.'

'That's all right. More important people than me to spend your time with.'

'Not really. I'd have loved to talk about the old days.'

'Well, Helena was planning to invite you to dinner on Saturday. Are you free?'

'No, sadly I'm not. I've got to go back to New York early, problems in the office. That old thing.'

'Oh. Right.' She could hear him digesting this, wondering what the problems could be, whether she was going to tell him about them. She didn't.

'So – it'll have to be next time, I'm afraid. Or of course you could come to New York.'

'I don't have time for trips to America. Someone has to keep the home fires burning.' His voice changed, suddenly. 'Well it's been lovely to see you, Barty. I've – missed you.'

What an extraordinary thing to say: Giles, who never expressed any kind of emotion.

'I miss you too, Giles. It's been too long.'

'Yes. Well – goodbye, then. Jenna's a nice little thing, I must say. Turned out very well.'

'Thank you. I think so, obviously. 'Bye, Giles. Don't leave it too long.'

The last call she made was to Celia who was at Cheyne Walk.

Barty had planned to go and see her that evening, to tell her about what she had done and why, but there was no time now. It could wait.

'Sorry it's so late. I hope you weren't asleep.'

'Asleep!' said Celia. 'Of course I wasn't asleep. It's only half past ten. Bunny's gone up to Glennings, that's why I'm here. I'm working in my study, as a matter of fact.'

Barty smiled, thinking of her in that study, her favourite room in the world, she always said. It overlooked the river and the street, she said the quiet at the back distracted her.

'I was thinking about you,' said Celia, 'thinking of that night when Jay was so ill, remember? And you heard the phone ringing while we were all asleep, got me up, got us over to the hospital.'

'Of course I remember,' said Barty. 'It was one of the first times I—' she stopped. She didn't want to upset Celia.

'You what?'

'I – I felt really part of the family.'

There was a silence; then Celia said, 'Oh dear. I never realised, you know, when you were small, how hard it was for you. I suppose I should have done.'

'It was,' said Barty, deciding that having started she should go on, 'very hard. But infinitely worth it, in the end. I know what a lot you did for me, Celia. I'll never forget it, I promise you.'

'Well' – the brisk voice softened suddenly – 'you did a lot for us as well.' Then, more herself, 'Jenna all right?'

'Absolutely. Down with Billy, happy as a—'

'A pig in muck,' said Celia interrupting her, laughing. 'She's a remarkable child, Barty. Really remarkable. You've done a very good job.'

'The raw material was pretty good, I think,' said Barty, 'but thank you. Goodbye, Celia. Thank you for everything.'

Barty lay in bed, thinking not about Charlie, as she had feared, but about Jenna and how proud of her she was, as everyone had told her she must be. Laurence would have been too, she knew; she had done well for him. It was a good feeling. She fell asleep easily, oddly happy. Her trip had done her good. She was so very pleased she had come.

Giles was working at his desk next morning when Helena phoned. She never disturbed him at the office; she sounded very strained.

'Giles – Giles, have you heard the news?'

'Of course I haven't heard the news,' he said irritably, 'we don't sit here listening to the wireless all day, you know.'

'No. No, of course not.' She was silent, then said, 'Giles something's happened. At least—'

'Yes? Helena, you're not making any sense. What's happened?

'A plane has crashed. Come down into the Atlantic. A BOAC plane, bound for New York. I think – wasn't that – wasn't Barty on it?'

CHAPTER 31

'Get out! Get out of here. Get out of this room. At once!'

'Jenna—'

'I said get out. This was my mother's room, you have no right to be in it.'

'But we need it—'

'You do not need it. I need it. You can't use it. Please, please just go away—'

Charlie threw his hands up in the air in a gesture of surrender and left. She stared after him, then got up from where she was sitting on the bed, shut the door firmly and locked it. Then she slid open the great sheet of window and sat on the wooden floor of the balcony, her arms hugging her knees, looking out at the ocean. God, she felt a mess. Such a mess. And so confused. One minute she needed Charlie, loved him, trusted him, the next she hated him, wanted him out of her life. Finding him in her mother's room at South Lodge with Mrs Mills, directing her to change the linen, had definitely been the latter.

She sometimes wondered if her mother had felt the same way about him. She would like to ask her. She would like to ask her a lot of things. But she couldn't. She could never ask her anything again. She was on her own, and she had to manage. She had learned that early, in the days following her mother's death.

It had been Joan who told her; she had come down to the paddock after lunch, where Jenna was riding Florian, Elspeth's horse, looking what Jenna could only describe to herself as fearful. Very white, her round face somehow narrower, drawn in, her eyes suspiciously large and dark-ringed.

'Jenna,' she called, and her voice was odd too, a bit shaky, 'Jenna, my lovely, come into the house, would you? I – I want to talk to you.'

She had known it was something: something serious, something big, that someone was ill, or angry, or terribly upset, and, rather slowly, instinctively frightened herself, she'd dismounted, tied Florian to the rail and followed

Joan into the kitchen. Billy was there too, his own face heavy, his eyes red-rimmed.

'What is it?' she said. 'What's happened?' and then Joan said, 'Jenna, dear, it's — it's your mother. It's Barty.'

'What?' she had said stupidly, 'what's the matter, is she ill?' And Joan had said very quietly and calmly, 'No Jenna, she's not ill. She's — well, she's dead, I'm afraid. Her plane crashed. I'm so, so sorry.'

She had sat down and held out her arms to Jenna; and, big girl that she was, she went to her, went into her arms, sat there on her lap, her head buried on Joan's shoulder, so shocked and shaken she had no idea what she was doing, not crying, not saying anything, hardly able to breathe.

'Oh Jenna,' Billy said, 'Jenna, I'm so sorry. It's terrible, dreadful—'

He pulled a handkerchief out of his pocket, blew his nose, wiped his eyes.

'She was so good,' he said, almost irrelevantly, 'such a good girl. Mum was so proud of her.'

Jenna looked at Joan. 'Are we sure? Are we quite sure? Sometimes they find people, where did it happen? Maybe—'

'We're quite sure,' said Joan, 'I'm afraid. It was over the sea. No survivors, that's what it said. There, there, my lovely, you have a good cry—'

The tears didn't really start then; just a few, rolling rather slowly down her face. It was all too awful to absorb, the thought of her mother falling into the sea, dying in the sea, her mother, who only last night had told her she loved her, to be careful on the tractor, her mother who she would never see or hear from again, as long as she lived.

She said she would like to go to her room and she lay there, on the bed, the same bed she had shared with her mother, just a week before, snuggled up, trying to keep warm, talking in whispers about how cold it was, giggling because they couldn't keep their coats from falling on to the floor. Now she was alone in the bed, alone in the room, alone in the world; it seemed absolutely impossible.

She knew she would feel better if she cried, anything would be better than this fierce, tight pain which seemed to be slowly spreading right through her body, needing to be let out; but she couldn't. She lay there for a long time, hardly thinking, icy cold; she could hear Florian whickering in the paddock, could hear Joan's voice talking quietly to Joe and Michael when they came in, heard the telephone ringing again and again.

Joan came up every now and again, to ask her if she'd like to speak to Celia, to Cathy, to Izzie, to Sebastian; she kept shaking her head, just staring at Joan, as if she was having trouble understanding what she said.

It got darker and still she lay there, growing colder, frozen with the pain and the fear of what lay ahead of her, a whole life without her mother; wondering how she could manage it, how she could carry on, without her to talk to and laugh with and be cross with and argue with and look up to – and love; and it seemed unthinkably hard.

It was Joe who released the tears for her; he came up and knocked at her door. She called to him to come in, and he stood there in the doorway, his hands twisting together, his dark eyes filled not with tears but with anguish for her.

'I'm so – sorry,' he said, speaking with obvious difficulty. 'I don't know what to say, not really, no more than that, I'm so sorry, Jenna.'

'That's all right,' she said, feeling a sob rising now in her throat, 'thank you. Thank you, Joe. Would you – would you come and sit on the bed for a bit?'

'Course,' he said, 'course I will.' And she could see he was terrified of it, of having to witness her grief, of not being able to find any of the right words, and his courage touched her deeply.

He sat down at the end of her bed, and just looked at her; then he sighed and said, 'She was a lovely lady, your mum. It doesn't seem right, she's not here no more.'

'It doesn't, does it?' said Jenna, her voice quite bright and calm. 'Not right at all. She should be here, right here, in the house, downstairs, I need her, Joe, I need her so much—'

'We'll do what we can,' he said simply, 'all of us. I will, any rate, I promise you that.'

And then he reached for her hand and took it, very awkwardly, and sat looking at it, as if he didn't quite know what to do next. Jenna tried to smile at him but found she couldn't, that it was quite impossible, and she started to cry. A great wave of pain, she could feel it, rose higher and higher, knocking her, tossing her, dragging her in its wake; Joe moved forward and put his arm around her and just sat there, letting her cry, not saying anything, anything at all. And when Joan came up, an hour or so later, he was still sitting there; they had hardly moved but Jenna had stopped crying, was leaning against him with her eyes closed, and the front of his shirt was dark with her tears.

'It's all right, Mum,' he said, very quietly. 'Just leave us be. That'd be best, just leave us be.'

The next day Izzie arrived with Celia; Jenna was glad, they were two of the people she liked best, could best cope with in this strange, sad new country she had found herself in. Celia was very quiet, clearly shocked, her voice frail with crushed tears. Izzie, like Joe, said very little, but what she did say was exactly right.

She hugged Jenna to her for a long time, sitting on the lumpy sofa in what Joan called the best room, just letting her cry; finally, she said, 'I know you must feel so alone, Jenna. But you're not. You've got us, you've got all of us. We'll look after you, as very best we can.'

'Thank you,' Jenna said, trying to smile at her. 'Thank you very much. But—'

'I know,' said Izzie, 'I know exactly. It won't be anything like the same, ever again, but we'll be there for you, whatever happens. You mustn't be afraid.'

Afraid was what she was, of course: afraid of being alone, without her mother, without anyone, anyone she could think of as hers. Of course there was Charlie, and there were all the Lyttons and there was Joe and Joan and Billy; they would be kind and do their best for her, but they all had other people of their own, they did not belong to her as her mother had, any more than she did to them.

'I'll – I'll try not to be,' she said, without believing it was possible; and Izzie hugged her tighter and said she knew how it was to be without a mother.

'Of course it wasn't so bad for me because I never had one. But I have always so longed for one, I've thought about having one so much, what we could do together, how we would be together. So I know about that sort of – blank in your life.'

'Yes, but you had a father,' said Jenna, 'a father who loved you. I haven't got that either. I'm just me, all alone. It feels terribly – bad. And I loved her so much. Who do I love now, Izzie, who?'

Later they sat in the kitchen, and Celia started talking about Barty; briefly at first, about what she had been like when she was a little girl. 'She was tiny, you know, so thin, but terribly strong, and so brave. She had a very difficult time with us in those early days, I didn't fully realise it, I'm afraid, and she missed her own mother dreadfully, but she managed, she won through in the end.'

And then, because it was so good to hear about her, Jenna asked Celia to go on. She talked for many hours, about Barty, about all the things she had done, how she had read Sebastian's first book to Jay all through one night in hospital, when he had nearly died, how she had done so well at school, won scholarships, worked so hard; how she had been Oliver's nurse when he came home from the war, reading to him for hours, and playing the piano to him, how she had fed him his first proper meal of soup, how proud she had been; how happy she and Giles had been together, best friends – 'He needed one, you know, with those dreadful twins lined up against him' – and about how brave she had been when her father had died, in the war, how she had kept Billy's spirits up when he had lost his leg. 'It was she who persuaded my mother to go and visit him in hospital, and that was the beginning of a very long story.' She told them about how Barty had been so good to Izzie – 'and I needed her,' Izzie said, 'Father didn't want to have anything to do with me, you know, for years.'

'Why?' asked Jenna curiously.

'Because I was responsible for my mother's death. As he saw it. By being born. He couldn't help it and, as you know, he came to love me in the end. But Barty was so good to me, came to visit me so often, I loved her very, very much.'

Celia told Jenna how Barty had done so well at Oxford, how proud she had been of her first flat, 'I couldn't understand it, I was quite cross at the time. She had a perfectly good home with us. Why go and live in some dreadful place where she had to share a lavatory? But of course I can see it now, and she was right, she needed to make her own way, she had a hugely independent streak.'

'And when – when her mother died,' said Jenna, 'who looked after her then?'

'I – did my best,' said Celia, 'and she was very brave, but so unhappy. Like –' she hesitated, then said, very steadily '– like you, she felt quite alone. Even though she had Oliver and me. They were very close, you know, she and Wol, as she called him. I think she felt he understood her better than I did, that he was less frightening.'

'She said she found you frightening when she was little. I didn't.'

Celia smiled at her. 'That's very good to know. I take it as a compliment.'

On and on they talked, until it was dark outside and Billy came in to light the fire; Celia was exhausted, but she talked on, undaunted by Jenna's relentless questioning and curiosity. She knew what she was doing; she was bringing Barty back for Jenna, bringing her alive again, not just as the strong, clever, loving adult Jenna had known, but the brave, stalwart child, who had lost her own mother not once, but twice, first when she had been taken away from her by Celia, and then when Sylvia had died, the child who had been lonely and frightened herself, but who had survived.

No one had quite known what to do about a funeral, what form it could possibly take. It was Sebastian who suggested a service of remembrance.

'And have it down at Ashingham, in the chapel. Jenna loves it there, feels safe, everyone will like that. It's important to say some formal goodbyes.'

And so they did; everyone came. The Lyttons arrived in great force, great numbers of them right across the generations.

Jenna, sitting in the front pew between Celia and Charlie, who had arrived two days earlier, was awed by the way they filled the little church; used as she was to her own tiny family. And the others too, of course, Sebastian, Izzie, the Millers, Celia's eldest brother Lord Beckenham and his family: all come to say goodbye to Barty, who they had loved so much.

The church was filled with flowers; but there was a dreadful emptiness at its heart; the coffin, in all its stolid poignancy, was not there, only an awful awareness of how completely Barty was lost to them.

It was a very simple service: Barty's favourite hymn since she was a little girl, 'Onward Christian Soldiers', just one lesson, read by Jay and chosen by Jenna, from the Sermon on the Mount, a few prayers, and then Sebastian rose to speak.

'We have come here today,' he said, his great voice filling the little church, 'to say goodbye to Barty, who we loved. All of us. It was her gift, to inspire love. We all have Barty stories, we could tell them until nightfall. I would like to tell you only one of my own. When I first met her, she was a little girl of nine or ten, I suppose; already a part of this great Lytton clan and yet still very much a Miller. I remember seeing her at the Lytton house in Cheyne Walk; Celia had the proofs of *Meridian* and had allowed her to read them.

'I had met her a few times, and had already come to admire her. She was always beautifully mannered, rather grown up for her age: old-fashioned, was the adjective I applied to her. I asked if she had read *Meridian*, a little nervously, I must admit. It was my first book, and authors are notoriously anxious. She looked at me solemnly and said that yes, she liked it very much, she thought it was very good and I was just breathing a sigh of relief, when she added, clearly feeling she must be absolutely honest, that it was almost but not quite as good as *Little Women*, which she advised me to read if I had not already done so. Suitably chastened, I left.

'It was not until she told me later that she was quite sure *Meridian* had saved Jay's life and that she didn't think that *Little Women* would have done the same job, that I felt confident enough to move forwards and write the sequel. I tell you that story because it illustrates Barty so well: she never became so very different from that little girl; she remained a quite extraordinary person: clever; clear-sighted; brave; kind; steadfast; loyal; and very, very honest.

'This is a dreadfully sad day for us all, and for Jenna in particular; but she should take comfort in knowing that her mother has handed on to her a most precious birthright – that of her own character. Indeed, I know of no one who disliked Barty, no one who was afraid of her, no one who did not admire her, no one, indeed, who had anything but good to say of her.

'She was, quite simply, unique: we were privileged to have known and loved her; and Jenna should be very proud of being her daughter.'

He finished, then took his place in the pew opposite Jenna, and smiled at her gently, before sitting with his head bowed. Izzie, realising that he was weeping, slid her hand into his; she was crying herself. She glanced anxiously across at Jenna, who was biting her lip, fighting back her tears, but managing nonetheless to sing the last hymn, chosen this time by Billy and Joan, 'Dear Lord and Father of Mankind', before breaking down completely and burying her face against Celia. And Celia, who had always prided herself on her self-control, who had never wept publicly, not at her mother's funeral, not at her sister-in-law's, not even at Oliver's, put her arms around Jenna and bent her head over her, her own tears falling on the lovely red-gold hair.

Charlie had been very good from the beginning. He had arrived looking perfectly dreadful. Jenna and Cathy, accompanied by Izzie, met him at Heathrow and took him back to Cheyne Walk where Celia received him graciously, giving no inkling that she knew the reason for Barty's sudden return to New York. It had, of course, occurred to her, as it had to Sebastian, that Charlie was, indirectly, responsible for Barty's death; she could tell by his embarrassment, his patent misery, that he felt it too.

She warmed to him that evening; he said very little, made an effort to talk and then fell awkwardly silent. Dinner was an uncomfortable meal; the girls were both tearful, Celia exhausted, Izzie subdued; only Lord Arden talked, bland, easy nothingness, about the weather, the shocking fact that not only non-hereditary peers but also women were being admitted to the House of Lords, about Lord Altrincham's outrageous criticism of the monarchy, about Prince Charles becoming Prince of Wales; no one was interested in what he was saying, no one even properly listened, but they were deeply grateful for it, releasing them as it did from making any effort themselves.

Next day, Charlie appeared at breakfast, looking very pale, and asked Jenna if she would like to talk; she said she would. She was touched by his obvious misery; in a strange way it helped. Here was the one other person to whom her mother's death was of immediate importance; everyone else, however sad, had their own lives, but Charlie's life, like hers, would never be the same again.

He told her how much he had loved her mother, how happy she had made him, how much Cathy loved her too. 'It wasn't easy, what she did, taking us both on, but she managed it. She managed most things, I guess.'

'Yes,' said Jenna, 'she was pretty special.'

He asked her, almost nervously it seemed, if she had any idea why Barty had flown back early; Jenna said it was because of work.

'She said there were problems in the office; I hate that office,' she said heavily, in a foretaste of the anger that was to come.

Anger which had poisoned everything for her for weeks, months even, had made ordinary activities almost impossible, friendship difficult, schoolwork unthinkable, even the fondest memories unhappy. She went over and over the events, savagely questioning her mother's need to leave without them, her insistence on putting her work first, her failure even to discuss with Jenna whether she minded, whether she would like to go too.

'She should have thought of me,' she would say, her small face ugly with grief when anyone – usually Charlie – tried to remonstrate with her, comfort her. 'She should have thought that I would be alone, that I would need her. She just went off without me, how could she do that?'

She was angry with Lyttons too, for the claims it had made on her mother, angry with the family for encouraging her to fly back alone.

'I expect they thought things might go wrong for them, if she had stayed, not sorted things out. They might have lost their precious jobs, they all depended on her, you know.'

And angry with herself, for not insisting that she went with Barty on the flight; she was told repeatedly by Celia, by Sebastian, that there had been no room, and reminded by Joan that she had said she was perfectly happy at the farm, but she said Barty should have waited until there was room. 'She shouldn't have risked it. I'd rather have died with her, much, much rather. I hate everything, hate it all.'

Charlie asked her what she would like to do, whether she wanted to stay in England, with Celia or the Millers; she shook her head.

'No, I want to go home. I want to go back to our home, mine and my mother's. Especially to South Lodge. She wouldn't have wanted me to live here, I know. Not even with Billy and Joan. And my father was American, he wouldn't have wanted it either. And besides,' she said to Charlie, with a rather feeble smile, 'I want to be with you. We can comfort each other.'

And so they left, a week after the memorial service, when time began to drag and they had too little to do except to grieve. Charlie, obviously happy at Jenna's desire to stay with him, given confidence by it, relaxed, visited everyone in the family in turn, thanking them for their support, assuring them he would take great care of Jenna.

'And I have no doubt he will,' said Celia to Venetia, 'there is no doubt that, for all his faults, he is genuinely fond of the child and she of him. I've been very impressed with the way he handles those girls. Really, they could both be his, there's no favouritism of any kind.'

'Well, it's no different from you and Barty,' Venetia said, slightly coolly. 'I don't remember you favouring us against her, rather the opposite.'

Celia said nothing; she was less inclined to argue these days, conserving her strength for more important things.

One of which, of course, and the one which was worrying all of them, with increasing urgency each day, was the future of Lyttons, without Barty; and in particular the future of Lyttons London.

CHAPTER 32

It was shocking, really, how swiftly grief became greed, Jay thought, as he sat in the boardroom at Lyttons listening to them all, Celia, Venetia, Giles, and himself to be sure, he could not excuse himself from this, discussing what could be done, what must be done.

Only two weeks ago, they had all been weeping in that little church, their hearts wrung with a sorrow which had been entirely genuine, over the loss of someone most dearly loved; now they were squabbling – and that could be the only word for it – over how they might benefit from that loss.

Celia thought they should try to buy back the entire company. 'It's ours by right anyway, it wouldn't exist without us.'

Giles said that was financially impossible. 'It would ruin us. We could never fund such a loan, it would run into many millions.' Venetia said they should re-acquire Lyttons London in its entirety: 'cheaper, simpler, more feasible'.

Jay said that, as far as he could see, they could do that: 'it's in the articles of association, it was agreed we have an option to buy the shares in the event of Barty's death or resignation as a director . . .'

'Well, clearly that is what we must do,' said Celia, 'it seems perfectly simple to me.'

'Apart from raising the money,' said Giles.

'I really can't see any problem with that. Any merchant bank would advance us the money for such a purpose.'

'Possibly.'

'Oh Giles, why do you have to be so negative about everything?'

'Not negative, mother, realistic.'

'Giles,' said Celia, 'this is a very important and successful publishing house. I would say, personally, that it's more unrealistic to assume we won't be able to raise the money. If you can't even recognise that fact, then perhaps I had better do the negotiations myself. If—'

'Look,' said Jay, slightly wearily, 'this discussion really is a bit premature. We should be talking to Harold Charteris about what we ought to be doing before we get too excited about raising the money. Who do you suppose the shares go to otherwise? Since Barty owned them personally?'

'Jenna, presumably,' said Giles. 'Into her trust fund.'

'Do we have any idea what was in the will?'

'None. Presumably there was one.'

'Of course there would have been,' said Celia, 'Barty was far too efficient, far too aware of Jenna's vulnerability to leave anything to chance. Believe me, every end will have been tied up, every t dotted. I mean crossed.'

She sighed. She was far from herself, Jay thought, she looked exhausted and her cough was very bad. She looked really old today, every moment of her age. How old was she now? She was blurring the edges of the years rather cleverly. She and Oliver had been married in 1904; she must be in her seventies.

'I think one of us should go to New York. Have a meeting with the board there,' she said. 'We're in limbo, we don't know who is supposed to be controlling Lyttons. For God's sake, this is a substantial company, it must be properly run. For all we know, that fool of a husband of hers will have a say in things in future.'

'Please God not,' said Venetia, 'is that actually a possibility?'

'I don't believe so,' said Celia. 'She would never have entrusted him with Lyttons. The only thing that might have happened is that she failed to make a new will when they were married. Which, again, is extremely unlikely.'

'What difference would that make?'

'A one hundred per cent difference,' said Giles. 'Remarriage negates an existing will. She would, in the eyes of the law, have died intestate. Which would mean, I think, in law, that half of her estate would go to her husband and half to Jenna. And that would include Lyttons.'

'God,' said Venetia, 'what an appalling thought. How can we find out?'

'We'll know soon enough,' said Celia. 'Charles Patterson certainly won't waste any time coming over here, claiming editorial control, if he thinks he can get it. He told me several times how much he would like to be involved, that he was hoping that he and Barty might be able to work together one day. I agree, Venetia, it is an appalling thought. I really think I should speak to someone over there. Jamie Elliott, he's one of Jenna's trustees. He'd probably tell me.'

'Or Kyle Brewer,' said Venetia, 'what about him? He's a trustee as well.'

'I would prefer not to get involved with that family,' said Celia coldly, 'they're a very – tricky bunch.'

'Mummy, the Brewers aren't tricky,' said Venetia, 'they're really very nice, and Felicity's lovely. You know Daddy thought a lot of her.'

'Indeed?' said Celia. 'I'm afraid I never realised that. A very silly woman, in my opinion. No, I shall speak to Jamie Elliott. He's a charming man, and most attractive. If Laurence was anything like him, I can quite understand why Barty fell for him.'

'Whatever's happened,' said Giles, 'it will take months. All those things, waiting for probate, getting the company valued, nothing will be settled for some time.'

'Yes, but we still need to know,' said Venetia, 'and we also need to know what we're all supposed to be doing. On a day-to-day basis, that is.'

'Carrying on as usual, obviously,' said Celia. 'I certainly have no intention of running to New York every time a publishing decision is called for. Barty trusted our judgement and interfered very little. I see no reason to suppose that will have to change. It would be outrageous if it did. Now if you will excuse me, I shall go and place a call to Jamie Elliott straight away.'

While she was in her office, composing herself (for she was still prone to absolutely unexpected waves of grief, stealing up on her), her secretary came in.

'Claridges Hotel phoned this morning, Lady Celia.'

'Yes? What on earth did they want?'

'Apparently, Miss Miller left a small jewellery box behind when she checked out. In the hotel safe. They've been trying to contact her—'

'Well how absolutely absurd,' said Celia, 'surely they realise – oh well, perhaps they don't.'

'They wondered if they could send it over to you, Lady Celia. Clearly they can't keep it there.'

'Yes, yes, of course. Tell them to send it to Cheyne Walk. I'll keep it for – oh dear.' The tears welled up again, pain caught her throat. 'So sorry, Patricia.'

'That's all right, Lady Celia, I understand. Shall I get you a cup of tea perhaps—'

'No, no, I've drunk far too much tea already today. Just put in a call to New York, would you? To Mr James Elliott, you have the number. And come and fetch me from the boardroom when you have him on the line.'

'Yes, Lady Celia.'

Jamie was politely unhelpful; he was unable to tell her anything yet.

'The contents of the will are not yet available, Lady Arden, even to the trustees. What's more, that could be some time ahead. Probate has to be granted, and as you know—'

'Yes, yes, I realise that. But are you at least able to assure us that there is a will?'

He hesitated. 'I am not able to tell you that at the moment, Lady Arden. As soon as we have formal notification, then I will pass it on.'

She sighed. 'Mr Elliott, you take my meaning, I am sure. I refer to a valid will, post-dating Barty's marriage.'

'I do take your meaning, Lady Arden, of course. But at the present time, I cannot answer that question. I'm so sorry.'

'It could make a great difference to us, you see.'

'I do see. And to others, I assure you.'

'Well – as long as you do let us know. As soon as possible. And perhaps we should be there when the will is read.'

'I'm sure that would be possible. In any case, all beneficiaries will be notified and invited to attend the lawyers' offices. But I do assure you, if you are unable to come, I will acquaint you with every detail relating to you.'

'Clearly a great deal will relate to us,' said Celia. 'Barty was part of this family and the major shareholder in Lyttons London.'

'Of course. And if there is any news, I will let you have it, naturally.'

'Thank you. I – don't know how much you saw of Barty,' she added, 'quite a lot, I imagine. I'm sure, like us, you are still very shocked.'

'Very shocked, Lady Arden, yes. It was – is a dreadful loss. Can I assure you that Jenna will be in very good hands here; we will all do our very best to take care of her.'

'I know you will. And – one has to say, she is clearly very fond of Mr Patterson and he of her.'

'Of course,' he said. 'Of course. But if the need arises, then there are several people in New York able to –' his voice shook briefly, he was clearly upset, '– to love and care for her.'

'Thank you, Mr Elliott. That is very good to know.'

Giles and Jay both felt there was nothing to be gained by going to see the New York lawyers or even the board of trustees in the immediate future.

'It would be a complete waste of time,' said Jay, 'but – my God, it will be a relief to know everything's in order. Imagine if we were at the beck and call of that idiot.'

He had taken against Charlie to a surprising degree.

'He's genuinely distressed, and it's very sweet that he and Jenna love each other so much,' he said to Tory. 'But he does stick in my craw. He obviously sees himself as a great corporate brain.'

'Well, I like him,' she said firmly, 'and I think he's very attractive. I'm not surprised Barty married him. He's wonderful with the children. I really can't think there's much harm in him.'

'Or much good either,' said Jay gloomily.

For four days more they agonised at the prospect of being under Charlie Patterson's control.

'If it happened,' Giles said to Jay, 'he'd be here all the time, telling us what to publish, what to buy, interfering in everything. He's that kind of man, a busybody, it would be quite ghastly.'

Celia went so far as to say she would resign if it happened; Venetia looked at her coolly.

'It's all right for you, Mummy, you're going to be retiring again in the foreseeable future anyway—'

'I don't quite see why you should think that.'

'Oh, all right. Let's say by the time you're eighty, then.'

'You know I never think age is relevant.'

'Mummy, stop arguing for arguing's sake. You know perfectly well what I mean. Some of us have rather longer ahead of us here than you do. People like Keir and Elspeth have a lifetime. Oh, it's unthinkable. Barty can't have been that foolish, she can't.'

'I'm sure she hasn't,' said Celia, 'she has Jenna to think of.' And wished she believed it.

They felt guilt about their unease as well; that they should be so concerned for themselves, for their own future. And added to that a certain unspoken hope that perhaps Barty might have given them back something of Lyttons, that she might have seen her death as an opportunity to return the company into its rightful ownership.

They all had trouble sleeping over the next few days.

So did Charlie Patterson.

Barty had ceased to discuss financial matters with him, except on the most domestic level and insofar as they affected his company. He had no idea what her plans might have been for him; her rage and misery had been so great during those last few days before she went to London, he would not have been surprised if she had completely cut him out of her will.

Of course she would not have expected it to be relevant for a long time; but she was immensely efficient, and she was given to acting with great decisiveness. He might even find himself no longer Jenna's guardian. Anything was possible.

Barty had said very little on the subject of her discovery about Meg; she had taken herself off to South Lodge as she always did in times of trouble, and when she had returned, had simply refused to discuss it. Even when they all left for England, she had merely said goodbye and given him a brief hug, for the girls' sake. And that was the last he had had of her. Ever.

Grief had not quite turned to greed for Charlie Patterson; but greed was certainly beginning to assert itself.

CHAPTER 33

It was the small, unexpected things which hurt the most, Jenna had discovered. You could grit your teeth each day, say yes, your mother had died, that it was terrible, dreadful, but you could survive, you had to survive. You got up in the morning, went through the motions, you got dressed, went to classes, talked to your friends, ate your lunch, even occasionally found something funny, or interesting or both, even more occasionally found yourself actually wanting to do something, like play in a match, read the latest *Seventeen* magazine, try a new hairstyle. And then you'd go into your dressing-table drawer and find a bracelet your mother had lent you, that you'd forgotten to give her back, that you'd sworn you had given back, that there'd been an argument over, and you'd sit there, hearing her voice, hearing her say, 'Jenna, you did not give me that bracelet back. Now go and look for it, please', and you'd sit staring at the bracelet, seeing it most vividly on your mother's wrist, her thin wrist, vividly at first, and then less so because the picture would be blurred by your tears.

Or there'd be a letter for her, lying on the mat, probably just a circular of some kind, or letters about shares or something, and you'd realise that to the people who'd addressed the envelope, typed her name, she was still alive, still able to pick letters up and open them and act on them, or throw them in the waste-paper basket, that she was not dead, not lying at the bottom of the Atlantic Ocean, out of reach for ever.

Or you'd be sitting in the dentist's waiting room, flicking the pages of some old society magazine, and there she'd be at a party, laughing, talking, holding a glass, her hair as always drifting slightly untidily around her face. 'Miss Barty Miller,' it would say, 'Chief Executive of the Lyttons publishing company with—' and you'd sit there shocked, looking at her there, quite alive, perfectly happy, about to leave the party and come home again, come home for supper and chat and arguments, instead of being gone for ever, removed from the magazines and the parties and the Lytton publishing company, never coming home any more.

Those were the worst things.

And all the first times, those were difficult: the first back-to-school, the first exeat, the first family birthday – Cathy's, it had been, early in April, and they'd all tried very hard, but Barty had always been so good at birthdays, she had not only given lovely presents, but had arranged fun outings or parties, found new games to play, that, try as they might, they all found themselves sinking suddenly into a dreadful aching silence, which had sent Jenna fleeing to her room in an agony of tears while Cathy and Charlie visited her one at a time to try to comfort her and failed absolutely.

And the first trip to South Lodge, their special place, hers and her mother's where, ever since she was the tiniest little girl, she had been taken, where she had spent her happiest times, where, in the house that he had built, she had felt somehow closer to the father she had never known, that had been awful: to go there without her mother, to walk on the shore without her, stand on the verandah and look down at the ocean, hear the wind in the grasses, taste the salt in the wind, all without her, it was like a long, dreadful dream from which there was no awakening.

Cathy had been great; Jenna forgave her everything in those first few weeks: her silliness, her vanity, her nonsensical flirtatiousness with Fergal and indeed anyone else. She was genuinely grief-stricken herself, they cried together, and she told Jenna how much she had loved Barty, how much she would miss her.

'I'm sorry,' she said to her, the very first night, 'so sorry I said mean things about your mother sometimes. I didn't mean them, she was so great.'

'I said mean things too,' said Jenna, touched by this confession, 'mostly to her. I'd give anything in the world to have her back so I could say sorry. All those fights we had. But –' her lip trembled '– but the last thing I said to her was that I loved her. That kind of – helps a tiny bit.'

'You see, I just can't remember my mother,' said Cathy. 'I was so small. I can remember what she looked like, and I can remember her being ill, having to go away quite a lot—'

'Away? What, to the hospital?'

'Yes. Like when she fell downstairs.'

'She fell downstairs?'

'Yeah, quite often.'

'Oh,' said Jenna, 'maybe she was just terribly weak.'

'Maybe. And I can just about remember sitting on her knee, and being hugged. But that's all. So – there's not so much to miss, I guess. And I did have my dad,' she added.

'Yes,' said Jenna, 'yes, you're so lucky, Cathy, in your dad.'

'Well – you get to share him,' said Cathy. 'I hope it helps a bit.'

'It does. Thanks, Cathy.'

It did help, of course: more than a bit. Charlie was great, not just kind, not just concerned, but wonderfully sympathetic. He seemed to know when one of the unexpected things had happened, he was extremely worried when they first went to South Lodge, even asked Jenna if she'd rather be there alone; he spent hours talking to her, listening to her – and when she wanted it, rather than when it suited him. He never minded if she told him to go away when she was crying, rather than asking for a cuddle, never took it personally, and was genuinely grieving himself. She found that comforting too: that he missed and longed for her mother so much. It seemed to her dreadful that they should have been separated for those last few weeks and she said so; 'It was so good of you, staying behind to take care of Mrs Norton. We all thought so. Did you speak to Mother before – before she left England that day?'

'No,' he said and sighed, 'no, I didn't. But I was all set to go and meet her at the airport and I was so excited, like a kid out of school. And then –' he stopped, his face working.

Jenna looked up at him and slipped her hand into his, gave him a kiss. 'It's so horrible isn't it?' she said.

He actually cried sometimes; she had heard him, alone in his study, late at night, a dreadful, painful sound, and he wept with her too, occasionally, holding her in his arms. She sometimes thought she could not have got through it at all without him, without knowing how much he shared her grief. Poor Charlie; life had been very cruel to him. Sally Norton had died; she had a second stroke very suddenly. Charlie went alone to the funeral; he said it would be more than the girls could bear. He came back looking rather pale and was very quiet, and they made a great fuss of him, cooked him his favourite supper, and then tactfully left him alone. Jenna thought she heard him on the phone later, arguing with someone; but she wasn't sure. In any case, she felt it best not to interfere.

Everyone tried to help, of course; some more successfully than others. A lot of people said too much, pouring sympathy all over her like treacle. Tory and Venetia, for example: she liked them both, but she just didn't need to be hugged and kissed and cried over. Izzie was wonderful, just quietly *there*. So was Noni, which was odd, seeing as how gushy she normally was, even more so than her aunt. Sebastian had been very untreacly, had asked if she'd like to come and see him, given her a giant hug on the doorstep and said he couldn't think of anything to say, but if she wanted to talk, he'd listen.

'Otherwise, we'll just try and get through it together, shall we? I need some help sorting out some old manuscripts, want to help?'

Back home, Mr and Mrs Mills had been a bit treacly, but clearly so upset themselves that she'd forgiven them. Maria had cried endlessly, but Jenna had expected that; on the other hand, she talked about her mother for hours, and that seemed to help, it was all so warm and loving and realistic, somehow. She'd talk about the bad things too, well not the bad ones, but how Barty had been so fussy with them both, got so cross when they were untidy, how badly she used to cook but would still insist on doing it. It meant sometimes they even ended up laughing.

Lucas astonished her by writing the most amazing letter: so warm and funny and kind, telling her stories about what her mother was like when she was young, how he'd loved her tales about being in the ATS during the war, when she'd worked on the big guns, how she'd let someone into the barracks one night when she was on guard duty, not demanded the password, and he'd turned out to be some colonel person. And how he'd tried to teach her to do conjuring tricks but she was absolutely hopeless, and how she tried to teach him to climb trees, but he was too frightened.

'She was so brave, always right at the top, and I'd be whimpering at the bottom, like the little weed I was.'

He'd been lovely after the funeral as well, came up to her and gave her a kiss and said he couldn't think of a single thing to say except how sorry he was and how much he'd loved Barty. When she'd burst into tears later on, while everyone was leaving and he and Noni were saying goodbye, he hadn't tried to pretend he hadn't noticed, and hurried away, he'd hugged her and just stood there, holding her, not saying anything at all because it clearly wouldn't work. He was a bit like Joe, she thought, in his own way; very quiet, but underneath the quiet, full of ideas and thoughts. Most of the family seemed to think he was awful; she really liked him.

And her uncle Jamie, he'd been absolutely lovely, so warm and unfussy and kind. She was always asking him if her father had been like him, and he said not in the least, he'd been much cleverer and more successful for a start, but she felt they must have had quite a lot in common, and it made her feel less alone, knowing he, at least, was there.

She now realised that she was, potentially at least, rather rich; Jamie had very gently gone through what her mother's death meant to her in practical terms, had assured her that her immediate arrangements would not change, there would be funds available to supply everything that she needed.

'But you don't know exactly what – well, what her will –' she stopped, her lip trembling '– what her will said.'

'No, I don't. Not yet. As soon as I do, of course, I'll tell you.'

'What about the houses, who will they belong to? Number Seven, and South Lodge?'

'I don't know. I'm sorry. But we'll get an idea very soon. I have to say I would be very surprised if they didn't stay with you.'

'Yes, I see.' She looked at him. 'So we don't have to move, or anything?'

'Of course not. Not the slightest chance. Unless you want to, that is.' He smiled at her, his warm, lovely smile.

'Of course I don't. And – what about Lyttons?'

'Well, as you know, your mother owned Lyttons personally. Fifty per cent is in trust for you, and the Lytton family have a thirty-two-per-cent share in Lyttons London. Now, that might change. The Lyttons have an option to buy the remaining sixty-eight per cent of those shares. That means that they have the right to buy those shares at a special price, to be agreed between their lawyers and ours and the trustees.'

'I see. Well – I expect they will. I hope so, anyway. There seems to be rather a lot to sort out.'

'There is quite a lot,' he said, smiling at her gently again, 'but you don't have to worry about any of it. Kyle and I and Martin Gilroy, we are still the trustees of your estate, as we have been for most of your life, and we'll look after it for you. We have a legal duty to act in your best interests, and to make sure that any decisions we take meet that test. And nothing is going to change for the time being, as I told you. You have plenty of money in your own trust fund, apart from what's in the will. Any questions?'

'No,' she said, 'except why did it have to happen, I guess. And – will Charlie get anything?'

'Once again, I'm afraid I don't know.'

'I hope he does. He ought to. I often thought it was kind of hard for him, having to accept everything from Mother.'

'Maybe,' said Jamie. He looked a bit odd as he said it, she thought. 'And of course he has his company now, his classic car company, which is his, to run as he likes.'

'Might he get something of Lyttons? That would be so nice. Could I do that anyway, give him some of my shares? I'd rather like him to be part of it.'

'Only if I and the other trustees feel it's in your best interests,' said Jamie.

'But they belong to me. Not the trustees.'

'They are yours. But you're a minor. Until you're twenty-one, we have to decide all that sort of thing for you.'

'But – why should you decide against it? Mother loved Charlie, they were really happy, I love him, he's helped me so much. If I want him to have some shares, why can't he, what harm could it do?'

'I – don't think it would do any harm,' said Jamie, 'I wasn't suggesting that, it was just that the trustees have to take all these decisions for you.'

'I see. Well, I can't see why you should refuse. Can I make a formal request for that, please?'

'Not yet,' said Jamie, 'we're waiting for something called probate. That means the will being effective, indeed legal. It could take some time.'

'How much time?'

'Oh – many months. At least nine months, I'd say, possibly even a year.'

'How could it, what's so complicated?'

He explained some of the intricacies: she listened carefully.

'OK. You know, I think I might be a lawyer, it quite intrigues me.

Anyway, the minute it's granted, probate I mean, I want Charlie to have some Lytton shares. OK?'

'OK, we'll consider it very carefully.'

'Jamie,' she said, and suddenly he saw Laurence in her, in the set of the neat little jaw, the hardening in the blue-green eyes, 'Jamie, it's not a lot to ask. I want that. If it's going to be my company, I want Charlie to have some of it. All right?'

'All right,' he said, 'I'll make a note, look, put it in the file ready for when we get probate. Then it can be discussed. I can't do more than that, Jenna, it's the law.'

'Oh for God's sake,' she said, and stood up, walked out, and slammed the door. He watched her. Sometimes it was hard to believe she was so young.

The Lyttons sat in the boardroom with Harold Charteris, the company secretary; he had had a call from Dean Harmsworth, the company secretary in New York, with whom he was on very good terms.

'It seems there is a valid will,' he said, 'made and registered after Mrs Patterson's marriage.'

'So Charlie Patterson won't get his hands on the company,' said Celia. 'Isn't that right, Mr Charteris?'

'Well – unless she decided to leave it to him.'

'Absolutely out of the question,' said Jay.

'I – wouldn't know,' said Charteris carefully, 'but it seems very unlikely.'

'Did he give you any idea of the contents of the will?'

'No. But he said he would as soon as possible. We may have to wait for probate to be granted unless the lawyers give us the details. They usually do. Probate will take a long time in my opinion, because of the complexity of the estate. And it's always more difficult with privately owned companies, because it's so much more difficult to establish the company's value. Then the IRS have to move in—'

'Who are the IRS?' said Venetia.

'The Internal Revenue Service. The US tax men. It's going to take many, many months. A year, possibly longer. But your option is there to buy the shares in Lyttons London, that has nothing to do with the will. There is a time limit on the option, namely exactly one year from the date of Mrs Patterson's death, and the American board must be notified that you wish to exercise your option, within that time limit. By my calculation, that takes us to the eighth of March 1959. After that, you have ten business days in which to pay for the shares. Failure to meet any of this timetable will mean you will lose the option. There is absolutely no leeway. I cannot stress enough how important this is. On the other hand, a year is a very generous timespan in which to exercise a share option.'

'One would have expected generosity,' said Celia, her voice just a trifle cool. 'Barty was, after all, one of the family.'

'Of course. Now, a notice in writing that you wish to exercise the option must be delivered to the company secretary of Lyttons New York; you can do that yourselves or our solicitors can do it for you. I would advise not delivering the notice until you are absolutely confident the funds are in place; after that, you will only have ten working days to obtain them.'

There was a silence; then, 'Well, I think we should be able to find the money in that sort of time,' said Giles.

'I hope so. The first thing we must do is brief a firm of chartered accountants to put a value on the shares. They must be an independent firm, obviously, and will act as arbitrators between you and the trustees in America. Who of course, together with the existing directors, are now, for all practical purposes, running the company.'

'What an appalling thought,' said Celia. 'What do the trustees know about publishing?'

'Kyle Brewer knows a bit,' said Venetia mildly. She couldn't resist it; her mother's antagonism towards the Brewers intrigued her.

Celia glared at her. 'Very little, I do assure you,' she said. 'I have met him fairly recently, and I was quite surprised by his lack of grasp of some of the most basic things.'

'I don't think you need worry, Lady Celia,' said Harold Charteris. 'The editorial board in New York will still be in charge of editorial matters, I feel sure. It would be madness to change those arrangements.'

'I'm sure Mr Charteris is right, Mother,' said Giles, 'and can I just say, Mr Charteris, we will work closely with you and the accountants. We'd better have a meeting with them as soon as possible.'

'Very well. Now, you realise we could be looking at a very substantial amount of money here.'

'Like – what?' said Jay.

'Obviously it's very difficult to say. The shares are privately held, they have no published value. Normally, of course, a price is arrived at by comparison with the shares of a similar-sized company, but I would say, at a very rough estimate, we would be looking at not less than two million pounds. It could be more, the New York board will naturally want to talk the price up. You could be looking at a very high valuation indeed.'

There was another silence; then, 'Well, we can raise that sort of money perfectly easily,' said Celia. 'There would be absolutely no problem.'

Charteris cleared his throat. 'Hopefully not, Lady Celia, but there could be. The company has been doing pretty well over the past couple of years, but it is far from rich. In cash terms quite the reverse. The risks would be high. And—'

'Mr Charteris,' said Jay hastily, seeing Celia's expression move from cold to icy, 'what steps should we take, exactly? To raise the money? I know we've got twelve months, but what with the valuation and so on, we really can't afford to waste any time.'

'Well it isn't entirely straightforward. If it was a public company, of course, there ought to be no problem finding a bank, to underwrite a rights issue. Small private companies such as this are in a much more difficult position. My advice would be to go to one of these outfits like ICFC. They—'

'I do so loathe this fashion for using initials instead of proper names,' said Celia. 'So sloppy, so—'

'Mother, please!' said Giles. 'Let Mr Charteris finish.'

'ICFC stands for the Industrial and Commercial Finance Corporation, Lady Celia.' Harold Charteris smiled at her.

He's got the patience of a saint, thought Jay, and just as well. He could see Celia scuppering any attempts at a deal if they weren't all very careful.

Celia nodded graciously at Charteris. 'Do go on.'

'They were set up with the precise purpose of encouraging entrepreneurial activity. To help small companies acquire capital. I would suggest a meeting with them at the earliest possible opportunity. They're very helpful, very helpful indeed. Although –' he hesitated, glanced at Celia rather warily, 'they will inevitably look at us with quite a beady eye. All money is loaned with a view to return on investment. And of course they want security.'

'Well, we can offer them that. Lyttons itself represents a great deal of money.'

'Not in terms they would understand, I'm afraid. A publishing company doesn't have any assets, you see, and—'

'No assets!' said Celia. 'Of course Lyttons has assets, this is one of the most successful publishing houses in the world—'

'By assets, Lady Celia, I mean tangible ones. Properties, equipment, machinery, that kind of thing.'

'He's right, Celia,' said Jay, 'our assets are our authors. Apart from this very nice building and the warehouse in Kent, a few typewriters and so on, we don't have anything we could actually put a price on. The true value of our company is impossible to calculate. It's angels on the head of a pin stuff.'

'I have never heard anything quite so absurd in my life,' said Celia. 'And I'm very surprised at you, Jay, even voicing such a view. Lyttons is a venerable publishing house, how can you possibly dismiss it as worthless?'

'Mummy he's talking about hard cash,' said Venetia, 'not our literary heritage. Please, Mr Charteris, do go ahead and arrange a meeting with these people. As soon as possible.'

'Absolutely,' said Jay, 'we'll make ourselves available whenever you need us. Now we have another immediate problem, in my view. Who are we supposed to report to?'

His answer came a week later, in a letter from Marcus Forrest to Giles.

'I think we should meet as soon as possible to establish a chain of command. Perhaps you or Jay Lytton might come to New York, or, if you prefer, members of our board and editorial staff could come to London.'

'Chain of command!' said Celia. 'Dreadful expression. I trust they are not going to try and suggest we are to be anywhere but at the front of such a thing.'

'I think they might,' said Jay.

Celia was at home having breakfast when the jewellery box arrived from Claridges. She nodded, took it from Mrs Hardwicke, and went upstairs to her room, where she sat looking at it for some time through a haze of tears. She had given it to Barty herself; it was very pretty, quite small, a travelling case, really, made of cedarwood. She tried to open it; it was locked. Just as well. Looking at Barty's jewellery, some of which she had undoubtedly given her, lying there unworn, in some strange way abandoned, would have been extremely painful. Odd how it was these small things which hurt the most. Well, there was no rush. She would put it in her own safe, and give it to Jenna, the next time she saw her. That was what Barty would have wanted. And maybe there would be a key at the American house; it would be a pity to force the lock. 'Oh Barty,' she said aloud, smoothing the inlaid lid with her hand very tenderly, 'oh Barty, I miss you so.'

Venetia looked at Adele, sipping tea and nibbling at cucumber sandwiches as if she was at a garden party, and thought how incredible it was that she should remember nothing of what she had been through during the last few hours.

She never did; this had been her third electric shock treatment, and each time Venetia expected her to come back from the treatment heavily traumatised, but each time she got the same rather vague smile, the same complaint of a 'bit of a headache', and then when they got home, the same polite acceptance of tea, of a piece of cake, and the same slightly vapid conversation.

Venetia always went with her; the first time Adele had been terrified, in spite of the doctor's encouraging words. He had been franker, but equally reassuring, with Venetia.

'Don't look so anxious, Mrs Warwick. She'll go into hospital – as my patient, into St Christopher's – in the morning, at about nine. First we would sedate her, then give her a muscle relaxant and so on, she won't even see the electrodes, they'll be on the trolley behind her. As soon as the anaesthetic is effective, we place the electrodes on her head. What we're doing is passing low voltage electricity through the brain, and the effect – to witness, anyway – is exactly like that of an epileptic fit.'

'It sounds ghastly,' said Venetia with a shudder. 'Are you quite sure she won't – won't suffer?'

'I'm quite sure. And please believe me, it should help her. Nobody knows quite how it works, but it does.'

'And – how quickly?'

'She'd have to have two, possibly three, treatments a week. Some people feel better immediately, some after four or five treatments. She'd probably have six altogether. After which most patients recover quite astonishingly from their depression, say they feel normal, in fact. It's remarkable to witness. I really would advise it, she's still very depressed, and she needs to face her past. It's actually her past which I think is causing her greatest problems, not her present.'

'Well – I'll talk to her about it.'

She did; Adele was fearful, but resigned. She had great faith in Dr Cunningham, and if he thought ECT was going to help her, then she was prepared to be brave and submit herself to it.

And so they went: together, of course. They might now be two very different people, but they were still identical twins, still almost telepathically close, still uniquely able to understand and identify with one another. Adele clung to Venetia's hand in the taxi, silent, white-faced with terror, and still begging that her sister be with her until she was unconscious. They agreed; Adele was wheeled away, and then returned to Venetia, and proceeded to sleep for a couple of hours. After that she was seen by Dr Cunningham and at tea time allowed to go home.

For poor Venetia, imagining her sister having wires attached to her head, then shocked into uncontrollable fits behind the closed door, the experience was far worse.

There was little effect the first three times; then after the fourth, Adele announced that she wanted to go to Woollands on the way home.

'I'm so sick of looking like a fright. Do let's. And have tea there.'

Venetia refused to allow that, but said they could go in the morning; Adele, a little subdued but otherwise cheerful, bought three suits, a dress and jacket and four pairs of shoes.

Dr Cunningham was delighted.

After the fifth session, she said she would like to take Venetia, her mother, Noni and Lucas out to dinner, 'to say thank you', and was able to discuss Barty's death tearfully but easily; after the sixth and last, she announced what she wanted to do most in the world was go out with her camera and take some photographs.

A week later she said she wanted to go to Paris to see Madame André; would Venetia go with her?

'I know that's what I've got to do, Venetia. I should have done it years ago. I've got to – well, lay some ghosts. I feel as if I've been running away from it all, from the memories, and what really happened, from why I did it. I think if I go back there, face it all, I'll feel better. I can't see Bernard Touvier, who wrote to tell me Luc had been shot, he's died. But Madame André is still there. Will you come, darling? Please?'

Venetia said she would; the next day Adele phoned her, her voice light with joy. Lucas wanted to go with them.

Jamie Elliott looked at Charlie, sitting in his office, clearly and genuinely distressed, his hands twisting together, his face pale and haggard, and felt considerable sympathy for him; while still noticing the perfectly cut suit, the fine lawn shirt, the Gucci loafers, the gold Rolex watch, and contrasting him with the Charlie Patterson he had first met, with his frayed shirt cuffs and down-at-heel shoes.

Charlie had suggested the meeting: 'To discuss Jenna's future. Just informally, of course, I don't want to involve anyone else at this stage. But you are her uncle, after all, and I thought therefore we should be in close contact.'

'Of course. But I don't see there's much of a problem at the moment,' said Jamie, 'she's a minor, we will continue to administer her trust fund until she comes of age. You, as her stepfather, will continue to have daily care of her. And I'm sure you will do that conscientiously. She's very fond of you, she was telling me that only the other day, when she came to have supper with me.'

'That's good to know,' said Charlie, 'and of course I'll do – I am doing – everything in my power to take care of her, and to help her through this.'

'I know you are. Now, in the immediate future, your own financial situation is, as I understand it, pretty straight forward.'

'Well – I have the income from my new company. Which is fairly puny.'

'Ye-es. But I mean the day-to-day stuff. You will clearly continue to take responsibility for her.'

He had been faintly surprised that Barty had not changed that arrangement, had not asked him – or Kyle – to take it on. But then, whatever else, Charlie was wonderfully good with Jenna, who loved him dearly. And, of course, she would hardly have expected a guardianship to come into play so soon. Poor Barty. He cleared his throat, fixed his eyes on Charlie.

'Of course I will. And I want her to have as little change as possible in her life. For instance, I would like her to stay at Dana Hall. The fees would presumably come out of the original trust fund? The one not subject to the will.'

'Oh, yes, they certainly would.'

'And – her day-to-day expenses, her clothes, her spending money, the upkeep of her pony, all that sort of thing?'

'Yes. All of it. Naturally, we would have to set up some kind of immediate system to enable us to pay all those bills direct, out of the estate, certainly until probate has been granted, but – yes. And the housekeeping, food and staff, that will come out of the trust fund too. Cathy's school fees and other maintenance, I imagine you will meet from your own funds, the salary you draw from your own company.'

'Yes, of course. Not that it is very lucrative at the moment. I've been forced to neglect it, obviously, what with other claims on my attention. But within the next few months, I hope I can nurse it back to life.'

'I hope you can, too,' said Jamie.

'What happens to the company? To Lyttons?'

'Lyttons?' Jamie managed to look as puzzled as Charlie himself. 'I don't quite understand.'

'Where will the shares go now? I'm very shaky on such matters.'

'Well, it is, of course, subject to probate. Half the shares are already in Jenna's trust fund, of course.'

'And the rest? Is there any chance they might go on the market? Once probate is granted, and the way ahead is clear?'

'I very much doubt it. Lyttons is not a publicly quoted company. Of course, the other trustees might feel now was the time to float part of the company, I believe that's an increasing trend in England at least. But that wouldn't happen in the foreseeable future.'

'Well –' there was a pause. Charlie was clearly thinking, or pretending to think. '– I am part of the family now. More than ever, it could be argued. Perhaps it might be possible for me to obtain a few shares?'

'It – might be,' said Jamie carefully, 'but I'm not sure how. Lyttons is a family company. The Lytton family have an option to buy the UK shares, which I understand they intend to exercise. That is not subject to the will. Anyone who takes those shares under the will takes them subject to that option. You could put in a request, when probate has been granted, to buy some of the US ones. I have no idea how we would value them. But I could put it to the board—'

'Yes, I see. Oh dear, we're rushing ahead, rather, aren't we?'

'I'm not,' said Jamie mildly.

'Well, as you say, it's all going to take time. There's no rush. But the thing is – I would like to think I had a few shares, was part of the Lytton family firm. As I am raising a member of the family. A very important member.'

For which you clearly feel you should get a few free shares, thought Jamie. Oh dear. Jenna might love Charlie, she undoubtedly did love him; she was certainly very dependent on him emotionally. And Charlie was her legal guardian. But he was not to be trusted. That much was very clear.

And there was still the ongoing matter of the forged cheques. Barty would still be alive but for that.

This was a chilling thought, which Jamie, like the handful of other people who knew the facts behind Barty's return, tried to dismiss. It had been a ghastly accident; nobody's fault. That was the only way to think about it. Otherwise they would all go mad.

Marcus Forrest smiled at Jay; Jay smiled back. They appeared to be two civilised, successful men, sharing a pot of excellent New York coffee. In fact they were gladiators, about to go into battle. A battle over editorial control of Lyttons London, and how far that control should extend. It was a difficult one.

'Perhaps we should start by looking at how you functioned when Barty was alive,' said Forrest. 'As I understand it, you discussed virtually everything with her: major purchases, of books, that is, and the subsequent contracts, promotional budgets, publication schedules—'

'Yes,' said Jay, 'that's correct. But—'

'Jay, let's not get involved in further detail at this stage. And then she, and the board of course, had approval of your twice-yearly budgets, any major expenditure, staff changes at a senior level—'

'Yes—'

'Right. Well, I see no reason for that to change, do you? You and I can work in exactly the same way.'

'I'm – not sure that's going to be possible,' said Jay. 'Not in quite the same way.'

Marcus Forrest raised his eyebrows. He had rather fine eyebrows, very thick and blond; he was rather fine looking altogether, very patrician, very East Coast, fair, with a narrow face, a long nose, and very light blue eyes. He was tall, thin, elegant and very witty, good company; Jay had always liked him. And admired him, had admired Barty's judgement in hiring him. He was clever, a brilliant editor, possessed of a good editorial instinct. Exactly like Jay. There was one big difference though; Forrest was an intensely hard worker.

'Why?' he said now. 'Why can't we go on like that? It seemed rather gloriously simple to me.'

'Because,' said Jay, 'if you will forgive me for speaking frankly—'

'Of course.'

'Barty had a very clear grasp of the British market. We didn't have to explain anything to her. She knew many of the authors personally, the old stalwarts, that is, she had met all the new ones; she knew the retail outlets, the major figures in English publishing, she had always been – in effect anyway – a Lytton.'

'I see. And does being a Lytton – in effect – bestow upon one some special powers of editorial judgement?'

'We like to think so,' said Jay, with a grin, 'although not always, of course. But – what I mean is, Barty was English. She absolutely understood the English market. Decisions could be quickly made. Explanations were inevitably brief. We had developed a shorthand. I think that to carry on in exactly that way would be difficult . . .'

Forrest nodded, as if in agreement; then he said, 'Would you say members of the family had ever been able to get around Barty?'

'No,' said Jay. 'Absolutely not.'

'It's a pretty formidable force you have over there. Headed by the redoubtable Lady Celia.'

'Hardly headed,' said Jay. 'I'm the editorial director, Celia is more of a figurehead these days—'

'Oh really? She seems very active in the company to me. Marvellous woman, I do admire her.'

'We all admire her,' said Jay carefully.

'But – she must be what – late sixties? Early seventies?'

'Something like that. Past retirement age.'

'Well – yes. Past it. But not actually retired. Barty had been trained by her. And brought up by her. Had grown up with all of you.'

'Yes. I don't quite see where this is leading.'

'It's leading me, Jay, to certain conclusions. That an old woman is a powerful force in that company. Too powerful, some would say. That the one person who should have been able to countermand her was – let us say – in awe of her.'

'Absolutely untrue,' said Jay.

'Indeed? I had observed a degree of deference in Barty when Lady Celia came over here.'

'She might have appeared deferential. But Barty would never have agreed to anything she didn't approve of.'

'I'm not so sure. Those military memoirs of General Dugdale's, for instance, you paid an absurd price for them. He was a friend of Lady Celia's, I believe.'

'Marcus, I don't quite like—'

'And I believe Lady Celia had expressed the view that you should republish the Buchanan saga?'

'Yes.'

'Barty didn't like that idea. She told me.'

'None of us was sure about it.'

'She also told me she was afraid she'd have to let it through; that she would trust Lady Celia's legendary judgement. Jay, I suggest to you that Barty was not completely in control of Lyttons London.'

'She didn't need to be,' said Jay. He was growing indignant now. 'She trusted us. We ran it.'

'I know that. With what amounted to insufficient accountability. In my view. Given your shareholding in the company I would like to see that accountability increased. As for any lack of knowledge of the London market, I can easily rectify that. I intend to spend a fair bit of time there, getting to know it intimately. Precisely so that any judgements I make are well-informed. I thought I would make my first visit in about a month's time. I have no intention of playing the heavy father, I assure you. Now, this new series about the queens of England by Lady Annabel Muirhead, is it really such a good idea? There are several rather similar works coming out next year and—'

Jay arrived back in London exhausted, and called a board meeting; he said it was absolutely essential they pressed on with exercising their share option.

'It's already, I'm sure I don't have to remind you, mid-April. And if we don't get control of the company we're just not going to survive.'

'Dear, dear Madame André. Oh, it's so wonderful to see you, I never thought I would, you know. Now this is my sister, my twin sister Venetia, and this is my son, Lucas. Can you believe it, Madame André, that little tiny boy you sent off with the toy cow in his hand is this young man?'

The fluent French stopped; Venetia had only understood half of it, but she was touched by Madame André's response, a tearful rush of affection, cries of '*Ma chère, chère Mam'selle Adele*', as she embraced first Venetia, then Lucas, commented on his height, his good looks – '*comme il est beau, Mam'selle*' – on how he had grown up in the intervening years.

And Adele stood there, tears streaming down her face, smiling at the same time, and Lucas put his arm round his mother's shoulders and stood there too, smiling, half embarrassed but quite clearly very moved, looking around him, at the dark poky room which was the last, the very last he had seen of Paris, almost twenty years earlier.

The name touched Adele more than anything: the name, the silly name which had first annoyed, then amused her, and that had finally been so powerful in its ability to evoke memories. She heard it again and again, spoken in Luc's voice, hundreds, possibly thousands of times, over their short, difficult history, as she met him, fell in love with him, bore his children – and left him. Without saying goodbye. And then received the last, final, sweet, sad letter from him, telling her that he was going into hiding, sent 'With all my love *ma chère, chère Mam'selle Adele*.'

Lucas was reluctant to leave; she was surprised. Like herself, he spoke perfect French; he questioned Madame André endlessly. Had she grown up in Paris? In what other districts had she lived? What had Paris been like during the occupation? What did she remember of him and his sister, and of course his papa, what could she tell him of him as a young man?

'Your papa found this place for your *maman*,' she said. 'He came here one evening and looked at it, and told me he was bringing his young wife here, that she was English, and expecting a baby. I told him it was not ideal to live on the top floor with a baby, but he said he knew she would love it. He was very handsome, Lucas; you look very like him. And very charming, and so excited, it was to be a surprise for your mother, you see, she knew nothing of it.'

'He gave me the key,' said Adele, smiling at the memory, 'over lunch at La Closerie des Lilas and then said he would take me to the door which it fitted. Or something like that.'

And then she stopped smiling as the memory began to hurt, and said it was time they left.

She sat in her room that first night at the small hotel where they were staying, just off the Boulevard St Germain, so dangerously near her memories, and felt at first that her heart would break. There she had lived with Luc, and their two small children, in what had, for the most part, been considerable happiness and there she had left him, driven away from him out of Paris, out of France, out of his life. Without – and again she thought it, forced herself to think it – without saying goodbye.

Lucas was going out with Venetia; Adele couldn't face it. Venetia was treating him to what she called a posh dinner at Maxims; he had his father's love of glamour, and was struggling not to appear too excited. Adele opened her window and looked out. It was still only seven and a perfect evening; Paris was bathed in the golden light which is its speciality, dancing on the tender young leaves of the chestnut trees, settling on the silver-grey rooftops. She could hear the car horns in the street below, the gendarme's whistles, the pigeons calling, the unmistakable sounds of Paris; suddenly, she knew what she wanted to do.

She called Venetia in her room, and told her where she was going; and then left the hotel. She walked along the Boulevard St Germain, up towards the Place St Sulpice, until she could hear the fountains; she turned the corner and there they were, the long, leaping, noisy row of them. She stood there staring at them and suddenly she was no longer Adele, middle-aged, lonely and unhappy, she was the Adele who was twenty-four again, young, hopeful, tender, and in love. She could feel the handles of the pram in her hands, the wheels bumping on the cobbles, could hear little Noni laughing, see Lucas's small face peaceful as he slept; she stopped at the corner, the corner of the street where she had lived all those years ago, and heard Luc calling her, laughing, breathless, trying to attract her attention, felt his arms on her shoulders, swinging her round to kiss her. It was safe, that life, that other happy life, safe in the past; she had not spoilt it by then, had not thrown it ruthlessly away, it was still hers to live and to savour.

She walked, more slowly now, into the shadows, along the rue St

Sulpice, stopped outside the door through which Luc had led her that first day, the door into the courtyard, and then the door to their home, up on the third floor, to the tiny apartment where they had lived together for three long years, as Paris moved from peace into war, and for her, from happiness into pain.

She rang the bell; Madame André opened the door, her old face smiling with happiness that she had come back. 'I was afraid, Mam'selle, I would not see you again. Certainly not today.'

She had aged a lot; she had seemed to Adele old at the time, in wartime Paris, but now she was really old, at least seventy, her face deeply lined, her grey hair sparse, but her dark eyes brilliantly alive.

'May I come in? I would so like to talk to you some more.'

'But of course. I am delighted to have a visitor, I am alone much of the time these days. But I am quite happy,' lest Adele should feel sorry for her, 'really very happy indeed.'

She made a pot of coffee, poured her some absinthe; the taste of the two together, the strong coffee, the liquorice-tasting aperitif that Adele had drunk so often to please Madame André, while disliking them both, took her back in time more vividly still, to when she would sit there in the dark little room, either too hot or too cold, while Noni chattered in the background and more often than not Lucas wailed on her knee . . .

It was hot that night; so hot that the window was open on to the street. They settled near it, in order to feel the faint breeze in the evening air, and Madame André smiled at her. 'So – you want to speak some more?'

'Yes,' said Adele, 'yes, Madame André, I do.'

Lucas studied himself in the mirror; he quite admired what he saw. Someone tall, slim, stylish (he hoped Venetia would agree to the silk shirt and admire the slightly pointed shoes); with the dark hair and eyes and slightly olive skin of his French ancestry. He was, he could see, very like his father; he had studied countless photographs. It made him feel, he wasn't sure why, slightly superior to the rest of the family. Well, more interesting, anyway.

He went to the drawer to get out his wallet; he intended to buy Venetia a drink before dinner. And then remembered his mother had never given him the francs she had promised. Damn. He phoned her room: no answer. He tried Reception; they told him she had gone out.

He went along to Venetia's room and knocked on the door; she opened it, still wearing her dressing gown.

'I'm not ready yet. Sorry. Lucas, you can't wear that shirt to Maxims. Nice shoes, though.'

Lucas sighed. 'I'll change the shirt,' he said. 'I was half expecting you not to appreciate it.'

'It's a lovely shirt. It's just not suitable.'

'Anyway, I know I'm early. Do you know where my mother is?'

'Yes, she went back to see Madame André again.'

'Oh – right. How long will you be?'

'At least half an hour. I did say eight.'

'I know you did. I'll be downstairs, then. Changed into a nice dull shirt.'

'Good.'

He looked at his watch; he'd have plenty of time. He did want the money; he'd feel such a kid if Venetia paid for everything. And he was sure his mother wouldn't mind. He set off briskly towards the rue St Sulpice.

The street was empty and very quiet now; everyone was out in the squares and cafés. As Lucas neared Madame André's house he could hear voices drifting out of the window, very clear on the still, evening air. Madame André's and his mother's.

Lucas had spent his life listening in to other people's conversations; it was how he had learned a great many crucial things. He had absolutely no scruples about it.

He stood there quietly, leaning on the wall near the window, totally out of sight, and lit one of the Gauloises that made him feel slightly sick but which he was determined to master. And listened.

'So, you have been married again, Mam'selle? You must forgive me, I must not continue to call you that.'

'Oh, Madame, please do. It's – well, it's important. Yes, I have been married. And now I'm getting divorced.'

'Mam'selle!' The brilliant eyes were soft with sympathy. 'You have not been lucky, I think.'

'I don't know, Madame. Maybe it's me. That's why I'm here, to try and find out what went wrong, why I did what I did.'

'Because you had to.'

'I did? Are you sure?'

'But of course. There was no other way.'

'But why? Because the Germans were coming? Others stayed, others were more loyal. After all this time, you know, I still feel so bad, so guilty, taking the children away—'

'No, of course it was not because of the Germans. It was because – may I be honest?'

'Please, please do.'

'Because of him. Because of the way he treated you. That was why you went. He – he was betraying you.'

'I know that. Of course I do. But – I should have talked to him about it, worked something out, not just rushed away as I did, leaving him here' – her voice shook – 'alone. I should have been braver, I should have been willing to stay.'

'I think you have forgotten, Mam'selle, how brave you were.'

'I was?' Adele was astonished.

'But of course. You know he wanted you to leave, he urged you to go home. And you longed to go, you told me so, home to your family and your mother, to have your children safe.'

'Oh.' She sat staring at her, across the dark, over-furnished little room, took a large sip of the absinthe and promptly regretted it. 'Did I really?'

'But of course. You refused, time and time again. You said your home was here and your place was with him and the children. Whatever the risk. I heard you arguing about it one day, the sound came down from your little balcony.'

'Oh.' She was silent, digesting this new, absolutely unfamiliar piece of her history, that was, nonetheless, so plainly true.

'I was very fond of you, Mam'selle. But I wanted you to go. To be safe. I was very afraid for you.'

'How did you know Luc was being unfaithful to me? He didn't – didn't bring her here?'

'Of course not. But I saw him coming home late, I saw his face sometimes, distracted, irritable as he rushed in. I saw your disappointment when arrangements were changed, cancelled. I am an old woman and, more to the point, I am French, we have a great instinct for these things.'

'So – it had been going on a little while, do you think? Well, I suppose I must have realised that.'

'A little while, I think, yes. A few weeks, maybe one or two months.'

'Oh.' She wondered then: wondered very sadly, if Luc had been pressing her to go home so that he could be rid of her, could return to his wife. He had been very duplicitous; it was perfectly possible.

'I was very fearful for you. And so very sad when I realised you had discovered it. Although it set you free to leave. I was glad of that at least. But you must believe me, Mam'selle, you were brave. Very brave and very true. For a long time.'

'Oh,' she said again. This was so different from what she had thought. She really had forgotten he had urged her to go: absolutely forgotten it. It made everything seem rather different . . .

Lucas left, swiftly, made his way back to the hotel, changed his shirt and apologised to Venetia for not having any money with which to buy her a drink.

'I really wanted to.'

'Lucas, it couldn't matter less. Honestly. It was sweet of you to think of it even.'

He seemed rather quiet, she thought, quiet and slightly distracted.

Perhaps meeting Madame André had upset him; Adele had been afraid it might.

★

'Who lives up there now?' Adele said suddenly, indicating the top floor.

'Oh – another young couple. With another baby.'

'*Plus ça change*,' said Adele, smiling. She felt much happier suddenly. '*Plus c'est la même chose*. That's an expression in England too, you know.'

'It is?' Madame André hesitated. 'Would you like to go up there, see the place again? I'm sure they would be pleased to show you.'

'Oh—' She flinched from that. 'Well – I'm not sure. Not sure if I'm brave enough.'

'You! Not brave? After what you did, made that journey all alone – come, I will ask them.'

And so it was that Adele stood once again in the small apartment, looking over the rooftops, and remembered not only happiness, not only love, but bitterness and the fierce, unbearable pain of betrayal. A betrayal, she now knew, that had actually rewarded courage, loyalty and selflessness. And she was able to look, finally, and with forgiveness, at herself and her flight from Paris, so many years ago . . .

CHAPTER 34

It was to be nearly all hers. It felt terrible; she felt terrible. She would have given anything not to have it: not just because of her mother, but because it felt so wrong, so − so overloaded, so uncomfortable. Like eating a huge meal, and being asked to sit down for two hours and offered another. She just didn't want it all. She really didn't.

Jamie had talked her through it. Explained that the lawyers had decided that everyone could be informed of their entitlements, since there were no great complications, there were ample funds for the taxes and death duties, and it at least enabled everyone to get on with their lives.

'Your mother left almost everything to you. In trust, that is. Most of her personal fortune, and Lyttons in its entirety. Apart from the thirty-two per cent of Lyttons London owned by the family.'

'And they're going to buy the rest?'

'They hope to.'

'Can't I just give it to them?'

'No, Jenna, you can't. It doesn't work like that.'

'But I want to.'

'Darling, you can't.'

She had been fiddling with a stapler on his desk; she suddenly threw it down, petulantly childlike, got up, and walked over to the window and looked out. He watched her. She was still very, very easily upset, trembled on the edge of her raw grief. She struggled, day by day, struggled to be brave, to cope with it all, to behave as she knew her mother would have wanted, but it was horribly hard. The grief caught her unawares; came out of nowhere, tore at her when she was doing the simplest, happiest things, riding, walking on the shore at Southampton, shopping, giggling with Cathy at a TV programme. It hurt even to watch her as he was now: quietly patient, waiting for her to recover herself. Again.

'It's so unfair,' she said suddenly, then managed one of her rather fierce smiles. 'So unfair. Tell me, is there anything for Mr and Mrs Mills?'

'Yes, there is. Ten thousand dollars. And the cottage for the rest of their lives. And five thousand for Maria.'

'That's really nice. I'm glad. What about the Millers? Billy and Joan. Lots, I hope.'

'Quite a lot. One hundred thousand dollars. Whatever that is in pounds.'

'That's really good. And – Charlie? What about him?'

'Well, first of all, your mother has appointed him as your guardian.'

'Well, of course she would have done. She knew how much we loved each other.'

'I know. But it still needed to be confirmed, legally. In her will. So he has day-to-day care of you.'

'Fine. And did she leave him any money?'

'She did. Two hundred thousand dollars.'

She smiled happily. 'That's great. I'm so very glad. He deserves it.'

She obviously felt, Jamie thought, in her touchingly childlike way, that it was a reasonable bequest, the sort of thing Charlie would be pleased about. Actually, of course, it was an insult.

He had been insulted: insulted and outraged. Jamie could see that. He had fought to keep it under control, had said how very generous, but he had left as soon as he politely could, his face white, his mouth set.

Difficult: very difficult. Of course it was sensible. Whatever Barty had left him, he would have run through in no time. For Jenna's sake it had been decided not to pursue the matter of the forged cheques, for which Charlie had been reluctantly grateful. But it would be very difficult: to be the widower of someone with a personal estate of around three million dollars, and to be the guardian of her extremely rich child, when all you had been left was two hundred thousand dollars. Jamie actually wondered why Barty had left Charlie anything at all, why he had even featured in her will; but of course all her affairs were in perfect order, they always had been, and she would not have risked his getting his hands on her fortune, however remote the chance might be.

How could she have done that, Charlie thought, walking so fast, so hard up Sixth Avenue that he kept crashing into people, almost knocking them over, angry with them as well as with himself. He thought he might laugh, at first: laugh out loud. At the sheer bloody ludicrousness of it. Two hundred thousand bucks. To him. To her husband. Out of an estate of – what? Three million easily, he had calculated. If you added in the houses and the shares and so on and so forth. Before tax, anyway. It was horrible: an insult. Worse than nothing, in a way. That would have been a drama, he would have attracted interest, sympathy, rather than the embarrassed looks he knew he'd get now.

That was how she rated him, as worth little more than her servants.

Look at him, her will said, look carefully, I want you all to see that he cannot be trusted with any more, he doesn't deserve it, he will waste it, lose it, he must not have it. OK, so he'd lied to her a little; he'd still loved her, cared for her, made her happy, made her laugh, and looked after her child, her grieving, broken child as if he had been her own father. Of course Barty hadn't expected that: hadn't expected to die, hadn't expected to leave him. But it still meant the same thing: that was how she rated him; very, very low. It would scarcely cover his loan repayment. He felt absolutely diminished.

He began to feel something entirely new that afternoon: only a tiny sliver of a thing, but most certainly there, drifting about in his head. He had been violently jealous of all the Lyttons for some time. That went without saying. But this was new and more dangerous than that: and it centred on Jenna.

There had been nothing of the company for the Lyttons; somehow they had all hoped, against the odds, that there might be. That she would give them a further percentage. Of course there were the share options and Barty had hardly expected to die so young, she had imagined growing old in the company, exactly as Celia had, and no doubt felt she had done more than enough for them. But – still. They had hoped.

To recover something that had been absolutely theirs, and had become absolutely hers, partly through her own efforts to be sure, but mostly by an accident, or a series of accidents, of chance meetings, love affairs, wars, deaths, bequests, going back into the mists of time, into the estates of the Elliotts.

It hurt Celia the most, of course; she felt it personally, felt it as a deliberate blow. How could she have done that? Barty, the child she had saved from poverty and cruelty and neglect, Barty, who had been educated and trained and groomed by her for the position she finally reached, Barty, who knew what Lyttons had meant to Celia, holding as much of her heart as any of her children. How could she not have felt bound to return it to her, and to her family, in the event of her own death? It was a very cruel final blow.

Lucas was different somehow. Adele couldn't quite work out how. He had been sweet to her for a long time now, thoughtful and affectionate; but since going to Paris, he had become somehow less arrogant, less inclined to criticise everyone, even his cousins, who had always been his targets. And he spent more time with Clio, which pleased her enormously, and actually wrote thank-you letters, without Adele having to nag him, and asked her what she would like him to wear for any social event to which he was accompanying her.

She didn't comment on it, of course, and he seemed perfectly happy; but she did wonder what might have brought it about. Maybe just meeting Madame André, feeling that part of his life less mysterious and confused. Or that he was closer to his roots.

She would probably never know; but she was certainly very grateful for it.

Jay was finding the delay in settling the company's affairs almost unbearable. Marcus Forrest was tightening his screws day by day; only the previous week he had blocked the purchase of a novel, which Jay had wanted very much to buy, and refused even to consider it, without really giving any explanation, apart from the fact he just felt it was overpriced and slight. Jay, who had encouraged the author and his agent into thinking he was certain to buy it, had to endure the humiliation of telling them that, after all, he must turn it down. The word was out all over London by lunch time, that Jay Lytton was now in the pocket of New York, and that his judgement wasn't worth the time of day.

He found himself increasingly at the receiving end of memos instructing him not to buy this, not to publish that, to wait for a decision while Forrest read something, which often meant he lost the book in question anyway. It was driving him mad. He was still capable of brilliant ideas, lateral thinking, following hunches against considerable opposition – his coup for the year had been his plan to publish a thriller in three parts, the first just out. He had fought the entire editorial board, apart from Celia, who backed him with huge enthusiasm, and had won. It had proved not only a great promotional success, attracting vast publicity, but a financial one; the bottom line would be three successful books for the price of one. The author was still reeling at his own naïveté.

After that, Jay had felt he might win more battles; but it proved to be a one-off. Forrest plainly regarded him as yesterday's man. Which was hard to take at the age of forty-four, when he actually felt he should have up to twenty years ahead of him. He didn't like to contemplate what would happen to him if they were unable to buy the company, if they couldn't raise the money, or the trustees decided to set the price too high, thereby enabling other, richer purchasers to get hold of Lyttons. He would probably find himself out of a job.

Jay was by nature optimistic; it was one of his most endearing characteristics. And the optimism was well-founded. The nickname Lucky Lytton, first bestowed on him at school, had followed him through university, a hugely dangerous war, and indeed for most of his career. Jay just never got caught. Where others were beaten for truancy or smoking or drinking, sent down from university for having girls in their rooms, trapped into marriage by unwanted pregnancy, wounded in battle, Jay Lytton, having run the same risks, emerged unscathed. He had a gloriously happy marriage, a beautiful family and a success that was partly, at least, quite unearned. But now it seemed, the famous luck was running out; fate was finally demanding her revenge.

Izzie and the boys had also been sent for by Jamie and told of their inheritance. Ten thousand dollars for Izzie, and five each for the boys 'to be invested in Neill & Parker,' Jamie had said, 'or whatever company Neill & Parker might become—'

'What, you mean like Neill, Parker & J.W. Thompson?' asked Mike.

'Something like that, yes,' said Jamie. 'The point is, it's for the company. Otherwise it reverts to Barty's estate.'

'It'll be invested all right,' said Nick. 'How amazing.'

Jamie smiled rather wearily. 'She was an amazing person.'

They went down to Chumleys, the three of them, and proceeded to get very drunk.

'I can't believe it,' said Izzie. 'I really, really can't. It's such a lot of money.'

'*You* can't believe it! How do you think we feel? Five thousand bucks apiece. All for Neill & Parker.'

'I know. It is so extraordinarily generous. Oh dear,' she smiled a shaky smile, 'I'd much rather she was here.'

They were silent, suddenly ashamed to be so openly celebrating their good fortune.

Izzie looked at them. 'Listen. It's fine,' she said, 'she'd be so pleased we were pleased. Anyway, it won't be ours for a long time. Years possibly, Jamie said. I quite like that, it makes me feel less – greedy.'

'Yeah. What do you think you'll do with your money, Princess?'

'I haven't the faintest idea. I thought I might buy a new rug.'

'Isabella Brooke,' said Nick, kissing her tenderly, 'you sure know how to live.'

It amazed her how much she loved him, and how much he loved her. They were, as he often said, quite appallingly happy.

Neill & Parker was also doing well: not brilliantly, but well. The bulk of their business was still books; and they weren't making enough to tell Joanie Morell to disappear up her own arse, which was Mike's most dearly held ambition. But the gallery account had grown, and so had another account, a stationery chain, and Izzie's idea for the gallery's radio campaign had led them into negotiations with a small record company. They were still in the same office, and the three of them still did all the work, but there was just about enough of both work and money to fund another employee if necessary.

The boys had been worried about never paying Barty back, but clearly she hadn't minded in the very least. She had bequeathed them her investment in the company as well as the money.

Izzie still missed Barty terribly, there was a huge gap in her life and always would be; but at least she and Nick both saw a lot of Jenna, invited her over to dinner, with Charlie and Cathy. Nick was less keen on Charlie than Izzie was, he said he wouldn't exactly trust him with his last cent, but he was happy to spend time with him, if that was what Izzie and Jenna wanted.

Of Geordie they heard nothing, apart from the letter he wrote to Izzie when Barty died, saying how sad he was, and how much he knew she would miss her, 'as indeed shall I. A very great loss to all our lives.' It was as if none of them had ever known him; Izzie found it rather disturbing.

He was still living in Washington, had published a new, very successful novel, and was reportedly having an affair with a young editor.

'Poor girl,' Izzie said, when she heard this on the literary gossip line. And meant it.

Noni told her he had never been back to England, never tried to see Adele; she was divorcing him. He never saw Clio, it was all very sad.

'But Maman is so much better, even beginning to take photographs again. And Lucas is really quite human! He went to Paris with Maman and met the old lady who was the concierge where they lived before the war; it seems to have been a very good experience for him, I don't know why. He's even talking of joining Lyttons if he's allowed, after National Service. Can you believe that?

'Clio seems all right, although I know she still misses Geordie dreadfully. She's started at a new school, and is very grown up. I've promised to bring her out to see you and Jenna next summer. Jenna says we can all go out to South Lodge.'

Izzie had liked that idea: very much. Taking care of Clio seemed to her a modest reparation for what she still saw as her sins.

She and Nick now lived in a very nice, if modest apartment, in the Village; very similar to the one Izzie had had, very close by, only a bit bigger.

Mike had taken over the lease on Izzie's old one. He said he needed to be near them, otherwise he didn't know how he would get by, what with having to breathe in and out on his own and so on. It was an act of course, and anyway, he had a very nice Jewish girlfriend now, whose only ambition was to marry him and have babies. Mike, who wasn't even sure about the marriage part, let alone the babies, was, as he put it, letting her wait a little for him.

Nick occasionally talked to Izzie about getting married, but she told him she wasn't interested.

'It's perfect how it is, why change it?'

'Most girls don't see it like that.'

'I'm not most girls.'

'I know that. I thank God for it. Well – we'll get married when there's a little Lady Isabella on the way. How's that?'

'Fine.'

It was her only worry: the only cloud on her golden happiness, that the awful abortion might in some way have affected her ability to have children. Celia's gynaecologist had assured her it shouldn't, but you never knew . . .

Anyway, that was far in the future. Well – quite far.

Giles was still very depressed. It was not unusual for Helena to find him slumped at his desk after dinner in the evening, not working as he had said he was going to do, but staring ahead, blankly miserable, as if contemplating a future he did not want.

He felt physically ill; he had a permanent headache, he couldn't sleep, and he felt nauseated much of the time.

Things were not going well for him at Lyttons, either; his mother, in her own grief, was particularly querulous and difficult, questioning his smallest decision, Marcus Forrest clearly thought he was a complete idiot, and ignored him as much as possible, his paperback list was failing (largely due, he knew, to lack of a promotional budget in the face of fierce competition from not only Penguin, but also from Pan and Fontana), and the purchase of their shares seemed as far away as ever.

But he had one thing which was relieving his misery: a book. It was an odd story: early that spring, just after Barty had died in fact, a woman had sent in a manuscript – some of it handwritten – about her life in the Highlands. She lived in a remote croft and was virtually a hermit; her main companions were the deer who roamed the hills.

The book was almost a diary of her life with the deer – 'You should call it *Deer Diary*,' Keir had remarked with a grin when he heard about it. Many of the deer were almost tame and she knew them by name.

It made surprisingly charming reading, and was not without drama. She found a seriously injured doe one day, caught up in some undergrowth, apparently shot by a stalker, and managed to get her home in her truck and nurse her back to health; another magnificent stag visited the croft every morning, ate the bundle of greenstuff she had prepared for him and then submitted himself to being stroked and talked to; a fawn, abandoned by its mother, was raised in the croft garden and grew up to be as faithful as a dog. There was a harrowing description of a fawn's breech birth, with the author acting as midwife, and another of the death of a doe, apparently from poisoning. All the creatures had names and personalities; there were breathtaking descriptions of the surrounding countryside; and some moments that were genuinely moving.

Joanna Scott was also something of an artist, and submitted a couple of watercolours with her manuscript; Giles was very keen to buy it, suitably extended, to commission several more paintings, and sell the book as a Christmas gift.

Jay was sceptical, and so were several of the editors, and Keir was hugely amused when he heard about it, but Celia thought it was a wonderful idea from the beginning.

'With the English love of animals, how can it fail? I'd back it, Giles, definitely. Get the woman down, make her an offer.'

Joanna Scott appeared in the offices a few weeks later; she was very tall, very thin, with a gaunt, weatherbeaten face and long, straggling grey hair, falling over the shoulders of her lumber jacket, and an accent so thick it was hard to understand her.

'Not much use for the publicity photographs,' said Jay.

'Oh, we can tidy her up. And anyway, we don't need to take a photograph,' said Celia.

'No – the public will want to see her, it's that sort of book.'

'Well, maybe they can't,' said Celia briskly, 'we'll get her to paint the croft instead. That will do.'

The book had been scheduled for the following Christmas: 'It's an absolute natural for a gift-book. And I'd be worried about other publishers poaching the idea if we postponed it too long.'

The whole thing amused the rest of the family: it was so unlike Giles and so unlike the sort of book he would normally want to publish.

'Whatever next, royal memoirs?' said Elspeth with a giggle. Like most publishers, Lyttons affected to despise the huge success of the memoirs of Marion Crawford, governess to the little princesses.

'Charlie, are you all right?'

He smiled at Jenna rather wearily.

'Yes, I'm all right.'

'You look awfully down. And tired.'

'I am a bit.'

'Why? Specially, I mean?'

'Well – my business isn't going too well, I'm afraid.'

'Oh Charlie, I'm sorry. So sorry. I suppose – well, I suppose it wasn't a very good time for you to launch it.'

'Not very, no. It was kind of hard to concentrate.'

'What can I do for you? Make you some tea, fix you a Martini?'

She had often heard him telling people that her mother made the best Martinis in Manhattan; Jenna was working hard at mastering the skill.

'A Martini'd be nice. Thank you, sweetheart. You're very good to me.'

'You've been pretty good to me.'

'The thing is,' he said, slowly, 'I'm going to have to sell it. The business,

I mean. It's just not paying its way. And I think – with a bit more time – it'd have been all right.'

'Charlie, that's terrible. You can't do that. I'll – I'll speak to the trustees.'

She knew already it was fairly hopeless; but she went on trying. She was beginning to grow very tired of Jamie and Kyle. They were so – obstructive.

They were obstructive that day. 'I'm sorry, Jenna,' said Kyle, 'but we can't touch the money in your trust fund. Not at the moment. Even if we wanted to.'

'Which you don't.' She glared at them. 'Well, I've got an idea. I can borrow against the fund. I've read about that, in the papers.'

She had taken to reading the financial pages; following the progress of her stock, studying other things which she could one day put her money into.

'Sorry, darling. You can't.'

'Why not? I can just go to a bank, or Charlie could ask them.'

'You can't, because you're a minor. Charlie can't, because the trust isn't in his name.'

'Oh –' She turned away, looked out of the window of Jamie's penthouse. It was a lovely day; the trees in Central Park were just turning gold, the sky was purest blue. How could she help him: how?

'I think you're so mean,' she said, 'Charlie's been so good to me, always. I want to help him. He's in real trouble, his business is failing, he hasn't been able to concentrate on it, he needs time. And he doesn't get the money from the will for ages—'

They looked at her; their expressions were identical, embarrassed, wary, closed.

'Look – couldn't you lend him some money, Jamie? I really want you to. I could pay you back, you could take it out of my trust fund. Or when we get this wretched probate thing. Why is it taking so long, anyway?'

'Because it's so complex. Because there are so many elements involved. Because—'

'Yeah, yeah. I heard all that. Look, isn't that an idea, you lending Charlie some money? It would mean so much to me, I hate to see him so worried and unhappy.'

'Jenna, we can't. Sorry.' It was Kyle; clearly wretched. 'We don't have money to pour into a failing business. Money we might not get back. Sorry, Jenna. The answer's no. It has to be.'

'Well, I think you're horrible,' she said. She was very upset, near to tears. 'I think you should do it in memory of my mother. She loved Charlie, she'd just hate to see this sort of thing going on.'

'She probably would,' said Jamie gently, 'but—'

'Don't say it again. That you can't do anything about it. I'll have to think of something myself.'

When she got home that day, Charlie was sitting watching TV. He looked very down.

'Hi sweetheart.'

'Hi Charlie. No good, I'm afraid. I've tried and tried to get Jamie and Kyle to help, but they just go on and on about the will and the trust fund. I'm so sorry.'

'That's all right, poppet. Thank you for trying.'

'I'll fix you a Martini. Where's Cathy?'

'Out with some boy.'

'Nice?'

'He seemed OK.' He watched her while she made the Martini, smiled bravely at her when she handed it to him.

'Thanks, sweetheart. Anyway,' – his voice was very casual – 'you know what I was thinking about?'

'No, I don't.'

'I don't know why, but – well, your – I guess they'd be your stepbrother and sister. The Elliotts . . .'

'Oh yes?' She was pouring herself a Coca-Cola.

'You never met them, did you?'

'No, never. I'm sure they wouldn't want to meet me. My father divorced their mother. And then married mine.'

'Yes, but there were a few years in between. What were their names, do you remember? And how old were they?'

'Well, the girl was called Kate. I can't remember what the boy's name was. She must be about – goodness, seventeen. Actually, that's right. I saw a photograph of her in one of the papers the other day. At the Infirmary Ball, I think. Or something like that. You know about all that social rubbish?'

'You know I do.' He looked put out.

'Sorry. Well anyway, she's very pretty. I'll see if I can find it—'

'Really? Yes, I'd like that. Anyway, what I was thinking of, was how odd it is that you had never met them. And they'd known your dad. It might be kind of interesting, don't you think?'

'Not really,' said Jenna, 'no.' She did feel quite strongly about that; the father she had never known was hers, she didn't want to share him with anyone. Especially his children, children who had actually known him, seen him, talked to him, sat on his knee.

'They must really be rich,' Charlie said.

'Think so?' She was rummaging through the pile of papers on the coffee table.

'Well of course. They got most of the money, didn't they? Your dad's money?'

'Not sure,' she said, and then her voice was suddenly sharper. 'It doesn't really interest me, Charlie, you know. I hate the whole subject of money. Especially at the moment. And especially who got what. Can we change the subject, please?'

'Of course. Sorry, honey. I didn't mean to – upset you.'

He looked remorseful. She felt bad. It had been tactless of her, talking like that about money, when he was so worried about it. She gave him a kiss.

'That's OK. I guess I'm a bit touchy. Anyway, here she is. Miss Kate Elliott. All done up in white. Look at those gross gloves. Oh, and here's the brother, Bartholomew, that's his name. He looks all right. Not a bit like my dad, as far as I can tell from the old pictures, but . . .' She handed him the paper.

'Thanks, darling.' He took it, studied the photograph; he seemed more cheerful all of a sudden. She was pleased. Although it was a funny thing to get cheered up by, the thought of some dumb girl's coming-out party.

CHAPTER 35

Elspeth wondered if it was all right to feel so happy. With the family – well, half the family – still so shocked by Barty's death.

Of course she hadn't known her very well. Barty had been living in New York since 1946 and had been away for much of the war; she'd been fond of her of course, but Barty's death had made very little difference to her life – apart from the presence of Marcus Forrest in the office from time to time and she actually rather liked that. It would have been more than her life was worth to say so, the others all hated him, but she thought he was quite a good thing. He was clearly very clever and he was also very charming and good-looking. He seemed light years younger to her than Giles and Jay, and he always made time to chat to her each time he came over. He would seek her out if she was in the office and talk to her about what she was doing, and when he called a general editorial meeting he always invited her. She had managed to persuade Keir to let her attend.

'Please,' she had said, smiling sweetly at him over the supper table, 'please, Keir. We can't afford to upset him. After all, he's very important to you, isn't he? What possible harm could it do to Cecilia, just one little meeting.'

Keir scowled at her, said there seemed to be a growing number of little meetings, and picked up the paper. But he didn't say any more about it. Elspeth took that as consent.

She sometimes felt she was walking a tightrope in her life; swaying this way and that, nearly losing her balance, righting herself just in time. It seemed very difficult and very dangerous, and if she did fall off it would be deadly, but she knew it was worth it.

She worked quite a lot these days; enabled to do so, not – of course – by a nanny, but by a nice woman called Mrs Wilson, who lived in some flats further down Battersea Park Road. Mrs Wilson came in initially to babysit, when Keir and Elspeth went out in the evenings, and expressed – to Keir as well as to Elspeth – a desire to see more of Cecilia. 'She's a beautiful wee thing.'

Elspeth said promptly that there could be no question of that, she liked to look after Cecilia herself; but over the next two or three months, she took to asking Mrs Wilson to come in occasionally while she attended an editorial meeting – Keir had reluctantly agreed to it.

The fact that the Wilsons were Scottish, that Donald Wilson taught in a primary school in Balham and could enjoy idealistic conversations with Keir about the iniquities of the English education system, undoubtedly helped Elspeth's cause. By that autumn, Mrs Wilson was coming in three times a week, the hours extending so gradually that Keir was scarcely aware of it, arriving after breakfast – when he had left for the office – and staying until Cecilia's bath-time.

It was wonderful to be working again, and she had such plans: a romantic thriller – rather like a latter day *Rebecca*, she explained to Jay, 'only more psychological, sort of Hitchcocky, really' – a series of children's books, 'but not expensive – paperbacks, twenty-six of them, about a series of little people who live under the pier at the seaside, each one with a name beginning with a different letter of the alphabet. The man who brought the first two in to show me is just so sweet and clever.' She had also commissioned a guide for women on cooking, sewing, decorating and gardening, called *Mrs Perfect*, 'but the title's tongue-in-cheek, it's for women like me who can't do anything practical, with really simple diagrams to follow'.

And she and Clementine were already working on a new novel about a girl who found out, at the age of nineteen, that she'd been adopted.

Like Celia, Elspeth felt brought to life by work; like Celia, she loved her family, but at the same time felt that if she wasn't working, she was somehow not properly functioning, only marking time, playing at life.

'I feel myself getting slower and slower, running down like a clock,' she said to Celia one day when she was in Lytton House with a manuscript; Celia smiled at her and said she had once made exactly the same remark to Lord Arden.

'But he doesn't understand, I'm afraid.'

'Keir understands, all right,' said Elspeth, 'he just doesn't like it.'

She supposed she was a little tired. The baby was due in another month – although it felt like years since she had thought she was going to be sick at Kit and Clementine's wedding – but she felt so well, so revitalised, that there was none of the drained exhaustion she had felt when Cecilia was nearly due. She looked back at the dreadful, miserable days in Glasgow with something close to disbelief: how had she endured that, why had she endured it?

Occasionally, when she had the time, she pondered on the future. Without being over-optimistic, or even arrogant, it looked rather good to her. She and Keir were, potentially at least, a great team: clever, talented and, as her grandmother often remarked, 'you remind me of Oliver and myself when we were young, your lives and your work are intertwined. It makes for a good partnership, Elspeth, you must nurture that.'

Celia continued to adore Keir; she was fiercely proud of him, of having her faith in him justified. And Marcus Forrest also thought a lot of Keir, listening to his opinions, taking a particular interest in everything he was editing, suggesting to Jay that Keir took over certain projects and books. Elspeth could see that this had its dangers. Giles certainly resented it, Jay was irritated by it, her mother had warned her that it could be counter-productive, especially Celia's adoration.

'I'm delighted, darling, of course. But Granny can't go on for ever, and he could be storing up a lot of resentment. Which will rebound on him when she does finally retire.'

'Oh, Mummy, do you really think it'll ever happen?'

'What, her retirement? God knows,' said Venetia with a sigh. 'I half dread it, half long for it. She's still so bloody good at her job.'

She seldom used strong language; Elspeth looked at her in surprise. She was edgy of course, they all were. Everything was difficult for them. Not just the business of the shares, but the arrival of Marcus Forrest in London every few months and the tension that created. He was increasingly exercising his editorial prerogative, vetoing purchases, promotions, even titles. It all made for an atmosphere which was the opposite of calm.

Forrest was Machiavellian in his management style; he worked with first one and then another editor, setting up with a chance remark here, a mild criticism there, a steady loss of the feeling of cohesion, of common purpose in the editorial team which Oliver and Celia had worked so hard to create. The utterly loyal editorial force that had been Lyttons was slowly becoming something more individually based and self-centred; Jay and Celia felt it was a bad thing, Elspeth and Keir, and a couple of the other younger editors, could see that it had its virtues, nurturing as it did a certain edgy creativity, a willingness to explore new ideas.

Certainly, Elspeth thought, she and Keir were the only members of the family who were secretly rather enjoying it all. They didn't admit it, of course, not even to one another.

They were both rather pleased by Lucas's suggestion, made to his grandmother, that perhaps he might join Lyttons, after his National Service. 'The more youth in the company the better,' Elspeth said, 'on the family side, I mean. And I believe his father was a brilliant publisher, so it ought to be in his genes in a big way.'

'What really ought to happen,' said Keir, 'is that it should stop being owned by the family. It should be made into a public company. When all this is over.'

She stared at him.

'But Keir – why?'

'Because it would bring some money in, that's why. Enable us to do what we need to do. The family company is a thing of the past, Elspeth.'

'Oh really?' she said. 'Well, that's very interesting. You haven't seemed to mind it yourself. Up to now.'

At which he told her she should wake up, that they all should.

'Remember the dinosaurs, Elspeth. I'm not saying any more than that.'

She told him he'd be wise not to; but later thought about what he had said, and even began to wonder if perhaps he wasn't right.

Celia's main preoccupation, apart from the share valuation, was General Dugdale's memoirs. Or rather, as she said to Sebastian, his memoir.

'He is appallingly slow. What I've read is marvellous, but—'

'And how much is that?'

She hesitated; then said, 'One chapter.'

'One! Celia, that's terrible. What's he doing?'

'I don't honestly know. Every time I ring up, Dorothy tells me he's working on them. But he won't let me go down and help. We'd hoped to publish them this summer, but I'm afraid now it's going to have to be later. It's the only big non-fiction book we've got. And you know that dreadful Marcus Forrest complained in the most unpleasant way about the advance.'

'I do seem to remember you saying something about it. Several times.'

Celia ignored this.

'I can see I'll have to go over there soon, just sit with him and try and work something up. But—' she sighed.

Sebastian looked at her.

'You look tired, my darling. I know you hate that, but you do.'

'I know,' she said, surprising him. 'I feel tired.'

'What does the doctor say? I suppose you haven't seen one?'

She looked at him. 'Actually, I have.'

'And?'

'And he's sending me to some chest man.'

'Oh,' said Sebastian. 'Oh, I see. Well – no doubt he'll put you right. Give you some medicine to take. You have stopped smoking, haven't you?'

'Sebastian, you know I've stopped smoking. It's dreadful. Hasn't done any good, either. I told them it wouldn't, they didn't take any notice.'

'Well . . .' he looked at her and there was great concern and love in his eyes. 'You see this chest chap. He'll know what to do, I'm sure.'

'I hope so,' she said, and sighed again, then visibly hauled herself together. 'Now let's talk about your new book, Sebastian. I hope that's not going to be late.'

'Of course it is. When did I ever deliver a manuscript on time? Except for the first one, of course. The important one.'

'The one that made you famous,' she said.

'No,' he said, taking her hand and kissing it, 'no, I mean the one that led me to you.'

Elspeth had been working on some proofs one late-September afternoon, when she was suddenly aware of a rather fierce pain in her back. She ignored it; she knew it couldn't be the baby, there were at least four weeks to go.

Half an hour later, it had grown rather worse; she stood up to try to ease it, felt a gushing between her legs, and looked down to see a large puddle forming on the floor.

She walked rather gingerly towards the door, opened it, and called Mrs Wilson; Cecilia toddled up and looked at the puddle behind her.

'Naughty Mummy,' she said.

'I know,' said Elspeth, and giggled; then as a stab of pain caught her somewhere rather more familiar than her back, she lost all desire to laugh and said, 'Mrs Wilson, I think – well, I'm sure – I'm in labour. Could you call the ambulance please?'

Three painful but blessedly brief hours later Robert Brown entered the world.

Keir was ecstatic. It was quite annoying how ecstatic he was, Elspeth thought. He hadn't been nearly as moved by Cecilia's arrival.

'It's because it's a boy, darling,' said Venetia, when Elspeth complained to her the next day. 'They're so utterly childish. I never could understand it. Daddy was just the same. They seem to think it proves their manhood or some such nonsense. He is a rather sweet baby, Elspeth, he looks just like you.'

'Do you think so? Granny said the same. Well, she said he was unmistakably a Lytton.'

'Granny says that about all the babies. Lovely to call him Robert, after Uncle Robert, I presume. He'll be thrilled, dear old darling.'

'I know, I thought so. Unfortunately, Keir thinks it's after his father. And he's already told him.'

'Well, that's all right. They'll both be happy. How do you feel?'

'Fine. It was all over so quickly. I feel as if I could get up and go straight back to work.'

'Well don't. Good heavens, Elspeth, who are those wonderful flowers from? That huge bouquet over there, all white? Make mine look very mean.'

'Oh,' said Elspeth carelessly, 'Marcus Forrest.'

'Goodness!' Venetia looked at her. 'Who's teacher's pet, then?'

'Me, I hope,' said Elspeth, with a dazzling smile.

★

454

A share price had finally been agreed: it meant that Lyttons London did indeed have to find two million pounds.

'Well that's fine,' said Celia, 'I see no problem with that. We can just send Mr Charteris off to those people, and Lyttons will soon be ours again.'

She was suddenly in high spirits, the tiredness and depression quite forgotten; Jay looked at her with a mixture of affection and incredulity. How could a woman of such sophistication, a woman who still entertained some of the greatest names in publishing at her dinner table – only last week he had dined there with Mark Longman, John Murray and Leonard Russell of the *Saturday Book*, marvelling at the way she could still charm and dazzle anyone she chose, and revel in being able to do so – a woman who had nurtured Lyttons for fifty years, virtually single-handed through two wars, be so absolutely naive about anything pertaining to business? He supposed it was one of her talents – always had been – to close her mind to anything disagreeable, to ignore difficulties, to concentrate solely on what she wanted and how she was going to get it. He wished he had the same ability.

'Harold Charteris suggests that we see these people ourselves, ICFC. Rather than rushing around talking to investors like—'

'Yes, yes, like bulls in china shops. Of course. Good idea. Can you fix that, Mr Charteris?'

Harold Charteris said he could.

ICFC were unable to help.

'They have a limited pot of cash, that's the simplest way I can describe it,' said Charteris, 'and at the moment, it's fully committed. However, all is not lost. They gave me the name of another outfit, more initials I'm afraid, Lady Celia, BISC, short for British Investors in Small Companies. Known in the trade, rather inevitably, as Biscuit. I've spoken to them, asked if they can help, and they were quite optimistic. The first thing they would want to do is send one of their researchers into the company, to see if we are the sort of outfit they would like to work with.'

'What you mean is snooping around, watching us work,' said Giles. 'Good God. I don't know that we'd like that very much, Mr Charteris.'

'I'm afraid, as the saying goes, you'll have to lump it, Mr Lytton. If you want to proceed with these people. I do assure you it's entirely standard. And then we need to have ready what amounts to a portfolio on the company: cash flow details, accounts for at least the past five years, list of assets, work in progress, all that sort of thing. We should get to work on that straight away. Time is running out on us. Only about three months left.'

Giles sighed. This was obviously going to be very hard work. His depression had not eased; he still felt literally heartsore. The only thing boosting his morale was the incredible success of *Deer Mountain*, as they had decided to call *Deer Diary*.

The book had proved, against all the odds, to be a huge success; the initial print order of twenty thousand had moved up to thirty, then fifty and finally, by late-November, an unthinkable seventy. It was clearly going to be the hit book of that Christmas; people literally stood in queues for it, put their names down for more copies. Venetia had launched a highly successful promotion, selling limited-edition prints of the illustrations with the book; a jewellery company had even suggested a *Deer Mountain* charm to go on charm bracelets. That had been too much for Giles.

'We're a publishing company,' he had said to Venetia, 'we're not in the novelty business.'

She had been very cross.

And now there was a children's version planned for the following year, and a possible sequel the year after that; the family had completely stopped sniggering about it. Even Marcus Forrest was impressed . . .

Izzie had spent a lot of time telling herself there was nothing to worry about. They weren't even trying to have a baby, for heaven's sake. It would have been a terrible idea, they were so busy building up Neill & Parker, they worked night and day, and they'd got the most wonderfully exciting new account, a small publishing company called McGowan Benchley.

They were the perfect client, young, innovative, and fun. As Mike put it, they had balls. They were staking everything on their launch; Bruce McGowan had remortgaged his house, and Johnny Benchley had sold his beloved Cadillac, his sailing boat and, as he put it, sent his children out to work. What he meant was he'd sent his wife out to work, which meant the children going into a crèche. They had found some premises on the West Side and seemed to spend twenty-four hours a day there. McGowan Benchley and Neill & Parker had clearly been made for one another.

Neill & Parker had pitched against a much bigger agency, who had given a brilliant presentation the day before they had, had spent a lot of money turning their boardroom into a bookshop, mocking up expensive posters and showcards. The word on the street was that they had got the account, that they were unbeatable. There was one thing they didn't have, though; and that was Izzie.

Izzie had come up with a copyline and a concept which, as Johnny Benchley put it, just blew them away. After two weeks of doing something that literally felt like beating her brains out, she had gone for a walk one day, partly to get away from the boys and the enraging sight of their eyes fixed hopefully on her every time she looked up. She had wandered into a thrift shop and found an old dictionary of quotations which she bought for Nick, who collected dictionaries of every kind. Flicking through it in the coffee shop at Macy's where she stopped for a rest, she had found a quotation by Mark Twain, from a speech he had made to a club in New York.

'A classic: something everybody wants to have read and nobody wants to read.'

She put it down, stared ahead of her for a bit, then read it again. And again.

Two days later, after thirty-six hours without sleep, they went, rather bleary-eyed, to McGowan Benchley's offices and presented her copyline: 'McGowan Benchley. For tomorrow's classics. The ones you'll want to read today.'

The account was worth quite a lot of money: a two-hundred-and-fifty thousand-dollar launch, which meant a fat fee. It was going to pay for a new office.

They were beginning to feel financially sound, even before Barty's gift to them. And that had turned Izzie's thoughts in the direction of all sorts of rather serious things. Like buying a proper place to live. Getting married. And – having babies. Just now and again, because she did know Nick wanted babies one day and wouldn't mind too terribly if they had an accident, she had – well, risked things a bit. The first time, she had been quite worried, because she was so sure it would work and she'd have to confess to Nick; the second, she tried not to think about it; the third, she was actually disappointed; and now, she was getting worried, because she was beginning to be sure it wouldn't work.

She thought about it more than she ought to, she knew. She couldn't help it. If she hadn't had the abortion it wouldn't even have crossed her mind. But the guilt of that, the anxiety because she had never told Nick about it, the fear of what he might say, the terror that she had been damaged in some way and so could never have babies: that guilt and fear not only crossed her mind, they criss-crossed it, backwards and forwards, again and again, wearing a groove in it.

Only, of course, it was silly. Very silly. But – she worried just the same.

One morning in late November Marcus Forrest called Elspeth into the office which he had made his own, saying he would like to speak to her. Elspeth went in, rather as if to a headmaster's study, her heart thudding, but Marcus smiled at her.

'Sit down, Elspeth. How are you feeling? I must say, you seem to have recovered very quickly.'

'Yes,' she said, aware, even as she spoke, that she was at least two sizes too large, that her hair hadn't been seen to for months, that her clothes were unfashionably loose-looking. 'Yes, I feel very well. He's an awfully good baby.'

'Good. And you're back with us, which is excellent.'

'Well—'

'I like that series of children's books you're doing; very clever. Was that your idea?'

'Half mine. I thought a series based on the alphabet like that would be good; then the author came in to see me with some rough ideas and we put them together.'

'Very clever. Good publishing. The sort your husband does so well. Nice young man, your husband, clever as well. Anyway, I want to make you a proposition.'

'Oh,' she said. She didn't feel quite up to propositions of any kind.

'I think you should be working for us full time. I think you're wasted with this rather vague arrangement of yours.'

'Jay's happy with it,' she said carefully.

'I'm aware of that. But I'm in overall charge of editorial arrangements here, and I don't think we're getting full value from you.'

'But it works perfectly well,' she said, panic rising, 'I get the work done, in fact I probably get more done, because I'm not wasting time travelling and I can see the authors when necessary, sometimes at home, sometimes here and—'

'Elspeth,' he said gently, 'I'm not criticising you. Or the arrangement. I think it's remarkable what you've achieved, given those arrangements and your two very small children. No, I'm offering you a new job. I want you to be one of the senior editors. I would like you to work on the main women's fiction list, reporting to Jay.'

'To Jay?'

'Yes. And ultimately, of course, to me.'

'I – see,' she said. Only senior editors reported to Jay. This was an extraordinary thing she was being offered. The room seemed very light and bright suddenly, she felt dizzy and slightly shaky. 'Yes, I see. Well – thank you. Thank you very much.'

'So I take it you'll accept?'

'Well – I –'

He looked at her and he was no longer smiling, no longer trying to be charming; the pale-blue eyes were quite hard.

'Now, there is a condition to this. Obviously you couldn't do that job in your present situation. You would have to be in the office, full time. You would be working very hard. It would be a very responsible position.'

'Yes, I see,' she said again.

'So – I'd like your answer as soon as possible. Obviously you'll have to discuss it with your husband.'

'Thank you,' she said, and then heard herself saying, while knowing it was dreadful, foolish, dangerous even, 'I will discuss it with my husband, of course. But I think you can take it that my answer will be yes. And thank you. Thank you very much. I'll try to justify your faith in me.'

'I have absolutely no doubt that you'll do that,' he said, and he was the other Marcus again, smiling, charming, easy. 'I'm really delighted, Elspeth. I think we'll enjoy working together.'

'No, no, no!' Keir's face was so changed by rage that she scarcely recognised him, his dark eyes blazing, his mouth a thin, angry line. 'No, you will not, Elspeth. You will not start working full time. I won't have it.'

'*You* won't have it! Well, that's very interesting. *My* wishes and ambitions don't come into it, it seems. You decide everything for me, do you, Keir? I'm sorry, I hadn't quite realised that.'

'Oh, don't start all that claptrap with me,' he said. 'You know perfectly well you're cheating on our arrangement, you have been for months, only I've been foolish and weak enough to turn a blind eye. You promise me this, that and the other, pretend you're doing what I want, when in fact you're doing the opposite. You're my wife, Elspeth, you're the mother of my children and you will stay at home and look after them, not go running around, indulging yourself and your ambitions and your ego. My God, when I think, when you first announced that you were pregnant, how you said of course you would do anything I said, anything I wished, if you could only keep the baby. When did you ever do anything I said, Elspeth? I would like to know that.'

'And why should I? I'm your wife, not your servant. And besides, I never said that, I said I would manage on my own if you hadn't been prepared to marry me, and I would have done. I could have—' she stopped. This was dangerous, dangerous ground.

'Oh, aye, you could have done.' He became more Scottish when he was upset. 'Of course you could, and perhaps you'd like to rub my nose in that a little more. Explain how you had to cut yourself down to size and live in the only way I could afford.'

'But I did,' she said, and she was shouting now, 'I did do that, lived in that horrible flat in Glasgow, all on my own, it was awful. I was lonely and miserable and bored, but I did it—'

'Very good of you,' he said, 'very good indeed. Well, I'm sorry if I'm such an unsatisfactory husband, Elspeth. Very sorry. But the fact remains. You do not do that job, and you can tell that smooth bastard so in the morning. Otherwise our marriage is over. That's my last word.'

In the morning, still angry, she went to see Marcus Forrest and told him that she would like a little more time to consider his offer, if that was all right.

He said it was: 'It's a big decision for you, I can see that.'

'Thank you,' said Elspeth. 'I'll try and let you have an answer very soon.'

Then she went to tell Keir what she had done. And thought she had never loved him less.

★

Charlie Patterson stared at Jonathan Wyley across his large desk. It was at least twice the size of a standard desk, with only one neat file, a pad of paper and a pencil, and an even neater pile of law books set at the back of it. Three-quarters of its vast expanse was clear of anything at all.

Jonathan Wyley was one of the most senior of all the senior partners at Wyley Ruffin Wynne; and Wyley Ruffin Wynne was one of the most important and successful of all the most important and successful New York law firms, while being young and high profile rather than old and discreet. That was why he'd gone to them, staking everything he had, all the money left in his classic car company account. He wanted a firm so hot, so clever, so clearly able to command respect, that no one, from the very beginning, could dismiss what was said on his behalf.

'So – you think we have a case?' he asked, and his voice had a tremor in it, so excited was he, so awestruck, so terrified that he might have heard wrongly.

Charlie waited, trying to distract himself; Wyley Ruffin Wynne's offices were on the sixty-third floor of a building on Sixth Avenue; just uptown from Radio City and the United Nations building. Behind Jonathan Wyley's head, he could see the great sprawling spatter of high-rise New York, the completed buildings, gleaming in the frosty sunshine, together with the cranes and scaffolding and labourers on those that were still unfinished. A few wispy clouds trailed across the intensely blue sky, in the distance a helicopter whirled on its self-important way.

Jonathan Wyley still said nothing, just stared at his pad of paper, at the notes he had made on it; Charlie stood up, unable to bear the tension any longer, walked over to the window, looked down, far, far down at the toy cars and people and trees, and wondered how much it really mattered.

'Do help yourself to coffee,' said Wyley, indicating the tray and the jug on a table beside him, and he reached for one of his books, flicking through the pages; his clock had a loud tick, an irritatingly loud tick, Charlie thought. Edgy clients would find that very intrusive.

Finally, Wyley pushed away the book and the pad and the pencil and leaned back in his chair, looked at Charlie and said, 'Oh yes. You – we – do most definitely have a case.'

'Oh my God,' said Charlie. 'Oh my good God.'

Just before Christmas, Marcus Forrest came over to London; Elspeth was sitting at her desk at home when he phoned her.

'Can I take you out to lunch one day? Or can't you tear yourself away from your children for that length of time?'

'Of course I can. I'd love to have lunch. Thank you.'

That'd be one in the eye for Keir; she'd be very sure to tell him about it. All about it.

In the event she didn't. Not all.

It started out perfectly all right; he'd booked a table at the Caprice in a rather secluded corner, was waiting with a bottle of champagne on ice at his side.

'I thought a Lytton girl like you would expect champagne.'

'Hardly a Lytton girl at the moment,' said Elspeth soberly.

'Oh what nonsense. You look more like your grandmother every day. That's a compliment, by the way, I've seen pictures of her when she was young and thought how beautiful she was. You have her talent, too.'

'I didn't mean that,' she said carefully.

'What did you mean, then?' His eyes on her face were intrigued.

'Oh – I'd better not tell you. Bit indiscreet.'

'Have some champagne. That usually induces indiscretion.'

She smiled and looked around her. She loved the Caprice, the curved banquettes, the tables spread with pink cloths, the atmosphere it had of a rather feminine drawing room.

'It's gorgeous here,' she said, sipping her champagne.

'I'm sure you often come here.'

'I – used to. When I was young.'

'And now, of course, you're so terribly old.'

'I feel it,' she said, 'sometimes. As if life is passing me by.'

'That's a terrible thing to feel.'

'Isn't it? Sorry, I'm not being very festive. This is so kind of you.'

'Not in the least kind,' he said, 'it's a piece of self-indulgence, actually. I like having lunch with pretty women.'

'Well,' she said, looking round, 'there are plenty here. My cousin Noni comes here a lot. With all her aristocratic beaux.'

'She really is beautiful. I could have sworn there was talk of her getting engaged.'

'There was. To some weedy peer. But it's all off, thank goodness. We didn't like him at all. She's going out with an actor now. Some friend of Tony Armstrong-Jones, who's done some pictures of her for *Vogue*. She was so thrilled about that, she says he's the most brilliant photographer she's ever worked with. She says he takes risks. He took one of her riding a bicycle, or rather just as she was falling off it. But so you could still see the clothes. She's such a success herself, Noni, we're all so proud of her—'

'Your family is full of success,' he said, 'it runs in its veins. You've got a very high percentage of it in your blood, I'm quite sure of that.'

'I – hope so.'

She smiled at him, thought how charming he was and how good-looking. He was wearing a perfectly cut suit with rather narrow trousers and a very pale pink-and-white striped shirt; he was exactly the kind of man she really liked, smooth, easy, interested in what she had to say. Not difficult and terse and bad tempered . . .

'You're not married?' she asked suddenly, pushing away her plate, only half emptied.

'No, I'm not. Is there something wrong with that? I can order you another—'

'No,' she said. 'No, it was delicious, I'm just not very hungry. I never am when I'm—' she stopped.

'When you're what?'

'Nervous, I suppose.'

'Now why should you be nervous?' he said, and his tone was astonished. 'If anything, it's me who should be nervous, having to entertain someone who must regard me as being as old as time.'

She laughed. 'Of course I don't. I was just thinking—' she stopped again.

'Elspeth, you have to start finishing your sentences. I'm finding it rather disconcerting. Now what were you thinking?'

She looked at him; very directly. The champagne had taken effect, she was dizzying up nicely, as Amy put it.

'I was just thinking you were exactly the sort of man I most liked,' she said.

They started to talk easily then; flirtatiously at first, then about Lyttons, about work, and more seriously. He wasn't married, no, he said, he was divorced. 'We had a very good marriage, at first. Then I discovered my mistress.'

'Your mistress!'

'Yes. Work. And devoted more time to that than to my wife. We had two children by then, she was very busy, it was rather easy to slip apart.'

'I know all about that,' she said.

'You do? I thought you were so devoted to your husband.'

'Devoted!' said Elspeth, and suddenly found her eyes filled with tears.

Marcus Forrest looked at her in horror then tactfully away as she rummaged in her bag for a handkerchief.

'I'm sorry,' she said, 'so sorry.'

'I'm sorry too. Not that you cried. Unlike most men, I rather like tears. But that you're not happy. Do you – do you want to tell me about it?'

'No,' she said firmly, managing to smile and then, 'why do you like tears?'

'I find them rather sexy,' he said unexpectedly, 'a letting go. And an indication of a tender heart. Of course they're not always, but—'

'I'm not sure that I have a tender heart,' she said, 'any more.'

'Oh, I think you do,' he said, and he reached out a hand and wiped a stray tear from her cheek. 'I'm quite sure you do. You'd be working for me if you didn't.'

She ignored the 'me'.

'I'm afraid not. Keir wouldn't allow it.'

'Wouldn't allow it?' He sat back, staring at her. 'That is just about the saddest thing I ever heard. That someone as talented, as ambitious as you, should be held back because of—' He stopped, then said, 'Is there anything I can do to help?'

'I'm afraid not. No. It's the marriage or the job.'

'So you chose the marriage. And you say you're not tender-hearted.'

'I feel very tough-hearted,' she said suddenly, plunging recklessly into a ravine of confession. Dangerous confession. 'I feel hurt and angry, all the time. I can hardly bear to think of him there, at Lyttons, doing all the things that I should be doing, I certainly can't bear to talk to him about it at the end of the day.'

'I'm so sorry,' he said, 'so very, very sorry. Is there nothing I can do about it?'

'No. Nothing. Nobody can.'

'Well, if you do think of some way I can help, just let me know. And now perhaps we should talk of happier things. Like – where should I take some very boring booksellers for dinner this evening? What shows should I see while I'm in London? Where can I buy a present for my daughter?'

'Well,' said Elspeth, 'you should take the booksellers to the Savoy. You should see *The Entertainer*. It's marvellous, with Laurence Olivier. And the present for your daughter, I can help with. Just go to Harrods. They have everything, absolutely everything, from dolls to roller skates to—'

'Pretty dresses?'

'Lots of pretty dresses.'

'Then let's go and choose a pretty dress together. If you have the time, that is.'

Elspeth met his eyes in absolute complicity.

'I have plenty of time,' she said.

The stores were spangled with Christmas lights, filled with people in holiday mood. Elspeth followed him, smiling, as he threw himself into a frenzy of shopping. He bought presents by the armful: toys, dresses for his daughter, and a cashmere sweater for the ex-Mrs Forrest. After a moment's hesitation, Elspeth bought an identical one for herself.

'Nothing for your husband?'

'No,' she said firmly.

He looked at her and laughed. 'He doesn't need presents to my mind. He has you.'

They visited Harvey Nichols as well, where he bought the ex-Mrs Forrest some scent.

'Arpège,' said Elspeth, 'how lovely.'

'What do you wear? Chanel? You seem like a Chanel girl to me?'

'Never tried it.'

'I shall buy you some, then.' He looked down at her and smiled. 'On one condition. You only wear it when you are with me.'

'Bit of a waste,' she said, laughing.

463

'Will it be?' he said, and his eyes were serious suddenly. 'If I had my way, Elspeth, you would wear it a great deal.'

She said nothing, but he opened the packaging and the bottle and dabbed some, very slowly, behind each of her ears.

It was an extremely erotic moment.

'Now,' he said, 'it's tea time. No point my going back to Lyttons now. Why don't we have tea at the Ritz? And look in on Hatchards at the same time, see how we're doing there.'

They took a cab to Hatchards in Piccadilly; wandered round looking at the displays.

'We're doing well, aren't we?' he said. 'That book of Jay's, the three-parter, it's selling like the proverbial hot cakes.'

'He's very clever, don't you think?' said Elspeth.

'Quite. Not as clever as your husband, though. Oh dear, how indiscreet of me.'

'I won't tell him,' said Elspeth briskly, 'don't worry.'

Deer Mountain was also doing extremely well, had a small table all to itself on the bend of the stairs.

'I was wrong about that,' Marcus said, 'it's reprinting for the fourth time, Giles tells me.'

'Yes. Did you like it?'

'I hated it,' he said, 'but it's a brilliant piece of work. Although there's something about it that makes me uneasy.'

'What?'

'I don't quite know. It's just a bit too – perfect. And where's the author?'

'She's a recluse,' said Elspeth, 'she doesn't want publicity.'

'Then why publicise her deer, her lonely mountain, her life? Someone will find her, they're bound to.'

'I think you're horrid,' she said laughing.

'Well, maybe. Let's go and have tea.'

They walked along Piccadilly, and settled in the Palm Court of the Ritz, spreading their bags out around them.

'I've never known a man to like shopping,' she said, looking at his packages.

'Oh I've always liked it,' he said, 'I'm very acquisitive, you see.'

'What do you like to acquire?'

'Oh – just about everything. Pictures. Antiques. Clothes. Pretty women.'

She smiled at him, utterly, dangerously relaxed. 'I suppose you have lots of those.'

'No,' he said, 'not many. Not many come up to my very high standards, you see.'

The harpist, seated by one of the biggest palms, was playing rather incongruously a medley from *West Side Story*, the waves of chatter from all the tables rose and fell, more and more people arrived, swooped on their friends and kissed them ecstatically. It was all deliciously excessive, she thought, and said so; 'I suppose you like excess?' she asked, smiling at him.

'Of course. I'm very greedy.'

Elspeth met his eyes directly; there was a silence, then, 'Me too,' she said. 'Could I have another glass of champagne? And another of those wonderful cucumber sandwiches?'

'Suddenly you've got an appetite. Does this mean you are no longer nervous?'

'Not nervous at all,' she said, and then impulsively leaned forward and kissed him on the cheek.

'I've had such a lovely time. Thank you so much.'

'It was entirely my pleasure,' he said and then, 'that scent suits you, really very well.'

He put his hand under her chin, kissed her back; only this time on the lips, very gently, but she still felt it, his warm mouth moving on hers, and – of course – her own responding, stirring just slightly, the sensation echoed in her, deep, deep within—

'Sir, Madam.' The Ritz waiter stood above them, deferentially disdainful. 'Some tea?'

'No thank you,' said Marcus Forrest. They both started to laugh.

CHAPTER 36

Christmas had been awful. The worst thing yet. She had known it would be, of course, but she hadn't expected anything quite so bad. Jenna had actually been planning to go to England, to spend it with the Millers. They had invited her, and she had thought it was absolutely the answer.

Charlie and Cathy had been sweet, encouraged her to go, said they'd be fine; and surely they would be, she thought, they could see other people, not just her and her friends and relations. She had written to Celia and said she was coming and asked if she could see her, and perhaps Adele and Venetia, and Celia had written the loveliest letter back, saying she would adore to see her, and to have her to stay for a few days if the Millers could spare her.

'I have something for you, too,' she wrote, 'it's waiting here for you. Something of your mother's. Best love, Celia.'

She had been really excited, and almost happy, especially about seeing the Millers. She had bought a few new clothes, presents for everyone, received lots of letters from them all, saying how much they were looking forward to seeing her.

They set off for the airport, a week before Christmas: and then it happened. Very suddenly, while they were checking her on to the flight, shocking her with its violence, a shaking, first hot, then icy panic, a sickness in her stomach, a pounding in her head, a need to run away: and a realisation that she absolutely could not get on an aeroplane.

'I – can't go,' she whispered to Charlie, clinging to his hand like a small child, trying to control herself, control the tremulous tears, the violent shuddering. 'I can't go, I'm too afraid, I can't, oh Charlie, I'm so sorry.'

He had been wonderful, had sat down with her on one of the seats and held her, cuddled her, kissed her and said it was all right, of course she mustn't go if she didn't want to, there was no need, it didn't matter.

She stood up, said she must go the lavatory, but then found her legs too weak to support her; Cathy put an arm around her and helped her in and she sat there, crying and shuddering, horrified at herself, at her lack of courage, at the mind-emptying power of her fear.

'I can't understand it,' she kept saying. 'I came back with you and Charlie. I didn't think about it then, why am I now?'

'I don't know,' Cathy said helplessly, 'but maybe you were so shocked then you didn't think about it properly, or maybe you had me and my dad. I don't know, Jenna, but it doesn't matter, you don't have to go. I was dreading you going, anyway,' she added with a rather shaky grin. 'We were going to be pretty lonely.'

Somehow that made Jenna feel better; even so, she felt dreadful about letting down everybody in England, and insisted on speaking to Joan and Billy herself.

'Don't you worry, my lovely,' Joan had said, 'we'll miss you, course we will, but there's always next year. It's natural you shouldn't want to get on a plane, I wouldn't either, horrible things.'

She phoned Celia too, afraid that she would be rather disapproving, but she was wonderful and told her she quite understood, and that it was just as well she hadn't got over to England and then not felt she could go back. 'Or perhaps that would have been better. I think I'd have liked that,' she added, and Jenna could hear her smiling. 'I quite understand, my darling. And so will everyone else. You've been so brave. You deserve a bit of a wobble.'

So they had gone home again. She and Cathy had arranged a Christmas dinner at lightning speed, with Maria's help, and invited Jamie and the Brewers for the evening, as her mother had always done; they had said they couldn't come, they already had a big party arranged, but invited them over there. It seemed a good idea and she had rushed out and bought lots more presents; Charlie had already got a tree and it stood where it always did, on the outside balcony of Number Seven, the lights shining out into the darkness, and she had thought maybe she was even glad she wasn't going to be in England. They would go to the midnight service at St Bartholomew's, she and Cathy were going carol singing with their friends and they would go skating on Christmas Eve, as they had always done, then walk home, all the way up the brilliant streets, savouring the day ahead . . .

And then Jenna realised what they had all done; they had arranged Christmas exactly as Barty had always done, because they didn't know any different way to do it, were spending exactly the same kind of day, doing exactly the same things, seeing exactly the same people – only without her. And suddenly every moment was dreadful, every moment a reminder, stockings without her, presents without her, pulling crackers without her, carving the turkey without her, going round to Jamie's without her, an aching blank where she should have been, an emptiness in the room so strong that she could see it, see her mother not being there.

★

Time was ticking on rather horribly, Giles felt. It was now January, they had exactly two months in which to find two million pounds and BISC were moving with dreadful slowness. Brian Gilmour of BISC had phoned Harold Charteris early in December to say he was sending in their specialists to have a look at the company, and to see if he felt he could recommend it to the board as an option for a loan.

'Two people will be coming. One of our financial people will want to have a look at your accounts department, talk to your accountant, take a look at your balance sheet, that sort of thing. He'll evaluate your building, see what he thinks that's worth, and the warehouse, of course. And then there's a very nice young fellow, name of Peter Phelps, I'm sure you'll like him, he knows quite a bit about your area, has looked at several publishing companies for me. He won't disrupt things too much, I hope, just make some enquiries in various departments, see what's happening, what you propose to publish over the next three years or so, what your sales figures have been over the past two or three years, and so on.'

This enraged Celia. 'I don't know what this person expects to find – that we are publishing pornography, perhaps? Everyone knows what we've published, and the sales figures are there for all to see. I hope they don't imagine we've been distorting them or something like that.'

'No, Lady Celia,' said Charteris patiently, 'of course not. But they do want facts. Facts and figures, that's what the whole thing is about. You can't expect someone to hand over this sort of money without being sure the company is sound.'

'Well clearly it's sound. We wouldn't be here if it wasn't.'

This was such a wildly inaccurate statement that Charteris chose to ignore it altogether.

'And how long is all this going to take? We're very busy at the moment, we can't afford to spend days on end with people answering stupid questions.'

'Gilmour tells me it'll take about two or three days. They will then put together a report for him, and he'll decide whether to recommend it to the board or not.'

The day before Peter Phelps arrived, Jay took Celia out to lunch. 'I know this all seems very tiresome to you, Celia, but it is essential. We can't proceed without these people. So it really is in our interest to be helpful.'

Celia looked at him. And then gave him her most conspiratorial smile.

'Of course I'm going to be helpful,' she said, 'whatever made you think I might not?'

Peter Phelps, on arriving the next day, found himself greeted in the foyer by Lady Celia Lytton personally; she swept forward, a rather dramatic figure in dark turquoise, with a large black hat on her head, trimmed with turquoise feathers, clasped his hand in both hers and said, 'Mr Phelps, how very, very good of you to come. You must let me know exactly what you would like me to do to help you in your work. And I would be most honoured if you would join us all for lunch at the Dorchester. My husband, Lord Arden, will probably be joining us.'

Peter Phelps, who lived in a small house in Pinner and spent his weekends birdwatching with his sister, managed to murmur that he was very grateful but he preferred to take a rather brief lunch hour, if Lady Celia wouldn't mind. 'Time is of the essence in our business, do please forgive me,' and he followed her to the boardroom. There she had set up a full display of every book published by Lyttons over the past three years, complete with sales figures, a range of catalogues, and a document outlining publishing plans for the next three years.

'I do hope this will be enough for you,' she said graciously, 'my nephew, Jay Lytton, and my son Giles will be with us shortly, to answer any questions you may have. I'm so sorry you aren't able to join us for luncheon, my husband will be most disappointed.'

As Lord Arden was up in Scotland shooting, this was fairly unlikely; but Peter Phelps was not to know that.

He was particularly interested in *Deer Mountain*. 'Such a wonderful book, I bought it for my mother for Christmas', and the prospective memoirs of General Dugdale. 'I would enjoy that very much. Are you expecting a large volume of sales from that, Lady Celia?'

'But of course. We publish in late summer and it should sell right through into the autumn. A second volume will follow next year. I shall see you are sent a signed copy. General Dugdale is a great personal friend of mine.'

'How kind,' said Peter Phelps.

He left at the end of the following day looking a little dazed, but with most of the small notebook he had brought with him filled with his neat, closely packed handwriting.

'I think that went rather well,' said Celia. 'I hope I behaved with enough grace, Jay.'

'Of course you did.'

She supposed it had been worth it; at least if it worked, she wouldn't have to do the awful thing.

It was very odd being an adulterous woman. You felt at one and the same time very good and very bad. Very good because you knew you were still attractive, still sexy. And bad – well it was obvious why you felt bad. Although rather glamorously bad. Most of the time, Elspeth felt as if she was watching a film about herself. It was very exciting.

She supposed she would have felt much worse, much more wicked, if Keir was being nice to her. But he wasn't; he was being foul. Cold, distant, argumentative; he had still never thanked her, or even expressed appreciation for turning down Marcus Forrest's offer. It wouldn't have hurt him, and it would have helped her a lot. In fact, it would have made all the difference.

All the difference when Marcus Forrest invited her for another lunch when he came back to London in January; all the difference when he had told her he had been thinking of her ever since he had left; all the difference when he reminded her to wear her Chanel No. 5; all the difference when, as he kissed her goodbye, having made no improper suggestion of any kind, he had said that if she would like it, he would certainly like to see her again; all the difference when some flowers arrived for her, thanking her for sparing the time to see him, and asking her to lunch again the next time he came – 'not for several weeks, I'm afraid, but I shall look forward to it greatly if you will agree.'

And certainly all the difference when he did come back in February, when Keir was away overnight (to address a conference of Scottish booksellers where it was thought his Scottishness would help) and Marcus invited her for cocktails at six at his hotel. It had turned out the cocktails were being served in his suite; after two, he kissed her and she responded in the most helpless, hopeless way, kissing him back in an agony of desire (while knowing it was the most stupid thing she could possibly be doing).

And then somehow she was lying on the bed, on Marcus's bed, and he was undressing her, kissing her, telling her how much he wanted her and how beautiful she was, dipping his finger in the champagne at his side and tracing first her face and then her nipples with it, then licking it off, slowly and deliciously. It was too late by then, far too late, to do anything except melt away beneath him, and let him lead her into the most glorious wonderful sex.

But when it was over, finally, when she had travelled so far and so high that she had to fall, fall endlessly into a deep, splintering, breaking delight, she lay, exhausted, absolutely terrified by what she had done.

'It's all right,' he said gently, over and over again, trying to soothe her, 'I understand. Of course you feel dreadfully disloyal and wicked, and – well, I had no right to do that. I feel ashamed.'

'Of course you don't,' she said fretfully. 'Why should you feel ashamed, I let you do it, I could have said no to lunch. I could have sent back the flowers, I could have refused the cocktails, I could have run from the room screaming—'

'I would have followed you,' he said gently, 'and I would have offered more cocktails and I would have sent you more flowers and bought you another lunch. I am quite hard to resist, when I have fixed my mind on something.'

And even then she kept thinking that if Keir had been nicer to her, if he had allowed her to take the job, if she had not been feeling so hurt and angry, then a second onslaught from Marcus Forrest, even a third, might have been possible to resist.

Just possible. He was very, very attractive she thought, on the way home to Battersea in the taxi, rehearsing her explanation to Mrs Wilson for her lateness (an important author suddenly arriving, demanding attention), checking her face again, reapplying her lipstick, smoothing her hair, wondering if it showed, if someone like Mrs Wilson could look at her and know that only an hour earlier she had been writhing about in bed with a man who was not her husband, crying out with pleasure and weeping with remorse.

Luckily, Mrs Wilson seemed not to be able to do that.

The funny thing was, it helped with Keir. Guilt made her less angry, fear made her more compliant. For the first time for weeks, she attempted – and managed – to seduce him (while wondering fearfully if she was in some way changed, if he could tell), and for the first time in weeks she asked him about his work, served him fish pie, sent him to sit down while she cleared away.

She felt better too; less used, more appreciated. She was under no illusions, she knew Marcus Forrest was not really in love with her – although he had whispered that he was falling in love as he undressed her, as she lay in his arms, afterwards, crying again with remorse. She knew that neither was she in love with him: she was merely attracted to him, flattered by him, and she liked him enormously.

She did feel ashamed: but not as much as she had expected. Which, of course, made her feel more ashamed. What was wrong with her? Was she a naturally wicked person, that she could sleep with the first man who had asked her after she was married, that a couple of champagne cocktails and a lot of honeyed words could persuade her into bed, when she had the serious responsibilities of a husband and two small children; and with a man who was, strictly speaking, her boss and her husband's boss, how stupid was that?

What dangers had she exposed herself to, as she kissed Marcus, told him she wanted him, went into his bed, what hope for her career now? He had (being not only a skilful seducer but a clever man) tried to reassure her on those things: 'Of course I'm your boss, of course I hold your husband's future in my hands – at the moment, anyway. Do you really think I'm so amoral as to exploit all that? If you do, then you should leave, Elspeth, leave at once, and we need never see one another or speak of what has happened again.'

And while she had not quite believed him, she had not disbelieved him either; as she got to know him better, she liked him more and more. He was kind, thoughtful, considerate of her anxiety, gentle with her fears.

'I am not exercising *droit de seigneur* either,' he said another day, kissing

471

her tenderly, 'the fact that you work for me has absolutely no bearing on the fact that I find you beautiful, amusing, clever and extremely stylish. I would have pursued you even if you'd been working for Macmillans. I can't say more than that.'

'I shall test you on that,' she said, kissing him in return, 'I shall leave Lyttons and go to Macmillans, and see what happens.'

'You will do no such thing. I still live in hope of your accepting my offer. But I tell you something else, Elspeth Lytton. For that is how I think of you. If you were free, I would be taking this thing very seriously. Very seriously indeed. I told you I was falling in love with you; I seem to have fallen quite a lot of the way in already.'

'Well Mr Lytton, just a call to say everything's in order.' Gilmour's dry, courteous voice gave nothing away. 'We have everything we need, a nine-page report has come in to me and now I have only to pass it on to the board.'

'Fine. Well –' Jay hesitated '– you don't have any – any indication of what their decision might be?'

'I'm afraid not. I can tell you that I have put in a recommendation that they should consider your case sympathetically, but beyond that, it's out of my hands now.'

'Yes. Yes, I see. And I don't suppose you can give me any idea of the timescale involved?'

'I'm sorry, no. Probably a couple of weeks.'

'A couple of weeks! That – that doesn't leave us much time to find someone else. If we need to.'

'I'm afraid not. Unfortunately you came to us rather late in your own timetable.'

'That couldn't be helped. We hadn't got the valuation before.'

'Of course not. Don't worry, Mr Lytton, I'm sure it will be very sympathetically considered.'

'Thank you,' said Jay. He put the phone down, feeling rather sick.

In the middle of February, General Dugdale was doing some final pruning of his fruit trees before spraying them with a tar oil wash; it made a diversion from writing his memoirs. He had put in a couple of hours that morning, but he had a mild headache which appeared to be worsening and felt that a break would ease it. He planned to return to writing during the afternoon.

He had done the most painstaking research, poring over old battle reports, both in the newspaper archives, and regimental records, and visiting old comrades – including Boy Warwick – and reliving with them the time in the desert, with its fierce discomfort and camaraderie. He had over a dozen exercise books on his desk, all filled with notes in his immaculate copperplate handwriting.

He also enjoyed the actual writing; Celia had not been mistaken when she recognised a rare talent for intriguing, informative and tightly packed prose. So many memoirs were rambling and repetitious; General Dugdale's were the reverse. They read like a thriller. Several newspapers, notably the *Observer*, had expressed a great interest in them; publication of the first volume of two was planned for late summer. There was only one problem: only about a quarter of even the first book was actually written. The General took great pride in his prose style, and spent many hours not just writing, but polishing and reworking, trying out different openings to chapters and paragraphs, reading sections aloud to his wife, looking for literary references which he could use both for chapter headings and within the text.

Celia phoned him at least once a week, to enquire how he was getting on and to ask if he needed any editorial guidance; he always told her it was all absolutely tickety-boo, or splendid, or going swimmingly, and realised, as he put the phone down, that he had moved forward very little from the last time she had called. He tried to speed up, but it was difficult; he began to find it rather stressful, and to sleep less soundly, rather, indeed, as he had slept in the desert, fitfully and lightly, waking every hour or so.

He supposed he should have told Celia that he was running behind schedule, but pride forbade it; he felt confident that he could make up for lost time if he really put his back into it.

It was a fairly warm day and the pruning shears seemed increasingly heavy; after about twenty minutes, the General felt unaccountably dizzy. He ignored it for a few moments, then realised he was actually quite unable to see the shears at all and walked rather unsteadily into the house, where he had some difficulty explaining to Mrs Dugdale what his symptoms were. Mrs Dugdale took one look at him and sent him to lie on the sofa in the drawing room – it was a measure of her concern that she didn't make him take his boots off. Then she telephoned the doctor.

The doctor examined the General carefully, diagnosed a mild stroke and said he must rest completely for the next forty-eight hours.

The following morning the General woke up very early, feeling much better, and decided to get up and make a cup of tea for himself and Mrs Dugdale. Halfway down the stairs, he felt dizzy again; a loud crash as he fell to the hall floor was Mrs Dugdale's first intimation of his second, and rather more serious, stroke.

Mrs Dugdale was reading to her husband when Celia telephoned; she explained what had happened, and said her husband had been worrying about the delay in finishing his memoirs. Celia was shocked, for she was very fond of the General but, feeling mildly panicky at the same time, managed to tell her that he mustn't even think about returning to his task until he was completely well.

'Just because the book is scheduled for the summer doesn't mean it can't wait. Tell him to concentrate on getting well.'

She put the phone down and decided to say nothing to Jay yet.

Mr Gilmour phoned Harold Charteris; could he come in and see him 'and perhaps the Lyttons as well. I have some news for you.'

'Of course,' said Charteris. His mouth was suddenly completely dry. The news was not entirely good. The board were persuaded that Lyttons was possibly a worthy company for investment, but the terms were going to be tough.

'How tough?' asked Jay.

'Well, as you know, we loan money at three per cent above bank rate. That is entirely normal for any investment company.'

'Yes, we knew that.'

'However, the board feel that they would want to take a larger share of the equity.'

'Yes?' said Giles.

'We would require a forty per cent share,' said Gilmour, 'or at least thirty-five per cent.'

'Forty per cent! But that's' − 'extortionate' he had been going to say, but stopped himself just in time − 'that's a rather large share, surely? We are seeking to retain control of our company, not lose it all over again.'

'Not so large a share, Mr Lytton, no. Not in a case like this. We feel, given the nature of your company, its inevitable volatility, and indeed its size, we do need to retain a considerable amount of control. It's a very small company, although fairly profitable, and as I say, it has no assets worthy of consideration.'

'Mr Gilmour,' said Celia, unable to bear this any longer, 'you are talking about one of the oldest and most respected publishing houses in the world. It is not a very small company, and it has assets very worthy of consideration. We publish some of the finest authors in the world, we have a backlist which is the envy of the entire industry, and I do rather feel you can't possibly know what you are talking about. Perhaps we should go elsewhere—'

'I appreciate your literary heritage,' said Gilmour, 'and Mr Phelps was deeply impressed by it. Particularly the very successful *Deer Mountain*, and the forthcoming military memoirs. But, as I explained, when a financial corporation talks about assets, it means assets it can realise.'

'Yes, of course,' said Giles. His face was white with tension; he felt extremely irritated and rather sick. This was all beginning to look, if not hopeless, then certainly very far from hopeful. 'Well − I think we would like you to press on, Mr Gilmour. At least come up with an official proposal.'

Mr Gilmour said he would press on.

'It's outrageous,' said Celia, 'of course we can't part with forty per cent of the company. Especially not to these people. I'd rather give up altogether. I will never agree to it. Never.'

Jay looked at her. 'Let's wait and see what they come up with, shall we? They know our feelings, maybe the offer will improve. It's unwise, I feel, to give up at this stage.'

She said nothing; he took her silence as assent.

It actually meant she was wondering if, at last, she had to do it. To do the awful, the unforgivable thing.

'Jay, I'm afraid I have some rather − difficult news.'

He looked up; she was looking nervous. Celia never looked nervous. It just didn't happen.

'What sort of difficult?'

'General Dugdale has only written − well, part of the book.'

'Oh God.' He pushed his hands through his hair. 'Well − let's get in what he's done, see if we can use that, or even ghost the rest.'

'I'm afraid that won't be possible.'

'Why not?'

'Because − because he's only written—'

'Written what, Celia? For God's sake, come on, tell me the worst. It can't be that bad.'

'It is bad, I'm afraid.' She took a deep breath, faced him very levelly. 'He's only written a little over a quarter of the book.'

'Oh God,' said Jay.

'That's appalling,' said Giles, 'that completely upsets the cash flow for the rest of the year. The one Gilmour's presented to his people.'

'I had realised that, Giles.'

'Is there no hope at all? Of his finishing it?'

'Apparently not,' said Jay. 'Old bugger's quite ill, it seems. Not allowed to work for several months. Can't anyway. Gone a bit gaga.'

'We'll have to revise the cash flow. It was quite optimistic, we can't possibly keep the lid on this. At least we won't have to pay him the second tranche of his advance. The one due on delivery of the manuscript. That was quite substantial.'

'Giles,' said Jay, sitting down opposite him, offering him a cigarette, lighting one himself, 'Giles, I'm afraid we already have.'

'What?'

'Yes, Celia authorised it, just before Barty died. He asked her if she could help, if he could have it early, as his elderly mother had to go into a nursing home. He's an old friend of hers, what do you expect her to do?'

'She'll just have to get it back,' said Giles. 'I'll speak to her myself. That is outrageous, what she's done, absolutely outrageous.'

Celia said it was out of the question that she should get the money back. 'I couldn't possibly worry Dorothy, she's so upset already. It was such a love match, you know, she adores him to this day and—'

'Celia, I'm delighted the Dugdales are still in love,' said Jay, 'but this leaves an enormous hole in our schedule. Not to mention our budget. Oh God, of all the times for this to happen—'

'I suppose you mean the money people. We don't need to tell them, surely.'

'I'm afraid we do,' said Jay.

'But why? This is a publishing matter, not a business one and—'

Giles sighed heavily. 'Of course they'll need to know, Mother, those memoirs represent a large part of our projected cash flow for the second half of the year. The trade are promising big orders. It would be fraudulent to pretend they're still in the schedule.'

'Well,' said Celia, 'I'd rather put the money into the cash flow, or whatever it's called, myself. In fact, I will, if you think it's so important. How would that be?'

Jay stared at her. 'That's extraordinarily generous of you. We might – might have to take you up on it. Let's see, shall we?'

God, the old girl must be rich, he thought, going back to his office. Tossing ten thousand pounds around as if it was petty cash. He'd personally be pushed to find ten pounds at the moment.

It seemed endless. Every day BISC seemed to need more information. A more detailed cash flow, fuller sales predictions, lists of authors, contracts, further publishing schedules. Greatly against his will, Jay had been persuaded to keep from Gilmour the news about the Dugdale memoirs.

'I still think it's absurd that he needs to know,' said Celia. 'We need the money in early March, the memoirs are due for publication in September.'

'August, Celia.'

'We'll find something else,' said Celia. 'I told you this sort of thing would happen, trying to work with people who don't understand publishing.'

'Oh, Celia, please!' Jay sounded most unusually irritated. 'They're trying to enable us to continue publishing. You seem to have trouble remembering that.'

'I suppose I do. I just find the process rather painful.' She smiled suddenly at him. 'I might even publish my own memoirs. They'd sell.'

'They certainly would,' said Jay.

He was to remember that conversation in the months ahead.

476

Douglas Marks was a keen young journalist, fresh from a long stint on the *Western Morning News*, and in only his second week at the *Daily Sketch* when he was told by the features editor to try to get an interview with the author of *Deer Mountain*, Joanna Scott.

'Not very exciting, I know, but our editor's mother-in-law bought the silly woman's book and loved it and wanted to read all about her. There must be many other readers who feel the same way. What we want is human interest, photographs of her with the deer, you know the sort of thing. The point is, nobody's managed to get hold of her yet, she won't give interviews, so it would be a scoop of sorts. Don't look like that, lad, takes all sorts to make a paper.'

It wasn't quite the sort of scoop Marks had envisaged when he came to Fleet Street from the provinces, but he was prepared to give it a go. Deer lady today, Prime Minister or Princess tomorrow. Maybe.

He phoned Lyttons and got a point-blank refusal from the publicity department. Mrs Scott, it appeared, was very shy and reclusive, and needed to protect the deer as much as herself. In that case, could he meet her in Glasgow or even Perth? Then the deer wouldn't need to be disturbed. This was also refused; a girl with a cut-glass accent told him she would send him what she called Mrs Scott's biography. Marks said he already had that and put the phone down.

He tried other leads, literary agents, bookshops, but always got the same answer; Mrs Scott would not see anybody, least of all the press. Would she talk on the phone? No, she didn't have a phone. Could he make a date for later in the year, not at the sanctuary, somewhere else, to be agreed by her? No, she wasn't prepared to do that.

'I'm beginning to think there's something fishy here,' he said to his fellow trainee-reporter, known to all and sundry as Jimbo. 'This is a smash-hit book, it outsold every other book on the market at Christmas, people literally queued up to buy it, it's still selling like hot cakes.'

'So?' said Jimbo, 'what's the big deal? She doesn't want to talk to the press. I wouldn't, if I was an old lady living on a mountain.'

'But if she's that much of a recluse, why write the book?'

'To make money.'

'Yeah, and to sell lots of copies. Otherwise, why write it in the first place? And if you write a book, you talk to the press. That's what authors do these days, successful ones who sell lots of books, that is. They do talk to the press. Just every now and again. It helps sales.'

'Maybe her sales don't need helping.'

'Sales always need helping. And now there's a children's version coming out later this year, in the summer, surely they'll want publicity for that.'

Jimbo shrugged. 'Clearly they don't need it.'

'No. There's something funny here. Look, this is a charming, attractive book, there's nothing disagreeable in it, no violence, nothing pornographic, why on earth won't the woman who wrote it agree to an interview?'

'I think you're getting worked up about nothing, Duggie boy. Why don't you get stuck into that story about this year's CND march? Bloody silly nonsense, if you ask me. But at least that's fact . . .'

'Yes, but then I've got to tell old Jacko I can't do what he wants with the deer woman. I'll look like a fool. It's not like they've asked me to interview Humphrey Bogart.'

'He's dead.'

'I know that, you bloody idiot. Actually, I think he might be easier to get hold of. No, I've just got to get her address. I've got a hunch about it, Jimbo. I just feel in my water it's a story.'

'Oh yeah? Where's your green eye shade, then?'

'Oh shut up. Look, want to come out for a drink? If you can make any sensible suggestions, I'll stand you a beer.'

'Make it lunch, and I'll promise to come up with something.'

As Douglas and Jimbo drank their way through dinner that night, following an equally liquid lunch, Fenella Woodward, the new (and very well-spoken) receptionist at Lyttons was telling her mother about the interesting phone call she had had that day.

'It was a Canadian, the son of one of Joanna Scott's best friends. You know, she wrote *Deer Mountain*. Anyway, his mother was absolutely thrilled to discover that her old school friend had done so well, and they want to look her up, apparently. The mother emigrated to Canada when she was quite young, and they're here on a visit, and longing to get in touch with her. He was so sweet, obviously a wonderful son, his mother is an invalid, she has some dreadful muscle-wasting illness, and this could be her last trip to England. He said he just knew it would make her feel so much better.'

'What would?'

'Well, being able to meet her.'

'What, on this mountain? With a muscle-wasting illness? Did you give him her address?'

'Yes, I did. I said he must write in and we would forward the letter. That's what we're told to say, but he said they were leaving in three days, and she has to go back into hospital. It just seemed so unkind not to help as much as I could. So I did – give him her address. Not of the sanctuary, of course, but the one where she collects her letters, in the village nearby. What harm can that do?'

'If I were you, Fenella,' said her mother slowly, 'I wouldn't tell anyone you did that.'

★

'I'm afraid,' said Jay, 'this cash flow still isn't looking good.'

'Well,' Giles replied wearily, 'maybe we shall have to leave the Dugdale memoirs in it. Find someone else to write the book, finish it quickly.'

'Giles, I've left it in.'

'Oh,' said Giles. 'Oh Christ.'

'There's another thing. They're questioning the need for this place. Couldn't we move to cheaper premises? Do we really need to be in the heart of the West End?'

'Yes, of course we do. It's essential. Everybody is.'

'I would argue with you on that, I think,' said Jay. 'Everybody isn't. This place must cost twice what Michael Joseph pays in Bloomsbury, or André Deutsch in Cumberland Place. I know it's beautiful, I know Oliver loved it, I know it's the only possible replacement for Paternoster Square. But paying these rates is commercial suicide. Maybe we should think about it: at least for the future.'

'Oh God,' said Giles. 'I'm hating all this.'

'It is rather – unfortunate,' said Charteris. 'We shall look – disorganised if we have to cancel the memoirs. And at precisely the time when we want to look the opposite.'

'It is the sort of thing that happens all the time in this business though,' said Jay, 'surely that must count for something?'

'I'm afraid not very much. It's precisely that fact that has made getting the money quite – difficult. The fact that this is a capricious, unreliable business. And we are becoming quite unusual in remaining a private company. Collins and Longmans have both sold public shares, and they are only two examples. They're all going down that road.'

Jay stared at him, a curl of excitement suddenly in his stomach. 'Are you suggesting—' It was almost unthinkable, certainly unsayable.

Charteris shook his head. 'Not at the moment, no. Even if we all agreed it was a viable option, this is no time to do it. In fact, it's virtually impossible. But if you had control of the company, then yes, I do most certainly think we should look at it very carefully.'

'Celia would never consider it,' said Jay.

She wouldn't, of course: but he would. Giles and Venetia might. The young ones, Elspeth, Keir, Lucas – if his new ambition to join the company materialised – they probably would see it as not only inevitable but desirable. They would recognise the need for change, for growth, for the money that such a course of action would provide, and see, too, that family businesses – with their inherent tangle of private agendas and prejudices – had almost certainly had their day. It was such a different world from the one in which Celia, Oliver and LM had developed Lyttons; not only tougher, but unimaginably wider. And they needed capital: so badly. To expand, to build a proper paperback list, establish foreign agents, and – of course – to buy and keep the best authors. If they reacquired the company, the matter should be properly and dispassionately aired and explored. They might even be able to pay themselves decent salaries.

The address which Douglas Marks had been given, School House, Tullydie (presumably some kind of *poste restante*, he thought, certainly no mountain hideaway), was in a village near Perth; he had to change trains to get to Perth and after that, it was a long bus journey to the village. He had brought a camera with him, loaned by the picture desk; just a small one, nothing obtrusive.

The village was small and drab, and surprisingly near a town. It had a pub, a school, a few houses, and a shop, all on one main street. Marks stood looking round him; this couldn't be right. There were some mountains in the distance; far, far in the distance. He would put them at twenty or thirty miles away. Long trip to collect letters. He took a couple of pictures, anyway.

The location of School House was not obvious, there was no street name, and there was quite clearly no school. Indeed there were none of the cosy landmarks to be found in an English village, no church, no village green, no pond. Clearly local knowledge was needed; he went into the shop.

A village shop: everything looking old and vaguely unsavoury, battered tins, creased packets, even the cheese, under its glass dome, looked as if it had been there for some time. A young girl was behind the counter; Marks asked her if she knew where School House was.

'Out of the village,' she said. 'Take the road towards Craigraich. At the first crossroads turn left, then it's about a mile up on the hill.'

'I don't have a car.'

She shrugged.

'Is there a local taxi service?'

'Taxi service?' She looked at him as if he had asked for a casino or a brothel. 'No. You could walk though.'

'And – is that where Mrs Scott lives?'

'Who?' she said.

'Mrs Joanna Scott?'

'Who wants her?'

It seemed an odd question.

'I'm a solicitor,' he said.

He had used this explanation effectively in the past; most people seemed to live in the hope, or even expectation, of solicitors arriving on their doorsteps with news of large bequests and opened their doors most trustingly.

But, 'A solicitor?' she said suspiciously. 'And you've no car?'

'I've come from London. By train and then bus.'

'Oh aye. Well, you'll have to walk, as I say.'

Marks walked.

The Lyttons and Charteris were in the boardroom, waiting for Brian Gilmour. It was 5 March.

'I would never have believed this could have taken so long,' said Giles wearily.

'Me neither,' said Venetia. 'I suppose it helps them tighten the screws.'

'What do you mean?'

'Well – they know we've got – what – three days left. How can we turn down any offer they make to us?'

'Oh, I don't think that's fair,' said Charteris mildly, 'these things do always take a lot of time. And most people aren't in quite the hurry we are.'

'I agree with Venetia,' said Celia. 'It seems absurd to me. Two months they've been poking their noses into our affairs, and nothing to show for it at all. I almost hope they turn us down. I can tell them what I think of them.'

'Please don't, Lady Celia,' said Charteris. 'It won't help and we might need them another time.'

'Pray God we won't.'

Brian Gilmour arrived in a self-important hurry, together with his assistant, a small nervous creature called John Peters. They accepted some coffee, waved away the plate of biscuits, and Gilmour pulled out some folders.

'Right,' he said, 'I hope you'll be pleased with what I have to tell you.'

They weren't: they were hugely disappointed. They could have the money: at 3 per cent above bank rate. They had expected the high rate; that was the good news. But BISC were adamant; they wanted a 40 per cent shareholding.

'We'll need to talk about it, of course,' said Giles wearily, 'if you could give us a few hours. Obviously we can't take much longer. But that is a very high percentage and we really need to be sure we are all happy about it. Or rather,' he added, unusually outspoken, 'that we can live with it.'

Gilmour nodded. 'Of course. Just give me a ring. If you're agreeable, then the paperwork can be done very quickly. I know you have a time problem. Get back to me before the close of business today, if you would; otherwise I have to tell you it's likely we might withdraw. We have another client most keen to accept our terms. But you have priority, at this stage.'

'It's absolutely out of the question,' said Celia. 'I will not part with forty per cent of Lyttons. That's all there is to it. And I'm sure you will all agree with me.'

Jay sighed. 'Not necessarily.'

She swung round to face him.

'What do you mean? What on earth do you mean?'

'Look, Celia, I'm sorry and I understand your feelings on this, but we've got to be realistic. There's no point resisting a further forty per cent stake when the Americans currently hold seventy per cent.'

'I don't quite follow you, Jay.'

'What I mean is, we only hold thirty-two per cent ourselves. New York have sixty-eight per cent. If we go with BISC, and get the shares, then we'll still be twenty-eight per cent better off. You must see that.'

'I don't. I think it's open to debate that we'll be better off. At least the Americans are Lyttons.'

'It's true,' said Venetia, 'at the moment we're only dealing with Lyttons New York. Who are at least publishers. We'd be going in with people who don't know a book when they see it. Unless it's full of figures. On the other hand, I really don't think I can face much more of Marcus Forrest. I'd go for these boys. We'd have a bit more control.'

'It seems to me,' said Giles, 'that whatever happens, the future's pretty bleak. I still think forty per cent is ruinous. I just don't think it's worth taking the offer. Swapping one set of dictators for another.'

'Giles, it's March the fifth,' said Venetia, 'if we give up on these people now, we'll never find anyone else.'

'I think that's right,' said Charteris. 'Not in the time, anyway. There is absolutely no leeway.'

'Well, I won't give my vote to it,' said Celia. 'And that is final. It would break Oliver's heart.'

'Oh Mummy, don't be so bloody melodramatic.' Venetia pulled out her cigarette case, passed it round. Jay took one. The others refused. It seemed oddly symbolic; dividing the group further. Venetia lit up, blew out a cloud of smoke; Celia promptly started to cough, waved the smoke away.

'Perhaps,' she said, 'you'd like to tell me in what way you consider I'm being melodramatic.'

'Daddy's not here. It might break his heart if he were, but it can't. And we're fighting to survive, could I remind you. Daddy would like that.'

'He wouldn't want this company in the hands of money people,' said Celia.

And so it went on. Finally, at five-thirty, Giles said, 'Look we have to tell them something this evening. We seem to have absolute stalemate. What do you want me to do?'

'Wait until tomorrow,' said Celia suddenly. 'Please.'

'Celia, we can't. We'll lose them.'

'I don't believe that. I'm sorry.'

Jay sighed. 'Could we take a vote on that? On our being prepared to risk losing the money?'

'I'd vote in favour,' said Giles, surprising everyone.

'So would I,' said Venetia. She smiled at her mother: a quick, warm smile. We've been through too much together, that smile said, to give up now.

'Very well,' said Jay. 'I think it's madness, but—'

Celia smiled at him.

'Thank you,' she said. And set off for home to do the awful thing.

Douglas Marks trudged along the bleak lane. It was a long way; it seemed much more than four miles. The air was freezing, and it was getting dim now, despite it only being three o'clock. He had gone to the pub first, a chilly, dispiriting place with a one-bar electric fire which seemed to have absolutely no heat in it and a landlord as unwelcoming as his premises.

School House was quite big; an ugly white rectangle, set against a hill.

A small hill. A mountain it certainly wasn't.

Marks pulled his camera out of his pocket and took another picture. It just might come out, despite the poor light. He walked up to the door, pulled a long metal bell handle. It jangled endlessly in the silent darkness behind the door. Nothing happened.

He tried again; then walked round the side of the house. There was a car, quite a new, smart-looking Vauxhall parked there; someone must be in. He went back, pulled the bell again, not too hopefully. And this time it happened.

Someone came, someone who could only be described as an old retainer, a small, grey-haired woman, wearing a drab grey dress and a white apron.

'Yes?'

'Good afternoon. I wonder if I might see Miss Scott. Miss Joanna Scott.'

'Miss Scott? Who are you?'

'My name is Douglas Marks. I'm a solicitor. From London.'

She shut the door again. Marks stood there in the cold darkness, feeling rather as if he was in a bad film.

Finally she opened the door again. 'You'd better come in.'

He stood there, waiting, for what seemed like a long time; it was oddly silent in the house, no sounds of people talking, or even moving about, no radio playing. But the house, or what he could see of it, was well-furnished, newly decorated, it seemed, with a thick carpet on the stairs, velvet curtains at the window. Obviously Joanna Scott had been spending her royalties on her house.

The retainer returned. 'Follow me.'

Marks followed her into a big room. It was less cold in here, there was a fire burning, and a thick rug in front of it; the curtains were closed. It was very dark.

'Mr Marks? I am Joanna Scott. You're from Rawlinsons, I presume. Is it about the settlement?'

Marks looked at her; her voice was quite refined, she was well-dressed, her hair immaculate, and she was at the very least in her late sixties. And she was in a wheelchair.

Celia stood in her room looking at herself in the long mirror, wondering if it was a little unsubtle to dress for the part as much as she had. To put on her most flattering dress, to make up her face with such care, to wear the diamonds Lord Arden had given her, which she had never really liked and had hardly ever worn. Well, she lacked the strength to change now; she would just have to be unsubtle. She took a deep breath and opened her door, set out along the corridor. She had been thinking about this for so long, wondering if she possibly could do it, shrinking from the insensitivity, the crudity of it, hoping against hope she wouldn't have to do it.

But – she couldn't bear to let everything go without at least trying. It would be a betrayal of Lyttons; a betrayal of everything she cared about.

Lord Arden was standing by the fire, smoking, drinking gin and tonic; he stubbed out the cigarette.

'Sorry my dear. Thought you wouldn't be down just yet.'

'That's all right, Bunny. I'll have a G and T, please.'

'You look tired. Feeling all right?'

'What? Oh, yes. Yes, I'm fine, thank you.'

She was tired; she was always tired these days. Maybe this new man her doctor was sending her to would be able to offer some help.

'Bunny,' she said, 'I want to speak to you about something.'

'Oh yes?' He was busy with the drinks tray; he didn't look at her.

'I—' Oh God, this was difficult; how could she do it, after the years of coolness, of indifference, of excluding him from her life. 'I – had hoped not to have to ask you.'

'For the money, you mean?'

She was astonished; so astonished that she sat down abruptly, feeling quite faint.

'You all right, my dear?'

'I'm fine. Yes, thank you.' She took the drink. 'I – I just didn't think you'd taken much of it in.'

'Celia, really. How absurd you are. You must consider me very stupid indeed.'

'Of course I don't. But—'

'I did wonder when you'd get around to it. Seemed to be taking an awfully long time.'

'Oh dear,' she said. Relief hit her; relief at not having to actually frame the words, face him with them.

'I'd love to help you, Celia. Love to help you get Lyttons back.'

'You would?'

More relief. She should have done this before, been tougher, braver. She smiled at him one of her brilliant, dazzling smiles. 'Oh Bunny—'

'Of course. I know what it means to you.'

'So much. Everything. Well' – she added, hastily tactful – 'almost everything.'

'But I can't.'

'You can't?' It didn't make any sense at first.

'No. I just don't have it. Nothing like it. Oh, I know, I've got all this land and property. I know everyone thinks I'm as rich as Croesus. But I'm not. Income tax is so frightful these days. Well, you know that, for God's sake. Dreadful, these people in control of the country now. No one would think there was a Conservative government in. No, I'm afraid I really am borrowed up to the hilt. Every acre is borrowed on, several times over. Nothing in the bank; in fact, if I died tomorrow, Coutts would be quite grateful. Huge overdraft there.'

'Oh,' said Celia. 'Oh, I see.' She felt rather dazed.

He looked at her. 'I'm sorry, old girl,' he said, coming over to her, putting his hand on her shoulder, 'so sorry. I kept trying to raise the subject, but you never seemed to want to talk about it. I'd like to be more involved in your affairs, you know, like to help you. I wish you wouldn't shut me out so much. Of course I can't help with the literary side, and I suppose I'm a lousy businessman, or I'd have some money in the bank. But I could listen to you, make the odd suggestion. I'm not entirely stupid.'

Celia looked at him; at this kind, infinitely generous man who she had married on a whim, an awkward, selfish whim, to whom she had seldom been more than courteous, often impatient, occasionally quite cruel, and she felt some rather unfamiliar emotions. Guilt. Remorse. Embarrassment, even.

And something else; something extraordinary. A kind of relief. Relief that she didn't, after all, have to abuse his good nature, take his money. He was too good for that, too innately generous. It would have been too much to ask. Or rather to take. Even if it had meant saving Lyttons.

'Of course I know you're not stupid, Bunny,' she said finally. 'And – I'm sorry. Sorry I shut you out. I always thought – well, that you wouldn't want to be bothered with my problems.'

'Well, I would,' he said, graciously ignoring the lie. 'It's all I can do for you, it seems. Listen to you. So – although I can't lend you the money, I might have a view on things. Why don't you tell me about it? While we have dinner?'

'Yes,' said Celia, 'yes, I think I'd like that, Bunny. Very much. Thank you.'

'This is a great story, lad. Well done. Lot of good stuff. I like the drab house outside and all the luxury inside. Some mountain. We'll give it a big splash at the weekend.'

'Not before then?'

'No, it's a natural. Certainly for the end of the week.'

Marks looked at his features editor.

'I think it's a bit of a risk. Someone else might get hold of it.'

'Oh, rubbish. It's only a few days. We'll run it on Thursday. You don't want it getting lost in some nonsense about the new Common Market, do you?'

'No, I suppose not,' said Marks meekly.

The following morning, Celia called a meeting in the boardroom.

'I think we should go with these people. I agree. At least we'll have some degree of control.'

Venetia looked at her in astonishment. Her mother was famous for never changing a decision; her mind, once made up, went into what Jay had once described as rigor mortis.

'Mummy! We're awfully glad, aren't we, Jay? But – why? What's altered?'

She sighed; she looked very tired. Looked her age, in fact, Venetia thought.

'Nothing's altered. Well, nothing that affects our situation I'm afraid. We should accept their offer. At least it's one in the eye for the Americans.'

'Well, that's marvellous,' said Jay. He spoke quite quietly. He felt as if he was walking on ice which was not just thin, but already cracking. 'I'm delighted.'

He smiled at her; even now, he could hardly believe it, felt terrified it was a sudden whim, that a serious argument presented to her now would make her swing away from her decision again.

'I'm not glad,' said Giles. 'I think you must have taken leave of your senses, Mother.'

He could hardly have said anything better calculated to confirm Celia's position; Jay felt like cheering.

'How very interesting,' was all she said.

'I shall go and call Gilmour immediately,' said Charteris.

He was afraid that the delay might have been fatal; but Gilmour said that with a little goodwill on both sides, they should be all right.

'Talk about a photo finish,' he said, 'but I think the Lytton head is just about in front.'

'Thank God,' said Jay.

★

The documents containing the Heads of Agreement arrived in Lyttons' offices on 7 March.

'Right, lad. Here's your big moment. First proper national story, eh?' Like to look over the page proof?

Marks nodded, took the page proof. It even had a picture of the School House. The snap he had taken had come out. It was a bit dark and smudgy, but it was unmistakable. The caption read 'Mountain or Mansion?'

He felt very happy.

The company secretary at BISC was about to add his signature to those of the chief accountant and the managing director on the Heads of Agreement, when his own secretary came into the boardroom.

'Excuse me, Mr Dolland—'

'Just a moment, Miss Curtis, I've got a messenger waiting downstairs for this.'

'But Mr Dolland—'

'I said just a moment.'

He signed the document, put it in the envelope, handed it to the post-boy who was waiting for it.

'Right, off you go. Hurry now, this is extremely urgent.'

'Mr Dolland—'

The post-boy had gone.

'Right, Miss Curtis. What is it?'

'It's this, Mr Dolland. I thought you ought to see it.'

She handed him the newspaper she was holding. He took it, glanced at it, then gripping it more tightly, sat down, read it very fast and said, 'Get that messenger back. Fast. Why on earth didn't you show me this before?'

'Publishers Humiliated.'

'Fraud Discovered.'

'Big Publishing Fraud.'

It seemed to be on every hoarding, that evening, the *Evening Standard*, and the *Evening News*, both carried it on their front pages as a teaser, both promised 'details inside'.

Giles sat with his head in his hands, refusing to see anybody; every time anyone told him it wasn't really so serious, it hadn't harmed anyone, he felt worse, sank deeper into his despair. It had harmed him, it had harmed Lyttons . . . and what Marcus Forrest would be making of it he dreaded to think.

More to the point, BISC had pulled out. A short, terse note to Harold Charteris expressing their regret that in view of the revelations in the press, they no longer wished to enter into a permanent arrangement with Lyttons.

'Anyone would think,' said Jay, throwing the paper down on the drawing-room floor that night, 'we'd been caught publishing pornography.'

Tory picked it up. 'Can I read it?'

'Of course.'

EXCLUSIVE: DOUGLAS MARKS

DOWN FROM DEER MOUNTAIN

I established today that the author of *Deer Mountain*, the book that was the best-selling title last Christmas, a book that has gripped the country's imagination, is not a tough, outdoors type, living on her own in a cabin on the mountains with only the deer for company, but a rich woman living in a large house in a village near Perth, and who has been in a wheelchair for twenty years. *Deer Mountain* was the brainchild of her daughter, Miss Fiona Scott.

Joanna Scott's grandfather was a ghillie; she used to visit him as a child, staying in his croft in the mountains, getting to know the countryside and its inhabitants, most notably the deer. She is a talented artist, and even as a small girl, used to make sketches of the deer and the mountainside.

She married a school teacher and together they ran the village school in Tullydie; her back was broken in a riding accident and she has been confined to a wheelchair ever since. Fortunately, she had family money which enabled her and her daughter to remain at the School House and live there in comfort for many years, after her husband died. But the money was beginning to run out.

Two years ago, they began to plan the book about deer. Mrs Scott could remember many of the individual deer clearly, and could recall stories told by her ghillie grandfather. Her daughter sent an outline, purporting to be Joanna's diary, to various publishers; Lyttons, the well-known family publishing house, bought it, and presented it to the public as a genuine story. It has sold in thousands, making a great deal of money both for the publishing house and for the Scotts. A children's version is planned for later this year.

A source at Lyttons disclosed that Mr Giles Lytton, who bought the book and who had met Miss Scott, claims he had absolutely no idea about the fraud. He never visited Tullydie and it was the daughter who presented herself to him as being Joanna Scott on her trip to the London office. Another member of the firm met her from time to time in Glasgow or in London.

Various members of the book trade said today they were shocked that Lyttons, always a well-respected house, should stoop to perpetrate fraud in this way.

'It is hard to believe they did not know,' said Mr Anthony Huntley of Better Books in the Charing Cross Road, 'although clearly the Scotts were a very cunning and devious pair. We will certainly be returning all our copies of *Deer Mountain*, feeling that we have been sold something under false pretences which we would not wish to pass on to our customers.

'What I can't understand,' said Tory, looking up at Jay, 'is how it didn't get out via her own community. This village where she's supposed to live . . . where she does live. There must have been some gossip, you know what villages are like—'

'Apparently, there was real affection for her there,' said Jay wearily. 'She'd been a very good teacher, she'd done a lot for the community, still does. She's put a fair bit of the money into a new village hall, there was a lot of sympathy when she broke her back, they're all very strongly behind her.'

'Well, good for them,' said Tory. 'I do like community spirit. It reminds me of the war, my darling, and meeting you.' She returned to the paper. 'I bet the shop will regret that,' she said suddenly. 'Returning the copies. I bet you'll sell more than ever.'

Jay stared at her. 'Do you really think so?'

'Of course. It's wonderful publicity, everyone will want to buy one now. You wait and see.'

'Even if you're right,' said Jay, putting his arms round her, giving her a kiss, 'and you could be, it won't get us our money, that's for sure.'

Keir took the same view as Tory. 'So bloody what?' he said to Elspeth that night. 'So Lyttons has been found guilty of fraud? Really serious fraud! For God's sake, it's hardly fraud at all, and if it is, it's piddling and it's brought us some wonderful publicity. *Deer Mountain* will sell more copies than ever, you mark my words. You're all looking at it the wrong way round.'

'Maybe,' said Elspeth rather vaguely.

Boy found it hugely amusing.

'What a brilliant con,' he said. 'Wish I'd thought of it. Maybe I could do one of my own. I could write a book about sheep. From the point of view of the humble shepherdess. I'll call it *Little Bow Creep*. Or how about *Little Boy Untrue*?'

'Oh do shut up, Boy,' said Venetia irritably.

Helena, while being sorry for Giles, was rather shocked.

'It is fraudulent,' she said, 'you must admit that Giles. Presumably this woman came in to the office at one point.'

'She did, yes,' he said. 'I met her. Well, not her, as it turns out. Her daughter.'

'And what did you think?'

'I thought she was a hugely disagreeable woman. But I thought the book was very clever.'

'Well it turns out you were right on both counts,' said Helena.

'Yes, I suppose so,' he said, encouraged by this faint praise.

'But I still think you should have checked on her more carefully. It can't be so very difficult.'

'Helena,' said Giles, and suddenly his face was white and taut with rage, 'when I ask you to come and do my job, you may. Until that day I would be grateful for your silence on matters of which you have absolutely no knowledge or understanding.'

Helena stared at him for a moment; then she said, 'Sometimes, Giles, you're so like your mother it is scarcely credible.'

The hurt he had inflicted on her was briefly eased; she left the room and most uncharacteristically slammed the door.

Celia, too, had bought the newspaper, but she did not have an opportunity to read it until she was on her way home from an appointment in Harley Street. The words meant very little to her; compared with the news she had just been given. The whole thing, indeed, seemed rather unimportant.

CHAPTER 37

There were lots of clichés about it: about electricity in the air, about charged atmospheres, about hostility which you could feel. Elspeth didn't think she had ever actually experienced it before. Faint echoes of it perhaps, when Marcus Forrest came into the office, changing arrangements, cancelling advertising schedules, even occasionally when Celia and Giles had one of their head-to-heads, as Keir called them. But not like this: when all the Lyttons were almost visibly circling one another, wary, watchful, distanced from one another, not meeting one another's eyes.

Keir was sitting slightly apart from the rest of them, very self-contained himself, not communicating with anybody, his brilliant dark eyes fixed on some papers he was leafing through, his almost-black hair untidy as always, his large hands clasped together in unmistakable tension.

Suddenly, as all married people do from time to time, Elspeth saw Keir quite differently, almost as a stranger, rather than the person she lived with, slept with, took entirely for granted, saw him not as her difficult, demanding husband but as an interesting, dynamically attractive man. He had changed physically since she met him, in those far-off days at Oxford: he was still only twenty-nine, but he looked in many ways much older. He had put on weight; he was heavily built like his father, no longer a skinny boy, but a big, powerful man, with broad shoulders and strong arms which still looked too long for his body. He worried about not getting enough exercise, said he was heading straight for a heart attack, desk-bound, over-stressed, eating too many good lunches. He had taken up boxing; went to train twice a week, at the Thomas à Becket gym in the Old Kent Road. He loved it, came back refreshed and better-tempered, his formidable energy released. And afterwards, he actually talked to her through supper, telling her about the men he had met there, many of them known to her by name at least, for it was where the pros went, people like Sugar Ray Robinson and Henry Cooper.

She was intrigued by this hobby, it seemed to her an interesting outlet for his aggression, and a return to his roots; one of his uncles had been a champion boxer in Glasgow, and Keir had often talked about him, of how brave he was and how strong, and how he could take on three men at a time in a street brawl and still win. When she said that it was hardly relevant to his life at Lyttons, he gave her one of his rare brilliant smiles and said she was wrong, physical fitness and courage were invaluable mental tools as well.

The expression on his face now, this stranger's expression, was intriguing, she thought: not equable, not even entirely pleasant, but ferociously intent; when he spoke it was quickly, impatiently, as if he could hardly get the words out fast enough in order to have a response.

He was not in the least like Marcus Forrest, for sure; people said you were always attracted to the same type of person, but it was hardly true in her case, they were at opposite ends of the spectrum, the one so perfectly polished and smooth, the other so deliberately awkward and coarse-grained. Marcus always dressed as if for a fashion photograph, Keir, as if he had dragged on some clothes dropped the night before on the floor; however many nice clothes she bought him (from her secret budget), however well-cut his suits and coats and jackets, however well-made his shirts, he looked the same, untidy, rumpled, careless. Marcus talked with charm and ease, Keir with directness and passion. Marcus flattered, smoothed; Keir was blunt and confrontational and often caused trouble. They were both formidably clever; but Marcus's intellect had been tamed, brought to order, Keir's was still wild, and intractable.

What was intriguing, Elspeth thought, was that they admired one another; and (she allowed herself to think very briefly) they both admired her. Perhaps that was the most surprising thing.

Her life with Keir was not comfortable; he appeared actually to dislike her much of the time these days, returning her smiles with scowls, greeting her chatter at the end of the day and over the supper table with a request for silence, while he read something or made some notes.

He had never tried to flatter her or to please her, but he used to tell her how much he loved her and why; he never gave the usual lover-like reasons, but said it was because she ate too fast, or talked in her sleep, or stuck her tongue out when she was concentrating on something, rather like a child. He admired her courage, he said, her stoicism in childbirth, and on the hunting field, as deeply as he deplored her passion for it, and her imperfections, her slightly crooked teeth, and what he called her over-rounded bottom. She couldn't actually remember, she realised, when he had last said anything like that, or indeed when he had told her he loved her; it was very sad. All that passion, all that literally irresistible love: gone.

No wonder she had taken a lover; but it was a dangerous road she was travelling, quite apart from the perils of being found out. Having a lover meant endless and odious comparisons, a careful refusal to find pleasure in the marriage, a reluctance to make any kind of effort, and what amounted to a watchfulness for slights, unkindness, lack of affection, providing, as they did, the excuse for infidelity . . .

Sometimes she wondered if Keir had some idea about her and Marcus, so hostile had he become. But if he had, he would not have kept his suspicions to himself; he'd have confronted her, shouted at her, quite possibly attacked her physically. And confronted Marcus as well, threatened him with violence, refused to work for him for another hour. She had no idea what might become of her; she tried not to think about it too much, to live for the moment as much as she could. But in spite of the excitement and pleasure of her affair with Marcus, its soothing, healing effect, she knew what she really wanted was something much simpler, much more rewarding, much more important. She wanted to work, to do what she was best at in the world; and she wanted to be happily married. She had gone into her marriage deeply in love, desperate to prove herself a good wife and mother; it had taken a great deal of unkindness and neglect to shift her from that ambition. She had been dangerously in need of comfort and affection when Marcus had first directed his formidable charm at her; that might be an excuse, but it was also true.

She saw Keir's eyes on her, thoughtful, brooding, and smiled at him; he didn't smile back. He really was—

Celia caught her eye, frowned slightly. She had noticed her grand-daughter's mind wandering; she didn't like that. Elspeth shifted on her chair, gave her her full attention; and wondered again what this was about.

Celia had called the meeting – without even hinting as to the reason – and had especially requested Elspeth's presence. Keir had made his usual heavy comment about the increasing number of meetings she was called to, but added that there was nothing he could do about it, since Celia had called it: and so she had gone. Marital disputes were hardly valid reasons for not attending meetings, least of all Celia's.

It had all started quite well; Celia had arrived, looking particularly glamorous in a pale-blue suit and very high-heeled beige shoes. It was extraordinary, Elspeth thought, looking at her, how real beauty survived age. Her skin was lined, her dark hair was streaked with a great white wing going backwards from her brow, and she was very thin. But the dark eyes were still large and brilliant, the mouth perfectly curved, the cheekbones high and finely etched, the neck still long and elegant, in the pearl and diamond chokers she had made her signature; and she wore such wonderful clothes, always in the latest cut and hem-length and fabric, she always looked so truly stylish. Elspeth planned to be exactly like her when she was old.

Celia sat down at the head of the boardroom table, told Giles to move from where he was sitting at the other end, to the chair on her right – there was no reason for this that anyone could see, except to emphasise his wretched position – and then made Keir fetch some water for her, told Jay to stop talking to Venetia, and Venetia to stop giggling, and began.

The announcement came at once; and its effect was almost as powerful as the previous one, made only six years before. It seemed longer. Lightning could not only strike twice, Elspeth thought, it remained as dangerous.

'I have decided,' she said, 'that the time has finally come for me to retire. And before any of you say or even think this is becoming tedious, I do assure you that this time I mean it. Don't look at me like that, Venetia, please. Any questions?'

'Well—' Venetia, half amused, half stung by the maternal admonition, put down her coffee cup and looked at her mother levelly. 'There's only one and we all ask it. Why?'

'It's time,' said Celia briefly.

'You said that last time.'

'I know. I was wrong. I misjudged it. This time I know. I shall leave Lyttons at once. After today, you will not be seeing me here. Unless you are kind enough to invite me to the occasional launch party, of course.' They were silent now, absorbing her words. In fact, Elspeth thought, it was more definitive than last time. The announcement of her retirement that day was overshadowed by that of her remarriage; you could feel the impact of it now, it dented the atmosphere, no longer light-hearted, but solemn and formal.

'Well – we're very sorry,' said Jay, and found to his astonishment that he was. It was one thing to wish her away, as he did every day of his life, quite another to find the wish granted, with such sudden and unseemly haste. 'I should be saying all sorts of gracious things and in due course, no doubt, I will, but that's all I can manage for now. From the bottom of my heart and indeed from all our hearts, I know. We shall miss you horribly.'

'Oh, I dare say,' she said, her smile rather brief, 'and I shall certainly miss you. But – don't worry,' her eyes danced with sudden malice, 'this time I won't be back. You know what they say: quit while you're ahead. I've always thought that a very sound philosophy.'

There's something else, thought Elspeth, some other reason we don't know yet. Perhaps it would emerge . . .

'Of course it could be argued that we are not ahead. We're still in thrall to the Americans, still forced to tug our forelocks to Mr Forrest. But we are doing well. As you know, that wretched business with the newspapers has had no effect on the sales of *Deer Mountain*, rather the reverse; I think we can breathe a sigh of relief on that one. Clementine's new novel is being very well received, and I have just commissioned – my legacy to you – a biography of Lillie Langtry. Fascinating creature, she has everything from the publishing point of view, she was an actress, a king's mistress, and one of the great beauties of her day. It will be published next autumn. General

Dugdale is also very much better and getting back to work.' Another pause; she looked very serious suddenly. 'Now – to business.'

'If that was the pleasure,' said Keir, 'I don't know that I can cope with the business.' He was looking more shaken than anyone; with good reason, thought Elspeth, he's losing his champion. Do him good.

'Oh nonsense. You'll like the next bit. It's about my editorial commitments. I want to hand them over to the right people. That is very important to me. I didn't do that last time. Probably significant.' A pause. God, she's milking this for all it's worth, Giles thought. Not missing a trick.

'I would like Keir, working with Elspeth, of course, to be in charge of what I have always called young fiction, the books by new, unproven writers. Many of those have become very well proven, as you know; but it is absurd for a woman of my age, or even an age approaching it, to be editing writers as young as my grandchildren.'

This was a point very often made by both Jay and Giles to her face and by several other editors behind her back; the fact was that she edited all fiction, by both young and old with a flair and vitality that was breathtaking. A hard act to follow, thought Elspeth, a lump suddenly in her throat: but we'll do our best for her, keep up her standards. She looked at Keir, smiled hopefully. He should be, he must be pleased, thrilled, even; but his face, meeting hers, was blank, his eyes stony. God, if he was going to fight this—

'Biographica, on the other hand –' Celia paused here, and the expression on her face was oddly touching; Biographica, perhaps the greatest imprint in autobiography and biography in English publishing, was something that was absolutely her own, she had created it as a young woman, before the twins were born, and she loved it passionately and possessively, almost as if it were another child. It would not be handed over lightly. '– I would like Jay to take Biographica on,' she said finally, and the smile she gave him was very sweet suddenly. 'If he felt able.'

That was good, Elspeth thought: very good. It would have been dreadful if she had not asked him; but she was more than capable of it, of dealing him the mortal blow.

And Jay, openly delighted, said that of course he felt able and that he would do his best to take care of it.

'I know you will. And I know it will be in the best possible hands. Don't let Marcus Forrest get his over-manicured ones on it.'

They were a bit over-manicured, Marcus's hands, Elspeth thought, she had often noticed them, just a bit too neat-looking, the nails perfectly filed and buffed; it was very American that, rather like his over-pressed suits and always new-looking ties . . .

'Celia!' said Jay. 'As if I would. I shall fight to the death to keep them in my own rather gnarled ones.'

495

Even Giles laughed; the tension suddenly eased. And then returned. Celia took a sip of water.

'And now, my shares.'

An absolute silence fell over the room; everybody so still it was as if they were not actually there at all, as if a photograph had been taken, freezing the moment in time.

'I have thought about this very hard,' Celia said, her eyes resting thoughtfully on each of them in turn, 'and it has not been an easy decision to make. Of course the shares are not very many in number; the days when Oliver and I, together with LM, owned Lyttons seem very far away. But times change. Within Lyttons London, they represent a degree of power. And although I am very aware that, in spite of what I said earlier, the company is going through a difficult time, that we are not our own masters, that we feel permanently unable to work with any degree of confidence, this is the wrong way to look at things. The Americans in general, and Mr Forrest in particular, may be making our lives difficult,' – her eyes rested on Elspeth: does she know, thought Elspeth, she must – 'but we have to remember one very important thing. They need us. They could not run Lyttons London without us.

'There is a very great deal of talent in this company. That is our power. And we have to hold fast, to fight for what we know is right, and never give in. At the moment it seems we will never recover our independence, but one never knows what is over the horizon. And when and if the time comes, we – I'm sorry, you' – she smiled, mischievously, her eyes dancing – 'must be absolutely ready.'

'Sounds like the Battle of Britain all over again,' whispered Jay to Venetia; she gave him a withering look and then suddenly choked into her coffee. Celia looked at them both very coldly.

'Perhaps you would like to share the joke with us all,' she said, 'otherwise, please concentrate on what I am saying. This is a serious meeting, and a serious matter.'

They were duly silenced; Venetia, looking down at her hands like a naughty little girl, Jay shifting slightly uncomfortably on his chair.

'I have tried,' said Celia, 'in making this decision, to look forward. That is what we must do, if Lyttons is to survive. It is very easy for older people,' – she can't bear to use the word 'old' Venetia thought – 'even middle-aged people, to look back, to cling to the past, if you will forgive the cliché, to refuse to welcome the future. That is extremely dangerous. And in passing my shares on, in the way I have chosen, I feel I am welcoming the future. That is why I hope you will feel able to agree that they are going to the right hands.' She stopped, smiled sweetly into the room, round the table. God, she's enjoying this, thought Jay, loving every moment, her last great performance, or even, possibly, her encore. 'I want them to go to someone who absolutely understands our traditions, but who is possessed at the same time with the courage for a new and innovative approach.' Another pause. Come on, come on, Giles thought, tell us, and please, for the love of God, let it be me.

'And I hope you will also feel able to agree with me that they should go not to just one person, but two.'

Another long pause; who, who? thought Venetia, her mind racing over the options, Giles and me? That would be kindest. Jay and me? That would be cleverest. Giles and Jay? That would be the most diplomatic—

'I give my shares, with complete confidence and my love, to Elspeth and Keir.'

Another silence: an almost frightening silence. Elspeth, feeling dazed herself, half thrilled, half tearful, smiled at Keir, reached across for his hand. He did not take it, just sat rigidly still, his eyes blank. So he was going to fight on against her: bastard. Absolute bastard.

Venetia struggled to smile, not to look – what? What did she feel? Put out, she supposed. It was too soon; they were too young. They hadn't worked long enough, battled enough, hadn't seen enough. Athough her parents had been just as young, when they had taken Lyttons into their control, shaped it exactly as they thought best: and with great success.

It seemed almost incredible now. And Elspeth and Keir would learn. They would not have it all their own way, rather the reverse. So – perhaps it was a good idea, given that there was plenty of time. And it was a clever option. Had she chosen one or the other, it would have been difficult, in all sorts of ways. This could heal the rift between Elspeth and Keir, force him to accept Elspeth's return to work, soothe his pride, smooth his path. She smiled at Elspeth, then at her mother.

Jay struggled harder; this was grossly unfair; Keir Brown, not a Lytton, not even very experienced, clever, yes, hardworking sure, talented certainly: but not a Lytton. Getting Celia's shares. Well, half of her shares. And was he himself really so far over the hill as not to be the next generation, the future Celia was so suddenly obsessed with, had he become, in his forties, the past? He could eventually have passed his own shares to Keir, that would have been fine. But for him to have them now, a young man in his twenties – it was very hard. Old witch; she'd always loved him, flirted with him, got him into the company. It was gross favouritism. All Jay's pleasure at being given Biographica faded away. This was going to be very hard to live with.

Giles felt only a sick, dull misery, a despair, a sense that it was over, that he had lost for ever any chance of running the company, of running even the 30 per cent which was left to them. That was all he had got after a lifetime of hard work, of disappointment, of humiliation at his mother's hands, and this was the final one: still only a small percentage of a small percentage.

He found it hard even to remain sitting at the table, so wretched did he feel . . .

'Well,' said Celia. She smiled brilliantly round the room, 'I think we should all have a glass of champagne, don't you? Toast Keir and Elspeth's future. And my rather delayed retirement. Giles, would you—'

But before Giles even had that satisfaction, of refusing to run to her bidding for the last time, one appalling last time, Elspeth stood up. Someone had to say something, she knew: and it should be Keir, he should have the grace, the good manners, the humility even. But he wasn't going to. He was angry: very angry. And she knew exactly why.

'Granny, I would like to thank you. Very, very much. Keir and I are both immensely grateful and immensely proud of the faith you're putting in us. We'll try very hard not to let you down, to earn that faith. And to wish you, of course, a very long and happy retirement. Will you all join me, please, in a toast?'

Venetia, watching everyone carefully, while helping Jay – not Giles, who sat slumped in misery – to serve the champagne, noticed two things. Two important things. That Keir had still not said a word, had not smiled, even. And that her mother's face, when Elspeth wished her a long and happy retirement was, beneath the warm, dazzling smile, infinitely and dreadfully sad. And the expression in her dark eyes, looking round the boardroom for what she had promised to be the last time, was oddly fearful.

CHAPTER 38

It was a dreadful loss to the office. Lytton House seemed sadly changed, less vibrant, without Celia – improperly dressed, as Keir put it. Jay had laughed, but it was true. Celia had lent not only her brilliant mind, her history, her unequalled associations with the industry to Lytton House, she had given it glamour. For weeks, they expected her to return, to hear her voice calling imperiously from her office, to see her tall figure, her still-lovely legs walking down the corridors, to look up and see her standing in front of their desks, with yet another idea, observation, suggestion, criticism. But it did not happen. And day by day they missed her not less, but more.

They speculated endlessly as to the reason for her departure: that Lord Arden might have finally put his long-suffering foot down, that she was weary of it all, that she was afraid of losing her edge, of not contributing as she should, that at last she had decided to make room for other things in her life. The arguments she had expressed, entirely reasonable and logical coming from anyone else, were simply unacceptable coming from her. The debate went on and endlessly on, not only in the office, but in restaurants, over dinner tables, in the boardrooms of other publishing houses.

It seemed astonishing afterwards, when they all knew, that no one had guessed the real reason.

Sebastian had known: from the very beginning. She had gone to see him, the day after she had seen the consultant, on the anniversary of Barty's death – and how appropriate that was, he thought. She had walked into his study, looking very pale, and stood in front of his desk. He looked up at her and smiled.

'Hallo, my darling. I wasn't expecting you today. You look tired.'

'Sebastian,' she said with a sigh, 'you should have learned by this time in your life that there is nothing more depressing for a woman than to hear that she looks tired. It's worse than being told she looks a fright. One can do something about that.'

'All right. You look a fright.'

'I know I do,' said Celia. She sat down. 'Hold my hand, Sebastian. I've had a bit of bad news.'

And Lord Arden knew; she told him as well, in her new affection and gratitude to him, told him what was happening to her, her tone very matter-of-fact.

'Sorry,' she said when she had finished, 'I'm going to be a bit of a nuisance, I'm afraid.'

Lord Arden looked at her for a long time, his expression, as usual, good-natured, slightly impassive. Then it changed; his lip quivered just for a moment, and his blue eyes filled surprisingly with tears. And then he went over to her and took her hand, bent and kissed it.

'Don't you worry about that, my dear,' he said, 'you're worth a bit of bother, I'd say. What do you want to do?'

'Bunny, would you mind very much, if I moved permanently into Cheyne Walk?'

'Of course I wouldn't. You've never really settled here. Want me to come with you?'

She didn't, of course; but in the most loving gesture of their entire marriage, she told him that she did.

Elspeth was having a hideous time; Keir had managed to remain silent until they reached home that day, and then he had rounded on her, savaged her, told her she must have known, that she and Celia had cooked it up between them, a clever ruse which would make it impossible for him to argue with her presence in the office, would force him to accept a proper role at Lyttons for her.

At first shocked, then angry, and finally deeply hurt, Elspeth stopped arguing with him, or trying to convince him. Nothing would persuade him otherwise, he said, he was sickened by the manipulativeness of it, by such a conspiracy against him and his beliefs. He could not live and work within such an open flouting of what was, to him, a deeply important principle of their marriage.

At first she had thought he would get over it, would come to terms with it; but as the days went by and became weeks and his anger remained, an anger against Celia as well as herself, she began to despair. She would not, indeed she could not, give in; it was unthinkable. Her pride and delight in her grandmother's gift was boundless. She felt capable of anything; her brain soared, teemed with ideas, she had a fierce new energy, a permanent sense of excitement. Rejecting the shares was simply not an option; and she saw Keir's hostility as a rejection of herself.

She offered him compromises (while wondering why she should): to wait until Robert was a little older, or to work a three- or four-day week until both children were at school, but he was adamant. Either she refused to accept her shares, her place on the board, continue as she had been, working from home as an editor, or he would leave Lyttons himself.

'Our marriage should come first,' he said, at the end of one particularly vicious row, 'and it clearly doesn't, as far as you are concerned. You may pursue your own ambitions, nurture your own appalling ego at the expense of your family if you wish. I will not be around to see it. Please make your choice. I will not be forced into compromising my principles, Elspeth, and that is all I have to say.'

Elspeth talked to Marcus about it; he said all the right things, of course, that Keir had no right to subject her to such emotional blackmail, that he was living in the past, that he could not deny her her rightful place at Lyttons, that he was dreadfully wrong to try to suppress her talents.

'But Marcus,' she said, loyalty to Keir rising rather surprisingly to the surface, 'you told me yourself that it was your career that broke up your own marriage. Don't you regret that?'

'I regret that my marriage is over,' he said, 'of course. But I couldn't have given up my career for it. I just couldn't. It would have been a betrayal of myself. And I think it would be the same for you.'

She found it quite sobering that he should speak in the same language as she had used to herself. It made her more thoughtful still about their relationship.

Celia was deeply distressed; that a gesture which she had genuinely thought would lead Elspeth and Keir out of the quagmire they had worked themselves into, should have proved so misguided. She tried to talk to Keir, but he refused to listen. He saw her as the chief architect of his misery, as much to blame as Elspeth; between them they had humiliated and diminished him, and it was not, he said, to be borne.

'I just don't know what to do,' Elspeth said, visiting her grandmother one morning in Cheyne Walk. 'I really think he means it, he's not going to give in.'

'And – are you?'

Elspeth looked at her. 'Of course not. How could I? You want me to have your shares, and I'm going to have them. It's a great honour and it's exactly what I most want in the world. This is about me, Granny, as much as the shares, it means the person I am is not the person Keir wants me to be. I think that's very serious. Ending my marriage suddenly seems the better option. No, I'm not going to give in.'

'Oh Elspeth,' Celia sighed. 'I really thought it was going to solve your problem. I thought it was such a clever idea. Poor Keir. He must be very unhappy.'

'I can't think why,' said Elspeth crossly.

'Darling, of course he's unhappy. No one behaves like that if they're feeling positive, and sure of themselves. Your grandfather was just the same. Absolutely impossible whenever he felt threatened.'

She looked steadily at Elspeth. 'You don't think – you don't think he's guessed? Or even found out for sure?'

'Guessed what?' said Elspeth quickly.

'Darling, I'm not a complete fool. And neither is Keir.'

Elspeth met her grandmother's eyes. She blushed.

'Are you terribly shocked?'

'Of course not. Just the same, I think you would be very wise to finish it.'

'Do you really? But Granny, Marcus understands me, he knows what I'm about, he values me, the real me. And you know why it started, because of exactly what I just said, because Keir doesn't. He wants someone who doesn't even exist. God knows why he thought I was that person.'

'I expect because he loved you.'

'But I've just told you, he doesn't love me. Not the real me. And he's been vile to me for so long, I can't even remember what it was like when he was nice.'

'I know all that. But he senses he's losing you. And he's very frightened. It's making his behaviour worse.' She stopped, looked intently at Elspeth. 'Do you love Marcus?'

The question took her absolutely by surprise, forced the truth out of her.

'No,' she said, 'no I don't. He's charming and thoughtful and funny and I do find him terribly attractive and – well, like I said, he knows and appreciates who I really am . . . But I don't love him, no. And he doesn't love me, either. I – I suppose I love Keir. I can't think why, but I do.'

'In that case, Elspeth, finish it. It may be a very glamorous and exciting affair, but it simply isn't worth it.'

Elspeth got up and walked over to the window, looked across at the river. 'May I ask you something?' she said. 'Something – very private? I so need to know.'

'You may.'

'Did Grandpa love the – the real you?'

'I suppose he must have done,' said Celia, and she smiled at Elspeth. 'Although the real me drove him almost mad. But I think he was more sure of himself than Keir. Keir clearly feels very beleaguered. Beleaguered by Lyttons.' She hesitated then said, 'You know, I did think of leaving my shares entirely to him. For that very reason.'

Elspeth stared at her. 'To Keir? Really? That would have made Giles cross! And Mummy.'

'Would it have made you cross?'

'No,' she said slowly. 'No, I don't think it would. I think I'd have been very pleased.' She smiled at her grandmother. 'I really must love him, mustn't I?'

'You must.' Celia kissed her. 'You'll do the right thing, Elspeth. You're my granddaughter, and more like me than any of them. Now, if you will excuse me, I must go upstairs and have a little rest before luncheon.' Elspeth was too involved in her own problems to find this remark odd.

Feeling more than slightly guilty, Izzie went to see a specialist in New York. Mary Desmond was not only a highly successful and brilliant gynaecologist and obstetrician, but she was also deeply involved in research into the new birth control pill and had done some very interesting trials on it.

She was impatient for its launch; mainly because it would bring an end to the dreadful agonies and scars, both physical and psychological, which thousands of young women like Isabella Brooke had had to endure.

She was particularly moved by Izzie in her anguish; she looked so young, little more than a child, with her long golden-brown hair and her pale face with its huge brown eyes. It was hard to believe she was twenty-nine.

She had listened to her carefully, to her fears about why she had not conceived, and asked her how long she had been working on it, as she put it, examined her, and then met Izzie's eyes very directly and said, 'I can't find any immediate reason why you should not conceive. Of course there are investigations we can make, but it seems a little early. I promise you, Miss Brooke, there is no real reason your abortion should have affected your fertility. You say there was no serious infection at the time, as far as you know – and I do assure you, you would have known about it – and therefore you have probably avoided the real danger.'

'How?' said Izzie, 'I mean, what would that have done?'

'Well, it could – only could, mind you – have blocked your fallopian tubes. There are three things you need in order to conceive: eggs, healthy sperm and unblocked tubes. I have no way of knowing how healthy your boyfriend's sperm is,' – her eyes twinkled at Izzie – 'but we can try to establish whether or not you are ovulating properly. What I want you to do is make a BTC for me.'

'What's that?'

'Sorry. We medics always forget we speak a different language. A basal temperature chart. I want you to take your temperature every single day. The temperature dips just before ovulation. It's surprisingly reliable. I presume you don't have any pain or discomfort around the middle of your cycle?'

'Not that I've noticed. Is that –' she hesitated '– is that a bad thing?'

'Of course not. It's just that some people do and it's an easier way of knowing that you're ovulating. Now, provided that's happening, and there really is no reason to think it isn't, that would be reassuring. We can also check your tubes, just to make sure they're not blocked. However, it isn't entirely pleasant, and it's usually done under anaesthetic. We can do it two ways, either with gas, which we blow through your uterus and thence up into the fallopian tubes – we can hear it, believe it or not – or we can do it with dye, inject it into your womb and then do an X-ray. It's called a tubal insufflation. But I wouldn't recommend it yet. It's far too early. Let's see how you're doing with the ovulation.'

'And what about my cervix? Might that have been damaged?'

'I certainly couldn't see any evidence of it.'

'But if it is—'

'Well, if it is, and as I say, I don't think it is, it might have become what we call incompetent. Which would mean there was a risk of miscarriage in the second trimester. At about fifteen or sixteen weeks. If that did happen then we could put a stitch in the cervix so that it wouldn't happen again.'

Izzie stared at her in horror, envisaging the longed-for baby lost again.

'Couldn't we do it anyway?'

'No. It's not done as a preventative device. There are risks attached, as with all medical procedures. But it would be there, as a second string. Literally,' she added, with her wide, warming smile. 'You do know, don't you,' she added, 'the best way of getting pregnant?'

'No,' said Izzie hopefully. Maybe she was going to say that you had to make love lying on your side, or under the kitchen table, or when the moon was full, something simple like that.

'Have lots and lots of sex and just enjoy it. Especially when you're ovulating, of course, but at other times as well. Mother Nature can be surprisingly perverse. Most infertility is the result of infrequent intercourse. Did you know that?'

'No,' said Izzie. 'No, I didn't.' And thought, smiling, how much Nick would like this particular piece of advice. She left Mary Desmond's consulting rooms feeling comforted. And stopped at a chemist on the way home to buy a thermometer.

Part of Mary Desmond's advice – to have sex often – was easy. Relaxing and not worrying about it, was not.

Three months had passed now, of careful temperature taking, careful timing; three periods had come and gone, three sets of raised hopes, sometimes for just a few hours, sometimes a few days, once a whole week. Nick didn't know, of course, she hadn't told him, it somehow made it worse, she didn't want him knowing how important it had become to her; all she had done was make a hole the size of a dime in her dutch cap. After all they still hadn't got a proper apartment, they still couldn't afford a baby; not really, not easily, not comfortably. He'd just laugh her anxieties away, tell her they had all the time in the world. And now, even the advice to have sex often was becoming difficult. She would take her temperature, find it was exactly the right time, and then set about seducing Nick. Without telling him why, this was often difficult. He worked erratic hours, they all did, often staying at their desks at Neill & Parker until midnight or later; then they would unwind with some wine, go and eat, then fall into bed at two or three in the morning. Izzie's ardour (usually feigned by this point) did not find a very enthusiastic response.

'Not now, honey,' he would say, kissing her, turning over away from her, 'tomorrow, that'd be great. Night, darling. Love you.'

And tomorrow would come and there would be another late night and by that time the precious lowered temperature would have risen and the priceless ready-to-go egg would have escaped so that when finally Nick did feel like making love to her she was disappointed and irritable.

'I'm sorry, Nick,' she said quite sharply one night, as he took her in his arms, started kissing and caressing her, 'I just don't feel like it.'

'But Princess, you felt like it last night.'

'Last night, yes, night before, yes, tonight I don't. OK? Now I'm really tired. Sorry.'

And then she would hear him, first silent with surprise, then snoring loudly and she would lie there, wide awake, grieving for yet another baby not conceived, already anticipating the pain both physical and mental that awaited her two weeks hence.

She went back to Mary Desmond, who had tried to reassure her, told her not to worry, studied her temperature chart, said she was obviously ovulating, that time, she was sure, would produce a baby.

'Yes, but you don't understand, I feel so miserable all the time, I can't think about anything else. And except when it's the right time, I don't even want sex. And I'm really snappy and horrid to Nick.'

'Have you discussed it with him?'

'No, I can't. He doesn't even know I've been trying.'

'I think you should. He'll be more understanding. Have you told him about the abortion?'

'No,' said Izzie in horror. 'He'd be so shocked, you don't understand. He's a really, really good person.'

'So are you. I would say.'

Izzie hesitated; then she said, 'No, I couldn't possibly. He'd – well, he'd never feel the same about me again. He'd think I'd been deceiving him all this time and—'

'Well, you have,' said Mary Desmond. Izzie looked at her; she was smiling. 'It's not a very serious deception, in my book. Perfectly natural, perfectly understandable. It was a horrific experience for you, you'd want to keep it from anyone. But I think perhaps you should tell him.'

'I can't,' said Izzie again, 'I simply can't.'

'Well, look. We still haven't investigated those tubes. Perhaps we should do that soon. We'll give it a couple more months and then have you in for a couple of days. But – try to relax, Miss Brooke. You're very young, you know.'

Izzie thought of twenty-six-year-old Elspeth with her two babies, of twenty-four-year-old Amy, pregnant with her second, and knew that she didn't feel in the least bit young.

Elspeth had decided to have a last try. If Celia was right, and Keir felt threatened, thought she didn't love him, then maybe she should try to convince him she still did. Maybe that would make all the difference. She waited until he seemed to be in a moderately good mood – as opposed to the really bad one that had become the norm, tried not to chatter through supper, cleared away while he read the paper and then went in with a jug of coffee. He frowned at her.

'I don't think I want any coffee. I'm sleeping very badly as it is.'

Not an auspicious start. She managed to look sympathetic – somehow.

'I'm sorry. Well, I shall have some. You know how well I sleep.'

'Indeed.'

'Keir, can we talk?'

'We can,' he said, putting down his papers. 'By which I presume you mean can you talk?'

'Keir,' she said, the easy tears rising, 'I'm trying to be – constructive. Please!'

He sat back in his chair, folded his arms, sat looking at her in a parody of patience.

'It seems very sad to me,' she said, 'that we can't talk any more. We used to talk all the time.'

'We did indeed. You had the time in those days.'

'So did you.'

He thought for a moment, then nodded. 'Aye. That's true.'

She was encouraged.

'You see – I think that's all that's wrong. Really. I still – love you.'

'You do?' His expression was dispassionate, almost disinterested.

'Yes. Very –' this was hard '– very much, Keir.'

'I see.'

'Is that all? All you have to say?'

'For the moment.'

'Don't you believe me?'

He sighed. 'I don't know what I believe any more. About anything.'

'All right. Try this. I really, really want our marriage to be a success. So much. Not this awful cold, dead thing.'

'Is that how you see it?'

'Well, yes. Don't you?'

He said nothing.

'I think back to the early days, when we were so – so together. When—'

She stopped. She was beginning to feel humiliated. When you wanted me, she had been going to say, when I wanted you. She did still want him; she wanted him a lot. She could hardly remember now when they had last made love, when she had known that strong, healing, complete pleasure. She sighed.

'Well, we were together then, Elspeth. We wanted the same things, we cared about the same things. It's rather different now, isn't it?'

'It is, yes. That's what I—'

'I'll tell you why it's different, shall I? Because now we want different things and care about different things. You want a career, you want success, you care only about yourself—'

'That's so unfair,' she said, and she was almost shouting, 'I do want a career, success is less important, but I care about the children—'

'So much that you're prepared to leave them every day.'

'That is a filthy distortion. I've already said—'

'Oh, you've said a lot of things. A lot of pretty things. You're not prepared to act on them though, are you? You say you love me. If you loved me Elspeth, you'd do what I wish, you wouldn't go against me all the time, belittling what I hold most dear. You wouldn't try to make me feel a fool, an old-fashioned fool for having ideals, about marriage, about where men and women should stand in marriage—'

'I have never tried to make you feel a fool.'

'You might not have tried, Elspeth. You've certainly succeeded. Oh, it was very clever, that plan of your grandmother's, forcing me to accept you working. Well it's not forced me. Don't talk about loving me, Elspeth. It makes me feel sick.'

He stood up, glaring down at her; she sat in her chair, crying, frightened by the passion she had apparently unleashed, hurt beyond endurance.

'I'll tell you what you're doing, you're destroying me. Me and everything I stand for and believe in. I loved you once, more than I can say. I fought it, you know, I fought loving you—'

'Why?' she asked, her tears halted.

'Because I knew it would lead to trouble. We're too different, our roots are too different—'

'Oh Keir! Really! That is just so absurd.'

'Oh, it's absurd, is it? I don't think so. My standards were not your standards, my ideals were not yours. They could never be. I should have seen that, I was a fool—'

'I see,' she said, very calmly. 'Well, I'm glad you realise it now. Clearly I was a fool as well. Good night. What a very interesting conversation this has been.'

She went to bed then, in the spare room; she fell asleep at once exhausted, and then woke at three and spent the rest of the night staring into the darkness, hurt and bewildered beyond anything, and wondering if there was anything she could do except give up on her marriage. Since Keir so clearly didn't love her any more.

She could never remember feeling so lonely. Not even in the flat in Glasgow.

'Darling, you seem awfully unhappy. Tense. Not the girl I used to know. Is there anything you ought to be telling me?'

'No. No, I don't think so.'

'You sure?'

'I'm sure. Yes.'

'Absolutely certain sure?'

'Oh Nick, for heaven's sake. I'm quite sure.'

'Good. Because I was beginning to wonder if there was something wrong with me. If I had BO or some other unmentionable thing.'

'Of course not,' said Izzie, 'don't be silly.'

'I'm relieved. You may be my sunshine, as the song said, but the clouds seem to be covering you over quite a lot of the time just now.'

'No,' said Izzie, 'no really. I'm fine.'

'And you still love me?'

'Of course I do.'

'Good. Because I have a little idea. Which just might make you happy.'

'What's that?'

'I think we should get married. And settle down to making babies. How'd you feel about that?'

Izzie burst into tears and rushed out of the room.

CHAPTER 39

'Oh my God!' She could hear her own voice, shaky, shocked, disbelieving. 'Oh my God!'

It couldn't be possible. Absolutely couldn't.

She sat down at the kitchen table, holding the letter, realising her fingers were trembling. In fact, she was trembling all over, she felt sick, she was going to—

Jenna, calm down. Just calm down. Nothing's happened yet. It was probably a mistake, a stupid, ridiculous mistake.

But – here it was. A letter addressed to Charlie, from some legal firm, about her. Lying on the top of the great untidy heap of stuff on his desk, where she'd been looking for a letter to school he'd promised to write about her doing extra riding next term; they'd phoned to say they hadn't had the letter yet and it was important.

Saying – she forced herself to be calm, to read it very slowly, half aloud, so that it made more sense – saying that she was entitled to one third of her father's estate. Or at least, that seemed to be what it was saying:

. . . just to confirm my advice to you as a result of our second meeting of July 9, 1959, re. the estate of the late Laurence Elliott:

1. That his afterborn child is entitled to an equal share of this estate, under Section 28 of the New York Decedent Estate Law. Provided, of course, that the mother did not waive any rights to a claim.

2. That we would need to take two actions in the Supreme Court. The first to establish that the claim is valid, and that Jeanette Elliott is the afterborn child, the second an order to account.

In plain language, that would mean that the trustees of the late Mr Elliott's estate, and the beneficiaries of that estate, would be called to account. This would be decisive in terms of Miss Elliott's entitlement. Perhaps you would be good enough to let me know whether you wish to proceed with the first action, and if so, when you could come in to see me again, so that you can acquaint me more fully with the details of the case. I sympathise with your reasons for the delay over the past six months, but in answer to your last question, I see no need for Miss Elliott to be involved until we have established the merits of this case.

Yours truly

Jonathan Wyley

Jenna put her head in her hands and burst into tears.

She had been feeling so much better. So much stronger, quite happy, even, a lot of the time. She couldn't help it; her life was moving on, and very pleasingly so. She felt guilty at first, feeling happy; like when they were all sailing out at the Hamptons, or having a barbecue with friends on the beach; or when she and Cathy were getting on well, instead of squabbling as they did a lot of the time now; or when she went back to school that summer and it was so great to see everyone and to be welcomed back and to realise how many good friends she had.

Then, she had been in the end-of-term play and that had made her happy too; she got the lead part in a musical called *Love From Judy* (based on *Daddy Long Legs*, one of her favourite books as a child). Of course there was some sadness in there as well, thinking of how proud her mother would have been, of how she'd have been cheering her from the front row, but Charlie had been cheering in the front row instead and that had been pretty nice.

Charlie had continued to be great: really great. So kind and loving, and for a whole year after her mother died, had never even gone out once without her, not even to have a drink or to the movies. She had dreaded him getting another girlfriend, it was one of the things which had most frightened her. Although she could see that it probably had to happen and maybe it wouldn't be so bad. He was, after all, very good-looking and very sweet, and he was clearly lonely. She and Cathy were away a lot, he was bound to want female company sooner or later. He had been out with one girl, who he'd met through his business, just for a drink; Cathy and Jenna had teased him so much about it, he said if he ever did it again, it would have to be in deepest secrecy.

'You couldn't do anything in secrecy,' said Jenna, giving him a hug.

But – it seemed he had.

They had come back from Southampton to get ready for the return to school. Charlie was out, at his small office – the showroom had gone – Cathy was away with a schoolfriend, and Jenna was at home alone, waiting for some friends to call. They called; she told them she couldn't make it that day.

She waited: for a long time. Finally, well after lunch, he came in; she heard him whistling as he threw his coat on to the chair in the hall – her mother had always got so cross when he did that – then running up the stairs. He was clearly on his way right up to the top floor to his study, but he saw her, sitting in the drawing room, watching him, and stopped.

'Hallo, sweetheart. I thought you were going out?'

'I – was. But then I needed to talk to you.'

'Oh darling. Well, I'm here. Want a drink or anything? Have you had lunch?'

She shook her head.

'No, I'm not hungry. Thank you.'

'Well, want to tell me about it? What's the matter?'

'Charlie, why did you go to see those lawyers? Wyley and whatever. About me? Without telling me?'

'Ah.' He sat down on one of the deep, lush sofas opposite her, and stared at her. He looked very pale, very shocked. He was clearly struggling to find an explanation. 'Yes. Well – well, how did you find out?'

'The lettter was just lying on the top of your desk. I saw it.'

'Jenna, you shouldn't go to my desk.'

'You never minded before. You always said it was fine. I was looking for a letter about riding lessons, they called to say they needed it. You shouldn't be so untidy, Charlie,' she added with a ghost of a smile.

'You're right. I shouldn't.' He returned the smile; more ghostly still.

'Well – I'm waiting. What is this, what is it all about?'

'Jenna, I don't even know how to begin. Where to begin. I feel – just so terrible that you should have found the letter. I must look such a – so devious to you.'

'Just a bit.'

'The thing is – oh hell, do you mind if I have a drink?'

'Of course not.'

She watched him as he poured himself a stiff bourbon and sank heavily on to the sofa again.

'It goes like this,' he said slowly. 'The thing is, I read a case, it was about someone like you, someone who's been born after their father dies.'

'The afterborn child,' said Jenna. Her expression had changed now; it was tougher, more thoughtful.

'How did you—? Oh, of course, you read the letter—'

'I read the letter.'

He waited, then said, leaning forward, his eyes fixed on hers, very candid, 'The thing is, sweetheart, I've always thought it was so unfair, those two getting all the money when you had nothing—'

'Hardly nothing, Charlie.'

'Nothing of his. Jenna, that estate must have been worth millions. Millions and millions—'

She said nothing.

'You have a right to it. An absolute right. I remember telling your mother that.'

'And—'

'She didn't want you to have it. She had her reasons, of course. But – it felt wrong to me. Anyway, I'd always thought there was nothing that could be done about it. The money was gone, willed away. And then – well, like I said, I read this article. I decided to do some research on your behalf. Jenna, there is no doubt. No doubt at all. As you could see from that letter. The money is yours. For the taking.'

'Yes,' she said, 'so you say. So Mr Wyley says. But the thing is, Charlie, I don't want to take it.'

This was the test, she thought, looking at him for the first time with suspicion; if he pressed it now, then his motives were not entirely unselfish. He was hoping to get his hands on at least some of the money. If only vicariously. He was very extravagant; that much she had observed.

Charlie looked at her and smiled; his sweetest smile. He held out his arms to her.

'Then, darling, of course I'll drop the whole thing. I wouldn't dream of pushing you into something you don't like. I was only thinking of you, I swear. We'll write to Mr Wyley together, right now, and tell him we don't want him to do anything. And you can post the letter,' he added, as she moved into his arms, sat next to him on the sofa, rested her head on his shoulder. 'So you know I'm not going to cheat on you.'

'Charlie! Of course not. Well – yes, let's write. I'd like that, like to get it settled. And – I'm sure you meant well, please don't think otherwise. It's just that – I so hate money.'

'I know you do,' he said.

But before they wrote the letter, the phone rang; and it was forgotten.

Izzie was lying on the bed when Nick came back; he had stormed out, they had just had a row. Another row. They kept having them these days; she was so edgy and miserable, and the sex thing had got worse not better, all she could think about the whole time was conceiving. She was tense and awkward where she had once been relaxed and joyful, and somehow every little thing just blew up first into bickering and then into a full-blown row. That night had been specially bad, he had come in with some flowers and they weren't very nice flowers, he had clearly bought them at the drugstore, not a florist. While once she wouldn't have given it a thought, today it irritated her; she'd tried, pretended, but as she was getting a vase, he bent to kiss her and she just couldn't help it, she'd turned her head away, and – well, he'd just gone. Stormed out. And now he'd come back; looking at her for the first time in their entire relationship with something close to distaste.

'Hallo,' she said.

He didn't even answer, but walked over to the sideboard and poured himself a drink. Then he turned and looked at her, his eyes hard.

'Who is he?' he said.

'What?'

'I said, who is he? Who's the other guy?'

'Nick, I don't know what you're talking about.'

'Oh, please,' he said, 'can we just get this over? Clearly, there's someone else. I'd kind of like you to tell me who it is, then I can clear out of here and not take up your time any longer. Maybe I should do that anyway, maybe I don't need to know. It's up to you, I guess.'

'Nick, there isn't anyone else. I swear to you.'

'Oh yeah? Is that really so? In that case, why have you gone off me? Why do you kind of cringe when I get into bed? Why do you make love to me, which isn't exactly frequent, as if you were fulfilling some tedious duty? Why don't you talk to me any more? Really talk, I mean? Why do you look at me as if you disliked me half the time? If all that doesn't add up to screwing someone else, Izzie, I seem to be seriously bad at arithmetic all of a sudden.'

'Oh God,' she said, sitting up, putting her arms round her knees, burying her head in them, 'Nick, don't. Don't talk to me like that.'

'But why not?' he said. 'Why shouldn't I?'

'Because it hurts,' she said, and she was shouting at him now, her voice harsh and angry. 'You don't know how much it hurts. I can't bear it, Nick, I really can't.'

'*You* can't bear it!' he said. 'Oh, now that is really rich. How about me, how about what I'm having to bear?' He stopped suddenly, stared at her. 'Is it that creep MacColl? Is it? I swear to God I'll kill the bastard if it is—'

'No,' she said. 'No, no, no. It isn't anyone, Nick, it isn't. It's you I love, really, really love, can't you get that into your head?'

He looked at her in silence for a moment, then, 'It's very hard,' he said, 'hard to get it into my head, I tell you that.'

'You'll have to try.'

He lit a cigarette, walked over to the window, turned to look at her. 'I am trying, for God's sake,' he said, 'just try telling me about it, huh?'

'I'm – I'm just feeling very tired,' she said, finally. 'Tired and upset.'

He shook his head wearily, walked over to the cupboard, and started dragging his things out of it.

'What are you doing?'

'What does it look like I'm doing? I'm packing. I'm leaving. Being tired and upset, that isn't enough. It just doesn't make a person act like you've been acting. Sorry.'

'But – but Nick, I told you. I love you. And there isn't anyone else.'

He sighed . . . pulled his suitcase out from under the bed, put a few things in it, then stopped suddenly and looked at her, his eyes infinitely sad.

'You'll have to do better than that,' he said.

Izzie stood up, facing him; her eyes were very large and dark, her hands twisting together behind her back.

'All right,' she said. 'I'll try.'

He sat and listened in absolute silence while she told him her sad, sorry, difficult story, standing there as if before a judge and jury, not flinching from anything, too frightened to meet his eyes. And when she had finished, he said, 'Look at me,' and his voice was different from anything she had heard before, somehow louder and harsher. Taking all her courage, she had looked at him, expecting to see anger and distaste, and saw instead only absolute tenderness and sorrow and saw, too, the reason for the changed voice: he was struggling not to weep.

'Come here,' was all he said, and she went to him. He put his arms around her, and kissed her, very tenderly, kissed her mouth and her eyes and her hair and finally said, 'And you went through all that quite alone?'

'Yes,' she said. 'Of course I did, I had to, there was no one else who could help me,' and he said, 'Dear, dear God, Izzie, and you thought I would be angry with you?'

And then somehow they were lying on the bed, and she was wanting him more than she had ever wanted anything in her entire life, and something happened between them then which was very swift and absolutely overwhelming.

In a flood of relief and tears and even laughter came love, love expressing itself more beautifully than she could ever remember: in a glorious softening and welcoming, reaching and flying and a bright intense explosion, then falling, falling into peace, and through the peace, Nick telling her how much he loved her.

And then through it came the sound of the phone ringing, on and on; and the peace was broken into with horrible abruptness and the happiness almost shattered.

Elspeth had gone to have lunch with Marcus Forrest; she had intended not to, to tell him finally that she didn't want to see him any more. Or at any rate, not for several months. Her life was difficult and dangerous enough without his presence in it; certainly until she had decided what to do about her marriage. The marriage was very bad indeed now; apart from the continual quarrelling and hostility there was no physical contact between them at all any more, she could hardly remember when Keir had last kissed her, even. She got into bed each night and he would join her hours later, after saying he had work to do; and when he did get in beside her, he lay very carefully and deliberately on his side of the bed and didn't even touch her except by mistake.

She was relieved in a way; you couldn't want someone who was so hostile to you, who you felt you hated sometimes in return, you couldn't want them to make love to you. It would be truly a violation, the very thought of it made her cold, closed up to him.

It was horrible; if it hadn't been for Marcus, she would have thought she had become completely frigid. Only that wasn't quite right either; sometimes, when she lay in the darkness against Keir's cold, hostile back, she felt a surge of wanting him, so strong that it actually hurt physically, and she would think perhaps, if they could only meet there in bed, perhaps things could still be mended. She tried, occasionally, put her hand out, felt for him, felt for a response, kissed the hostile back even, pressed herself close, but it was hopeless, he never responded, never stirred; then she would turn away, and cry herself, very silently, to sleep. And wake up angrier and colder than ever.

Somehow, because she was so lonely and unhappy, when Marcus did arrive in London, when he phoned her to ask if she would like to have lunch, to say that he had missed her, that he couldn't wait to see her, it was so literally heart-warming, to be wanted, to be found desirable, that she had not said no, it was out of the question, that the whole thing had to end; but had heard herself, instead, saying feebly that yes, that would be lovely, lunch anyway, and she had missed him too, and couldn't wait to see him either. Maybe she could say something today.

Mrs Wilson was just putting the children into their coats and hats after lunch, ready for a trip to Battersea Park, when the phone rang. She was half tempted to ignore it, and probably would have done had Cecilia, who had developed a penchant for telephone conversation, not picked it up and said, 'Hallo.'

'Hallo, my darling. It's Noni.'

'Hallo, Noni. Come and see me.'

'I can't, darling. Is Mummy there?'

'No. Only Wilson.'

This was her rather grandiose name for Mrs Wilson; the 'Mrs' had eluded her, while the rather easier name of Wilson had stuck. Nobody minded, certainly not Mrs Wilson, but Keir felt it smacked of snobbery.

'Can I speak to Wilson?' said Noni.

Mrs Wilson was rather nervous of the telephone; she had never used one before going to work for the Browns. She took it and shouted, 'Hallo?' into it.

'Hallo, Mrs Wilson. It's Noni here, Noni Lieberman. When will Mrs Brown be back?'

Mrs Wilson was even more in awe of Noni, with her exquisite clothes and her fame, than she was of Celia. She virtually curtseyed into the phone.

'Tea time,' she shouted.

'Ah. Well, can you get her to ring me, please?'

'Let me get a piece of paper.'

Mrs Wilson wrote down the message very slowly and carefully in capital letters.

'And tell her I saw her at lunch time at the Ritz with the lovely Mr Forrest.'

'Mr who?'

'Mr Forrest. No need to write that down, Mrs Wilson, probably best not. Just tell her, all right? Thank you so much. 'Bye for now.'

Mrs Wilson wrote the second half of the message down anyway. It might be very important, a lot of Mrs Brown's messages were. And anyway, she might forget to tell her.

Venetia was working on her autumn schedule for Marcus Forrest when Lord Arden phoned. She was surprised when her secretary announced him, he had never phoned her in the office before.

'Hallo Bunny. How are you?'

'I'm very well. But—'

Venetia listened, half her mind initially still on her budget; five minutes later, eyes huge in her white face, she walked into Giles's office.

'Whatever you're doing,' she said, 'it can wait.'

She went into Keir's office as well, told him and said where she was going.

'And get hold of Elspeth, for God's sake. She'll want to be there.'

Keir phoned home; and was told that Elspeth was still not back.

'Not back from where, Mrs Wilson? I thought she was working at home today.'

Mrs Wilson felt very pleased with herself; as she thought the second part of the message had proved important after all. 'Oh, no, Mr Brown. She's having lunch. At the Ritz. With Mr – excuse me just a moment, Mr Brown, while I look – oh, yes. With Mr Forrest.'

'So you see, Marcus, I really really think perhaps this ought to end, it's been perfectly lovely, I've adored every minute of it, but – well, my life is so difficult and Keir is so impossible and—'

'My darling Elspeth, I thought that was the whole point. I thought that was how I had managed to persuade you to – well, to yield to me.'

She giggled; one of the things she most loved about Marcus was his absurd turns of phrase. She decided she would just enjoy the day and discuss it all further next time.

'You do a lot for my insomnia, you know,' he said, smiling at her. 'I fall sweetly asleep every night, counting your various assets. Modesty forbids my telling you quite what I count, here in this public place, but it is a most formidable list, I do assure you. Now then, eat up? Or are you feeling nervous?'

She laughed and said she wasn't; somehow being with him made her feel so much better about everything. She was in the middle of telling him exactly that, toying with the stem of her wine glass as she did so, when she looked up and saw Keir standing in front of the table.

Expecting abuse, she received none; braced for rage, she saw none; ready for violence, she felt none. Only Keir's face, harrowed with pain, only his voice, heavy with grief: as he told her that Celia had been in surgery all morning to remove part of her right lung, riddled as it was with cancer, that the cancer had been far more extensive than the surgeon had expected, that she was still unconscious and although she had forbidden Lord Arden to tell anybody, he had acted on the surgeon's advice to notify her family without delay.

CHAPTER 40

Charlie insisted on going with her; Jenna was grateful, really, although she kept telling him that she'd be all right, that she'd have Izzie to look after her, but he insisted; having witnessed her last panic attack, he said, he was afraid of it happening again.

'I won't be a nuisance once we're there, I promise,' he said. 'I'll keep out of the way, unless you need me.'

'Of course you won't be a nuisance. And – it would be nice,' she said with a feeble smile.

She was very shaken; she might not have known Celia very well, but as far as she was concerned, she was almost her mother's mother, almost her own grandmother, one of the people in whom her own rather sparse personal history was rooted.

And Celia had been very important to her. She had been the only English Lytton at her mother's wedding to Charlie, a wonderful comfort and strength when her mother had died, an example of courage ever since. She loved the way Celia's personal history was woven into Lyttons, working there, fighting for it, caretaking it during two world wars; it was just as much her creation and achievement as her family. And now it seemed she was going to leave them: leave her family, leave Lyttons, leave everyone who loved her.

'Why didn't she tell us she was ill?' she said to Izzie, clinging to her hand as well as to Charlie's, her teeth chattering as the plane rose into the air, seeking to distract herself from the hot panic, the cold nausea.

'She wouldn't,' said Izzie, 'she'd hate to have to tell us, she was never ill, she disapproved of it, she thought it was feeble. She wouldn't even let anyone be tired.'

'My mother was like that,' said Jenna. 'How strange. When they weren't even properly related.' She released Charlie's hand, but continued to hold Izzie's, took a deep breath. 'I feel a bit better now. Now we're up here. What were we saying? Oh yes, I guess some of all that just rubbed off on my mother. God, it's like a bad dream, all happening again.'

'I know, Jenna,' said Izzie, 'I know. I'm so sorry.'

'I just hope we get there in time. In time to tell her goodbye. I'll never get over not saying goodbye to my mother.'

Izzie looked at her helplessly.

'I'm sure we will,' was all she could say.

Nick and Mike had both come to see them off; Nick had offered to come too, but Izzie felt it was best he wasn't there, that in a way she would rather deal with it on her own, and help her father through what would be quite dreadful grief.

'OK. If you say so. I'd have rather liked to bid her farewell.'

'I'll do it for you.'

'It's so sad. She was the greatest lady I ever met.'

'She was the only lady you ever met,' said Mike.

'That's not very nice. Don't insult my girlfriend,' said Nick. 'Goodbye, Princess. I love you. Call me if you can. And keep looking up at the stars.'

She was crying so hard when she said goodbye to him that she could hardly see his long, lugubrious face through her tears. But she had to pull herself together for Jenna. Poor, poor little Jenna.

Venetia and Adele sat side by side in the waiting room; they were holding hands, little girls again in this great crisis of their adult life, communicating in their truncated language. 'Do you—?'

'Didn't think—'

'Should we—'

'Let's ask—'

'He mightn't—'

'But you never know—'

On and on it went, irritating Giles almost beyond endurance. How could they not have guessed, he wondered, how, when it had been the first thing they had all thought of the first time, the first time she had announced her retirement? Especially as they all knew she had been ill. But somehow – it seemed too obvious, too likely. Or maybe they had assumed she would have told them this time; would wish to avoid any misunderstandings, another set of mistaken rumours.

They should have known better, should have read her more clearly. But she had always been so very hard to read.

Kit and Clementine had arrived; Kit sat motionless, holding Clementine's hand, only releasing it when she hurried from the room white-faced, and returned a little later, looking better. Nobody knew why, until she confided in Venetia that she was pregnant. Venetia smiled with pleasure.

'We must tell Mummy. She'll be so pleased.'

And then became silent as she realised they might never tell her mother anything ever again.

Sebastian sat in a corner of the room, silent, quite motionless, hunched over a book; every time the door opened he looked up, an agony of fear in his eyes, and every time it wasn't a doctor or a nurse, he returned to the book. He had not said anything at all, except to greet Kit and Clementine when they arrived. Adele, looking at him, wondered how he was going to bear it.

Lord Arden was also there; pale, but quite calm, greeting people courteously as they arrived, rather as if they were coming to dinner.

She can't die, she can't, she can't, Elspeth kept thinking: over and over again, like a mantra, feeling somehow, absurdly, that as long as she kept it up, Celia would remain with them, where she was needed, where she was loved. The prospect of life without her was so unlikely, it was not really a prospect at all, it was a bad dream, a ghostly fear, a dreadful unreality.

She was sitting next to Keir, holding his hand, clinging to it, as she had been, ever since he had told her, standing there in the absurd over-gilded dining room of the Ritz, apparently unsurprised to see her sharing a table (and clearly quite a lot more) with Marcus Forrest. Suddenly, in that moment, the misery and misunderstanding and anger of the past few months were wiped out in a great sweep of grief and shock and fear; retribution, she knew, would come, must come, but for now, the situation was too urgent, too extreme to allow for anything else.

They went together to the hospital. It seemed quite late; but she was not aware of being either tired or hungry, simply lost in a white-out of emotion which she supposed was fear. Every so often she would catch her mother's eye and they would smile at one another, but they had not spoken, apart from when she arrived; no one was saying anything, the silence as absolute as the fear.

None of her brothers and sisters were there; it was agreed there might be too many, that they would all drive one another mad.

Boy was to meet Izzie and Jenna at the airport; they would arrive late that night. She has to live till then at least, Elspeth thought; she has to, they have to be able to say goodbye to her.

And then it happened; the door opened, and Mr Cadogan, the surgeon, came in, no longer in his gown. Nobody moved, nobody spoke; only Sebastian rose, very slowly, his face haggard.

'Well,' Cadogan said, and unbelievably, almost shockingly, he smiled. 'Good news. At least – better news. She has regained consciousness, in fact, she's quite alert. Asking to see people, even . . .'

He seemed surprised; her weary and traumatised family were less so. Celia could confound most predictions, get the better of most things. Including, at the moment it seemed, death.

'And – can we?' asked Venetia tremulously. 'See her, I mean?'

'Very, very briefly. And only immediate family. Of course, with an operation like this, there are no guarantees, and –' he sighed portentously, lest they might not take his news entirely seriously '– and of course the fact remains that she does have lung cancer. We have not been able to remove all the tumours, and she is extremely frail. However, for the time being, she appears to be out of danger. Lord Arden, if you would like to follow me—'

Lord Arden looked round at them all apologetically; Adele gave him a gentle push. 'Go on, Bunny. Give her our love.'

Sebastian spoke for them all; heaving first a tumultuous sigh, then breaking into his sudden, radiant grin.

'Old she-devil,' he said.

The twins were allowed in, just for a moment, and then Giles and Kit. Celia was surprisingly alert, demanding to see everyone else. The nurse said she had had quite enough for one day: 'Tomorrow, perhaps.'

They were told to go home, after their brief visits.

'You all live nearby,' the surgeon said, 'we can contact you at once if there is – well, if there is any need.'

Gratefully, with a slight sense of anti-climax, they went.

Only Lord Arden and Sebastian said they would stay, refused to be dismissed; Elspeth, leaving the room reluctantly, for she had not been allowed to see her grandmother, looked at the two of them and thought how extraordinary it was that they could be there, keeping vigil together, without hostility, without jealousy even, simply and determinedly stating the same desire: not to leave Celia, under any circumstances, not to risk her dying alone, but to be with her until their respective duties as her husband and her lover were properly and finally done.

It had been decided that Izzie, Jenna and Charlie would stay at Berkeley Square. Izzie should not be alone in her father's house, and Jenna didn't want to be parted from her.

'There's plenty of room, and we'll all be together,' said Venetia. 'Then if – well, if we have to go suddenly to Wimpole Street, it will only take minutes. Adele is coming too, aren't you darling?'

Adele nodded. 'Of course.'

'Now I've got something for you, Jenna.'

'For me?' She appeared half asleep, exhausted by the long flight, by fear and sadness; holding Charlie's hand, as they sat in the Warwicks' vast drawing room, Charlie drinking whisky, Jenna and Izzie – rather surprisingly – hot chocolate.

'I know you don't think you want it, Jenna,' said Venetia, when the housekeeper brought it in, 'but it's the most comforting thing in the world, and it'll do you both good. Just try.'

'You'd better,' said Izzie. 'She always used to make me drink it, got really cross if I didn't.'

Jenna sipped it, not wanting it at all, wanting to be at the hospital, then found the sweet richness surprisingly comforting.

'Are you quite sure we shouldn't be there?'

'Quite, quite sure. I just phoned. She's a little better, she's sleeping. She could go on like this for days. Sebastian is there, of course, and Lord Arden, but we were just getting in the way in the end.'

'Does Father know I'm here?' said Izzie.

'Of course he does. Now, Jenna, this is it, what Mummy wanted you to have. Apparently it was the last thing she said to Lord Arden as they were leaving for the hospital. Just in case anything' – her voice shook – 'happened to her. She said it was very important. He remembered while we were there, said he'd have it sent over.'

'What is it?'

'It's your mother's jewellery box. She – well, she left it behind, when – oh, darling, I'm sorry, I'm so, so sorry. Come here, darling, darling Jenna, there, it's all right, cry as much as you like, how stupid of me, I should have thought—'

She was distraught herself, most unusually so. Venetia, who was always so calm and in control, always saying and doing the right thing.

Jenna managed to stop crying and even to smile at her. 'It's all right, I do want it, of course I do, it's lovely to have it. It was just – just a bit of a shock. I'll – I'll look at it by myself, if that's all right. Up in my room.'

'Of course it is. Charlie, more whisky?'

'Yes, please,' said Charlie.

Sebastian looked at Lord Arden; and spoke for the first time for hours.

'I hope this is – all right,' he said. 'My being here.'

Lord Arden had been dozing, propped against the wall; he squinted across at Sebastian, shifted himself upright. Centuries of self-control and English breeding spoke.

'Of course it is,' he said, 'of course. My dear chap, how could I possibly object?'

'Quite easily,' said Sebastian, managing a smile, 'I would have thought.'

'Good Lord, no,' said Lord Arden. He smiled back and they continued to sit there, two old men in love, oddly at peace with one another.

An hour later, Charlie was just settling into bed when there was a knock at the door.

'Come in.'

'It's me.' Jenna's face was apologetically anxious. 'It's this box, Charlie, I can't open it. And I really want to.'

'Here, give it to me.'

He took it; pushed at the lid. It was locked. Firmly. Surprisingly firmly for such a small box.

'No key?'

She shook her head.

'You got a hairpin?'

'A hairpin! Charlie, you are funny. Why would I have a hairpin? And what do you want it for?'

'You're a female, aren't you? What about Izzie? She's got long hair.'

Izzie did have a hairpin; she had a fistful and was just, in fact, pinning her long mane of hair up, about to have a bath.

Jenna took one to Charlie.

'OK. Here we go.' There was a minute or so's silence; then the lock clicked and he eased the lid up gently.

'Charlie, wherever did you learn to do that?' Jenna's voice was awed.

'Let's just say it was one of the more useful things I learned at my school.'

'Your school!'

'Well – yes. Anyway, sweetheart, there you are. All right?'

'Yes, thank you. I'll – I'll open it on my own, if you don't mind.'

'Of course I don't mind.'

Lord Arden and Sebastian were both half asleep again when a nurse came in.

'Lord Arden!' She spoke to him; he was, after all, the husband. What the other man was doing there she had no idea. 'It's your wife. She's asking for you.'

'Me! You sure it's me?'

It seemed to her an extraordinary question. 'Yes,' she said firmly. 'Quite sure.'

'How is she?'

'She's doing as well as can be expected.'

He followed her; Celia had woken from quite a long sleep. She was very drowsy with the morphine, as well as the other drugs she had been given; but she managed to smile.

'Bunny, hallo.' She took his hand.

'Hallo, my dear. Feeling all right?'

'Oh yes. Fine.' Even in her confusion, she managed to smile at the absurdity of the question.

'They say you're doing pretty well.'

'Good. I just wanted to thank you, Bunny. For everything.'

'Me? What have I done?'

'Oh, Bunny.' She smiled at him rather feebly. 'A lot. Put up with me, for a start.'

'Not a lot to put up with. I can truthfully say it's been a pleasure.'

523

'I doubt that.' She smiled again, tried to take his hand, failed. 'Sorry. Bit sleepy. Is – is Jenna here?'

'Yes. She's with Venetia.'

'Did you – give her—'

'Yes, I did. Everything's under control. She'll be along in the morning when you're awake.'

She nodded, drifted off; then roused herself again with an immense effort.

'I am awake.'

'Yes, of course you are, my dear.'

Her eyes closed again, for quite a long time; then: 'Sebastian?' she said.

'He's outside. Shall I get him?'

'Would you mind?'

He was relieved by the prospect of escape, of some kind of action.

'Of course not,' he said. 'Stay there, don't run away.'

'Try not to.'

The nurse was very resistant to Sebastian's being allowed in.

'I've been told only next of kin,' she said.

Lord Arden looked at her rather sadly.

'I do assure you, my dear young lady, that gentleman is closer to her than any kin in the world. You let him in, there's a good girl. Do her far more good than I can. Don't worry, I'll sort Matron out if there's any trouble.'

Very doubtfully, the nurse allowed Sebastian in.

She was propped up quite high in the bed; she opened her eyes and smiled at him. 'Oh, Sebastian.'

'Oh, Celia.' He picked up her hand and kissed it.

'You all right?' she said.

'I'm fine. How about you?'

'All right. I love you, Sebastian.'

'I love you too, Celia.'

'I just wanted to tell you.' The voice was slightly slurred, but the dark eyes on his were brilliant just the same.

'I'm glad you did.'

'I've been very lucky,' she said, 'haven't I?'

'Yes, I think you have.'

'Lovely about Clemmie. The baby.'

'Lovely.'

'Everything I wanted, really. Except for Lyttons.'

'Ah.'

'She should have given it back, Sebastian. She really should.'

'I know, my darling.'

'It should be ours. It should.' She was quite agitated; he reached out and stroked her cheek.

'I know it should. And – maybe she planned to give it back, she wasn't expecting – well what happened.'

'I know. Oh dear. So sad.' Two tears rolled down her cheeks. He looked at the skin; it was very fine, almost papery, etched with dozens of tiny lines. It was a long time since he had seen her without make-up. He reached out, gently wiped the tears away.

'Oh, my darling. Don't cry.'

'Sorry.' Another silence, then, 'So sad,' she said again.

Sebastian sat there, looking at her, as she slept. After a while, the nurse told him he must leave.

Jenna opened the box very slowly and cautiously. Her hands, she noticed, were shaking slightly. She felt almost afraid: of how she would feel, at this last, late link with her mother. It was so very personal, jewellery, it belonged so absolutely to its owner, as intimate a part of her as perfume.

It was only a small box: she had seen her mother pack it a dozen times. It had a tray, divided into small sections, for rings and earrings, and a bigger one for necklaces and bracelets.

There wasn't much in it; a silver bracelet that Barty had always loved, which Giles had given her when she was very young; her best watch, which Jenna had always thought was made of diamonds when she was a little girl, but was actually that odd thing called paste; a pair of gold bangles that Barty had told her were from her father. She was pleased to see those, she had wondered occasionally where they were. And, most wonderfully, a ring which Jenna knew had been her grandmother's and which her father had had sized for her mother. It was a flower of jewels, an aquamarine set in diamonds.

'Jonathan Elliott, your grandfather, gave it to Jeanette, he said the aquamarine exactly matched the colour of her eyes. As it does yours, Jenna. You have those same extraordinary eyes,' her mother had told her.

Laurence had given it to Barty the day he went away to France. The last time he saw her. Jenna wondered why she had left that behind; she loved it, wore it almost all the time. She must really have left in a great hurry. Jenna slipped it on her finger; it fitted perfectly. She smiled at it; it brought her mother somehow close. She would wear it always, from now on.

That was all: she was about to close the box, when she realised there was a leather base, removable by way of a narrow piece of ribbon.

Jenna pulled at the ribbon, eased the base up: and saw two envelopes inside.

'Keir, is that you?'

'What?' His voice was slurred, stupid with sleep. 'Yes, who is it, is it the hospital?'

'No. It's me, Jenna. I'm so sorry to wake you. But I have to speak to Elspeth.'

'Why, is Celia worse?'

'No. That is – I don't know. Please get her, Keir. Please.'

There was a pause; she heard a door shut, then open again, heard Elspeth's voice, wide awake, frightened.

'Jenna, it's me. What is it?'

'Can you come round? To Venetia's?'

'What, now?'

'Yes. Please, Elspeth, it's really important. I'd come to you if I could, but there's no one to bring me.'

'Of course I'll come. But why?'

'I've got a letter for you.'

'A letter! Who from?'

There was a pause; then Jenna said, clearly speaking with difficulty, 'From my mother.'

'Think I'll push off,' said Lord Arden, 'just for an hour or two. Jolly tired.'

'Good idea,' said Sebastian. 'I'll stay, anyway. Just in case.'

'You don't think I should—'

'No. Not at all. They say she's out of danger, she's sleeping quite soundly, at least that was my last report from that dragon of a sister. Good time to go, I'd say.'

'Glad you think so. Right-oh, then. Give her my love if you see her before I do. Tell her I won't be long.'

'Of course,' said Sebastian. 'Don't worry, I'm sure it's perfectly all right to go. See you in a few hours.'

'Yes. Thank you, Brooke. Jolly good of you.'

He walked out slowly, pulling on his jacket. He looked exhausted.

In her room, Celia stirred. She didn't feel very well. Well of course she wouldn't. She'd had major surgery and she'd got cancer. Of course she wouldn't feel – well. But she didn't feel as well as she had an hour ago, or whenever it was Sebastian had been with her. It was hard to define, exactly how she felt. A bit of a headache. A bit – sick. And shaky. Literally. And dizzy. Odd to be feeling dizzy, lying down. She debated ringing for the nurse and then decided against it. She would only start fussing and checking everything and moving her about. Which hurt. She just wanted to lie still. Quite still. Maybe if she went back to sleep she'd feel better again when she woke up.

'Shall we go now?' said Elspeth.

'What, to the hospital?'

'Yes.'

Jenna debated this in silence for a moment. She was terrified of Venetia or Boy waking up, taking over this momentous piece of news, saying they must do this, that or the other. When it was theirs, their excitement, their gift for Celia. She still couldn't quite believe it. Neither could Elspeth. They were sitting on her bed, taking it in turns to read the letter, over and over again. Izzie was there too, roused from her bed to hear about it, to see the letter, read the document for herself.

'It's like a midnight feast,' Jenna whispered, and in spite of everything, probably because of everything, the heightened emotion, the seriousness of it all, they suddenly got the giggles.

Jenna had been waiting on the doorstep when Elspeth arrived in her little car, put her finger on her lips, ushered her upstairs into her room. She watched Elspeth open the letter, saw her skin change from being pale to a dark flush of excitement, and then grow pale again, watched her read it, over and over again, said, 'Should we look at the other bit, do you think?' Elspeth hesitated for a moment and then said, 'Yes, I think we should. The letter's for me, but the envelope isn't addressed to anyone, just says what it is.'

They had looked at it, awestruck, and then Jenna had looked at Elspeth and said, 'My God. All for you.'

'Not all,' said Elspeth, 'just whoever's still there. Which is everyone, isn't it?' And then, taking her cue from Jenna, said, 'Oh my God. Oh Jenna. Oh my God.'

That was when they woke Izzie.

'Yes,' said Jenna, finally, 'we should go. Definitely. Even if they won't let us see her now, we'll be there, the minute they do. Come on, Izzie, let's get dressed.'

'Am I coming too?' asked Izzie.

'Of course you are,' said Jenna, 'you're family, aren't you?'

They reached the hospital at two; it was extremely dark and quiet-looking. Elspeth's courage began to fail her, but Jenna took over, ran up the steps, pressed the night bell, and when no one came, pressed it again. A night porter came to the door.

'What do you want?'

'We want to come in,' said Jenna. 'We have a relative who's a patient here and we have some absolutely crucial news for her. Please let us in.'

'I'm sorry,' he said, and even in his indignation he was obviously mildly amused, 'but we don't allow visitors this time of night. You'll have to leave and come back in the morning.'

Jenna looked up at him: and her voice was suddenly lower and more authoritative, her expression autocratic.

'Well, I'm sorry too,' she said, 'but this is a legal matter. If you wish, I can show you the documents. It's of the utmost importance that we see

527

Lady Arden at once. I wouldn't like to answer for the consequences if we don't. Now, do please let us in.'

The porter hesitated; he was not used to being ordered about by young girls. But this one was certainly different from most. Finally, he opened the door and let them into the hall.

'Wait there,' he said, 'I'll see if I can find a night sister.'

Sebastian had been asleep; he woke with a start, an appalling pain in his left shoulder. He sat up, rubbed it hard, stood up, and stretched slowly and carefully. His right leg had gone to sleep as well. God, he felt awful. He'd give a lot to go home, be in his own bed. But – he couldn't go. Couldn't leave her. Not yet. She might need him.

He decided to go for a walk. The leg was beginning to come back to life, with appalling pins and needles; his head ached too, quite badly. Maybe he could go out just for a moment, find somewhere, a hotel possibly, where he could get a cup of coffee. He walked down the corridor, looked in through the doorway, to where Celia lay; she appeared to be asleep. The nurse in the ante-room put her finger on her lips.

It would be all right, then; just for half an hour.

She felt worse; very, very faint. And a sick whirling dizziness, she felt as if she was going to fall off the bed. There was a strange feeling in her ears and an odd sound; and a pressure in them. It was all a bit – frightening, really. She was rather breathless too. Almost reluctantly, she pressed the bell.

'Good God,' Sebastian looked at them all, standing in the hall. 'What on earth are you lot doing here?'

'Sebastian! Oh, thank God. We have to see Celia, at once.'

'Well you can't, she's asleep.'

'Is she still all right?'

'Well –' his voice was cautious, he couldn't have them thinking Celia was going to recover completely, go home, be herself again. 'She's recovering from the operation. She's a little better. At the moment, anyway. But – why do you want to see her?'

'Look,' Elspeth held out the letter. 'If anything's going to make her better, it's this.'

He read it: sat down on a chair in the hall, pushed his hand through his hair, read it again; and then smiled at them, a glorious, happy smile.

'She has to be told,' he said, 'she has to be told the moment she wakes up.'

'Can we come and see her?'

'Well, you can come up to the waiting room. They won't let you in if she's asleep. But – we can wait together. Or do you want to go home?'

They looked at him in horror.

'Go home! Of course we're not going home,' said Jenna. 'We wouldn't dream of it.'

Sebastian's expression, as he looked at her, was very sweet and contemplative. Then he said, 'She was a very special person, your mother.'

'I know it,' said Jenna.

'How do you feel now, Lady Arden?'

'Not very well.' She could hear her own voice, less clear. If only the dizziness would ease; it was very, very bad. And she felt a bit breathless and still very faint.

The nurse took her temperature; it was within the normal range, given that she'd had surgery. Major surgery. She took her pulse; it was a little faint, a little slow, rather than fast. But again, she was an old lady, she'd been through a lot that day. She patted Celia's hand, said she would sit by her bed for a bit.

'If you don't feel better in a while, I'll get Sister. Or a doctor.'

Celia closed her eyes; she felt horribly in danger of falling off the bed.

The nurse was just going to fetch Sister, walking rather fast; she had taken Lady Arden's blood pressure and it seemed to be very low. She didn't look too good either; she was a dreadful colour and appeared confused.

'Ah, Nurse. How is Lady Arden?' It was the man: the other one, not her husband. He looked familiar but she couldn't think why.

'She's – she's fine. But her blood pressure is a little low. I'm going to fetch Sister.'

'Can I go in and see her? Please.'

'Absolutely not. No. I'm sorry. Please. Wait in the waiting room.'

A crawling fear invaded Sebastian; some deep sense told him this was not good.

He went back to the waiting room, tried to smile at the girls.

'She's just having a few checks done.'

They nodded; only Izzie, who knew him best, recognised his anxiety. She sat down next to him, slipped her hand into his.

Suddenly, he couldn't bear it any longer. He got up, walked down the corridor; the nurse was coming out of Celia's room. He looked over her shoulder; he could see two more people bending over the bed.

'How – how is she now?'

'Look,' she said, 'please. Please leave us alone. Lady Arden isn't very well, and we're doing all we can for her. Please wait in the waiting room, you're just making things worse—'

'But I have to go in. I have to tell her something, something crucially important. I—'

Sister appeared; she looked flushed and anxious.

'I don't know who you are,' she said, 'but it's most important you leave Lady Arden alone. She isn't at all well. She can't be visited at the moment. We have to—' she stopped.

'Have to what?' said Sebastian.

She hesitated, then said, 'Take her back to theatre. As soon as Mr Cadogan arrives.'

'But why?'

'I can't tell you that, I'm afraid.'

'For God's sake,' he said, 'for God's sake, why not? What do you think I'm going to do, stop you doing whatever is best for her?'

She looked uncertain; then relieved as a doctor came out of Celia's room.

'Dr Smythe. Could you tell this gentleman he cannot see Lady Arden at the moment? He's being very insistent.'

Dr Smythe looked at Sebastian; and against every possible likelihood, hurried, anxious as he was, he recognised him.

'You're Sebastian Brooke, aren't you?'

'Yes, yes I am. For what it's worth.'

'I thought so. My son loves your books more than anything in the world, you're his hero. Good Lord.' He appeared transfixed, far more interested in Sebastian than in the drama going on around him. 'Good God. What – what can I do for you?'

'Let me in to see her,' said Sebastian, indicating Celia. 'Let me in quickly, before it's too late. I have to – have to tell her something, something desperately important. It will – I promise you – it will only take a moment. And make her very happy.'

Dr Smythe hesitated. Then he said, 'Matron would kill me for doing this. But – yes, go on. It can't do her any harm, not now. Just for a moment. While we wait for Mr Cadogan.'

Sebastian went in, very quietly. Celia's eyes were closed, her hands clasped together. She looked ghastly.

He took one of the hands, and kissed it.

'Celia?'

She turned her head.

'Sebastian?' Her voice was very faint, very weak.

'I want to tell you something. Something important, something wonderful. Can you hear me?'

She frowned. 'Just. Only just. Horrible sort of noise in my head. I feel so dizzy, Sebastian. So dizzy.'

'Hold on to me. I'll keep you safe. And listen very carefully. Barty has given Lyttons back. She made a codicil to her will. It was in her jewellery box, Jenna found it. It's yours again, my darling. Lyttons is yours.'

Not hers really, he could see that: not for very long. A few hours at the most. But for that moment it was: Lyttons was hers, and all was well for her again, all was as it should be. Her world had been set to rights, by Barty's final gift to her: brought to her just in time. And as he looked at her, she opened her eyes and they were quite, quite clear and comprehending, and she looked back at him and smiled a smile of purest joy.

'How lovely,' she said, 'how absolutely lovely.'

And then she closed her eyes again, and, still smiling, seemed to move away from him, into some strange other country where he could no longer be with her. Her hand in his grew limp, her head turned away and settled into her pillow and she sighed a small, light sigh: and he could see that he had done all he could for her, that all the long years of knowing her and loving her were finally over, and longing, yearning to follow her, he lost her at last.

Part Three

CHAPTER 41

It was Helena who found them. So harmless-looking, so innocently intriguing: so very, very dangerous.

It was a week after the funeral; which had been small, confined to the family, held at Chelsea Old Church, so comfortingly near to the house, to be followed in the autumn by a large memorial service. This was Kit's suggestion and the rest of the family had agreed. It would be far easier to bear, a quiet funeral, with only one another to witness their grief. It had been simple as well as quiet; just some of Celia's favourite music and hymns, readings by her grandchildren, and not even an address by the parish priest.

This, again, had come from Kit. 'She didn't know him, there's nothing she'd have hated more than a lot of bloody silly religious platitudes, and I personally would find it unbearable. I'll say a few words if you like,' he added, surprising everyone, for he was notoriously reluctant to expose himself to the danger of public emotion; and he did, speaking in his lovely voice of the brilliance and beauty they had lost, and the inspiration she had left behind.

Because they were alone, all together, the day was not as difficult as it could have been, everyone felt able to mourn, to weep, even to laugh at some of the more outrageous memories and stories. Venetia recounted the moment when she had opened the great door of Lytton House in Paternoster Square, 'doubled up with my contractions, half London on fire outside, bombs everywhere, and there she was in her tin hat on cook's bicycle, hugely irritated because I'd been so long answering the door'. And Giles, unusually forthcoming, described his mother's behaviour after Oliver's stroke: 'Every doctor in the land said he would never move or speak again, and she had him doing both in weeks. Talk about bullying. Poor old Father wasn't even allowed to have his food without saying something first.'

Celia had never recovered consciousness that night; the immediate cause of death was a massive haemorrhage in the lung cavity. 'Not unknown after surgery of this kind, I'm afraid,' Mr Cadogan had said, 'but of course she was extremely ill and the prognosis was very poor.' The family had all agreed quietly that she would have far rather died that way, than struggled on for months in increasing pain and helplessness.

Lord Arden was patently, and very touchingly, heartbroken. 'He genuinely loved her, no doubt about it,' said Adele, 'and he was filled with remorse at not having been with her.' Sebastian, thoughtful even in his own grief, assured him almost truthfully that she had died in her sleep, and knew nothing about any of it, which Lord Arden seemed to find greatly comforting. Drawing his own comfort from having been with her at her end, Sebastian withdrew entirely from everyone, even Izzie, for several days, moving from his bedroom to his study and back again, walking endlessly on Hampstead Heath, and only reappearing at the funeral, where he seemed surprisingly strong and told his own stories of Celia's ferocity as an editor and the dreadful fear he lived in every year when he delivered his manuscript.

'Once she made me rewrite the first two chapters at proof stage; Oliver was furious. It was very expensive but she said it would be much more expensive if they lost sales because the book was bad, which it undoubtedly was. I had twenty-four hours in which to do it; I told her I'd worked all night and she said she hoped I didn't think that was a reason for not carrying on the following day. She was right, of course; the book was far better for it.'

Any more personal memories he kept to himself, partly out of deference to Lord Arden, partly because, as Izzie said, they were what he clung to now, all he had, and were not to be shared.

Izzie asked him – of course – to come back with her to America, to stay as long as he liked, and Jenna had said, with a most touching thoughtfulness, that he could go to South Lodge and be there on his own, if he would like that; he said he would stay in London for the time being, that he had a new book to write, which would be better therapy than anything else he could think of, but later in the year he might very well accept both invitations. 'Only I must be here for the arrival of Clemmie's baby. Maybe after that.'

He was rather sweetly excited about the baby; for more reasons than one. Izzie found it a little hard to bear.

Charlie did not go to the funeral; he said he would feel like an intruder and they were grateful and not a little surprised by such sensitivity. He had volunteered to be at the house afterwards, to help Mrs Hardwicke and Lord Arden's butler 'have things ready'. There was clearly no need for this, but again, they were so grateful that they allowed him to think there was.

He was very agreeable at the luncheon, making it his prime objective to look after Jenna, but disappeared shortly after that, saying he had an appointment with someone; no one could imagine who, but again, they sensed he was simply being thoughtful.

He left two days later; Jenna assured him she would be absolutely fine, flying back with Izzie – 'I've broken my jinx, honestly, you go.'

She wanted to spend some time with the Millers and various other members of the family; she had been hoping to see something of Lucas, but apart from his being very sweet to her at the funeral and chatting to her at the lunch, she was disappointed. He had broken a holiday with friends in France and although he was returning to spend some of the long vacation at Lyttons, it would be after her return to New York.

The solicitors had requested a copy of Celia's marriage certificate to Lord Arden: to establish beyond all legal doubt that she had in fact married him, had become the Countess of Arden. They said that of course they could get a copy, but it would be a great help to have the original in the complex legal procedures that had to be gone through before sorting out her estate.

It was not among all the other papers in her desk, not with the certificates of her birth and her first marriage and all the other myriad things pertaining to her complex life, and Lord Arden was unable to find it, said that Celia had always kept such things filed.

'I was pretty hopeless at organisation,' he said apologetically. 'Still am, of course.' He went on to volunteer the freedom of his London house and the help of his butler to search further for the certificate. 'I'm off to Glennings for a bit, try and get over it all.'

Adele, who had volunteered to conduct the search and an initial round-up of her mother's things said she might take him up on it later, but she would carry on looking in Cheyne Walk for a while first.

'There's so much to sort out there, such a mass of stuff, I'm sure I'll find it.'

But she did not. She found all sorts of other things: things which made her cry: four pairs of tiny first shoes, four milk teeth, locks of hair from their first haircuts, bundles of letters from Oliver at the Front in the First World War, letters from Giles and Kit at school, from Giles in Italy during the war, from Barty in New York, letters from Paris, from herself, letters from the Warwick children and Izzie at school, and – most heartbreaking of all – a fairly small collection, tied up with red ribbons and labelled simply 'From Sebastian' and underneath his name a kiss. She took those straight to him, watched him struggling to control himself, and then when he failed, went in search of a strong whisky for him. When she brought it back, he was sitting, staring at the letters, the ribbon still tied.

'I'm so sorry, Sebastian,' she said. 'So very sorry.'

'Oh, my darling, it's all right. I'll survive. We had a pretty good run, she and I. You have to learn to live off your memories when you're as old as I am, you know.'

'Sebastian,' said Adele, gently, 'I do know. I do it now.'

537

He looked at her, startled for a minute, then smiled.

'I expect you do. Are you all right, Adele?'

'I'm fine. Yes. Much, much happier. We just have to get on with everything. As she would have wanted, of course.' She smiled. 'Every time I find myself sitting down and crying, I think of what she'd say to me if she saw me, and that gets me going again, I can tell you.'

She was planning to move into Cheyne Walk herself in due course. Celia had told her that was what she wanted, delighting and surprising her in that last, swift, sad meeting, and it made sense; Giles and Venetia and Kit all had substantial houses and plenty of money and she did not, and the memories of Montpelier Street were not happy ones. She could fit out another studio for herself at the top of the house, the views from up there were glorious and she could sell Montpelier Street and invest the proceeds. She had not yet told the children; she felt sure Noni and Lucas would be delighted, they loved the house, and it would affect them very little. But Clio might be reluctant to move, she was six now, a sweet, charming child, but she had never quite recovered from the abrupt departure of her beloved father and his failure ever to reappear. It manifested itself in a hatred of change, a suspicion of new people in her small world.

Geordie had written to Adele to say how sorry he was to hear about her mother, and had sent an enormous bouquet of flowers for the funeral, but no more; any thought that he might attend was dashed by a further note saying he was afraid his presence would be more of an embarrassment than a help. What it actually meant, as she said to Venetia, was that he was a coward, as well as a bastard, and afraid to come. She drew considerable pleasure from the fact that she really didn't seem to mind very much.

The certificate, however, had not materialised; it was Helena who suggested to Giles that it might be in the office.

'Why should it be there? It was a personal thing, it would have been at home.'

'Well it doesn't seem to be, does it? I think you should look. I will if you won't.'

And there, indeed, she did find the marriage certificate; in the bottom drawer of Celia's desk, along with some pictures of the wedding, a sorry testimony, she thought, to a marriage entered into on a whim and regretted every day of her life since.

'None of them were ever put on show or framed, were they?' she said, showing them to Giles. 'Just stuffed away, out of sight, rather like he was. Poor man. What a fate—'

'Helena,' said Giles, his voice almost sharp, 'my mother only died a week ago. Please don't speak of her in that way.'

'Sorry,' said Helena quickly. 'Sorry, Giles. Well, there you are. You'd better phone the solicitors. I wonder what's in there,' she added, looking at the small, black safe in the corner of the room. 'Anything else we ought to know about? Any other valuables, or secrets?'

'I don't know. It's been there for ever. I think she kept manuscripts in it. It's probably empty now.'

'Probably. But you never know. Do you know the combination?'

'Yes. She thought I didn't, but I did. More than my life's worth to open it, of course, but – well, all right. It's 10617. Our birthdays.'

'You don't mind?'

'Of course not. Look, I'm going next door to see the others. They're all trying to do a normal day's work. Come and find me, would you, when you've finished.'

But Helena had still not reappeared when an hour and a half later Giles decided he was hungry and wanted lunch; faintly intrigued, he walked back into his mother's office. And found Helena sitting entirely motionless on the floor, surrounded by dozens of small leather-bound volumes, two or three of them in her lap, several more set neatly on Celia's desk, above her head.

'Look, Giles,' she said in a voice so quiet, so awed, that it almost shook; 'look. These are your mother's diaries. Kept for every day of her life, ever since she was five years old. Just look at them, Giles, just read one or two, this one, here, and this. Did you have any idea she was keeping them?'

'No,' he said, uncomfortable at this intrusion into his mother's most personal life. 'I didn't. And I would really rather not read them. They're very – private, surely.'

'Oh no,' said Helena, and her eyes meeting his were brilliant, 'well, of course they may be private. But they concern all of us. And some of what they have to say is – well, it's absolute dynamite, Giles. I've only dipped into them, but every other page there's something. About Jay's father, and LM – and your father too, quite unbelievable. You've got to read them, absolutely got to.'

Giles said he would look at them when he had time and told her to put them back in the safe. Clearly reluctant and more than a little put out, she did as she was told.

Things were in turmoil at Lyttons; once the initial euphoria had passed, there was a need to put it in order, draw up new lines of management, restructure the company financially, form a new board. The most satisfying thing had been telling Marcus Forrest; Jay suggested that Giles should do it.

'Go on. It'll give you the most pleasure.'

And it had: he did it in writing, at the lawyers' suggestion, informing him that under a codicil to Barty's will, entirely and indisputably legal, drawn up by a London solicitor, signed, witnessed, and dated, the remaining 68 per cent share of Lyttons London was to revert to family control.

Forrest wrote a stiff note back, saying that he was delighted for them and they should meet as soon as possible, for what he called a debriefing; they could imagine his chagrin all too clearly. He might be the editorial director of Lyttons New York, but in London he had been – as Venetia had nicknamed him – the *oberführer*. It was a delicious thing to contemplate his demotion.

Nobody knew quite why Barty had done what she had; they could only be grateful. And not just the family, but the entire company were pleased; everyone had suffered from the American interference, from the overturning of decisions, from the odd double-think that Marcus Forrest had indulged in, from the perception of the outside world as well as within Lytton House, that they were not their own masters, not properly in control of their own publishing destiny.

Giles called a board meeting as soon as it seemed decently possible, forty-eight hours after his mother's death. After all, he said, only slightly apologetically, neither Barty nor Celia would have wanted such an opportunity to be squandered.

It was agreed that their shareholdings should remain proportionately the same; he and Jay and Venetia would hold 25 per cent each, with Elspeth and Keir holding their percentage between them. Elspeth had gone to him privately after the meeting and said that she and Keir had some matters to resolve between them, before they could formally take up their holding; he had accepted this and told her to take her time.

Giles had, already, Elspeth noticed, in just a few days, become at the same time more relaxed and more authoritative. His grief at his mother's death had been genuine, he had never ceased to love her (while quite frequently hating her at the same time), and had longed, above everything, to please her; now at last the great burden of her disapproval had been lifted.

Elspeth's own situation was rather more complex.

It had seemed odd to them all at first, that Barty's letter should have been addressed to her: the youngest and least important member of the family and the publishing house. But then they realised that, of course, Barty had been looking ahead many years, decades even, she had obviously not expected to die for a long time: by then, Celia would surely have left Lyttons, and quite possibly Giles, Jay and Venetia too.

It had been a very sweet letter:

Dear Elspeth,
    I am writing to you as the representative of what (at the time of

writing) is the new, young Lytton family, in the hope that you can see my wishes are carried out satisfactorily. You seem to be an extremely competent person, and climbing the ladder very fast; possibly by the time you get this you will even be in Celia's chair! It certainly wouldn't surprise me.

I have made a codicil to my will, which will be with my lawyers in New York, as will this letter, stating that on my death, the shares in Lyttons London should revert, in their entirety, to the family. It is where I want them to be and indeed where they should be. Look after them and Lyttons well!

With my love,
Barty

'I wonder why she didn't tell you – or us – at the time,' Venetia had said thoughtfully.

'I can see exactly why,' said Elspeth. 'It would potentially have been dynamite. Everyone waiting to get their share, squabbling over who would get what and when, who was going to be in control; it would have been awful. I mean, it was fine then, with Barty in control, she was family, anyway.'

'Yes,' said Venetia coldly, 'I suppose in a way she was.' Elspeth looked at her interestedly; she had always detected a hostility between the twins and Barty, and this was further evidence of it. She wondered why: jealousy, perhaps. Ever since she could remember, Celia had adored Barty, talked about how clever she was, how wonderfully well she had done; it had probably been quite – irritating. As indeed, it had been for her, hearing her grandmother extolling Keir and his talents endlessly.

'Anyway,' said Venetia just a little too carelessly, 'we won't be seeing any more of your friend and mentor, Mr Forrest, will we? You'll miss him, I expect.'

God, thought Elspeth, does she know, too? Did the whole place know? Was it possible that Keir had not known?

'Yes,' she said, meeting her mother's eyes very levelly, 'yes, I will miss him, I have to say. I liked him. And he cheered me up.'

'Well, he didn't cheer me up,' said Venetia. 'He made me want to jump out of the window.'

Giles had decided to keep the diaries to himself for the time being; they troubled him, deeply. He had taken a few home to read, and then taken them back, locked them up in the safe once more.

Helena was disturbed by his secrecy; she felt the diaries were too important – and too revealing – to be hidden away. She felt the family should know they existed and decide together how to deal with them. A lifetime of unpleasantness and humiliation at Celia's hands had left her utterly cynical about her mother-in-law, with no desire to protect either her or her memory. Giles, however, felt a strong desire to protect her: and, given their content, the whole family. By keeping the diaries secret, he was doing that. He told himself – and indeed Helena – that he was simply waiting, waiting until the drama of Celia's death and the initial grief had passed, before deciding what to do; in fact, a very strong instinct told him they should never be read by anyone. Which, as Helena pointed out, was a bit like discovering a body and deciding not to mention it, in case someone got into trouble. It was arrogant, she said, and it was wrong, a decision he had no right to make. But she had been a good wife for too long to disobey; she respected the decision, and kept silent.

The diaries were horribly frank and full not only of reminiscence, but of observation. Reading them, Giles felt, was like having his mother sitting beside him, talking, or rather whispering in his ear, a rush of confidences and observations, some of which were familiar to him, some revelations. They made him feel very uncomfortable, voyeuristic; reading them was not in any way a pleasure.

On the other hand, he couldn't keep them secret for ever. They weren't his. Not that they were anybody's except hers. More than once he had decided to burn them, but that seemed wrong too; besides they were a most extraordinary social document. He had never realised, for instance, and he was sure no one else in the family had, that his mother had actually met Hitler, dined with Goebbels, and during that period was full of praise for them both. That was when she had been so friendly with Lord Arden, who in turn had been very close to Oswald Mosley. Giles was hugely relieved – after leafing quickly and guiltily through that section of the diaries – to find that they had only been friends. Having a lifelong affair with Sebastian Brooke was one thing (also well-documented, he felt sure); a sexual liaison with someone deeply enamoured of the Nazis was something else entirely.

There was another entry that shocked him: in the year she had married his father. He had always been intrigued by their marriage, by how she had met Oliver and decided to marry him. She was the daughter of a titled landowner, reared to marry someone of her own class and genre. Oliver Lytton was neither. She had met him, it seemed, at a rather bohemian London luncheon party given by a friend of her older sister's and had fallen completely in love with him: what shocked Giles, though, was that having realised her parents would never agree to a marriage with someone so unsuitable, she set out to seduce him and become pregnant, thus forcing the issue.

He had never even suspected such a thing: had simply assumed he had been born nine months after their marriage, that being how things were in those days. *Sexual intercourse, absolute bliss*, read the entry for May 9 1904, *Great fun working on baby-making!*

He scarcely slept that night; it was after that he decided to keep all the diaries under lock and key. After all, they were doing no harm. Nothing like the harm they would do if they were read by the rest of the family. Or – and that did make his blood run cold – by a wider public.

Giles was no fool and he had been in publishing all his life. He knew a sensational read when he saw one; he trembled to think what would happen if another publishing company – or even worse, a newspaper – got hold of these diaries. They were, as Helena had said, potential dynamite.

'Elspeth,' said Keir. His tone was quite conversational; it did not sound in the least threatening.

'Yes?'

'I haven't asked you before. I didn't feel I could and besides, we were both upset. But I have to now: what were you doing at the Ritz with Forrest?'

His tone was still quite mild, only half interested; she smiled at him, quickly, said, 'Having lunch.'

'I could see that, Elspeth.' Slightly heavier tone now, eyes getting harder, 'but why were you having lunch?'

'Don't be silly. I work for Lyttons – when you let me . . .' – mistake that, Elspeth, don't antagonise him – 'he wanted to talk about various projects with me—'

'Oh yes? Anything wrong with the office?'

He still sounded quite mild; Elspeth kept her voice steady.

'Well – he liked to get out sometimes. You know what it's like there, always something interrupting you—'

'Right,' he said. 'Let's stop this, shall we? How many times have you had lunch with Marcus Forrest? Have you had – anything else with him?'

'Like what, Keir? Tea once, actually, at the Ritz—'

'You and he seem to enjoy the Ritz. Does he stay there?'

'No,' she said, 'he stays at—' and then stopped, seeing she was walking fast into his trap.

'Stays where?'

'At Claridges. You know he does, everyone knows that—'

'Indeed? Do you know, I don't think I did. Well, maybe I did. But I don't see why you should have known.'

'Oh for God's sake,' she said, 'Celia told me, she's met him there, Venetia, Jay, they all know—'

'And does he have a suite there? Or just a room?'

'I haven't the faintest idea. Why are you asking me all this, anyway?'

'You know perfectly well,' he said, 'perfectly well. I want to know if you've been to his room or his suite and if so, what went on there? Have you been having an affair with Marcus Forrest, Elspeth? Have you?'

'Oh don't be so ridiculous,' she said.

'Have you been to bed with Marcus Forrest?'

And then, because she couldn't lie to him, couldn't look into his eyes and lie, he knew her too well, there was no point, she said finally and very quietly, 'Yes. Yes, I have. I'm – I'm sorry, Keir. Very sorry. I do regret it terribly.'

'Right,' he said, 'well, I'm glad you're sorry. And I'm glad we've established it as an absolute fact. I know where I stand now.'

And he turned on his heel and walked out of the room; a few minutes later she heard the front door slam.

He didn't come back until the following morning; when he did, he told her he was leaving her.

'And I shall be leaving Lyttons, too. I won't be an embarrassment to you any longer. Maybe you can continue your relationship with Mr Forrest. Although it might be a little difficult, now that he won't be coming to London quite so often.'

Elspeth was silent; there really seemed nothing at all that she could say.

CHAPTER 42

'Jenna—'

'Yes?' She spoke absently, she was leafing through some books.

'Can I maybe talk to you about something?'

'Of course you can.' She looked at Charlie; he was clearly embarrassed. 'What is it?'

'Well – the thing is, I'm – I'm in a bit of a jam. Financially.'

'A jam? How could you be? Oh, you mean with your business. I thought that was better, now you'd cut back, got the small office, just deal in the cars—'

'No,' he said, 'not just the business. I – the thing is, Jenna, I have debts now. I couldn't worry you with them before, I never wanted to, I was hoping the money from the will would come through. But it's taking such a time.'

'I know that,' she said, 'and I've asked Kyle and Jamie to help, so many times, you know I have. If I could lend you the money myself I would, but I can't.'

'Darling, I know that. You've been absolutely sweet and wonderful, and I couldn't be more grateful. But – the fact remains, I'm in debt.'

'But – why? I don't understand.'

'I lost a lot of money, selling the cars. You should never sell anything quickly, you get a lousy price. And then – well, I don't know, I found myself having to borrow money. From the bank. For this and that.'

'Yes, but for what, Charlie? As I understand it, the trustees pay all the money you need to keep us, the upkeep of the houses, Maria and Mr and Mrs Mills, my school fees. They've put it up twice, they told me.'

'Yes, that's exactly right. But – that doesn't cover my own expenses. Or Cathy's. She's developed some pretty expensive tastes over the years; the school fees are high, she has to keep up with her school friends, do the extras. Then there's her clothes, all that stuff – anyway,' he looked down at his hands, 'it's got so bad I'm going to have to take her away from Dana. She'll have to leave after this term.'

'Oh Charlie, no, that's terrible.'

'It would – it will be. The two of you being like sisters all this time.'

She was silent; then, 'I'll ask the trustees again. I think they might make an exception over that.'

'Well – from past experience they won't. I guess that's why I – well, never mind. There's more, though.'

'More? Oh, Charlie, what?'

'I – well, I did something a bit stupid.'

'What?'

'I borrowed some money. At a very high rate of interest.'

'What from a – a moneylender, someone like that?'

'Someone like that. And now they're after me. I've been trying to fob them off, I sold a few things, a watch your mother gave me—' He stopped, bit his lip.

Jenna sighed. 'Oh, Charlie, I can't bear this.'

'Sweetheart, neither can I. But you know I do need a little money of my own. Just to – well, to buy drinks for friends, clothes, that sort of thing. And I don't have any. That's quite – hard.'

She nodded. 'Of course.'

'I mean, I can only spend what comes with the monthly cheque. And there isn't much left over. You girls don't come cheap.'

He managed to smile at her. 'Anyway, that's how it all began. Me lying awake worrying, wondering what to do, when I could tell Cathy about leaving school, these guys virtually sending in the heavies—'

'You should have gone to Jamie, and told him.'

'I tried. He made it pretty plain he wasn't going to help.'

'I just find that so hard to believe,' said Jenna.

'Sweetheart, it's true.'

She sighed. 'I'll go and see him again.'

This time, and very reluctantly, moved by her distress, Jamie agreed that he would ask the other trustees to take over Cathy's school fees.

'Thank you. And – what about Charlie's debts?'

'I'm afraid those are his affair. Nothing to do with me or you.'

'Of course they're to do with me. You don't seem to understand. Charlie has looked after me, all this time. I don't know what I'd have done without him. Nobody else has been anything like as good to me.'

'Jenna, listen to me—'

'No. You listen to me. Jamie, do you really think my mother would approve of what you're doing to Charlie, and therefore to me? Do you think she'd want me worried and upset, do you think she'd want her money to be just sitting there in some lousy bank account while I was worrying about Charlie being beaten up?'

'Beaten up? Jenna, don't be ridiculous.'

'You don't understand. He's had to go to some kind of moneylenders.

OK, I can see you think that was a dumb thing to do. How else was he going to cope? Can't you see, just living with me, looking after me, exposes him to expense. And now he can't pay these people back and they're threatening him. I just can't stand this, it's really getting to me, getting in the way of my studies. If my mother knew about it, knew I was so upset, she'd be absolutely furious. With you, I mean, not Charlie. Does that make you feel good? I don't think so. Now will you please, please do what I ask. There's enough money there, for God's sake, bloody millions—'

'Jenna!'

'I'm sorry. But I'm just so upset. If Charlie wasn't so good to me I'd kind of understand how you felt. But he's never, never let me down, not for a moment. And I won't let him be let down in return.'

Deeply reluctant, but persuaded by her anguish, Jamie agreed to see Charlie and, 'possibly make him an advance.'

'Not possibly, Jamie. You'll make him one. I really need you to do this. Please don't let me down.'

Jamie met her eyes, and saw Laurence; heard him too, in Jenna's clear voice, in the words and phrases which Laurence would have been proud of, a mixture of high emotion and tough logic. Where had she learned that: where and how?

'Yes, all right, I'll put it to the trustees,' he said.

Keir had left Lyttons. He had gone to see Giles and told him he was leaving Elspeth and that it would be too painful and awkward for him to stay. Giles and Jay agreed there was no point holding him to his notice period, it was only going to increase the problems with Elspeth. She was so miserable.

She had absolutely forbidden anyone to let word get out to Marcus Forrest; the last thing she wanted was him feeling responsible, and offering to marry her. She didn't think he would, and she was sure he wouldn't want to, but he was such a gentleman, he might feel he had to. And she had enough to worry about.

Venetia, torn between sorrow for her and a conviction that it was the best thing in the long run, found herself unable to help very much, apart from offering to have her and the children to stay. 'You don't want to be alone all the time.'

Elspeth said she seemed to have been alone for years, and it wasn't going to make much difference; 'I'm thinking of getting a live-in housekeeper. That way I can work more easily. Although I don't want to disappear all day and every day suddenly; the children have lost their father, they shouldn't lose their mother too.'

Her sense of having only herself to blame didn't help. 'It was hardly rape,' she said to Amy, who was commiserating with her one day, 'I encouraged Marcus, I can't pretend I didn't.'

'Yes, and you had every reason for it. I'd have had an affair if I'd had a husband like Keir.'

'He was a very good husband,' said Elspeth fretfully, 'just not right for me.'

'I don't think he was a good husband at all. Think how mean he was when you were up in Glasgow. Honestly, Elspeth, I think you're deceiving yourself. And blaming yourself too much. I think you did awfully well, sticking it out for so long.'

She missed Keir horribly. Even his brooding, scowling presence was better than no presence at all; in contemplating a life without him, she felt, above all, panic. It was one thing to complain about a husband, wish him away, even; quite another to find the wish granted.

During the first few days after his departure, she did feel a certain relief; life was simpler, she could do what she liked, go to Lyttons, plan her future. All without fear of complaint, interrogation, contradiction. But it didn't last very long. Then she found herself lonely, and quite frightened.

She could see, in spite of everything, that she did still love him: she had loved him so much and so fiercely in the early days; such a feeling was not to be easily dissipated. You simply could not love someone, marry them, bear their children, share every intimacy of life with them, and then walk away, say right, that's over, nice while it lasted, gone wrong now, though.

Her very self had changed, become part of Keir, too much had been shared, enjoyed, endured; and even if her marriage was over, her feelings for him, however mixed, were not, they were still passionate, strong, even violent. And she felt a dreadful sense of failure as well as regret, remorse as well as anger: it was a second bereavement, the death of her marriage, as fierce and as painful as that of her grandmother. She missed Celia terribly, her clear-sighted wisdom, her tough common sense, the uncritical love she had always given her.

During the last few months, Celia had been totally accessible to her, a swift walk away, across Albert Bridge. Elspeth had leaned on her more and more, drawn from her strength, sought her out, far more than she had her mother. Looking back, she was shocked to think how much she had taken her for granted.

Keir was in his bedsit in Balham, wondering if there was a publisher left in London he had not already approached about a possible job, and wondering, also, if even at this stage, he might be forced to consider a change in his career, when there was a tap at his door.

'Mr Brown? Telephone.'

'Oh – thank you, Mrs Dudley. I'll be right down.'

Who was it? Very few people had his phone number, only Elspeth, in case there was a crisis with the children, and his parents. He didn't want to speak to either of them; Elspeth because he was still so angry and sickened by her, and his parents because they had been very reluctant to take his side.

'Takes two hands to clap, laddie,' his father had said, 'she's a good lass, she put up with a lot on your account. She was very, very plucky. You should ask yourself why she went off with this man.'

It was not what he had expected.

'Hallo?' he said cautiously, now.

'Keir? Sebastian.'

'Sebastian!'

'Yes. Look I—'

'How did you get my number?'

'From Elspeth.'

'I see. Well – what can I do for you?'

'I'd like to see you. Buy you a drink or something.'

'What for?'

There was a silence; then Sebastian said, 'I've had more gracious responses to an invitation.'

'Sorry. But I'm not feeling very – gracious.'

'I can tell that.'

Another silence.

'Well – would you be kind enough to meet me or not? I've got a message for you.'

'Can't you give it to me on the phone?'

'No, it's a bit more complex than that.'

'In what way?'

'Look,' said Sebastian, then stopped; after another moment or two the phone went dead.

He had obviously hung up. Silly old bugger. If he thought he could put in a word for any of the Lyttons, he could think again. His overriding emotion, apart from hurt, was a fierce near-hatred of the Lytton clan and the way they had tried to manipulate him.

Sebastian stalked into the kitchen, pulling on his coat.

'I'm going out, Mrs Conley,' he said, 'and if there's a call from a Mr Brown, tell him I have nothing to say to him. Rude young bugger. She's well shot of him, I'd say.'

Mrs Conley agreed; she had never liked Keir, he was what she called a rough diamond, and on the rare occasions when she had seen them together, she had been very struck by the way he treated Elspeth. He seemed to be permanently cross with her.

Sebastian was still shaking with rage when he reached the ponds at Hampstead Heath an hour later. All he'd wanted to do was help the stupid young fool. Celia had been wrong about him; he was a bad lot. Poor little

Elspeth. She deserved better. Although, if it was true about her and Marcus Forrest, she deserved better than him as well . . .

Celia's memorial service was to have been held at St Bride's Fleet Street, the journalist's church and one of Celia's favourites. It was going to be an occasion of immense grandeur; the invitation list read like *Who's Who*. Not only all the great names of the publishing world, Jonathan Cape, Jock Murray, Michael Joseph, André Deutsch, the brilliant young publisher George Weidenfeld, Celia's own authors, Lady Annabel Muirhead, Nancy Arthure, and, of course, the great Sebastian Brooke, but others who had been her friends, John Betjeman, Somerset Maugham, Dame Edith Sitwell and Dame Jean Conan Doyle. Then there were the booksellers, Basil Blackwell, Christina Foyle, and the venerable John Wilson of Bumpus.

The family alone would fill several pews; apart from the English branch, the American Lyttons would be coming, including Jack and Lily from California, and all the American associates, the Brewers, Jamie Elliott, Mike Parker and Nick Neill, of course. The Millers must also come and Jenna, obviously, and therefore, Charlie and Cathy. As the list grew, as everyone added names, declared it was essential that so and so was invited and such and such attended, it became clear that St Bride's would simply not be big enough and someone suggested it be moved to St Martin-in-the-Fields. Celia had loved it there too, had always gone to the candlelight carol service, accompanied by her ever-growing band of grandchildren.

This caused a further delay, St Bride's had been booked for September, but it was November before a suitable date could be found for St Martin's. It needed to be early, rather than late in the month, since Clementine's baby was due at the beginning of December.

The form of the service caused considerable argument. What music, which readings, how many of them, who should read, which representatives of which generation? The young being, of course, as important as the old. Weekly meetings were held from August onwards, chaired by Giles and the twins; all suggestions were considered, none cast aside without careful discussion. Thus a suggestion from Clio that she read from *Alice in Wonderland*, the first book her grandmother had read to her, and from Lucy that she read 'The Owl and the Pussycat' for the same reason, led to the rather charming agreement that there should be an anthology, read by the young – young being defined as anyone under sixteen: several short pieces rather than one long one.

Another suggestion that the leading authors should read from their own works was dismissed as verging on the narcissistic, but clearly there must be a major reading from *Meridian* and this great honour fell to Rupert Lytton, Tory and Jay's younger son, an angelic-looking child of nine. And then there were the eulogies: who would give them? Sebastian was an obvious choice, and yet his position was slightly delicate; Kit was another, but he had said he would find it impossible.

'And this time, I mean it, I simply could not stand up there in front of all those desperately important people and talk about her,' he said, 'sorry.'

Jay, for all his easy social charm, was not a natural speaker, said he would rather not; and Giles said that he himself would be hopelessly stiff and nervous.

'You two?' he suggested to the twins; they considered it carefully but rejected it again.

'We'd just sound silly. Girls shouldn't do that kind of thing.'

'Of course they should,' said Giles, 'you're supposed to be modern and forward-looking.'

'I think,' said Venetia, 'we should have two eulogies. One from someone quite young, and one from someone quite old. Which means it could be Sebastian. Somehow, if he wasn't the only one, it wouldn't be so – difficult. And I know he'd love to do it, he's such an old ham.'

'And the young?'

'Goodness, I don't know. Elspeth, maybe?'

'Possibly. If she'd do it. She's a bit fragile at the moment.'

'Is Keir coming?'

'He's been invited, obviously. You're not suggesting—'

'Of course not. I just wondered.'

'I think it should be a woman, Giles is quite right. She was such a champion of women. And Elspeth's the only suitable Lytton. The others are too light-weight—'

'Even Noni?'

'Even Noni.'

'I'll ask Elspeth,' said Venetia.

Elspeth said she couldn't possibly.

'I might, if everything was all right, but I feel a bit – on shaky ground. People will sit looking at me, thinking I've been abandoned by my husband—'

'I'm sure they wouldn't.'

'Mummy, they would. I'd think they were, anyway, which is what matters.'

'Have you heard from him?'

'He wrote and thanked Giles for inviting him to the service.'

'Good,' said Venetia brightly.

'Well – not really. He doesn't feel he can accept.'

'That's understandable, I suppose. Unusually sensitive, under the circumstances.'

'Mummy—'

'Sorry. Any other news?'

'No. Except that he's found a proper flat, in Fulham, not just that awful room in Balham—'

'Good.'

There was a silence; then Elspeth said, slightly tentatively, 'I have got one suggestion for the young person.'

'Yes?'

'Jenna.'

'Jenna! But she's not even a Lytton.'

'Well – she is, in a way. She's Barty's daughter. Barty was an honorary Lytton, she was brought up with you. She was more of a Lytton than Sebastian. I think she should be represented. And she's very impressive. Jenna, I mean. Hugely self-confident, has that wonderful voice, sort of husky, like Barty's—'

'I'll think about it,' said Venetia, 'and maybe ask the others. But I don't think they'll like the idea.'

To her surprise, after the initial shock, they did: Jenna was a great favourite, she cut a swathe right through all the family complexities, she had been one of Celia's pets.

'But she might not agree,' said Giles.

'Well – we'll write and ask her, shall we, Dell? Ask her from both of us. That'll make it easier to say no, if she doesn't feel she can cope.'

'Why?' said Giles.

'It just—' said Venetia.

'—will,' said Adele.

Jamie Elliott and Kyle Brewer faced Charlie across Kyle's office. It was plain from both their expressions that they were finding the situation distasteful.

'We understand from Jenna,' said Jamie, 'that you have financial problems.'

'That is correct.'

'And that you might have to take your daughter away from Dana Hall.'

'Also correct.'

'Jenna is finding this rather distressing,' said Jamie.

'I think that's natural, don't you? It distresses me and she's quite fond of me, you know. Cathy is like a sister to her—'

'Of course. We appreciate all that. And she has asked us to help you. Financially.'

'She didn't have to do that,' said Charlie earnestly.

'She didn't?' said Kyle, his eyes gimlet-hard. 'I'm afraid I rather think she did. Having heard of your plight. She's a very tender-hearted, very loyal girl. It might have been better if you hadn't told her—'

'Oh, for fuck's sake,' said Charlie, dropping his guard suddenly, 'I was married to her mother. I'm her legal guardian. I've been looking after her ever since Barty died. It hasn't been easy.'

'We're aware of that. And of how fond of you Jenna is. And, incidentally, what a very good job you have done.'

'Well, thank you so much,' said Charlie, his voice heavy with sarcasm. 'Clearly I'm not all bad. Even by your impossibly high standards.'

'Charlie, we want to help you—'

'No you don't. You absolutely hate the thought of helping me. You want to help Jenna. Well, that's OK by me. Help is help, however you dress it up.'

'Indeed. Now, it has been agreed by the trust that it will pay your daughter's school fees, and her attendant expenses there, these to be defined in writing very carefully.'

'Oh really? How do you mean, exactly?'

'Well, her extra lessons, her clothes, her travel, that sort of thing. We would want receipts, obviously, from you—'

'To make sure I won't be slipping any gold watches in, handmade suits, that sort of thing? You guys disgust me. What kind of generosity is that?'

'Charlie, I would advise you not to start cutting up rough,' said Kyle, 'it really isn't very sensible.'

'Yes, Sir. Sorry, Sir. Would you like me to lick both your asses, or just one of 'em?'

They ignored this.

'We are also prepared,' said Kyle, 'to pay off your debts. We understand you have got into the hands of some rather unpleasant people—'

'Yeah!' said Charlie. 'They have something in common with you guys.'

Kyle looked steadily at him.

'Charlie, I do warn you, we could still change our minds about this.'

'No, you couldn't, Jenna wouldn't let you.'

'She doesn't actually have the choice. Anyway, we are prepared, out of Jenna's trust fund, to pay off those debts. We will do it for you, we want all the details, names, addresses, bank accounts—'

'You mean you're not letting me get my hands on anything really dangerous. Like the money.'

'That's about the size of it, yes. This to be set against your inheritance from Barty's will.'

'What?'

'You heard,' said Kyle.

There was a long silence: then Charlie said, 'Jesus, you guys do take all. Fucking millions in that fucking fund and the guy who's done most for Jenna over these past two years gets fucking peanuts out of it.'

'Charlie—'

'Oh for God's sake. Listen to me, you two sanctimonious pricks. Two things here: one is that my debts are rather larger than my inheritance, as you call that chicken feed Barty's chucked at me. The other is that unless you pay this honestly and fairly, that is to say, without setting it against any fucking thing, I'm off. Leaving. Turning my back on that poor benighted kid, leaving her at the mercy of that anally retentive tribe in England, and indeed you two charming heaps of shit. What do you think that'd do to her? She really does care for me, you know. I keep her going. She'd be pretty well done for if I went. That plucky little heart of hers would break. Oh, and by the way I do care for her too. A lot.'

'We do – realise that,' said Kyle. He spoke with difficulty.

'Oh, you do? And you're not prepared to do anything for me in return? I see.'

'Charlie, please.'

'No. I won't please. I want what's due to me, what anyone with an ounce of decency could see that I should have. OK? So do I get it or not? Huh?'

'Would you give us a moment, please?' said Jamie.

'Sure,' he said, suddenly more himself again, 'sure. I'll wait right here. I've got nothing else to do. My business has collapsed. Largely because I had to sell it in a hurry, thanks to you. No, you go ahead, take as many moments as you like.'

Ten minutes later they came back and told him they would unconditionally clear his debts, and that his legacy from Barty would be unaffected.

Charlie thanked them, gave them the information they had asked for and left.

At the corner of the street, using a public box, he put in a call to Jonathan Wyley.

'I'm sorry I never answered your last letter,' he said, 'family problems. I've decided though, I'd like to go ahead. If you're quite sure there's no need for Miss Elliott to be involved at this stage.'

'Absolutely no need. Provided you can give me written evidence that you are indeed her guardian. I'm delighted. Shall we make a date for you to come in, then?'

'Yes, fine. I'll call you when I'm home, and have my diary. Thanks.'

Charlie walked the several blocks home. Half relieved that his debts were to be settled and he'd get the loan off his back, half so angry still he could hardly see.

He'd show those fuckers. All of them. Lyttons, Elliotts, Brewers, the whole fucking lot of them. He wasn't quite sure how, but he would.

CHAPTER 43

Giles was finding his mother's diaries the most addictive thing he had ever read. He read them every night now, before he went home, drawn to them like a rather lugubrious bee to a honeypot, opening the safe when everyone had finally left, and working through them methodically, one by one.

It was not entirely pleasurable; certain incidents, particular revelations were more than uncomfortable, they were actually distasteful to him, and even shocking. He felt deeply awkward reading them, it was like watching his mother, his father and Sebastian, spying on them, listening to their conversations, observing their actions, unseen and unheard.

Giles also discovered that there were three missing. One was for the current year, which was understandable. She would hardly have come to the office to deposit it in her safe when it was only half finished. But the two others were more of a puzzle. One was for 1909, and the other, exactly ten years later, 1919. The first was the year before the twins were born, when Barty joined the family, and the second the year before Kit's birth; the diaries simply weren't there. It intrigued him greatly; if there had been many others missing, he might have assumed they had got lost, but every other year was there, neatly filed in order. Why not those?

He tried desperately to remember the significance of 1919; he had been fourteen, away at school and – what else? It was so hard to pinpoint memories. Barty would have been twelve. But there was one memory, and it increased his anxiety: memories of a half-comprehended drama, involving Barty, dreadful scenes taking place two floors below him at Cheyne Walk. He had never really discovered what happened that night; his mother had forbidden, and Barty firmly discouraged, any discussion about it. He remembered her dreadful distress, of course, over something she had refused to divulge, remembered her being hysterical, crying hour after hour and also the appalling scene when Celia had found the two of them lying on his bed, as he tried to comfort her, could still hear Barty screaming at her, saying dreadful, violently hostile things.

After that, doors had been slammed shut, entry barred; and he had never known any more. It had seemed to involve Sylvia Miller, Barty's mother, who had just died, and Celia herself; beyond that there was nothing.

The more he thought about it, the more likely it seemed that this episode must be the missing link; he could find nothing else in the diaries which he had read remotely relating to or resembling it. He tried to tell himself that perhaps his mother had not kept diaries for those years, that she had been too tired or too busy; it was unlikely but possible.

But certainly the entry for 1 January 1910 sounded as if it followed on from something else: *Such an exciting new year. We go into it with one child and will leave it with three. I am very tired this morning, hardly surprising after the party last night, but feel very well indeed. Next appointment with Dr Perring tomorrow. I so hope he's as positive as last time . . .*

No, that was not the first entry after a long break.

So – where was it? Where was 1909? With 1919 and 1959: but where? He checked the beginning of 1920 for clues. That was the year Kit was born. The first of January was a very positive entry: *A wonderful evening, everyone here. Baby very active! So different from last New Year, when we were beginning to worry about losing Lyttons.*

No, it didn't sound as if she'd missed out a year's diary-keeping there, either. There must be a link: the one explaining the other . . .

There were other, dreadful things too, relating episodes from his father's life at the front, during the First World War, one so dreadful it kept him awake all night, and after that a revelation so intimate, so personal, he felt sick and ashamed to have read it at all. For weeks after that he left them unread, swearing to read no more; but found himself compelled back to them again.

It was not all dark, not all revelation, of course; there were wonderful stories about the early days at Lyttons, about Celia and LM running it almost single-handed during the war, the truly touching story of LM's love affair with Jay's father, and of how Celia had arrived just in time to save Jay from adoption; the inspiring story of Billy Miller and Lady Beckenham, how she had rescued him from the despair of being eighteen years old and a victim of war, having lost not only a leg, but the will to live. Lady Beckenham had taken him on as a stable lad and given him his life back.

And the best thing of all, Celia had written, *is that I can face Barty again. She had lost faith in us entirely.*

Much more about Barty and how much Celia had loved her; more, he felt sometimes, and quite bitterly, than about himself.

She is truly precious to me, one entry ran, *I feel I have created her as much as I have my own.*

And then there was Celia and Sebastian: on and on it went, year after year, the story of that absolute love, fierce, loyal, unswerving, surviving so much; he reached March 1920 and read through, his eyes blurred with tears: *Kit is here and he is ours, mine and Sebastian's, and nothing can ever take that from us.*

Sometimes I hate Sebastian, sometimes I am so angry with him I would like to kill him; sometimes I think I never want to see him again. But whatever I feel for him, I love him. More and more. It is as simple as that.

And even the sorrow and outrage he had felt for his father was muted, somehow lessened. Indeed the entry when Oliver died explained and excused much about that love affair and about how the three of them had conducted their lives within its confines. *Oliver is dead and my heart feels quite broken. Were it not for Sebastian, I would want to die.*

They could not be destroyed, these diaries; they were infinitely precious.

Keir was so cold towards her; it hurt so much. Nothing, it seemed, could crack that coldness; not even asking him to stay for a meal, to discuss things, to make plans, even, to tell her what he was doing. He simply said they had nothing to say to one another.

Elspeth saw him every week, because every weekend, he came to take the children out. There was no doubt that Keir adored his children. And they him. Watching them greet him, Cecilia with whoops of joy and shouts of 'Daddy, Daddy,' Robert with his wide, heart-hurting grin, holding out his plump arms, seeing them cry when he left them again at the end of the day. It was all very painful. But not as painful as when he nodded to her briefly, before he turned away and said 'Next Saturday, then', and left without a further word. Not even, 'How are you?' or 'Is everything all right?' She marvelled at his hardness, his cruelty. He was a little mad, it seemed to her; he must be. He was utterly convinced of his own moral superiority – which was, she supposed, in absolute terms, superior indeed; whatever marital crimes he had committed, of neglect, of withdrawal of affection, of diminishing her, they could hardly be compared with adultery. She really did only have herself to blame.

There was one huge consolation, of course, and that was her work. She now spent three days a week at Lyttons, absolutely revelling in it. She had her own list (since Keir had left the firm), her own office, even her own staff, a secretary and an editorial department: two junior editors, one of them only a little younger than she was, and a trainee. It was wonderful. She was not only looking for novels to publish, and then buying them, with a sureness of touch which surprised even Jay; she was constantly having ideas for new fiction as well. She spent a lot of time discussing them with Clementine, who said talking about books was all she was fit for at the moment: 'I can't imagine having the energy to write anything ever again.' She was very pregnant and realising, as she confided to Elspeth, that she was going to be looking after not just one child but two.

'I adore Kit, of course I do, but he is immensely demanding, he's been spoilt all his life and I'm afraid he's not going to take kindly to second place when the baby arrives.'

'Tough,' said Elspeth, 'he's going to have to.'

But for all her brave words and her visionary ideas, she was without her own overgrown child; and she missed him horribly.

Clementine was actually very large indeed.

'I'm almost glad Kit can't see me, I look so hideous.'

'Of course you don't, you look beautiful,' said Elspeth.

'Oh really? I don't think so. I never could quite buy this idea that women were never more lovely than when carrying three stone extra on their stomachs. And it is nearly three stone, I've just gorged my way through it. It's been quite nice, though.'

'How does Kit feel about the baby?'

'Well, obviously he's thrilled. Although every so often he says something sad about not being able to see it. I can understand that. He's a bit down altogether at the moment, still so upset about his mother. He feels terrible about missing all that time when he was sulking about her marriage, you know. So this baby has quite a lot of work to do.'

'I'm sure it will manage,' said Elspeth cheerfully.

Lucas was working at Lyttons while waiting for his National Service call-up; he was enjoying it enormously. He was only allowed to perform very menial tasks, which he didn't seem to mind in the least; his favourite being working in the post room. Elspeth was astonished, remembering the arrogant Lucas of only a few years earlier, but he told her he was intending to take the company over one day and there was a proud tradition of chairmen starting their days in the post room.

'You get to know everyone, you get to study the hierarchy, and you find out what everyone's really like. I have great plans for the company already.'

'Oh you do, do you?' said Elspeth. 'Are we allowed to hear them?'

'Of course. My main observation so far is that we're very undercapitalised. We need a lot more money. And that's easily dealt with, we should go public. Do a rights issue. We could still retain overall control and we'd have the funds to expand. It's got to happen, everyone in publishing is doing it.'

'It wouldn't be hard to talk me into it,' said Elspeth, 'I've thought it myself, and so has Keir. And I think Jay might be persuaded. But Mummy and Giles – never!'

'Well, that would be three against two,' said Lucas.

She stared at him. 'Lucas, you're not on the board, you don't have any shares. Don't be ridiculous.'

'Oh, I'll get some,' he said confidently.

Still a little arrogant then. She looked at him thoughtfully. There really was a new generation of Lyttons; it would be very interesting to see how they worked out . . .

The following Saturday Elspeth spent the day at Cheyne Walk, they had all been helping Adele settle in.

'Got any nice young ladies at the moment, Lucas?' asked Elspeth, taking a cocktail from him. He was rather proud of his expertise with cocktails.

'Dozens, of course. Queuing up outside my room every night.'

'Izzie thinks Jenna's got a crush on you.'

'Good,' he said, cheerfully, 'I think she's very sweet. I tell you, in about three or four years, that girl is going to be quite glorious-looking. Those eyes, and that hair! And I really admire her, she's got such guts. She'll have to wait a few years, though, it'd be cradle-snatching at the moment.'

'Lucas, you are so arrogant,' said Noni, 'why should she wait a few years for you?'

'Because I'm irresistible,' he said, 'so charming and amusing and so romantic-looking.'

The trouble was, Noni thought, punching him hard, it was true. At least these days he was nice . . .

It dropped on to Annabel Elliott's breakfast table like a stick of dynamite. A stick of dynamite with the fuse alight. A letter to her solicitor from some Manhattan attorneys. She had thought, at first, it was a letter asking her to be on some charity board or other and was pushing it aside, when the words began to sink in:

> . . . will petition Under Section 28 of the New York Decedent Estate Law to attain an order against the trustees of the Laurence Elliott Trust to show cause why they should not provide the equal share of your late husband's estate to Miss Jeanette Elliott, born March 17, 1945, to which she is entitled . . .

'Oh my God,' said Annabel Elliott, and reached for the telephone to ring Gregory Pollack, her lawyer.

Pollack was initially reassuring, saying he had felt it was a try-on, a desperate measure by a greedy family and that he would look into it further; by the time Annabel reached his office two days later, he had become rather less sanguine.

'I'm afraid that they do have a case. We can dispute it, of course, but under the law, she is indeed entitled to a third of the estate.'

'But − she wasn't even mentioned in Laurence's will.'

'Presumably because he could not have known about her. He was killed before she was born. God knows why the wife's chasing the money now. Possibly she's in financial trouble, she only got the houses, and a small share portfolio as I recall, and that type of person tends to let money go to their head.'

'She's dead,' said Annabel Elliott.

'Dead!'

'Yes. I read about it in the paper. She was killed in a plane crash, about eighteen months ago, flying back from England. You remember she was English?'

'Yes, of course. How very interesting. So who is the child's guardian?'

'Obviously someone with an eye to the main chance.'

'So it would seem. Well, I'll write to Wyley Ruffin Wynne and tell them we shall contest their petition.'

'Can we do that?'

'Of course. They have to prove that she is indeed Mr Elliott's afterborn child—'

'Not very difficult, I imagine. What else?'

Pollack hesitated.

'Not a lot else, is there, Mr Pollack? As I understand it. This child – Jeanette, named after Laurence's mother, incidentally – has a right to a third of the estate. Quite simple. What sum of money are we talking about, I wonder? Somewhere in the region of thirty million dollars, wouldn't you say? I hope the trustees have looked after it carefully.'

'On that score, Mrs Elliott, you need have no worries at all. The estate has increased in value quite dramatically, as you know. And there are a lot of arguments we can present yet. For one, why wait till now? The law doesn't like delay. Although' – he hesitated – 'I have to say Wyley Ruffin Wynne are extremely clever lawyers. I would love to know who has instructed them. There must be a very canny guardian involved.'

'The children aren't going to like this,' said Annabel Elliott, 'they aren't going to like it one bit.'

'Would you like a drink, Keir? You look terribly tired.'

He did; exhausted. Of course looking after two small children all day wasn't exactly restful, but he looked what her mother called 'tired tired'.

He hesitated. 'No. No, I don't think so. Thank you. I have to get back.'

'What on earth for? It's Saturday. Or are you going out this evening?' That thought hurt.

'No,' he said. 'No, but I have a lot of work to do.'

He was very subdued; less hostile. She took heart from this.

'For Wesley?' He had started there two weeks earlier; there had been a lot of publicity in the trade press about it. 'Honestly Keir, if Granny knew you were working for Wesley, she'd send down a thunderbolt. She hated them so.'

'All the more reason for moving there,' said Keir. But he smiled: just faintly. Elspeth saw the smile and struck.

'Go on, stay for a drink. You can help me put the children to bed.'

'Yes, yes!' Cecilia started clamouring, jumping up and down.

He sighed.

'All right. Just for a bit.'

He had never helped her bath the children, in all the years since Cecilia was born; they were hugely over-excited by it. A rather wet hour later, Robert was in bed and Cecilia eating scrambled egg; Elspeth fetched a bottle of wine.

'Or would you rather have whisky? Like a true Scot?'

'Aye, I would.'

He poured himself a very large one; she opened the wine for herself.

'I've learned to do all sorts of things since you left, you see. How is it at Wesley, anyway? Is it as wonderful as Kit always said?'

'They're very good publishers. Yes. I'm enjoying it.'

'Will – will you be coming to the memorial service?'

'I – don't think so.'

'Oh Keir, why not? You should. You know how Granny loved you, what a lot she did for you. She'd have been so hurt.'

'Well, she won't know, will she?'

'That's not a very nice thing to say.'

'I – really don't feel I could, Elspeth. To be honest. Your family must think very badly of me. Turning down her gift, I – well, I don't feel I could face them.'

'I think they think quite badly of me,' she said soberly, 'but you should come, Keir. Promise me to think about it.'

'I – I will think about it. Yes.'

'Thank you.'

'And how is it at Lyttons at the moment? I suppose you're working full time, are you? Now that you've got rid of your jailer?'

'No,' she said steadily, 'only three days a week. I said I wouldn't leave the children yet and I haven't.'

'Oh,' he said, looked slightly discomfited, 'oh, yes, I see.'

'I think, Keir,' she said, her eyes meeting his very steadily, 'you really have got me rather wrong. I'm not the harsh, power-crazed woman you seem to imagine.'

'Elspeth,' he said, 'Elspeth, I—'

Robert started to cry; she got up, 'Excuse me, please.'

When she came back, he had his coat on.

'I must go,' he said. His voice was hostile again. 'Really. I have a lot to do.'

It was only after he left that she realised there was a letter on the window-sill, with an American stamp on it. It was actually from Izzie, but he had no doubt thought it was from Marcus. Damn. Damn, damn, damn. Just when they might have been getting somewhere.

'This is such an honour!' said Jenna to Cathy. She was reading a letter. 'I absolutely can't believe it. This is from Venetia and Adele. They've asked me to speak at Celia's memorial service. Me! Not even a relation. She's got hundreds of proper grandchildren, and they're asking me.'

'Wow! Let me see. Oh, my God, Jenna. What will you wear?'

Jenna was still very fond of Cathy, and always would be, but they were definitely growing apart. She was learning to accept that and not fight it. If she wanted to talk hair and clothes and boys, Cathy was great; if she wanted to discuss politics, or travel, or art, there was no point even trying.

Of course Cathy had been wonderful about her mother, just the best friend, wonderfully supportive and always ready to talk or listen, or cry with her, and that had made an unbreakable bond, she would never forget it or stop being grateful for it. But a soulmate Cathy was not.

'I – don't know,' she said now. 'I'll have to think about it. All of it. I'm not even sure I'm brave enough to do it.'

'Oh Jenna, of course you are. You'll be wonderful.'

'I hope so.'

It would be terrifying. Absolutely terrifying . . . which was no reason not to do it; her mother had taught her that. 'If you know something's important to you,' she had said to Jenna once, 'then you owe it to yourself to try. However frightened you are.'

She would be doing it for her mother as well as for herself. She could talk about Barty, say how Celia had brought her up, done so much for her, all that kind of thing. And say how much Celia had helped her when her mother had been killed. It wouldn't be easy, though; she could feel the tears rising even at the thought of it.

Adele and Venetia had said there was plenty of time for her to think about it, although they'd like to know quite soon. 'We have just over four weeks. If it's no, we'd like to know as soon as possible, because we have to find someone else.'

No, she must do it. She would write at once and tell them so, before she could change her mind. She smiled at Cathy.

'Yes, I'm going to say yes.'

'You'll be great. So – what *are* you going to wear?'

Jenna looked at Cathy thoughtfully, smiling almost indulgently. She felt much older than her in lots of ways: although Cathy had left Jenna far behind in one respect; she was most definitely not a virgin, she had slept, to Jenna's certain knowledge, with three boys since the gardener.

'Cathy Patterson isn't fast,' one of her classmates at Dana Hall had remarked, 'she's the speed of light.'

She was absurdly pretty, with her vast blue eyes and neat little turned-up nose, a china doll of a girl, very small, but with a bosomy figure and beautiful legs. She was simply a honeypot to boys; they flocked to her. It was well known that if you wanted to have a good time you didn't go out with Cathy Patterson in a foursome. You'd be left watching miserably all night while she flirted with both of the boys.

Jenna worried about Cathy, about her sleeping around; it wasn't just the risk of her getting pregnant (although Cathy assured her she wouldn't), it was what it would do to her reputation, make everyone think she was cheap. That was something no one could afford. Cheap girls just got used.

And there was something else: Cathy drank, quite a lot. Not just at parties, when everyone did, but before she went out, always at mealtimes, and sometimes she would sneak to the sideboard or the fridge at home and pour a slug of vodka into a jug, then top it up with orange, so it looked like she was just drinking orange juice while she watched TV.

Her father had once questioned her about this, had asked her quite seriously if she had been drinking his vodka, it went down so fast; Jenna listened and watched, incredulous and even impressed while Cathy's blue eyes filled with tears and she reproached her father for even thinking she would do such a thing. He always believed her . . .

Jenna didn't like alcohol, but she did like boys; in fact, that summer, after she got back from England, slightly disappointed about Lucas, she had been in love for the very first time, and it had been just so wonderful and exciting. He was called Tommy; he was seventeen years old and summering at Southampton. He hadn't just been trying to get her to neck with him all the time, he'd liked talking and he'd been really funny, really fun, and so good-looking as well. He was a terrific sailor and they'd been out on the beach one night, having a barbecue, a whole load of them, and Tommy had asked her to go for a walk with him, and he'd suddenly stopped and she'd thought here we go, only he didn't try to get his hands up her T-shirt, he said he wanted to tell her that he loved her. She'd been so surprised and so happy that she'd thrown her arms round him and told him she loved him too before letting him kiss her, really kiss her, and for the rest of the summer they'd been inseparable. Only then he'd gone back to school, he was at Choate, and although he'd been really good about writing at first, the letters had tailed off and she realised this wasn't for life after all. She managed to put it behind her; and look forward to seeing Lucas at the memorial service in November.

'There is one thing,' said Jonathan Wyley. 'Are you quite sure that Mrs Elliott did not specifically waive any rights to a share of the estate for her child? That would be a powerful argument against our claim; indeed, it would entail a trial on the claim itself.'

'I – don't know,' said Charlie, and his heart seemed to have stopped beating entirely, 'but surely if she had, they wouldn't waste any time telling us?'

'Of course. Which is why I think it unlikely. But there will be documentation left with her own lawyers, or it might conceivably be linked in some way with her will. Although that would have come to light by now, I would have thought. Anyway, it needs to be confirmed before we go to court.'

'So?'

'So, you have to check on that. They could demand absolute proof that the second Mrs Elliott did not waive her rights to the money, given the time that has elapsed since Mr Elliott's death and the ample opportunity she had to make the claim. It would save a lot of time. Mrs Elliott's lawyers would know, without doubt. She would have had to go to court to waive the claim.'

'It's a question I would find difficult to ask them.'

'I don't see why. It's very straightforward. Because, if she did waive the claim to those rights, then it would be a waste of time and money trying to proceed.'

'Could anyone else waive them on her behalf at this point?' He wouldn't put that past Jamie Elliott, if he got wind of this.

'No. Only the mother. And once we've put this process into motion, nothing can stop it. It's inexorable. And as Jenna's guardian, you do have the right to do that. But as I say, we can't go forward without this information.'

'Yes, all right,' said Charlie. 'I'll see what I can do.'

'Jenna says she'd be proud and happy to accept,' said Venetia to Giles.

'Good. I'm delighted. Does she want any help with what she'd like to say?'

'Knowing Jenna, I would think that very unlikely,' said Adele. 'I have never known a girl more sure of her own mind. Now, where is she going to stay? At Cheyne Walk? That would make the most sense.'

'You don't mind?'

'Of course I don't mind.'

'It would mean having Charlie and Cathy as well.'

'I like Charlie,' said Adele firmly. 'I think you've all got him wrong. I'd love to have him to stay. And Cathy's quite sweet and she certainly can't be left under the same roof as Fergal again, Venetia.'

'Oh, Fergal's in love,' said Venetia, 'with a girl he met during Cowes week. She's perfectly sweet, Boy and I adore her.'

'Must be very well connected then,' said Adele, winking at Giles.

Venetia's snobbery had become as great, possibly greater, even, than her mother's.

★

Again and again, Giles wondered what he should do with the diaries; the burden of the secret was increasingly intense. He worried desperately about them being discovered, worried they would somehow fall into the wrong hands – although how he could not imagine – worried that he was wrong to keep them to himself. Wouldn't Sebastian love to have sight of them, to read of that lifelong passion; didn't the twins have a right too, and Kit, perhaps, as well?

But then he thought of the darker side of the stories: of the dreadful sadness of Izzie's and Kit's love affair, of Boy Warwick's unfaithfulness, of Adele's humiliation in Paris, her escape from France, Luc Lieberman's dreadful end. Were they not best buried, these things, safe in the care of those they belonged to, revealed only by choice and reshaped and retold, even to one another, as their owners saw fit?

But what right did he have to decide the fate of the diaries? To say they should be preserved or destroyed, revealed or kept secret? They weren't his, they were his mother's; what would she have wanted for them? And should not all her children share in that decision?

He had reached no conclusion as the family began to arrive for his mother's memorial service.

CHAPTER 44

Charlie was getting desperate. As he understood it, all that stood between him and roughly thirty million dollars was a piece of paper that might not even exist. If it did exist, then the thirty million dollars was staying in the Elliott bank account; if it didn't, then it would come winging over into his. Well, Jenna's, anyway. Give or take a few months and maybe a couple of million either way.

He was fairly sure that if Barty had waived her claim, she would have filed a copy away herself, even if it was also with her lawyers. He had never known anyone so obsessed with copies and filing. Every damn letter she'd ever written, certainly about Jenna, was filed away; if there was anything about this, then he'd find it. Just pray God he didn't.

So far, he hadn't; there was nothing at Number Seven, anyway. A weekend at South Lodge, sifting through the rather meagre papers she had kept there, revealed nothing more intriguing than the document confirming her membership of the sailing club, a few receipts for donations to the Parrish Art Museum, copies of letters she'd written to the local paper and the various local residents' associations. He'd even asked Mr and Mrs Mills if they knew of anywhere she might have kept documents; they said no, although there were some boxes of papers in the loft he might like to look through. He spent several hours looking through boxes of old English newspapers, mostly about the last war; his spirits rose with every hour.

'What if it can't be found, this thing?' he said to Wyley. 'Surely that means it doesn't exist?'

'Of course not. I really don't understand your problem. There will be records. You simply have to check it out with her lawyers.'

The thing was, Charlie was scared of doing that. They'd tell the trustees; or they might. Martin Gilroy, one of that grisly trio of trustees, was a lawyer himself, although not with the firm Barty had generally dealt with. They'd tell him about it without a doubt.

He was in the bath after another long evening sifting through all the papers for the second time when he had the brainwave: it was so simple and yet so bloody clever . . .

'You're a genius Patterson,' he said aloud.

'Jenna darling, I need to know something. For a form I have to fill in.'

'I don't suppose I can tell you.'

'You might. Could I just ask you?'

'Sure. If, after that, you'll listen to my speech.'

'Of course I will. Honeybunch, you know that rather sorry business, just before Celia died, when I wanted to find out if you were due any more money from your dad?'

'Yes, of course. Charlie, you're not—'

'Of course I'm not,' he said, his voice and eyes very hurt.

'Sorry. Sorry, Charlie.'

'But I do need to know something, God knows why.'

'What's that?'

'Well it's not me, it's the IRS. The income tax people. They need to know if your mother officially waived any claim to that money.'

'Why on earth should they need to know that?'

'God knows. But they do. It seems that in some way it could be considered a potential asset. Your share, I mean. If she didn't waive the claim.'

'How odd. An asset of yours?'

'Well – as your guardian, yes. I suppose they think I could claim it.'

'Why don't you ask the trustees? They'd know.'

'And risk another earful from them? I don't think so.'

'Charlie, I thought they were being nicer to you now. That they'd helped you last time.'

'They did, darling. But they gave me a hell of a lecture first. About how I should be able to manage on what I got from them, all that stuff. As if I was a kid of sixteen.'

'Oh God.' She looked at him, then went over and put her arms round his neck. 'Charlie, I'm so sorry. They are horrible.'

'No, they're not. Of course they're not. They're doing their job, safeguarding your interests.'

'And you're not, I suppose? God, they make me so angry.'

'Well – do you think you could ask them that? Without mentioning me?'

'Sure. If it's important. I'll see what I can do.'

She phoned Jamie; she didn't really want to see him, she was too angry.

'I need to know something. You know my father's estate, apparently I could be due a lot more from it.'

'You could?' He sounded wary. 'Who told you that?'

'I read about a similar case, Jamie. In the paper. Nobody told me.'

'I see. Well – what about it?'

'Do you happen to know if my mother waived the claim to my share?'

'Does it matter?'

'I'd like to know, that's all. Anything wrong with that?'

'No. You're not – thinking of claiming it, are you?'

'Of course I'm not.' Her voice was scornful. 'You know how I hate that whole thing. I hate everything to do with money, and I certainly hate what I have to contend with, all the rubbish about the trust and not being allowed to do what I want with it. Not even help a friend.'

'Jenna, we have helped Charlie. If that's what you mean.'

'Yes, sure, and gave him a lecture into the bargain, I hear.'

There was a silence; then Jamie said, 'Jenna, did Charlie ask you to get this information for him?'

'Jamie,' she said, and her voice was outraged, 'I find it shocking you should even think such a thing. I just want to know. And if my mother didn't write, waiving this claim, then I want you to. She'd hate me to be going after that money, as much as I would. OK?'

'I really don't think we're empowered to do that, Jenna. But I'll look into it, and let you know.'

'Oh God,' she said, and he could hear her temper rising, 'I can't tell you how glad I'll be when I'm in control of my own affairs, do what I know is best for me.'

'I'm sure you will,' said Jamie. 'Anyway, I'll check this out for you. 'Bye Jenna.'

He put the phone down and looked at it thoughtfully. Then he picked it up again and spoke to Kyle.

'I think that bastard's up to something. And he's using Jenna to help him. We need to talk to Gilroy.'

Gilroy was clearly shaken.

'I imagine this is about Jenna's right to a share of her father's estate. As his afterborn child. And of course unless the claim was waived, she's entitled to one third of it. Even now.'

'Serious money,' said Kyle. His eyes were thoughtful.

'Very serious indeed. And Charlie has an absolute right, as her guardian, to petition for it. Moreover, as her guardian, he would have control of it, if he got it. He could administer the funds, on her behalf.'

'Jesus, what a thought.'

'Absolutely.'

He came back twenty-four hours later.

'I've made some enquiries. Our friend has been to see Jonathan Wyley, of Wyley Ruffin Wynne.'

'Christ. That must have cost him a bit.'

'I imagine he thought it would be worth it,' said Jamie.

'Well – it could be,' said Gilroy, 'it's interesting, isn't it?'

'It could be more than interesting,' said Kyle, 'it could be an absolute bloody nightmare. So – he could actually get his hands on this money?'

'In theory. As I said, he is her legal guardian.'

'Why Barty appointed him, I'll never know.'

'We talked about that,' said Jamie, seriously, 'the fact is, and she admitted it, he is wonderfully fond of Jenna. In lots of ways he's been terribly good to her. And she loves him in return. Don't forget, Barty had no anxieties on the financial front, she knew his hands were well and truly tied. Plus, of course, it didn't seem to her very crucial. As everyone keeps saying, she didn't expect to die, she was a young woman. I guess she thought she'd sort it out sometime.'

'She sorted Lyttons out in time,' said Kyle.

'I know she did. But I think they were two completely different matters in her mind. Anyway, what shall I tell Jenna?'

'Oh, tell her we're making enquiries. It's perfectly true. And it might take a few days. Mr Patterson will have to be patient.'

'Difficult for him under the circumstances.'

'Poor little Jenna,' said Jamie. He felt genuinely upset.

'Charlie? It's about that thing, you know—'

'What thing is that, darling?'

'You know, the claim, whether my mother had waived it or not.'

'Oh – yes. I'd forgotten all about that. And—'

'Kyle Brewer just phoned me. They're checking it out. They're going to let me know as soon as they can. Is that OK? Charlie are you OK? You look terrible.'

'I'm perfectly all right,' said Charlie.

'Can I get you anything?'

'No, you can't.'

'Not even a drink?'

'No. Just leave me alone, Jenna, would you? I have work to do. I need a bit of peace.'

He was so rarely even irritable with her, she felt near to tears.

The memorial service was on the tenth of November. Izzie was arriving in London on the third, and the boys were following five days later: 'We can't leave the shop for too long, darling. Sorry.'

'That's all right,' said Izzie, 'I can spend some time with father, on my own. He'll like that.'

They were all three to stay at Primrose Hill; Kit and Clementine were also staying for a few days. Mrs Conley was very excited.

'It'll do Mr Brooke all the good in the world,' she said to Mrs Morrison, who now came in to what she called 'help her with the cleaning', and Mrs

Conley called 'taking over'. 'It'll take him out of himself a bit. That and the baby, all heaven-sent.'

Mrs Morrison, who didn't know the history, couldn't quite see why Mr Brooke should be so excited about someone else's baby, and said so; Mrs Conley put her right.

'Mr Brooke is a very kind and generous gentleman,' she said, 'and Mr Kit is Lady Celia's son and therefore a very good friend.'

'Funny, you know,' said Mrs Morrison, 'I often think Mr Kit looks rather like Mr Brooke.'

'Really?' said Mrs Conley vaguely, 'I hadn't noticed.'

'She's very large, isn't she, Mrs Kit?' said Mrs Morrison, 'she's going to have a bad time, that's for sure.'

Mrs Conley agreed. 'Terribly small hips. And she'll have her work cut out, looking after a baby *and* Mr Kit. He's very nice, and he manages wonderfully, but my goodness is he spoilt!'

Mrs Morrison said it was natural, she supposed, given his problem, and went upstairs to make the beds.

Izzie was longing to get to London; she was very tired, and it would be a relief to have some time on her own. It was very nice, working with Nick, but it did make for a rather non-stop relationship. Which again was wonderful, when things were going well at Neill & Parker; when they weren't, it was very exhausting. And she was longing to see her father, and Kit and Clementine – she had heard Clemmie was huge – and everyone else. Much as she adored New York, she did occasionally feel a physical yearning for London.

She supposed New York was now her home; there was no way she and Nick could settle in London. He was rooted in New York, and Mike too, trying to resettle them in London would be impossible; rather like moving rockery plants into a water garden and expecting them to thrive.

She worried about her father endlessly; all alone as he was, in what seemed suddenly such a big, quiet house. Of course Celia hadn't lived in it with him, but she had been there so much, and she had made sure the others visited him too. Izzie had a horrible feeling they'd all slowly drift away without Celia's vigorous nagging. He'd coped with the shock of her death very well at first but, later on, when the drama was over, the grief really began to set in.

'Poor Father,' she said suddenly with a heavy sigh to Nick, as she packed her case, the night before she left. 'He hasn't had much luck in his life really. His personal life, I mean.'

'Oh I don't know. He had a lifetime of Celia—'

'She wasn't his. Not really.'

'I think she was. He had her heart.'

She smiled at him. One of the things she most loved about Nick was the way he put new perspectives on things, quite ordinary things. 'I suppose so.'

'And he had you for – what? Twenty-nine years. More than I've had. Although I plan to try and catch up now.'

'Oh Nick.' She went over and kissed him. 'I do love you. I'm sorry I've been so – mean, lately.'

'I wouldn't call it mean. And if you promise to keep loving me, I could even handle mean. You've been fine, Princess. Just a bit – down. I know you're tired. You've had a lot to cope with.'

She kissed him again and suggested they went out for dinner. After that, they could make love; it wasn't anything like the right time, but it would be nice anyway . . .

It was to be in the afternoon at three o'clock, a little unusual for a memorial service, but it meant they could entertain the chosen many, as Boy put it, for drinks afterwards, and the family could then relax over dinner.

The changes were still going on with only a week to go; a third and final programme had just been proofed. There had been much argument over the music and in particular what would be played before the service.

'Mummy wasn't religious, she just loved beautiful words and music, of all sorts,' said Venetia. 'I think we should have lots of lovely Bach and Brahms, all that sort of thing, and maybe even some Mendelssohn. We've got the hymns, after all, and—'

'But this is a service, it's in a church, for God's sake.'

'Giles, so what? We're not suggesting a bit of swing.'

At which point Lord Arden intervened; his personal request for the service was '*Panis Angelicus*' and it was decided that this should precede Sebastian's address.

'But I've been thinking, I would also like something of Fauré's *Requiem*,' he said, adding slightly apologetically, 'if that would be all right and not too late. It's so uplifting, despite being a requiem.'

'Of course it would be all right,' said Adele, kissing him, for she was, of all of them, the most fond of him, 'and actually, why don't we have that before the service, Giles? It's so lovely, and I know Mummy would approve. Nice and long too, in case people are late.'

Lord Arden said surely they wouldn't be late, but Venetia said he didn't know the publishing world very well, if he thought that; Lord Arden turned amused blue eyes on her and said that indeed, no, not very well at all.

'I was never allowed to, she kept me well away from it.'

That had made them feel dreadful. Venetia asked him what else he would like, even at this late stage: he said he knew it was a little corny, but he would like St Paul's Letter to the Corinthians. 'I do think it is quite the most beautiful piece of writing in the English language.'

'Would you like to read it yourself?' asked Venetia.

He turned quite pink with pleasure and said that it would be marvellous if they really thought he should.

'Oh, Bunny, of course. It's just that you said before you didn't want to play a very big role.'

'Well, there are roles and roles. I certainly couldn't speak off the cuff.'

'In that case, please do read it. We can have a run-through in the church later.'

Jay then said he was sorry to suggest something else new at the last minute, but if there were changes being made, he and Tory had been at a funeral that weekend and the absolute highlight had been the singing of 'Where E'er You Walk'; 'I think Celia would like that, it's so like her . . .'

And so it went on; a fourth version of the programme was run off by Lyttons own printers with only twenty-four hours to spare, and Giles said that if his mother came to him in a vision and requested a change now, he would have to tell her she couldn't have it.

The twins gazed at him in blank and silent astonishment.

'You wouldn't dare,' said Venetia.

'No I wouldn't,' said Giles.

For the hundredth time he debated telling them about the diaries; for the hundredth time he decided not to. Not yet.

The Brewers and Jamie Elliott were staying at Claridges; Venetia had offered to have them, but they said no, there must be so much family to accommodate and indeed, it was true. Apart from the Warwicks themselves, the Millers were arriving at Berkeley Square the morning of the service, and would be staying that night, and Jack and Lily would be with them too.

A week before, there was a surprise call from Marcus Forrest; they had invited him but he had refused, to everyone's relief. Suddenly, now he said he would like to come after all.

'Celia and I had our differences, but I admired her so much and I would like to think that Lyttons New York would be represented.'

Since Lyttons New York was already being very well represented, because the entire board was attending, this was slightly surprising, but it was felt they could only express delight.

'You can look after him,' said Venetia to Elspeth, with a slightly cool smile. Elspeth, with a still cooler one, said it would be a pleasure.

She was very upset that Keir was not coming; partly because she had hoped he would on her account, but mainly because she felt it was an appalling slight on his part towards her entire family and the memory of her grandmother in particular. All right, he didn't believe in an afterlife, nor did she. She didn't think, as Lord Arden clearly did, that Celia would be sitting up on her cloud looking down at them – and probably, as Venetia said, noting what she didn't like in order to complain about it later. But she would be there very much in spirit, everyone would be thinking about her, talking about her, remembering her, bringing her back to life; it was outrageous that he should sling this insult into what was above all a loving and respectful occasion.

She had told him so, several times, but it had done no good; she was so angry with him, she could hardly speak when he came to collect the children the Saturday before. By the time he returned with them, however, she found it hard to stop.

'I hope it goes well,' he said, 'on Thursday.'

'Oh really?' she said. 'If you wanted it to go well, you'd do your bit to support us, rather than turning your back and walking away from it. I think perhaps you've come to think of your publishing success as being entirely earned by your own hard work. The actual facts are rather different, as I recall. I don't think Macmillans or John Murray invited you to join them when you left Oxford, did they? Or – who else was it you applied to – oh, yes, Heinemann, I think, and Michael Joseph. Goodness, it was a long list. Goodbye, Keir. I shall try not to think of you while it's going on. It would completely spoil it for me, I'm afraid.'

In the event, she was able to think of very little else.

'Do you think there's something wrong with Dad?' said Cathy.

'Don't know. Why?'

'He seems so – edgy. All he does is snap at me. It's unlike him. I'm worried.'

'He snapped at me the other night too. And I know he's not sleeping, he was in his study about three this morning, when I got up to get a drink. That's unlike him too. He does love his sleep.'

'Maybe he's just worried about this trip, meeting all your grand relatives.'

'Maybe. Poor Charlie. He said right at the beginning, when the invitation came, he was excited about it.'

'Or maybe he has money worries. He used to get like this when big bills came in.'

'Poor Charlie,' said Jenna again.

Charlie felt worse every day. There was no news from the trustees. It was a nightmare. A real nightmare. He couldn't ever remember feeling so helpless. Every day he decided to instruct Wyley to approach the lawyers direct and every day he decided against it. He had to keep this low-key. He couldn't risk Jenna getting wind of the fact he was making his own enquiries. If all went well, and they could proceed, he'd have to find some way of breaking the news to her. But he wasn't having her needlessly upset at this stage. He just had to wait.

When he had been a small boy, the nuns had taken them to a funfair, as a great treat, and while the other boys were larking around on the carousel, Charlie had played doggedly with one of those Grab-a-Gift games. He had spent over an hour and all this money there, juggling with the hook, trying to pick up the trashy toys at the bottom of the case; every time, as he put his ten cents in, he thought this time, this time he would do it, and the hook would swoop down and he'd think he was in control and nearly, so nearly, grab something and then time would run out and the hook would stop moving and he'd be left with nothing yet again. He felt rather like that now. Only he had no control over the hook at all.

Jenna still didn't like flying; but she had discovered the trick was to be terribly busy, to have lots and lots to do; with that in mind she had brought along the script of *Noah* which the school was doing for Christmas and in which she was Mrs Noah. She also had a huge stash of magazines and, of course, she had her speech to worry about. She was still fiddling with it.

She was very nervous; every time she thought of the huge church, filled with distinguished people, she felt sick.

'Hey,' said Cathy, looking up from one of the gossip pages, 'hey look, it's that guy, your half-brother, you know. Bart Elliott, they call him here. Says he's going to be twenty-one next year and he's giving a party for five hundred people on some island, and jetting himself there in his own plane. How about that? He's quite cute looking, Jenna, think you could introduce me?'

'I hope I never meet him myself. I think he must be absolutely dreadful,' said Jenna.

'Me too,' said Charlie.

He smiled at her. And thought that, if he had his way, Mr Bart Elliott would have just a little more trouble financing his plane than he was expecting.

Charlie was feeling better; he wasn't sure why. Maybe it was just getting out of New York, away from it all for a few days. Maybe with every day that passed, without the documentation turning up, he felt more confident.

Whatever the reason, he was going to enjoy London. He had a good feeling about it.

'I hope you girls don't mind being up here on the top floor,' said Adele, apologetically, 'but we're getting rather full. Maud, Uncle Robert's daughter, and her husband Nathaniel — sorry, Charlie, very confusing — have suddenly announced they're not coming on their own but are bringing their two children. So I have to find room for them as well. Anyway, I've put you in the room that was your mother's, Jenna, I thought you'd like that.'

★

She had actually visited the room before, high up, above the tree tops even, with a wonderful view of the river, had sat on the bed, thinking of her mother there as a small child, feeling lost and frightened, growing up there, doing her homework, reading. There was even Barty's little desk, and her wardrobe and chest of drawers; it made her feel very close to her.

'I would like it,' she said, 'thank you.'

'You've met Maud, haven't you?' asked Adele.

Jenna said she had, a few times; 'But she and my mother were never very close. Maud never seemed to quite approve of her.'

'More fool her,' said Adele lightly. 'Now, I have a message for you, Jenna, from Lucas, he says he's really looking forward to seeing you, and he'll be here tomorrow afternoon.'

'Really?' Jenna flushed with pleasure.

'Really. And I'm going to give a dinner tomorrow night, an American dinner, for all you lot, Uncle Robert and the Brewers and Jamie, of course—'

'That sounds just great,' said Charlie, 'I think that's really charming of you, Adele. Shall we sing the "Star-Spangled Banner"?'

'Charlie, you're so vulgar!' said Jenna. But she was laughing at him and reached up to give him a kiss.

She's so fond of him, Adele thought, and he obviously adores her. She couldn't understand why so many people in the family didn't like him. She felt a sense of sadness herself, that she would be very much on her own, haunted by the ghosts of her two husbands. Well, not even two husbands, one and a lover. She really didn't seem to be very good at relationships. She had even, for a wild moment, considered sending Geordie an invitation, but rejected it almost at once; it would hurt too many people, including his own small daughter, and it would outrage too many more. It was just that once – so long ago it seemed – he had been very much part of the family, Celia had been very fond of him, and he of her. As fond as Geordie MacColl was of anyone except himself . . .

Cathy was in a strop over the Warwicks not coming to the dinner.

'But Cathy, the whole point is it's an American dinner,' said Jenna, 'and the Warwicks are English. It's a lovely idea of Adele's, I think.'

'Yes, well, it's all right for you, you've got Lucas to make eyes at. Who have I got? More elderly relations. I mean, like this old couple from California, how exciting, I don't think.'

'Oh Cathy, I don't make eyes. And this old couple, as you call it, are really fascinating. Lily Lytton was an actress once, a showgirl in London and then in Hollywood, I think that would be quite exciting, actually.'

'Well, you can talk to her, then. And I'll chat to Lucas.'

'Yes, all right,' said Jenna with a sigh, 'but anyway, he's so grown up now, he's twenty-one nearly, he's not going to bother with us.'

'Oh right! Well I'll get through it somehow, I s'pose. I can't wait to see Fergal, I thought we might go out to a nightclub maybe, after the dinner.'

Izzie and the boys were also invited to the American dinner; 'You can come if you like,' Adele said to Sebastian, 'I don't want you feeling left out, but—'

'My darling, I shall revel in feeling left out. Thank you for thinking of me, but I shall enjoy a quiet evening. I have a great deal to do.'

Adele had only just come back from having her hair done, immediately after lunch next day, when she saw a taxi pulling up outside; Jamie Elliott got out.

She looked at him in horror. She liked Jamie very much but she still had an inordinate amount to do, including making arrangements for Maud's children – every bit as dreadful as she had expected, real free-range American brats, as Boy had said. Maud expected them to be invited to the dinner, but Adele had politely refused: 'It's a grown-up dinner, Maud, they'll just be bored.'

'Not at all, they're very used to adult company. Zara is, after all, nearly eleven, and a very good conversationalist. She has very strong views on all sorts of things and Nathaniel and I always include both the children in our social arrangements. So—'

'Well, I'm sorry, but there just isn't room,' said Adele firmly. 'Mrs Hardwicke will make them a really nice supper and they can watch TV. They'll be much happier, don't you think?'

Maud clearly didn't, but she could see she was beaten. Increasingly, the twins seemed to her to resemble their mother.

'Hallo, Jamie,' Adele said now, 'do come in. I'm afraid you're a little early.'

'I know that,' he said, 'but I thought maybe I could be useful.'

'Well—' The thought of a stranger to the house, trying to help, asking where everything was, was hideous.

'I'm sure everything's under control. But it struck me that there might be something I could do. And if not – well, I'll go away again. Where is everyone, anyway? It seems very quiet.'

'Yes, it is. Jenna and Cathy have gone shopping. Charlie's out sightseeing. Maud and Nathaniel have taken their children—'

'Their truly dreadful children,' he said, meeting her eyes and smiling. 'You'd noticed?'

'Noticed? Adele, I've watched them grow ever more dreadful. She's my half-sister, don't forget. I'm the ghastly Teddy's godfather, for my sins. Now – is there anything at all I can do? Or shall I just get out of your hair?'

'Well –' she hesitated '– you could sort out the wine. That's the one thing I still find hard. Not having a butler, you know—'

'Oh I do know. Can't get one myself. Mind you, I am looking for a female one. Of course I will, Adele, it's one of the very few things we men can cope with. Lead me to your cellar, I'll do the rest. And I bet it is a real cellar, isn't it?'

'Yes, it is,' she said. 'Down here. There's plenty of everything, I think, fridge in the pantry through there, corkscrews and decanters in the dining room on the sideboard. That would be marvellous, Jamie, thank you so much.'

'And what's on the menu? Better know that, don't you think?'

'Goodness, you really do sound like a butler. Clam chowder, then steak, then pecan pie or cheesecake.'

'Very, very American. This is so sweet of you. Anyway, I'll know what to get up now. Don't worry about me, I'll be fine.'

How nice he was, she thought, going into the kitchen and filling half a dozen vases with water; and so very handsome. As her mother had often said, if Laurence had been anything like that, and she supposed he must have been, she could certainly understand Barty falling for him.

'Jenna, hallo. You look very – grown up.'

It was Lucas; smiling down at her. He seemed taller than ever. He really was so handsome, she thought. Well not exactly handsome, but terribly romantic-looking, with his deep-set dark eyes, his mop of black curls, his rather pale thin face. He was wearing a camel-coloured duffel coat, with a big shaggy jumper under it, and he was carrying an armful of books.

'Hi,' she said quickly. Wishing she had brushed her hair and got a bit of make-up on.

'When did you arrive?'

'Oh – two days ago. Your mother's been great.'

'She is great. Where is she, do you know?'

'In the dining room. She's—'

'Lucas! Hi. Oh my God, you're so tall.' It was Cathy, Cathy in tight jeans and a shirt, open one button too many, her hair tied up in a ponytail with a bright red ribbon, her big blue eyes, carefully mascara'd, sparkling up at him, her perfect mouth slicked over with pink pearly lipstick. 'I love the duffel coat. Do I get a kiss? As your honorary cousin, or whatever I am? How annoying Jenna got to you first. I want to hear all about Oxford, it must have been so wonderful there, I'd so love to see all those beautiful buildings and Jenna said you'd been on one of those ban-the-bomb marches, I think that is just such a wonderful thing to do.'

On and on she went, with Lucas looking down at her and smiling; Jenna felt she would like to slap her. Extremely hard.

Jamie looked round the cellar in amazement. It was vast, running the whole width and length of the house; there was the usual clutter of trunks and boxes at one end, a couple of bicycles, and a rather fine rocking horse, but at least half of it was given over to wine, great racks set from floor to ceiling, white on one wall, red on the other, with a smaller set for brandy, port, and champagne. It was like a cellar in a film. Years and years of dust had settled on the bottles, cobwebs draped over the furthest shelves. They had probably not been disturbed since Oliver died. What a treasure trove: there was an absolute fortune sitting here. If it was auctioned, it would raise thousands. Better not let Charlie Patterson get his hands on it . . .

He wandered along the racks, looking at the labels: all the classics were here, Margaux, Latour, Lafitte, some of them going back to the Twenties, one bottle of Lafitte so old it almost creaked as he touched it: dated 1905. Wonderful whites as well, not quite so grand, Puligny-Montrachet – he might take a couple of those for this evening – and three bottles of Sauternes, Château d'Yquem, dated 1905, he could almost taste its rare sweetness, just looking at the bottles. And the champagne: magnums, even a couple of jeroboams, Krug, Roederer, Dom Perignon, all vintage, of course, as old and dusty as the Lafitte, several 1910s, a handful – or rather an armful – dated from the Twenties. He was getting drunk just looking at them. There were Napoleon brandies, over a hundred years old, and port too, vintages as far back as the Twenties, and beyond – it was quite incredible. Which to choose? Was it actually quite the thing to haul up from your hostess's cellar bottles of wine which could be priced in tens, possibly hundreds of pounds? Probably not; he should go for more modest options, and perhaps go for broke on the brandy and port. That would be fun.

He began to rummage; spiders scuttled irritably away, outraged at having their territory disturbed, cobwebs got caught in his hair. He pulled out an armful of reds, set them down on the floor, simply to sort them: they were rather randomly stacked, the rare with the not so rare. This was going to be more of a task than he had expected . . .

'Marcus, hallo!' He was standing in her doorway. She smiled up at him, genuinely pleased to see him. She had forgotten, in her early misery over Keir, how altogether charming Marcus was. Now that all she felt for Keir was rage and outrage, a smiling, appreciative man seemed suddenly irresistible. 'It's lovely to see you.'

'Lovely to see you too. You're looking wonderful.'

'Thank you.' She knew she wasn't, she'd forgotten he was coming in, had dragged on a skirt and sweater, was having her hair done later. She wasn't even sure she'd put on any proper make-up that morning.

'May I?' He bent to kiss her, then pulled back, shaking his head disapprovingly. 'Dear oh dear, Elspeth.'

'What?'

'No Number Five.'

She laughed. 'Sorry. I didn't know you were coming. And I wouldn't wear it for anyone else. Obviously.'

'How busy are you? Any chance of dinner? Or tea? At the Ritz of course?'

'Well – tea would be nice. But I'm afraid we have a surfeit of relations here, as you can imagine; I have to be at my mother's for dinner, and then tomorrow it's entirely family—'

'Of course. I understand.'

'It's nice to see you. Now' – she'd better tell him, get it over – 'there's something I have to tell you.'

'Yes?'

'Keir and I have – separated.'

'Separated!' There was an expression of absolute shock in his eyes: shock and something like fear. She just managed to be amused by it.

'Yes. And he's left Lyttons. Gone to Wesley.'

'My God! I had no idea. Why, how – oh, Elspeth, I'm so sorry.'

'Well – the marriage was pretty well over.'

'I know but—'

A faint relief moved into his eyes; he hadn't known anything of the sort, not really, he'd thought he was a diversion, an amusement . . .

'It just couldn't go on. And once he'd left me, well, he had to leave Lyttons, really.'

He was silent; clearly very shaken. Terrified she was going to make some claim on him, cite him, perhaps, even try to get him to marry her. She felt irritated: she'd expected better from him than this.

'I'm so sorry,' he said again. 'If only I'd known.'

'And if you had, Marcus?' she said, unable to resist it, 'what would you have done? Rushed over here to comfort me?'

'Oh, Elspeth,' he said, and she could see him very carefully feeling his way, just beginning to relax. 'Of course I would. Of course. Let me start today. Better late than never. Four at the Ritz, then.'

'Lovely,' she said.

'How are you getting on?' It was Adele, smiling at him through the gloom. 'It's amazing down here, isn't it?'

'Absolutely amazing. Your father was obviously an incredible connoisseur.'

'Some of them were my grandfather's.'

'Good God. Well, there are certainly a lot of wines here much older than you are. Look at this, I've just been stroking it, a Château Margaux, 1912. Premier Grand Cru.'

'Not older than me, I'm afraid. Tiny bit younger.'

'It doesn't look it.'

She laughed. 'Well, don't just stroke it, let's drink it.'

'Adele, you can't cast pearls like that before swine like us. It would be a crime.'

'Oh – well, all right. Maybe another night, when there's not so many of us. How would that be? Not much point it sitting down here.'

'Not really. That might be fun. Anyway, I've made a bit of a selection, do you want to vet it?'

'Heavens no, just do whatever needs doing to it. I trust you absolutely. Let's have a nice brandy, though. I do love brandy. Although I mustn't have a hangover tomorrow, must I?'

'Preferably not.' He looked around him, indicated the rocking horse. 'I see a few relics from your childhood over there.'

'Yes, he's lovely, isn't he? He's rather valuable. Mummy would never let us have him for our children. I can't think why not, we were allowed to ride him. And there's a dolls' house somewhere – over here, under those sacks.'

'A dolls' house! I rather like dolls' houses. I always think they first inspired my ambitions in the property market. My father had a scale model of Elliott House made once. We weren't allowed to play with it, obviously, but it was a remarkable piece of work. And then Robert had one made for Maud, of Sutton Place. Is yours a model of this house?'

'No, it's just an ordinary dolls' house. But it's very pretty.'

'Can I see? Would you mind?'

'Of course not. Bit hard to get at, though—'

'Let me help. Right – here we are. If I can just ease it out.' He reached in, pulled the house out, removed the sack carefully. It was quite large, about three feet tall, Georgian-style, with curtains at the windows and a real brass door knocker.

'Isn't it lovely?' said Adele. 'We adored it, Venetia and I. Oh – now there's a shame, the chimney's come off. I wonder if it's there . . .'

'I probably pulled it off with the sack. Sorry. Shall I look—'

He bent down, worked his way into the corner; the ceiling was lower there, and the light was very dim.

'You haven't got a torch, have you?'

'Yes, here. Someone's moved that house recently, there are tracks in the dust, see.'

'So there are. Someone pretty determined, I'd say. Now then, I – ah. Here it is. One chimney. Very fine. And some window boxes, look. I'll stick them all back on for you, if you like.'

'I would, very much. If you have time.'

'I do. I'll just – good heavens. Did you know there's a little wall safe here?'

'No. How exciting. Do you think it leads to Narnia?'

'Might do. Very intriguing. I wonder if it's locked. I can't find a handle or anything.'

'Oh, do let's try,' said Adele. 'It's really exciting. I suppose there can't be anything in it of value, but it would be fun to look.'

'I'm trying to find something to open it with. I can't—'

'Let me look. I'm smaller than you.'

'Sure.' He eased his way out backwards, dusted himself down.

'Oh dear, you're filthy.'

'Doesn't matter. Let me hold the torch for you.'

She wriggled in, felt the safe with her fingers. There was a lock, she could feel it, but she could just get her nails under the door, and – it eased open very slowly.

'It's not locked,' she called to Jamie. 'Can I have the torch?'

Feeling rather like Howard Carter, opening the tomb of Tutankhamun, she pulled the door open slowly and peered inside.

'The flight was wonderful.' Lily Lytton lay back on Venetia's sofa, stretched out her still-shapely legs, and smiled with pleasure. 'Absolutely wonderful. So smooth and quiet.'

'Nonsense,' said Jack, poking at his ears. 'It was dreadful. Can't get my hearing back. Dreadful things, those planes. Wish we'd come on the boat. Only good thing, air hostess looked after me, pretty little thing, got me an extra gin to calm my nerves.'

'One gin too many,' said Lily briskly. 'That's why you don't feel too good, Jack, you've got a hangover.'

'You both look marvellous,' said Venetia, and indeed they did, Jack so straight and slim still and extremely dapper, dressed in a blazer and flannels, his old regimental tie a little battered, but perfectly knotted, Lily alarmingly pretty, her once-red hair now dark blonde, perfectly coiffed, her huge brown eyes carefully made up. They were both in their seventies, but if it hadn't been for Jack's gnarled finger joints and Lily's stiffness they could have passed for fifteen years younger.

'California obviously suits you.'

'Well, it's such fun!' said Lily. 'We have a wonderful time, you know, lots of parties, we have so many friends there, and the climate is perfect for us. Of course we miss the family, and' – she lowered her voice – 'Jack's hearing isn't what it was, makes him bad-tempered.'

He glared at her. 'You talking about me?'

'Of course not. I was saying how much I was looking forward to Adele's American dinner party tonight.'

'Don't know that I'll be able to face it,' said Jack, 'not after that flight.'

'Well, you stay and rest, dear,' said Lily, 'I'll go. Venetia was telling me there will be lots of young there—'

'Very pretty young,' said Venetia. 'You should see Jenna, Barty's daughter, she is just heaven, and then there's Noni, now the international model that she is, and – oh, excuse me. The phone. It never stops at the moment.'

She came back looking rather upset.

'I'm so sorry. That was Adele. She's got a – well, a bit of a problem. She wants me to go round there for an hour or so. Would that be all right? Mrs Hardy will get you anything you need. And if Jack doesn't want to go tonight, we'll be here—'

'Of course he wants to go,' said Lily, 'he just said he thought a good meal might make him feel better. What he means, of course, is a pretty girl or two. No, you run along, Venetia, we quite understand.'

'Thank you. We'll have the car ready at seven-thirty. It's not far, you'll remember the house, of course.'

'Of course,' said Jack, 'beautiful old place. So glad Adele's got it. Pretty little thing, she was.'

'She still is,' said Venetia firmly; and set off to see her.

Adele had been crying; she led Venetia upstairs and into her bedroom, shut the door.

'Look at these. I found them in the cellar. In an old wall safe. They're Mummy's diaries.'

'Diaries! I didn't know she kept diaries.'

'Well, she did. And they're – oh Venetia. They're so – so dreadful to read.'

'Why dreadful?'

'You'll see. I mean it's strange, reading them, anyway. It's like getting part of her back. You can hear her voice, and of course some things are happy, but some – well, come here, sit down, look, this is for 1909. You wouldn't believe the things that are in it, I've marked the place, it's so sad. And so – so shocking. And then this one is—'

'Look,' said Venetia firmly, 'go and fetch us a cup of tea. I'll read this one and then I'll at least know what you're talking about. Don't cry, Dell darling, it can't be that bad.'

But when Adele got back, Venetia's own eyes were huge with shock, and wet with tears. She held out her arms to Adele, put them round her.

'Oh Dell. I see what you mean. How awful it must have been. She was so young, when you think about it. And – writing it down. How could she do that, risk anything so dangerous?'

'Well,' said Adele, blowing her nose, wiping her eyes on the back of her hand, 'you know Mummy, never frightened of anything, if she thought it was right. But, yes. Anyone could have found it, anyone.'

'Although not down there.'

'Oh, I don't think it's been down there that long,' said Adele. 'If you ask me, it's a new hiding place. It was quite clean inside the little safe, it was behind the old dolls' house, you know, and the diaries weren't dusty. I bet there are lots more. But – where, Venetia? Where are they?'

'God knows. Maybe she destroyed them. Oh, Dell, look at this. The very last entry.'

'I hadn't got that far.' Adele looked. Looked through more tears:

If this is the end, rushing at me, then so be it. I would almost prefer it that way; I hate the alternative. I said goodbye to my darling this afternoon; just in case. He gave me great courage: as always. No one else knows yet. Except Bunny, of course. He's been very sweet. I should have been nicer to him. I should have been nicer to everyone. My only regret, I think . . .

The twins sat there, crying, reading the fragments of a great love story: and learning things about their mother they would never have believed in a thousand years.

CHAPTER 45

Secrets have a chameleon-like quality: changing in form and character as they move from place to place, from person to person. Thus an exquisite love story becomes a torrid affair; an act of mercy becomes a crime; innocent love becomes incest, fidelity fraud, generosity fecklessness, discretion cowardice.

Useless for the first informant to say no, no, you don't understand, it wasn't like that. The secret, once released, runs out of control, gains a life of its own, travels faster and faster, taking on ever more dangerous forms, becoming ever more unrecognisable . . .

All these things Giles Lytton knew, almost without realising it; and his painstaking protection of Celia Lytton's diaries, his infinite discretion, his agonised caution, were justified within just a very few hours, as the secret was ripped out of his careful hands and thrown recklessly away.

The twins telephoned Sebastian, thinking that, as the great repository of Celia's secrets, he must know, might have the missing diaries himself; he sighed and said yes, of course he had known: 'I never read them, of course, she never let me − apart from the ones you've got there. She showed me those, that last day −' His voice shook, there was a pause. 'And I warned her it was dangerous, writing everything down. But it was a sort of addiction. She did it every night, said she couldn't sleep until she had.'

'So Daddy must have known?'

'Oh yes, she said he worried about them even more than I did, although I don't think he realised how − how detailed they were. How did you find them?'

'Dell was in the cellar, helping Jamie get out some wine. He wanted to see the dolls' house. It was an amazing chance. I suppose she put them there.'

'No,' he said, 'I did.'

He had been to see her the day before she went into hospital; 'I think she knew it might be − final. And she was worried about a few things. A bit feverish, quite unlike herself. Worried about Clemmie's baby, made me promise to see she had it in the London Clinic, with her gynaecologist, not in what she called some dreadful public hospital. I said I would. As if anyone could tell that girl what to do. Worried about Jenna, too, said she didn't trust Charlie, that I was to keep an eye on things there.'

'Not surprised,' said Venetia.

'You're all so horrid about Charlie,' said Adele, 'anyone can see how much he loves Jenna and she him, for that matter.'

'Maybe. Anyway, she was also terribly worried about Elspeth and young Keir, that they were going to break up. Said she'd made things worse, and wanted to say she was sorry to him. And she gave me a message to deliver to him in – well, in case.'

'Did you tell him that?' asked Venetia.

'I tried. But not until he'd left Lyttons and Elspeth, and he was being so bloody awkward. He was really quite rude to me on the phone. I thought he could stew in his own juice. Maybe I should have persevered. Oh dear –' he looked distressed.

'Don't worry about him,' said Venetia. 'He's well able to take care of himself.'

'I think so. And then, she was worried about the diaries. Not most of them, just these three volumes. Well you can see why, I suppose, only it's so long ago – as I say, she was feverish, and upset – anyway, she'd brought them from the office and she gave them to me, told me to put them in that safe down in the cellar. She said she'd have done it herself, only she didn't have the strength to move the dolls' house. I said why couldn't I destroy them, but she said no, no one would ever find them there. God knows how you two did, you really are clever girls. She was thinking of turning the whole lot into a book, radically edited of course, but she thought those two would be just too dangerous in the wrong hands. Fortunately, they're still in the right ones.'

'Yes,' said Adele, smoothing the leather with her hands. 'It's what I shall do in my twilight years, Sebastian,' she said, 'or twilight months, anyway. It'll be a lovely project and you can help me.'

'Just a minute,' said Venetia, 'did you say they were in the office?'

'Yes, in that safe in her room. You know, the one she kept all the manuscripts in and a few old contracts.'

'And – nobody knew?'

'No. No, I'm certain. I never told anyone, and she certainly didn't.'

'Now hang on,' said Venetia, 'Giles said he'd cleared out that safe. The day he found her marriage certificate to Bunny. So – my God. The bastard. The bastard—'

Giles was making notes for a speech he was going to make when he looked up and saw the twins. They were so clearly extremely angry that he actually shrank back in his chair, every bit as afraid of the pair of them as he had been as a small boy, confronted by a threat to tell their mother something wrong that he had done, or even a joint beating up, which could be quite painful, four wiry little arms, four tough little feet, two sets of sharp little teeth.

'Where are the diaries?' said Venetia.

'Why didn't you tell us?' said Adele.

'What's in them?'

'Who else knows about them?'

'What gives you the right to decide what to do about them?'

'Have you told anyone?'

'What about Kit?'

On and on it went, fierce, ferocious questioning, their voices rising, identically querulous, their eyes brilliant, identically angry.

'Oh stop it,' he said wearily, 'just stop it, please.'

'Why should we?' said Adele.

'Why can't you answer us?' said Venetia.

'Because you won't bloody well let me.'

'We're letting you now.'

He was silent for a moment, just looking at them; then he sighed and said, 'I'm sorry. Very sorry. I just didn't know what to do.'

'Oh really? And why didn't you ask us?'

'Because I was so worried. Afraid of what would happen, if word got out.'

'Oh, that's charming,' said Adele.

'Really touching,' said Venetia.

'I mean we'd have sold them to the highest bidder wouldn't we, Venetia?'

'Of course. Is that what you were afraid of, Giles, us telling someone, talking to the press?'

'No,' he said wretchedly, 'no, of course not. But they are – highly inflammatory.'

'Well, we can see that. Although we've only read three.'

He looked at them. 'Three?'

'Yes, the unfinished one, just before she died, 1919, and, oh, Giles. The year she – well, the year Barty's mother had that baby.'

'What baby?'

'Oh God,' Venetia sat down suddenly. 'You haven't seen that one, have you?'

'No. How could I? It was missing.'

The twins looked at each other.

'Look,' said Adele, after a moment, 'I have guests arriving in an hour. I must go home.'

'Does anyone else know?'

586

'Sebastian. But he knew anyway. And Jamie.'

'Jamie Elliott?'

'Yes.'

'Oh Christ. Why tell him? This is exactly why—'

'Do shut up, Giles,' said Adele, 'he was with me when I found them. He only knows they're diaries, not what's in them. Don't worry.' She started to walk out of the door, then turned and said, with a smile on her lips, 'I'll tell you what I am going to find difficult this evening. Looking at the saintly Felicity Brewer in quite the same way.'

'Why?' said Giles.

'She and Daddy had an affair. Mummy found out. Now at least we know why she was always so frosty about her.'

'Oh God,' said Giles, 'this is getting worse and worse.'

'Not at all,' said Venetia. 'Don't you think he deserved it?'

'You look gorgeous,' said Marcus Forrest. 'Absolutely gorgeous.'

Elspeth smiled at him.

'Bit better than earlier.'

'No, just different.'

He looked different too: more relaxed. She supposed he'd got used to the idea.

'I should hope so. A small fortune's difference. Spent at Monsieur Rene's in South Audley Street.'

'And what does he do? Nothing too French, I hope.'

She always forgot how he made her laugh.

'Depends what you mean by French. He does my hair.'

'That's allowed. And –' he leaned forward and kissed her cheek – 'not Number Five?'

'No,' she said, 'I didn't think it was appropriate.'

'Elspeth! Why not?'

'Things have changed, Marcus, haven't they? It's not quite the same as it was.'

'I – suppose not.' He hesitated. 'It's a little early, I suppose, to ask you if you have any plans?'

'Very early. I have no idea.'

'Well, that's natural. You must be feeling very confused.'

'I am. Yes.'

'I was wondering if you were going to proceed with a divorce.'

Obviously still worried he was going to be cited.

'I – don't know. I don't think I have any grounds, actually.'

'But—' he stopped. Keir had grounds; that was clearly what he had been going to say. She wasn't going to let him get away with that.

'But of course Keir does.'

'I – suppose so, yes.'

There was a silence. He was looking very uncomfortable again.

'I'm so sorry,' he said, 'so very sorry. For my part in it. I feel very guilty. I really do.'

Well, that was something.

'Thank you,' she said, 'I don't think you need to, though. Feel guilty, I mean.'

'You don't?' The relief on his face was almost funny.

'No. I don't. I don't think it would have happened if I'd been happier.'

That hurt his vanity, if nothing else.

'It can't have helped,' he said, 'and I wish you'd told me before. I hate to think of you going through it all on your own.'

'And what would you have done, Marcus?' she said for the second time that day. She couldn't resist it. 'Got on a plane, come over to comfort me?'

'Possibly.'

He smiled at her rather awkwardly. He was clearly finding her mood difficult to read. She decided to put him out of his misery. It had served its purpose.

'No, honestly, Marcus, I really don't think you should blame yourself. I was miserable, everything was going wrong, you were a lovely diversion.'

'Yes,' he said, 'yes, I see.'

Relief was struggling now with hurt pride; it was quite funny, really. One minute he'd been afraid she'd land him in court, or turn up on his doorstep with her two children, the next he was upset because she obviously would do neither.

It was a shame, really; it would have cheered her up, to continue their affair. But she just didn't want to. She suddenly saw Marcus quite clearly; he lacked reality. He was a very good actor playing a smooth, well-dressed charmer. A self-absorbed charmer, watching himself carefully all the time. Making sure he did everything right: he even made love as if he had had lessons. Oh, he did it very well, no doubt about it, carefully, considerately, asking her if she liked what he was doing.

When Keir had made love to her, he just – well – just loved her. It was something they had shared so passionately and so all-consumingly that it would never have occurred to either of them that it might not be what the other wanted.

But – Keir was gone. He had left her and her life. He was harsh, critical, hostile, and arrogant. He had taken what she and her family had given him and thrown it back at them, deliberately and without a gracious word; what place could he have in her life now? God, she was a mess; God, she was lonely.

But at least she knew about Marcus. She kissed him on the cheek.

'I've got to go now. I'm so sorry. I'll see you tomorrow. And thank you for tea.'

Her message, she knew, was perfectly clear.

★

'Mr Patterson is being very patient, wouldn't you say?' said Jamie to Kyle. They were sitting in the lounge at Claridges, having tea.

'Very,' said Kyle.

'I think the information should turn up quite soon now, don't you?'

'Oh I should think so. Quite soon.'

'Perhaps while we're here even.'

'Perhaps.'

'It would be a nightmare if—'

'God yes. Absolute nightmare.'

They sat there, contemplating a future where Charlie Patterson had control of Jenna's vast fortune. It was indeed a nightmare.

Lucas had planned to go away for a long weekend the day after the service; to stay with friends in the country, with a very pretty girl called Florence who had been in his tutor group. After all, he was about to be locked up in barracks for weeks at a time. But – now he felt he might stay at home. His mother seemed a bit over-excited. His older sister was leaving early the following day, for a modelling assignment in Milan, his small sister was always overjoyed to have him at home; and while he wasn't exactly enjoying the great influx of Lyttons, he found some of them, and particularly the Americans, interesting. That old girl Lily, once a Gaiety Girl as far as he could make out, was wonderful, he could have talked to her for hours, and he really liked Jamie Elliott and Kyle Brewer. He was of half a mind to try to spend some time in New York. He might even chat up that guy Marcus Forrest who everyone was so rude about. He seemed OK to Lucas.

And then there was Jenna; he was greatly intrigued by Jenna. Not just by her beauty, and the vibrant sexuality of which she was quite unaware – unlike her horror of a stepsister – not even by her obvious interest in him, but by her courage and her self-assurance. Not many girls her age would even contemplate standing up to speak in a vast church filled with famous and distinguished people; Jenna was, although terrified, as she told him cheerfully, facing her ordeal with great fortitude.

'It's such an honour. And I know my mother would have wanted me to do it, so I couldn't turn it down. But boy, will I be glad to sit down again.'

'I'm terribly impressed,' he said, smiling at her, 'how long are you speaking for?'

'Oh, not very long. Around five minutes, Giles said. But I don't know if you've ever spoken in public, five minutes is quite long.'

'I know it is. I once spoke at the Union.'

'Goodness.' She had heard of the Oxford Union from her mother, knew its debaters often ended up ministers, sometimes even prime ministers. She sighed. 'So you're another person to be worried about.'

'What do you mean?'

589

'Every single person in that church seems to be famous or distinguished, or has a history of public speaking. I'm going to feel so pathetic.'

'Of course you're not. You'll be wonderful, I know you will. And we'll all be rooting for you. You know what they told us at school?'

'No.'

'You just fix on one person, imagine you're speaking to them. Just till you settle down. Got notes?'

'Well yes. But I won't need them, I know every comma off by heart.'

'Still, have 'em with you. That way you won't even think about drying up. And remember, everyone's on your side. You won't get heckled.'

She laughed. 'I hope not.'

'And if you do I shall personally hit the person on the nose for you. Honestly, Jenna, you'll be fine. Now I must go, got to make a phone call. I'll see you at dinner.'

'Fine.'

She watched him go out into the morning room, where the phone was, thinking how wonderful it would be, if she were sitting next to him.

Lucas picked up the phone and was about to dial Florence's number when he heard his mother's voice on the extension in her room, asking Clementine if she could speak to Kit. Lucas was a greatly reformed character but he still had undesirable traits, to which he admitted cheerfully; one of them was listening to other people's phone calls. Especially when they sounded interesting. And this did; Adele seemed breathless, over-excited, even for her. He put his hand over the mouthpiece, to muffle the sound, and listened.

Noni was looking at herself in the mirror when Lucas came in; Clio was by her side at the dressing table, holding out her jewellery. They both smiled at him.

'Hallo, baby brother.'

'Hallo, big brother.'

'Hallo, beautiful sisters.'

'Hair up or down, do you think?' said Noni. 'I thought down, Clio says up.'

'I agree with Clio. Clio, my darling, how would you like to make yourself useful? And get me a glass of water. With ice in it. Ask Mrs Hardwicke if you need help.'

'Of course I don't. She's in an awful bait, though.'

'Why?'

'Those children, the American ones, are driving her mad, she says. They keep walking into the kitchen and asking her for fresh lemonade.'

'Oh dear.'

'They're absolutely awful. Especially Teddy. Pity me, I have to spend the evening with them. Watching TV.'

'We'll keep visiting you, won't we, Noni? Go on, sweetheart, get my water, there's a good girl.'

'OK.' She smiled and left. Noni looked up at her brother.

'You're such a lazy toad, Lucas. Why not get your own water?'

'Because I want to tell you something. Something quite *intéressant*. And you'll never guess what, in a million years . . .'

It had all gone rather well, Adele thought; everybody seemed happy. The pecan pie had been an inspiration: everyone loved it. The wines had been fantastic; Jamie had acted as butler, had even given a little rundown on each wine as he served it, not boringly, but bringing them alive. She did like Jamie. She had done a last-minute switch of place names, had put him, instead of Kyle, next to her; she noticed with amusement that Lucas had done the same, had switched Cathy for Jenna. Cathy was now sitting in between Mike and Jack, clearly mildly put out, but still flirting furiously with both of them. Jack obviously thought he had found himself in paradise, beaming down her cleavage, nodding at her chatter, and, every so often, taking her arm and whispering God knew what in her ear, at which she would go into peals of mirth. She was rather sweet, really, Adele thought. Like her father. He was a really nice man. She just didn't care what anyone said, Charlie was courteous, thoughtful, very appreciative – and obviously incredibly proud of his girls as he called them.

There was one thing, though, Adele noticed: Cathy drank a lot. By the time they went into dinner, she had downed three glasses of champagne and was flushed and giggling furiously up at Lucas; her father caught her eye and frowned at her, and a little later on, leaned over and said something to her but she took no notice. It was rather alarming at her age, she even drank the red wine unwatered. Adele watched to see how much Charlie drank, these things were often hereditary, she knew, but he drank very sparingly. Maybe Cathy was just nervous.

Izzie seemed to like Charlie too; Adele had put her next to him and they were swopping stories about Manhattan characters: there was someone called Moondog, they said, who stood on the corner of the CBS building every day, dressed in full Viking regalia, with horns on his head.

'I've tried talking to him,' Izzie was saying, 'but Nick says I'm wasting my breath.'

'Absolutely right,' said Charlie, 'he just ignores you. I don't know how he can stand that gear in the summertime.'

'I heard a very good story about La Guardia the other day,' said Jack. 'He was one of the great mayors of New York,' he added, 'for those of you who don't know. You boys would know if it was true. Apparently, he was in court and someone came up in front of him for stealing, and he fined everyone in the court.'

'Absolutely true,' said Nick, 'he'd stolen from the deli, the guy, because his family were starving and La Guardia said he was fining the whole court for tolerating a society that allowed such a thing to happen.'

'Quite right,' said Lily, 'and how very American.'

'Do you feel English, Mrs Lytton,' asked Charlie interestedly, 'or American?'

'I feel both, I think. My body is English, that's for sure, but my head seems increasingly American. And do please call me Lily.'

'OK, I will. Thank you. And you were a film star, Lily, I believe?'

'Oh yes.' Lily embarked on the largely fictitious story of her film career; Charlie listened, nodding attentively.

It was all turning out to be rather fun; the only irritant was Maud, dressed rather sternly in bottle-green. She had become an absolute nightmare, Adele thought, remembering rather sadly the sweetly serious little girl she and Venetia had been genuinely fond of, and wondering rather helplessly how she could shut her up. So far she had delivered her views on publishing and lamented its increasing commercialism, delivered a short lecture on how no one with any sense at all could be influenced by advertising, deplored the fact that photographic modelling had come to be regarded as a career, and had then turned her attention to photography, telling Adele which camera she should buy, and what wonderful results she herself had achieved with it.

Felicity was on the other side of Charlie; they had clearly enjoyed one another. She was still very beautiful, Adele thought: her fair hair silvery now, but the gentle face, with its high cheekbones and curvy mouth, seemed almost unchanged. Maybe that was part of growing older yourself; you didn't recognise the ageing of other people. But – goodness, it was interesting to study Felicity. To think of her having an affair with her father. She decided it had probably been mostly talk anyway. Felicity was very good at talk: and very good at talking to men, soothing and flattering them, finding them interesting, very much the sort of woman her father would have enjoyed. And everything which her mother was not: gentle, pliant, soft-voiced, quietly humorous. And of course she was a wonderful poet. On the other hand, Oliver had been quite the opposite of flirtatious; it was hard to imagine how it could have begun. No doubt the diaries would reveal that. As well as a great deal more.

And then Izzie: Izzie looked so lovely. She was wearing a black satin shirt dress, buttoned – or rather unbuttoned – quite low, with a wide belt, emphasising her tiny waist and her lovely hair caught up in a rather complex heap of curls. Every time Nick looked at her, he smiled proudly.

She was clearly very happy with him. But sparkle as she might, there was a sadness about her, a shadow behind the lovely brown eyes; Adele wondered what it was. Nick clearly adored her. It couldn't be that . . .

They were both so funny, those boys, they were like a comedy turn, they could make a fortune on television, have their own show. And she loved the way they talked about Izzie, as if she belonged to both of them; she didn't seem to mind. Adele found she was very glad Izzie was happy; and that she had completely forgiven her for sleeping with Geordie. It was odd that. She supposed it was because she had just been able to accept Izzie's version of it. And Izzie had, after all, saved her life. Oh God. Geordie. Geordie and the diaries. That would be there too. And Izzie too. All her sad story, spelt out no doubt, her love for Kit, her almost running away . . . What were they going to do with those things, what could they do, to keep them safe . . . ?

'A toast to our hostess.' Jamie was on his feet, smiling down at her. 'It's been a wonderful evening, so thoughtfully planned and so beautifully executed, and I would like you all to raise your glasses. Adele, thank you.'

Slimy bastard, Charlie thought, obediently raising his, smiling. God, he hated him. And Kyle Brewer as well, so pink-faced and pompous, holding forth about the literary scene as if he was Nelson Doubleday himself . . . He was only a fucking agent, for God's sake, a parasite.

He smiled at Kyle across the table. 'I love these publishing legends. Barty told me once that Nelson Doubleday's office was so huge he used it as a golfing green.'

'Well, that's almost true,' said Kyle, smiling back, 'a putting green, anyway.'

'My favourite story of Mother's was about Dick Snyder,' said Jenna. 'She said he got promoted so often that his business cards were always out of date. I was really impressed by that.'

'Would you like to go into publishing?' asked Lucas.

She hesitated, then said, 'No, I don't think so. I don't think I have the right sort of brain. I'm really interested in being a lawyer at the moment. I like the exactness of it. You can't – bend it about, or fix the law.'

'Oh, you'd be surprised,' said Kyle. 'It's full of loopholes, for people to clamber through. The most open-and-shut cases often turn out to be stuck at just about halfway.'

Charlie looked at him; was he insinuating something? But Kyle's expression was bland as he smiled at Jenna.

'Yes, well, that wouldn't happen in my office,' she said quite sharply. Everyone stared at her; there was obviously some hostility there, thought Adele. How odd.

'Adele, dear, I think, if you will excuse us, we might take ourselves off,' said Felicity, 'it's been quite a long day and it will be a longer one tomorrow. John, come along dear, and Kyle, or are you going to stay with the other young?'

The other young! thought Lucas, winking at Jenna, refilling her glass. Is that fat old chap supposed to be young?

'No, no,' said Kyle, 'I need to get my head down. Lovely evening, Adele, thank you so much.'

'We must go too, Jack, come along,' said Lily, hauling Jack's gaze away from Cathy's cleavage. 'To think, this afternoon, you felt too tired to come at all . . .'

Gradually they left; Jamie kissed Adele at the bottom of the stairs, and thanked her again.

'And don't worry about the diaries,' he said quietly, 'I won't tell a soul.'

If Cathy had not been dancing past them, on her way to renew her make-up in the hope that at least now she would get a little of Lucas's attention, the next few days might have turned out rather differently.

They all went into the drawing room, Izzie and the boys, Lucas and Noni, Jenna and Cathy.

'Phew,' said Lucas, 'that was hard work.'

'Oh I don't know,' said Jenna, 'I enjoyed it.'

'Yes, and we all know why,' said Cathy sweetly. Jenna scowled at her.

'I thought it was the best fun,' said Izzie.

'It's not over yet,' said Lucas, 'shall I put some records on?'

'Yeah!' said Cathy. 'Do you have any Elvis?'

'Think so,' said Noni. 'They're all in the playroom. Want to come and help me look?'

They returned not only with Elvis, but Johnnie Ray, Frank Sinatra and Little Richard; Cathy took to the floor with Lucas. She was, of course, a superb dancer. As Jenna watched him, laughing down at her, swinging her round, pulling her back and forwards through his legs in true rock-and-roll style, she felt sick with jealousy and suddenly terrified about the next day. Then Mike appeared, bowed in front of her.

'May I have the honour?' he said.

He was an even better dancer than Lucas . . .

An hour later Adele appeared, looking pale and rather tense.

'I would like you to be quiet now. *If* you don't mind. The whole house is shaking. And I'd like to remind you that tomorrow is a very important day.'

She disappeared again; they all looked at each other.

'Dear, oh dear,' said Lucas, 'naughty us. Six of the best.' He sat down next to Jenna, took her hand, patted it. 'You OK?'

'Just.'

'She's fine,' said Cathy, 'how about we have some more wine.'

'Good idea,' said Lucas, 'I'll get it.'

He came back with a bottle of white wine and one of brandy.

'This bottle looks older than God. Anyone like to join me?'

'I'd like some champagne, personally,' said Noni.

'You and your champagne,' said Lucas. 'Honestly, she has to have it for breakfast.'

'Oh, very amusing. I'm going to find some.'

'Down in the cellar? Mind what else you find down there.'

'Shut up, Lucas,' she said quickly, 'you know you promised.'

'Sorry. Well, I'm hitting the brandy.'

He was already quite drunk. Cathy looked at him interestedly. Then she said, 'What's in the cellar, then?'

'Oh' – he took a big swallow of brandy – 'wine. More wine. More and more wine—'

'And—'

'Oh – nothing. Curiosity killed the kitten, young Cathy.'

'This house makes you curious. It's full of secrets,' she said, taking a glass of wine from Nick.

'Oh Cathy, of course it's not,' said Jenna.

'Yes, it is. People whispering in corners, shutting doors tight, crying—'

'Who was crying?'

'Adele.'

'When?' asked Izzie anxiously.

'This afternoon. We'd just got back from shopping, hadn't we, Jenna, and she was crying.'

'Really? I wonder why.'

'She's upset about Granny, I expect,' said Noni quickly. She had come back into the room, was struggling to open a magnum of champagne.

'Of course she is,' said Izzie, 'Celia was her mother, don't forget.'

'Sorry,' Cathy flushed. 'I didn't think. Sorry.'

She drained her glass, held it out for more.

'You sure do put it away, young Cathy,' said Mike. 'This bottle's dry. I'll get another.'

'You should have some of this brandy, Parker,' said Lucas, 'it's fantastic.'

'I'd rather go for the Krug, if you don't mind.'

'Oh, I'll have some of that,' said Cathy.

'Cathy—' said Jenna.

'What?' She looked at her fiercely.

'Nothing. Sorry.'

'That's OK. Now, then, what next? Charades?'

'Oh spare me,' said Noni, 'GGM's charades at Christmas, I'll never get over them.'

'Who was GGM?' asked Nick.

'Great-grandmama,' said Noni. 'Lady Beckenham. Granny's mother.'

'You ever feel you walked through the looking-glass?' Nick said to Mike.

There was a silence; Cathy spoke into it.

'Anyone know anything about some diaries?' she said.

Lucas had said far too much, Noni thought, lying in bed afterwards, wishing the room would stop spinning round. Far far too much. If he hadn't been so drunk; if they hadn't all been so drunk . . .

But somehow, he'd started, saying a bit; then, in trying to shut him up, she'd said still more; he'd said she didn't know what she was talking about, he'd heard the phone call, for God's sake; and by the end of the conversation, what had emerged was that Celia's diaries had been found and they were full of every single family secret there ever had been; a few of them were in the house, and the rest were in a safe in her office, and Giles was terrified they'd fall into the wrong hands.

'So what if they did?' Cathy interjected at this stage.

'You don't understand,' Noni had said, 'this is quite a well-known family. Everyone has heard of my grandmother. And Sebastian. And Kit too. And quite extraordinary things have happened to us. Like my mother and my brother and I had to escape from occupied France, in a stolen car—'

'It wasn't stolen.'

'Well – it wasn't really hers. And our father was shot, by the Nazis. And then Barty being adopted—'

'She was never adopted properly,' said Izzie. It was the only thing she had said; she had been growing quieter and quieter, stiller and stiller, clinging to Nick's hand.

'Well, all right, taken away from her family. And doing better than any of us, owning all of Lyttons.'

'And then giving it back,' said Jenna just slightly defensively.

'Of course.'

There was a long silence; then Izzie said, 'I think we should go, boys. If you don't mind.'

'Of course. It's been great. A really great evening. Can we thank you, Noni and Lucas, as your mother isn't here?'

'Of course,' said Lucas, adding rather belatedly, 'you won't talk about those diaries, will you? It's quite – private stuff.'

'Of course not,' said Nick.

'Of course we won't,' said Mike.

'Any of you, I mean?'

Jenna said nothing, just shook her head; she was clearly disturbed by the whole thing herself. Cathy's big blue eyes met Lucas's in outraged innocence.

'Of course not,' she said.

CHAPTER 46

Keir woke up very early, and lay awake staring into the dark morning, gathering his courage together. He had decided to go to the memorial service. The more he thought about not going, the more cowardly it seemed. There was no reason, really, why he should feel unable to face the Lyttons. It had been his decision, after all, to leave; he hadn't been fired, rather the reverse, he had nothing to be ashamed of, it had been Elspeth who had committed adultery, not him – he had come to regard his fling with the girl in Birmingham as a moment of foolishness which Celia had taken the most disgraceful advantage of – but if he didn't go, then he would be guilty of bad manners and ungraciousness.

He did feel bad about one thing, and that was his rudeness to Sebastian on the phone. Several times he had tried to write a note to apologise, but then found it impossible, torn it up; he told himself it had been Sebastian who had put the phone down on him, but he knew that was no excuse.

It was just that in his misery, his isolated misery, at being without Elspeth, knowing she didn't love him any more, contact with Sebastian had been the last thing he could face. Sebastian had been hand-in-glove with the Lyttons, part of the family, in more ways than one, certainly part of the publishing house; there was nothing he could say to Keir that would not be biased, probably a further attempt at manipulation.

Just the same, he could have written a very brief note, apologising, but every day that passed made that seem more difficult. Now, swept up in the general emotion of this day, he felt he would be able to do it. And it would have the great advantage that Sebastian would be too busy to want to talk to him.

He still had his invitation to the service; they were surely not going to tell him he couldn't go in? He could slip in at the back, when all the Lyttons had arrived, and make the briefest contact with them afterwards; everyone would be terribly busy, including Elspeth, and then he could find Sebastian and say his bit and leave. After that he could walk away from them all with a clear conscience. And carry on being utterly miserable.

He wondered if he ought to buy a new tie.

Venetia's very first thought on waking was of the diaries. She had slept badly and had had troubled dreams; twice Boy had shaken her awake, her face wet with tears, her head full of shadowy, threatening thoughts.

'What do you think we should do?' she said, as he held her and comforted her.

'Burn them,' he said, 'they're very dangerous, and a dreadful temptation for anyone who gets hold of them.'

'Are we really that interesting, though?'

'I'm afraid we are. Think of that business with your mother meeting Hitler, just for starters. And the episode with Barty's mother's baby. I mean, if that got out it would be a sensation.'

'I know. It must have been so ghastly for her. Poor Mummy, poor, poor Sylvia. Oh dear.'

'Yes. Now she *did* have a hard life. And then her daughter comes to rule Lyttons. Astonishing. What a story it is,' he added, 'all of it, I mean. What a family I married into. Good God. My father would be turning in his grave.'

She looked at him and smiled for the first time: a curvy, sexy smile.

'Do you think it's all there, Boy? All of it?'

'If you mean my misdemeanours, I expect so. I'd say from what you told me, everything is. Including our rather sudden marriage.'

She shuddered. 'If you ever find me taking up diary writing, stop me straight away. Oh, Boy. What a mess.'

Izzie also woke up thinking about the diaries; she had thought of little else all night and slept hardly at all. As far as she could make out they were painstakingly thorough; there was every possibility that it would all be there, her and Kit, her and Henry – and her and the baby. And the abortion.

'Oh God,' she said, and sat bolt upright, pushing her hair back. Nick looked up at her.

'Whatever is it? It must be terribly early.'

'It is. Sorry. Bad dream. Go back to sleep.'

'You OK?'

'I'm fine.' Thank goodness she'd told him; how terrified she would be now if she hadn't. Just the same, all the other things—

She got up, went quietly downstairs into the kitchen. She would make a cup of tea and—

'Hallo, Isabella.'

'Father! Hallo.'

'I couldn't sleep. What with one thing and another.'

He looked at her and tried to smile; his dark-blue eyes were very sad. She went over to him, and put her arms around him.

'Poor Father. Not an easy day for you.'

'No. She seems very – near, suddenly. And very far.'

'I'm so sorry. So very sorry.' She hesitated, then said, 'Father, I know about – about Celia's – the diaries.'

'You do!' He looked very shocked. 'Who told you?'

'Lucas.'

'How the hell does he know about them? Adele promised she wouldn't say a word—'

'I – think he heard her on the phone. And it came out quite slowly, in dribs and drabs, he was very drunk, we all were.'

'All? Who was in on this briefing?'

'Rather a lot of us, I'm afraid.'

She told him; he pushed his hand through his hair.

'Dear God. What a nightmare. Cathy, of all people. And Lucas isn't much better. Stupid young fool. I've a good mind to—'

'Father, don't say anything to him. Please. It can't help. The secret's out and that's all there is to it; you can't lock it up again.'

He sighed. 'No, I suppose you're right. Oh, Isabella. I don't like to over-dramatise this, but those diaries are very dangerous. I think we should destroy them, I really do.'

Clementine woke up feeling dreadful. The baby, this vast child she was carrying, seemed to have invaded the whole of her, not just her womb. Its legs seemed to be wrapped in some way round her ribs, its head pressing down into her thighs, its feet and hands to be engaged night and day pummelling her stomach, her bladder, even her breasts. It was awful. She was never doing it again. And she felt so sick all the time, she'd never really stopped feeling sick: and she was so, so tired.

Actually, yesterday she'd been feeling much better, had a burst of energy and had gone for a walk with Kit; but today she felt exhausted again. She wished they'd gone up to London last night, so she could have recovered from the journey; the thought of sitting first in a taxi then on a train and then in another taxi, and all that before lunch, was horrible. When was she going to fit her rest in, for heaven's sake?

She was so, so glad Kit couldn't see her; apart from her huge stomach, her ankles and hands were swollen, and even her face was puffy. They said it was all right, quite normal, but she had begun to worry.

Then there was this wretched business of the diaries: Kit had been terribly shaken by that. She could see why, in a way; it was one thing to know your father was your mother's lover, and that you had been in love with your half-sister, but quite another to have it written down in black and white for all the world to see. Not that all the world would see it. She kept telling Kit that, but he seemed convinced something might happen to them. 'It's such a temptation,' he kept saying, 'anyone who got hold of them, anyone at all, would see they were dynamite.'

'Are you sure? Why would they matter so much? We're not film stars or anything.'

'Clemmie, have you seen the list of who's coming to that service tomorrow? We may not be film stars, but my mother was extremely well-known and for a few days, will be even more so. Then there's Noni, face on every magazine cover, name in every gossip column. My father is a household name. And Lyttons have also been in the news lately, one way or another, regaining the company, Barty's will, all that rubbish about the deer woman – no, I think some newspaper or magazine would love to publish the diaries. Or some other publishing company.'

Jenna woke up feeling absolutely petrified, her entire mind a white-out of fear; how was she going to survive today? Even the morning's rehearsal, with all the family there, was going to be terrifying, never mind the thing itself. All those people, about four or five hundred of them, famous, clever, distinguished people, all sitting there, looking at her, listening to her, she – God, she was going to be sick. She leapt out of bed, got to the bathroom, emerged white and shaking to see Charlie on the landing.

'You all right, my darling?'

She managed to smile at him.

'Not really.'

'Scared?'

'Not scared, terrified. I really do feel like running away. Charlie, I can't do it, I can't, all those important people, I shall just dry up, fluff my lines, be sick again—' she started to cry.

'Hey, hey,' he said, taking her hand, leading her into his own room, sitting down on the bed with her, putting his arm round her. 'You just listen to me, Miss Jenna Elliott. You are going to be fantastic and you know why?'

'No.'

'You're going to be fantastic for your mother. She would have so loved to see you today, hear you today, know you'd been chosen. So proud. Almost as proud as me.'

She leaned her head on his shoulder. 'Oh Charlie. You're so sweet.'

'And I tell you something else. There are all these people, sure, all these grand, important English people. But you are very important too, today. Just as important as any of them. You're saying a lot about Celia, just by being there.'

'How?'

'You're saying that she did something wonderful, taking your mother home with her that day, bringing her up, doing all she did for her. She saw something very special in Barty. And you're the proof of it. You've got that specialness too. Now, I don't know what your dad was like, I'm sure he was a great guy, but you certainly seem very like your mother to me.

Brave, clever and strong. And beautiful, of course. Mustn't forget that. All right? Understand?'

She nodded, managed to smile.

'You'll be just fine. You'll be more than fine. And I'll be there, rooting for you, cheering you on. I loved your mother very much, Jenna, and I love you, too. You're not going to let either of us down. I know it.'

'Oh, Charlie. Thank you. Thank you so much. And no, I won't let you down. Of course I won't.'

Elspeth woke up rather late; she and the children had spent the night at her mother's house. Venetia had invited Lord Arden to dinner, not wanting him to feel left out of the great rush of Lytton activity; it had been a full six-line whip, as her father called it, everyone there, the whole noisy, argumentative mob. Lord Arden had clearly enjoyed himself immensely, and then before he left, Jack and Lily had arrived home full of stories of their own dinner party at Adele's. Jack and Lord Arden had started swopping a whole lot of new stories, about the First World War, and somehow it had been one in the morning before they had all got to bed.

And throughout it all, chatting determinedly to Lord Arden, greeting her brothers and sisters, running through the arrangements for the next day, listening indulgently to tales of derring do from the trenches, she kept thinking of Marcus Forrest and his suggestion that they see more of each other, now that she was free.

It should be easy, of course, easy and delightful: to enter into a proper relationship, with a charming, handsome, amusing, hugely attractive, if distinctly shallow, man, who found her not only desirable, but extremely clever. Not just easy but irresistible. But – somehow it wasn't. It was very difficult. And at the bottom of her heart she knew why. It was because of another man, not conventionally charming or handsome, certainly not amusing, but bad-tempered, authoritative and selfish, but who she could only assume that, in spite of everything, she still loved. Only he didn't love her any more; that was the point. The awful, miserable point.

Joe and Billy were milking, very early. They had to leave by nine, Joan had said, she wasn't having them being late. Although Billy said if they left at nine, they'd be there by twelve, a bit early for a service at three, she said they had to find Venetia's house; she had very kindly offered to give them lunch, so they had to be there by then anyway.

'And then we've got to get tidied up, I've got to get my hat on—'

'Tidied up!' said Billy. 'We'll be tidy enough as it is.'

Joan had had the foresight to write to Venetia and ask her what they should wear: Venetia had written back and said just a smart suit or dress and coat and a nice hat for her. 'The men will mostly be in morning suits, but some will come in dark suits, of course.'

Joan knew what that meant, they'd nearly all be in monkey suits, and she'd insisted they got them, all three.

'We can afford it, goodness knows, with what Barty left us, and I'm not having everyone looking down on us, calling us the poor relations.'

Billy had said why not, since they *were* the poor relations, and Joan said rubbish, they were quite rich relations now, by anyone's standard and they owed it to Barty to look it.

'Wonder if she's changed,' said Joe thoughtfully. 'Jenna, I mean. I expect she'll be real grown-up and smart and that.'

Billy looked at him. 'You're not holding a torch for her, are you son?'

'Dad! She's my cousin.'

'I know. Perfectly legal of course, for cousins to marry.'

'I don't want to marry her, Dad. You've got it all wrong. Anyway, I've got Sarah now . . .'

Sarah was at university with him, also doing veterinary studies, a sweet, rather manically cheerful girl, a perfect antidote to Joe's silent shyness. 'But she's real special, Jenna is. I'd like to go on being her friend. Only I'm scared she might have got all fancy airs and graces.'

'I doubt it,' said Billy, 'I doubt it very much. She's a Miller, don't forget, through and through, not a Lytton. And you did a lot for her, the night her mum died. She'd never forget that.'

'She's an Elliott as well, Dad.'

'I know that. But if ever Barty was born again, it's in Jenna. Might not look like her, but my word, she thinks like her, talks like her, even if it is with an American accent.'

'I wonder what he was really like,' said Joe, adjusting the cups on a couple of cows' udders, 'her dad.'

'Well, Barty loved him, that's for sure. We'll never know no more 'n that.'

'That's good enough for me then,' said Joe.

Giles's role in the service was modest; he was reading the first lesson. He had chosen the 52nd Psalm. It was one of his own favourites, and for the sheer beauty of its language, so precious to his mother, infinitely suited to the occasion. But he was aware that of all the people speaking and reading that day, his voice was the least musical, he was the least charismatic figure and he feared that, compared to Sebastian Brooke or Jenna Elliott or even small Rupert Lytton, he would seem – as always – dull, dry stuff. There was to be a run-through without music at the church that morning; like Jenna, he was dreading it almost as much as the actual thing.

Lucas woke up with a severe hangover. Bloody stupid, getting so drunk last night. That brandy had been a real killer. Very fine, no doubt, but . . . He groaned, turned over in bed, holding his stabbing head, details of the evening rushing back at him.

Pretty stupid of him, spilling the beans as he had, about the diaries. Unforgivable, really. He could only hope it hadn't been too dangerous. After all, they were all more or less family – and none of them were likely to go rushing off to Fleet Street to sell them to the highest bidder. And anyway, he felt everyone was getting a bit over-excited about their value. What could be in them, for heaven's sake, apart from a few details about a handful of long-finished affairs? And who would care about them anyway? As Noni kept saying, they weren't film stars . . .

God, he felt awful. He'd have to go in search of some Alka Seltzer and some fresh air. Thank goodness the service wasn't in the morning. He wondered how Noni was feeling; she'd been pretty drunk. And that little Cathy, she could put it away.

Cathy: she was the one person in that room he wouldn't have trusted. But – what was she going to do about the diaries? And why should she want to, anyway?

He was worrying too much. They were all worrying too much . . .

He eased himself out of bed, wincing at the pain in his head, and went in search of a cure.

Charlie was reading *The Times* in the morning room when Cathy came in.

'Hi darling. You all right?'

'Yes, sure. You?'

'I'm fine. Wouldn't mind a bit of fresh air. Want to come for a walk with your old dad?'

'Yes, OK. I'll just get my coat, it's freezing out there. Mustn't be too long, though, Adele said I could go to the rehearsal.'

'We needn't be long.'

She looked fine, he thought, smiling at her; maybe he'd imagined how much she'd drunk last night. He was probably over-sensitive about it. Hardly surprising.

'You have fun after I went to bed?' he said as they set off along the River Walk, her arm tucked into his. It was very cold; cold and very grey, with a heavy mist on the river. The noises of the morning were muffled, except for the screeching of the gulls, wheeling greedily overhead; the cars all had their lights on, driving slowly along the Embankment. It was a foggy day in London town, as the song said; and exactly as he had always imagined a November London to be.

'Yeah, great fun. Noni found some records and we were dancing. Until Adele came down and ticked us off for making a noise.'

'Cathy!'

'Well, it wasn't just me. And then—' she looked round, over her shoulder, as if she was afraid of being overheard. He smiled at her.

'What's this? Spy story or something?'

'Nearly as exciting. Can you keep a secret?'

'I'm wonderful at keeping secrets, I promise you.'

'Good. OK.' She looked round again and then said, 'Apparently they've found these really amazing diaries that Celia kept.'

They had all gone off to the rehearsal; Charlie had declined. He said he'd get too nervous and he wanted to enjoy the service in all its glory that afternoon.

'Unless you'd rather I came?' he said to Jenna. But she shook her head.

'No, I feel much better now. Thanks to you.'

'That's my girl.'

He waved them all off and then went back to *The Times*; until he was sure Mrs Hardwicke and the daily woman were both safely upstairs, doing the bedrooms.

Then he walked very casually across the hall, opened the door leading to the cellar and went down the dusty steps.

Right. Behind the dolls' house, she'd said. Dolls' house, dolls' house – yes, that must be it, under those sacks. And you could see the trail on the floor where it had been dragged out the day before.

OK; best make sure he didn't make fresh ones. Pull it in the same direction exactly. Now. Torch shining on the wall: somewhere here – Lord, these people were extraordinary. That wine! Must be worth thousands and thousands. What they'd had last night, of course, had been pretty good. That idiot Elliott seemed to know his wine. And wanted them all to know he knew it. Smug bastard. Chatting up Adele like that. Well, she was very pretty. And nice. He really liked her . . .

As for Brewer, with his wobbling chins and his red face, getting redder by the minute, he wasn't fit to be let out in polite society. Barty had really liked him, though. Said he'd been wonderfully kind to her when she'd first arrived in New York. Oh well. Her judgement altogether hadn't been too good . . .

There it was. Little safe in the wall. Not even locked. Like taking candy from a baby.

He only wanted to take a look at the damn things out of curiosity. He was quite sure they were nothing like as important as Cathy had said. Just details of the social life of a rich old lady; which the family had no doubt inflated into some great drama.

'Lucas said they thought it would be really dangerous if they got into the wrong hands,' Cathy had said.

So they put them back in an unlocked safe in a hiding place two dozen people already knew about. Not very clever . . .

He tucked them into his pockets and pushed the dolls' house back into position.

Elspeth was on her way home to Battersea to get ready for the afternoon and leave her children with Mrs Wilson; halfway along the Embankment Cecilia said she wanted the potty.

'Won't be long, darling, nearly home. Hang on.'

'Can't, can't, can't.'

'Sweetie, please. Only about five minutes.'

'Can't wait. It's coming, it's coming now—'

'Oh Cecilia –' she sighed. It would be at least ten minutes before she crossed the bridge, parked the car and reached the bathoom in the flat; on the other hand, Cheyne Walk was wonderfully just in front of her. She swung the car across the road, pulled up in front of the house, opened the door and dragged Cecilia out.

'Come on quickly. Into Granny's house, run—'

It was too late; by the time she had got Robert out of the back, a large puddle had formed round Cecilia's small feet. She started to cry. 'It's all right, poppet, it doesn't matter. Come on, we'll go in and get you all cleaned up. Take my hand.'

She rang on the door; no answer. Of course, they were all out at the rehearsal. But Mrs Hardwicke should be there, and the cleaner – still no answer; Cecilia was crying harder.

Elspeth actually had a key to Cheyne Walk; her grandmother had entrusted her with it, so that she could use her library if she was out. But did she have it with her? She rummaged in her bag. Yes. Yes, here it was.

She opened the front door, ushered her children into the hall; as she did so, the cellar door opened and Charlie Patterson emerged.

'Hi,' he said, grinning at her easily. 'You've caught me. Guilty of a fearsome crime.'

'What's that?'

'Checking out your grandpa's wine cellar. We had such wonderful stuff last night, I thought I'd go and have a browse.'

'Yes, I see.'

She liked Charlie, he seemed extremely nice and charming; she couldn't see why at least half the family was so down on him.

'Sorry,' she said, 'can't wait. We've had an accident, as you can see—' she indicated the dripping, shivering Cecilia.

'Oh, I do see. Well look, let me help. Want to give me the little fellow while you go and hose her down? It's all right,' he added, laughing, as she looked at him doubtfully. 'I'm used to kids.'

'He might cry.'

'That's OK. I'm used to that too. Come on, young man. Let's go find some cookies, huh?'

And Robert, who normally screamed at the mere approach of strangers, allowed himself to be carried into the kitchen, giggling cheerfully while Charlie tickled his tummy. What a treasure, Elspeth thought; maybe he could be hired as a nanny.

She was just returning downstairs with a dry and smiling Cecilia when she heard the phone in what had been her grandmother's study and answered it.

It was Jamie Elliott.

'Hi, Jamie. It's Elspeth.'

'Is Charlie Patterson there?'

'Yes. Shall I get him?'

'Please.'

'Charlie,' she called down the stairs, 'telephone call for you. It's Jamie.'

No answer; she ran down the stairs, went into the kitchen. Charlie was sitting at the table, feeding Robert biscuits and playing Round and Round the Garden with him. She smiled.

'You really are a wonderful babysitter. Let me take him. There's a call for you. It's Jamie. You can take it upstairs, if you like, in my grandmother's study. Know where that is?'

'I – think so. Thank you.'

His expression didn't change; but his colour did. It went from a normal healthy shade to one she could only describe as ghastly: a sort of greenish-white.

She watched him anxiously as he left the room. Obviously half expecting some bad news.

But when he came back, he was smiling, although he seemed a little on edge.

'Sorry about that. Family business. Look – you'll have to excuse me, I'm afraid. I have to write some letters.'

'Honestly, it's fine. We're going back to my flat now anyway. Thanks for all your help. I'll see you later.'

'Sure.'

It couldn't be. It just couldn't be. The baby wasn't due for three-and-a-half weeks. The consultant had said, last time she saw him, that the head wasn't even engaged. And he should know.

And first babies were notoriously late. Everyone knew that. She was famous in the family for being three weeks late herself. Although if this baby was another six-and-a-half weeks arriving, Clementine would go completely mad.

Anyway, she obviously wasn't going into labour today. She couldn't be. All that was happening was one of those practice contractions the consultant had warned her about. Added to a very vigorous bout of kicking. Anyway, it had gone now.

She took Kit's hand.

'We're there,' she said, 'come on, let's go and find a taxi.'

The bastard. How he had loved it. Absolutely loved it. Telling him, in that bland, courteous voice, that he had the information he needed to do his tax return. Knowing, of course, exactly what he was saying, what he was doing to him. 'Yes?' he'd said and he really had thought he was going to faint, standing there, staring out of the window at the fog, holding the phone so hard his knuckles were white, the nails of his other hand digging into his palm, so deeply that when he looked at it later the imprint was clear.

'You're OK,' said Jamie. He'd tried to work out quite what that meant, and he'd had plenty of time to think because the whole conversation, time itself, seemed to be going in slow motion. Did he mean he was OK, that the claim hadn't been waived? No of course not. Elliott wouldn't put it like that. Or would he? Was it just possible?

'It's good news, I think.' Another pause. Come on, you bastard, come on. Get it over with, tell me.

'You won't be liable for any extra tax.'

'Oh I won't?'

How did his voice sound so normal?

'That's what you were worrying about, wasn't it?' said Jamie.

'Yes. Yes of course.'

'Because we've heard back from Barty's lawyers. There's no question of Jenna getting any further money. Barty had waived the claim on her behalf, in court.'

'Oh really?' He could hear his own voice, so easy and relaxed. Even with a hint of relief in it. 'Oh that's good.'

'Yes. So I hope that's helpful.'

And then, because there was no point pretending any more, and because Jamie so clearly knew and because he felt so dreadful, with a pressure in his head so great he really thought he might faint, Charlie said, 'You're really enjoying this, aren't you Elliott?'

'No,' said Jamie, and his voice sounded genuinely puzzled, 'no of course not. Well, I must go now. I'll see you this afternoon, no doubt. Good morning, Charlie.'

So that was it; the end. Of all his hopes, his plans, his careful, clever solution to his problems. Over. The requisite bit of paper had been found; and he would continue to get nothing, nothing at all. Except a load of shit from the lot of them.

It had taken them long enough. Pretty incompetent lawyers, taking around two and a half weeks to find a document. Jenna ought to get rid of them. He suddenly wondered if they'd guessed, or if they'd known all along, and delayed telling him, watching him suffer, thinking of him squirm. They probably had. It would have given them great pleasure. The bastards. He felt sick; sick and so angry, he couldn't contain it. He wanted to smash things, destroy them, destroy everything that these people had. Self-righteous, vindictive, devious, greedy people: given so much, giving so little. All he had ever wanted was what was due to him: as Barty's husband, Jenna's guardian. Not vast wealth, not riches, he would never have even considered trying to get at that money if they'd treated him decently, given him just – enough: enough to live with dignity, without the humiliation of having to scrabble around, borrowing here, begging there. How dared they, how dared they take so much from him and offer nothing in return. He was only good enough, it seemed, to look after the child, to attend to the tedious daily business of her care – not that he resented that, she was worth ten, a hundred, of every single one of them. But: some reward, some acknowledgement, some thanks, even, would have helped.

He sat down on his bed; he was shaking, he realised, and absurdly near to tears. He looked at the clock: quarter past twelve. They'd be back for lunch at one. Including Elliott and Brewer. Bastards. How was he going to sit opposite them at the table, knowing they knew, knowing they must know by now that he knew and—

He felt in his pocket for his handkerchief; and his hand found one of the diaries.

The rehearsal – or rather the run-through, no one was allowed to call it a rehearsal – had gone really well. Jenna hadn't said the actual words she was going to use, simply what they were going to be about; the important thing had been the organisation, who would sit where, what music or words would prompt the next person to stand up and so on.

There was a printed programme anyway; none of it was left to you to work out for yourself.

She had another panic attack just before she got up to do her own bit, longed for Charlie to be there. But he wasn't, and she'd clung to Cathy's hand instead and Cathy had been really great.

So now, she could go back and tell Charlie that so far she'd been fine; and this afternoon he'd be there. She certainly couldn't do it without him.

Charlie sat on his bed, staring at the closed books; shaking now for a different reason, no longer angry, but acutely excited.

Here was revenge: sitting in his hands. He was quite literally holding it. It was an extraordinary sensation.

He really hadn't expected very much of the diaries. But – they would be a distraction, he thought, walking slowly up the second flight of stairs to his room. And it would be kind of interesting to read about life in the nineteen hundreds.

Much of the early months were just – charming. Celia taking up good works, under the auspices of the Fabian Society, visiting Sylvia Miller – Barty's mother – every week, in the two wretched rooms where she lived, to study how she was faring on the pound a week her husband Ted earned. A pound a week: and she'd already had six children. Some of them sharing their parents' bed, others lying under the table, the baby – that had been Barty at the time – in a drawer. *She has to fetch water from a tap in the yard for the washing and to bath them all,* Celia had written, *and heat it on the range. Poor, exhausted, frail woman that she is. And Ted has to walk an hour a day to his job at a factory where he earns just twenty-three shillings a week. And by the standards of the neighbourhood, that is quite good. How can this be, in this day and age? It makes me so angry I can hardly bear it.*

He remembered Barty's outburst, the night he had said he felt poor. Suddenly it seemed very vivid; her outburst then had meant nothing compared to this, this living, almost breathing, document. Later, *Poor Sylvia tells me she has fallen again, as she puts it, the baby due just before Christmas. Seven children there will be then, in those two rooms: and I have the gall to complain about my back aching and Nanny not ironing Giles's petticoats properly. I feel truly ashamed.*

There were some early comments about Barty, how sweet she was, and how pretty: *Her hair is the colour of a lion's mane, and she's so quick on her little feet. And she has a lovely neck, so thin and delicate. Definitely my favourite: and she seems to like me too.*

And, *Poor little soul, she has to be literally tied up much of the day, for her own safety, to the leg of the table, lest she pulls the boiling water on the range down on herself. She's so lively and busy, it's like being in a prison cell for her.*

Then Celia had discovered the baby she was expecting was twins: and decided to keep the information from Oliver, so that she could continue doing what she wanted. *I feel so perfectly well, and he'll just start fussing. Anyway, I have to be there for Sylvia's baby. She needs me. It's worth any risk. I have so much and she has so little.*

Courageous old bird she had been, even then, especially as she seemed to have had a miscarriage the year before. That was why Oliver had insisted she should leave Lyttons; that was why she had taken up her good works. Manipulative and duplicitous then too: Barty had often told him that.

But then – and at this he had sat bolt upright on his bed – then Sylvia had her baby. Celia was there:

It was six weeks too early. I went with a Christmas hamper for them all and a shawl for the baby and she was in labour when I arrived. Ted was sitting on the steps, said she'd asked if I'd go in and be with her. Oh dear. This is so hard to write. I stayed with her, held her hand all the time. It was quite quick, she was very brave.

The baby was a girl. But – she was dreadfully deformed. Her legs twisted round each other and she had some sort of horrible open wound on her back. But so beautiful, just the same, a sweet, peaceful little face. We thought she was dead. Sylvia was so very, very upset, I felt so useless. The midwife had tried to revive her, but – no good. It seemed. She wrapped her in a towel, and gave her to me to hold, then went to fetch some more towels and newspapers from her own house.

Sylvia asked if she could hold the baby, and I put her in her arms. 'Thank God she died,' she kept saying, 'thank God,' and at the same time she was crying, crying with grief. I kept thinking, stupidly, how much nicer it would have been if the baby had been wrapped in the shawl.

It was very dark in the room, just the candlelight. That's why I couldn't be sure, not at first. But I am now. I am sure and I'm very clear about what happened. The baby breathed: not just once but two or three times and then she gave a little sigh and her eyelids fluttered. Sylvia said, 'Oh God. Oh dear God, no,' lying there, staring at her, kissing her poor, sweet little head. After that she looked at me, quite alert suddenly, and said, 'Will you help me?' Of course I did. I was her friend and I had to help her. I fetched a pillow and I really can't remember clearly what happened next, but we did what had to be done. It did have to be done. She was so deformed, suffering so much. Her brain must have been damaged too, not breathing for so long. In a rich household perhaps, but in that one – God help her. God help them all.

We wrapped her in the shawl I had brought, and Sylvia held her, so sweetly and tenderly, and we knew this time she was quite safe.

The guilt will be with me for the rest of my life. But it did have to be done. And I was proud to have helped her to do it.

'Sweet Jesus,' said Charlie aloud. 'Dear sweet Jesus.'

'Clemmie, my darling, are you all right?'

'What?' She was concentrating, trying to work out if it had been painful, or just the usual discomfort. Just the usual, she decided. Definitely. And it was ages since the last one. At least half an hour.

'I said, are you all right? You seem very – distracted.'

'Sorry, Sebastian, I am a bit. The baby's beating the hell out of me. But – no, I'm fine. I'd like to lie down for half an hour or so, if that would be all right.'

'My darling, of course it would. Do you want some food? Or a drink?'

The thought of food was horrendous; where could it go? With her stomach a punch ball, squashed up somewhere near her shoulders. She smiled at Sebastian.

'Food no. A drink yes, some warm milk would be lovely. Mrs Conley knows how I like it.'

'Fine. I'll go and tell her. Kit, what about you?'

'Oh I'll have a whisky, I think. I need some Dutch courage.'

'What on earth for? You haven't got to do anything.'

'I know, but it's still going to be quite – difficult. Isn't it?'

'I'm afraid so,' said Sebastian with a sigh.

'Charlie, are you coming down to lunch? It's all ready.'

His voice sounded strange, shaky and strange.

'I – don't think I will, if you don't mind. I've got a terrible headache, I'm trying to get rid of it before this afternoon.'

'Oh, I'm sorry. Can I come in?'

'Of course.' He was lying on the bed; he did look terrible, she thought, very pale and sort of – upset.

'Oh, Charlie.' Jenna suddenly felt awful, filled with a wild, selfish panic. 'You're not going to be too ill to come, are you? I couldn't do it without you.'

'Of course not. That's exactly why I'm having a rest. I'll be fine, darling, we don't have to go for an hour and a half. I've found some codeine, I feel better already. Just tell the others how sorry I am, will you? And I'll be downstairs at half past two, don't worry.'

'Promise?'

'I promise. I won't let you down. How was this morning?'

'Fine. Absolutely fine. I feel much better now. I wish you did.'

'I will do. Off you go, darling. I'll see you later.'

'OK.'

Half an hour later, Cathy appeared.

'You OK, Dad? Jenna said you weren't feeling well.'

'I – wasn't. But I'm fine now.'

He didn't feel fine; he felt shocked, dazed with what he had learned and what he had read. And at the power he held so unexpectedly and so literally in his hands.

CHAPTER 47

Keir was one of the first in the church: so worried had he been that they would send him away, say there was no room, after his discourtesy in ignoring the invitation. But of course they did not; they showed him to a pew, halfway down the aisle, with great courtesy, gave him an order of service. One of her favourite quotations was on the front cover under her name: 'rich with the spoils of time . . .'. It suited her so well. He sat reading, smiling: they were doing her very proud. And so they should. Children, grandchildren, husbands, lovers: all playing their part. He suddenly and rather surprisingly wished he could do something for her too.

The Millers arrived quite early as well; they had said they would like that, like to have a look around the church. Really, they were longing to get away from the Warwicks. They were all very nice but, as Billy put it, they didn't seem much to do with Barty.

'But we're not here for Barty, Bill,' said Joan firmly, 'it's Lady Celia's day.'

'I know that, but – well, we wouldn't be here if it weren't for Barty. She was part of them all. I wish you hadn't said we'd stay the night.'

'Well, I did. It was kindly meant. And it means we can see Jenna. She's coming over, Venetia said. So stop grumbling. Most people'd be glad to spend the night in a house like that.'

'Well I wouldn't.'

'Too bad. Look, here we are. Joe, tidy your hair, looks like you haven't brushed it for days. You too, Michael. Come along now, in we go. And remember, we're here for Jenna.'

Elspeth didn't see him at first; she was shown straight to a pew right at the front and she sat looking round her. If she was looking for anyone it was for Marcus Forrest. She saw several friends, watched poor Clemmie waddling in – really there was no other word for it – with her arm through Kit's, following Sebastian. She didn't look at all well, poor girl. She was obviously having a horrid time. Elspeth waved and smiled at her and

Clemmie waved back. She looked a bit worried, Elspeth thought, as well as ill; probably about Kit. He'd been very upset about all this.

And then she saw him: saw Keir, sitting about half a dozen rows back: looking at her. Just looking. And suddenly she wasn't there in St Martin-in-the-Fields, an about-to-be-divorced woman with two children, and an ex-lover, mustn't forget that, an ex-lover – she was twenty-one again, and a virgin, in the Bodleian, making notes on *Paradise Lost*, while those eyes, those dark, probing eyes met hers. And however much she might look away, as she was doing now, frown slightly, as she was also doing now, pretend it meant nothing to her, and carry on with what she was doing, he went on looking at her. A few minutes later, exactly as she had done then, she looked again, and the slightest smile touched the corners of his mouth as he recognised the fact. And she felt it, just as she had done then, disturbed, touched in some remote corner of herself, and deny it as she might, the sensation stayed with her, uncomfortable, important, impossible to ignore. After her sisters arrived to sit with her, and her brothers; after she shifted along to make room for other people and half hoped that, if she looked around, her view of him would be blocked by one of the great pillars; through the music, the lovely, lovely requiem soaring through the church; through the murmurs of excitement as this distinguished person and that one arrived, politicians, actors (there were the Oliviers and the Redgraves), and even minor – well, quite minor – royalty (the Duchess of Kent, and was that the Mountbattens?); even after she had finally seen Marcus Forrest, walking in with the rest of the Lytton New York contingent (and sinking just a little too reverently on to his knees), she was aware of Keir there, looking at her. Then, and in spite of everything, she was so very glad and grateful that he had come.

Jenna walked in, very pale but composed, with Charlie and Cathy, followed by Lord Arden; as she passed the Millers' pew she saw Joe and smiled at him with such joy that everyone who saw it was touched and smiled too. Joe smiled back at her, then flushed scarlet and looked down at his over-large feet. The sight seemed to afford him some comfort.

The twins came in together, almost last; they looked stunningly beautiful, and remarkably like their mother. They were dressed not identically, but very similarly, in black dresses and coats, each wearing one of the pearl chokers which Celia had made her trademark. Adele was sitting next to Lord Arden; he smiled at her tenderly. She took his hand and held it, and as she did so, the years rolled away as they had done for Elspeth and she was on a ship with him again, the last ship to sail from Bordeaux, riding the dangerous seas up the coast towards England, the target of German bombers and mines, cheering and encouraging one another while her children played on the deck in the sunshine quite unaware of the extraordinary piece of history they were living through.

'We are gathered here today, to celebrate the life of Lady Arden' – it was the rector of St Martin's, speaking in a rich voice, so well-suited for the occasion – 'to celebrate it in the presence of her beloved family . . .'

There it went again; that sharp, painful tug. It was unmistakably pain that time; Clemmie cautiously looked at her watch. Exactly fifteen minutes since the last one. Exactly. That was what was frightening her, the preciseness. Not random pain, not even quiet, steady discomfort but neatly timed orderly spasms. They didn't hurt much yet; but she could see that they could. That they would. So maybe she was in labour. That was all right. Labour took a long time, hours and hours; there was no way she was going to have the baby here, in this church, in the middle of Celia's memorial service. No, as soon as the service was over, and it was only going to last a little over an hour, then she would tell Venetia or Adele, or maybe someone a little less involved, Elspeth perhaps, or Izzie, and an ambulance could be called and she would be taken to hospital and, if she was very lucky, her baby would be born that day. Much more likely actually it would be born tomorrow . . .

She realised everyone else was standing up and so heaved herself up as quickly as she could. Goodness, she was uncomfortable. She took Kit's hand again, and smiled at Sebastian. They were both obviously near to tears. The last thing she should do was worry them about a baby that looked as if it just might be born tomorrow . . .

They had sung the first hymn: Giles, white as death, was walking towards the lectern. His hands shook as he smoothed down the page, adjusted the ribbon which marked the place; he cleared his throat, looked round him desperately, afraid he was not going to be able to utter a word. Then something extraordinary happened; he looked at Helena and she smiled at him. A warm, brilliant smile: of encouragement and, no doubt about it, affection. And Giles too, was suddenly in another place, not in the church, watched by dozens, hundreds of distinguished people, but leaving home alone, in absolutely equal terror, for life in the army, not as an officer, because he had failed at his selection, but as a private soldier. She had been smiling at him in exactly that way then, in encouragement and love, and now he smiled back at her, as he had then, with a flash of unmistakable gratitude, his courage suddenly found. And he began to read, his voice ringing through the church, strong and moving, not flat and dull as he had feared. '. . . The days of man are but as grass: for he flourisheth as a flower of the field . . .'

As she had indeed been, Sebastian thought, so lovely a flower, for so many years, her beauty unfaded for so long, her head unbowed, her face lifted always to the sun. He saw her now, perfectly clearly, as she had been that very first day when he had walked into her office with his manuscript. She was sitting at the desk; he had read to her from it and had known even then that he had found love, and knew that she had found it too, astonishing, joyful, and impossible to deny. She had fought it, as only she could, angrily, fiercely:

'I want you to tell me you love me,' he had said one day.

'I can't,' she'd said, 'I really can't.' Struggling to remain faithful to Oliver, but it had done no good.

He remembered how she sent him finally away, refusing to leave Oliver, remembered her grief and his, seemingly unbearable. He remembered visiting her in hospital when Kit had been born, when, despite all the other people in the room, she seemed to be alone in it, alone with him and their son, an extraordinary and palpable closeness; and he remembered going to her the night Pandora died, when her love for him overcame all her grief, all her jealousy at his own marriage and how he had found with her the only comfort there was for him in the world.

And he remembered her dying, that he had been able to be with her, and it suddenly seemed the greatest gift of all.

'*Panis Angelicus*', one of the loveliest anthems; Lord Arden felt it sustaining him as he walked up to the lectern. The bible was ready, open at the Letter to the Corinthians; all he had to do was read it. Not very difficult, he could manage that; but then somehow something more seemed to be required of him and to his absolute astonishment he found he was able to do it.

'I would just like to say a few words,' he said, hearing his own voice quite strong and very clear, and everyone who had known how nervous he was even of reading, let alone speaking, was astonished. 'A few words about Celia before I read the lesson. St Paul wrote to the Corinthians about charity, but what he meant by that was love. That is why I have chosen it. Celia's greatest gift was her ability to love. She loved unconditionally, and in a great many different ways. She loved her husband, her children, her grandchildren and her friends –' at this point his eyes rested on Sebastian and he briefly smiled '– she loved Lyttons, she loved her work, she loved words, she even, I think –' and at this point his old eyes twinkled '– she even managed to love me. Certainly she made me very happy for the few years we had together . . .'

'The old sweetheart,' whispered Adele to Venetia, her eyes filling with tears.

'I hope she did,' Venetia whispered back. And then St Paul spoke to them: '. . . with the tongue of men and angels . . . charity suffereth long and is kind . . . beareth all things, believeth all things, hopeth all things, endureth all things . . . now abideth faith, hope and charity and the greatest of these is charity.'

There was a long silence after he had finished; even music would have seemed an intrusion.

It was really hurting now; Clementine felt quite shocked by the ferocity of the next pain. Longer too, rising to a peak, then fading blessedly away; if this was going on for twelve hours or whatever, she hoped she was going to be able to be brave enough. As it faded again, she eased her hand away from Kit's, looked at her watch; only ten minutes that time. This was speeding up rather fast. Of course it was still all right, plenty of time, but a bit worrying. She relaxed into herself, as they had taught her to do at the hospital, breathing deeply, and tried to concentrate on Clio introducing *Alice in Wonderland* – 'which was the very first thing my grandmother ever read me, and which has been my favourite ever since' – and then on Lucy and 'The Owl and The Pussycat', and then, of course, on Rupert, with his golden curls and his serious self-assurance, launching into the first chapter of the first book of *Meridian* – 'Once upon a different time, there was another country, in another world, not far away from this one . . .'

Oh, no. Not again. Was it really ten minutes? They had been quite long readings. Have a look, quickly, hand disengaged from Kit again, look at the watch – Oh, God, this was pain all right, this was real pain, relax Clemmie, deep breaths – look at the watch. Eight minutes. Eight very short minutes. What next? What was she going to do, what on earth was she going to do?

Izzie sat listening to *Meridian* with her own special memories. Of a little girl, a sad, lonely little girl who had heard her frightening, stern father weeping during the night, and who had gone bravely (very bravely, for she was extremely frightened of him), to enquire if he was all right.

And how that little girl had given him her own thoughts about *Meridian*, and had seen those thoughts become a story; thoughts which had brought them together, had helped him to forgive her for taking her mother away from him.

She loved him so much; so very, very much.

She smiled a smile of sheer glorious happiness at him, and hoped he would understand.

Sebastian caught the smile and returned it; it gave him courage and strength. Only thing was, Arden, the old bugger, had taken his theme: about Celia and love. Of course he had much more to say, but the sweetness and the spontaneity of those few words made his own seem rather ponderous and theatrical. Well, he could improvise a bit: just as Arden had. Of course he had an absolute right to do it, he was her husband after all and – and then he heard a muffled gasp, and looked sharply at Clementine. He saw her biting her lip, white-faced, saw her hands clenched at her sides, her eyes suddenly wild and afraid and realised at once what was happening to her and what he must do.

'Come along,' he whispered to her, taking her hand, half standing up. 'Time to go, I think. You all right?'

She nodded, feebly, breathing deeply, visibly easing back into herself; it was over for now.

'It's all right,' she said, 'I'll be—'

'No,' he said, 'come on, now! Do as you're told.'

A few people had noticed, were staring; obediently she stood up, whispered to Kit that she was fine, and followed Sebastian meekly down the aisle. Halfway down, another pain; the effort of trying not to bend double was absolutely monumental.

Outside, he took her arm; 'Come along, my darling. By happy chance, there's a hospital just there, two hundred yards away. We can walk there. Next pain, just lean on me and breathe very, very deeply.'

'Sebastian, no, you're about to speak,' she said, 'get someone else, please, and go back in.'

'No,' he said, 'absolutely not. That will waste time, and besides, what do you think Celia would say to me if I left you to bear our grandchild with some stranger? Now, this way—'

'Oh!' She almost cried out with the pain this time; violent, tearing at her, longer, rising faster, fading more slowly. 'Oh, Sebastian—'

Somehow he got her there, walked her into the admissions hall, stayed with her while they put her into a wheelchair and, stroking her hair, told her not to be afraid, she would be all right, she would survive, went with her into the lift and along the corridors, walking beside the chair, holding her hand, even made her laugh once – 'What would that old fruit in the church have said if you'd had it there? On his rather over-polished flagstones.'

'Jenna, you'll have to speak now,' Giles's voice was very calm, very authoritative, as the strains of the next hymn finally faded. 'It doesn't look as if Sebastian's coming back. All right?'

She took a last look at Charlie, her eyes very large and scared, and he gave her the briefest kiss on her cheek and then she stood up and walked very steadily to the lectern and began.

God, he was proud of her. So proud. She looked beautiful standing there, her large eyes looking round the church, speaking to them all with a sweet half-childish authority.

'I am not quite related to Lady Arden,' she said, and there was only the mildest tremor in her voice, 'or rather to Celia, which is what she told me to call her. But my mother, as most of you know, was brought up by her. That is why I am here. I represent my mother, who loved her very much, and I loved her very much too. She was, it seems to me, a shining example to everyone. Certainly to me: I hope to grow up and live long enough to be very like her. Not in quite the same way, but to be clever, and brave and greatly loved, and also to set the kind of examples which even the youngest person can follow . . .'

They had allowed him to stay. He was there with her through it, through the almost shockingly short but fierce labour, soothing her, helping her, bathing her face, giving her sips of water, holding the mask for her when she tried to push it off, encouraging her to push, push her daughter, her red-faced, furious, wailing, flailing daughter, into the world. 'We must call her Pandora,' Clementine said, 'how lovely, how lovely—'

Jenna had finished; with a sweet, final tribute to Celia, which had brought a choke of emotion to almost everyone in the church: 'She helped me so much when my mother died. She talked to me about her as much and as often as I wanted, no matter how tired she was or how upset herself. She brought her alive for me again, sitting with me hour after hour, comforting me with stories of my mother, stories I had never heard, but will never forget. I call that courage, and I call that love. I am very proud to be her honorary granddaughter.'

She smiled then, very sweetly, and returned to her seat. Charlie put his arm round her shoulders and hugged her and Cathy squeezed her hand; 'Well done,' whispered Lord Arden; 'Very well done,' both the twins said; and everyone around her was smiling at her and Noni was blowing kisses to her across the aisle and, after a few moments, Lucas did the same; and further back, Joan's face was streaming with tears, and Billy was blowing his nose very hard.

And Elspeth turned and looked behind her to smile at Keir; only to see that he was not there.

A few hundred yards away, Sebastian watched, first puzzled and then anxious, as Clementine's face, so serene and so happy, suddenly distorted with pain again, and she cried out. And, as the final anthem soared in the church, a second baby was born, a boy; and no anthem, Sebastian thought, laughing and weeping at the same time, no eulogy, no words that he could possibly have spoken, could have been a better celebration of Celia's life and his place in it than twin grandchildren, born in his presence, to him and to her.

CHAPTER 48

Where had he gone? Why had he gone?

The hurt, the disappointment, was almost unbearable. She had really thought he had come back, had decided he might be able to forgive her. Now it was over again. And he was gone.

Elspeth sighed heavily, turned to pick up her things, smiled brilliantly and bravely at everyone, and followed the rest of the family out of the church.

Outside, it was almost dark, and the fog was coming in again, swirling around the lights of the buses and cars in Trafalgar Square; everyone was talking at once, saying how lovely it had been, how wonderful Jenna had been, how touching Lord Arden's words had been, and, of course, above all, where were Clemmie and Sebastian, was she all right?

Sebastian was walking out of the lift and into the reception area of the Charing Cross Hospital, feeling exhausted and slightly shaken now as well as elated, his mind fixed firmly on a drink, when he saw Keir, sitting by the door, looking nervous.

'Hallo,' he said, rather warily.

'Hallo, Sebastian. Is she – is she all right?'

'She's fine. Two babies. Two healthy babies.'

'Two!'

'Yes. Boy and a girl. Wonderful, isn't it?'

'Wonderful. Congratulations.'

'No reason to congratulate me,' said Sebastian firmly. 'She did all the work. Now I must go and find Kit. How did you know I was here?'

'I – followed you. When you left the church.'

'Oh yes?'

'Yes. I wanted to speak to you. Then I realised you had more important things to worry about—'

'Just slightly—'

'So I waited.'

'Right. Well, I can't stop now.'

'No. Of course not. But this won't take long. I wanted to say I was sorry. For being so rude, when you phoned. I really am very sorry.'

Sebastian stared at him. In all the time he had known Keir he had never known him express any kind of apology for anything. It was quite unexpected.

'Oh – that's perfectly all right,' he said, 'you were upset. I understand.'

'It's very nice of you. Thank you.'

'Look,' said Sebastian suddenly. 'Look, there was a reason for my phoning. I had a message for you. From Celia.'

'From Celia?'

'Yes. But – it might require a bit of explanation. Especially as it's reaching you a bit late. I've got to go to this damn fool dinner at Venetia's tonight. But I don't intend to stay very long. Why don't we meet for a drink after that. Like to come to my club? The Reform. At say – ten.'

'Well – yes,' said Keir. 'Yes, thank you. Thank you very much.'

'Good. Well I must go now. They probably visualise Clemmie having her baby in the gutter somewhere or other.'

'He must have taken her to hospital,' said Venetia. 'Don't worry, Kit, she'll be perfectly safe with him, it's just a question of finding out where.'

'He'll let us know as soon as he can,' said Adele, 'probably the best thing is to go home, where he can phone us.'

But Kit was distraught, said they must not leave, Clemmie might come back, looking for them, Sebastian might come for him, take him to her, he simply must stay.

Boy volunteered to go home to wait for news there, Jamie to visit all the hospitals in the vicinity, Jay to go to the nearest police station and put in a call to all the hospitals which might, he said, be quicker, Kyle to telephone Clementine's consultant in London and see if he had any news.

Only Charlie said nothing and did nothing; just stood there, frustrated by the delay, longing for them all to disappear, to go to Venetia's, so that he could plead a worsening headache and a need to go back to Cheyne Walk. Then make his way to the completely deserted Lytton House. And Celia's office. And Celia's safe. And the rest of Celia's diaries.

'Look,' said Jenna, pointing. 'Look, there he is. There's Sebastian.'

And there he was, striding through the thickening fog, waving cheerily, smiling, looking suddenly years younger.

'Kit,' he shouted, 'Kit, she's fine. She's – you've – got twins.'

'Twins!' said Kit, and he looked not pleased but shocked, almost stricken. 'My God, girls, boys—'

'One of each. Not a repetition of your sisters, thank God. Both well. No wonder she was so huge, poor darling.'

'It must have been terribly quick,' said Adele.

'Is she really all right?' said Venetia.

'How big were they?'

'What's she going to call them?'

'Stop it, you two, for heaven's sake. Your mother always said you never knew when to stop talking. Clemmie's fine. Very pleased with herself. It was quick, the doctor said, exceptionally so. Even he didn't realise it was twins, until the second one decided to arrive. Something about one lying on top of the other so he couldn't hear the second heartbeat. She did wonderfully. You'll have to ask her the rest of your questions yourselves. Now they might let Kit in, but not the rest of you. Plenty of time for that. Come on, old chap, take my arm. We'll come to your place, Venetia, in a little while. OK?'

'Of course. Of *course*. Oh – let me give you both a kiss. Congratulations, both of you. It's truly wonderful.'

They watched them go off together, through the fog, father and son, arm in arm, to inspect the new generation; it was an oddly touching sight.

'How lovely,' said Adele, 'how very, very lovely.'

'Come on then,' said Venetia, 'our guests await. Where are the cars, Boy? Oh, there, come on, everyone, pile in.'

Charlie released Jenna's hand.

'Sorry, sweetheart. I'm feeling pretty rough. My headache's come back with a vengeance. Would you mind if I didn't come to Venetia's – at least not until this evening? I need to get my head down.'

'Oh, Charlie. I'm so sorry. Shall I come with you?'

'No, no, of course not. You go and have fun. Everyone will want to congratulate you. And so they should. 'Bye, darling. I'll see you later.'

He hailed a cab and directed it to Grosvenor Square.

'Oh, and is there a medical suppliers we could call in on the way? I'm a doctor, I need to buy a new stethoscope, I'm not at all familiar with London. And while we're about it, I need a holdall. Any suggestions for that?'

The cabby said he certainly had, John Bell & Croydon in Wigmore Street for the stethoscope, Selfridges for the holdall, and swung his cab round. Charlie looked back; people were still pouring out of the church as they drove away, a great mass of rich, glossy, well-dressed, self-important people, all talking, no doubt, about Celia and her wonderful life and family. He wondered what they would say if they knew she had once conspired to murder a baby.

There was a large crowd at Venetia's; Jenna, flushed with excitement, found herself in the centre of it, kissed, hugged, congratulated. But only two of the tributes meant anything to her.

'You were marvellous,' said Lucas. He put his arms round her and hugged her. 'I'm not just saying it, either, you really were. I was very, very proud of you.'

And, 'Well done, Jenna,' said Joe, smiling at her awkwardly, blushing furiously, 'you were really very good. Very good indeed.'

'Very good,' said Billy, kissing her, 'given a lot to have your mum hear you, I would. Eh, Joan?'

Joan was speechless, flushed with excitement, her eyes brilliant; all she could do was hug Jenna and kiss her on both cheeks.

It was nice to hear from all the others, but it meant very little to Jenna. She settled herself in a corner with Joe and said she wanted to hear all about his veterinary training. A lot of other people had said that to him today: like Jenna, he felt very few of them meant it. But she did. He launched into a day-by-day account; she listened intently, her eyes fixed on him, occasionally asking a question. From across the room, Lucas watched them and felt a stab of something he recognised quite clearly as jealousy. He told himself it was absurd, she was only talking to her cousin, her dull, acutely shy, country bumpkin of a cousin. He didn't feel any less cross.

Elspeth still felt quite horribly upset. Upset, angry and incredibly foolish to have thought, as she had, that Keir had come back. What a fool she was; she hoped no one had noticed, her sitting there all alone, so conspicuously alone, craning her neck round, looking for Keir, smiling foolishly at the place where he had been.

Keir, who so obviously, so publicly, didn't love her any more.

'Hallo, Elspeth. You're looking lovely. Can I get you a glass of champagne? Nobody seems to be looking after you.'

It was Marcus Forrest.

'I'm used to that,' she said. And smiled at him. At least he would save her from being alone.

'Thank you for today, Helena,' said Giles.

'What did I do?' She sounded genuinely surprised.

'Gave me my courage back.'

'Oh.' She smiled again, remembering. 'Good. You were marvellous, Giles. I was so proud of you.'

'Thank you.' For the first time since he could remember, he felt a little proud of himself.

He had them. It had been absurdly easy. The safe had been child's play; they were there, the diaries. Now they were all in the very nice leather holdall he had bought at Selfridges. Good thing it was so big; it was quite a haul. He was desperate to read them.

Charlie hailed a cab, driving slowly and cautiously through the fog.

'The Savoy Hotel, please,' he said.

He didn't know many London hotels, but he'd been to the Savoy and he'd noticed some very good, quiet telephone kiosks there, away from the main reception area, where you could sit and talk in peace. They even had a ledge for writing. And of course space at your feet for your bag. That was what he needed: a good, quiet telephone kiosk. That was all he needed now, in fact.

Venetia had decided on a buffet dinner for the evening; there were too many people to sit round a table and it would make moving around, making sure everyone was all right, much easier.

Elspeth felt, therefore, that her request that Marcus should stay was not unreasonable; there was no table plan to disturb, no numbers to upset. Her mother did not, however, see it like that.

'I'm sorry, Elspeth, but I don't want him here. I don't particularly like him as a person and he caused great distress when he was in charge of Lyttons London, not just to me, but to Giles and Jay and several of the other editors. This is a family gathering and, quite apart from anything else, it would show disrespect to your grandmother's memory if you failed to attend.'

Elspeth said that she had every intention of attending, walked out of her mother's room and slammed the door as loudly as she dared. Which wasn't very loudly at all; at the age of twenty-six, she was still in awe of her mother. Venetia had felt much the same about Celia, to the day she died.

She went to find Marcus; he was chatting to Kyle about the success of two best-sellers, *Lolita* and *Lady Chatterley's Lover*.

'We are obviously becoming a more permissive society,' Kyle was saying. 'I'm delighted, of course, but I do wonder where it will end. I suspect we shall see a vast boom in books like this thing everyone in the business is talking about, *The Carpetbaggers*. You had a sight of that yet?' Marcus said he had; 'I tried to buy it, but we couldn't afford it of course. Simon & Schuster paid an absurd price for it. Although I dare say they'll get it back. Funny he's gone that way, I thought that Harold Robbins was a serious writer once. I loved *A Stone for Danny Fisher*, I thought it was a great book.'

'There's more money in sex,' said Kyle, and then saw Elspeth and smiled.

'Hallo, darling, you OK?'

'I'm fine. What was that about sex?'

'I said there was money in it.'

'Certainly seems like it. Lyttons are still a bit virginal, I'm afraid.'

'Would you have wanted to publish *Lady Chatterley*?' asked Marcus, laughing.

'Of course I would. Wouldn't you?'

'I guess I would.'

'We'll have to find a new D.H. Lawrence, I suppose. Kyle, would you be awfully sweet and come and talk to dear Billy Miller and his wife. He's Barty's brother, you know, and they're a bit out of their depth.'

'Sure, honey. Lead the way.'

'I'll be back,' Elspeth hissed at Marcus over her shoulder, 'don't go away.'

'As if I would.'

Five minutes later, half despising herself, she had arranged to meet him for a drink later that evening: 'Say about ten? I'll leave here early, say I've got a filthy headache.'

'Not too filthy, I hope?' he said.

She knew she'd asked for it, but she found the remark offensive at such a time; she found it hard to smile.

This was incredible; absolutely incredible. If he did have to sell – and he really didn't want to – these would be worth a fortune. A small one, anyway. Of course the diaries were worth more to the Lyttons than they were to anyone else, but either way it would pay a few bills.

He'd found out why 1919 had been hidden away with 1909. It had been quite a year, he thought: Celia pregnant with Sebastian's baby, planning finally to leave Oliver, Lyttons in serious danger of financial ruin. But it was also the year Sylvia had died, of acute septicaemia. She had been at Cheyne Walk, delirious: *She thinks she is having the baby, that baby, and she's said some rather dangerous things, which Barty has heard. I pray it makes no sense to her.*

It seemed it had: *Barty went to see Mrs Jessup, the midwife, to make some enquiries of her own. And came back here distraught, understandably so, and accused me of killing the baby. It was dreadful. Only Oliver was able to calm her, persuade her that it had been, in fact, an act of mercy; they have a very close relationship, painful for me to observe. She said some very harsh things to me, many of which, I have to admit, are true.*

It was that intervention, it seemed, Oliver's passionate defence of Celia and what she had done, that had persuaded her to stay: *I cannot leave him now, in spite of everything. It would be too great a betrayal.* Barty had never told him any of that: too painful, he supposed, although every other story about her was familiar to him, even those that did her discredit, like renewing her relationship with Laurence while her fiancé, John Munnings, was away in Italy during the war and her machiavellian trouncing of the Lyttons.

'Boy,' said Charlie aloud, ordering a second whisky from the hovering waiter, 'they certainly lived, these people.'

He found other things, wonderful stories: a trip booked on the *Titanic's* maiden voyage, only missed because Barty contracted pneumonia; Oliver, the supposedly saintly Oliver, having an affair with that irritating other saint, Felicity Brewer; Celia's involvement with the Fascist movement in England, before the Second World War, actually dining with Hitler – 'A marvellously inspiring man' – he was only dipping into it, there was no time for more, but every week, almost every page yielded something. And then finally poor old Lord Arden, Bunny to his intimates, who she had married in the full knowledge he was impotent: all written down, with an almost nonchalant detachment.

How dreadful it would be for them, if this came out. Charlie drained his glass, and picked up the bag. Time to make the phone call . . .

'Oh Kit, I wish you could see them. They're both so tiny—'

He was sitting by her bed, holding Pandora, occasionally reaching out to take Clementine's hand.

'But not too tiny, I hope.'

'Of course not, I told you, five pounds each, they'd be in an incubator otherwise; no wonder I was so uncomfortable. Both with lots and lots of red hair—'

'Which has more?'

'Sebastian. Feel—' she took his hand, passed it over the other baby's head.

'Both with big blue eyes. And both so hungry already. I hope I can cope.'

'And do they look alike?'

'Well – they're both babies. But not very alike, no. Pandora's much longer and skinnier, and she has a very full mouth, Sebastian's kind of chunkier—'

'Chunkier! How can a baby be chunky? Here, take this little one and let me hold him. He doesn't feel any different.'

'Well, he is. You'll have to believe me. And his face is – rounder. I think he's going to look exactly like you.'

'That's fine. And if Pandora looks like you, then everyone will be happy.'

'Yes.' She was silent for a while, then said, 'Your father was so kind, Kit. I couldn't have done it without him. He really is the most wonderful person.'

'I know it.'

'Kit—'

'Yes?'

'Kit, I think we should move back to London. To be near him.'

A silence: then, 'If that's what you want.'

'It is.'

'Fine by me. I worry about him too.'

'And I know Oxford is lovely, but so is Primrose Hill—'

'Primrose Hill! That sounds a little too near.'

'Why not, Kit? Just tell me why not.'

There was a silence; then Kit smiled and said, 'I don't think I can.'

Jamie was telling Adele about the house he was thinking of buying on the coast of Maine – 'It's absolutely lovely, what they call a cottage, built of clapboard and right on the ocean. You'd love it' – when Boy came over to him.

'Sorry to disturb you, Jamie. Phone call for you. It's Charlie. Charlie Patterson.'

'Oh, I'm sorry.'

'Not your fault. Apparently he's hoping to come over later, feeling better, very apologetic but – he wants to talk to you.'

'Please excuse me, Adele.'

'Of course.'

She watched him leave the room, wondering why he had told her she'd love his cottage in Maine, as if it would matter, while reproaching herself for thinking that yet another man she hardly knew could become really important to her. It was Geordie all over again. She had married him much too quickly and look where that had got her. And why was she thinking about marriage, for goodness sake? She'd only really got to know Jamie over the past two or three days, it was pathetic.

She looked round the room, saw Lucas laughing with Jenna, he was besotted with that child, it was really rather sweet, then noticed that Joe, on the other hand, was looking helplessly awkward and lonely, and went across to introduce him to Lucy. Lucy could literally talk to anyone for ever.

'Elliott?'

'Yes. Where are you? Jenna was worrying about you.'

'I'm at the Savoy.'

'The Savoy. What on earth are you doing there? I thought you were ill.'

'No. Never better, actually.'

Jamie sighed. God, he was irritating.

'Well – what can I do for you?'

'Quite a lot, actually. I've got the diaries.'

'The diaries?' Jamie could hear his own voice sounding quite normal, only mildly interested. As if the importance of what Charlie was saying hadn't quite registered. Maybe it hadn't.

'Yes. You know, Celia's diaries.'

It was beginning to register now; somewhere in his stomach rather than his brain.

'I don't quite understand. Why have you got them?'

'Because I wanted them. I thought they could be useful to me.'

This was getting nasty; icily, creepily nasty.

'I – don't quite see why.'

'You don't? I'll explain, shall I?'

Jamie said nothing. A tight band had settled round his head, a very hot, tight band.

'I want to sell them to you.'

'Oh, now don't be ridiculous, Patterson. They're not yours to sell.'

'I think that's open to discussion. Possession being nine tenths of the law. I've got them. Right here. At my feet.'

'How? How have you got them?'

'Irrelevant at the moment, I'd say.'

'Not really,' said Jamie, his brain beginning to move out of its straitjacket, to function more efficiently. 'How do I know you've got them? They're in a safe. In Celia Lytton's office.'

'Not any more, they're not. They're in a really very fine leather bag. I'm looking at them right now. Shall I read you an excerpt? Let me see. Oh, now this is quite a nice one: 16 June 1916. *Darling Jack, home on leave. Such fun to see him. So different from Oliver, so gay, so full of life. And so beautiful. There was some very serious temptation this evening, which I admit to. He started to kiss me, really kiss me, and I really kissed him back. I longed and longed for him and so very nearly took him upstairs. Not quite – but it was a very near thing. My own husband's brother. Oh dear.*

'Now, I couldn't have made that up, could I, Elliott? Or – here's another. This is quite long, you'll have to be patient: November 1916. *Oliver home on leave. He told me a dreadful story this evening, of how a moment of sheer terror on his part cost another man his life. They were leaving the trenches to go over the top and Oliver suddenly lost his nerve; he hesitated, and this man, Barton, sneered at him, said, "You're not afraid, are you sir?" Clearly recognising that he was. And who would not have been, sometimes? Oliver pulled himself together and followed him out, but Barton paid for that few seconds' delay; a shell that would have caught Oliver hit him instead, ripped his leg off, and his arm too. He died in agony after many hours. Oliver wrote to his family, told them as he has to tell all the families, that Barton had died instantly. He said he would blame himself for ever.*

There was a pause; then Charlie said, 'How would Barton's family feel, I wonder, reading that? Couldn't have made that up either, could I?'

Jamie was completely silent, transfixed with terror himself; he waited until he felt slightly calmer, then took a deep breath and said, 'So – how did you get them? I still don't understand.'

Charlie chuckled; 'Oh, if you grow up the way I did, Elliott, with the sort of friends I had, you learn a lot of useful things. Cracking a very old safe is one of them. And of course the first three were put back in their hiding place at Cheyne Walk. Very odd thing to do, that. I got them out this morning. Ask Elspeth, if you don't believe me, she saw me coming up from the cellar.'

'Yes. Yes, I see. So – where is this leading? I still don't quite understand.'

'Of course you do. I want some money. If it wouldn't pain you to part with it too much. Barty's money.'

'Jenna's money.'

'Yes, all right. Jenna's money. There's plenty there, I'm not intending to make her destitute. I wouldn't dream of it. But I reckon you could let me have a million dollars. Without anyone noticing too much.'

'I don't think I could.'

'OK. Two million.'

Jamie was silent for a moment; then he said, 'Charlie, this is ridiculous.'

'No it's not. It's completely reasonable. And one million would be fine, actually. Just joking then. And don't suddenly start calling me Charlie, as if we were best buddies. You hate and despise me, as much as I hate and despise you.'

'You are not going to get a million dollars,' said Jamie, trying to sound confident.

'Well, if I don't get it from you, I'll get it from someone else. Another publisher, maybe. Or a newspaper. I think the press would be delighted with these diaries. They've got everything. Sex. Power. Incest. Murder—'

'Oh don't be absurd,' said Jamie, 'you know that's not true.'

'I think you'd find it was, if you'd read them all. A good editor could easily make it seem true. The newspaper placards certainly would. Anyway – it's up to you. But look, I don't want to put any pressure on you. I'm not in any great hurry. Although I've booked myself on to a flight tomorrow evening. I'd like it settled by then. You'll want to talk to some of the others, I expect. That tight-assed lot you seem to get along with so well.'

'Charlie, they are Jenna's family.'

'No, they're not,' he said, and his voice was suddenly angry, '*I'm* her family. I looked after her when she was broken-hearted over her mother. I've cared for her through it all, sat with her hour after hour, listening to her, drying her tears, helping her through it. I really have. That's what makes people family, Elliott, care and love. And none of them spent much time worrying over my own loss. That was fucking hurtful, I can tell you. It's possible, you know, to love someone rich and successful while you're poor and a failure. Nobody seems able to believe it.'

He stopped.

Jamie was silent; just for a moment, he felt a flash of remorse. It didn't last. 'So, you're so fond of Jenna that you're prepared to drag her family into the gutter? Is that right? Sell all their secrets. At a time when they're trying to come to terms with their own grief?'

'Yes,' said Charlie, 'yes, if you want to put it that way. I am. But I trust it won't be necessary. I trust you'll do it my way. And just in case you're thinking of telling the police, I really wouldn't. The publicity – and I'd make sure there was a great deal – would be pretty unpleasant.'

Jamie realised the telephone was slippery with his sweat. He could feel something running down his face. More sweat. And he felt sick.

'Of course we'll need to talk about it,' he said, hoping his voice didn't sound as shaky to Charlie as it did to him, 'I presume you're prepared to give us a little time.'

'Yeah. Within reason. Oh, and there is something else.'

'Yes?'

'If one word of this gets out to Cathy or Jenna, those diaries go straight to the *Sunday Times*. Or the *Daily Mail*. Or whichever paper will give me the most money. I don't want them caught up in this, I don't want them hurt. Understand?'

Jamie actually laughed then; at the sheer hideous double-thinking.

'Yes, I understand,' he said finally. 'I can't think how you imagine you're going to get away with this, and not involve them, but – yes, I understand what you're saying.'

'Good. Now can I speak to Cathy, please?'

'Sure,' said Jamie. He put the phone down and stood up; his limbs felt very heavy, it was difficult to move them at all. He walked slowly back into Venetia's dining room, looked around for Cathy. She was standing very close to Fergal, gazing up at him, her eyes fixed on his; as he got closer he heard her say, 'I'd just love to go out dancing. Any hope of slipping out, would you say?'

'Cathy,' he said, and was amazed at how normal he sounded, 'your dad's on the phone. He wants to speak to you.'

'Hi, Dad. Where are you? Aren't you coming over?'

'No, sweetheart, I can't. I tried, I got all dressed up even, but I feel really bad. I'm going to go to bed, try and sleep it off. I'll see you in the morning. You having fun?'

She hesitated. 'Not much.'

'That's a shame. Now listen, there's something else. Something's cropped up with my business, I have to fly back tomorrow. You and Jenna can follow on at the weekend, as arranged. That OK?'

'Sure,' said Cathy.

'Good. Now give my love to Jenna and tell her again she was great, won't you?'

'Sure, Dad. I love you. Sleep well.'

'Love you too, darling.'

'What on earth was that about?' asked Boy. 'You look dreadful. Want a drink?'

'Oh God. Yes, please. A stiff one. Thanks. Boy – we need to talk. How soon can we do that?'

'Who's we? If you mean me, right now. I've had quite enough of this lot. Any port in a storm and all that.'

'No, I mean the family. You, Giles, the twins, Kit, if possible. Can we get him over here? And Sebastian, definitely. Is he still here?'

'No, he's gone to meet someone at his club. Said it was important. What is this, can't it wait till tomorrow?'

'No, I don't think it can. If I told you it was to do with those diaries and Charlie Patterson, would you wait till tomorrow?'

Boy's face changed. 'Christ. Probably not. Look – I'll see what I can do. And we'll try and get rid of everyone. Give me half an hour.'

'Mummy, I'm going to go, if you don't mind. I'm very tired and the fog's awful.'

'You can't drive in this, Elspeth. Why don't you stay?'

'I can't possibly stay, I have two children at home. Not everyone has live-in nannies, you know.'

'You sound like that wretched husband of yours,' said Venetia irritably. 'But all right. Leave your car here, though, I'll get someone to find you a taxi. Everything seems to be breaking up, anyway.'

'Oh – all right. Thank you. Well done, Mummy. Lovely evening.'

'Cheers,' said Sebastian. He raised his glass to Keir and smiled. Keir looked around him: the Reform was everything he disapproved of, a bastion of blue-blooded privilege, from its grand staircase and its marble pillars, its book-lined walls and vast leather chairs, to the rather grand humility of its staff and the opulent silence. He tried to ignore a feeling that he quite liked being there.

'Cheers,' he said.

'I mustn't be long. I'm rather tired.'

'I expect you are.'

'This message. From Celia.'

'Yes?' Keir looked nervous.

'It's twofold. I should have written you a letter about it, really. Sorry, Keir.'

'Oh – please don't apologise. I asked for it.'

'Yes, but it's important. I imagine. Anyway, here goes. First thing was, she asked me to tell you that she'd thought of leaving all her shares to you. Not to the two of you. But she decided against it.'

'To me?'

'Yes.'

'Good God.'

'Well – there you are. And when she told Elspeth, later on, Elspeth said she would have liked that.'

'Elspeth would have liked me to have the shares?'

'That's what Celia said.'

Keir stared at him in complete silence; he felt rather as if Sebastian had spoken in a foreign language and he was called upon to translate it. Finally he spoke. 'So it wasn't something they cooked up between them?'

'My dear boy, I have no idea. I'm simply the messenger. I can't interpret for you. I shouldn't have thought so, but I really don't know. I may have spent half a lifetime close to Celia, but I never really understood her. Nobody did. Oliver certainly didn't.'

'He didn't?'

'No, of course not. What husband does understand his wife? I didn't, neither of mine. That's what makes the whole thing so interesting, don't you think? Not understanding them, I mean. All we can hope for is to make them as happy as possible. And that they will do the same for us.'

Keir looked at him rather doubtfully.

'Is that really what you think?'

'It certainly is,' said Sebastian. 'There's a bit more to it than that, of course, but that's the crux of it. I didn't manage to make my first wife happy, unfortunately, and she booted me out in the end, but I was learning, with Pandora. Although not for long enough.'

'No. That must have been very – dreadful.' Keir felt awkward; he didn't usually have this kind of conversation. But it seemed important.

'It was dreadful. Yes, of course. But – one slowly learns to live with even the greatest grief. I shall learn to live with this new one, I dare say. At least I have Kit and Clemmie and now the babies. And Izzie – to an extent. I miss her horribly, but she's very happy over there. Anyway, I'm getting maudlin. Now the second message was – now what was it? Oh yes. Didn't mean a thing to me, but it might to you. She said she had never mentioned Birmingham to Elspeth. She seemed to think it was important you knew that.'

'Yes. Thank you.'

That seemed less extraordinary and Keir realised he had taken it for granted; and thought now what a high regard he must have had for Celia's discretion. He was beginning to feel very uncomfortable.

Sebastian yawned. 'Excuse me. Well, that's it. All done. Sorry it's taken so long. She'd have been awfully cross if she'd known. Must peel off, old chap. Terribly tired. Will you be all right getting home? In this fog?'

'Oh – yes. Yes, of course. It's not that thick. What about you?'

'I'm going to stay here. Tell me, are you enjoying working at Wesley? They publish Kit awfully well, I think.'

'Not as much as I enjoyed working at Lyttons,' said Keir.

'Feeling better?' said Marcus tenderly. They were in the bar at Claridges.

'Yes. Much. Thank you.'

'Good. You just needed a little cherishing. You clearly don't get enough these days.' He refilled her glass.

'I certainly don't,' said Elspeth, 'not even from my mother.'

'I suspect your mother doesn't like me.'

'You suspect right.'

'Does she – know?'

631

'Oh yes. And it really annoys her. Mostly because you annoyed her. When you were in charge of Lyttons London.'

'Pity. I like your mother. She's beautiful and intelligent. Like you.'

'Oh dear.' Elspeth sighed.

'What was that about?'

'For a beautiful and intelligent person I'm not doing very well. Made a complete mess of my life in almost every direction.'

'Well – you must let me help you get it in order again.'

'Yes.' She looked at him and tried to feel more enthusiastic. This had been a mistake. It wasn't working.

'And – I can't – persuade you to come and relax in my suite for a little while?'

'No. I'm sorry. I really have got to get back to the children. And – it doesn't seem quite appropriate somehow. After today.'

'Of course not. I understand.' He always understood. It was all part of his charm. Wasn't it? Of course it was. And he was being very sweet about it all. She had led him to think she was about to tumble into bed with him. She had thought she was. She had thought it would help. But – it wouldn't.

She hadn't wanted it – or him – at all. What she wanted had been looking at her across the church; what she wanted never told her she was beautiful, and seldom that he was pleased to see her; what she wanted did not express a desire to cherish her, or to help her get her life into order; but what she wanted clearly didn't want her.

She made a huge effort, put that other person out of her mind, kissed Marcus and said, 'I'm so sorry, but now I really must go.'

'Of course. I'll see you to your car.'

'I didn't come in my car,' she said, 'the fog's really thick. I came in a taxi.'

'Then I'll see you into a taxi. And look forward to tomorrow.'

They walked to the entrance of Claridges; the traffic was crawling down Brook Street at about five miles an hour.

'That's hideous,' he said, 'I can't let you go out in that.'

'Of course you can. I really do have to get home. Mrs Wilson can't stay after midnight.'

'Then I'll come in the cab with you.'

'No, Marcus, honestly, it's fine.'

'It's not fine. I wouldn't sleep. I'll see you safely to your door. And don't worry, I won't try and force an entry.'

She smiled. And tried to tell herself it was nice to be treated with such care.

'OK,' said Jamie, 'that's the situation. What are we doing to do? Just tell me what you all think.'

He looked around the group sitting on the vast sofas either side of the fireplace in the drawing room. They looked, above all else, exhausted. And beyond that, Adele was tearful, Venetia flushed and angry, Sebastian, who had been contacted at his club, was brooding, Kit fearful and Giles completely stunned.

Giles spoke first. 'I feel so dreadful,' he said, 'I should have destroyed them immediately. Or at least put them in the bank or something. I shouldn't have kept them. Whenever I think of any of our children reading them, I feel quite sick. Never mind the public at large. I knew they were dangerous, a – a kind of time bomb, sitting there, I blame myself terribly—'

'Giles,' said Adele gently, 'don't be silly. They've been sitting there for about fifty years, you can't blame yourself. And you tried to do the right thing, you kept them to yourself, it was only – God, only yesterday, we even knew they existed. If anyone's to blame it's me, dragging the others out of their hiding place.'

'Look, we're not going to get anywhere by going down this road,' said Boy. He sounded impatient. 'It's absolutely nobody's fault, with the possible exception of Celia, writing the bloody things all those years. Now I'm a simple sort of fellow. It seems to me we either give Patterson the money or we don't. If we don't, I think he'll do what he says. He's very angry, and clearly a bit unbalanced, and those diaries are temptation beyond endurance for him. I'd say give him the money, but it's not for me to decide.'

'I think he probably is unbalanced,' said Adele, 'and I know this is going to make me very unpopular, but I do feel rather sorry for him. He has had a horribly difficult time, I think he really did love Barty—'

'Oh, Dell! How can you say that?'

'Quite easily. He was absolutely shattered at her funeral. He's also been wonderful to Jenna, and none of us has expressed any appreciation for that at all.'

'Oh, for God's sake Adele,' said Kyle, 'he's had a ball, ever since he married Barty. He's had the run of South Lodge and Number Seven, he's bought boats, lodges, clothes, cars, a business—'

'Kyle,' she said, and her voice was very quiet, 'I know all that. I also know that if you're very unhappy and very angry, things like clothes and cars don't help very much.'

They all stared at her; Jamie looked at his hands, twisting his fingers this way and that, Kyle glowered into his glass.

'Well,' said Giles finally, 'we all know which way you're going to vote. You'd better go and hand over the money yourself, Adele, give him a nice soothing cuddle into the bargain, suggest he goes for some analysis.'

'Giles,' said Venetia, seeing Adele's face pale, her eyes swim with tears, 'that isn't fair. I can see exactly what Dell means. She's only trying to get at what's behind this. And she's right, we haven't been very – thoughtful towards him.'

'Oh for goodness sake,' said Boy, 'the man's a crook.'

'And a confidence trickster,' said Kyle. 'You don't know the half of it, I'm afraid.'

They all stared at him.

'What do you mean?' said Giles.

Kyle told them.

Keir walked out of the Reform Club and stood staring into the fog; he felt very odd. His father had once taken him to Blackpool for the day and they had gone on the Big Dipper. He had come off it feeling as if he had been turned inside out, not sure where he was, what his feet were doing, what he could possibly do next.

He felt like that now. He had been so sure, so absolutely sure, that Elspeth had been interested only in her own progress, her own success; that he had become a minor consideration to her, that his departure from her life had been little more than an inconvenience, a convenience, indeed, in many ways, enabling her to do exactly what she liked with the rest of her life. That had hurt him, in fact, far more deeply than her affair with Marcus Forrest. And now he had learned, and there was no doubt that it was true, that she would have been happy for Celia to give him all the shares, to have none for herself. Nothing could have contradicted more firmly all his stubborn preconceptions, nothing could have told him more clearly he had got everything absolutely wrong.

And nothing could have made him realise more clearly how much he still loved her. He wanted to see her. More than anything else in the world.

'Can you give him a million dollars anyway?' said Giles.

'Is there a million in Jenna's trust fund?'

'Oh yes,' said Jamie.

'And – it wouldn't leave her – hard up?' Kit's voice was tentative, quite anxious.

'Absolutely not.'

'Because if it did, then we should try and find the money. Or some of it. I mean, it seems very unfair, that she should have to buy us out of trouble.'

'Kit!' said Giles. 'That's a bit harsh.'

'I don't think so. Having the diaries published would hurt us far more than it would hurt her. She'd be safely in New York, she's an Elliott, after all, not a Lytton, it's hardly Jenna's problem—'

'What is? What's not my problem?'

Jenna was standing in the doorway, looking round the room, smiling at them; intrigued and just very slightly anxious at the same time.

It took over half an hour for the taxi to travel from Brook Street to Albert Bridge Road; Elspeth sat willing it to go faster, longing for the journey to be over, trying to respond to Marcus's kisses, feigning a greater concern over both the fog and her children than she actually felt.

'This is so, so good of you,' she said, as they finally reached her block, 'I'm truly grateful. I'd ask you in, only Mrs Wilson would be shocked and anyway, I think you probably ought to get back. Good night, Marcus, and thank you for everything. Ring me tomorrow.'

'I will.'

She had disappeared through the main door that led in from the street when Marcus realised she had left her fur stole behind. Well, it was as good an excuse as any. She might even have left it on purpose.

He told the cabbie to wait, and ran across the road after her. Keir Brown, approaching in his own cab from a different direction, saw his unmistakably tall, stylish figure disappearing through the front door.

Boy, the most practised liar, spoke first.

'We were just saying that it must be difficult for you. Having family on both sides of the Atlantic. Not knowing quite where you belonged. And Kit was saying that wasn't exactly a problem. Rather the reverse, in fact.'

There was a silence, while she looked at them all; then she said, 'No you weren't. You weren't saying anything like that. I don't know what it was, but it wasn't that.'

Jamie looked at her carefully.

'We were talking about your money, Jenna. Saying it wasn't exactly a problem. Although I know you see it as one. In a way.'

She was silent, her eyes moving over them, one by one, trying to evaluate what was actually going on.

'But why were you talking about it now? All of you? I don't understand.'

'People always talk about money, Jenna, on days like today,' said Sebastian firmly. 'It's a rather nasty by-product of death.'

'Yes, but why my money? What's my money got to do with Celia's death? Unless she left me some. I thought you'd gone home, Sebastian,' she added.

'Well she did,' said Venetia, grabbing gratefully at this straw, and indeed it was true. 'Leave you some money, I mean, quite a small bequest, actually, and one of her pearl collars which she thought you'd like.'

Jenna smiled with pleasure.

'Really? How lovely. She was so good to me. And one of those gorgeous collars, that is just – well, the best. Goodness, I can't wait to try it on. Oh well – I must get back to the others. We're dancing, I hope it isn't making too much noise.'

'No, no, it's fine,' said Boy. 'What did you come down for, anyway, darling?'

'Oh – some lemonade. Everyone's so hot and thirsty.'

'I'll make a big jug and bring it up,' saiu Venetia quickly, 'and Lucy really ought to go to bed, she's so much younger than the rest of you.'

'Oh, but she's having a ball,' said Jenna. 'Don't worry, nobody's doing anything unsuitable. And I'll get the lemonade myself. You look as if you're awfully busy down here. Thank you. Lovely evening, Venetia.'

She went into the kitchen, made the lemonade and fetched some glasses, then as she went past the drawing room with the tray, put her head round the door, smiled, and said, 'Come up and join us, why don't you?'

And then, seeing them relax, smiled at them all again, closed the door quite firmly, and walked to the first floor, into the room that was Boy's study, closed that door, and picked up the phone. She was not Laurence Elliott's daughter for nothing. She knew how to deceive when she wanted to. And she knew a lie when she heard it.

Keir paid off the taxi, and started to walk through the fog. He had no idea where he was walking, he just needed to keep moving. To get away from Battersea, from Marcus: and from Elspeth. He walked and he walked, first across the bridge, and then in a zigzag across Chelsea, taking first left then right turns, doubling back on himself, almost wanting to be lost, so that he had something else to think about, to worry about.

Getting lost was not difficult that night; there is something about fog that distorts direction, confuses distance. After half an hour he had no idea where he was. Some of the streets were wide, some narrow; at one point he thought he was in St James's, at another he seemed to be approaching Buckingham Palace, and then, almost illogically, he was at Hyde Park Corner. It was all a swirling, freezing blur. He felt numb, he was so cold, not just his hands and feet but his entire body, it was oddly hard to force his legs to keep moving; his brain began to get mercifully numb, too. He would just go on like this, walking all night if necessary, and wouldn't be able to think, wouldn't be able to remember anything at all. Least of all seeing Marcus Forrest running into what was, after all, his own front door.

'Mrs Hardwicke? It's Jenna. I'm sorry to ring you so late, but could I possibly speak to Mr Patterson? He might be asleep, I know he's not well, but it's really important. Yes, thank you, I'll wait.'

She waited, sipping at the iced lemonade, tapping her foot, trying to keep calm. If Boy came in now—

Mrs Hardwicke sounded apologetic.

'I'm sorry, Jenna, but Mr Patterson's not in his room.'

'Not in his room? But – well, is he in the drawing room, maybe, or the snug? Pardon me, the morning room? Would you mind checking?'

Mrs Hardwicke checked; no, Mr Patterson definitely wasn't there.

'He – you don't think he had to go and see a doctor, do you? He had a terrible headache earlier.'

'I don't know, Jenna. I haven't seen him at all. I'm sorry.'

'Oh – OK. Can you ask him to call me when he does get in, do you think? Leave a note out for him, if you're going to bed. I'm at Mrs Warwick's house. No, I'm sure they won't mind. Thank you, Mrs Hardwicke.'

She opened the door cautiously; no sound from the drawing room. She went quickly upstairs, deposited the tray of drinks on the floor outside the playroom, and put her head round the door, beckoning to Cathy. Cathy came out reluctantly; she had been dancing with Fergal.

'What?'

'When you spoke to Charlie, where was he?'

'At Adele's, of course.'

'Are you sure? Did he say that's where he was?'

'I suppose not. But he said he wasn't well, he was going back to bed. Where else could he have been?'

'I don't know. But he's not there, and as far as I could make out from Mrs Hardwicke, he hasn't been there all evening. It's a bit odd.'

'Oh, I'm sure he's fine,' said Cathy, 'he's old enough to take care of himself. Maybe he's gone to get some fresh air, maybe he's gone to a bar somewhere. Look, come on, Jenna, let's get back to the party. It's such fun.'

'Yes – all right,' said Jenna.

Alan Stewart had had a rather good evening: drinking with his mates in a bar in Soho. One of them was getting married on Saturday; this was his stag night. The last time Alan had seen him, he'd been sitting in the gutter in Windmill Street, holding an empty bottle of champagne, pretending it was a guitar, and singing 'Lipstick on Your Collar'. Alan had wondered if maybe he ought to have stayed with him, but a couple of the other lads were still around, even if they were pretty legless as well; and Peckham was quite a long way away. In this fog, and on his motorbike, it was going to take a while.

Rather unsteadily, he waved to them all and wove his way in the direction of Piccadilly.

Charlie decided he'd had enough of the Savoy. He'd had a very good dinner, in anticipation of his new wealth, and he wanted to get his head down. He had a lot to work out: and no doubt a lot of crap to listen to. He'd been very careful not to drink too much. Plenty of time for that, when he was safely back in New York.

He picked up the holdall, and made his way out to the Savoy courtyard. The fog was so thick it looked completely impenetrable. There was not a taxi to be seen.

★

It really wasn't his fault, Alan told himself over and over again as he sat in casualty, waiting to have his arm bandaged. Nothing much wrong, just a bad cut. But the chap he'd hit, he obviously wasn't so good. They'd taken him off somewhere. He'd just walked straight out in front of Alan. Off the pavement and into the road. At Hyde Park Corner of all places. Just hadn't looked at all. Not that you could see much in the fog. But Alan had had his lights on and he'd been going really slowly. And yes, he'd had a few drinks, but not so many he didn't know what he was doing. The road being icy hadn't helped, he'd slammed his brakes on, but he'd skidded, on and on. That was really how he'd hit the bloke. He'd just skidded into him. He'd felt the blow, the heavy shuddering thud as he hit him. He'd remember that for the rest of his life: the thud and the cry. And then the silence.

But – it was going to be all right, surely. He hadn't killed him or anything, had he? Had he? Oh God. Oh dear, dear God.

CHAPTER 49

He supposed he should let them know. He didn't want the girls worried. And they might be, if they found he wasn't at Cheyne Walk. He would phone and tell Elliott that he was staying at the Savoy for the night, that he'd be back at the house in the morning, and to tell the girls. It was an absolute bitch, this fog. It looked set for days. It would mean his flight would probably be delayed as well. Which would be OK, but not exactly comfortable. Very uncomfortable, in fact. Maybe he should just stay at the Savoy.

He picked up the phone and asked for the Warwicks' phone number.

It was Giles who seemed to have found the solution. The wonderfully simple solution.

'I think,' Boy had said, 'we're going about this the wrong way altogether. We should call his bluff, tell the police, get him arrested. He's committed a burglary, for God's sake. We're just assuming we've got to go along with him, play it on his terms. Why should we do that?'

'Because, as he said, there'd be some pretty unpleasant publicity,' said Jamie, 'he's only got to make a song and dance when he's removed from the house, or worse still at the airport, and the press would be on to it. On to the fact that the diaries exist. Some scandalous diaries. That in itself is dangerous. And he'd be let out on bail, almost certainly, and God knows what he'd do then.'

And that was when Giles had said it. 'I've just realised,' he said, and he looked quite surprised himself, 'he can't possibly sell them.'

'Why on earth not?'

'We're being utterly stupid. We know the law of copyright, for God's sake. We've completely failed to realise a very important fact.'

'Which is?' said Boy.

'No newspaper can publish those diaries. They're copyright. The copyright of the person who wrote them. It's out of the question.'

'You're right,' said Kit. 'Of course. Why on earth didn't we think of that? We're all panicking. Giles, you're a genius. Let him have them, let him do his worst.'

There was a silence; they all digested this, panic briefly eased. Only briefly.

'That may be right, of course,' said Adele.

'It is right.'

'Fine. But do you really think that's all there is to it?' She was white, trembling, seemed near to tears.

'What else is there? It's perfectly simple. No one can publish the things.'

'So what? Do you really think that's the end of it?'

'Yes, of course. Calm down, Adele, for heaven's sake, you're being hysterical.'

'No,' said Sebastian, 'she has a point. There are other things Patterson can do, I'm afraid. He can talk. To all manner of people. A clever journalist could make a pretty good article out of that, hearsay or not. With all kinds of meaningful phrases like "impeccable source" and "a close friend of the family". And I believe you can use two hundred and fifty words, or something like that, it's fair usage, without impinging on copyright. Nicely illustrated with family photographs. Specially ones of Celia.'

'Oh, Christ,' said Giles.

'And just think of that,' said Adele, 'think of those two hundred and fifty words. What exactly do you think they might say? Quite a lot. Most of it, I would say. All our most private and personal lives, dragged into the public domain. Oh dear. I don't think I can bear this.'

She got up, started pacing the room, tears streaming down her face. Venetia went over to her, put her arm round her.

'Dell, come on. It's not so bad.'

'It is, it's awful, horrible.'

'She's right, I'm afraid,' said Giles slowly, 'apart from the personal aspect, Lyttons just can't afford any more scandal. We've had enough of it. I still have nightmares about *Deer Mountain* and what that did to us.'

There was another long pause; panic was rising again in the room, almost palpably.

'Of course,' said Kyle, 'you could always take out an injunction. That will stop him. He won't be able to do anything then.'

They all stared at him.

'Of course,' said Boy, beaming. 'Of *course*. There's our answer. Kyle, you're a genius. Why on earth didn't we think of that before? We bloody well should have done. Shall we ring the police now?'

'Hold on, hold on,' said Sebastian. 'Let's just think about this a bit. It isn't that easy to get an injunction. You have to show a judge you've got a pretty good reason for doing it. That you're going to be very seriously damaged by publication.'

'Sebastian,' said Giles testily, 'I do know about injunctions. I – we – have been involved in a few in my time. And of course it's not easy. But I think we could get one. Especially as he's stolen the damn diaries.'

'What do you actually have to do to get one?' said Boy.

'You have to go with your solicitor to a judge and make your case. Swear an affidavit. You can do it very quickly, once the judge has agreed, but he has to agree.'

'So – the first thing is to talk to our solicitor?'

'Yes.'

'Should we telephone him now?' said Kit.

'Seems a bit drastic,' said Venetia.

'Venetia, this is more than a bit drastic.'

'I don't think we need do it tonight,' said Giles finally. 'It's very late, Patterson thinks he's got us where he wants us, and he certainly can't do anything. Half the country's ground to a halt with this fog. I'd suggest we speak to the lawyers in the morning. Plenty of time.'

'And the police,' said Kit, 'have him arrested?'

'I think,' said Adele, 'that would be unnecessarily cruel. To the children, I mean. Think what it would do to them, waking up to find him being led off in handcuffs.'

'But Adele—'

'I think that's right,' said Sebastian. 'If we can stop him with an injunction, it's far cleaner, less distressing for everyone.'

'Yes, but we don't know we can. Not for sure.'

'Well, if we can't, then arresting him won't necessarily stop him, either. I agree with Adele, I hate the idea of some brutal arrest. Especially in her house,' he added with a grin. 'No, we've got the might of the law behind us. Let's rely on that.'

It was Jenna who heard the phone first: she had been listening for it, waiting for Charlie to ring. She fled down the top flight of stairs, made Boy's study just in time. She thought.

'Hallo?'

'Hallo? Hallo, who is this?' It was Boy's voice, on the phone in the hall, charged with anxiety. 'Boy, it's all right. It's for me. Sorry, so sorry.'

'Jenna? Who on earth is ringing you at this time of night?'

'It's – well, it's a friend.'

'A friend?'

'Yes. Boy, I'm so sorry. I rang him earlier and gave him this number. I met him the other night. I'm really sorry.'

'I should hope so. Funny sort of behaviour, ringing you in a strange house at nearly midnight. Get him off the phone straight away, will you?'

'Yes. Yes, I will.'

She waited; the extension clicked off.

'Charlie?' she said, very quietly. 'Wherever are you?'

Elspeth was playing with the children: a very complicated game of hide and seek. Whoever was hiding had a bell and they had to keep ringing it till they were found. It was a very persistent bell, on and on; she could not find Cecilia anywhere, she was somewhere out there in the fog, it was getting quite worrying, and the bell was still ringing – she woke up with a jump. The phone! At this hour! At – she looked at her luminous alarm clock – at two in the morning. What on earth had happened? She got out of bed, went out to the hall, shivering, cursing Keir for the hundredth time, for refusing to have a phone by the bed.

'Hallo?'

'Mrs Brown? Mrs Elspeth Brown?'

'Yes.'

'I'm sorry to disturb you in the middle of the night like this, Mrs Brown. This is St Anthony's Hospital, Old Brompton Road. I'm so sorry to bring you bad news, but your husband has been brought in, knocked down by a motorbike—'

At about three in the morning a stiff breeze started up in the English Channel; by three-thirty it had reached the outskirts of the capital, flying up the river, whipping at the fog, tearing it to shreds. By five, the air was almost clear, sound and sight restored to the city. Jenna had been awake most of the night, staring at the lightless window; as her open curtain suddenly fluttered, she leapt out of bed, looked out. She could see the streetlights, see the river; she could go.

Elspeth paced up and down her room, imprisoned by the fog, knowing no one could help her, not her parents, not even Marcus, drinking endless cups of tea, arranging for a neighbour to mind the children, making phone call after phone call, to silent taxi ranks, willing them to answer, terrified that Keir would die without her, without knowing she loved him, making bargains with God – if he was all right, if she got there in time, even, she'd give up work, never go near Lyttons again, go back to Glasgow, to that terrible flat, have six more babies . . . and then she heard the breeze suddenly in the trees outside her window and looked out. She could see the street; she could even see the park opposite. She could go.

Jenna knew she had to turn left out of the house; after that she was a bit hazy. She had hoped to find a cab, but there weren't any. The city might no longer be blind, but it was resting. She walked on. She knew she had to stay by the river; that way she couldn't go very wrong. She had asked Lucas, casually, where the Savoy was, and he had said by the river, towards the City. So – she'd be all right. It just might take rather a long time.

Elspeth decided to walk; if she saw a cab on the way, she could hail it, but it wasn't so very far to the Brompton Road. She could walk it in half an hour. Run it in less. And mostly she ran.

Charlie Patterson had woken up very early; he had slept rather badly. Not surprising, really, he supposed. It was a miracle he'd slept at all. He got up, pulled his curtains aside and looked out. It was half past five. The fog had gone. Completely gone. He could see lights moving on the river, hear the occasional car moving along the Embankment. Thank God. He could get his plane after all.

He had decided not to go back to Cheyne Walk. He had what he needed with him; he had the diaries, he had his wallet, he had his air ticket and his passport. The girls knew he had to go back to New York on business, they wouldn't worry. And he'd feel a lot safer at the airport. He might even get an earlier flight. You never knew what that lot might do. They might even call the police. He didn't think so, but they might.

Yes, that's what he'd do. He'd check out as soon as he could and make his way to London airport. He lifted the phone and ordered breakfast – he could get used to this life very quickly – and started to run a bath.

'Yes? Can I help you?' She didn't sound as if she wanted to help, sitting there in Casualty reception, looking officious.

'My name's Mrs Brown. Mrs Elspeth Brown.'

'Yes?'

'Mrs Keir Brown, actually.'

'Yes?'

'My – my husband's here. He was brought in last night?'

'Well he won't be here now. We don't keep people overnight here. This is Casualty. He'll either have gone or be in a ward.'

'He certainly hasn't gone,' said Elspeth. This was rather like a slap in the face, bringing her round from a faint. 'Could you tell me where he might be, please? Which ward?'

'What name did you say?'

'Brown. Keir Brown.'

'We've got a lot of Browns,' said the nurse severely, rather as if Elspeth should apologise.

She ran her finger down a list of names; finally it stopped. She looked at Elspeth in silence. He's died, Elspeth thought, it's too late, I'm too late, he's dead.

'You all right, young lady?'

It was a policeman; walking towards her, looking rather frightening in his helmet and heavy boots.

'Yes,' said Jenna, 'yes, I'm fine, thank you.'

'What are you doing out on your own?'

'Just – going for a walk.'

'At not quite six in the morning. Funny time for a walk. Not running away from anyone, are you?'

'No, of course not. Really, I'm fine. I was hoping to find a cab, but—'

'Don't get many cabs this time of day. You from America?'

'Yes. Yes, that's right.'

'And – where are you walking to?'

'The Savoy Hotel. How am I doing?'

'The Savoy? Well, you're nearly there. But you've taken a bit of a detour.'

'Have I? Oh dear.'

She was afraid of that. She had reached Parliament Square, had recognised it, of course, but had walked straight ahead, down Whitehall, away from the river. And wasn't sure how to find it again.

'Yes. But at the end of this street, you'll find Trafalgar Square. Turn right up the Strand and you're nearly there.'

'Oh, thank you. Thank you very much.'

She smiled up at him; but he didn't get out of her way. He stayed there, looking rather stern, frowning down at her.

'What's at the Savoy Hotel, then?'

'My – my stepfather.'

'Oh yes? And why isn't he with you?'

'Well, because – because he doesn't know I'm coming to see him. I was staying with friends last night. Relatives, I mean.'

'Which? Friends or relatives?'

'Both. Actually. Yes.'

'Dear oh dear. I'm not sure I can allow this. You walking around all on your own in the dark.'

'But – but I really need to get there. It's important.'

'So's your safety. How old are you?'

'Six – seventeen,' said Jenna staunchly.

'Oh yes. And my name's Father Christmas. Where's your mum?'

'She's – she's dead,' said Jenna and burst into tears.

Charlie lay in the bath, contemplating his future. It was going to be pretty good, but there would be problems. He hadn't really thought them all through. Hadn't had an opportunity, really. Diplomatic relations with the trustees would definitely be broken off; Jenna was very cute, she'd work out that things had changed. He might even leave New York, move over to the West Coast or something, where he could really start again. Jenna was growing up fast, she'd be going to college soon, and she was so independent, much more so than Cathy. She wouldn't need him. She wouldn't need anyone. He didn't like that thought very much. But it was true. And there were all those Lyttons and Millers, and Elliotts, of course,

644

they'd look after her. She'd be fine. Wouldn't she? Of course she would. There was a knock at the door; he felt his stomach lurch. Who could that be, at six in the morning?

He got out of the bath, saw a newspaper pushed under his door. That was all right then. But he realised he was actually feeling a bit jumpy. All his icy cool of the day before seemed to have deserted him. They'd had a while to think now, to plan; who knows what they might do? Maybe he'd cut breakfast. Just check out, take a cab, head straight off to the airport, see if he could get on an earlier flight.

Yes, that's what he'd do.

'Right, I've located him for you. But you won't be able to see him. Not now.'

Elspeth licked her dry lips. The morgue, she was going to say the morgue, of course she wouldn't be allowed to see a corpse, a corpse that was − had been − Keir . . .

'He's on Men's Surgical.'

'So − he's not − not dead?'

'Dead? Of course he's not dead. They wouldn't keep him if he was, we have quite a lot of pressure for beds you know.'

'Of course,' said Elspeth humbly, 'I'm sure you do. Er − where is Men's Surgical?'

'It's on the second floor. But you won't—'

Her voice tailed away; Elspeth was gone, running towards the lift.

Izzie woke up feeling terribly sick. She knew why she felt sick, it was excitement. This was the day she was going to see Ann Thynne, to arrange to have her tubes checked. She might even be able to do it in the next day or two. And Nick had agreed to come with her, to meet Mrs Thynne so that she could explain to him exactly what the situation was, and what Izzie's chances were. Nick wasn't exactly looking forward to it, he said he preferred the old way, of babies flying in with the stork, but if it was going to make Izzie happy, then he'd do whatever she wanted. Especially, he added, if it meant extra sex.

She turned over to him, kissed him.

'You all right, Princess?'

'I'm fine. Yes. Well—'

'What?'

'I feel a bit sick. I need a cup of tea.'

'That'd be nice. Make one for me while you're about it, would you?'

'Nick! I thought you might get it. Just for once.'

'OK.' He sighed. 'OK. Just give me a minute or two. Do I get a reward for it?'

'If you mean what I think you mean,' said Izzie, kissing him again, 'you might. Providing I feel better.'

'You're a hard woman, Miss Brooke.'

'I know.'

'Very hard.'

'Well – you knew that when you took me on. Please, Nick. And could you bring me some water as well. I'm really thirsty.'

'Anything else? Cookie, peanut-jelly sandwich?'

She shuddered.

'No thanks.'

Five minutes later Nick reappeared with the tea. Izzie took a gulp of it, stared at him for a moment and then fled to the bathroom. She came back looking rather green.

'Sorry. It must have been that salmon mousse of Venetia's last night. I thought it was very rich. I'll be all right in a minute.'

'No reward then?'

'No reward, sorry. But I do feel better. Maybe later. Let's go back to sleep.'

'Tell you what,' said the policeman.

'What?' said Jenna warily.

'I'll come with you. To the Savoy. See you safely in. See you right up to your stepfather's room.'

'Oh, but—'

'It's either that, or I take you to the police station, get you sent back to your folks. Or your friends, or whatever they are.'

'All right,' she said with a sigh, 'thank you. Thank you very much.'

'Good morning,' Elspeth smiled at the nurse; she did not smile back. She was very young and carrying a jug of water and a bedpan; she looked harassed.

'You shouldn't be up here,' was all she said.

'Shouldn't I? I've just been told my husband's here. He was brought in last night, after a motorbike accident, I've only just heard, couldn't I see him, just for a moment?'

'Would that be Mr Brown?'

'Yes. Yes that's right.'

'I really can't allow that, I'm afraid.'

'Oh please! Please, please. I don't even know what happened, just that he was hit by a motorbike.'

'Well, I can tell you that. He's got a fractured femur—'

'What's that?'

'Thigh bone.'

'Oh my God.'

'Yes, quite nasty. He had to have it set in theatre. And he's got a broken wrist as well, and a few cuts and bruises. But he's fine. Nothing to worry about. You can come back and see him at visiting time, I'll tell him you were here.'

'When's that?'

'Six o'clock.'

'Six! What, this evening? But that's nearly twelve hours away.'

'I know that,' said the nurse patiently, 'but those are the rules. I'm sorry. I'll tell him you came, shall I? Now—'

'Nurse Hall! Quickly please. Mr Jackson needs that bedpan urgently.'

'Yes, Sister.'

Nurse Hall flashed Elspeth an apologetic smile and moved off for the delights of Mr Jackson and his bedpan.

Elspeth could hear what must be official footsteps approaching along the corridor; she looked wildly round, saw a sign that said 'Gents' and shot into it. An elderly man in pyjamas sat in one of the open cubicles, smoking. He whipped the cigarette behind his back.

'You a nurse?' he said anxiously.

'No,' said Elspeth, 'don't worry, I won't tell. Er – are you on Men's Surgical?'

'Yes. That's right.'

'My husband came in last night. He's called Keir Brown. He's quite – young. Broken leg. Do you know him?'

'Oh yes. Nice young chap. Lost his temper with Sister, though, when she wouldn't let him have a cup of tea soon as he came round. Not a good idea.'

'That sounds like Keir. Well – where is he? In the ward, I mean?'

'Oh – by the window. Right-hand side. You going in?'

'Yes.'

'Well, you'd better watch it. Sister'll have you in terrible trouble. Take you to Matron, I wouldn't wonder.'

'I think I can handle that,' said Elspeth. She opened the door again, slipped out and looked into the ward. By the bed, which she now knew contained Keir, stood a doctor and someone who was clearly Sister; she ducked back quickly into the Gents.

'Not quite the right time,' she said. 'Could I possibly have one of your ciggies? I'll bring you in a whole pack this evening.'

Charlie tried to cancel the breakfast, but they said it was too late, it was already on its way. Well – he could use a coffee at least. And they weren't really likely to try and arrest him or anything. In fact, it was extremely unlikely. He held too many of the cards.

There was a knock at the door. Another lurch of the stomach; he opened it slowly. He was beginning to feel very nervous. The waiter trundled in the trolley, started removing the lids of salvers as if he was doing conjuring tricks, revealing sausages, bacon, eggs; and then there were small rolls of butter, toast, fruit juice, marmalade.

It was a terrible temptation, but – it would all take time. He should never have told Jenna where he was last night—

He signed for the breakfast, seized a couple of the pieces of toast and made a bacon sandwich, took a gulp of coffee and picked up the leather bag. He wanted to get out of here. Fast.

'Well, where is she, for heaven's sake?' said Venetia. 'She can't have just vanished in the middle of the night.'

Since this was exactly what had happened, Cathy felt rather irritated.

'I don't know,' she said again.

'Does anyone know?'

Cathy shrugged. 'I don't know, I haven't seen anyone else, have I? Why don't you ask them?'

She was a lot less sweet when her father wasn't around.

Venetia glared at her and slammed the door, went along the corridor, knocking on doors. Where was Jenna, did anyone know, had anyone any idea? No, she wasn't downstairs, yes, she might have gone for a walk, but surely not at six-thirty in the morning and without leaving a note, yes, she was sure there was no note.

She went downstairs to tell Boy; he said they should maybe give it another thirty minutes and then phone the police. He was just picking up the phone to do so when Lucas appeared.

'I think she might have gone to the Savoy,' he said.

They had pulled the curtains round the bed; she slipped in, looked at him. He was lying on his back, his eyes closed, frowning. He looked terrible. His face was bruised, there was a cut on his forehead, his left arm was encased in plaster up to the elbow, his leg was in some kind of pulley arrangement, attached to the bed.

She sat down very gingerly on the edge of the bed; he frowned more ferociously, turned his head away from her. 'I will not take that disgusting stuff,' he said, 'I want something for the pain and I want some tea. It's not a lot to ask. I—'

'It's the way you ask it, though, Keir,' said Elspeth, 'that's what makes the difference, don't you think?'

He opened his eyes, saw her, frowned, clearly trying to focus, to establish whether she was really there or if he was hallucinating. She smiled at him, picked up the good hand, and kissed it, then leaned over him and kissed him very tenderly on the lips. And then sat back smiling at him. He continued to frown.

'We don't have long,' she said, 'so before I get thrown out by Sister, I want to tell you two things. I love you. And I'm very sorry.'

'My God,' he said slowly. 'Oh, Elspeth, if you only knew—'

'I don't want to know,' she said, 'anything at all. It's all irrelevant. Except this.' And she kissed him again, felt his mouth move under hers, felt a great surge of love, and – rather surprisingly, under the circumstances – of longing. Well, that would have to wait awhile.

'I love you,' she said again.

The curtains were whisked aside. An outraged Sister stood there. Anyone studying her expression would have assumed she had caught them *in flagrante*, at the very least.

'What is going on here?' she said. 'How dare you come into this ward, out of visiting hours, interfering with routine and important medical procedure. This is a seriously ill patient. I must ask you to leave at once. At once.'

The seriously ill patient spoke.

'She's just going,' he said. 'It's all right. But I have to tell her something first. Two things. And then I'll take that disgusting muck of yours. I love her too. Very, very much. And I'm very sorry too.'

It was only a hunch, Lucas said, but suddenly last night she'd asked him where the Savoy was, how far away and was it too far to walk. She'd seemed a bit agitated, he said, but once she'd looked out at the fog again, seen that there wasn't even a single car or taxi on the street, she'd calmed down.

'I'll ring them,' said Boy, 'see if Mr Patterson's there. If he is, we'd better get over fast. God knows what he might be up to now.'

He had paid the bill, was standing in the courtyard, waiting for the doorman to get him a taxi. It might take a bit of time, the doorman said, there still weren't many around.

And then he saw the policeman. Turning into the Savoy courtyard. Walking rather purposefully.

'Shit,' said Charlie, 'oh shit.'

And because there seemed nowhere else to go, he turned back into the hotel and headed for the cloakrooms.

He had been in there for about ten minutes, wondering how long it might be before he could risk going out again, when another man came in; a man who had been in the restaurant the previous night.

'Great goings-on out there,' he said to Charlie, 'policeman, asking all sorts of questions, staff running about hither and thither, looking for someone. And a young girl crying. Crying her eyes out.'

'What – what does she look like? The girl?'

'Oh, pretty litttle thing. Sixteen or so, I'd say. Got red hair.'

Charlie hesitated: only for a moment. Then he walked out of the cloakroom, and up the steps into the main reception area. Jenna saw him and stopped crying, absolutely and at once. She went up to him and put her arms around him.

'Hallo, Charlie,' she said, 'thank goodness you're here. I'm *so* pleased to see you.'

'You OK now, Princess?'

'I'm fine. Yes. Thank you.'

'Good. Mike, we'll see you later. Got any plans for the morning?'

'I thought I'd go for a walk on Hampstead Heath. Now the fog's gone. I hear it's really lovely.'

'Great idea. If you see a stork, have a word with it for me, would you? I'd still kind of prefer it their way.'

'Sure,' said Mike.

Sebastian walked slowly up the road towards his house; he felt very tired suddenly. And rather alone. Very alone, in fact. God, he was going to miss her. Miss them all.

There was a house for sale, just two down from his own; it had been for sale for some time. It was very pretty and exactly like his own, only with a bigger garden. There was a man outside it, hammering an 'Under Offer' sign over the 'For Sale' sign. He supposed it had been bought by some young family. He hoped they would be nice: and friendly. He had no sooner had the thought than he realised he had never in his entire life taken any interest whatsoever in his neighbours, and certainly not to hope they'd be friendly. Rather the reverse.

He stopped, looked up at the house; it needed a lot of work done to it. The man hammering the sign up looked at him.

'Morning.'

'Good morning,' said Sebastian.

'Nice place, isn't it?'

'Very.'

'You live round here?'

'Yes. Just two houses along.'

'Well you've got some very nice new neighbours.'

'I have?'

'Yes. Young man came in, put the offer down on it just this morning.'

'Really?'

'Yes. Charming, he was.' He paused, stood back, looked at his handiwork, then said, 'Sad, though.'

'What was?' asked Sebastian patiently. He was beginning to wonder if he did want friendly new neighbours.

'Well, he was blind. Managed wonderfully, though, considering . . .'

650

They were sitting in the River Room, Jenna having had breakfast and Charlie a great many cups of coffee, when they saw Boy walking across the lounge. Followed by Lucas and Venetia. All looking rather agitated. Jenna saw them, and stood up, went over to them.

'I'm really sorry,' she said, and her voice was oddly authoritative. 'But would you mind leaving us alone a little while longer? I'm perfectly all right, as you can see. And Charlie and I have rather a lot to talk about.'

'Right,' said Ann Thynne. She looked at Izzie and Nick, who were sitting side by side in her consulting room. She sounded very serious. Izzie reached out for Nick's hand. Her mouth was very dry.

'Now, we do have a bit of a problem here.'

'Oh,' said Izzie, very quietly. 'Oh, I see.'

That was it: she was going to tell her it wasn't even worth examining her tubes. Clearly she had discovered something just then, while she was doing her examination, something they had missed before. She was never going to be able to have a baby. Never.

'The thing is,' she paused, looked at her notes, 'I can't do this examination until after your next period. As I told you.'

'No,' said Izzie, 'I know.'

'And that was due – when?'

'Well – like I told you. Almost a fortnight ago. Just before I left New York. But what with the journey and then the memorial service, and we've had a bit of family drama –' she realised she was rambling '– and I suppose that's held it up. Maybe I should book in to have it done in New York, instead of with you. It was just that I'd prefer it here.'

'Yes. Maybe. How do you feel in yourself?'

'Oh – fine. Absolutely fine. Yes.'

'Sweetheart, you were sick this morning,' said Nick.

'Yes, I know, but that was only Venetia's mousse.'

Ann Thynne looked at her, and her lips twitched. She tried to retain her rather serious, cool expression, but she couldn't. She suddenly burst into peals of laughter.

'Izzie,' she said, 'may I call you that?'

'Yes, of course. But—'

'Izzie, I would say that it is extremely likely that you are pregnant.'

'Pregnant! But I can't be pregnant, I—'

'Darling, we've been doing all the right things,' said Nick mildly.

'I know, but – but—' She remembered reading anxiety could inhibit conception. And ever since she'd told Nick about the abortion she'd felt quite different . . .

'It's very early days, I know,' said Ann Thynne, 'but if your period really is a fortnight late, and you've been sick – well, it doesn't require a very extensive gynaecological training to make a tentative diagnosis. And your breasts certainly look very active.'

'She has active breasts?' said Nick. 'Good God.'

'Yes, she does. That is to say, they're very veined, and I managed to coax a little colostrum out of them just now. I don't suppose you noticed.'

'No. I just wished you wouldn't squeeze them. It hurt.'

'Well, then. More proof. Now, what I want you to do is to give me a urine sample, and I'll send it along to the lab for a pregnancy test. But I really don't have many doubts.'

She sent Izzie off with a small phial and looked at Nick; he was sitting back in his chair, his eyes fixed on the ceiling.

'What are you doing?' she said, smiling.

'I'm lying here in the gutter,' he said, 'looking up at the stars.'

Two hours later, Jenna arrived back at Cheyne Walk in a taxi; she looked very calm, very determined.

Adele had been standing at the window with Jamie, watching out for her. She went into the hall.

'Hallo Jenna.'

'Hi Adele. I'm so sorry if you were all worried about me. Could I have a word with Jamie, please? Alone?'

'Of course.'

Jenna followed Jamie back into the drawing room. She closed the door.

'Jamie,' she said, 'I want you to pay one million dollars out of my trust fund and into Charlie's bank account. Today. Please.'

'Jenna, I can't do that.'

'Of course you can. I know you can. You and the trustees can just decide it's in my interests. Which it is. Mine and Charlie's.'

'But—'

'I'm sorry, I don't want any more buts. I want that money for Charlie.'

'What did he tell you?'

'Not a lot. He didn't need to. I have the diaries. Out there in the hall. I hope you won't be disgusting enough to count them, but you can if you like.'

'And – where is Charlie?'

'On his way to New York. Well, sitting at London airport, actually. Now is that all quite clear, or do we need to run through it again?'

'You know I absolutely can't agree to that.'

'Oh, but I know you absolutely can. Charlie deserves that money and I want him to have it. There's a very great deal more besides. All right?'

'Jenna—'

'Jamie, would you just listen to me? I love Charlie. I love him very much. I don't know how many more times I have to say this, but let's run through it again. I couldn't have survived since my mother died without him. He's loved me and cared for me and sat up all night with me sometimes and dried my tears and made me laugh and cheered me on and always, always been there whenever, *whenever* I've needed him. And I don't think you can put a price on that. OK, it was a funny way of asking for it. I don't care. It's my money, not yours. Why won't you let him have it?'

'Jenna—' Jamie hesitated; he seemed to be about to say a great deal more, but then he stopped. She looked at him and half smiled.

'If you were going to tell me things about Charlie you think I ought to know, please don't. In the first place, I don't want to hear them and in the second place – well—' She paused and smiled at him and it was Laurence's smile suddenly, and even Laurence's tone of voice.

'Jamie,' she said, 'did you really think I hadn't worked a whole lot of it out for myself?'

She went upstairs after that and stood at the window, looking out. Wondering how many times her mother had done the same thing, stood at the same window, looked down at the same view. She felt very close to her suddenly. Happily close.

Later that day, Lucas asked her if she'd like to go for a walk with him; she said she'd love it. It was a brilliant afternoon, the fog quite gone. They set out along the River Walk; the water was shining in the sunshine, seagulls wheeling noisily overhead, people bustling along, smiling, as if almost surprised to be able to see one another again. Lucas suddenly stopped and gave her a hug.

'You OK?'

'Yes, I'm fine.'

'Good. I just – wondered. It can't have been exactly easy for you.'

'Not exactly.'

He took her hand, and they started walking again.

'You were really great today,' he said. 'You dealt with them all so well.'

Jenna looked up at him and smiled.

'I wasn't exactly dealing with them,' she said, 'I just wanted to sort things out. For Charlie, I mean.'

'You really like Charlie, don't you?'

'Yes, I do. Well actually, more than like, of course. I love him. Very much.' She hesitated, then said, 'I mean I know he'll probably waste a lot of that money, get in a few more messes. But it really doesn't matter to me. I just want him to have it. Because I think he should.'

'I can understand that,' said Lucas. 'Just about.'

'I was thinking,' she said, after a pause, 'about something my mother once said to me. We were alone together one night, she'd been talking about my dad. It's very odd, you know, never to have known your dad.'

'I hardly did either,' he said. 'I was only a baby when we left Paris. So I do know how – odd it is. Unsettling, wouldn't you say? Only to know what people tell you.'

'Yes. Yes, that's exactly right.'

'Maybe that's one of the reasons we get along so well.'

'Maybe.'

He grinned at her. 'Anyway, tell me what your mum said.'

'She said how he was wonderful in many ways, but he wasn't perfect, nobody was perfect. And then she said, "that's what love is. Still loving someone, in spite of knowing the bad things." She said I should never forget that. And I know I never will. Never. Not for as long as I live.'